DATE DUE			

UNDER THE EDITORSHIP OF

Wayne C. Minnick

THE FLORIDA STATE UNIVERSITY

Oral Interpretation

FOURTH EDITION

Charlotte I. Lee
NORTHWESTERN UNIVERSITY

Houghton Mifflin Company · Boston
NEW YORK · ATLANTA · GENEVA, ILL. · DALLAS · PALO ALTO

Library of Congress Catalog Card Number: 76–139801

ISBN: 0–395–04776–5

Contents

Contents

Preface

This text on oral interpretation is based on the twofold conviction that the study of literature is in itself a rewarding and challenging experience, and that sharing the results of such study with an audience gives motivation and focus to analysis, and pleasure and satisfaction in performance. Interpretation is built on scholarship, technical know-how, sensitivity, and the desire to share. It demands total synthesis.

Interpretation, as we shall use the term and as it has been accepted in academic circles, goes several steps beyond a mere vocalization of silent reading. It requires an appreciation of one's material as a work of literary art and the ability to communicate that work of art through voice and body. It demands both intellectual and emotional response from the interpreter, and a control and channeling of the understanding and emotion to elicit the appropriate response from the audience. It is with such completeness of understanding and skill in communication that this book is concerned.

The interpreter is an artist, revivifying one art through another. As a musician translates the written notes into sound and thus conveys the achievement of the composer to the listener, so the interpreter brings to life the printed symbols which have preserved the ideas and experiences of mankind for centuries. Interpretation is thus an art of *re-creation*. The instruments of communication are voice and body. But voice and body are *merely* instruments, and while they must be used with skill and ease, they must always be controlled by an alert and informed mind.

With a view to developing the necessary understanding and appreciation, this book lays considerable stress on analysis of organization, structure, style, and the various devices which writers use in prose, drama, and poetry — from simile to cadence, from paragraph to rhyme. It attempts to help the student evaluate materials in terms of literary worth as well as audience appeal. It suggests ways to analyze pieces of literature and to examine similar selections comparatively. And it offers suggestions for preparing and presenting material to an audience.

The word "suggestions" must not be overlooked. There is great danger in being too specific or too dogmatic. Every piece of literature presents its own challenges and must be approached with an open, albeit informed, mind. There is no magic "how-to-do-it" formula. The basic principles of analysis and preparation presented in this book have proved useful, but they will vary in degree of usefulness from one work to another.

The aim of the analysis is awareness, appreciation, and response. Awareness and appreciation increase one's critical ability and give a firm foundation for literary evaluation. Response is threefold. The first step is understanding the writer's response to the experience he is sharing. The second is allowing the writer to "have his way" and responding fully to all the clues he gives. The third, of course, is sensing audience response, whether the audience is one person or a thousand, in the classroom or outside. Total response to the total experience is essential.

The student who is strongly performance-oriented will find that analysis gives him greater confidence in what he may have sensed intuitively and increases his flexibility in handling various kinds and moods of material. The student who is not primarily interested in performance but rather in the processes of literary examination will find that his performance and his audience's reaction are valuable tests of his thoroughness. Thus, although this book is certainly slanted toward oral performance, it does not deny the value of interpretation as a method of literary analysis and criticism.

The process of analysis set forth here takes into account, at least by implication, the so-called modal approach. This approach emphasizes the writer's relationship to his readers and the position he takes in recounting an experience, whether his own or that of some character he has created. The concern for stylistic analysis and awareness of organization is highly compatible with the rhetorical approach, which centers on the effective use of words in speaking and writing to influence or persuade. And attention to *persona* or speaker in a piece of writing capitalizes on some elements of the dramatistic approach. The more ways one looks at a piece of literature the more facets of its aesthetic qualities are revealed and the richer the experience of the literature becomes.

Part One is concerned largely with the selection, analysis, and oral interpretation of material. Chapters 1 and 2 establish broad fundamental principles common to all kinds of literature and thus serve as background for a more detailed examination of the various literary types in the sections which follow. Chapters 3 and 4 deal respectively with the aspects of body and voice which the interpreter must bring under control if he is to communicate effectively.

Part Two is devoted to the interpretation of prose. The first chapter examines the elements common to prose, with particular attention to nondramatic writing such as essays, biography, history, and letters. The second chapter deals with the function and dimensions of description. The third discusses the problems and advantages of narrative writing, and ends with a brief unit on Chamber Theatre.

Part Three is concerned with drama. The first chapter deals with the general characteristics of the genre. The second gives attention to technical problems and suggests ways of communicating motivation and individual traits. In these chapters, an attempt has been made to face squarely some of the technical problems which arise in the interpretation of drama: using (or not using) overt action, handling stage directions, picking up cues, and the like. In addition, Part Three reflects some of the current interest in "anti-plays," as well as in the increasingly popular group interpretation of drama known as Readers Theatre.

Although numerous verse selections appear in earlier parts of the book, the interpretation of poetry *per se* is not discussed until Part Four. Experience shows that students are apt to distrust their ability to communicate poetry to others and to shy away from it until they have first "found" themselves in prose and drama. There is some justification for this feeling, since poetry carries structural discipline, rhythm, cadence, and condensation of emotion and idea to a higher degree than any other form of writing. Hence, in dealing with poetry the student encounters refinements of problems met in less complex form in prose and in drama. In Part Four, he learns how figures of speech function in a poem; how rhyme, tone color, and rhythm enhance meaning; how meter and cadence complement poetic language – in short, how the elements of poetry work together to produce a whole greater than the sum of its parts. Equally important, he learns that synthesis must follow analysis if the poem is to be re-created as a work of art.

The "Selections for Analysis and Oral Interpretation" at the end of each chapter were chosen with several considerations in mind: the interests of college students today; the challenge inherent in the selections – whether the interpreter would feel a sense of personal achievement in presenting them orally; a certain standard of literary excellence; breadth and range – whether the selections would enlarge the student's understanding and introduce him to literature of many types and periods. The aim was to strike a balance between the well-known writers who are part of our literary heritage and those who are writing out of the experiences of our day. The humorous selections were included to demonstrate that neither the world nor the oral interpretation class need be a thoroughly solemn, sober place.

Suggestions for further reading are included at the ends of chapters where they seem relevant. They are selective rather than exhaustive and are intended to encourage the superior student to examine the ever-widening fields of literary criticism, linguistics, and aesthetics which are of particular interest to the interpreter. The books mentioned are easily available in most college libraries; in fact, the majority of them are now available in paperback editions as well.

The success or failure of this text depends in large measure on two elements which cannot be put down on the printed page. The first is the interest and enthusiasm of the individual student, without which any course is doomed from the beginning. The second is that invaluable and indefinable something which only an enthusiastic and dedicated teacher can give to any body of knowledge. If this text can serve as a guide and encouragement to student and teacher alike, it will have been well worth the hours spent in preparing it.

I am indebted to my colleagues throughout the country, and to their students, for sound criticism of previous editions of this text. The Fourth Edition reflects many of their opinions and critical judgments. My own students, too, made their contribution by asking intelligent questions which helped to clarify my thinking on theory and its practical application.

I am also indebted to the proprietors of copyright materials reprinted in this book. Detailed acknowledgment is made to them elsewhere in these pages.

CHARLOTTE I. LEE

Basic Principles

Part One

Chapter 1

*Interpretation is the art of communicating to an audience a work
of literary art in its intellectual, emotional, and aesthetic entirety.*

The Definition Analyzed

Interpretation is the art of communicating . . . By its very definition, art
implies skill in performance. It requires discipline and training in the use
of the appropriate tools, intelligence, experience, and the ability to order
both experience and response into meaningful form. The writer of a
literary selection is the creative artist. He orders his ideas, words, sounds,
and rhythms into a particular form. The interpreter, in turn, takes the
symbols on the printed page and brings his own experience and insight to
bear on the clues the author has given him. He then submits his experience and responses to the order imposed by the creative artist and
assumes the responsibility of re-creating the literary entity. This demands
thorough analysis, painstaking rehearsal, and strict discipline in the use
of voice and body. The oral interpreter's art, then, is comparable to that
of a musician playing the work of an artist-composer.

The truest and finest art is disarming in its *seeming* simplicity. It
makes its observers aware of the result, not of the means used to attain
the result. Technical display is not art. Art implies the systematic application of knowledge and skill in effecting a desired result, and the
desired result in interpretation is precisely the same as that of any other
phase of speech — communication.

A Beginning and an End

It is the perfect tribute when the members of the audience are so held by the material that they cannot immediately break the spell to applaud. If an audience says, "What a beautiful voice!" or "What graceful gestures!" the interpreter has failed. When the audience's attention is held by the effect of the material presented, the interpreter has succeeded. But this unobtrusiveness on the interpreter's part does not result from casual preparation or from a feeling that, since the literature is the important thing, he need do no more than face his audience, open the book, and open his mouth. On the contrary, it is the result of a preparation so thorough and a technique so perfectly coordinated that the audience cannot see the wheels go around.

. . . *communicating to an audience* . . . An audience may be one person or several thousand. No matter what the size or caliber of the audience, the interpreter's responsibilities are the same. He must communicate as skillfully as he can what is on the printed page, making intelligent use of every detail to achieve the organic whole. The listeners' the form in which it is presented, depends to a large degree on the interpreter's ability to discover these elements himself and to project them satisfactorily in their proper relationship.

How are these elements communicated to the audience? They are communicated by voice and body, working together and controlled by understanding of and concentration on the material. Consequently, the interpreter trains his voice and body so that they will respond unobtrusively to the requirements of the literature. He strives to eliminate mannerisms which may distract his audience. He is aware of the effect of posture, muscle tone, and general platform presence. He disciplines his physical action so that it aids his communication and in no way calls attention to itself. He works with his voice during practice periods so that he may be heard and understood. He is aware that he needs flexibility in range, force, stress, and volume if he is to do justice to the writing and bring out whatever strength and beauty the author has achieved through the sounds and relationships of the words. His concentration on communicating — that is to say *sharing* — the material at hand must be strong and continuous. During early rehearsals he will stop to work on difficult segments like a pianist fingering a complicated passage. In later rehearsals, when the selection is thoroughly in mind, he will begin to turn his attention out to an imagined audience, being careful not to let his attention wander from *what* he is sharing with them.

The modern interpreter often chooses not to memorize his materials completely. The time that would be consumed in committing the words to memory might be better spent in study and in perfecting the techniques of communication. Technically speaking, it does not matter in the least whether the material is completely memorized or not. If it is, the interpreter must concentrate on communicating the total effect rather than on the act of remembering. If he has chosen not to memorize completely, he must be free enough of the text to concentrate on communicating with the audience rather than on reading. By the time the material has been analyzed in detail, put back together again, and practiced conscientiously, it will be so firmly implanted in the interpreter's consciousness that an occasional glance at the page should suffice.

Whether he memorizes his selection or not, the modern interpreter has his book — or a typescript of it — with him during performance. Its presence serves two important purposes. First, it establishes the interpreter as the intermediary between the author and the audience. This is not to imply, however, that the interpreter has no more important part than to open his mouth and let the words from the printed page come out. His is the satisfaction of re-creation.

When we speak of the printed page, we are speaking of a tool, a medium. For neither the pages in a book nor the words on the page are the literary work of art. The printed page is merely a means of preserving word symbols through which an author once set down as precisely as he could certain thoughts, emotions, and attitudes. The printed page is the record — what the interpreter works from — but it is not the thing itself. Through his voice and body the symbols on the page are revivified, and the ideas and experience they symbolize are re-created.

The second purpose the presence of the book or manuscript serves is an aesthetic one. It alerts the members of the audience to the fact that the emotions presented are not in reality those of the person standing before them. Realizing this, they can respond without embarrassment. Thus, the book allows the audience to keep enough psychic and aesthetic distance from the reader to respond to the literature out of their own experience without feeling they are eavesdropping on a fellow human being. It enables them to respond to the literature instead of the performer. We have all, unfortunately, seen performers so emotionally involved that we are uncomfortable. The presence of the book or manuscript can *help* to avoid this, though the interpreter himself must keep his attention on *sharing* the *author's* response rather than demonstrating it or exhibiting his own intense sensitivity.

   . . . *a work of literary art in its intellectual, emotional, and aesthetic entirety.* . . . The interpreter's concern is to communicate the total effect of the literary work of art. This does not mean that he must present only complete works, or that he cannot use excerpts. Neither does it mean that his listeners will always receive the full impact of the author's achievement. For instance, they may be able to respond to a complex contemporary poem only in a general way. The fullness of their response will depend on their backgrounds and their familiarity with the work. But the interpreter must strive always to present the literature in its "intellectual, emotional, and aesthetic entirety," or the general feeling will be largely confusion. The elements of literary art work so interdependently in good writing that to ignore or eliminate any one of them is to misread the work. All the various qualities which contribute to the total effect must be held in their proper relation to the whole.

   For purposes of analysis, it is convenient to break a work down into its parts, but it should always be kept in mind that such arbitrary division is only a device to facilitate understanding. We may conveniently speak of content and structure, of logical meaning and emotive quality. But this separation is useful *only* in the sense that it provides a way of getting at full understanding. Content and structure do not in fact exist as separate entities; they form one organic whole. They must always be examined in relation to each other in an attempt to arrive at the total achievement of the writer, undeniably more than the sum of its various parts. The interpreter must constantly put the material back together after each step in analysis.

   Difficult as it is, then, to isolate and discuss separately certain aspects of a work of art, a full appreciation of the whole is enhanced by careful analysis of the particulars. In a general way, we may begin such an analysis by distinguishing the content from the structure of a piece of literature.

   In the broadest sense, content has to do with what is being said; structure with the way it is said. Content has two aspects. The first is the *intellectual* or *logical aspect*, which is simply what the material "says." It is addressed to the mind, and involves understanding the meanings of the words and the relationships between words and groups of words. The other aspect of content is its *emotive quality*, the capacity of the meaning *and* sound to arouse pleasure or pain, to stimulate to activity or repose through association. But because words seldom have meaning independent of association, or emotion-arousing qualities without meaning, for all purposes except analysis the logical and emotional qualities of a work of art can never be divorced. Since understanding takes place on the intellectual and emotional levels simultaneously, the skilled interpreter must find out what the author is saying, experience emotionally what is said, and communicate his total response — mental and emotional — to the audience.

Structure is so closely interwoven with content that it is difficult to discuss either without doing violence to both. Structure embraces the organization and expression of the ideas, the choice of words, the relationship of the parts to each other and to the whole. It is concerned with the manner of expression, from simple lucidity to the most complex ornamentations of language. In prose, for instance, it includes, among other things, the pattern of individual sentences as well as the effect created by several sentences in combination; in drama, the rhythm of the characters' speeches, the structure of the sentence or the poetic line, and the interrelationship of the speeches, scenes, and acts of the entire play; in poetry, all the contributions to the sound patterns, including stanzaic structure, scansion, rhyme, and length of line. These elements will be examined in more detail as each of these types of writing is discussed in later chapters.

. . . *aesthetic entirety* . . . embraces all the qualities which must be considered in appreciating a piece of writing as a successful work of literary art. These elements must always be evaluated in relation to each other and to the whole.

"Aesthetic entirety" includes all the matters we have touched on above, plus many more which we shall talk about throughout this book. Aesthetics deals with the theory of the fine arts and the individual's response to them. Though it includes all areas of art, our concern will be, of course, primarily literary art. As a study, it concerns itself with the ordering of the parts of a work of art as well as with the response of the beholder, or in our case, the interpreter and his listeners. Some books in this field are listed in the bibliography at the end of this chapter. At the moment, we need only be aware that there are aesthetic standards for the way the parts work together to create a literary whole, and that it is this *whole* which must be communicated to the audience with all its elements intact and correlated.

In short, it is the task of the interpreter to perceive and to communicate to his audience the intellectual, emotional, and aesthetic qualities of his material, not as separate entities but as a unified and coordinated whole. His aim is to present the material in its totality. His responsibility is to communicate the work of another, not to exhibit his own talents, sensitivity, or erudition. The writer is the creative artist; the interpreter, the re-creative artist. He is, however, an artist. His is the privilege of choosing an adequate example of literary art and bringing it to an audience with its aesthetic qualities intact. His introduction, transitions, and program arrangement also become part of *his* artistic product, which, though it owes its first responsibility to the creative artist, becomes, in fact, a creative act of the interpreter. He is conductor, director, arranger, and performer, all in one.

His introduction and transitions will be dictated by what he has discovered in analysis and what he thinks this specific audience needs by way of preparation or linking. He does not tell them what the material is going to say. The properly communicated selection will take care of that. Neither does he tell them what to look for and what he himself has found. Rather, he focuses their thoughts on what is to come, creates a harmonious mood, and begins to transform them from a group of people into an audience.

Sources of Material

The interpreter has an almost unlimited range of material to choose from. He may use prose, poetry, or drama. He need only consider the literary worth of the selection, its suitability for his audience, and his own interests. From the experienced interpreter's point of view, this freedom of choice is a distinct advantage, but it may present the beginning student with his first problem. From the wealth of available material, how is he to select something for his early assignments?

The first question, obviously, is where to look. Anthologies provide helpful short cuts in the search for material. The interpreter will find collections of prose — essays, short stories, humorous and satirical pieces, biographies, letters, diaries, even novels, and so on through the entire range of prose writing. He will find poetry classified by kind, as lyric, narrative, humorous, didactic; by period or nation, as Elizabethan, Victorian, modern American, and the like; and by subject or spirit, as poems about nature, Christmas, protest, patriotism. If he decides to try drama, there are numerous volumes which include entire plays, both one-act and full-length, or selected scenes. There are also anthologies which cut across these classifications — chronological surveys of a literature or anthologies of regional writing, for example; and of course there are volumes of selected works of individual authors. Dozens of useful anthologies are available in inexpensive editions in any bookstore or in hardback editions in any library. They are especially valuable to the beginning student of interpretation because they offer a wide selection in a single volume. After the first few assignments, he will have a better idea of the kind of material that appeals to him and where to look for it.

The student interpreter should begin by asking himself what interests him most. Is it the city or the country? Some exotic part of the world or his own home state? Perhaps he is much more interested in people than in places. What kind of people? In what circumstances? Has he been excited about a book he has read recently? If so, he should go back and read it again. An excerpt from it may do nicely for his first assignment.

Choosing the Selection: Three Touchstones

The advice to choose material for the first assignment because of its interesting subject matter does not imply that no effort should be made to evaluate its literary worth. On the contrary, throughout this book there will be constant concern with evaluation through analysis of material.

Most of us are attracted first to a piece of writing by what it says — its content. As our sophistication increases, we appreciate more fully the complexities of the relationship between meaning and structure. Though there are numerous ways to treat any subject, some are more effective than others. Probably you are very fond of certain poems, plays, or stories because of early associations. No one expects you to give them up. But you cannot impose them on an audience which does not share your associations unless your selections are also successful as works of literary art. Neither, of course, should you reject a piece of writing as "bad" because the author did not do what you wish he had done. If you do not enjoy a selection, you certainly need not choose to read it. But be careful not to limit yourself to what you have always liked and known. Be willing to broaden your horizons. The important thing is not so much to know what you like as to establish criteria for evaluating the literary artist's success or failure. It is important to admit why you do or do not wish to study a certain selection. Even though you may not come to like it, you may learn to respect its qualities as literary art.

Let us assume that you have made a tentative choice of material, or have narrowed the possibilities down to two or three selections equally appealing as far as content is concerned. Before making a final decision, you wish to evaluate the choices as pieces of literature. As the first touchstones, you will do well to consider three factors — universality, individuality, and suggestion.

Universality does not mean that the material will immediately appeal to all persons regardless of their intellectual or cultural backgrounds. It means, rather, that the idea expressed is potentially interesting to all people because it touches on a common experience. The emotional response it evokes is one most readers (or listeners) have felt at one time or another — love or hate, hope or fear, joy or despair.

Literature draws its material from life, but literature is not *exactly like* life. A writer selects and controls attitudes and motivations. He imposes order on the flux and change of human existence. And he gives us clues to direct us in relating our own experience to the order he has selected. Even deliberately distorted events can have relevance to our existence. When writing has universality, the interpreter will be able to call on his own background and experience to help him respond to such writing. When he communicates all the levels of meaning to his audience, they in turn will have a basis for identification with their own experiences.

The second touchstone of good writing is *individuality* — the writer's fresh approach to a universal subject. It is revealed in his choice of words, his images, and his method of organization. To decide whether or not the author has handled his subject with individuality, the interpreter needs to have some acquaintance with a wide variety of literature. It takes time and experience to be able to recognize individuality. Gradually, however, the student will see that it results in large part from the author's selectivity and control and is reflected in both content and structure. We shall take a closer look at this quality when we compare two poems later in the chapter.

The subtlest and most rewarding writing is characterized by *suggestion*. It leaves the reader something to do: it does not tell him quite everything. This does not mean that the writing is obscure. It means rather, that the author has chosen references and words which allow the reader to enrich the subject matter from his own background. There must, however, be enough clear suggestions for the imagination to follow. Frequently, considerable analysis will be necessary to find and properly use these directions; but once the possibilities for relevant association are realized, the writing continues to grow in meaning and in emotional impact for the interpreter and his audience. We shall touch on this aspect, too, in our comparison.

It is obvious, of course, that these three touchstones — universality, individuality, and suggestion — are closely related and serve to enhance and balance each other in effective writing: the idea is drawn from an experience which all men are able to share; the method of expressing the idea is different from that used by other authors; and the suggestion of associated ideas and responses points the way for the imagination to follow and allows for continuing enrichment of the various levels of meaning. Sometimes these touchstones are not present in a selection in equal force, nor is it necessary that they should be. But if any one of them is totally absent or patently weak, the interpreter will do well to look elsewhere for material if he wishes to interest and move his audience.

By way of illustration, let us look at two brief poems, one by Helen Hoyt and one by Emily Dickinson. Each contains an intensely personal experience and is written in the first person.

The Sense of Death

Since I have felt the sense of death,
Since I have borne its dread, its fear —
Oh, how my life has grown more dear
Since I have felt the sense of death!
Sorrows are good, and cares are small,
Since I have known the loss of all.

Since I have felt the sense of death,
And death forever at my side —
Oh, how the world has opened wide
Since I have felt the sense of death!
My hours are jewels that I spend,
For I have seen the hours end.

Since I have felt the sense of death,
Since I have looked on that black night —
My inmost brain is fierce with light
Since I have felt the sense of death.
O dark, that made my eyes to see!
O death, that gave my life to me!

HELEN HOYT

Before we look at the second poem, a word of explanation may be in order. Miss Dickinson did not give her poems titles and indeed never readied them for publication. Consequently, there are several versions of some of the poems, each differing in punctuation and even in word choice. Furthermore, Miss Dickinson's use of capital letters and dashes is thoroughly unique. She frequently capitalizes all the nouns and uses dashes instead of commas. Whether this had some mysterious symbolism or was simply an eccentricity of a strongminded lady, it is impossible to tell. Nevertheless, we shall accept it as it appears. The dashes, at least, seem compatible with interrupted or suspended thought units.

I Felt a Funeral

I felt a Funeral, in my Brain,
And Mourners to and fro
Kept treading — treading — till it seemed
That Sense was breaking through —

And when they all were seated,
A Service, like a Drum —
Kept beating — beating — till I thought
My Mind was going numb —

And then I heard them lift a Box
And creak across my Soul
With those same Boots of Lead, again,
Then Space — began to toll,

As all the Heavens were a Bell,
And Being, but an Ear,
And I, and Silence, some strange Race
Wrecked, solitary, here —

And then a Plank in Reason, broke,
And I dropped down, and down —
And hit a World, at every Crash,
And Got through knowing — then —

EMILY DICKINSON

The universality of the fact of death or the effect of death cannot be denied. However, these two poems present this universal experience in markedly different ways. In the first place, Miss Hoyt is talking about the aftermath of *having sensed* death — probably physical death. Miss Dickinson is talking about the period of the *sensing* — and probably about despair, a kind of spiritual death so numbing and soul-shattering that it became a "funeral" in her brain. Miss Hoyt uses straightforward language and sentences loosely linked together without a steady progression of thought. Miss Dickinson also uses straightforward language, but she introduces an extended metaphor which gives pace and progress to her writing. Finally, Miss Hoyt draws definite, even moralistic, conclusions. Miss Dickinson merely describes the experience and draws no conclusions.

Miss Hoyt obviously wishes to place death and a resultant acute appreciation of life in sharp contrast. A quick count reveals that half the lines are concerned with death and half with life — a very comfortable balance. And yet the distinct impression remains that this poem is more about death than life.

She asks us to take "Since" in the sense of "after" as well as in the sense of cause and effect. She repeats her title as six of the eighteen lines of the poem, and approximates it by parallel construction in three more. Such repetition could be most effective in creating a driving, insistent impact. However, the phrase "felt the sense of death" does not cut into our consciousness with much force. The word "sense" implies recognition or perception. It is quite possible to "feel" a "perception," of course, but let us look at the details she has chosen to give us this perception of death. Death is characterized by "dread," "fear," "forever at my side," "the hours end," "black night" and "O dark." None of these references is fresh or individual. Each has been used in the same connection for so many centuries that it has become trite. Taken separately and skillfully developed, each could have a wealth of suggestion, but Miss Hoyt gives us no time or incentive to establish an individual identification with what the "sense" of death was for her, or indeed might be for us.

Admittedly, Miss Hoyt's insistent use of "Since" in nine of the eighteen lines clearly tells us that the experience of sensing death led her to a new awareness of the value of life. Unfortunately, her references to life are equally vague and familiar. Life is referred to in "grown more dear," "Sorrows are good," "cares are small," "world has opened wide," "hours are jewels that I spend," "inmost brain is fierce with light," "eyes to see" and "gave my life to me." "Sorrows" is so inclusive and allows for such a weight of personal association that we cannot fix on the paradox of sorrows being "good" before we are whisked on to "cares" which are "small." Presumably, this line is intended to set up a balance, but it does not quite come off, partly because of the inclusiveness and permissiveness of "sorrows" and "cares," and partly because even small cares are not "good" as she asks us to believe sorrows have become. The use of the singular "sorrow" and "care" would at least have allowed us to accept these terms in a more abstract sense, and hence to identify more easily with the emotional implication. There is, too, a disturbingly familiar ring in "hours are jewels" and in the verb "spend." Though it may be quibbling to say that one does not "spend" jewels unless one lives in a medieval economy, nevertheless the association here is strained. The phrase "inmost brain is fierce with light" is probably the strongest line of the poem, particularly since Miss Hoyt has carefully set it against "black night." But again, it goes nowhere — except back to the already quite familiar refrain.

Further study of this poem will reveal little individuality, either in the selection of details or the way they are expressed. The element of suggestion is also poorly established — beyond the basic premise that after one comes close to death, whether in the actual physical sense or in having been made aware of its omnipresence, life becomes more precious. The words and figures of speech chosen to develop this premise lack the force, freshness, sharpness of focus, and emotive quality to make us feel that the poet has said something important in a way we have never quite thought of before.

Miss Dickinson also begins her poem with "I felt," but the clear positioning in time past and the implied completion of the event put it firmly in perspective without the vague, continuing "Since I have . . . ." Moreover, we are at once drawn into strong suggestion with "funeral." A funeral carries such a complex weight of values and images that we are bombarded by an association of grief, dignity, ritual, the presence of the body, and a mixture of respect and grim, formal, finality. To *feel* a funeral goes beyond merely attending one. And to feel a funeral in the brain goes still further. We are immediately aware of a new and individual approach to the universal subject of death — of spiritual death which destroys the life of the senses, crushes hope, and even denies the power of the soul.

We are given time to develop the complexity suggested here, our focus sharpened by the mourners going to and fro and by the sound they make "treading — treading." We are then returned to sensation in the last line of the first stanza. Two suggested interpretations of this line, rather than being contradictory, provide a thin thread of suspense, strengthened by "till it seemed." On one level "Sense" may be taken to mean the mind bending under the strain of the "treading." This interpretation is strongly suggested by "Brain" in the opening line. But Miss Dickinson may also mean that awareness — "Sense" — had become so acute that the sensation was unbearable. These two interpretations are not mutually exclusive, and both can well operate here in a deliberate and disturbing ambiguity.

The balancing of the concrete elements of a funeral service with the sensation felt in the brain continues to the last line of the third stanza. It is held together and kept vivid by a strict chronological progression, as well as by constant references to sound, already prepared for in "treading — treading." Sound reaches an almost unbearable intensity as "Space — began to toll," and becomes overwhelming in the opening lines of the next stanza. Our attention is snatched from this climax of sound by "and Silence," which by its very contrast is equally deafening.

At the same time the mourners and the pallbearers disappear abruptly, leaving the senses "solitary." But the experience does not stop there. It continues in a swift downward pattern, suggesting the lowering into the grave and much more. The breaking "Plank in Reason" suggests a wealth of associations and adds still another dimension to the horror of the drop "down, and down — " which culminates in the highly graphic "hit" and "Crash" in the next to last line. The repeated use of "and" involves us in this swift and helpless dropping.

The last line, like several of the others, carries deliberate ambiguity and moves on more than one level. "Got through" may mean *finished* knowing in the human manner, as well as *broke through* into a super-human or mystical knowledge possible only after death or a great spiritual crisis. The " — then — " functions on more than one level also. It completes the chronological progression; it terminates the immediate recorded experience; it teases us with a hint that there was more. A skilled interpreter can convey this multiplicity of meanings to his audience.

In our brief analysis of Miss Hoyt's poem, we criticized the lack of strength in her balancing of life and death. Miss Dickinson is not talking about life and death as contrasting states, but she manages very skillfully to keep us aware of the world of the living. The reference to those who are attending the "funeral" which she felt in her brain is strong through the first three stanzas, but held constantly within the framework of her point of view. Even in the sensation responses there is a quality of living awareness. "Sense," "Mind," "Soul," "Being," "Ear," "Race," and "Reason" all relate to but do not parallel "knowing" in the final line. There is also an alive, human quality in "hit a World," and "every Crash," because they are so essentially physical.

Thus from the opening line we are aware of a fresh, individual approach to the sensation Miss Dickinson is writing about. It catches and holds our interest because it is an unusual but certainly acceptable way of talking about a subject whose universality cannot be denied. It is a succinct, compressed statement which cuts into our awareness and increases our understanding.

During the discussion of Miss Dickinson's poem we mentioned the term "deliberate ambiguity." Ambiguity is sometimes confused with lack of clarity, but the term as it is used in modern literary criticism means "having more than one possible meaning, all of which are relevant and congruent within the organic whole of the piece of writing." Ambiguity may result in some obscurity, but it must not defy careful study or split the literary selection into incompatible segments. The kind of ambiguity we have been discussing is one of the richest sources of suggestion for the very reason that it does not narrowly circumscribe the experience of the poem.

Miss Hoyt used outworn and too-familiar references to suggest the terror of death and the glory of life. Miss Dickinson used images which stirred the senses and caused us to respond emotionally and physically. At the same time, she engaged our minds by juxtaposing unexpected and strongly suggestive words. Almost any line will serve as an example, but two of the most striking are the opening line and the reference to "a

Plank in Reason." At its best, then, suggestion takes us beyond the poem without taking us out of the poem. Suggestion and individuality go hand in hand.

There are numerous matters which we have completely ignored in our evaluation of these two poems. We shall refer to them in succeeding chapters when we work with analysis. It was not our intention — although it was a temptation — to do more than illustrate how the three touchstones of universality, individuality, and suggestion can operate within a piece of literature.

Bibliography

As we mentioned within the chapter, there are innumerable anthologies, many of them in inexpensive editions, in which the interpreter will find a wealth of material to choose from. Also, most of the current textbooks listed at the end of the Appendix contain a wide variety of selections. Two anthologies in particular, however, are designed explicitly for the interpreter.

Bacon, Wallace A., and Robert S. Breen. *Literature for Interpretation.* New York: Holt, Rinehart and Winston, Inc., 1961.

Brooks, Keith, Eugene Bahn, and L. LeMont Okey. *Literature for Listening: An Oral Interpreter's Anthology.* Boston: Allyn and Bacon, Inc., 1968.

The student will find help in clarifying terms and in understanding the various approaches to criticism and analysis in the following books. Each contains an extensive bibliography.

Barnet, Sylvan, Morton Berman, and William Burto. *A Dictionary of Literary Terms.* New York: Little, Brown and Company, 1960.

A *paperback of brief definitions and cross references.*

Beckson, Karl, and Arthur Ganz. *A Reader's Guide to Literary Terms.* New York: Farrar, Straus and Company, 1960. The Noonday Press, N203.

Similar to the title above but somewhat more complete.

Butcher, Samuel Henry. *Aristotle's Theory of Poetry and Fine Art, with a Critical Text and Translation of the Poetics.* Fourth Edition. New York: Dover Publications, 1951.

Readable translation of Aristotle's classic study with an essay on Aristotelian criticism by John Gassner.

Crane, R. S. (ed.). *Critics and Criticism.* Chicago: University of Chicago Press, 1952. Phoenix Books Edition, abridged, P15, 1960.

A *collection of essays by eminent critics of the "Chicago school" of criticism.*

Frye, Northrop. *The Well-Tempered Critic*. Bloomington, Indiana: Indiana University Press, 1963.

A look at some of the diverse approaches to literary criticism currently in vogue. Contains sound and workable conclusions.

Gardner, Helen. *The Business of Criticism*. New York: Oxford University Press, 1963.

A defense of the historical method of criticism and a plea for the re-alliance of criticism with scholarship.

Gilbert, Allan H. (ed.). *Literary Criticism*. Vol. 1, Plato to Dryden; Vol. 2, Pope to Croce. Detroit: Wayne State University Press, 1962.

Brief, helpful comments on excerpts from the great critics. Extended bibliographies for each period plus a general bibliography. Carefully indexed for cross-reference.

Hall, Vernon, Jr. *A Short History of Literary Criticism*. New York: The Gotham Library, 1963.

A survey of the history of literary criticism from Plato to the New Critics. Separate chapters on the literary thought of Marx, Darwin, and Freud.

Hyman, Stanley Edgar. *The Critical Performance: An Anthology of American and British Literary Criticism of Our Century*. New York: Vintage Books, 1956.

Essays by outstanding contemporary critics.

Kaplan, Charles (ed.). *Criticism: Twenty Major Statements*. San Francisco: Chandler Publishing Company, 1964.

Representative essays on criticism from Plato to T. S. Eliot.

Shipley, Joseph T. (ed.). *Dictionary of World Literature: Criticism-Forms-Techniques*. Second Edition. New York: Philosophical Library, Inc., 1945.

A complete, scholarly sourcebook of terms and writers.

Smith, James Harry, and Edd Winfield Parks (eds.). *The Great Critics: An Anthology of Literary Criticism*. New York: W. W. Norton and Company, Inc., 1951.

Brief excerpts and comments on the theories of critics from Aristotle to the mid-twentieth century.

Wimsatt, W. K., Jr., and Cleanth Brooks. *Literary Criticism: A Short History*. New York: Alfred A. Knopf, Inc., 1957.

A clear, succinct account of the development of the field of literary criticism.

Chapter 2

In the preceding chapter the three touchstones of universality, individuality, and suggestion were used in comparing two short poems. Even so brief an examination revealed some differences between the two and served as a starting point for the interpreter who needs to know how to choose a selection to which he can respond and which will satisfy his audience by providing a fresh look at a rich universal experience.

After making his selection, the interpreter must thoroughly investigate everything to be found within the particular piece of literature itself. He must know precisely what the author has given him to work with. Only when he fully understands the author's achievement can the interpreter decide how he will use his technique to re-create that achievement for his audience.

The public speaker must be constantly concerned with the selection, arrangement, and expression of his ideas in order to win a desired response. In interpretation, the author has already taken care of those matters. The interpreter must, however, accept the responsibility for discovering and making proper use of the author's organization and method of presentation.

First, of course, the interpreter must make every effort to find out precisely what the author is trying to say. He may easily understand the general meaning of a selection and yet find some specific lines or phrases that are not wholly clear. If so, he must look up the unfamiliar words and references; he cannot afford to gloss over them. The word or allusion is there because the author felt that it best expressed exactly

Analyzing the Selection

what he wished to say. For the author, it was not *almost* the right word; it was *precisely* the word he wanted. Consequently, the interpreter cannot hope to achieve the author's full purpose if he has only a vague idea of the definitions or connotations of the words. In fact, he may even distort an idea if he mistakes the exact meaning of a word or phrase.

The dictionary is, of course, the first source the interpreter should consult when he is unsure of a word. The dictionary gives primarily *denotative* meanings — what the word means *explicitly*. For example, it *defines* "funeral" as "the ceremonies connected with burial or cremation of the dead; obsequies."[1] And it defines "obsequy" as "a funeral rite or ceremony."[2] But of course we all know perfectly well what a funeral is.

Nevertheless, as we looked at the word in Emily Dickinson's poem in the preceding chapter, a cluster of associations began to grow out of our experience with "funeral." Gradually, the word began to mean more than the bare dictionary definition. The "more" is the *connotative* meaning. To connote means to "suggest or convey (associations, overtones, etc.) in addition to the explicit, or denoted, meaning. . . ."[3] Thus connotative meaning is an associated meaning and is often based partially on subjective values. The successful writer gives his reader enough clues

[1] *Webster's New World Dictionary of the American Language,* College Edition (Cleveland and New York: The World Publishing Company, 1959), p. 587.
[2] *Ibid.,* p. 1013.
[3] *Ibid.,* p. 311.

to the way he wants the word taken so that the connotative meaning is not *entirely* subjective. We must remember that the definition says "suggest or convey . . . *in addition* to," not "instead of." We will have more to say about connotation when we examine the various ways it operates in the major types of literature. It is most important in a consideration of the emotive quality of content, but it must not be overlooked or misunderstood in getting at logical content as well. When a writer selects a particular word from several possible choices, he does so because that word conveys something over and above what it "means." What that something else is, what special flavor it adds to the whole, is for the interpreter to ferret out and convey to his audience.

Closely allied to connotative meaning is the function of allusions. Allusions are references to persons, places, or events, real or mythological, which call up relevant associations. They are useful because in a word or phrase they can establish an entire complex of connotations. Tennyson's "Ulysses" (page 73) and Auden's "Musée des Beaux Arts" (page 48), for example, are both based on allusion. Ulysses immediately calls to mind the great adventurer and leader of *The Odyssey*. The somewhat archaic and classical implication of the museum in Auden's title fits perfectly with his references to the "Old Masters" and helps establish the continuum of suffering from their time to ours.

Organization of Ideas

After making sure of the meanings of the words, the interpreter must then examine the organization of ideas. Most material divides rather easily into three parts: the introduction or "lead-in" portion, the body of the material, and the conclusion or "tying-up" unit. Obviously, the body of the material contains the main point the author wishes to make. However, the selection and arrangement of details and ideas in the introductory unit is important as preparation for the audience as well as for the interpreter.

Authors use various means of catching and holding a reader's interest in the introductory sections. It is the interpreter's responsibility to discover what method the author has used and through his technique to make it work in performance. The writer may tell a story to introduce the situation. He may begin with a description or use a purely explanatory or expository introduction. In any case, the interpreter must ask himself, "How does the author lead into the main point he wishes to make?" "Where does the lead-in end and the main point begin to emerge?"

The same questions need to be asked about the conclusion. Where has the author made his point, and to what use has he put the material which follows this focal point? He may conclude with a summary, or he may end with narrative or description. It is the interpreter's responsibility to discover the purpose of each unit of the material and use it effectively.

When the interpreter has discovered the divisions and progressions of thought within the material, he must then examine the details of organization within each separate unit. This is important if the listeners are to perceive each section in its proper relation to every other section.

Within each unit there are "key" sentences or phrases upon which the thought progression depends. They may contain a new idea or another aspect of an idea introduced previously. The interpreter must know the position and function of each "key" so that he can establish it clearly in the minds of his audience, in its proper relationship to all the other phrases and sentences and to the whole unit.

Climax

As the interpreter discovers the "key" details within the introduction, body, and conclusion of the selection and evaluates each one in its relationship to the whole, he will be aware that they vary in degree of importance. Occasionally they will merely implant an idea or clue which will become important later in the development of plot or action. Frequently, however, they indicate a high point of logical development or of emotional impact. When this is true they may be considered as climaxes. There are often several minor climaxes leading up to and/or following the major climax. A climax may be the culmination of the logical content, the high point of emotional impact, or a combination of both. Thus we may speak of *logical* climax and *emotional* climax, remembering again that this separation is *only* for convenience in analysis and that ultimately we shall put them back together as they operate within the whole.

In a play or story, the logical climax is often called the crisis. It is that point at which the conflict becomes so intense that a resolution must occur, after which only one outcome is possible. In an essay, the logical climax occurs when the writer makes his main point with such clarity that his conclusion is inevitable. In a poem, it is the point at which he completes the logical development upon which the emotional content is based.

The emotional climax is the moment of highest emotional impact and involvement for the reader. If this seems to be a completely subjective matter, we must not forget that the writer gives us clues to follow. If our analysis has been careful and we are letting the author have his way, we will seldom fail to be moved most strongly at the point of emotional climax. The important consideration here is to be sure that we are taking into account the *whole* of the selection in our response. There are many degrees of emotion. The emotional climax may be as gentle as those in the two Frost poems at the end of this chapter or as dramatic as that found in Sophocles' *Oedipus* (page 293). If only part of a long selection is to be used, locating the climax or climaxes within that unit is especially important if the audience is to feel that it has received a complete, unified experience which reached a point of fulfillment.

Sometimes the highest emotional intensity will coincide with the logical climax. Often, however, this is not the case. The logical climax may precede the emotional high point and prepare for it. This will be true, for instance, when the emotional climax depends on a character's or speaker's response to a completed cycle of events. On the other hand, if the outcome of events depends on an emotional reaction, the emotional climax will precede the logical one, as it does in Miss Dickinson's poem: the impact of space, silence, and solitude precedes the completion of the fall.

This dual aspect of climax may seem difficult to handle, but complete understanding reinforced by experience will enable the interpreter to cope with the problem. The logical climax, for instance, will probably need a particularly high degree of mental directness. On the other hand, if the interpreter is driving too hard at the listeners' minds, the emotional climax may suffer. The audience will receive the full emotional impact only if the interpreter himself is responding as he reads. This does not mean that he pulls out all the stops and bursts into tears or shakes his fists in fury. He must, however, train himself to respond in such a way that his muscle tension is in harmony with what the words are saying. It is important to remember that literature moves on several levels and consequently may achieve its high point of logical development in one place and its emotional climax in another, although neither may be said to be independent of the other. The interpreter must always remember to put the material back together after each step in analysis, so that he may look again at the whole as a guide to the use of his own techniques.

Attitude

Attitude is a way of thinking or feeling about something. It reflects experiences and sense of values. In literature there are often two attitudes at work, the author's and that of a character or speaker whom the author has used to express his ideas.

Sometimes the author speaks in his own person, as in lyric poetry and autobiography (see Robert Frost's "For Once, Then, Something," page 37). When this is clearly the case, some knowledge of his life, his experiences, and his other writings will be useful. Nevertheless, bio-

3/28/74 For Trudy Scott

2 copies (XEROX) of each of the following pages:

pg. 38
pg. 90
pg. 109
pg. 110
pg. 118-119
pg. 127
pg. 182
pg. 371

Thanks,

Joanne

graphical details and critical writings are not infallible guides to understanding any particular example of his work. Authors, like other people, change their minds and their moods. One has only to examine the two sonnets by William Shakespeare at the end of this chapter to be aware that they exhibit quite different attitudes!

Often, however, an author uses a speaker or *persona*, a character created outside himself, to communicate his idea. When this is true, of course, his own attitude can be traced through his interest in and evaluation of such a person in a particular situation. But the interpreter's primary concern is with the attitude of the character or speaker. The speaker may closely resemble the author in his mental and attitudinal traits, as he does in Browning's "Andrea del Sarto," or he may be quite different, as in the same author's "Soliloquy of the Spanish Cloister" (page 434).

We shall have more to say about this problem in later chapters where we consider how it relates to specific types of writing. At the moment we shall concentrate on discovering how the author reveals his attitude — whether he is speaking in his own person, is thinly veiled by a compatible mouthpiece, or has created a speaker entirely outside himself.

One of the most important clues is the title. Usually a writer will indicate quite clearly in his title where he wants the focus of attention, as does Clayton Long in "Deer in the Surf" (page 40). Robert Frost gives up his conclusion in the title "For Once, Then, Something" (page 37). W. H. Auden suggests a possible inspiration for his poem, as well as a symbolic level of meaning, in the title "Musée des Beaux Arts" (page 48).

The author reveals his attitude in large part by the words he chooses. Sometimes they are filled with connotative meaning, so that the reader's natural response to the situation is heightened and carefully channelled in a particular way. Sometimes they are incongruous with the subject matter, and the reader becomes aware that the author is making a comment or value judgment as he progresses. This is true of the two fables by James Thurber at the end of this chapter. Thurber obtains much of his humor from his matter-of-fact treatment of preposterous events. Emily Dickinson chooses "cordial" social words to describe her encounter with death in "Because I Could Not Stop for Death" (page 155) in contrast to the harsh, heavy words in "I Felt a Funeral" (page 11). Robert Frost blends scientific words with informality as he addresses the star in "Choose Something Like a Star" (page 37). In short, when considered in relation to the universal implications of the subject matter, the author's style, which includes his choice of words and the way he puts them together, helps to indicate whether his attitude is one of serious high purpose, deep emotional involvement, detachment, bitterness, gentle amusement, broad humor, or satire.

An author's attitude, whether he is speaking for himself or not, influences and consequently is partially revealed by his method of organizing ideas. The way he groups words into phrases, clauses, and sentences indicates what he considers their relationship to be. The ideas put together in paragraphs or in stanzas of poetry, as a means of explaining, expanding, or limiting a key sentence, also gives us clues to attitude.

In addition to inferring the author's attitude from the "internal evidence" of the selection, it is often helpful to learn something about him as a person — to see the individual selection in the light of his whole experience. Biographies and introductions to collected works are very useful in the case of established authors. With a relatively unknown author, conclusions must often be based on nothing more than assumptions made from reading as much of his work as possible. The interpreter must be very careful, however, not to become so involved in details of the author's life that he loses sight of the specific piece of literature he is examining. His sharpest focus must be on the selection he is working with, not on the footnotes gathered together from miscellaneous sources.

The important thing to remember is that the interpreter must be concerned with the attitude of the author as nearly as it can be discovered from his title, his style, his way of life, and his other writings. It is the *author's* attitude that must come through, not the interpreter's.

Intrinsic Factors

So far we have been concerned largely with a general view of the material the interpreter chooses to use. Now we shall turn our attention to the details that work together to produce certain clearly discernible factors in a work of art. These factors, which we shall call the *intrinsic factors*,[4] will be found in varying degrees in all successful writing. But our interest here will go beyond illustration to an examination of how they function for the interpreter's more complete understanding, and how the matters we have discussed thus far relate to the effectiveness of these intrinsic factors.

The intrinsic factors are unity and harmony, variety and contrast, balance and proportion, and rhythm. They have been termed "intrinsic" because they are clearly discernible within the selection on the printed

[4] For a fuller discussion of intrinsic factors, see C. C. Cunningham, *Literature As a Fine Art* (New York: The Ronald Press, 1941). Some critics use *intrinsic* with a slightly different meaning (René Wellek and Austin Warren, for instance, in their *Theory of Literature* [New York: Harcourt, Brace & World, 1966]). Our use will follow Cunningham's, which is more limiting than Wellek and Warren's but not irreconcilable.

page and because they appear the same to all qualified judges; appreciation of them does not depend on the uniqueness and range of personal experience but on judgment of the thing itself. Since they are evident in content and structure, particularly in the relationship between the two, the interpreter will need to know exactly how they function within his own selection. He will also come to appreciate the author's skill in handling them and thus acquire another standard by which to make critical judgments.

These intrinsic factors must not be thought of as separate entities; they must be considered in relation to all the other qualities of the selection if they are to make their true contribution to the total effect. They have bearing on and are affected by the arrangement and organization of the material and also its logical meaning and emotive qualiy. After the material has been thoroughly analyzed in terms of these factors, it must, as always, be put back together again. The audience must never be aware of any one of the factors in itself, only of the total effect. As a matter of fact, analysis will show that none of them can be completely separated from the others. They overlap, correlate with, and affect each other, and many elements in the writing may contribute to more than one of them within a simple selection. Yet each makes its subtle contribution to the whole. We shall discuss the intrinsic factors very briefly and then identify and examine them in a piece of writing.

UNITY AND HARMONY

Unity is the combining and ordering of all the parts that make up the whole. It consists of those elements of content and form which hold the writing together and keep the reader's and listeners' minds focused on a total effect.

Unity may be achieved in a number of ways: through a character in a play or story, the narrator of a story, or a discernible speaker in a poem. It may also be achieved through attitude. A character, speaker, or narrator may serve as a unifying core by remaining relatively unchanged while others develop around him; or he may go through a clear and unmistakable process of development, which in itself holds the material together. Again, unity may be strengthened by singleness of setting. It may depend on the limitation or progression of time. Many stories, for example, take the characters and incidents in chronological sequence, with an implied or explicit time progression in transitions like "and then," "next," "a few hours later," "after this," and so on. Miss Dickinson used this method most skillfully in the poem we examined in the preceding chapter. Of course, such transitions are closely related to method of organization. Within the larger framework of organization numerous details contribute subtly to the unification of the overall effect. It is impossible to list all the things to be found in this category. The interpreter must approach each piece of literature as a new problem and by careful analysis find everything the author has provided for holding the selection together.

Harmony is the appropriate adjustment of parts to one another to form a satisfying whole. In literature it is the concord between the idea and the way that idea is expressed. Harmony is achieved in part through the author's choice of words, his sentence structure, and the relationship of phrases and clauses within the sentences. Obviously, then, it depends to a large extent on elements of style. In poetry, structural elements serve to enhance it. Another important source of harmony is the selection of details to set up associations in the readers' minds. Thus harmony is paired with unity. Although they differ somewhat in definition, they are clearly interdependent and must function together if the writing is to achieve its intended effect.

VARIETY AND CONTRAST

A picture all in one color or a musical composition with only one repeated melody is, except in rare cases where a special effect is achieved through monotony, dull and uninteresting. In the same way, a piece of literature which lacks variety and contrast is not likely to hold attention for long.

Variety is provided when two things of the same general kind differ from each other in one or more details. For example, several characters of the same age, sex, and social background may agree essentially but express themselves differently. Or one character at two or more points of his development may retain his unifying qualities but demonstrate his reactions in varying ways.

Contrast implies a sharper differentiation. It is concerned with the opposition or unlikeness of associated things. One character may be set against another by his responses to a situation or by his actions and motivations. He may be contrasted in appearance, age, wisdom, emotion, or any number of other attributes. One place or time may be contrasted with another. Quiet may be set against noise, dark against light, hope against despair, positive elements against negative. This is the basic effect Miss Hoyt was trying for in "The Sense of Death."

Thus variety and contrast are closely related. They function together to provide a change of emphasis or to heighten an effect. They are extremely effective in holding attention. The interpreter will find them invaluable in the clues they give him for vocal and physical vividness. At no time, however, must either the writer or the interpreter allow variety and/or contrast to become so strong that the proper relationship of the parts to the whole is destroyed. These two factors must always be held within the bounds of unity and harmony.

BALANCE AND PROPORTION

Balance and proportion are less easy to evaluate than the other intrinsic factors we have discussed. The test to be applied is the effectiveness with which they implement the other factors and contribute to the effect of the whole.

Since *proportion provides balance,* the two must be considered together. A seesaw or teeter-totter balances when the middle brace is exactly the same distance from each end of the board. When equal weights are placed at each end, that balance is retained. But when a heavier weight is placed on one end of the board than on the other, the balance is destroyed. Balance can be restored by an adjustment of proportions — either by moving the brace toward the end on which the heavier weight rests or by moving the heavier object closer to the point on which the board rests.

When equal weights or quantities lie at equal distances from a central point, the balance is said to be symmetrical. Identical candlesticks for example, placed equidistant from the center of a mantelpiece provide symmetrical balance. Perfect balance is satisfying to the senses, but sometimes the asymmetrical or unequal balance achieved by an adjustment of distances, weights, and masses may be more interesting and effective. Instead of the candlesticks on the mantel, there may be a tall plant at one end and a low bright-colored bowl at the other. These two objects do not agree in size and shape, but the bulk or weight of the one is somehow balanced by the intensity of the other.

Balance also exists within a piece of literature. It is brought about by the intensity or the proportion of content on either side of the point at which the entire selection seems to pivot and change direction. This point of balance occurs at the crisis in a story or a play. In a poem we call it the *fulcrum* because a poem, especially a lyric poem, does not use conflict in the same way a play or a story does. This fulcrum or point of balance may or may not coincide with either the logical or the emotional climax.

The principle of point of balance is even more important in the consideration of brief, compact selections than in longer units, and the interpreter will find it particularly helpful in poetry. For example, in the twelfth line of "I Felt a Funeral" attention shifts from the funeral and the things of the earth to space. This, then, is the fulcrum of the poem. One of the requirements of an Italian or Petrarchan sonnet, for instance, is that its thought turn after the eighth line, and we find that "Deer in the Surf," to mention only one example, does exactly that—although it departs, as do many modern sonnets, from the classic rhyme scheme.

Some selections seem to reach their balance point almost exactly in the middle—that is, there is about the same amount of material leading up to and following the fulcrum. This is the case, for example, in Anne Sexton's poem about her brother (page 41). The first twenty-four lines are about him as a child, the last twenty-two about him as a soldier. Such symmetrical balance gives the interpreter a fairly easy problem. He need only be sure that he builds to the proper point and does not allow the interest to sag thereafter. If the author has arranged his material so that such handling is achieved without too much difficulty, he may be considered successful in his use of symmetrical balance.

Frequently, however, especially among modern writers, the balance will be off-center. In many cases, the greater proportion of the total material will precede the fulcrum. This is certainly true in Kunitz' "I Dreamed That I Was Old" (page 46). Such asymmetrical balance is effective in producing sudden shock or a feeling of unrest. It is effective, however, only when the author has been careful to weight the smaller proportion of material with enough vividness and intensity to enable it to hold its own against the greater number of words it must balance. When this has been taken care of in the writing—as it should be—the interpreter need only make use of the clues the author has given him and add the proper amount of emotional intensity, emphasis, and stress to the smaller unit to achieve perfect balance in his performance.

RHYTHM

Rhythm in literature is usually thought of as an element of poetic structure, such as the relationship between stressed and unstressed syllables. But it is an important aspect of content as well. Rhythm of content is to be found in both logical and emotional content as they operate together. We shall delay a discussion of structural rhythm until the later chapters on prose style and poetic structure.

Rhythm of content may be established in numerous ways in both prose and poetry, and it will begin to emerge as the interpreter studies details of organization and style. For example, in Dickinson's "I Felt a Funeral" there is a steady alternation between references to the speaker in the poem and to "them." In "Choose Something Like a Star" the attention shifts back and forth from the speaker to the star, with an up-and-back-down pattern. In "Deer in the Surf" attention shifts from "her" to "we," as suggested in the first line ("her tracks . . . astonished us"). Both participants are kept in focus. The briefer the selection, the more important this factor is likely to be.

The selection from Genesis I at the end of this chapter is a very clear example of rhythm of content in prose. Here the style so clearly underscores the progression of events that the effect is one of a steady build to the climax — the creation of man. Each step in the process leading up to it — the creation of the firmament, the waters, the trees and plants and animals — has its own introduction, its own point of completion, and its own conclusion. Each step is introduced by a low-keyed declaration of God's intention. Immediately the command is given, with the full assurance that it will be carried out. The act is performed and God's approval is stated. Thus each unit builds to its own minor climax, and each of the succeeding steps increases in importance until we reach the creation of man.

Rhythm of content is also established by the location, frequency, and intensity of emotional builds and minor climaxes. This is certainly the technique in Genesis I. It is also a factor in "I Felt a Funeral," as we shall see when we reach our detailed analysis of this short poem later in this chapter.

Drama has a rhythm set up by its acts and scenes as well as by the dialogue within the scenes. In addition to shifts in focus of attention from one character to another and the builds and drops in emotional content and tension, scenes alternate (not necessarily exactly, of course) between the active and the static. Some scenes will suspend the main plot for the development of a subplot or humor. Shakespeare uses this technique with particular skill.

Thus the recurrent shift of attention from one character to another or from one place or time to another, or the alternation of description and narration or dialogue and exposition can set up a rhythm of content. The rhythm of emotional quality can be measured by the increased and decreased intensity of the reader's response and becomes evident as the minor climaxes are discovered. As we analyze more deeply, we shall discover innumerable ways of identifying and expressing this factor.

Rhythm of content is important to an interpreter because it is closely related to holding an audience's attention. Most people are able to concentrate fully and exclusively on an idea for only a brief span of time. The skillful writer allows for this fatigue or wavering of attention and permits the reader to relax from time to time. By understanding and conveying this rhythm of concentration, the interpreter can do the same for his audience.

Furthermore, listeners cannot be held at a high emotional pitch for very long at a time. In spite of themselves, and in spite of the interpreter's best efforts, they experience a sense of relaxation following the high points of emotional response. The wise writer and the informed interpreter will provide for this relaxation so that the emotional climaxes may be more effective, especially if they depend on accumulation of feeling. Rhythm is also, as we have seen, an excellent device for keeping variety and contrast in control.

The interpreter will receive a great deal of help from the intrinsic factors within a piece of literature. His problem is how to go about finding them and using the understanding gained from this analysis in his preparation and performance. Each selection will differ from every other in the degree of importance which must be attached to the various factors. The interpreter must let the author have his way, using what is actually *in* the writing rather than trying to fit it to a preconceived pattern. His first step should always be to look at his selection carefully and discover everything he can that the author has given him to work with. Then and *only then* should he concern himself specifically with unity and harmony, variety and contrast, balance and proportion, and rhythm. A careful consideration of these intrinsic factors will help him put the piece of literature back together so that all the elements operate within the organic whole.

A Sample Analysis

In the previous chapter we observed that Miss Dickinson's poem ranked somewhat higher than Miss Hoyt's when we measured them against the touchstones of universality, individuality, and suggestion. Let us look again at Miss Dickinson's "I Felt a Funeral" to discover how some of the details operate to insure the intrinsic factors as well. Since it is so brief, we shall repeat it here and number the lines for easier reference.

1	I felt a Funeral, in my Brain,
2	And Mourners to and fro
3	Kept treading — treading — till it seemed
4	That Sense was breaking through —
5	And when they all were seated,
6	A Service, like a Drum —
7	Kept beating — beating — till I thought
8	My Mind was going numb —
9	And then I heard them lift a Box
10	And creak across my Soul
11	With those same Boots of Lead, again,
12	Then Space — began to toll,
13	As all the Heavens were a Bell,
14	And Being, but an Ear,
15	And I, and Silence, some strange Race
16	Wrecked, solitary, here —

17   And then a Plank in Reason, broke,
18   And I dropped down, and down —
19   And hit a World, at every Crash,
20   And Got through knowing — then —

There are probably no words in this poem that need to be looked up in the dictionary. In our earlier discussion, we touched briefly on the connotation of some of them. We shall come back to this matter later — indeed it is impossible to avoid it in a selection so filled with suggestion — but for the moment we shall move on to organization.

The first line gives the complete opening situation. We know that she "felt" rather than saw a funeral and that she felt it in her brain. Immediately the possibility opens up that this poem is not about an actual funeral but about a sensation instead and, in a highly poetic way, an analogy. It may be the sense of death. It may be despair. It may be both. In any case, it is sensation within the rational part of one's body. That is a paradox in itself. Miss Dickinson takes two stanzas to establish this essential paradox, which we may consider as the introduction. The third and fourth stanzas take us from the tightly enclosed earthly "place" to space and the almost intolerable tolling followed by silence. On the opening line of the final stanza, we begin the descent and the conclusion of the experience. Thus the organization is really very simple and unified, and the logical climax is located in the last line, where the experience reaches its only possible outcome.

Though each stanza has its own emotional build, the major emotional climax coincides with the fulcrum, where heaviness is suddenly replaced by space and sound swells to sudden silence. The poem turns from earth, in a sense, to space in the final line of the middle stanza. After the weight of the box, the "creak across my Soul," which strongly suggests a creak across a floor, and the "Boots of Lead," we are suddenly confronted with the sharply contrasting vast and empty expanse of space. This is, as we have said, the fulcrum. It is approximately in the center of the poem and causes no trouble as far as balance and proportion of stanzas is concerned. Our next step will be to look closely at some details to see how they contribute to the intrinsic factors.

The poem gives us a sense of continuing development, and yet without real speed except for lines 19 and 20, where the drop occurs. This is achieved in part by the structure. The effect of steady continuation first suggested in "to and fro" is strengthened by the connectives "and," "till," "and when," "and then." It is interesting that the "and's" increase sharply in the last stanza so that the drop picks up speed and the experience is terminated with the final "then."

The verb forms also help to create this effect. Though the entire poem is in the past tense, there is a subtle variation within it. The repetition in "Kept treading — treading" and "Kept beating — beating" and "down and down" and the imperfect tense of "was breaking," "was going" give a feeling of action continuing over a period of time. It is interesting to notice, however, that at the fulcrum there is a shift into the infinitive with "began to toll," followed immediately by a subjunctive form throughout the entire fourth stanza ("As" in line 13 certainly implies "as if"). The subjunctive is used when we speak of an hypothesis or a condition contrary to fact. The final stanza returns to the simple past with "broke," "dropped," "hit," and "Got through" — about as completed a past as one can have!

We have already mentioned the use of "I felt" in the opening line. Taking the first person singular "I," we find that we move from "I felt" to "I thought," "I heard," "And I, and Silence" to "I dropped," "[I] hit," and "[I] Got through." Though the first four are evenly spaced one to a stanza, the last three occur in quick succession in the last three lines. Our attention is focused on the "I" at the opening of the poem, and then we are quickly introduced to the mourners. The rhythm of attention alternates, although not with perfect regularity, until the twelfth line, when space is introduced. We have no references to the mourners or to the funeral after that, and the next reference to "I" is "I, and Silence." A look at the funeral references will reveal that they continue at least by implication through line 13 with "toll" and "Bell," but it is really space that begins to toll and the heavens that are a bell.

When a writer returns often to a specific set of references, that set of references is called a *motif*. A motif in music, design, or literature is any detail repeated often enough to become significant. In music, it may be a phrase of melody or a set of chords. In design, it may be a leaf, a flower — a *fleur de lys* for example. In literature, the repeated reference need not be an exact repetition. It may be recurring references to the elements, such as storms, clouds, or sunshine, or to things related to each other, such as colors, nature, or trades.

The first line refers to "my Brain," and this reference is strengthened and at the same time delimited three lines later by "Sense," which we discussed in Chapter 1 as we talked about suggestion. Thus we go from "my Brain" to "it seemed," "Sense," "I thought," and "My Mind." This mental motif is not present again until the final stanza, which opens with a reference to "Reason" and closes with "knowing." We are very carefully returned to the poet with "I" in line 15 and "Reason" and "knowing" are in identical positions with "Brain" and "Sense" in the opening stanza. Though psychologists might quibble, "heard" in line 9 is more physical than mental. The next reference is to "Soul," then to "Being," and then to "Race," a large, general, abstract category rather than a specific personal reference. Moreover, the race is "strange," "Wrecked," and most important, "solitary." Even more subtle is the use of "Ear" with "Being." Thus lines 9 through 16 form a unit which differs from the rest of the poem in motif. As we have remarked, there is also a shift in verb form, and it is the only place where the sentence continues past the stanza break without being broken by a dash.

A simple listing by line (see following page) will make this discussion more graphic. We must remember, however, that a list is not a poem. It is useful only as a step in analysis. In the interest of clarity we shall omit the capitals.

Remembering that the intrinsic factors are closely related and that a detail may contribute to more than one of them, let us see how what we have found relates to unity and harmony, variety and contrast, balance and proportion, and rhythm.

The use of "I" and "my" is a strong unifying factor. It is clearly established in the first ten lines and returned to in line 15 and throughout the final stanza. The connectives and the simple progression of events also help to hold the poem together. The mental motif opens and closes the poem and is constant throughout, except for the middle portion where it is weaker but still operating in "heard" and "as [if]." The sound motif with the contrasting silence is heavy in the beginning, reaches a high level at the fulcrum, is somehow strengthened by the sudden silence, and returns with force in the final stanza. A feeling of weight and heaviness begins in the first stanza, reaches its peak in "lift a Box" and "Boots of Lead," and recurs in "Plank . . . broke" in lines 18 and 19.

Harmony cannot be fully appreciated until we have examined poetic structure, but certainly the heaviness just referred to and the continuing, unbroken downward progression are harmonious with such a sensation as is here described. "Drum" suggests funeral drums; and a tolling bell, also associated with funerals, prolongs the mood. "Wrecked," "broke," and "Crash" help to suggest the destruction following the tolling of space. Careful examination will reveal a remarkable harmony between what is being said and the connotation and sound of the words with which it is said.

Within the unity of this brief poem, we find enough variety and contrast to hold our interest. A look at the funeral motif and the sound motif indicates that Miss Dickinson used very subtle variety indeed. Too much variety within so brief a poem would seriously threaten unity, especially since contrast is so sharp. The poet's isolation is contrasted with the multiplicity of people in "Mourners" and "they all," until the isolation reaches its culmination in "I, and Silence . . . solitary." Their actions are contrasted with her immobility and numbing sensations. Space and the heavens are set off against weight and the tangible things of earth. Silence is set against a crescendo of sound. It is, in fact, because of contrast that the fulcrum operates so successfully.

Balance and proportion offer no real problem here since there are almost

Line	Persons	Mental and Physical Motifs	Connectives	Verb Forms	Funeral Motifs	Sound and Silence
1	I my	I felt my brain		I felt	funeral	
2	mourners		and		mourners	
3	they (implied)	it seemed	till	kept treading treading it seemed		treading treading
4	my (implied)	sense		was breaking		
5	they (mourners)		and when	were seated		
6					service drum	drum
7	I	I thought	till	kept beating beating I thought		beating beating
8	my	my mind		was going		
9	I them (mourners)	I heard	and then	I heard lift	box	heard them
10	them (implied) my	my soul	and	creak		creak across
11	their (implied)				lead	boots of lead
12		space	then	began to toll	toll	toll **FULCRUM**
13		heavens		as [if] . . . were	bell	bell
14		being ear	and	as [if] . . . were (implied)		ear
15	I and silence	race	and . . . and	as [if] . . . were (implied)		silence
16				as [if] . . . were (implied)		solitary
17		reason	and then	broke		plank broke
18	I		and . . . and	dropped		
19	I (implied)		and	hit		crash
20	I (implied)	knowing	and then	got through		

an equal number of lines and amount of emotional weight on either side of the fulcrum. The build to the fulcrum is steady. Immediately after the point of balance is reached, the action ceases momentarily so that even though the emotional and logical climaxes fall in the second portion of the poem, they do not overbalance the heaviness and familiarity of the funeral motif in the first section. Moreover, the emotional climax is controlled by the abstractions ("the Heavens," "Being," and "strange Race"). After the emotional climax, the speed picks up, and the repeated use of "and" tightens the progression to the conclusion.

Rhythm of content is strongest in the shift from the poet to the mourners which we mentioned earlier, and in the focus on their actions and then on her responses. Again, there is not enough time for a very elaborate pattern of rhythm of content in twenty short lines. As we continue to look at the poem, however, we are aware that both the variety and the contrast make a rhythmic contribution, as do some of the elements in unity.

There are innumerable small details which also contribute to the intrinsic factors. We cannot resist calling attention to the remarkable spacing of "treading," "creak across," and "Plank," all of which suggest floor boards, and to the positioning of "heard" and "Ear" and "Silence." The use of the already familiar "I" with "heard" controls the unity, and "heard" prepares us for "toll," "Bell," "Ear," "Silence," "Plank . . . broke," and finally "Crash."

Now the question arises of what the interpreter does with all this discovery. The answer is that he uses it fully and with complete confidence in his author. Whether or not the writer was conscious of using all the elements, or indeed of the intrinsic and extrinsic factors as such, is beside the point. It is the interpreter's responsibility to find everything the writer has given him to work with. He then goes about the difficult task of synthesis. It is here that he begins his work as an artist. Slowly, step by step, he puts all the parts together again so that the selection is once more an ordered work of literary art and not a mere listing of details. An analysis like the one we have just completed usually results in increased respect for and confidence in the author. If he has not been completely successful, the interpreter will realize where the writing is weak and thus have additional criteria for literary judgment.

The approach used for this brief poem may also be used for longer poems and for prose. Of course, in a longer poem or piece of prose the writer has more time to develop his material; therefore the fulcrum or crisis may not be as compact as it is in Miss Dickinson's poem. Furthermore, every selection, whether prose or poetry, will differ from every other in the relative importance of the extrinsic and intrinsic factors. Sometimes unity and harmony will be less important than variety. As we have seen, in "I Felt a Funeral" variety is less significant than contrast. In any case, the interpreter cannot begin to evaluate the intrinsic factors until he has found out what is in the material he has chosen.

As the interpreter begins to work on the material aloud in preparation for sharing it with his audience, he will find that the things he discovered in analysis serve as a guide to the use of his voice and body. He knows what unifies the material. He knows where the variety is and can use it to hold attention without letting it violate the essential unity and harmony. His awareness of rhythm of content and of the location of the fulcrum becomes a guide for climaxes as well as for progression. In other words, he knows where the selection is going and exactly how it gets there.

Frequently, as the interpreter works on the literature aloud, he gains new insights and hears new melodies. Thus it is wise for him to begin oral preparation well in advance of performance. He needs to let the writing work on him as he works on it. He should start with the whole selection each time he begins a rehearsal session. After two or three readings of the whole, he should turn his attention to details and how they operate for unity and harmony. Then he should put the material back together. Finally, he should consider the other intrinsic factors, returning each time to the total achievement.

The interpreter must remember that his audience does not want a reading of his analysis; it wants to share the experience of the literature. If the analysis has been thorough and the preparation sound, the interpreter may trust his author and himself. But unless he knows exactly what the author has done, he cannot possibly re-create his work.

Selections for Analysis and Oral Interpretation

Each of these selections must be analyzed thoroughly. Do not try to make them follow the pattern of the Dickinson poem, however, because every piece of writing differs from every other. Look at all the details we have discussed and then decide which ones contribute to unity and harmony, where variety and contrast exist within the unity and harmony. Find the fulcrum and climaxes, and consider balance and proportion. Look carefully for rhythm of content. Remember that details may contribute to more than one of the intrinsic factors. Start with the whole poem and let it work on you until you feel comfortable with it. Then move into objective analysis. After each step, go back to the complete poem and see how the pieces fit together. Remember that your audience wants the whole poem, not the separate pieces.

The word choice in this Frost poem was mentioned within the chapter. Notice how the address to the star works with the poet's comment to us to set up a rhythm of content. Watch for the shift from "you" to "us."

Choose Something Like a Star . . . / ROBERT FROST

O Star (the fairest one in sight),
We grant your loftiness the right
To some obscurity of cloud —
It will not do to say of night,
Since dark is what brings out your light.
Some mystery becomes the proud.
But to be wholly taciturn
In your reserve is not allowed.
Say something to us we can learn
By heart and when alone repeat.
Say something! And it says, 'I burn.'
But say with what degree of heat.
Talk Fahrenheit, talk Centigrade.
Use language we can comprehend.
Tell us what elements you blend.
It gives us strangely little aid,
But does tell something in the end.
And steadfast as Keats' Eremite,
Not even stooping from its sphere,
It asks a little of us here.
It asks of us a certain height,
So when at times the mob is swayed
To carry praise or blame too far,
We may choose something like a star
To stay our minds on and be staid.

Frost displays quite a different attitude in this poem. Compare the sentence lengths with those in the poem above. The final questions will take careful handling. He is asking both himself and us. Neither of us can say for sure — but there was "something" beyond just a surface reflection of himself.

For Once, Then, Something / ROBERT FROST

Others taunt me with having knelt at well-curbs
Always wrong to the light, so never seeing
Deeper down in the well than where the water
Gives me back in a shining surface picture

From *Complete Poems of Robert Frost*. Copyright 1923, 1949 by Holt, Rinehart and Winston, Inc. Copyright renewed 1951 by Robert Frost. Reprinted by permission of Holt, Rinehart and Winston, Inc.

Me myself in the summer heaven godlike
Looking out of a wreath of fern and cloud puffs.
Once, when trying with chin against a well-curb,
I discerned, as I thought, beyond the picture,
Through the picture, a something white, uncertain,
Something more of the depths — and then I lost it.
Water came to rebuke the too clear water.
One drop fell from a fern, and lo, a ripple
Shook whatever it was lay there at bottom,
Blurred it, blotted it out. What was that whiteness?
Truth? A pebble of quartz? For once, then, something.

The next two Fables For Our Time *present similar problems in balance and proportion in handling the "moral." Watch carefully for clues to attitude in the word choice and grammatical structure.*

The Little Girl and the Wolf / JAMES THURBER

One afternoon a big wolf waited in a dark forest for a little girl to come along carrying a basket of food to her grandmother. Finally a little girl did come along and she was carrying a basket of food. "Are you carrying that basket to your grandmother?" asked the wolf. The little girl said yes, she was. So the wolf asked her where her grandmother lived and the little girl told him and he disappeared into the wood.

When the little girl opened the door of her grandmother's house she saw that there was somebody in bed with a nightcap and nightgown on. She had approached no nearer than twenty-five feet from the bed when she saw that it was not her grandmother but the wolf, for even in a nightcap a wolf does not look any more like your grandmother than the Metro-Goldwyn lion looks like Calvin Coolidge. So the little girl took an automatic out of her basket and shot the wolf dead.

Moral: It is not so easy to fool little girls nowadays as it used to be.

The Unicorn in the Garden / JAMES THURBER

Once upon a sunny morning a man who sat in a breakfast nook looked up from his scrambled eggs to see a white unicorn with a gold horn quietly cropping the roses in the garden. The man went up to the bedroom where his wife was still asleep and woke her. "There's a unicorn in the garden," he said. "Eating roses." She opened one unfriendly eye and looked at him. "The unicorn is a mythical beast," she said, and turned her back on him. The man walked slowly downstairs and out into the garden. The unicorn was still there; he was now browsing among the tulips. "Here, unicorn," said the man, and he pulled up a lily and gave it to him. The unicorn ate it gravely. With a high heart, because there was a unicorn in his garden, the man went upstairs and roused his wife again. "The unicorn," he said, "ate a lily." His wife sat up in bed and looked at him, coldly. "You are a booby," she said, "and I am going to have you put in the booby-hatch." The man, who had never liked the words "booby" and "booby-hatch," and who liked them even less on a shining morning when there was a unicorn in the garden, thought for a moment. "We'll see about that," he said. He walked over to the door. "He has a golden horn in the middle of his forehead," he told her. Then he went back to the garden to watch the unicorn; but the unicorn had gone away. The man sat down among the roses and went to sleep.

As soon as the husband had gone out of the house, the wife got up and dressed as fast as she could. She was very excited and there was a gloat in her eye. She telephoned the police and she telephoned a psychiatrist; she told them to hurry to her house and bring a strait-jacket. When the police and the psychiatrist arrived they sat down in chairs and looked at her, with great interest. "My husband," she said, "saw a unicorn this morning." The police looked at the psychiatrist and the psychiatrist looked at the police. "He told me it ate a lily," she said. The psychiatrist looked at the police and the police looked at the psychiatrist. "He told me it had a golden horn in the middle of its forehead," she said. At a solemn signal from the psychiatrist, the police leaped from their chairs and seized the wife. They had a hard time subduing her, for she put up a terrific struggle, but they finally subdued her. Just as they got her into the strait-jacket, the husband came back into the house.

"Did you tell your wife you saw a unicorn?" asked the police. "Of course not," said the husband. "The unicorn is a mythical beast." "That's all I wanted to know," said the psychiatrist. "Take her away. I'm sorry, sir, but your wife is as crazy as a jay bird." So they took her away, cursing and screaming, and shut her up in an institution. The husband lived happily ever after.

Moral: Don't count your boobies until they are hatched.

An analogy operating in this poem establishes its unity and harmony as well as its rhythm of content. It emerges clearly after the eighth line, where the fulcrum begins.

Deer in the Surf / CLAYTON LONG

(Olympic Peninsula: 1957)

Her tracks were what astonished us at first.
Down by the surf, looking toward the sea,
What was that deer about? What did she see?
From green of trees, rushing to be immersed
In paler green, we'd come with turn of dawn.
So she, with other purpose, and otherwise,
Found the shore where twisted driftwood lies.
We thought, but got no good conclusions drawn.

The hounds she knew were of a fiercer kind
Than grumbled in our chastened blood. Some chance
Encounter, a forest shadow out of place,
Loosed the flashing hounds within her mind,
Spread those great eyes wide with frightened grace,
And struck the forest to her maddened dance.

Anne Sexton is often spoken of as a poet of the "confessional" school. This
poem is an outgrowth of her actual experience in an institution, but her skill
takes it beyond fact. The long sentence with its nursery rhyme construction
of clauses must be used as a connected unit. The last sentence is an important contrast. The speaker's mental disturbance must not be overplayed.
She is perfectly and detachedly in control of her logic.

Ringing the Bells / ANNE SEXTON

And this is the way they ring
the bells in Bedlam
and this is the bell-lady
who comes each Tuesday morning
to give us a music lesson
and because the attendants make you go
and because we mind by instinct,
like bees caught in the wrong hive,
we are the circle of crazy ladies
who sit in the lounge of the mental house

and smile at the smiling woman
who passes us each a bell,
who points at my hand
that holds my bell, E flat,
and this is the gray dress next to me
who grumbles as if it were special
to be old, to be old,
and this is the small hunched squirrel girl
on the other side of me
who picks at the hairs over her lip,
who picks at the hairs over her lip all day
and this is how the bells really sound,
as untroubled and clean
as a workable kitchen,
and this is always my bell responding
to my hand that responds to the lady
who points at me, E flat;
and although we are no better for it,
they tell you to go. And you do.

This poem by the same author is in quite a different style and tone. Notice the return to and variation on some of the lines in the first stanza as they appear again after the fulcrum.

For Johnny Pole on the Forgotten Beach / ANNE SEXTON

In his tenth July some instinct
taught him to arm the waiting wave,
a giant where its mouth hung open.
He rode on the lip that buoyed him there
and buckled him under. The beach was strung
with children paddling their ages in,
under the glare of noon chipping
its light out. He stood up, anonymous
and straight among them, between
their sand pails and nursery crafts.
The breakers cartwheeled in and over
to puddle their toes and test their perfect
skin. He was my brother, my small

Johnny brother, almost ten. We flopped
down upon a towel to grind the sand
under us and watch the Atlantic sea
move fire, like night sparklers;
and lost our weight in the festival
season. He dreamed, he said, to be
a man designed like a balanced wave . . .
how someday he would wait, giant
and straight.

Johnny, your dream moves summers
inside my mind.

He was tall and twenty that July,
but there was no balance to help;
only the shells came straight and even.
This was the first beach of assault;
the odor of death hung in the air
like rotting potatoes; the junkyard
of landing craft waited open and rusting.
The bodies were strung out as if they were
still reaching for each other, where they lay
to blacken, to burst through their perfect
skin. And Johnny Pole was one of them.
He gave in like a small wave, a sudden
hole in his belly and the years all gone
where the Pacific noon chipped its light out.
Like a bean bag, outflung, head loose
and anonymous, he lay. Did the sea move fire
for its battle season? Does he lie there
forever, where his rifle waits, giant
and straight? . . . I think you die again
and live again,

Johnny, each summer that moves inside
my mind.

The following excerpt from a novel about an ancient Greek actor whose father
was also a famous actor could be begun or ended after paragraph nine if it is
too long for practical classroom use. Remember that all the women's roles
were played by men and that masks were used. There are several minor climaxes which still would have some effect on the man remembering them. Let

them build so that the deliberately undercut comments which follow them bring us and the actor back to his present maturity.

FROM *The Mask of Apollo* / MARY RENAULT

At three, I was Medea's younger son, though I can't remember it; I don't suppose I knew I was on a stage. My father told me later how he had brought home his Medea mask beforehand, in case it frightened me; but I only stuck my fingers through its mouth. It is hard to make actors' children take masks seriously, even the most dreadful; they see them too soon, too near. My mother used to say that at two weeks old, to keep me from the draft, she tucked me inside an old Gorgon,[1] and found me sucking the snakes.

I do remember, though, quite clearly, playing Astyanax to his Andromache. I was turned six by then, for Astyanax has to work. The play was Euripides' *The Women of Troy.* My father told me the plot, and promised I should not really be thrown off the walls, in spite of all the talk about it. We were always acting out such tales as a bedtime game, with mime, or our own words. I loved him dearly. I fought for years to go on thinking him great.

"Don't look at the Herald," he said to me at rehearsal. "You're not supposed to know what he means, though any child would that was right in the head. Take all your cues from me."

He sent me out in front, to see the masks as the audience saw them. Climbing up high, above the seats of honor, I was surprised to find how human they looked, and sad. While I was there he did his part as Cassandra, god-mad with two torches. I knew it by heart, from hearing him practice. It was his best role, everyone agrees. After that he changed masks, ready for Andromache. This is the play where they bring her in from the sacked city on a cart piled up with loot, her child in her arms, just two more pieces of plunder. A wonderful bit of theater. It never fails.

I was still small enough to be used to women's arms; it was odd to feel, under the pleated dress I grasped at, the hard chest of a man, holding each breath and playing it out with the phrases, the rib cage vibrant like the box of a lyre. If one thinks, I suppose most men's sons would die of shame to hear their fathers weep and lament in the voice of a woman. But as he never missed his exercises, I must have heard them from the first day I drew breath: old men, young men, queens and booming tyrants, heroes, maidens and kings. To me it was the right of a man to have seven voices; only women made do with one.

[1] The mask of Medusa, whose hair was snakes.

When the day came, I was still aggrieved there was no mask for me, though I had been told again and again children did not use them. "Never mind," said my father, "the time will come." Then he pulled his own mask down, the smiling face going into the solemn one. He was in the prologue as Athene.

Outside the parodos[2] the cart was waiting, drawn by four oxen, with the gilded spoils of Troy. At last came the call boy, and my father in the pale mask of the shorn-haired widow. He clambered up, someone hoisted me after, he settled me on his knee, and the oxen started.

Out beyond the tall gateway was the great curve of the theater. I was used to the empty tiers. Now, filled with faces, it seemed vast and unknown, murmuring and dangerous as the sea. My father's voice whispered, "Don't look at the audience. You're scared of strangers. Think how they chopped up your poor old granddad. Lean on me."

This is not how I myself would direct Astyanax. He is Hector's son; I like him alert and bold, thinking no evil till the time. But my father knew his business too. Even the men were sighing as we came slowly on into the orchestra; I could hear the little coos and cries of the women, floating on this deep bass. Suddenly it took hold of me. My father and I, by ourselves, were doing this with fifteen thousand people. We could carry them all to Troy with us, make them see us just as we chose to be. I can taste it still, that first sip of power.

Then I felt their will reach out to me. It was like the lover's touch, which says, Be what I desire. All power has its price. I clung to Andromache my mother and leaned upon her breast; but the hands I answered to were Artemidoros the actor's. As they molded me like wax and sculptured us into one, I knew the many-headed lover had caught him too; I felt it through both our skins. Yet I felt him innocent. He did not sell, but gave freely, love for love.

The Herald came, with the news that I must die. I remembered I was not supposed to heed him; but I thought I should look sorry for my mother's grief, so I reached up and touched the mask's dead hair. At this I heard sighing and sobbing rise like a wave. It was coming from the block where the hetairas[3] sit; they love a good cry more than figs. But it was a few years yet before I knew enough to look for them.

When the Herald bore me off to die, I thought everyone backstage would be there to pay me compliments; but only the wardrobe master's assistant came in a hurry, to strip me naked and paint on my bloody wounds. My father, who had exited soon after me, ran over to pat my bare belly as I lay, and say, "Good boy!" Then he was off; it's a quick change from Andromache to Helen, what with the jewels and so on. It is always a splendid costume, meant to show up against the other captives'. The

2 A raised area behind a fortification which would be part of the set for this play.
3 The women in the audience, usually courtesans, who sat in a special section.

mask was most delicately painted, and had gold-wreathed hair. He went on, and I heard his new voice, bland and beguiling, answering angry Menelaos.

Soon after came my cue to be brought on, dead. They stretched me out on the shield, and a couple of extras lifted it. The day was warm, but the breeze tickled my skin, and I gave my mind to lying limp as I had been told. The chorus called out the dreadful news to my grannie Hecuba; lying, eyes shut, while the Herald made a long speech about my death, I prayed Dionysos not to let me sneeze. There was a pause which, because I could not see, seemed to last forever. The whole theater had become dead silent, holding its breath. Then a terrible low voice said just beside me:

"Lay down the circled shield of Hector on the ground."

I had been well rehearsed for this scene, but not with Hecuba. I had nothing to do but keep still; and this was Kroisos, the leading man. He was then at the peak of his powers, and, fairly enough, did not expect to tutor children. I had seen the mask, and that was all.

I had already heard him, of course, lamenting with Andromache; but that is her scene, and I had my own part to think of. Now, the voice seemed to go all through me, making my backbone creep with cold. I forgot it was I who was being mourned for. Indeed, it was more than I.

No sweetness here, but old pride brought naked to despair, still new to it, a wandering stranger. At the bottom of the pit a new pit opens, and still the mind can feel. Cold hands touched my head. So silent were the tiers above us, I heard clearly, from the pines outside, the murmur of a dove.

I was not seven years old. I think I remember; but no doubt I have mixed in scraps from all sorts of later renderings, by Theodoros or Philemon or Thettalos; even from my own. I dreamed of it, though, for years, and it is from this I remember certain trifles — such as the embroidery on his robe, which had a border of keys and roses — glimpsed between my eyelids. When I think of these dreams it all comes back to me. Was it Troy I grieved for, or man's mortality; or for my father, in the stillness that was like a wreath of victory on Kroisos' brow? All I remember for certain is my swelling throat, and the horror that came over me when I knew I was going to cry.

My eyes were burning. Terror was added to my grief. I was going to wreck the play. The sponsor would lose the prize; Kroisos, the crown; my father would never get a part again; we would be in the streets begging our bread. And after the play, I would have to face terrible Hecuba without a mask. Tears burst from my shut eyes; my nose was running. I hoped I might die, that the earth would open or the skene catch fire before I sobbed aloud.

The hands that had traced my painted wounds lifted me gently. I was gathered into the arms of Hecuba; the wrinkled mask with its down-turned mouth bent close above. The flute, which had been moaning softly through the speech, getting a cue, wailed louder. Under its sound, Queen Hecuba whispered in my ear, "Be quiet, you little bastard. You're dead."

I felt better at once. All I had been taught came back to me. We had work to do. I slid back limp as his hands released me; neatly, while he washed and shrouded me, he wiped my nose. The scene went through to the end.

The sharply off-center balance is of great importance here as we mentioned within the chapter. The emotional build of "wept" and "bitter longing" must be used fully and the turn at the fulcrum is abrupt. Be sure you understand the allusions in line eight.

I Dreamed That I Was Old / STANLEY KUNITZ

I dreamed that I was old: in stale declension
Fallen from my prime, when company
Was mine, cat-nimbleness, and green invention,
Before time took my leafy hours away.

My wisdom, ripe with body's ruin, found
Itself tart recompense for what was lost
In false exchange: since wisdom in the ground
Has no apocalypse or pentecost.

I wept for my youth, sweet passionate young thought,
And cozy women dead that by my side
Once lay: I wept with bitter longing, not
Remembering how in my youth I cried.

This familiar story of the creation of the world has a climax within each unit. These climaxes build up to the high point of the creation of man. It is interesting to compare this modern version with older versions and with James Weldon Johnson's poem "The Creation" (page 75).

Genesis I: 1–16 / THE TORAH

When God began to create the heaven and the earth — ²the earth being unformed and void, with darkness over the surface of the deep and a wind from God sweeping over the water — ³God said, "Let there be light"; and there was light. ⁴God saw that the light was good, and God separated the light from the darkness. ⁵God called the light Day, and the darkness He called Night. And there was evening and there was morning, a first day.

⁶God said, "Let there be an expanse in the midst of the water, that it may separate water from water." ⁷God made the expanse, and it separated the water which was below the expanse from the water which was above the expanse. And it was so. ⁸God called the expanse Sky. And there was evening and there was morning, a second day.

⁹God said, "Let the water below the sky be gathered into one area, that the dry land may appear." And it was so. ¹⁰God called the dry land Earth, and the gathering of waters He called Seas. And God saw that this was good. ¹¹And God said, "Let the earth sprout vegetation: seed-bearing plants, fruit trees of every kind on earth that bear fruit with the seed in it." And it was so. ¹²The earth brought forth vegetation: seed-bearing plants of every kind, and trees of every kind bearing fruit with the seed in it. And God saw that this was good. ¹³And there was evening and there was morning, a third day.

¹⁴God said, "Let there be lights in the expanse of the sky to separate day from night; they shall serve as signs for the set times — the days and the years; ¹⁵and they shall serve as lights in the expanse of the sky to shine upon the earth." And it was so. ¹⁶God made the two great lights, the greater light to dominate the day and the lesser light to dominate the night, and the stars. ¹⁷And God set them in the expanse of the sky to shine upon the earth, ¹⁸to dominate the day and the night, and to separate light from darkness. And God saw that this was good. ¹⁹And there was evening and there was morning, a fourth day.

²⁰God said, "Let the waters bring forth swarms of living creatures, and birds that fly above the earth across the expanse of the sky." ²¹God created the great sea monsters, and all the living creatures of every kind that creep, which the waters brought forth in swarms; and all the winged birds of every kind. And God saw that this was good. ²²God blessed them, saying, "Be fertile and increase, fill the waters in the seas, and let the birds increase on the earth." ²³And there was evening and there was morning, a fifth day.

²⁴God said, "Let the earth bring forth every kind of living creature: cattle, creeping things, and wild beasts of every kind." And it was so.

²⁵God made wild beasts of every kind and cattle of every kind, and all kinds of creeping things of the earth. And God saw that this was good. ²⁶And God said, "Let us make man in our image, after our likeness. They shall rule the fish of the sea, the birds of the sky, the cattle, the whole earth, and all the creeping things that creep on earth." ²⁷And God created man in His image, in the image of God He created him; male and female He created them. ²⁸God blessed them and God said to them, "Be fertile and increase, fill the earth and master it; and rule the fish of the sea, the birds of the sky, and all the living things that creep on earth."

²⁹God said, "See, I give you every seed-bearing plant that is upon all the earth, and every tree that has seed-bearing fruit; they shall be yours for food. ³⁰And to all the animals on land, to all the birds of the sky, and to everything that creeps on earth, in which there is the breath of life, [I give] all the green plants for food." And it was so. ³¹And God saw all that He had made, and found it very good. And there was evening and there was morning, the sixth day.

Be sure you know the allusion upon which the last eight lines depend. The length and structure of the sentences are interesting. Keep them operating as units of thought with the variety carefully contained within them.

Musée des Beaux Arts / W. H. AUDEN

About suffering they were never wrong,
The Old Masters: how well they understood
Its human position; how it takes place
While someone else is eating or opening a window or just
    walking dully along;
How, when the aged are reverently, passionately waiting
For the miraculous birth, there always must be
Children who did not specially want it to happen, skating
On a pond at the edge of the wood:
They never forgot
That even the dreadful martyrdom must run its course
Anyhow in a corner, some untidy spot
Where the dogs go on with their doggy life and the torturer's horse
Scratches its innocent behind on a tree.

In Brueghel's *Icarus*, for instance: how everything turns away
Quite leisurely from the disaster; the ploughman may

Have heard the splash, the forsaken cry,
But for him it was not an important failure; the sun shone
As it had to on the white legs disappearing into the green
Water; and the expensive delicate ship that must have seen
Something amazing, a boy falling out of the sky,
Had somewhere to get to and sailed calmly on.

*The episodes which immediately precede this excerpt have to do with a period
of time which the author spent as a bellboy in a hotel in Jackson, Mississippi.
Although his education in Jim Crow living began much earlier, it took on a
particularly bitter form during those months when he was growing into ado-
lescence. The literary style here changes swiftly to reinforce attitude. Keep in
mind that the incidents related are not presented because they are important
in themselves but rather as steps in his education in "ethics."*

FROM *The Ethics of Living Jim Crow* / RICHARD WRIGHT

I had learned my Jim Crow lessons so thoroughly that I kept the hotel
job till I left Jackson for Memphis. It so happened that while in
Memphis I applied for a job at a branch of the optical company. I was
hired. And for some reason, as long as I worked there, they never brought
my past against me.

Here my Jim Crow education assumed quite a different form. It was no
longer brutally cruel, but subtly cruel. Here I learned to lie, to steal, to
dissemble. I learned to play that dual role which every Negro must play if
he wants to eat and live.

For example, it was almost impossible to get a book to read. It was
assumed that after a Negro had imbibed what scanty schooling the state
furnished he had no further need for books. I was always borrowing
books from men on the job. One day I mustered enough courage to ask
one of the men to let me get books from the library in his name. Surprisingly, he consented. I cannot help but think that he consented because
he was a Roman Catholic and felt a vague sympathy for Negroes, being
himself an object of hatred. Armed with a library card, I obtained books
in the following manner: I would write a note to the librarian, saying:
"Please let this nigger boy have the following books." I would then sign
it with the white man's name.

When I went to the library, I would stand at the desk, hat in hand,
looking as unbookish as possible. When I received the books desired I

From pp. xxvii–xxx in "The Ethics of Living Jim Crow" from *Uncle Tom's Children*
by Richard Wright. Copyright 1937 by Richard Wright. Reprinted by permission of
Harper & Row, Publishers, Inc.

would take them home. If the books listed in the note happened to be out, I would sneak into the lobby and forge a new one. I never took any chances guessing with the white librarian about what the fictitious white man would want to read. No doubt if any of the white patrons had suspected that some of the volumes they enjoyed had been in the home of a Negro, they would not have tolerated it for an instant.

The factory force of the optical company in Memphis was much larger than that in Jackson, and more urbanized. At least they liked to talk, and would engage the Negro help in conversation whenever possible. By this means I found that many subjects were taboo from the white man's point of view. Among the topics they did not like to discuss with Negroes were the following: American white women; the Ku Klux Klan; France, and how Negro soldiers fared while there; French women; Jack Johnson; the entire northern part of the United States; the Civil War; Abraham Lincoln; U. S. Grant; General Sherman; Catholics; the Pope; Jews; the Republican Party; slavery; social equality; Communism; Socialism; the 13th and 14th Amendments to the Constitution; or any topic calling for positive knowledge or manly self-assertion on the part of the Negro. The most accepted topics were sex and religion.

There were many times when I had to exercise a great deal of ingenuity to keep out of trouble. It is a southern custom that all men must take off their hats when they enter an elevator. And especially did this apply to us blacks with rigid force. One day I stepped into an elevator with my arms full of packages. I was forced to ride with my hat on. Two white men stared at me coldly. Then one of them very kindly lifted my hat and placed it upon my armful of packages. Now the most accepted response for a Negro to make under such circumstances is to look at the white man out of the corner of his eye and grin. To have said: "Thank you!" would have made the white man *think* that you *thought* you were receiving from him a personal service. For such an act I have seen Negroes take a blow in the mouth. Finding the first alternative distasteful, and the second dangerous, I hit upon an acceptable course of action which fell safely between these two poles. I immediately — no sooner than my hat was lifted — pretended that my packages were about to spill, and appeared deeply distressed with keeping them in my arms. In this fashion I evaded having to acknowledge his service, and, in spite of adverse circumstances, salvaged a slender shred of personal pride.

How do Negroes feel about the way they have to live? How do they discuss it when alone among themselves? I think this question can be answered in a single sentence. A friend of mine who ran an elevator once told me:

"Lawd, man! Ef it wuzn't fer them polices 'n' them ol' lynch-mobs, there wouldn't be nothin' but uproar down here!"

Make full use of the direct discourse in this poem without breaking the unity. Notice how carefully the stanzas are balanced. Identification of the persona or speaker's age and attitude is essential for the humor.

When I was one-and-twenty / A. E. HOUSMAN

> When I was one-and-twenty
> I heard a wise man say,
> "Give crowns and pounds and guineas
> But not your heart away;
> Give pearls away and rubies
> But keep your fancy free."
> But I was one-and-twenty,
> No use to talk to me.
>
> When I was one-and-twenty
> I heard him say again,
> "The heart out of the bosom
> Was never given in vain;
> 'Tis paid with sighs a plenty
> And sold for endless rue."
> And I am two-and-twenty,
> And oh, 'tis true, 'tis true.

This brief poem is packed with nouns which reflect the title. Notice, however, the turn at the fulcrum where, without breaking the sentence, our attention is drawn to "dust from the walls of institutions" with which the last five lines are concerned. The dust becomes the epitome of all the other references.

Dolor / THEODORE ROETHKE

> I have known the inexorable sadness of pencils,
> Neat in their boxes, dolor of pad and paper-weights,
> All the misery of manilla folders and mucilage,
> Desolation in immaculate public places,
> Lonely reception rooms, lavatory, switchboard,

The unalterable pathos of basin and pitcher,
Ritual of multigraph, paper-clip, comma,
Endless duplication of lives and objects,
And I have seen dust from the walls of institutions,
Finer than flour, alive, more dangerous than silica,
Sift, almost invisible, through long afternoons of tedium,
Dropping a fine film on nails and delicate eyebrows,
Glazing the pale hair, the duplicate grey standard faces.

This modern translation of an ancient myth provides an excellent opportunity for variety. The author's attitude is also important and is reflected in his choice of words, especially in the dialogue.

FROM *Paris and Helen* / ROBERT GRAVES

Now, just before the birth of Paris, Hecabe had dreamed that she brought forth a faggot from which wriggled countless fiery serpents. She awoke screaming that the city of Troy and the forests of Mount Ida were ablaze. Priam at once consulted his son Aesacus, the seer, who announced: 'The child about to be born will be the ruin of our country! I beg you to do away with him.'

A few days later, Aesacus made a further announcement: 'The royal Trojan who brings forth a child today must be destroyed, and so must her offspring!' Priam thereupon killed his sister Cilla, and infant son Munippus, born that morning from a secret union with Thymoetes, and buried them in the sacred precinct of Tros. But Hecabe was delivered of a son before nightfall, and Priam spared both their lives, although Herophile, priestess of Apollo, and other seers, urged Hecabe at least to kill the child. She could not bring herself to do so; and in the end Priam was prevailed upon to send for his chief herdsman, one Agelaus, and entrust him with the task. Agelaus, being too soft-hearted to use a rope or a sword, exposed the infant on Mount Ida, where he was suckled by a she-bear. Returning after five days, Agelaus was amazed at the portent, and brought the waif home in a wallet — hence the name 'Paris' — to rear with his own new-born son; and took a dog's tongue to Priam as evidence that his command had been obeyed. But some say that Hecabe bribed Agelaus to spare Paris and keep the secret from Priam.

Paris's noble birth was soon disclosed by his outstanding beauty, intelligence, and strength: when little more than a child, he routed a band

From *The Greek Myths* by Robert Graves. Reprinted by permission of Collins-Knowlton-Wing, Inc. Copyright © 1955 by Robert Graves. Also reprinted by permission of the author and A. P. Watt and Son.

of cattle-thieves and recovered the cows they had stolen, thus winning the surname Alexander. Though ranking no higher than a slave at this time, Paris became the chosen lover of Oenone, daughter of the river Oeneus, a fountain-nymph. She had been taught the art of prophecy by Rhea, and that of medicine by Apollo while he was acting as Laomedon's herdsman. Paris and Oenone used to herd their flocks and hunt together; he carved her name in the bark of beech-trees and poplars. His chief amusement was setting Agelaus's bulls to fight one another; he would crown the victor with flowers, and the loser with straw. When one bull began to win consistently, Paris pitted it against the champions of his neighbours' herds, all of which were defeated. At last he offered to set a golden crown upon the horns of any bull that could overcome his own; so, for a jest, Ares turned himself into a bull, and won the prize. Paris's unhesitating award of this crown to Ares surprised and pleased the gods as they watched from Olympus; which is why Zeus chose him to arbitrate between the three goddesses.

He was herding his cattle on Mount Gargarus, the highest peak of Ida, when Hermes, accompanied by Hera, Athene, and Aphrodite, delivered the golden apple and Zeus's message: 'Paris, since you are as handsome as you are wise in affairs of the heart, Zeus commands you to judge which of these goddesses is the fairest.'

Paris accepted the apple doubtfully. 'How can a simple cattleman like myself become an arbiter of divine beauty?' he cried. 'I shall divide this apple between all three.'

'No, no, you cannot disobey Almighty Zeus!' Hermes replied hurriedly. 'Nor am I authorized to give you advice. Use your native intelligence!'

'So be it,' sighed Paris. 'But first I beg the losers not to be vexed with me. I am only a human being, liable to make the stupidest mistakes.'

The goddesses all agreed to abide by his decision.

'Will it be enough to judge them as they are?' Paris asked Hermes, 'or should they be naked?'

'The rules of the contest are for you to decide,' Hermes answered with a discreet smile.

'In that case, will they kindly disrobe?'

Hermes told the goddesses to do so, and politely turned his back.

Aphrodite was soon ready, but Athene insisted that she should remove the famous magic girdle, which gave her an unfair advantage by making everyone fall in love with the wearer. 'Very well,' said Aphrodite spitefully. 'I will, on condition that you remove your helmet — you look hideous without it.'

'Now, if you please, I must judge you one at a time,' announced Paris, 'to avoid distractive arguments. Come here, Divine Hera! Will you other two goddesses be good enough to leave us for awhile?'

'Examine me conscientiously,' said Hera, turning slowly around, and displaying her magnificent figure, 'and remember that if you judge me the fairest, I will make you lord of all Asia, and the richest man alive.'

'I am not to be bribed, my Lady. . . . Very well, thank you. Now I have seen all that I need to see. Come, Divine Athene!'

'Here I am,' said Athene, striding purposefully forward. 'Listen, Paris, if you have enough common sense to award me the prize, I will make you victorious in all your battles, as well as the handsomest and wisest man in the world.'

'I am a humble herdsman, not a soldier,' said Paris. 'You can see for yourself that peace reigns throughout Lydia and Phrygia, and that King Priam's sovereignty is uncontested. But I promise to consider fairly your claim to the apple. Now you are at liberty to put on your clothes and helmet again. Is Aphrodite ready?'

Aphrodite sidled up to him, and Paris blushed because she came so close that they were almost touching.

'Look carefully, please, pass nothing over. . . . By the way, as soon as I saw you, I said to myself: "Upon my word, there goes the handsomest young man in Phrygia! Why does he waste himself here in the wilderness herding stupid cattle?" Well, why do you, Paris? Why not move into a city and lead a civilized life? What have you to lose by marrying someone like Helen of Sparta, who is as beautiful as I am, and no less passionate? I am convinced that, once you two have met, she will abandon her home, her family, everything, to become your mistress. Surely you have heard of Helen?'

'Never until now, my Lady. I should be most grateful if you would describe her.'

'Helen is of fair and delicate complexion, having been hatched from a swan's egg. She can claim Zeus for a father, loves hunting and wrestling, caused one war while she was still a child — and, when she came of age, all the princes of Greece were her suitors. At present she is married to Menelaus, brother of the High King Agamemnon; but that makes no odds — you can have her if you like.'

'How is that possible, if she is already married?'

'Heaven! How innocent you are! Have you never heard that it is my divine duty to arrange affairs of this sort? I suggest now that you tour Greece with my son Eros as your guide. Once you reach Sparta, he and I will see that Helen falls head over heels in love with you.'

'Would you swear to that?' Paris asked excitedly.

Aphrodite uttered a solemn oath, and Paris, without a second thought, awarded her the golden apple.

By this judgment he incurred the smothered hatred of both Hera and Athene, who went off arm-in-arm to plot the destruction of Troy; while Aphrodite, with a naughty smile, stood wondering how best to keep her promise.

Word choice in this poem was mentioned within the chapter. It provides an interesting contrast to the Dickinson poem analyzed earlier.

Because I Could Not Stop for Death / EMILY DICKINSON

Because I could not stop for Death,
He kindly stopped for me;
The carriage held but just ourselves
And Immortality.

We slowly drove, he knew no haste,
And I had put away
My labor, and my leisure too,
For his civility.

We passed the school where children played
At wrestling in a ring;
We passed the fields of gazing grain,
We passed the setting sun.

We paused before a house that seemed
A swelling of the ground;
The roof was scarcely visible,
The cornice but a mound.

Since then 'tis centuries; but each
Feels shorter than the day
I first surmised the horses' heads
Were toward eternity.

The following two sonnets by Shakespeare offer an interesting contrast to each other. You will need to be sure you understand the grammatical structure of the sentences to have the references clear when they are read aloud.

Sonnet 18 / WILLIAM SHAKESPEARE

Shall I compare thee to a summer's day?
Thou art more lovely and more temperate:
Rough winds do shake the darling buds of May,
And summer's lease hath all too short a date:

Copyright 1942 by William Allan Neilson and Charles Jarvis Hill. From *The Complete Plays and Poems of William Shakespeare*, edited by William Allan Neilson and Charles Jarvis Hill. Reprinted by permission of Houghton Mifflin Company.

Sometime too hot the eye of heaven shines,
And often is his gold complexion dimm'd;
And every fair from fair sometime declines,
By chance, or nature's changing course untrimm'd;
But thy eternal summer shall not fade,
Nor lose possession of that fair thou ow'st,
Nor shall death brag thou wander'st in his shade,
When in eternal lines to time thou grow'st;
   So long as man can breathe, or eyes can see,
   So long lives this, and this gives life to thee.

Sonnet 130 / WILLIAM SHAKESPEARE

My mistress' eyes are nothing like the sun;
Coral is far more red than her lip's red:
If snow be white, why then her breasts are dun;
If hairs be wires, black wires grow on her head.
I have seen roses damask'd, red and white,
But no such roses see I in her cheeks;
And in some perfumes is there more delight
Than in the breath that from my mistress reeks.
I love to hear her speak, yet well I know
That music hath a far more pleasing sound:
I grant I never saw a goddess go;
My mistress, when she walks, treads on the ground:
   And yet, by heaven, I think my love as rare
   As any she belied with false compare.

Be sure you understand all the unusual words in this poem. Take particular care in handling the grammatical structure so that all the long, involved sentences are clear.

The Snow-Storm / RALPH WALDO EMERSON

Announced by all the trumpets of the sky,
Arrives the snow, and, driving o'er the fields,
Seems nowhere to alight: the whited air
Hides hills and woods, the river, and the heaven,

And veils the farm-house at the garden's end.
The sled and traveller stopped, the courier's feet
Delayed, all friends shut out, the housemates sit
Around the radiant fireplace, enclosed
In a tumultuous privacy of storm.

Come see the north wind's masonry.
Out of an unseen quarry evermore
Furnished with tile, the fierce artificer
Curves his white bastions with projected roof
Round every windward stake, or tree, or door.
Speeding, the myriad-handed, his wild work
So fanciful, so savage, nought cares he
For number or proportion. Mockingly,
On coop or kennel he hangs Parian wreaths;
A swan-like form invests the hidden thorn;
Fills up the farmer's lane from wall to wall,
Maugre the farmer's sighs; and at the gate
A tapering turret overtops the work.
And when his hours are numbered, and the world
Is all his own, retiring, as he were not,
Leaves, when the sun appears, astonished Art
To mimic in slow structures, stone by stone,
Built in an age, the mad wind's nightwork,
The frolic architecture of the snow.

Be sure you understand the references to the sights a "Pagan" would see. The sections of the sentences set off by semicolons must be kept related to the whole. They are grammatically dependent on each other. The fulcrum is abrupt and strong. Give yourself and your audience time to make the adjustment.

The World Is Too Much With Us / WILLIAM WORDSWORTH

The world is too much with us; late and soon,
Getting and spending, we lay waste our powers:
Little we see in Nature that is ours;
We have given our hearts away, a sordid boon!
This Sea that bares her bosom to the moon;
The winds that will be howling at all hours,
And are up-gathered now like sleeping flowers;
For this, for every thing, we are out of tune;

It moves us not. — Great God! I'd rather be
A Pagan suckled in a creed outworn;
So might I, standing on this pleasant lea,
Have glimpses that would make me less forlorn;
Have sight of Proteus rising from the sea;
Or hear old Triton blow his wreathèd horn.

Bibliography

Many of the following books deal with the evaluation of art in various forms, but they are applicable to the art of literature as well.

Beardsley, Monroe, Robert Daniel, and Glenn Leggett. *Theme and Form.* Englewood Cliffs, New Jersey: Prentice-Hall, Inc., 1956.

   Brief essays on the structure of the various modes of literature combined with an anthology arranged according to themes.

Geiger, Don. *The Sound, Sense, and Performance of Literature.* Chicago: Scott, Foresman and Company, 1963.

   The interpreter of literature is the special interest of this book, built on the premise that oral interpretation is in itself an act of criticism.

Langer, Susanne K. *Philosophy in a New Key.* Cambridge, Massachusetts: Harvard University Press, 1942.

   Discussion of art as cognitive discourse.

Pepper, Stephen. *The Work of Art.* Bloomington, Indiana: Indiana University Press, 1955.

   Propounds his theory of funding and fusion in response and contains a clarification of object and vehicle.

Richards, I. A. *Principles of Literary Criticism.* New York: Harcourt, Brace and Company, 1925.

   One of the classics of modern literary criticism.

Vivas, Eliseo, and Murray Krieger. *The Problems of Aesthetics.* New York: Holt, Rinehart and Winston, Inc., 1935.

   Essays on the nature and problems of aesthetics as a discipline and criteria for judgment.

Wellek, René, and Austin Warren. *Theory of Literature,* Third Edition. New York: Harcourt, Brace and World, Inc. (Harvest Books), 1966.

   Discussion of the nature and function of literature with helpful notes and good bibliography.

The fields of linguistics and semantics also have bearing on the interpreter's study of literature. The following books are good introductions to the two fields.

Hayakawa, S. I. *Language in Thought and Action.* New York: Harcourt, Brace and Company, 1949.

The basic principles of semantics as they relate to speech and literature.

Sapir, Edward. *Language: An Introduction to the Study of Speech.* New York: Harcourt, Brace and Company, 1921. Harvest Books edition, HB7, 1949.

A clear exposition of the principles of linguistics and their application to literary study.

Chapter 3   The Use

The interpreter's first problem, as we have seen, is to find suitable material which will be worth the time and effort he must spend in preparing it for performance. After he has chosen his selection, his next responsibility is to gain as complete an understanding as possible of all its elements — its logical meaning, its emotional overtones, and its qualities of literary craftsmanship. Finally, when he feels that he thoroughly understands the material, he must turn his attention to the most effective way of communicating it to the audience. It is at this point that control of the twofold instrument of body and voice becomes important. Just as a musician cannot give a satisfactory performance without having first perfected the handling of his instrument, so an interpreter, who is both instrument and instrumentalist, cannot do justice to the selection he has chosen unless he devotes some attention to technique.

The term "technique" does not imply artificiality in the use of voice and body. In fact, the finer the technique, the less apparent it is to the audience. Technique may be defined as style of performance. The style of performance in the art of interpretation must be unobtrusive if the interpreter is not to call attention to what he is doing and thus distract the audience from the material. Display of vocal or physical virtuosity as an end in itself has been outmoded since the decline of the "mechanical" school of elocution in the nineteenth century. Such display is considered in poor taste today, and is interesting only to the degree that an exhibition of calisthenics or a recital of scales and arpeggios would be

of the Body in Oral Interpretation

interesting. The interpreter develops and uses technique as a means of communicating the material, not the material as a vehicle for displaying technique.

The modern interpreter develops vocal and bodily technique as a pianist practices scales, so that his muscles may respond without apparent prompting or effort to the demands he makes on them. Only then can he hope to achieve a total response from his audience. Overt attention to technique belongs to the rehearsal period and has no place in performance. During a performance the interpreter's attention should be concentrated on his material and on the response of his audience to that material. If his preparation has been adequate, the muscles of the vocal mechanism and of the entire body will respond according to the habits set up in rehearsal. As skill increases through experience, this habitual response will become more dependable.

Since oral interpretation obviously implies the use of the voice, it would seem that the vocal mechanism should be considered first. It is a mistake, however, to overlook or underestimate the subtle but very significant role of the body in oral interpretation. As a matter of fact, the body begins the process of communication even before the voice is heard. From the moment the audience is aware of the physical presence of the interpreter, he is arousing a response, establishing in them what the psychologists call a "set," or condition of mental readiness, toward what they are about to hear. It is true that he does not begin to communicate the *specific* material until he starts to speak, but by his bodily action he gives intimations of his mental attitude toward himself, his audience, and his material. His state of physical tension or relaxation reflects his emotional state, which in turn is often indicative of his confidence in himself and in the selection he has chosen.

An audience is quick to resent an overbearing or cocky attitude and is equally quick to question the authority of a speaker who seems unsure of his ability. The interpreter will strike a happy medium when he is confident that he is adequately prepared, that his material is well chosen, and that his audience is capable of understanding and responding to that material. When he has doubts on any of these points, his uncertainty will be reflected in his physical bearing, and the audience will sense his insecurity and unconsciously share his discomfort. It is important, then, for the reader to avoid any mannerisms that may give an unfavorable impression, whether of virtuosity, arrogance, or lack of self-confidence.

Thus through bodily carriage and physical actions the interpreter sets up definite attitudes in the audience toward himself and his material, quite apart from the specific content of that material. But the body performs an even more important function in relation to the specific content. The physical reaction of the interpreter to his material, accompanying and indeed springing out of his mental response, is a vital factor in drawing a complete response from the audience.

Not only does bodily action in all its aspects give clues to the audience about the interpreter, but it is of vital importance in suggesting character and reflecting author and/or *persona* attitude. We have all seen speakers whom we did not believe for a moment because something in what we saw belied what we heard. In drama, the way a character moves and the tone of his entire body often reveal as much as or more than the words he uses. The visual and the oral work together as the interpreter communicates his own thoughts or those of another.

Bodily action may be defined as any movement of the muscles of the body. This movement may be a full gesture, or it may be merely a relaxation or tension of the small muscles around the eyes or mouth, across the shoulders and back, in the legs, or a combination of any or all of these. It includes the approach to and departure from the platform, movements of the head, arms, shoulders, hands, torso, and legs, change of posture, facial expression, and the muscle tone of the entire body. The modern interpreter has no desire to establish or call upon a set of rules for posture and gesture. He knows that the test of bodily action is its effectiveness in the communication of the literature at hand, rather than its conformity to technical rules. Bodily action is effective only when it is completely suited to the material and thus helps to elicit the desired response; when it is so unobtrusive as to go unnoticed except insofar as it contributes to that response; and when it is free of personal mannerisms which would distract the audience.

Posture

The basis of effective bodily action is good *posture*, which is primarily a matter of proper positional relations among the various parts of the body. Good posture is that arrangement of the bones and muscles which puts the body in its perfect natural alignment so that each unit does its job of supporting and controlling the bodily structure without undue tension or strain. When this is accomplished, the entire body is balanced, flexible, responsive, and coordinated. Barring physical defects, good posture requires nothing more complicated than standing straight and easy from the ankle bone to the crown of the head so that the various parts of the skeletal structure fall naturally into place. This is not as easy as it sounds, however, if bad posture has been allowed to develop.

Because the muscles of the body are easily trained and adjust themselves rather quickly, tensions and strains may not be apparent after bad posture is firmly established, even though they continue to exist. For example, one of the most prevalent errors in posture is to allow the spine to sway in at the center of the back. This causes the neck to be thrust forward and the pelvis to be tipped out of natural alignment in order to preserve the balance of the skeletal structure. Such posture, which produces tight muscles in the throat and across the base of the ribs, interferes with natural voice placement and inhibits proper breath control. At the opposite extreme, when the spine is allowed to curve out so that the shoulders droop, the chest sags and the pelvis tips forward, causing the stomach to protrude. Such posture crowds the important diaphragm muscle and cuts down on the breath capacity, besides giving an impression of lack of energy and enthusiasm.

Gesture

A *gesture* may be defined as any clearly discernible movement which helps express or emphasize an idea. In the usual sense, gestures are overt actions of the hands and arms — and occasionally the head and shoulders. These parts of the body do not function as separate entities, however, but involve a "follow-through" which both affects and is affected by the degree of muscular tension in every other part of the body. Thus it is impossible to treat gesture apart from an awareness of posture and of muscle tone in general.

Unlike the oral interpreter trained in the theories and practices of the last century, when books on "elocution" and "expression" devoted several chapters to detailed study of gesture, the modern reader is little concerned with gesture as a separate, specific part of his training. Rather he believes that gesture is an integral part of bodily action, that it grows out of his response to his material, and that it must aid in complete communication. If an action does not help communicate the material, it is not a gesture; it is only a distracting and extraneous movement which violates the basic principle that no action by an interpreter should call attention to itself. This is not to say that gestures are not to be used. It *is* to say that their use must be dictated by the needs of the material being presented.

The interpreter's use of gestures normally depends on two considerations. The first, as we have said, is his material. The interpreter will use whatever bodily action is necessary to make the meaning clear to his audience and to convey the emotional quality effectively. He is attempting to create a total impression in the minds of his listeners and thus help them re-create what the author has experienced. Too many or too specific gestures are likely to call attention to the person of the interpreter and hence distract from the material.

The second consideration in the use of gestures is the personality of the speaker. Some interpreters respond physically to their material with greater ease than others. If gesturing is difficult for the interpreter and makes him self-conscious, he should forget about it and concentrate on empathic response and muscle tone. He should use whatever gestures he wishes in rehearsal until he can handle them effectively when he needs them, but he should never let gestures as such become an issue when he is before an audience. When the interpreter's concentration shifts in performance from his material to the problem of gestures, his audience will be quick to sense his preoccupation.

However, since a responsive body is such an important factor in the total process of communication, he would do well to work conscientiously on this problem during his rehearsal periods. It is often helpful to use large, exaggerated gestures in the early phases of preparation for a performance, or to move freely about the room, responding consciously and overtly to all the empathic cues and muscle imagery in the selection. This overt response during preparation is the basis of muscle memory, discussed more fully in the second chapter on drama (pages 320–380), where it is basic to character suggestion. The muscles will "remember" the big action, and muscle tone will reflect this "remembering" even after the specific overt gestures are discarded or modified.

If, on the other hand, the interpreter has a tendency to "talk with his whole body," he should use whatever gestures make him feel at ease and help him communicate his material. It is important, however, to keep in mind both facets of this advice — "make him feel at ease" and "help him communicate." There is the danger that what makes the interpreter feel at ease may distract his audience and thus actually block communication.

Perhaps the interpreter has developed certain habitual physical actions which are not gestures at all, in the sense that they do not help express the idea. He may be using a repetitious movement, such as a constant raising and lowering of one hand, a tilt of the head, or a shrug of the shoulders. Such personal mannerisms, called autistic gestures because they grow out of the interpreter's own personality, direct attention to the interpreter himself and prevent the audience from concentrating on his material.

Under ordinary circumstances, it is inadvisable for the interpreter to work before a mirror; by doing so he is likely to divorce bodily action from its proper function of communication. If, however, he suspects that he has a too-regular pattern of movement, an occasional checkup before a large mirror will help call this fault to his attention.

As we have noted, the modern interpreter does not plan specific gestures. Though he sometimes follows an explicit pattern of physical movement in the middle stage of preparation, in performance he abandons the large, explicit movements and goes forward into the realm of suggested action. He never marks passages as a reminder to execute a carefully worked out movement at a particular place. Rather, he strives for such complete understanding of the material that he will be able to respond to it fully — his gestures an integral part of that response.

A good gesture conforms to no rules except the rule of effectiveness. It is effective when it helps to communicate, is unobtrusive, and does not result in distracting mannerisms. It depends on and grows out of the reader's total response to the material. Like every other aspect of technique, gesturing must be the result of the interpreter's mental and emotional response to what is on the printed page. As such, it will be a powerful force in engendering the desired response in the listeners.

Muscle Tone

We have already referred to muscle tone in our discussion because it is impossible to talk about any effective bodily action without considering it. It happens as a result of muscle memory, complete response to the material and the interpreter's concentration on sharing that material with his audience. Usually we are not aware of it as a separate aspect of bodily action and need only to be reminded occasionally that it must not distract from or negate the other aspects of performance.

Muscle tone refers to the degree of tension or relaxation present in the entire body. It is an extremely important consideration in projecting material to an audience, because an audience responds to what it sees as strongly as to what it hears. Muscle tone can reinforce or detract from the total impression the interpreter wishes to convey.

When the posture is good, the body is in a state of controlled relaxation, with no undue muscular strain or tension. The properly poised body is flexible and responsive, and moves with coordination and fluidity. It is "all of a piece." Controlled relaxation is not to be confused with apathy or lack of physical energy. The interpreter who looks as if he is too tired, depressed, or bored to stand up straight communicates an unfortunate impression to his audience — and draws an undesirable response from them. For they reflect in their own muscle tone his sense of weariness, depression, or boredom. Relaxation is an easing of tension; it is not total disintegration. The degree of relaxation is controlled in the interest of dignity and poise, and is partly determined by the requirements of the material to be presented.

Muscle tone is affected by the mental attitude of the speaker as well as by his control of the physical aspects of posture. It will vary from obvious tension to assured, controlled relaxation in direct proportion to the interpreter's confidence in himself, his material, and his audience. Any performance will carry with it a degree of excitement which is translated into physical tension. The secret is to be able to channel that tension so that it becomes an asset instead of a hazard. The "butterflies" in the stomach are not a sign of fear but of excitement, which, properly understood and controlled, communicates itself to the audience in terms of a vital, stimulating performance. Too frequently, however, the inexperienced performer attributes this tension to stage fright — and immediately sets up a fear pattern. If the material is acceptable and preparation has been adequate, then the "butterflies" are a good sign. They are the result of excitement and involvement without which no performance can possibly succeed. Of course, if the interpreter has prepared inadequately and is really unsure of his ability, or at least is not sure that he has done the best he could, then there is no help or sympathy for him. He cannot hope to solve his problem until he is willing to put more time and effort into careful and complete preparation.

Two types of "sense imagery," which will be discussed again in the chapter on description (pages 184–214), should be mentioned in this chapter as well. They are the *kinetic* and *kinesthetic* images found in words and phrases which appeal directly to the so-called motor sense. *Kinetic* refers to a large, overt action such as "ran," "jumped," "sat," "walked," or "threw." Clearly, from what we know of muscle tone, these actions are invariably accompanied by tension or relaxation. Rarely in literature do you find a kinetic action without a clear indication of how one ran or jumped or sat or walked or threw. *How* the action was performed is *kinesthetic* — the degree of tension or relaxation which goes along with the kinetic. There is a difference between "I was terrified and I ran" and "I ran for the sheer joy of being young in summer." Or between "She sat primly waiting" and "She sat dozing in the sun." But a kinesthetic image, unlike a kinetic one, can stand alone, as in "She was drowsy and relaxed" or "I stayed perfectly still, dreading to hear the sound." A kinesthetic response is the usual response to references to height and distance. It is closely akin to emotional response and so much a part of empathy as to be considered basic to its implementation.

Empathy

One of the interpreter's most powerful tools is his control and use of empathy. Although its roots are in the classic Greek, *empathy* is a term borrowed from modern psychology. Meaning literally a "feeling into," it is defined as both "the imaginal or mental projection of oneself into the elements of a work of art" and "a mental state in which one identifies or feels himself in the same state of mind as another person or a group."[1] This "mental projection of oneself" into a piece of literature implies, of course, emotional response to the writing in addition to logical comprehension.

Every writer who deals with emotions, no matter to what degree, uses words and phrases in such relationship that they cause some mental disturbance, which may take the form of pleasure or pain, activity or repose. The interpreter responds mentally to these words and phrases as he prepares the material. If he has not experienced precisely what the author is describing or creating, he can usually recall some parallel or approximate situation which once called up in him a comparable response. As he responds emotionally to the written material, his muscles tighten or relax, usually without his conscious effort. This tightening or relaxing of the muscles affects the tone of the entire body.

The *interaction* of *emotional* and *physical* response is the basis of empathy as it concerns the interpreter. The following experiment will clarify this interaction and show how it works:

1. Shut your mind to your immediate surroundings and recall some occasion or experience which made you feel happy and exhilarated. It does not matter in the least what the experience was, as long as it made you feel particularly pleased with yourself and with your world. Spend as long as you wish in recapturing the circumstances and the accompanying emotion.

[1] H. C. Warren, ed., *Dictionary of Psychology* (Boston: Houghton Mifflin Company, 1934), p. 92.

2. Next, turn your thoughts to a set of circumstances which made you violently angry. Concentrate on every detail and allow yourself to become thoroughly resentful. This is the chance to say all the things you thought of after it was too late. Work yourself up into a state of complete irritation.

3. Now go back to the pleasant situation. Recapture the experience as completely as you can. As you allow your mood to change and the happy memory to take over, notice what is happening to your muscles.

4. Keeping your muscle tone exactly as it is, go back to the anger you felt before. Don't let a muscle tighten or change. It is clearly impossible to be as thoroughly angry as you were when your muscles were responding freely, if unconsciously.

Physical response and emotional response are inseparable and each serves to intensify the other. Try this exercise several times until you are fully aware of this interaction. It is the basis of empathy as the interpreter uses it.

A word of warning is advisable at this point. The muscular response is in itself a result of inner or mental activity. The outward or physical signs are an indication of that inner activity, never a substitute for it. The mental and emotional response must come first; the muscular response must follow.

Empathy works for the interpreter in three distinct but interdependent steps: *from* the literature to the interpreter, *from* the interpreter to his audience, and *from* the audience back to the interpreter.

As we read a piece of literature we relate to it actively. We have all had the experience of coming out of a movie or play or of finishing a book and being physically exhausted, not because we have been uncomfortable but because we have participated so thoroughly that our muscles are tired. This participation, which combines mind, emotions, and muscles, is the first step in empathy. It is partly what makes us choose a selection to read in the first place. The interpreter may lose this empathic response in the middle phases of his preparation when he is trying to balance climaxes, the fulcrum, the intrinsic factors, and all the other elements he finds in analysis. But as he gets the material back together again and looks forward to sharing it with an audience, the empathic response will come back, strengthened by his increased mastery over the parts which make up the whole. Thus the first step is the interpreter's response to the stimulus given him by the literature itself. Without this response the second step is impossible.

The second step in empathy has to do with the audience's response to the interpreter's material. This usually takes the form of an unconscious imitation of the speaker's muscle tone. When the interpreter is responding empathically to his material, he gives physical cues to his hearers, who in turn respond by muscular imitation. This muscular imitation helps intensify their emotional response. It is the same phenomenon which causes us to frown and feel depressed or irritated, to smile and feel happy, to yawn and feel tired or bored because someone else is frowning, smiling, or yawning.

The true interpreter will be aware of the value of empathy even in the way he approaches the platform. During his introduction he will use it to help establish an emotional readiness in his audience. If his selection is brief and intense, like the Dickinson poem in Chapter 2, he will find that his audience moves with him much more surely if he makes proper use of empathy. His own mental and emotional state of readiness will affect the tone of all his muscles. And the audience, by unconscious imitation of what it sees, will adopt the physical tone he is projecting.

The simple exercise on pages 67–68 shows how a contradictory muscle set can inhibit emotional response. By imitating the interpreter's physical tone, the audience puts itself into psychic readiness for the response he wishes to elicit. By unconsciously or subconsciously imitating what they see, they prepare the emotional threshold for their own response. And, of course, what they see in the interpreter is the result of his own response to the material he is bringing them.

The third step in empathy is the interpreter's ultimate reward: the audience sending back an empathic response by its concentration and its alternating tension and relaxation. Thus the cycle becomes complete: from the printed page to the interpreter, out to the audience, and back to the interpreter.

Psychologists have a complex scientific framework within which they study empathy, with varying theories to explain its source and effects. We as interpreters, however, are primarily concerned with how it works in the delicate but basic problem of interaction among the literary selection, the interpreter who presents that selection, and the members of the audience. In its simplest physical terms, empathy involves a sympathetic or imitative tension or relaxation of the muscles. As it immediately concerns the interpreter, it is at once his own muscular response to the sense and spirit of what he is reading and a means of eliciting physical and emotional response from the audience. Hence he needs sufficient control over the muscle tone of his body to enable him to react appropriately to his mental and emotional responses. The interpreter must work conscientiously to develop a flexible, responsive body so that he may make full use of all his muscles to achieve complete communication from the printed page to his audience. Understanding the principle of empathic response is vitally important to the interpreter. By a bare reading aloud, without preparation and without projecting himself into the material, he may manage to transfer the essential logical content from the printed page to the minds of his audience, but he cannot lay claim to the name of interpreter unless he makes full and artistically honest use of empathy.

Selections for Analysis and Oral Interpretation

All the following selections have a strong suggestion of physical action. In preparing them for oral interpretation, let your muscles respond completely, taking time in some cases to work out specific action, which you may or may not use in performance, to help you achieve the proper empathy. Since voice and body must work together, many of the selections at the end of the next chapter will also provide opportunities for bodily action, although they were chosen primarily because of their vocal demands.

Remember that each selection must be analyzed for organization, attitude, and the factors of art, as well as for suggested bodily action.

Be sure you understand all the allusions in this first selection. The action described is obviously not that of the speaker, but kinesthetic imagery is very strong.

The Second Coming / WILLIAM BUTLER YEATS

Turning and turning in the widening gyre
The falcon cannot hear the falconer;
Things fall apart; the centre cannot hold;
Mere anarchy is loosed upon the world,
The blood-dimmed tide is loosed, and everywhere
The ceremony of innocence is drowned;
The best lack all conviction, while the worst
Are full of passionate intensity.

Surely some revelation is at hand;
Surely the Second Coming is at hand.
The Second Coming! Hardly are those words out
When a vast image out of *Spiritus Mundi*
Troubles my sight: somewhere in sands of the desert
A shape with lion body and the head of a man,
A gaze blank and pitiless as the sun,
Is moving its slow thighs, while all about it
Reel shadows of the indignant desert birds.

The darkness drops again; but now I know
That twenty centuries of stony sleep
Were vexed to nightmare by a rocking cradle,
And what rough beast, its hour come round at last,
Slouches towards Bethlehem to be born?

This selection may profit from the use of some carefully timed gestures. The timing will be dictated by the author's attitude, which in turn is enforced by the style. Watch carefully for a rhythm of content set up by alternating action and comment.

FROM *The Complete Book of Absolutely Perfect Housekeeping*
ELINOR GOULDING SMITH

The first step in proper bedmaking is to strip the bed completely and air out the room. This is easily done by opening a window, or, if it should be too cold outside, blowing a few times. Next the mattress is turned. This is correctly done by grasping the mattress firmly at the side by the loops provided and flipping it lightly over. If, as you do this, you hear something snap and find that you can't straighten up again, you haven't got the knack. Keep practicing. As soon as the mattress is turned, get out a file and smooth off your broken nails before going on to the next step. You don't want to snag the sheets, do you? You may also, if you wish, apply some liniment to your right shoulder.*

The next step is to put on the mattress pad or mattress cover, and this should be done now as it will be very hard to do it later.

The bottom sheet is put on next. This is important. If you mix up the sheets and accidentally put the top sheet on the bottom and the bottom sheet on top, no one will get any sleep at all that night since they will all be suffering from vertigo. The bottom sheet must not only be put on the bottom, but also it is urgent that it be put on upside down and inside out to insure even wear. You see, the top sheet, which is *always* put on top (this is an absolute *rule*) is put on right side out and upside up. Then, when the sheets are changed, the top sheet is put on the bottom (this is an exception to the rule above) it is then put on inside out and upside down and the new sheet is put right side out and upside up. You must understand, however, that right side out for a top sheet is actually inside out, while inside out on the bottom sheet really means right side out. The reason for this is obvious — when you turn the

* You may now find it necessary to apply liniment to the mattress, too.

top of the top sheet down, you want the turned-down part to be right side out, not inside out. (However, don't ever turn the bottom of the bottom sheet up as this would result in utter confusion.) If this is not clear, the simplest thing to do is to change both sheets at once, or, better still, provide a nice clean pile of sweet-smelling hay or straw which can be thrown out from time to time and replaced as needed.

We are now going to place the bottom sheet on the mattress. Some women throw the sheet over the mattress any old way, and then walk around and around the bed, tugging the sheet this way and that and smoothing it out and pulling it up and down till all the life has gone out of it. This is highly imperfect bedmaking. The proper way is as follows. Take up the sheet in the hands. Grasp the sheet by the selvage at the side. Make sure the top of the sheet is toward the bottom of the bed and that the sheet is inside out (that is of course actually right side up). Also be sure the sheet is more or less centrally located, lengthwise. Now stand by the side of the bed, with your feet parallel and toes pointing straight ahead. Hold your back straight, head up, chin in, etc. Now, with one small flick of the wrists the sheet should place itself on the bed, straight, centered and smooth. If it didn't, you didn't get the flick right. Try again tomorrow. But above all, don't touch it again now. If you start tugging it about, you will never learn the right flick.

The bottom sheet must be tucked in all around before even considering the top sheet. Some women do the head and foot first and then the sides. This is inefficient. The correct way is to start at the nearest corner, *miter it firmly no matter how it struggles,* and continue once around the bed, tucking in the sides and mitering corners as you go. When you have reached the starting place, DON'T LOOK BACK.

The placing of the top sheet is exactly like the placing of the bottom sheet (except that it is now right side up, which means inside out, and with its top facing the head of the bed). The top sheet is tucked in only at the bottom. Isn't that lucky? Do not tuck it too far in, as you may then pull out the whole business, bottom sheet and all, when you withdraw your hands. If you tuck it *too* far in, you may be trapped there and never get your hands out at all. Keep your enthusiasm in check at all times.

You may now place the blankets on the bed, using the same flick of the wrist. This is a very tricky business, because it sometimes happens that at this exact moment the cat suddenly decides to take a nap on that very bed and lands in the middle just as the blankets are settling down nicely into place. In this case it is best to remain calm. Continue to make the bed *around* the animal. This may leave an unsightly bump in the center of the bed, but eventually she is certain to get hungry and will leave of her own accord. Should she fail to do this, *call a veterinarian at once* as a healthy animal is always hungry, and she may be coming down with some obscure type of cat ailment. On the other hand, she may not be suffering from cat enteritis at all, but is simply having a litter of kittens. In this case, your best bet is to sleep in a semi-circular position so as not to disturb the kittens until they are six weeks old and strong enough to make their way to somebody else's bed.

Once the blankets are on, you may fold down the top of the top sheet nicely over the blankets, and then proceed to tuck in the sides and miter the bottom corners. Some authorities believe that a fold should be made at the bottom of the bed to allow room for feet. I don't go along with this theory at all. There is no necessity for people to sleep on their backs with their feet sticking straight up. It is conducive to snoring. They should learn to sleep on their sides, with their feet nice and flat or folded well up toward the middle of the bed where there is more room. Or, better still, they can sleep on their stomachs with their toes curled down over the end of the mattress. There's *plenty* of room for their feet if they lie in the proper positions.

Many women, after making up the bed, cover it all up with a bedspread. In certain cases, this may well be the wisest maneuver. Do not forget to place the pillow (having first shaken it well) neatly at the head of the bed as placing it at the foot will only confuse things further.

During the period in which you are acquiring the flick of the wrist and using the proper self-control in regard to straightening and tugging, there may be a certain amount of complaining on the part of your family. Don't let them get away with this. Explain to them that you have made the beds in strict accord with the finest authorities (that's me) and that if the sheets are wrinkled it is no doubt due to *improper entering of the bed* on their part. If they're just going to climb in any old way, you can't be blamed for wrinkles.

In time you will acquire the knack of absolutely perfect bedmaking. Or they will become accustomed to wrinkles. (Tell them to think of their bed as a little nest.) Either way.

Muscle tone and posture will help suggest the power and strength of this Greek hero. These qualities are more important than his age. His memories of past actions and his hope for future ones will be strongly kinesthetic as he considers them, and they set up a clear rhythm of content.

Ulysses / ALFRED, LORD TENNYSON

> It little profits that an idle king,
> By this still hearth, among these barren crags,
> Matched with an agèd wife, I mete and dole

Unequal laws unto a savage race,
That hoard, and sleep, and feed, and know not me.
I cannot rest from travel; I will drink
Life to the lees. All times I have enjoyed
Greatly, have suffered greatly, both with those
That loved me, and alone; on shore, and when
Through scudding drifts the rainy Hyades
Vexed the dim sea. I am become a name;
For always roaming with a hungry heart
Much have I seen and known — cities of men,
And manners, climates, councils, governments,
Myself not least, but honored of them all, —
And drunk delight of battle with my peers,
Far on the ringing plains of windy Troy.
I am a part of all that I have met;
Yet all experience is an arch wherethrough
Gleams that untraveled world, whose margin fades
Forever and forever when I move.
How dull it is to pause, to make an end,
To rust unburnished, not to shine in use!
As though to breathe were life! Life piled on life
Were all too little, and of one to me
Little remains: but every hour is saved
From that eternal silence, something more,
A bringer of new things; and vile it were
For some three suns to store and hoard myself,
And this gray spirit yearning in desire
To follow knowledge, like a sinking star,
Beyond the utmost bound of human thought.
    This is my son, my own Telemachus,
To whom I leave the sceptre and the isle, —
Well-loved of me, discerning to fulfil
This labor, by slow prudence to make mild
A rugged people, and through soft degrees
Subdue them to the useful and the good.
Most blameless is he, centred in the sphere
Of common duties, decent not to fail
In offices of tenderness, and pay
Meet adoration to my household gods,
When I am gone. He works his work, I mine.
    There lies the port; the vessel puffs her sail;
There gloom the dark broad seas. My mariners,
Souls that have toiled, and wrought, and thought with me, —
That ever with a frolic welcome took

The thunder and the sunshine, and opposed
Free hearts, free foreheads, — you and I are old;
Old age hath yet his honor and his toil.
Death closes all; but something ere the end,
Some work of noble note, may yet be done,
Not unbecoming men that strove with Gods.
The lights begin to twinkle from the rocks;
The long day wanes; the slow moon climbs; the deep
Moans round with many voices. Come, my friends,
'Tis not too late to seek a newer world,
Push off, and sitting well in order smite
The sounding furrows; for my purpose holds
To sail beyond the sunset, and the baths
Of all the western stars, until I die.
It may be that the gulfs will wash us down;
It may be we shall touch the Happy Isles,
And see the great Achilles, whom we knew.
Though much is taken, much abides; and though
We are not now that strength which in old days
Moved earth and heaven, that which we are, we are;
One equal temper of heroic hearts,
Made weak by time and fate, but strong in will
To strive, to seek, to find, and not to yield.

Rhythm of content and empathy work together to build climaxes in this Negro "sermon." The juxtaposition of folk phrases and Biblical style is interesting. Notice that the poet has not used dialect. You must reflect empathically the tremendous scope of the actions being performed. Both kinetic and kinesthetic imagery are at work here, although the kinetic is not that of the speaker.

The Creation / JAMES WELDON JOHNSON

And God stepped out on space,
And he looked around and said:
I'm lonely —
I'll make me a world.

And far as the eye of God could see
Darkness covered everything,

From God's Trombones by James Weldon Johnson. Copyright 1927 by The Viking Press, Inc., 1954 by Grace Nail Johnson. Reprinted by permission of The Viking Press, Inc.

Blacker than a hundred midnights
Down in a cypress swamp.
Then God smiled,
And the light broke,
And the darkness rolled up on one side,
And the light stood shining on the other,
And God said: That's good!

Then God reached out and took the light in his hands
And God rolled the light around in his hands
Until he made the sun;
And he set that sun a-blazing in the heavens.
And the light that was left from making the sun
God gathered it up in a shining ball
And flung it against the darkness,
Spangling the night with the moon and stars.
Then down between
The darkness and the light
He hurled the world;
And God said: That's good!

Then God himself stepped down —
And the sun was on his right hand,
And the moon was on his left;
The stars were clustered about his head,
And the earth was under his feet.
And God walked, and where he trod
His footsteps hollowed the valleys out
And bulged the mountains up.

Then he stopped and looked and saw
That the earth was hot and barren.
So God stepped over to the edge of the world
And he spat out the seven seas —
He batted his eyes, and the lightnings flashed —
He clapped his hands, and the thunders rolled —
And the waters above the earth came down,
The cooling waters came down.

Then the green grass sprouted,
And the little red flowers blossomed,
The pine-tree pointed his finger to the sky,
And the oak spread out his arms,
The lakes cuddled down in the hollows of the ground,
And the rivers ran down to the sea;

And God smiled again,
And the rainbow appeared,
And curled itself around his shoulder.

Then God raised his arm and he waved his hand
Over the sea and over the land,
And he said: Bring forth! Bring forth!
And quicker than God could drop his hand,
Fishes and fowls
And beasts and birds
Swam the rivers and the seas,
Roamed the forests and the woods,
And split the air with their wings.
And God said: That's good!

Then God walked around,
And God looked around
On all that he had made.
He looked at his sun,
And he looked at his moon,
And he looked at his little stars;
He looked on his world
With all its living things,
And God said: I'm lonely still.

Then God sat down —
On the side of a hill where he could think;
By a deep, wide river he sat down;
With his head in his hands,
God thought and thought,
Till he thought: I'll make me a man!
Up from the bed of the river
God scooped the clay;
And by the bank of the river
He kneeled him down;
And there the great God Almighty
Who lit the sun and fixed it in the sky,
Who flung the stars to the most far corner of the night,
Who rounded the earth in the middle of his hand;
This Great God,
Like a mammy bending over her baby,
Kneeled down in the dust
Toiling over a lump of clay
Till he shaped it in his own image;

Then into it he blew the breath of life,
And man became a living soul.
Amen. Amen.

The action in this poem was clearly shared by the speaker although it also is strongly kinesthetic in recall. In the third stanza he candidly and directly demands a contrasting pair of physical reactions.

Dulce et Decorum Est / WILFRED OWEN

Bent double, like old beggars under sacks,
Knock-kneed, coughing like hags, we cursed through sludge,
Till on the haunting flares we turned our backs,
And towards our distant rest began to trudge.
Men marched asleep. Many had lost their boots,
But limped on, blood-shod. All went lame, all blind;
Drunk with fatigue; deaf even to the hoots
Of gas-shells dropping softly behind.

Gas! Gas! Quick, boys! — An ecstasy of fumbling,
Fitting the clumsy helmets just in time,
But someone still was yelling out and stumbling
And floundering like a man in fire or lime. —
Dim through the misty panes and thick green light,
As under a green sea, I saw him drowning.
In all my dreams before my helpless sight
He plunges at me, guttering, choking, drowning.

If in some smothering dreams, you too could pace
Behind the wagon that we flung him in,
His hanging face, like a devil's sick of sin;
And watch the white eyes writhing in his face,
If you could hear, at every jolt, the blood
Come gargling from the froth-corrupted lungs,
Bitter as the cud
Of vile, incurable sores on innocent tongues,
My friend, you would not tell with such high zest
To children ardent for some desperate glory,
The old Lie: Dulce et decorum est
Pro patria mori.

There are strong contrasts in empathy here between the power of God's grandeur and the tenderness of nature's freshness. Make the most of both of them, allowing the sounds of the words in combination to help you achieve the lift on which the poem opens and closes in order to balance and control the heaviness of the middle lines.

God's Grandeur / GERARD MANLEY HOPKINS

The world is charged with the grandeur of God.
   It will flame out, like shining from shook foil;
   It gathers to a greatness like the ooze of oil
Crushed. Why do men then now not reck his rod?
Generations have trod, have trod, have trod;
   And all is seared with trade; bleared, smeared with toil;
   And wears man's smudge and shares man's smell: the soil
Is bare now, nor can foot feel, being shod.

And for all this, nature is never spent;
   There lives the dearest freshness deep down things;
And though the last lights off the black West went
   Oh, morning at the brown brink eastward springs —
Because the Holy Ghost over the bent
   World broods with warm breast and with ah! bright wings.

This excerpt from a novel affords an opportunity to contrast the ease and sense of well-being Li'l Joe feels at the opening with his terrified tension in the later section. His posture and kinetic response offer clear contrasts to the two young assailants. David, the nephew he reared and who married a white girl, has now become a successful lawyer able to fulfill Gramp's lifelong dream of seeing Africa.

FROM Five Smooth Stones / ANN FAIRBAIRN

Li'l Joe was restless. Seemed as though a man had a right to be, he thought; couldn't expect a man seventy years old to sit back and fold his hands when he had a passport to Africa in his pocket. David had warned him over and over: "Watch that passport, Gramp. Don't you go carrying it around with you. Ambrose's got a safe in his taxi office. Keep it in there." But he couldn't do that. How was a man going to convince folks he was really doing something like to go to Africa unless he had something to show? He knew his people. "That's what Li'l Joe say — that's what he say — that he's going to Africa." They'd ought to have some of the needles the doctor at the health department had stuck into him, last week or two. Sick as a dog, a couple of them had made him. Man who hated needles bad as he did wasn't going through all that for nothing.

Li'l Joe thought that when he went to New York to take the plane, just before Christmas, he'd go by train. Get himself a roomette and take it easy, nothing to worry about; the Timminses were going to take care of Chop-bone, see that he stayed in the house at night, let him out in the morning, see he got fed and all. Maybe he'd even spend the money to put Chop-bone in one of these fancy cat kennels while he was gone. He didn't know just yet where he'd be landing over the water. David was taking care of that — David and Sara. He wouldn't be able to bring her to his home, and that was bad, or their children. Li'l Joe wouldn't be seeing any great-grandchildren round the house; he supposed he'd have to go where they were. "There won't be any children," David had said. "That's me talking, and I mean it. If it was a hundred years from now — maybe. But not now. Sara doesn't feel that way about it, but she doesn't know the kind of hell we'd be letting them in for. After all, could be we might have to come back over to the United States and settle down —"

Li'l Joe grinned at Chop-bone, curled in one of his favorite places, beside the clock on the mantel. "David sure talks big," he said to the cat. "Boy sure talks big. I knows that girl. Does she want chilren — chilren's what they gonna have —"

Shucks, he couldn't stay home; even though he'd be leaving in a little bit more'n a month it was still an uneasy thing, knowing David was going so far away again tomorrow. He changed his clothes, gave his shoes a brisk polish, and put on a soft tan cashmere pullover that David had brought him, under his coat. Couldn't risk catching a fresh cold, not now. Might go into complications, just when he had to be feeling good for the trip.

He knew there was a lot of talk, a lot of worry, about the school trouble and the bad things that were happening, but he hadn't realized how much tension there would be everywhere he went; he could feel it even on the streets, where there seemed to be less people than usual. He listened to stories from his friends of some of the things that were happening because a little Negro girl was trying to enter a white school, and he knew the truth of them. He knew, too, that few, if any, of them would ever see print, and that was a damned shame. World ought to know, he thought, the whole world ought to know how some of these folks can treat a li'l chile just because she's black.

Not everyone he talked with was in agreement about the school trouble. Listening to them, he wondered if he'd have had the courage to send David to a white school, if the same situation had existed when David was a child. He didn't think he would have; it would be worse for a boy.

A little boy, even if he was still chubby and round-eyed, would make the whites madder than what a little girl would. 'Saiah had been right when he'd used that old-fashioned phrase, "Days of trouble coming."

Over a beer, Li'l Joe told his favorite bartender: "I ain't going to live to see it, and you ain't either, but the time's coming it won't be like this. But there's going to be blood running first. I said it before and I says it again — "

And the bartender replied: "Don't do to talk that way, Li'l Joe, not right now. They got ears, those walls have. Can't even trust some of our own. You know that."

"Been knowing it — "

But there had been some who were glad to have something to talk about besides the school hassle, and he showed them his passport and they talked of his trip and what he would see and learn, and because he was Li'l Joe Champlin they wished him well and smiled without envy at his straight, slim back when he left them. "Sure glad for him," they said to each other. "No better man around than Li'l Joe. Sure glad — "

As he started for the bus stop, tired now, knowing he would sleep when he got home, he turned a block off his course; he'd drop in on Pop and Emma Jefferson for a cup of coffee, say hello to Ambrose if he was at his taxi office next door.

Just ahead was the building that used to be Guastella's bootleg club in the days of Prohibition and the depression. He seldom passed it he didn't remember the night years before when he had found ten dollars on the floor of the men's toilet, and how he'd gone home thinking about the things the ten dollars would buy that he and Geneva had needed so bad.

There hadn't been a night since Geneva had passed, all those years ago, he hadn't thought of her on his way home, half convincing himself a lot of times that she'd be there, just like tonight when he could almost see her, good as real, in the kitchen, happy in the new house, happy with the things he'd bought for her, smiling happy with the boy, with David.

It was when he started across the street at the corner where Guastella's used to be that footsteps behind him entered his conscious mind. That wasn't anything new. Lawd! some whites thought it was funny to follow a colored man, make him nervous, just, he supposed, so the colored man would know the whites were still around, watching everything he did. Best thing to do was stay near the curb, cross the street, and head for an all-colored bar and go inside and mingle till whoever it was had gone by; they'd be laughing, more'n likely.

But now, hearing the footsteps, remembering the stories he'd heard earlier, feeling the tension in the street, he knew an old fear, and quickened his steps, his breathing faster, shorter, under the pressure of fear, the controlled hurry.

The footsteps did not stay behind him, came abreast of him, one on each side, and he rolled his eyes quickly from right to left and saw two young men in sports shirts, sweaters, and jeans, both fair-haired, fair-skinned, with duckwing haircuts, distinguishable from each other in Li'l Joe's eyes only because the one on the right was taller.

The taller one spoke first, over Li'l Joe's head, to the other. "He's a scrawny li'l ol' nigger — "

"Yeah. Too old to bother with — "

"Hell, man, we've got him. What'll we do with him?"

"Turn him loose. He's under the limit." They both laughed.

These boys were just trying to give him a bad time; Li'l Joe told himself that, knew it to be true; they were just acting smart, but there was fear in him tonight, so much had been happening, and the fear was a heaviness in his chest and belly, a weakness in his legs. He found words, fighting off the shortness of breath, the weakness. "Ain't you young uns got nothing better to do than bully an old man?"

"We ain't bullying you, boy. You come along with us — "

"Let him alone. People are looking — "

"Hell, no. We said we'd show those black bastards what we thought of 'em, didn't we?"

Li'l Joe heard a "snick," saw metal gleam in the taller boy's hand. They were getting closer now to Ambrose's; in a minute he'd risk the metal and make a break for it. "You come along with us peaceable," the tall youth was saying. "Real peaceable." He snickered. "Hell, you ain't fit for much more than kindling wood. Not enough fat on those bones to make a good fire — nothing but spindly ol' kindling."

Somewhere inside Li'l Joe a child was screaming — "Ma! Ma! — My daddy didn't burn! Did he, Ma? Ma! Ma! *Mamma!*" and then the pain came, blotting out the little boy, tearing his chest in two, searing his arm and lancing into his mouth — came and went and came again, worse then, and he didn't have any legs, and the pavement rose and struck him and he lay there, gasping, while from somewhere a long way above him someone said, "Run! For Christ's sake, get going — " There was the sound of metal hitting the pavement beside him; then there were only the pain in his chest and the gasping struggle for the air that wasn't there. Strong arms cradled him, and a familiar voice said, "Li'l Joe. Li'l Joe! — Hey, you guys, call an ambulance! Li'l Joe, it's Ambrose. Can you hear me, Li'l Joe?"

Now he was forcing words out, each word a mountain to be pushed across a desert of hot pain: "David — David — tell David — needs — needs David — "

"All right, Li'l Joe; all right, now. Easy — easy — David'll come — *Christalmighty! He's gone — "*

But he hadn't gone, not for the space of another gasping breath, not for the length of time it took for the words to reach him through the fog of pain. "David'll come." What came after didn't matter because he couldn't hear the words as the pain gave over to peace.

The strong rhythmic identification within each unit of this single-sentence poem will help you achieve the needed variety. Each unit has its own minor climax and comes to its own minor conclusion. Nevertheless, the punctuation warns you that the poem must not be broken into completely isolated sections but must build from the first invocation to the climactic final unit. Carefully preserve the balance between the great strength and dignity of each unit and the gentle details. The changes in empathy are important.

For My People / MARGARET WALKER

For my people everywhere singing their slave songs repeatedly: their dirges and their ditties and their blues and jubilees, praying their prayers nightly to an unknown god, bending their knees humbly to an unseen power;

For my people lending their strength to the years: to the gone years and the now years and the maybe years, washing ironing cooking scrubbing sewing mending hoeing plowing digging planting pruning patching dragging along never gaining never reaping never knowing and never understanding;

For my playmates in the clay and dust and sand of Alabama backyards playing baptizing and preaching, and doctor and jail and soldier and school and mama and cooking and playhouse and concert and store and Miss Choomby and hair and company;

For the cramped bewildered years we went to school to learn to know the reasons why and the answers to and the people who and the places where and the days when, in memory of the bitter hours when we discovered we were black and poor and small and different and nobody wondered and nobody understood;

For the boys and girls who grew in spite of these things to be Man and Woman, to laugh and dance and sing and play and drink their wine and religion and success, to marry their playmates and bear children and then die of consumption and anemia and lynching;

For my people thronging 47th Street in Chicago and Lenox Avenue in New York and Rampart Street in New Orleans, lost dis-

inherited dispossessed and HAPPY people filling the cabarets
and taverns and other people's pockets needing bread and shoes
and milk and land and money and Something — Something
all our own;

For my people walking blindly, spreading joy, losing time being
lazy, sleeping when hungry, shouting when burdened, drinking
when hopeless, tied and shackled and tangled among ourselves
by the unseen creatures who tower over us omnisciently and
laugh;

For my people blundering and groping and floundering in the dark
of churches and schools and clubs and societies, associations
and councils and committees and conventions, distressed and
disturbed and deceived and devoured by money-hungry glory-
craving leeches, preyed on by facile force of state and fad and
novelty by false prophet and holy believer;

For my people standing staring trying to fashion a better way from
confusion from hypocrisy and misunderstanding, trying to
fashion a world that will hold all the people all the faces all
the adams and eves and their countless generations;

Let a new earth rise. Let another world be born. Let a bloody
peace be written in the sky. Let a second generation full of
courage issue forth, let a people loving freedom come to growth,
let a beauty full of healing and a strength of final clenching
be the pulsing in our spirits and our blood. Let the martial
songs be written, let the dirges disappear. Let a race of men
now rise and take control!

*Langston Hughes is able to condense the history of his race from its begin-
nings through the first quarter of the twentieth century in this brief poem.
The repetitions are, of course, a strong unifying factor, as are the motifs. Be
careful that they do not obscure the variety and progression. The pride and
strength in the poem should influence empathy and muscle tone.*

The Negro Speaks of Rivers / LANGSTON HUGHES

I've known rivers:
I've known rivers ancient as the world and older than the flow of human
blood in human veins.
My soul has grown deep like the rivers.

I bathed in the Euphrates when dawns were young.
I built my hut near the Congo and it lulled me to sleep.
I looked upon the Nile and raised the pyramids above it.
I heard the singing of the Mississippi when Abe Lincoln went down
   to New Orleans, and I've seen its muddy bosom turn all golden
   in the sunset.

I've known rivers:
Ancient, dusky rivers.

My soul has grown deep like the rivers.

*The old lady whose words we hear in this poem obviously once loved being
alive and physically responsive. Her memory of the joy of her body must be
used when it appears. Note the inner strength and fire suggested in the two-
line stanza. Rhythm of content reflects the rhythm of her life—as she remem-
bers the past, is frozen in the present, and yearns for what is to come.*

Old Lady's Winter Words / THEODORE ROETHKE

To seize, to seize, —
I know that dream.
Now my ardors sleep in a sleeve.
My eyes have forgotten.
Like the half-dead, I hug my last secrets.
O for some minstrel of what's to be,
A bird singing into the beyond,
The marrow of God, talking,
Full merry, a gleam
Gracious and bland,
On a bright stone.
Somewhere, among the ferns and birds,
The great swamps flash.
I would hold high converse
Where the winds gather,
And leap over my eye,
An old woman
Jumping in her shoes.

If only I could remember
The white grass bending away,
The doors swinging open,
The smells, the moment of hay, —
When I went to sea in a sigh,
In a boat of beautiful things.
The good day has gone:
The fair house, the high
Elm swinging around
With its deep shade, and birds.
I have listened close
For the thin sound in the windy chimney,
The fall of the last ash
From the dying ember.
I've become a sentry of small seeds,
Poking alone in my garden.
The stone walks, where are they?
Gone to bolster a road.
The shrunken soil
Has scampered away in a dry wind.
Once I was sweet with the light of myself,
A self-delighting creature,
Leaning over a rock,
My hair between me and the sun,
The waves rippling near me.
My feet remembered the earth,
The loam heaved me
That way and this.
My looks had a voice;
I was careless in growing.

If I were a young man,
I could roll in the dust of a fine rage.

The shadows are empty, the sliding externals.
The wind wanders around the house
On its way to the back pasture.
The cindery snow ticks over stubble.
My dust longs for the invisible.
I'm reminded to stay alive
By the dry rasp of the recurring inane,
The fine soot sifting through my south windows.
It is hard to care about corners,

And the sound of paper tearing.
I fall, more and more,
Into my own silences.
In the cold air,
The spirit
Hardens.

This cutting from the first few pages of Kafka's novel admittedly does grave injustice to the work as a whole, but it is nonetheless an interesting problem in bodily action for the interpreter. The moments of physical struggle and tension interrupted by Gregor's comments provide a rhythm which must be handled carefully so that the unity is not lost. The audience must feel empathy resulting from the helplessly moving legs and grotesque bulk of the body.

FROM *The Metamorphosis* / FRANZ KAFKA

As Gregor Samsa awoke one morning from uneasy dreams he found himself transformed in his bed into a gigantic insect. He was lying on his hard, as it were armor-plated, back and when he lifted his head a little he could see his dome-like belly divided into stiff arched segments on top of which the bed quilt could hardly keep in position and was about to slide off completely. His numerous legs, which were pitifully thin compared to the rest of his bulk, waved helplessly before his eyes.

What has happened to me? he thought. It was no dream. His room, a regular human bedroom, only rather too small, lay quiet between the four familiar walls. Above the table on which a collection of cloth samples was unpacked and spread out — Samsa was a commercial traveler — hung the picture which he had recently cut out of an illustrated magazine and put into a pretty gilt frame. It showed a lady, with a fur cap on and a fur stole, sitting upright and holding out to the spectator a huge fur muff into which the whole of her forearm had vanished!

Gregor's eyes turned next to the window, and the overcast sky — one could hear rain drops beating on the window gutter — made him quite melancholy. What about sleeping a little longer and forgetting all this nonsense, he thought, but it could not be done, for he was accustomed to sleep on his right side and in his present condition he could not turn himself over. However violently he forced himself towards his right side he always rolled on to his back again. He tried it at least a hundred times, shutting his eyes to keep from seeing his struggling legs, and only desisted when he began to feel in his side a faint dull ache he had never experienced before.

• • • • •

His immediate intention was to get up quietly without being disturbed, to put on his clothes and above all eat his breakfast, and only then to consider what else was to be done, since in bed, he was well aware, his meditations would come to no sensible conclusion. He remembered that often enough in bed he had felt small aches and pains, probably caused by awkward postures, which had proved purely imaginary once he got up, and he looked forward eagerly to seeing this morning's delusions gradually fall away. That the change in his voice was nothing but the precursor of a severe chill, a standing ailment of commercial travelers, he had not the least possible doubt.

To get rid of the quilt was quite easy; he had only to inflate himself a little and it fell off by itself. But the next move was difficult, especially because he was so uncommonly broad. He would have needed arms and hands to hoist himself up; instead he had only the numerous little legs which never stopped waving in all directions and which he could not control in the least. When he tried to bend one of them it was the first to stretch itself straight; and did he succeed at last in making it do what he wanted, all the other legs meanwhile waved the more wildly in a high degree of unpleasant agitation. "But what's the use of lying idle in bed," said Gregor to himself.

He thought that he might get out of bed with the lower part of his body first, but this lower part, which he had not yet seen and of which he could form no clear conception, proved too difficult to move; it shifted so slowly; and when finally, almost wild with annoyance, he gathered his forces together and thrust out recklessly, he had miscalculated the direction and bumped heavily against the lower end of the bed, and the stinging pain he felt informed him that precisely this lower part of his body was at the moment probably the most sensitive.

So he tried to get the top part of himself out first, and cautiously moved his head towards the edge of the bed. That proved easy enough, and despite its breadth and mass the bulk of his body at last slowly followed the movement of his head. Still, when he finally got his head free over the edge of the bed he felt too scared to go on advancing, for after all if he let himself fall in this way it would take a miracle to keep his head from being injured. And at all costs he must not lose consciousness now, precisely now; he would rather stay in bed.

But when after a repetition of the same efforts he lay in his former position again, sighing, and watched his little legs struggling against each other more wildly than ever, if that were possible, and saw no way of bringing order into this arbitrary confusion, he told himself again that it was impossible to stay in bed and that the most sensible course was to risk everything for the smallest hope of getting away from it. At the same time he did not forget meanwhile to remind himself that cool reflection, the coolest possible, was much better than desperate resolves. In such moments he focused his eyes as sharply as possible on the window, but, unfortunately, the prospect of the morning fog, which muffled even the other side of the narrow street, brought him little encouragement and comfort. "Seven o'clock already," he said to himself when the alarm clock chimed again, "seven o'clock already and still such a thick fog." And for a little while he lay quiet, breathing lightly, as if perhaps expecting such complete repose to restore all things to their real and normal condition.

But then he said to himself: "Before it strikes a quarter past seven I must be quite out of this bed, without fail. Anyhow, by that time someone will have come from the office to ask for me, since it opens before seven." And he set himself to rocking his whole body at once in a regular rhythm, with the idea of swinging it out of the bed. If he tipped himself out in that way he could keep his head from injury by lifting it at an acute angle when he fell. His back seemed to be hard and was not likely to suffer from a fall on the carpet. His biggest worry was the loud crash he would not be able to help making, which would probably cause anxiety, if not terror, behind all the doors. Still, he must take the risk.

When he was already half out of the bed — the new method was more a game than an effort, for he needed only to hitch himself across by rocking to and fro — it struck him how simple it would be if he could get help. Two strong people — he thought of his father and the servant girl — would be amply sufficient; they would only have to thrust their arms under his convex back, lever him out of bed, bend down with their burden and then be patient enough to let him turn himself right over on to the floor, where it was to be hoped his legs would then find their proper function. Well, ignoring the fact that the doors were all locked, ought he really to call for help? In spite of his misery he could not suppress a smile at the very idea of it.

Let your muscles respond to this famous speech on the seven ages of man. Keep the progression firm and unified, but allow time for the physical and mental transitions.

FROM *As You Like It* / WILLIAM SHAKESPEARE

Act II, Scene 7

JAQUES.   All the world's a stage,
And all the men and women merely players.
They have their exits and their entrances,
And one man in his time plays many parts,
His acts being seven ages. At first the infant,
Mewling and puking in the nurse's arms.
Then the whining school-boy, with his satchel
And shining morning face, creeping like snail
Unwillingly to school. And then the lover,
Sighing like furnace, with a woeful ballad
Made to his mistress' eyebrow. Then a soldier,
Full of strange oaths, and bearded like the pard,
Jealous in honor, sudden, and quick in quarrel,
Seeking the bubble reputation
Even in the cannon's mouth. And then the justice,
In fair round belly with good capon lin'd,
With eyes severe and beard of formal cut,
Full of wise saws and modern instances;
And so he plays his part. The sixth age shifts
Into the lean and slipper'd pantaloon,
With spectacles on nose and pouch on side,
His youthful hose, well sav'd, a world too wide
For his shrunk shank, and his big manly voice,
Turning again toward childish treble, pipes
And whistles in his sound. Last scene of all,
That ends this strange eventful history,
Is second childishness and mere oblivion,
Sans teeth, sans eyes, sans taste, sans everything.

You will need to know the story of Orestes and his pursuing Eumenides to understand this poem fully. The speech phrases and the sentence lengths are very important in suggesting and controlling pace and emotional impact. The kinetic and kinesthetic imagery is basic.

XVI: *The Name—Orestes* / GEORGE SEFERIS

Again, again into the track, once more into the track!
How many turns, how many laps of blood, how many black
Circles of faces watching: the people watching me
Who watched me when, upright in the chariot,
I raised my hand, brilliant, and they roared applause.

The froth of horses beats upon my flesh. When will the horses
Weary? The axle shrieks, the axle glows. When will the axle
Seize up in flame? When will the rein break?
When will the whole hooves tread
Full on the ground, on the soft grass, among
The poppies where in spring you picked a daisy?

They were lovely, your eyes. You did not know where to look with them
Nor did I know where to look, I, without a country,
I who struggle on this spot — how many turns and laps! —
And I feel my knees failing me above the axle,
Above the wheels, above the savage track.
The knees fail easily when the gods will have it so.
No one is able to escape; no strength will do it, you cannot
Escape the sea which cradled you, for which you turn and search
In this moment of contest, among the breathing of horses,
With the reeds that used to sing in autumn to a Lydian Mode,
The sea that you cannot find again, run as you may,
Turn as you may, lap after lap, in front of the black
Eumenides who are bored and cannot forgive.

Bibliography

The current textbooks all contain some discussion of the use of the body in oral communication. The books listed below are more technical and specialized in their treatment but contain much that will be of interest to the serious student of interpretation.

Birdwhistell, Ray L. *Kinesics and Context: Essays on Body Motion and Communication.* Philadelphia: University of Pennsylvania Press, 1970.

An expansion of one of the early basic studies in the relationship between kinesics and oral communication.

Blackmur, R. P. *Language As Gesture*. New York: Harcourt, Brace and Company, 1952.

Detailed analysis of specific poems to illustrate the theory of poetry as language of gesture.

Burke, Kenneth. *The Philosophy of Literary Form: Studies in Symbolic Action*. Revised Edition. New York: Vintage Books, Inc., 1957.

Essays on rhetoric and poetics but basically a discussion of the theory of symbolic action.

Katz, Robert L. *Empathy: Its Nature and Uses*. New York: The Macmillan Company, 1963.

Emphasis on the dynamics of empathy and its social and aesthetic uses.

Ruesch, Jurgen, and Weldon Kees. *Non-verbal Communication*. Berkeley, California: University of California Press, 1956.

The relationship between digital and analogical communication with a strong recommendation for the development of the latter.

Stewart, David A. *A Preface to Empathy*. New York: Philosophical Library, 1956.

Empathy examined as identification and as a creative process.

Chapter 4   Voice

In the preceding chapter we gave most of our attention to the development of a flexible, responsive body. From time to time, however, we touched upon the effect of bodily action on vocal technique. Body and voice are a twofold instrument, and the modern interpreter learns to control them both so that they work together in perfect combination to communicate whatever the literature demands. The body makes its own special contribution; but it is the voice, of course, which is basic to oral interpretation. Unless the interpreter can be heard and understood, muscle response and appropriate gestures will be of little value.

Most people speak adequately for general conversation and informal communication. But the oral interpretation of literature requires additional flexibility and special control. The fact that the interpreter uses his speaking voice every day and has done so since he was a child is no guarantee that it is an adequate instrument for artistic re-creation. The interpreter needs to know first of all just how his voice functions and how it can be controlled and developed in order to provide wider range in pitch, greater flexibility in volume and stress, richer variations in quality, and finer degrees of subtlety in duration and rate. Once he understands how these factors can be controlled, he must work to develop his voice no less consciously than does the singer. As his voice control improves, he should be increasingly able to meet the demands of the various types of literary material with intelligence and sensitivity.

Perhaps it should be pointed out that the discussion in this chapter has to do with the normal speaking voice, not with any type of speech

Development for Oral Interpretation

defect. Speech defects are in the province of the speech therapist and as such do not come into consideration here. This discussion and the suggested exercises that accompany it are entirely concerned with improving and enriching the normal voice, which may need some attention to make it sufficiently flexible, strong, and responsive to play its part in the artistic communication of literature to an audience.

The student who has had voice training may find the following discussion useful only as a reminder of things he already knows. An effort has been made, however, to apply some of the principles to specific problems facing the interpreter. A few moments spent on the exercises will be most valuable during rehearsal periods when he is working on a particularly demanding selection.

Breath Control

The first concern of anyone interested in voice improvement should be breath control, because without adequate breath properly controlled the production of good vocal tone is impossible. Proper use of the normal breathing mechanism is simple. Any difficulties are due to bad habits which may be the result of physical or psychological tensions. An understanding of the muscles involved in the breathing process and of the functions they perform may help locate and release some of these tensions.

In inhalation — intake of air — the major concern is with the amount;

in exhalation — outgo — it is with varied control. The whole process of breathing rests on two basic physiological and physical principles: the balance of tension and relaxation in opposing sets of muscles which serve to control the creation of a vacuum.

When we inhale and pull in a quantity of air into the body, the diaphragm — the large dome-shaped muscle at the floor of the chest — lowers and pushes downward against the *relaxed* abdominal muscles; thus the lengthwise expansion of the chest is increased. As this action is taking place, the muscles between the outer surfaces of the ribs lift and extend the rib cage, and the side-to-side and front-to-back expansion of the chest is accomplished. This increase in size creates a vacuum inside the chest cavity. Atmospheric pressures force air into the vacuum so that the pressure inside and outside the body is equalized. The air is forced down through the windpipe (trachea), on through the bronchial tubes, and finally comes to rest in the flexible air sacs in the lungs in which the bronchioli terminate. The air sacs in the lungs inflate as the air enters, and when the lungs are thus extended the process of inhalation is complete. Obviously, then, breathing is an active muscle process.

When the mechanism is ready for the process of exhalation to take place (following the exchange of oxygen and carbon dioxide in the blood), the muscles in the diaphragm relax and the diaphragm rises into the dome-shaped position again. The muscles on the outside of the rib cage relax as the ones between the ribs on the inside contract. This action pulls the extended rib cage inward. All this pressure upward and inward acts on the elastic lung tissue containing the air forced in during inhalation; the elastic tissue begins to collapse, and the air is forced out of the lungs, up through the bronchial tubes, through the windpipe, and finally out of the nose or mouth. Thus one cycle of respiration is completed.

In exhaling for speech, however, there is frequently another action in addition to the relaxing of the diaphragm in the lower chest area. This action is the firm contraction of the abdominal muscles which are relaxed for inhalation. As they contract for exhalation, they support the action accomplished by the relaxing of the diaphragm, and in this way help to control the outgo of air. This process is known as "forced exhalation" — a term somewhat misleading, perhaps, because the contraction of the abdominal muscles should be an easy and natural process, particularly for a trained speaker who wishes "support" for a tone projected by sustained exhalation. It is simply an additional action, or rather a continuation of action, in the process of exhalation during silent breathing.

Now, where should the student of voice begin his exercises so that he will have greater breath capacity and better control over exhalation? He will want these muscle processes to function effectively so that he may give smooth interpretation to long flowing lines of poetry, for instance, or force a swift exhalation for command or expression of emotion in dramatic dialogue.

The first thing to remember is that proper breathing is possible only when the posture is good. If each muscle is to perform its assigned function, the body must be in a state of controlled relaxation — that is, in a state of nicely balanced relaxation and essential tension. Wrongly induced tension inhibits the flexibility of muscles that control the intake and the outward flow of air. One of the most frequent errors in breathing practice is forcing the muscles of the rib cage and the abdomen into a rigid position. These muscles must be firm, but they cannot function if they are locked. If the muscles below the ribs are "tucked in" after a full inhalation, they will be ready to help in the important function of support and control.

In exercises for improved breathing habits it is particularly important, when standing, to have the weight easily and comfortably supported by the feet and legs, to have the spinal column erect but not forced into position, the shoulders level, and the muscles that support them free from tension. Strong lifting of the shoulders, a common error in inhalation, serves only to put tension in the wrong area, with consequent effect on the vocal tone if phonation is to take place with the exhaled breath.

A simple exercise to demonstrate the proper balance between tension and relaxation in the special muscles of respiration will be profitable. This exercise also tends to show *where* concentration of energy should be — at the "beltline" rather than in the throat.

1. Take a deep, comfortable breath and hold it. Contract the abdominal muscles *sharply* and force the air out of the chest on a single vocalization such as "Ah — h — h," much as if sighing. Hold the contraction of these muscles an appreciable instant, then *suddenly* release the tension. Notice that the air rushes into the chest and fills the lower portion (perhaps more) of the lungs upon the release of the tension. Exhale by forcing air out of the chest with the gradual contraction of the abdominal muscles as the diaphragm relaxes and returns to its dome-shaped position.

2. Repeat the process described in Exercise 1, and as the air rushes in on the release of tension in the abdominal muscles, make a conscious effort to lift the upper rib cage slightly (careful — *not* the shoulders!) so that more space is created in the upper chest, and the whole chest is well extended and can accommodate a large intake of air. The upper portion of the lungs should be filled now, as well as the lower. Exhale, pushing the air out with the relaxing of the diaphragm and the gradual contracting of abdominal muscles and

lowering of the rib cage. (Don't collapse and let the shoulders sag!)

3. Repeat the process described in Exercise 2 as far as the sudden exhalation followed by the easy full inhalation. Now, as you start to exhale the full breath, begin to vocalize by counting aloud. As you begin to run out of breath for vocalizing, begin gradually to contract the abdominal muscles (*not* the upper chest ones) as you continue counting. You are now utilizing "forced exhalation." When you can no longer force air out of the chest by the strong but comfortable contraction of the abdominal muscles, stop the vocalized counting. Don't sacrifice a good quality of tone in the effort to "squeeze out" more sound. This will only result in undue tension in the upper chest and throat muscles — the very thing you want to avoid.

This exercise is basic to developing good breath control and should be used as a starter for any period of exercise. Most instructions say: "Breathe in," *then* "breathe out." This one suggests breathing out first, in order to empty the chest of air at the beginning of the exercise. In this way, a "stuffing" of the chest is avoided. Then comes the breathing in, followed by the controlled breathing out — the inevitable order whether "exercising" or not, for no one can go on holding his breath forever.

The student should not work steadily at this or any other exercise when he begins to feel tired. Until he grows used to a changed method of control or a marked effort to increase capacity, he should go back for a "rest" to his usual manner of breathing. It should become increasingly clear, however, as he follows this type of exercise, that the sooner he can make this method automatic, the easier will be his whole breathing process.

As he is able to take in larger amounts of air with ease and to continue forced exhalation to support the tone, he should be able to count more numbers on one breath. He should try with each exercise period to say a few more, being careful always that there is no strain in the throat, no forcing of the tone or sacrifice of quality. He should count at what seems an easy volume (loudness) for him, and at a pleasing level of pitch; that will accustom him to using his voice with proper breathing.

The student interpreter should try his breath control on the following passage, keeping an unbroken flow of sound to the end of each sentence, without, of course, doing violence to the meaning and connotation of the words.

FROM *The Pied Piper of Hamelin*

And out of the houses the rats came tumbling.
Great rats, small rats, lean rats, brawny rats,
Brown rats, black rats, gray rats, tawny rats,

> Grave old plodders, gay young friskers,
>> Fathers, mothers, uncles, cousins,
> Cocking tails and pricking whiskers,
>> Families by tens and dozens,
> Brothers, sisters, husbands, wives —
> Followed the Piper for their lives.

ROBERT BROWNING

It is obviously impractical to attempt to complete the long sentence on a single breath, except as an exercise. Such a procedure would threaten the clarity of the thought and the relationship of the phrases to one another. Some of the phrasal units will need to be separated by pauses of varying lengths when the material is read aloud. During these pauses the speaker has an opportunity to replenish his supply of breath. He must take care not to let the pauses break the continuity of thought. The position and duration of the pauses must always grow out of the relationship of the phrases to each other and to the complete thought being expressed. The interpreter will learn to breathe where he must pause, not pause in order to breathe. It will usually be impossible to get a capacity breath except in the major pauses which complete the units of thought. Therefore, the final step in control of breathing is to learn to inhale quickly and unobtrusively, while still using the proper muscles.

Frequently a speaker will be inhaling properly and using his full capacity for breath but still not be able to sustain a long flow of sound. Here the problem is not one of an insufficient supply of air but of inadequate control of exhalation. This is one of the major causes of "dropping" final words or syllables so that they do not carry to the last row of the audience. A simple exercise will help determine whether or not the control muscles collapse instead of exerting steady pressure as they relax:

> Inhale a full, comfortable breath. Be sure the shoulders are relaxed. Hold a lighted match directly in front of your lips as close as your profile will allow. Start to count aloud in full voice. You should be able to continue until the match burns down. If you blow the flame out, check the state of control of the muscles in and around the rib cage. Most of us exhale more than we need to on certain sounds, such as "*two*" or "*three*" or "*four*." Light another match, take another deep breath, and try the exercise again, speaking very softly with conscious control of the rate of relaxation of the muscles involved. You will feel as if you may explode, but you won't, and you will be made aware of where the control must be exercised. As you gradually increase your volume to normal, you will find that the flame flickers but that you will not extinguish it by a sudden uncontrolled spurt of air.

Volume and Projection

These two inseparable factors in communication are so important that they must always be of utmost concern to the reader, actor, or speaker. Anyone who has been in an audience of any size and found to his distress that he could not hear the speaker knows the immense importance of sufficient volume and good projection. The interpreter's purpose is, after all, to share his material with his audience. If he cannot be heard, he has obviously failed in his primary objective.

Actually, "volume" and "projection" are sometimes used interchangeably, and indeed they are both part of the interpreter's ability to be heard and understood. For greater clarity in this discussion, however, let us consider *volume* as degree of loudness and *projection* as the act of directing the voice to a specific target.

Of course, the interpreter must be able to make his voice fill the room in which his audience is gathered. He must learn to control his volume in order to fill the space easily without distorting his voice, or blasting down the back wall if his space is limited. He must know how much volume is required and how to achieve the greatest possible flexibility within that requirement. His understanding of the entire breathing process is basic to his control of volume.

Mere loudness, however, is not enough. It is, unfortunately, not unusual to encounter an amateur speaker who can be heard but cannot be understood. Obviously, this touches on the problems of pronunciation and articulation, which will be considered later in this chapter. Being understood, however, depends to a degree on the speaker's control of projection.

The first requirement of adequate projection is enough volume and support so that the tone will carry as far as the material and situation demand. The second requirement is the right mental attitude. This applies to the speaker with good control of volume as well as to the one who is less expert. For good communication, and hence projection, is a product not only of breath control but also of the speaker's constant awareness of the listener. Such awareness is often spoken of in the theater as "audience sense." Though this sense is a difficult thing to explain, it has its base in the speaker's attitude of reaching out toward an audience with every line he wants to communicate. These lines may be a robust and sturdy utterance, such as Ulysses' address to his fellow mariners. They may be as delicate, subjective, and personal as those that shape Maxwell Bodenheim's "Death" (page 127). Regardless of the energy of idea or feeling, the reader or actor with a fine sense of "audience participation" must have a psychological "set" that will help him reach out to the audience with his voice. The interpreter as well as the actor should keep in mind the old adage of show business and "play to the balcony." In other words, he should keep the back row of his listeners in mind and be sure that his words reach them. This advice is sound whether his audience is composed of a few people grouped around a fireplace or hundreds gathered in an auditorium or theater.

This mental attitude toward communication has an indirect but observable effect on the physiological control of projection. Thinking *to* as well as *of* his listeners, wanting to be sure that they hear and share the full effect of the literature, the speaker will tend to keep his posture erect and his head lifted slightly so that his throat is free from tension.

FOCUS OF PROJECTION

It is sometimes helpful to think of the voice as a tangible thing — a thing to be aimed and thrown at a target. This trick of "throwing the voice" may smack of ventriloquism, yet it is a practice everyone uses at times. The child calling to attract the attention of his playmate down the street sends his voice down to him; the football fan shouting advice to the players on the field directs his voice without conscious thought to the exact spot where his attention is focused. When the adult is carrying on a conversation in a room full of people, he may project across the room to answer a remark or add his bit to a conversation. When he wishes to be confidential, he lets his voice drop and his circle of mental directness narrow so that he fills only the desired area.

These exercises for focus of projection can be most effectively practiced in a large room. They are conceived primarily in terms of an imagined concrete situation, so that by thinking specifically of *what* to do, and using any words that come to mind, the interpreter can concentrate on the volume and focus suggested.

1. You are seated at a desk in the center front of the room. You see a friend at the door; you call an easy greeting. He waves and goes on. You think of something that you ought to tell him. You call his name quickly, but he apparently doesn't hear, for he keeps on going. Without leaving your place, call again; have a good full breath as you start to call and direct the sound at his fast-disappearing back. Do the same thing again with more volume and longer sounds supported by forced exhalation. Be sure you catch him this time.

2. You are giving directions to a group of people about to work out a diagram. The room is large, and everyone must hear. Direct your remarks to various places, thinking of certain people who might be there. After you have given instructions and the group starts to work, a question arises down front. You shift your focus of projection, reduce your volume, and answer the person who asked the

question. You then decide that others might need that special information, too. You raise your volume and expand your area of projection to attract everyone's attention, then repeat to the group what you have said to the individual. As you do this, take care to direct your voice to the various parts of the room so that all will hear.

When you have made some progress in projection through such exercises as these, move on to practice with literary material.

An interesting problem in projection is to be found in Shakespeare's *Julius Caesar*. As Brutus goes up into the pulpit to make his famous speech to the crowd, he addresses a single remark to those near him. On the opening sentence try to get the feeling of first speaking to those who stand beside you and then including the several hundred citizens who are milling around the Forum. It is necessary to quiet them during the early part of the speech.

> BRUTUS: Be patient till the last. Romans, countrymen, and lovers! hear me for my cause, and be silent, that you may hear; believe me for mine honor, and have respect to mine honor, that you may believe; censure me in your wisdom, and awake your senses, that you may the better judge. If there be any in this assembly, any dear friend of Caesar's, to him I say, that Brutus' love to Caesar was no less than his. If then that friend demand why Brutus rose against Caesar, this is my answer: Not that I lov'd Caesar less, but that I lov'd Rome more.

In the following lines from the famous trial scene of *The Merchant of Venice*, two characters are speaking. Our concern at the moment is not primarily with the difference in their voices or mental attitudes, but rather with the changes in focus and consequent projection in their speeches. (The parenthetical stage directions are inserted for this specific exercise. They do not appear in the text of the play.) The Duke speaks to Portia at close range on his greeting and first question and on the opening line of his second speech. After "take your place," it is assumed that she moves away from him so that his question,

> Are you acquainted with the difference
> That holds this present question in the court?

must carry over a greater distance than his first remarks but still be addressed directly to Portia. His order to Antonio and Shylock to "stand forth" may be thought of as carrying even farther, since they are probably among a group of people outside the judge's area. Practice the Duke's speeches until you can place them where you want them, and then follow the same procedure in Portia's speeches.

> DUKE: Give me your hand. Come you from old Bellario?
> PORTIA: (*To Duke as she gives him her hand*) I did, my lord.

DUKE: You are welcome; take your place.
Are you acquainted with the difference
That holds this present question in the court?

    PORTIA: (*From her place a few feet away from the Duke*) I am informed throughly of the cause.

    (*To the assemblage*) Which is the merchant here, and which the Jew?

    DUKE: Antonio and old Shylock, both stand forth.

    PORTIA: (*To Shylock after he has stepped forward from the crowd*) Is your name Shylock?

In working to develop volume and projection, the interpreter is concentrating on one of the basic requirements of all speech: that it reach its audience. Volume depends largely on adequate breath supply and proper support in exhalation. Projection combines these physical aspects with the psychological aspect of mental directness.

Pitch and Quality

Although pitch and quality are different attributes of sound, they are so closely related in origin and control in the human voice that they may be considered together. The way the vocal bands vibrate determines basically both the pitch and the quality of the vocal tone — the pitch by the rate, the quality by the complexity of the vibration.

The *pitch* of a sound is its place on the musical scale. It is located very generally in terms of the scale range, as high, medium, or low pitch. Skill in using pitch is of considerable importance to the interpreter in suggesting shades of meaning and in reflecting attitude. Changes in pitch give variety and richness to the material being read and help to hold the attention of the audience. Since a change of pitch produces *inflection,* a speaker's *inflection range* is the entire pitch span between the highest and lowest tone of which he is capable.

Any pattern in the variation of levels of pitch results in melody. When there are no discernible changes of pitch, the result is a monotone. Melody is an asset to the interpreter, but it can also become a problem. Most individuals have in their daily speech a characteristic pattern of inflections which is a part of their own personalities. This is highly commendable, and certainly it is to be expected that some of that pattern will be carried over into their work before an audience. It often happens, however, that the reader's pattern is so marked as to call attention to itself and thus get in the way of re-creation of the material. For example, in reading poetry, which tends to be patterned by design, one of the most common and annoying vocal patterns permits each line or each new thought to start on a high pitch and drift to a low tone at the close. The following lines are an example of poetic structure in which this problem must be controlled.

> Fair flower, that dost so comely grow,
> Hid in this silent, dull retreat,
> Untouched thy honied blossoms blow,
> Unseen thy little branches greet:
>   No roving foot shall crush thee here,
>   No busy hand provoke a tear.
>
> PHILIP FRENEAU, *The Wild Honeysuckle*

And again, in less conventional poetry:

> I hear America singing, the varied carols I hear,
> Those of mechanics, each one singing his as it should be blithe
>   and strong,
> The carpenter singing his as he measures his plank or beam,
> The mason singing his as he makes ready for work, or leaves
>   off work . . .
>
> WALT WHITMAN, *I Hear America Singing*

Quality, more difficult to define distinctively, can best be described as that characteristic of a tone which distinguishes it from all other tones of the same pitch and intensity. It is sometimes called timbre, or to use the German word, *Klang*, meaning the "ring" of the tone. In describing quality, one frequently uses words that suggest *color* — a "golden" tone, a "silver-voiced" orator, a "blue" note.

Quality of tone is perhaps most closely associated with mood and feeling. Connotation and emotional response will have a strong effect on quality, and empathy plays its part in the degree of tension or relaxation it imposes on the vocal mechanism. Vocal quality will be influenced by the interpreter's empathic response to whatever elements of emotion, strength, and beauty are inherent in the material. Whether he exclaims with Hecuba, "Ah woe! . . . For what woe lacketh here?" or shouts with an early celebrator, "It's gonna be a great day!" his sensitive response to the mood, together with his understanding of the connotation of the words used, should help him to communicate fully the feeling in the material. The interpreter who is true to his art will never adopt a certain quality and impose it on the selection. A display of "rich" quality or of a variety of qualitative effects, like every other display of technique for its own sake, is in poor taste and violates the fundamental rule of unobtrusiveness.

We may conclude this discussion of quality by presenting a portion of a famous example of harmony between sound and feeling — that is, between quality and emotion. In the lines from *King Lear* in which Lear,

old, enraged, and embittered, defies the storm on the heath, the interpreter will appreciate the contribution to the mood of angry defiance
made by the actual sound of the words, in addition to their connotation.
It is also a good exercise in projection.

> LEAR: Blow, winds, and crack your cheeks! rage! blow!
> You cataracts and hurricanoes, spout
> Till you have drench'd our steeples, drown'd the cocks!
> You sulph'rous and thought-executing fires,
> Vaunt-couriers of oak-cleaving thunderbolts,
> Singe my white head! And thou, all-shaking thunder,
> Smite flat the thick rotundity o' the world!
> Crack nature's moulds, all germens spill at once
> That make ingrateful man.

Pitch and quality working together, then, are invaluable in helping the
interpreter bring out the universality and suggestion in a piece of literature. He must pay particular attention to the control of these two aspects
of vocal technique because they contribute so much to the communication of the emotional content.

Rate and Pause

The *rate* at which a person speaks is often habitual, a part of his personality and his entire background. It probably serves him very well for
ordinary conversation, but he may need to adjust his habitual rate to do
justice to an author's style and purpose. As with the other elements of
vocal technique, the interpreter must train his ear to hear himself in rehearsal and in conversation. There is no magic formula for slowing a
too-rapid pace. It requires constant attention. The selection of material
which by its style and connotation encourages a slower pace will be helpful. Very frequently the mere physical process of forming a sequence of
sounds will affect the rate at which a sentence can be read intelligibly
and effectively. Thus the interpreter will do well to make certain that he
is forming every sound accurately and controlling his rate so that this is
possible.

Within the overall rate will be opportunities for subtle variety. Emotion, connotation, suggestion, and the combination of vowels and consonants will all provide the clues.

Rate is not only the speed with which sounds are uttered in sequence,
but also the length and frequency of pauses separating the sequences of
sounds. Of course, the interpreter will long since have recognized the
phrasal pause which clarifies the relationships of words in phrases to convey units of thoughts. The pause may also become one of the most

effective tools for building suspense and climaxes and for reinforcing emotional content.

The beginner is usually afraid to hold the pause long enough for its dramatic effect to register with his listener. If a pause is motivated by real understanding, by identification with the feeling suggested, it may be sustained for a much longer time and with greater effect than the beginner realizes. He need only be sure that something relevant to the material is going on during the pause, first in his own mind and consequently in the minds of his listeners. The pause must stay within the total concept of the selection and supply whatever transition or suspense is needed. He should work not only to use pauses in the most effective places, but to vary and sustain the lengths of the pauses as the material demands. Punctuation is used on the printed page to signal the eye. It guides the reader in establishing the relationship of words and phrases and their division into sentences. The interpreter can sometimes use change of pitch, quality, or emphasis, or a combination of these, to signal the ear of his listeners. He need not always use a pause. Moreover, it must be remembered that rules and fashions change in punctuation as in everything else. Thus the interpreter's full understanding and response, together with his sense of responsibility to his audience, are the final determinants in the use of pauses.

In the following scene from *Cyrano de Bergerac*, Cyrano is speaking of his monstrous nose and its effect on his entire being. The interpreter must make exquisite use of pause here. As he works on the interpretation, he will realize also that the tempo of the scene begins to change with "Oh, not that ever!" He will see how this change to a faster, more smoothly flowing rate is effected, and will realize that it goes hand in hand with Cyrano's struggle to turn from his romantic, self-revelatory mood to his customary half-comic acceptance of his nose.

> CYRANO: My old friend — look at me,
> And tell me how much hope remains for me
> With this protuberance! Oh I have no more
> Illusions! Now and then — bah! I may grow
> Tender, walking alone in the blue cool
> Of evening, through some garden fresh with flowers
> After the benediction of the rain;
> My poor big devil of a nose inhales
> April . . . and so I follow with my eyes
> Where some boy, with a girl upon his arm,
> Passes a patch of silver . . . and I feel

Somehow, I wish I had a woman too,
Walking with little steps under the moon,
And holding my arm so, and smiling. Then
I dream — and I forget. . . .
                              And then I see
The shadow of my profile on the wall!
   LEBRET: My friend! . . .
   CYRANO: My friend, I have my bitter days,
Knowing myself so ugly, so alone.
Sometimes —
   LEBRET: You weep?
   CYRANO: (*Quickly*) Oh, not that ever! No,
That would be too grotesque — the tears trickling down
All the long way along this nose of mine?
I will not so profane the dignity
Of sorrow. Never any tears for me!

To develop additional skill with rate, the interpreter should work
on selections demanding basically different rate patterns. As he reads
the material aloud with feeling, he will realize that the "quantity" or
length of the individual sound, whether vowel or consonant, must be
effectively observed, as well as the length of pauses between sounds. He
will probably conclude that often, in a prevailing rapid rate, the sounds
as well as the pauses are short, and that the converse relation is true in
a slower rate. Many of the lyrics of the Gilbert and Sullivan operettas
are wonderful examples of the way sound suggests rate, particularly the
fast-moving "Nightmare Song" from *Iolanthe*:

> When you're lying awake with a dismal headache,
>   And repose is taboo'd by anxiety —
> I conceive you may use any language you choose
>   To indulge in, without impropriety . . .

Intelligibility of Speech

We have already had occasion to note that speech, to fulfill its basic
function of communication, must be understandable or intelligible, and
hence that it must be heard. But to be fully intelligible, speech must be
not only audible but also distinct and accurate. The listener cannot keep
his attention on the material if he is constantly called upon to "translate"
slovenly speech sounds or mispronunciations. Therefore the interpreter
will want his speech sounds to be correct as well as distinct and pleasing.
It is true that nothing is more irritating to the listener than a speaker's
self-conscious, overly careful mouthing of vowels and consonants. It

smacks of affectation and insincerity. Moreover, it violates the cardinal rule of interpretation because it draws attention to the reader and his technique and away from the material. On the other hand, if the reader cannot be understood, he certainly cannot communicate. Consequently, he must learn to pronounce and articulate with such clarity and accuracy that any audience will be able to understand him.

A distinction between pronunciation and articulation may be helpful. *Pronunciation* refers to *the correctness of sounds and accents* in spoken words; it is not immediately concerned with shaping the sounds. *Articulation,* on the other hand, refers to *the shaping of the sounds* by the speaker's lips, teeth, tongue, and hard and soft palates. Sometimes it is hard to decide whether a fault is a matter of pronunciation or of articulation. When someone says "He kep' it" for "He kept it," is it faulty pronunciation or slovenly articulation? The listener will probably decide in this instance that the trouble is, by definition, faulty pronunciation. On the other hand, when he hears a lisping sound, as "thithter Thuthy" for "sister Susy," he has no hesitation in deciding that the difficulty is faulty articulation.

Pronunciation is considered acceptable when all the sounds of a word are uttered correctly in their proper order and with accent (stress) on the proper syllable. Current good usage is the guide to correct pronunciation, with a standard dictionary the final authority. It is not always the unfamiliar polysyllables that trip up the reader. Since he will be likely to distrust himself on them, he will probably look them up in the dictionary. The real pitfalls are the common, everyday words which he may have fallen into the habit of pronouncing incorrectly. Hence the interpreter will want to check his pronunciation of ordinary words to avoid this type of error. A mispronunciation can ruin a fine oral line. In addition, it may so distract a listener that he momentarily loses the thought. When this happens, communication suffers.

If the reader knows what correct pronunciation is and has checked his own everyday speech, he may profitably turn his attention to improving the formation of sounds and to strengthening their projection. Faulty projection of distinct sounds is closely related to the position of the sound in the word or phrase. The end of the word or phrase may often be slighted or left off, even though the preceding sounds are distinct enough. In the exercises for control of sustained exhalation, it was pointed out that adequate control is needed to complete fully the ends of lines or sentences. This control and the accurate shaping of end sounds are of course closely allied. The failure to finish words is one of the faults that interfere most with good communication. Particularly is this so if the interpreter or actor is performing in a large auditorium or theater.

The consonant sounds that help most in achieving distinctness are *p, b, t, d, k, g.* These sounds are called *plosives* because the release which completes their formation is a sudden, sharp "explosion" in the air. It is this plosive element that promotes their carrying power. The interpreter should practice common words, alone and in combinations, until he is sure that his sounds, especially the final ones, are distinct. Words like *drop, cab, eight, good, gig, slept, cribbed, asked,* and *sixths* are examples. "Tongue twisters" using these and many other sounds are too numerous to mention, and are the property of all who know Peter Piper and his ilk. Such jingles provide excellent practice in accuracy and flexibility.

The fricative sounds, *f, v, s, z,* etc., so called because they escape the speech mechanism with a slight "hiss" of friction, also demand accurate formation. Sometimes, as was suggested in the brief exercise for control of exhalation, the vigor of the escaping sound needs to be toned down. The sound that gives the most trouble in this respect is the ever-present *s* and *z* pair of sibilants. Actually, *s* and *z* are among the most frequently used consonants in the English language. No wonder that the noise made by a large group of people talking has been called the "hissing of geese"! (Nor need the company be entirely feminine to create this effect.) The interpreter should check the sound of *s* as he articulates it in lines like these:

Choric Song

There is sweet music here that softer falls
Than petals from blown roses on the grass,
Or night-dews on still waters between walls
Of shadowy granite, in a gleaming pass;
Music that gentlier on the spirit lies,
Than tired eyelids upon tired eyes;
Music that brings sweet sleep down from the blissful skies.
Here are cool mosses deep,
And thro' the moss the ivies creep,
And in the stream the long-leaved flowers weep,
And from the craggy ledge the poppy hangs in sleep.

ALFRED, LORD TENNYSON

If the sound is too prominent or sharp — a "whistled" *s* — a slight relaxing of the groove in the tongue, which directs the sound against the teeth, should help. Or perhaps what is needed is a definite shortening or cutting off of the sound by stopping the outgo of air more quickly. If the sound of *s* seems "slushy" or unclear, increased effort should be made to direct the stream of air sharply over the center of the tongue, to expel it centrally between the closely aligned edges of upper and lower teeth.

If there is a marked deficiency in the *s*, or in any other sound for that matter, a speech therapist should be consulted.

After he has checked on individual sounds and words, the interpreter should occasionally test his progress by trying pieces of material that involve difficult combinations of sounds. Even the most experienced interpreter will profit from an occasional session in which he listens for any carelessness which may have crept into his articulation. Such attention to vocal technique of course belongs in rehearsal periods. In performance his concentration must be on the literature he is sharing, not on his diction.

Selections for Analysis and Oral Interpretation

In analyzing these selections, pay particular attention to the vocal problems each presents. Almost without exception they require more than the normal supply of breath, either because of long, flowing sentences or unusual demands of volume or force. Some have interesting problems in projection. They all require maximum flexibility of range to communicate the richness of sounds which help them achieve their full effectiveness when they are read aloud. As is often the case, they also demand an awareness of bodily response as well.

Probably the classic example of the value of sound combinations is to be found in this familiar nonsense poem.

Jabberwocky / LEWIS CARROLL

> 'Twas brillig, and the slithy toves
>   Did gyre and gimble in the wabe:
> All mimsy were the borogoves,
>   And the mome raths outgrabe.
>
> "Beware the Jabberwock, my son!
>   The jaws that bite, the claws that catch!
> Beware the Jubjub bird, and shun
>   The frumious Bandersnatch!"
>
> He took his vorpal sword in hand;
>   Long time the manxome foe he sought —
> So rested he by the Tumtum tree,
>   And stood awhile in thought.
>
> And, as in uffish thought he stood,
>   The Jabberwock, with eyes of flame,

Came whiffling through the tulgey wood,
    And burbled as it came!

One, two! One, two! And through and through
    The vorpal blade went snicker-snack!
He left it dead, and with its head
    He went galumphing back.

"And hast thou slain the Jabberwock?
    Come to my arms, my beamish boy!
O frabjous day! Callooh, Callay!"
    He chortled in his joy.

'Twas brillig, and the slithy toves
    Did gyre and gimble in the wabe:
All mimsy were the borogoves,
    And the mome raths outgabe.

This relatively long selection will divide into smaller units for purposes of attention to vocal techniques. There are opportunities for vocal variety in the opening dialogue as well as in the quarrel. Moreover, the separate memory units require some consideration of rate and pitch.

FROM 91 *Revere Street* / ROBERT LOWELL

"A penny for your thoughts, Schopenhauer," my mother would say.

"I am thinking about pennies," I'd answer.

"When I was a child I used to love telling Mamá everything I had done," Mother would say.

"But you're not a child," I would answer.

I used to enjoy dawdling and humming "Anchors Aweigh" up Revere Street after a day at school. "Anchors Aweigh," the official Navy song, had originally been the song composed for my father's class. And yet my mind always blanked and seemed to fill with a clammy hollowness when Mother asked prying questions. Like other tongue-tied, difficult children, I dreamed I was a master of cool, stoical repartee. "What have you been doing, Bobby?" Mother would ask. "I haven't," I'd answer. At home I thus saved myself from emotional exhaustion.

At school, however, I was extreme only in my conventional mediocrity, my colorless, distracted manner, which came from restless dreams of

being admired. My closest friend was Eric Burckhard, the son of a professor of architecture at Harvard. The Burckhards came from Zurich
and were very German, not like Ludendorff, but in the kindly, comical,
nineteenth-century manner of Jo's German husband in *Little Men,* or in
the manner of the crusading *sturm und drang* liberal scholars in second
year German novels. "Eric's mother and father are *both* called Dr.
Burckhard," my mother once said, and indeed there was something en-
dearingly repellent about Mrs. Burckhard with her doctor's degree, her
long, unstylish skirts, and her dramatic, dulling blond braids. Strangely
the Burckhard's sober continental bourgeois house was without golden
mean — everything was either hilariously old Swiss or madly modern.
The Frau Doctor Burckhard used to serve mid-morning hot chocolate
with rosettes of whipped cream, and receive her friends in a long, un-
carpeted hall-drawing room with lethal ferns and a yellow beeswaxed
hardwood floor shining under a central skylight. On the wall there were
large expert photographs of what at a distance appeared to be Mont
Blanc — they were in reality views of Frank Lloyd Wright's Japanese
hotel.

I admired the Burckhards and felt at home in their house, and these
feelings were only intensified when I discovered that my mother was
always ill at ease with them. The heartiness, the enlightenment, and the
bright, ferny greenhouse atmosphere were too much for her.

Eric and I were too young to care for books or athletics. Neither
of our houses had absorbing toys or an elevator to go up and down in.
We were inseparable, but I cannot imagine what we talked about. I
loved Eric because he was more popular than I and yet absolutely *sui
generis* at the Brimmer School. He had a chalk-white face and limp, fine,
white-blond hair. He was frail, elbowy, started talking with an enthusiastic
Mont Blanc chirp and would flush with bewilderment if interrupted.
All the other boys at Brimmer wore little tweed golf suits with knicker-
bockers, but Eric always arrived in a black suit coat, a Byronic collar,
and cuffless gray flannel trousers that almost hid his shoes. The long
trousers were replaced on warm days by gray flannel shorts, such as were
worn by children still in kindergarten. Eric's unenviable and freakish
costumes were too old or too young. He accepted the whims of his
parents with a buoyant tranquillity that I found unnatural.

My first and terminating quarrel with Eric was my fault. Eventually
almost our whole class at Brimmer had whooping cough, but Eric's seizure
was like his long trousers — untimely: he was sick a month too early.
For a whole month he was in quarantine and forced to play by himself
in a removed corner of the Public Garden. He was certainly conspicuous
as he skiproped with his Swiss nurse under the out-of-the-way Ether
Memorial Fountain far from the pond and the swan boats. His parents
had decided that this was an excellent opportunity for Eric to brush up

on his German, and so the absoluteness of his quarantine was monstrously exaggerated by the fact that child and nurse spoke no English but only a guttural, British-sounding, Swiss German. Round and round and round the Fountain, he played intensely, frailly, obediently, until I began to tease him. Though motioned away by him, I came close. I had attracted some of the most popular Brimmer School boys. For the first time I had gotten favorable attention from several little girls. I came close. I shouted. Was Eric afraid of girls? I imitated his German. *Ein, swei, drei*, BEER. I imitated Eric's coughing. "He is afraid he will give you whooping cough if he talks or lets you come nearer," the nurse said in her musical Swiss-English voice. I came nearer. Eric flushed, grew white, bent double with coughing. He began to cry, and had to be led away from the Public Garden. For a whole week I routed Eric from the Garden daily, and for two or three days I was a center of interest. "Come see the Lake Geneva spider monkey!" I would shout. I don't know why I couldn't stop. Eric never told his father, I think, but when he recovered we no longer spoke. The breach was so unspoken and intense that our classmates were actually horrified. They even devised a solemn ritual for our reconciliation. We crossed our hearts, mixed spit, mixed blood. The reconciliation was hollow.

This poem will require particular attention to control of inflection and emphasis to make the important pun clear and meaningful when it is heard rather than seen on the page.

A Hymn to God the Father / JOHN DONNE

1623

> Wilt thou forgive that sin where I begun,
>   Which is my sin though it were done before?
> Wilt thou forgive those sins through which I run,
>   And do them still, though still I do deplore?
> When thou hast done, thou hast not done,
>   For I have more.
>
> Wilt thou forgive that sin by which I've won
>   Others to sin, and made my sin their door?
> Wilt thou forgive that sin which I did shun
>   A year or two, but wallow'd in a score?
> When thou hast done, thou hast not done,
>   For I have more.

I have a sin of fear, that when I've spun
    My last thread, I shall perish on the shore;
Swear by thyself at my death thy Sun
    Shall shine as it shines now, and heretofore;
And having done that, thou hast Donne.
        I have no more.

"Wild Grapes" calls for considerable variety of projection and volume. The narrative lines, of course, must be directed to the audience. The brother's first instructions are delivered as he stands beside the little girl; his "loud cries" are directed to her as she hangs suspended in the air.

Wild Grapes / ROBERT FROST

What tree may not the fig be gathered from?
The grape may not be gathered from the birch?
It's all you know the grape, or know the birch.
As a girl gathered from the birch myself
Equally with my weight in grapes, one autumn,
I ought to know what tree the grape is fruit of.
I was born, I suppose, like anyone,
And grew to be a little boyish girl
My brother could not always leave at home.
But that beginning was wiped out in fear
The day I swung suspended with the grapes,
And was come after like Eurydice
And brought down safely from the upper regions;
And the life I live now's an extra life
I can waste as I please on whom I please.
So if you see me celebrate two birthdays,
And give myself out as two different ages,
One of them five years younger than I look —
One day my brother led me to a glade
Where a white birch he knew of stood alone,
Wearing a thin head-dress of pointed leaves,
And heavy on her heavy hair behind,
Against her neck, an ornament of grapes.
Grapes, I knew grapes from having seen them last year.

One bunch of them, and there began to be
Bunches all round me growing in white birches,
The way they grew round Leif the Lucky's German;
Mostly as much beyond my lifted hands, though,
As the moon used to seem when I was younger,
And only freely to be had for climbing.

My brother did the climbing; and at first
Threw me down the grapes to miss and scatter
And have to hunt for in sweet fern and hardhack;
Which gave him some time to himself to eat,
But not so much, perhaps, as a boy needed.
So then, to make me wholly self-supporting,
He climbed still higher and bent the tree to earth
And put it in my hands to pick my own grapes.
"Here, take a tree-top, I'll get another.
Hold on with all your might when I let go."
I said I had the tree. It wasn't true.
The opposite was true. The tree had me.
The minute it was left with me alone
It caught me up as if I were the fish
And it the fishpole. So I was translated
To loud cries from my brother of "Let go!
Don't you know anything, you girl? Let go!
But I, with something of the baby grip
Acquired ancestrally in just such trees
When wilder mothers than our wildest now
Hung babies out on branches by the hands
To dry or wash or tan, I don't know which,
(You'll have to ask an evolutionist) —
I held on uncomplainingly for life.
My brother tried to make me laugh to help me.
"What are you doing up there in those grapes?
Don't be afraid. A few of them won't hurt you.
I mean, they won't pick you if you don't them."
Much danger of my picking anything!
By that time I was pretty well reduced
To a philosophy of hang-and-let-hang.
"Now you know how it feels," my brother said,
"To be a bunch of fox-grapes, as they call them,
That when it thinks it has escaped the fox
By growing where it shouldn't — on a birch,
Where a fox wouldn't think to look for it —

And if he looked and found it, couldn't reach it —
Just then come you and I to gather it.
Only you have the advantage of the grapes
In one way: you have one more stem to cling by,
And promise more resistance to the picker."

One by one I lost off my hat and shoes,
And I still clung. I let my head fall back
And shut my eyes against the sun, my ears
Against my brother's nonsense; "Drop," he said,
"I'll catch you in my arms. It isn't far."
(Stated in lengths of him it might not be.)
"Drop or I'll shake the tree and shake you down."
Grim silence on my part as I sank lower,
My small wrists stretching till they showed the banjo strings.
"Why, if she isn't serious about it!
Hold tight awhile till I think what to do.
I'll bend the tree down and let you down by it."
I don't know much about the letting down;
But once I felt ground with my stocking feet
And the world came revolving back to me,
I know I looked long at my curled-up fingers,
Before I straightened them and brushed the bark off.
My brother said: "Don't you weigh anything?
Try to weigh something next time, so you won't
Be run off with by birch trees into space."

It wasn't my not weighing anything
So much as my not knowing anything —
My brother had been nearer right before.
I had not taken the first step in knowledge;
I had not learned to let go with the hands,
As still I have not learned to with the heart,
And have no wish to with the heart — nor need,
That I can see. The mind — is not the heart.
I may yet live, as I know others live,
To wish in vain to let go with the mind —
Of cares, at night, to sleep; but nothing tells me
That I need to learn to let go with the heart.

*Walter de la Mare's familiar poem calls for considerable attention to volume
and projection. Be careful not to let the projected calls become so strong that*

they overbalance the quiet contrast. Don't neglect the "outdoors-indoors-out-doors" rhythm of content.

The Listeners / WALTER DE LA MARE

"Is there anybody there?" said the Traveler,
　　Knocking on the moonlit door;
And his horse in the silence champed the grasses
　　Of the forest's ferny floor.
And a bird flew up out of the turret,
　　Above the Traveler's head:
And he smote upon the door again a second time;
　　"Is there anybody there?" he said.
But no one descended to the Traveler;
　　No head from the leaf-fringed sill
Leaned over and looked into his gray eyes,
　　Where he stood perplexed and still.
But only a host of phantom listeners
　　That dwelt in the lone house then
Stood listening in the quiet of the moonlight
　　To that voice from the world of men:
Stood thronging the faint moonbeams on the dark stair,
　　That goes down to the empty hall,
Hearkening in an air stirred and shaken
　　By the lonely Traveler's call.
And he felt in his heart their strangeness,
　　Their stillness answering his cry,
While his horse moved, cropping the dark turf,
　　'Neath the starred and leafy sky;
For he suddenly smote on the door, even
　　Louder, and lifted his head: —
"Tell them I came, and no one answered,
　　That I kept my word," he said.
Never the least stir made the listeners,
　　Though every word he spake
Fell echoing through the shadowiness of the still house
　　From the one man left awake:
Aye, they heard his foot upon the stirrup,
　　And the sound of iron on stone,

And how the silence surged softly backward,
    When the plunging hoofs were gone.

Be careful that you understand all the allusions and "theatre jargon" in this poem. When a poet as sophisticated as T. S. Eliot pays such careful attention to obvious rhyme, we must certainly take our cue from him and enjoy it fully.

Gus: The Theatre Cat / T. S. ELIOT

Gus is the Cat at the Theatre Door.
His name, as I ought to have told you before,
Is really Asparagus. That's such a fuss
To pronounce, that we usually call him just Gus.
His coat's very shabby, he's thin as a rake,
And he suffers from palsy that makes his paws shake.
Yet he was, in his youth, quite the smartest of Cats —
But no longer a terror to mice and to rats.
For he isn't the Cat that he was in his prime;
Though his name was quite famous, he says, in its time.
And whenever he joins his friends at their club
(Which takes place at the back of the neighbouring pub)
He loves to regale them, if someone else pays,
With anecdotes drawn from his palmier days.
For he once was a Star of the highest degree —
He has acted with Irving, he's acted with Tree.
And he likes to relate his success on the Halls,
Where the Gallery once gave him seven cat-calls.
But his grandest creation, as he loves to tell,
Was Firefrorefiddle, the Fiend of the Fell.

"I have played," so he says, "every possible part,
And I used to know seventy speeches by heart.
I'd extemporize back-chat, I knew how to gag,
And I knew how to let the cat out of the bag.
I knew how to act with my back and my tail;
With an hour of rehearsal, I never could fail.
I'd a voice that would soften the hardest of hearts,
Whether I took the lead, or in character parts.
I have sat by the bedside of poor Little Nell;

When the Curfew was rung, then I swung on the bell.
In the Pantomime season I never fell flat,
And I once understudied Dick Whittington's Cat.
But my grandest creation, as history will tell,
Was Firefrorefiddle, the Fiend of the Fell."

Then, if someone will give him a toothful of gin,
He will tell how he once played a part in *East Lynne*.
At a Shakespeare performance he once walked on pat,
When some actor suggested the need for a cat.
He once played a Tiger — could do it again —
Which an Indian Colonel pursued down a drain.
And he thinks that he still can, much better than most,
Produce blood-curdling noises to bring on the Ghost.
And he once crossed the stage on a telegraph wire,
To rescue a child when a house was on fire.
And he says: "Now, these kittens, they do not get trained
As we did in the days when Victoria reigned.
They never got drilled in a regular troupe,
And they think they are smart, just to jump through a hoop."
And he'll say, as he scratches himself with his claws,
"Well, the Theatre's certainly not what it was.
These modern productions are all very well,
But there's nothing to equal, from what I hear tell,
    That moment of mystery
    When I made history
As Firefrorefiddle, the Fiend of the Fell."

Much of the humor in this memory of a traumatic experience results from "stage directions" for the use of vocal variety.

from *Ring Out, Wild Bells* / WOLCOTT GIBBS

When I finally got around to seeing Max Reinhardt's cinema version of "A Midsummer-Night's Dream," and saw a child named Mickey Rooney playing Puck, I remembered suddenly that long ago I had taken the same part.

Our production was given on the open-air stage at the Riverdale Country School, shortly before the war. The scenery was only the natural scenery of that suburban dell, and the cast was exclusively male, ranging

Reprinted by permission of Dodd, Mead & Company from *Bed of Neuroses* by Wolcott Gibbs. Copyright 1936 by Wolcott Gibbs.

in age from eleven to perhaps seventeen. While we had thus preserved the pure, Elizabethan note of the original, it must be admitted that our version had its drawbacks. The costumes were probably the worst things we had to bear, and even Penrod, tragically arrayed as Launcelot in his sister's stockings and his father's drawers, might have been embarrassed for us. Like Penrod, we were costumed by our parents, and like the Schofields, they seemed on the whole a little weak historically. Half of the ladies were inclined to favor the Elizabethan, and they had constructed rather bunchy ruffs and farthingales for their offspring; others, who had read as far as the stage directions and learned that the action took place in an Athenian wood, had produced something vaguely Athenian, usually beginning with a sheet. Only the fairies had a certain uniformity. For some reason their parents had all decided on cheesecloth, with here and there a little ill-advised trimming with tinsel.

My own costume was mysterious, but spectacular. As nearly as I have ever been able to figure things out, my mother found her inspiration for it in a Maxfield Parrish picture of a court jester. Beginning at the top, there was a cap with three stuffed horns; then, for the main part, a pair of tights that covered me to my wrists and ankles; and finally slippers with stuffed toes that curled up at the ends. The whole thing was made out of silk in alternate green and red stripes, and (unquestionably my poor mother's most demented stroke) it was covered from head to foot with a thousand tiny bells. Because all our costumes were obviously perishable, we never wore them in rehearsal, and naturally nobody knew that I was invested with these peculiar sound effects until I made my entrance at the beginning of the second act.

Our director was a man who had strong opinions about how Shakespeare should be played, and Puck was one of his favorite characters. It was his theory that Puck, being "the incarnation of mischief," never ought to be still a minute, so I had been coached to bound onto the stage, and once there to dance up and down, cocking my head and waving my arms.

"I want you to be a little whirlwind," this man said.

Even as I prepared to bound onto the stage, I had my own misgivings about those dangerously abundant gestures, and their probable effect on my bells. It was too late, however, to invent another technique for playing Puck, even if there had been room for anything but horror in my mind. I bounded out onto the stage.

The effect, in its way, must have been superb. With every leap I rang like a thousand children's sleighs, my melodies foretelling God knows what worlds of merriment to the enchanted spectators. It was even worse when I came to the middle of the stage and went into my gestures. The other ringing had been loud but sporadic. This was persistent, varying only slightly in volume and pitch with the vehemence of my gestures. To a blind man, it must have sounded as though I had reck-lessly decided to accompany myself on a xylophone. A maturer actor would probably have made up his mind that an emergency existed, and abandoned his gestures as impractical under the circumstances. I was thirteen, and incapable of innovations. I had been told by responsible authorities that gestures went with this part, and I continued to make them. I also continued to ring — a silvery music, festive and horrible.

If the bells were hard on my nerves, they were even worse for the rest of the cast, who were totally unprepared for my new interpretation. Puck's first remark is addressed to one of the fairies, and it is mercifully brief.

I said, "How now, spirit! Whither wander you?"

This unhappy child, already embarrassed by a public appearance in cheesecloth and tinsel, was also burdened with an opening speech of sixteen lines in verse. He began bravely:

> "Over hill, over dale,
>   Thorough brush, thorough brier,
> Over park, over pale,
>   Thorough flood, thorough fire . . ."

At the word "fire," my instructions were to bring my hands up from the ground in a long, wavery sweep, intended to represent fire. The bells pealed. To my startled ears, it sounded more as if they exploded. The fairy stopped in his lines and looked at me sharply. The jingling, how-ever, had diminished; it was no more than if a faint wind stirred my bells, and he went on:

> "I do wander every where,
> Swifter than the moone's sphere . . ."

Here again I had another cue, for a sort of swoop and dip indicating the swiftness of the moone's sphere. Again the bells rang out, and again the performance stopped in its tracks. The fairy was clearly troubled by these interruptions. He had, however, a child's strange acceptance of the inscrutable, and was even able to regard my bells as a last-minute adult addition to the program, nerve-racking but not to be questioned. I am sure it was only this that got him through that first speech.

My turn, when it came, was even worse. By this time the audience had succumbed to a helpless gaiety. Every time my bells rang, laughter swept the spectators, and this mounted and mingled with the bells until everything else was practically inaudible. I began my speech, another long one, and full of incomprehensible references to Titania's changeling.

"Louder," said somebody in the wings. "You'll have to talk louder."

It was the director, and he seemed to be in a dangerous state.

"And for heaven's sake, stop that jingling!" he said.

I talked louder, and I tried to stop the jingling, but it was no use. By the time I got to the end of my speech, I was shouting and so was the audience. It appeared that I had very little control over the bells, which continued to jingle in spite of my passionate efforts to keep them quiet.

All this had a very bad effect on the fairy, who by this time had many symptoms of a complete nervous collapse. However, he began his next speech:

> "Either I mistake your shape and making quite,
> Or else you are that shrewd and knavish sprite
> Call'd Robin Goodfellow: are you not he
> That . . ."

At this point I forgot that the rules had been changed and I was supposed to leave out the gestures. There was a furious jingling, and the fairy gulped.

"Are you not he that, that . . ."

He looked miserably at the wings, and the director supplied the next line, but the tumult was too much for him. The unhappy child simply shook his head.

"Say anything!" shouted the director desperately. "Anything at all!

The fairy only shut his eyes and shuddered.

"All right!" shouted the director. "All right, Puck. *You* begin *your* next speech."

By some miracle, I actually did remember my next lines, and had opened my mouth to begin on them when suddenly the fairy spoke. His voice was a high, thin monotone, and there seemed to be madness in it, but it was perfectly clear.

"Fourscore and seven years ago," he began, "our fathers brought forth on this continent a new nation, conceived . . ."

He said it right through to the end, and it was certainly the most successful speech ever made on that stage, and probably one of the most successful speeches ever made on any stage. I don't remember, if I ever knew, how the rest of us ever picked up the dull, normal thread of the play after that extraordinary performance, but we must have, because I know it went on. I only remember that in the next intermission the director cut off my bells with his penknife, and after that things quieted down and got dull.

This excerpt from a novel makes an amusing companion piece to Mr. Gibbs's memory. There is great opportunity for vocal variety here. Allow the young "interpreters" to enjoy the "elocutionary" aspects of the selections.

FROM *The Little Girls* / ELIZABETH BOWEN

Thick cream glazed blinds were pulled most of the way down. Failing to keep out the marine sunshine, they flopped lazily over the open windows in the hot June breath rather than breeze haunting the garden. St. Agatha's had been a house, IV-A classroom probably the morning-room. The blinds were lace-bordered. There was a garlanded wallpaper — called to order by having on it a bald, pontifical clock, only a size or two smaller than a station one, a baize board clustered with lists and warnings, and sepia reproductions of inspiriting pictures, among them "Hope," framed in oak. Of oak were the desks, to which were clamped high-backed seats. An aroma of Plasticine came from the models along the chimneypiece, and from jars of botanical specimens near a window whiffs of water slimy with rotting greenery were fanned in — the girl in charge of the specimens being absent with one of her summer colds. Chalk in the neighbourhood of the blackboard and ink thickening in china wells in the desks were the only other educational smells.

A dozen or so girls, most of them aged eleven, some ten, some twelve, sat at the desks. All wore their summer tunics of butcher-blue. By turning their heads, left, they could have seen strips of garden, parching away, between restless lace and stolid white window sills. Politely, however, most of them faced their teacher; this they could do for Miss Kinmate, if little else. This was the first lesson after mid-morning break with its milk and biscuits — even the slight feast had thrown IV-A into a gorged condition. But this also was the Tuesday poetry hour, to which Miss Kinmate attached hopes. Each girl (the idea was) chose for herself the short poem or portion of longer one which, got by heart, she was to recite.

One more of them had just taken the stand.

> "There *was* a time when meadow, grove and stream,
> The earth and — "

"Stop!" cried Miss Kinmate. "Before we begin, not *too* much expression. Wordsworth was not as regretful as all that."

"I thought he was. Like some old, fat person saying, 'There *was* a time when I could jump over a ten-foot wall.'"

"That would be silly."

"Well, this is silly, in a way."

"Your old, fat man would not be speaking the truth. Have you any idea how high a ten-foot wall is?"

"Yes."

"I wonder whether you have. Because, even a Greek athlete could probably not jump over that." (From a back desk, a hand shot up.) "*Yes*, Olive?"

"How high could a Greek athlete probably jump?"

"That would depend."

The child Clare, during this intermission, stood stonily contemplating her audience — hands behind her, back to the blackboard, feet planted apart, tongue exploring a cavity in a lower molar. At a moody sign from Miss Kinmate, she went on:

> " — and every common sight,
> To *me* did seem
> Apparell'd in celestial *light*,
> The glory and freshness of a dream.
> It is *not* now as it has been of yore; —
> Turn whereso'er I may,
> By night *or* day,
> The things which — "

"Stop! Oh dear, what are we to do?"

"I thought — "

"Well, don't — *try!* Otherwise, go and sit down. Ruining that beautiful poem!"

"Yes, Miss Kinmate."

"And don't make eyes at the others. Next time, choose a poem you understand."

"I do know another. Shall I try that?"

Miss Kinmate looked at the clock . The whole class (but for Sheila Beaker, who couldn't be bothered, and Muriel Borthwick, who having picked at a good big scab on her arm now dabbed blotting-paper at the resultant blood) did likewise, in an awed, considering way. "Very well," Miss Kinmate conceded. "Go on, Clare — though remember, there are others to come."

The child, having drawn a breath twice her size, launched with passion into her second choice:

> "Last night among his fellow roughs
> He jested, quaff'd and swore:
> A drunken private of the Buffs,
> Who never look'd before.
> Today, beneath the foeman's frown,
> He stands in Elgin's place,
> Ambassador from Britain's crown,
> And type of all her race.
>
> Poor, reckless, rude, low-born, untaught,
> Bewilder'd and alone,

A heart, with English instinct fraught,
He yet can call his own.
Ay! tear his body limb from limb,
Bring *cord,* or *axe,* or *flame! —*
He only knows, that not through him
Shall England come to shame.

Fair Kentish hopfields round him seemed
Like dreams to come and go;
Bright leagues of cherry blossom — "

"Stop! Time's up, I'm afraid. A pity, because you were doing better." Miss Kinmate's eye roved round. "Diana, try and not sit with your mouth open — wake up! What is the name of the poem Clare's just recited?"

" 'The Drunken Private of the Buffs.' "

"Not exactly. — Well, who and whose poem next? Muriel: you!"

"I think I'm bleeding too much."

"What, cut yourself?"

"Not exactly."

"Better go and find Matron."

Gory Muriel left. Miss Kinmate had to cast round all over again. "*Sheila,* then. Sheila, we'll hear you now."

Southstone's wonder, the child exhibition dancer, rose, tossed back her silver-gold plaits, and habituatedly stepped forward into the limelight. An ornate volume, open at the required page and gildedly looking like a school prize (which it was, though not awarded to her), was bestowed by her upon Miss Kinmate, with what was less a bow than a flowerlike inclination of the head. She then half-turned, with a minor swirl of the tunic, and, facing the footlights, glided three steps sideways into the place of doom left vacant by Clare. Here reality struck the prodigy amidships. Bewitched, since she rose from her desk, by her own performance, she had lost sight for that minute or two of her entrance's true and hideous purpose. She was to be called upon not to spring about but to give tongue. A badgered hatred of literature filled her features. She did deliver her poem, though in the manner of one voicing, with wonderful moderation, a long-nursed and justifiable complaint:

"Up the airy mountain,
Down the rushing glen,
We daren't *go* a-hunting
For fear of little *men;*
Wee folk, good folk,
Trooping all together;
Green jacket, red cap,
And white owl's feather!

> Down on the rocky *shore*
> Some make their home;
> They *live* on crispy pancakes
> Of yellow tide-foam;
> *Some,* in the reeds
> Of the black mountain-lake,
> With frogs for *their* watch-dogs,
> *All night awake.*
>
> High on the hill-top
> The old *King* sits.
> *He* is now so old and grey
> He's nigh lost . . . ?
> . . . his bridge of white wits?
> . . . his mist of white wits?
> . . . *his* bridge?
> . . . *his* wits . . . ?"

She ran down, ticked over uncertainly, gave right out, and turned on Miss Kinmate a look as much as to say: "Well, there you are. What else would you expect?"

"Never mind," Miss Kinmate hastened to say. "It went nicely so far. Though a little mournful — fairies are gay things, aren't they?"

Sheila had no idea.

"And one word wrong in your second line. It should be 'rushy,' not 'rushing.' How could a glen rush?"

"I thought it meant they were all rushing about," said Sheila Beaker, still more deeply aggrieved.

"Sheila chose a delightful poem, at any rate," Miss Kinmate informed the class — who knew to a girl whose the choice had been: Mrs. Beaker's.

There is great subtlety in the repeated sounds in these companion war poems. Your diction must be accurate to make use of all the complex tone color. Do not underestimate their simplicity of sound pattern.

Love Note I: Surely / GWENDOLYN BROOKS

> Surely you stay my certain own, you stay
> My you. All honest, lofty as a cloud.
> Surely I could come now and find you high,
> As mine as you ever were; should not be awed.

Surely your word would pop as insolent
As always: "Why, of course I love you, dear."
Your gaze, surely, ungauzed as I could want.
Your touches, that never were careful, what they were.
Surely — But I am very off from that.
From surely. From indeed. From decent arrow
That was my clean naïveté and my faith.
This morning men deliver wounds and death.
They will deliver death and wounds tomorrow.
And I doubt all. You. Or a violet.

Love Note II: Flags / GWENDOLYN BROOKS

Still, it is dear defiance now to carry
Fair flags of you above my indignation,
Top, with a pretty glory and a merry
Softness, the scattered pound of my cold passion.
I pull you down in my foxhole. Do you mind?
You burn in bits of saucy color then.
I let you flutter out against the pained
Volleys. Against my power crumpled and wan.
You, and the yellow pert exuberance
Of dandelion days, unmocking sun:
The blowing of clear wind in your gay hair;
Love changeful in you (like a music, or
Like a sweet mournfulness, or like a dance,
Or like the tender struggle of a fan).

The delicacy of sound and action in this poem will require considerable vocal control. Kinesthetic imagery and total empathic response are also important and will help dictate both quality and pace.

Death / MAXWELL BODENHEIM

I SHALL walk down the road.
I shall turn and feel upon my feet
The kisses of Death, like scented rain.
For Death is a black slave with little silver birds
Perched in a sleeping wreath upon his head.
He will tell me, his voice like jewels
Dropped into a satin bag,

How he has tip-toed after me down the road,
His heart made a dark whirlpool with longing for me.
Then he will graze me with his hands
And I shall be one of the sleeping silver birds
Between the cold waves of his hair, as he tip-toes on.

There are several "stage directions" for vocal changes in this selection. Make use of them for the climaxes and the variety and contrast.

Daniel, Chapter Five / THE OLD TESTAMENT

Belshazzar the king made a great feast for a thousand of his lords, and drank wine before the thousand. Belshazzar, while he tasted the wine, commanded to bring the golden and silver vessels which Nebuchadnezzar his father had taken out of the temple which was in Jerusalem; that the king and his lords, his wives and his concubines, might drink therefrom. Then they brought the golden vessels that were taken out of the temple of the house of God which was at Jerusalem; and the king and his lords, his wives and his concubines, drank from them. They drank wine, and praised the gods of gold, and of silver, of brass, of iron, of wood, and of stone.

In the same hour came forth the fingers of a man's hand, and wrote over against the candlestick upon the plaster of the wall of the king's palace; and the king saw the part of the hand that wrote. Then the king's countenance was changed in him, and his thoughts troubled him; and the joints of his loins were loosed, and his knees smote one against another. The king cried aloud to bring in the enchanters, the Chaldeans, and the soothsayers. The king spake and said to the wise men of Babylon, Whosoever shall read this writing, and show me the interpretation thereof, shall be clothed with purple, and have a chain of gold about his neck, and shall be the third ruler in the kingdom. Then came in all the king's wise men; but they could not read the writing; nor make known to the king the interpretation. Then was the king Belshazzar greatly changed in him, and his lords were perplexed.

Now the queen by reason of the words of the king and his lords came into the banquet house: the queen spake and said, O king, live for ever; let not thy thoughts trouble thee, nor let thy countenance be changed. There is a man in thy kingdom, in whom is the spirit of the holy gods; and in the days of thy father light and understanding and wisdom, like the wisdom of the gods, were found in him; and the king Nebuchadnezzar thy father, the king, *I say*, thy father, made him master of the magicians, enchanters, Chaldeans, and soothsayers; forasmuch as an excellent spirit, and knowledge, and understanding, interpreting of dreams, and showing of dark sentences, and dissolving of doubts, were found in the same Daniel, whom the king named Belteshazzar. Now let Daniel be called, and he will show the interpretation.

Then was Daniel brought in before the king. The king spake and said unto Daniel, Art thou that Daniel, who are of the children of the captivity of Judah, whom the king my father brought out of Judah? I have heard of thee, that the spirit of the gods is in thee, and that light and understanding and excellent wisdom are found in thee. And now the wise men, the enchanters, have been brought in before me, that they should read this writing, and make known unto me the interpretation thereof; but they could not show the interpretation of the king. But I have heard of thee, that thou canst give interpretations, and dissolve doubts: now if thou canst read the writing, and make known to me the interpretation thereof, thou shalt be clothed with purple, and have a chain of gold about thy neck, and shall be the third ruler in the kingdom.

Then Daniel answered and said before the king, Let thy gifts be to thyself, and give thy reward to another; nevertheless I will read the writing unto the king, and make known to him the interpretation. O thou king, the Most High God gave Nebuchadnezzar thy father the kingdom, and greatness, and glory, and majesty: and because of the greatness that he gave him, all the peoples, nations, and languages trembled and feared before him: whom he would he slew, and whom he would he kept alive; and whom he would he raised up, and whom he would he put down. But when his heart was lifted up, and his spirit was hardened so that he dealt proudly, he was deposed from his kingly throne, and they took his glory from him: and he was driven from the sons of men, and his heart was made like the beasts', and his dwelling was with the wild asses; he was fed with grass like oxen, and his body was wet with the dew of heaven; until he knew that the Most High God ruleth in the kingdom of men, and that he setteth up over it whomsoever he will. And thou his son, O Belshazzar, hast not humbled thy heart, though thou knewest all this, but has lifted up thyself against the Lord of heaven; and they have brought the vessels of his house before thee, and thou and thy lords, thy wives and thy concubines, have drunk wine from them; and thou hast praised the gods of silver and gold, of brass, iron, wood, and stone, which see not, nor hear, nor know; and the God in whose hand thy breath is, and whose are all thy ways, hast thou not glorified. Then was the part of the hand sent from before him, and this writing was inscribed.

And this is the writing that was inscribed: ME-NE, ME-NE, TE-KEL, U-PHAR SIN. This is the interpretation of the thing: ME-NE; God hath numbered thy kingdom, and brought it to an end. TE-KEL; thou art weighed in the balances, and art found wanting. U-PHAR SIN; thy kingdom is divided, and given to the Medes and Persians.

Then commanded Belshazzar, and they clothed Daniel with purple, and put a chain of gold about his neck, and made proclamation concerning him, that he should be the third ruler in the kingdom.

In that night Belshazzar the Chaldean king was slain. And Darius the Mede received the kingdom, being about threescore and two years old.

Although this poem was written during the nineteenth century, it is certainly relevant to the world today. Its strength lies in the quality of mind and attitude it reflects. The final sentence must be carefully controlled vocally to keep the last part of the stanza from overbalancing the important plea for fidelity.

Dover Beach / MATTHEW ARNOLD

The sea is calm tonight.
The tide is full, the moon lies fair
Upon the straits; — on the French coast the light
Gleams and is gone; the cliffs of England stand
Glimmering and vast, out in the tranquil bay.
Come to the window, sweet is the night-air!
Only, from the long line of spray
Where the sea meets the moon-blanched land,
Listen! you hear the grating roar
Of pebbles which the waves draw back, and fling,
At their return, up the high strand,
Begin, and cease, and then again begin,
With tremulous cadence slow, and bring
The eternal note of sadness in.

Sophocles long ago
Heard it on the Aegean, and it brought
Into his mind the turbid ebb and flow
Of human misery; we
Find also in the sound a thought,
Hearing it by this distant northern sea.

The Sea of Faith
Was once, too, at the full, and round earth's shore
Lay like the folds of a bright girdle furled.
But now I only hear

Its melancholy, long, withdrawing roar,
Retreating, to the breath
Of the night-wind, down the vast edges drear
And naked shingles of the world.

Ah, love, let us be true
To one another! for the world, which seems
To lie before us like a land of dreams,
So various, so beautiful, so new,
Hath really neither joy, nor love, nor light,
Nor certitude, nor peace, nor help for pain;
And we are here as on a darkling plain
Swept with confused alarms of struggle and flight,
Where ignorant armies clash by night.

Although the speaker in this poem is repeating the instructions of another,
we must be constantly aware of his voice in order to preserve the unity and
convey the intended effect of the last two and a half lines of each stanza and
the final stanza where both threads are woven together. Make full use of the
contrasts.

Naming of Parts / HENRY REED

(to Alan Michell)
Vixi puellis nuper idoneus
*Et militavi non sine gloria**

Today we have naming of parts. Yesterday,
We had daily cleaning. And tomorrow morning,
We shall have what to do after firing. But today,
Today we have naming of parts. Japonica
Glistens like coral in all of the neighbouring gardens,
    And today we have naming of parts.

This is the lower sling swivel. And this
Is the upper sling swivel, whose use you will see,
When you are given your slings. And this is the piling swivel,
Which in your case you have not got. The branches

From *A Map of Verona*, copyright 1947 by Henry Reed. Reprinted by permission
of Harcourt Brace Jovanovich, Inc. Also used by permission of the author and Jonathan
Cape Limited.
    * "I was but now still meet for ladies' love, and fought my battles not without
glory." (Guterman)

Hold in the gardens their silent, eloquent gestures,
    Which in our case we have not got.

This is the safety-catch, which is always released
With an easy flick of the thumb. And please do not let me
See anyone using his finger. You can do it quite easy
If you have any strength in your thumb. The blossoms
Are fragile and motionless, never letting anyone see
    Any of them using their finger.

And this you can see is the bolt. The purpose of this
Is to open the breech, as you see. We can slide it
Rapidly backwards and forwards: we call this
Easing the spring. And rapidly backwards and forwards
The early bees are assaulting and fumbling the flowers:
    They call it easing the Spring.

They call it easing the Spring: it is perfectly easy
If you have any strength in your thumb: like the bolt,
And the breech, and the cocking-piece, and the point of balance,
Which in our case we have not got; and the almond-blossom
Silent in all of the gardens and the bees going backwards and forwards,
    For today we have naming of parts.

This poem is devastating in the cold simplicity of its literary style. The word choice and the stark syntax, as well as the stanza division counting off the three "places," underscore the attitude of the persona. Keep the quotations within this unity of attitude.

Her Story / NAOMI LONG MADGETT

They gave me the wrong name, in the first place.
They named me Grace and waited for a light and agile dancer.
But some trick of the genes mixed me up
And instead I turned out big and black and burly.

In the second place, I fashioned the wrong dreams.
I wanted to dress like Juliet and act
Before applauding audiences on Broadway.
I learned more about Shakespeare than he knew about himself.

But of course, all that was impossible.
"Talent, yes," they would tell me,
"But an actress has to look the part."
So I ended up waiting on tables in Harlem
And hearing uncouth men yell at me:
"Hey, momma, you can cancel that hamburger
And come on up to 102."

In the third place, I tried the wrong solution.
The stuff I drank made me deathly sick
And someone called a doctor.
Next time I'll try a gun.

The "new" black speaks with a balance of contempt and pride of identity in
this poem. It must be handled firmly so that the first seven lines carry the
force of constantly repeated admonitions building to command proportions on
the three exclamations. Be careful that the last stanza has its own kind of
strength to insure the balance and achieve the climax.

The Key / JEANNETTE SMITH IRVIN

The key, they said, to freedom's door
Was to learn and save; walk and talk right;
GET EDUCATED!
MOVE UP!
BE ACCEPTED!
The key, they said, to Democracy
Was to act "white" and think you were free.

I have turned that key;
Strained against the door.
Now I have broken the key.
I do not want it any more.

Bibliography

The following books have specific exercises on voice and diction. The interpreter will wish to consult them for any minor problems which may need
attention.

Akin, Johnnye. *And So We Speak: Voice and Articulation.* Englewood Cliffs, New Jersey: Prentice-Hall, Inc., 1958.

Anderson, Virgil A. *Training the Speaking Voice.* Second Edition. New York: Oxford University Press, 1961.

Fairbanks, Grant. *Practical Voice Practice.* New York: Harper and Row, 1964.

Aimed specifically at audibility, intelligibility, and flexibility. A book designed for the normal voice with minor problems in the above areas.

Fisher, Hilda. *Improving Voice and Articulation.* Boston: Houghton Mifflin Company, 1966.

Hanley, Theodore D., and Wayne L. Thurman. *Developing Vocal Skills.* New York: Holt, Rinehart and Winston, Inc., 1962.

Heinberg, Paul. *Voice Training — For Speaking and Reading Aloud.* New York: The Ronald Press Company, 1964.

Especially designed to provide an application of current scientific knowledge for the student of speech and drama.

Recordings are very useful to help train your ear. The following book has an annotated list of recordings of prose, poetry, and drama.

Roach, Helen. *Spoken Records.* Second Edition. Metuchen, New Jersey: The Scarecrow Press, Inc., 1970.

The Interpretation
of Prose

Part Two

Chapter 5

Up to this point we have discussed matters of analysis common to all types of writing and the way the interpreter uses the knowledge he gains through analysis in his preparation and performance to make certain that his voice and body serve the demands of the literature. In this section we shall be concerned specifically with prose, and in the two following sections with drama and poetry respectively. We have seen that all literature has certain elements in common and that the basic principles of analysis and interpretation apply to all types. But it is equally true that each form imposes special problems and demands varying degrees of emphasis on one or more aspects of technique in preparation and presentation.

For example, the oral interpreter uses the same basic approach to poetry as to any other type of material, but he must also give special attention to condensation, sound patterns, and whatever strictures of stanzaic form, meter, and rhyme the poet has imposed. Drama requires special emphasis on character, time, place, and situation, and on the relationship among these elements which sets up the essential conflict, in addition to awareness of the form, which may be either prose or poetry. On the other hand, prose which is primarily nondramatic may nevertheless contain passages calling for attention to character and setting, and thus present problems similar to those found in drama. Or it may be highly suggestive and come very close to poetry in its use of imagery. Therefore, this division of material into prose, drama, and poetry, and further subdivision under these headings, must be regarded only as a convenience. For the concern of the modern interpreter is not with literary labels, except as they help him

Some Aspects of Prose

analyze his material. His interest is, rather, in the selection of suitable material and in the complete understanding of the piece of writing he wishes to communicate to his listeners. Classification can serve only as a starting point for a detailed analysis. It is the interpreter's responsibility to discover the problems and advantages in each type, and then to go beyond this generalization to the specific, individual variations within the particular selection he has chosen. For always, regardless of its form or type, each selection must be approached as an individual example. Before we consider the various kinds of writing, it would be well to review some aspects of literary style found in all prose writing.

Style is the channel through which the author relates his outlook on life to what he has to say in a given instance. It is the concrete, physical mode of written expression as it appears on the page. It embodies such technical considerations as overall organization of ideas, which we touched on in Chapter 2 in our analysis of the two poems; the steps in development of the central idea as they are evident in the major thought units, which are stanzas of poetry, acts and scenes in drama, and paragraphs in prose; the syntactical characteristics of the sentences within these major thought units; and choice of words and their relationship to each other within the sentence. The interpreter, since he will be communicating the "written symbols" orally, will also be concerned with the way the sentences will be broken up into *speech phrases*, the relationship of the *sounds* of the words as they are combined and the location of *stresses* which will be necessary for clarity. As Arnold Bennett says, "When a writer conceives an idea he conceives it in a form of words. That form of words is his style. . . ." It is shaped by the kind of person he is, by his general philosophy of life, and also by the culture and age in which he lives. It is dictated by his attitude toward his subject matter and toward his intended audience, his readers. Style is the heart of the intrinsic factor of harmony and is basic in establishing the tone of any selection. It is a tremendous help in getting at a character in drama and always offers important clues to attitude of the author or the speaker he has chosen to use in any type of writing.

Paragraphs

The first step in examining style is, of course, to become aware of the general organization of the whole selection. The next step is to discover how the elements which make up the whole are organized and arranged. In prose this involves a consideration of the major thought units, the paragraphs.

Paragraph structure is important to the interpreter because each paragraph is a unit in the thought progression. The length and complexity of the unit, and of the sentences which make it up, reflect the author's approach to the thought and the pace at which he is moving. Short, simple sentences and paragraphs indicate a direct, often relatively uncritical, approach and suggest immediacy of experience; long, complicated sentences and paragraphs suggest a more sophisticated and evaluative approach, perhaps an intellectualiztion of experience. The interpreter needs to be sensitive to these nuances of style and to reflect his awareness of them in his oral reading.

Moreover, the writer has indicated degrees of relationship and importance by what he has put together in the paragraphs. For instance, he may have included several relevant examples of a key idea in one unit, or he may have given each a separate paragraph, thus adding to their individual importance by setting them off from each other. A paragraph is a distinct subdivision of the main thought, dealing with a particular point and terminating only when that point has been developed. It usually has a slight climax of its own where a logical point or emotional level emerges and prepares the way for others to follow. They are large stepping-stones to the main climax and the conclusion.

Sentences

The way the author handles the sentences within the paragraphs is of practical concern to the interpreter, whose responsibility it is to make each segment of the total meaning clear to his audience. He must pay attention to length and grammatical construction as clues to attitude and tone in his analysis and as a guide to the use of his techniques of pause, rate, emphasis and inflection in performance.

The way a writer combines words into sentences is an important element of his style. The simple sentence (a single independent clause) and the compound sentence (two or more independent clauses) are most characteristic of a simple, direct style. The complex sentence (one independent clause and one or more dependent clauses) and the compound-complex sentence (two or more independent clauses, and one or more dependent clauses), on the other hand, are the mark of a more involved and complex style. The interpreter must, both in evaluating style and in interpreting orally, not only note these elementary grammatical distinctions; he must also consider sentence length, position of subordinate elements, order of words, and use of such effects as parallelism and balanced construction. The syntax of a sentence is a way of grouping the words to show their relationship and to point up degrees of importance. For example, contrast the syntax in these two phrases: ". . . all the marigolds and pinks in the bungalow gardens were bowed to earth with wetness" and "Drenched were the cold fuchsias. . . ." In the first example, the order is normal and leads easily to the completed thought. In the second phrase, however, "Drenched" is given strong emphasis by its position at the beginning of the sentence.

The writer in the following excerpt is describing his sensation on landing his plane after a dangerous and fantastic flight. He feels unable to reflect on the experience he has been through and to translate it through his intellect into an ordered pattern, and the succession of short sentences combining statements, questions, and an exclamation gives an almost breathless sense of his emotional exhaustion, the impossibility he feels of putting his experiences into words.

> Had I been afraid? I couldn't say. I had witnessed a strange sight. What strange sight? I couldn't say. The sky was blue and the sea was white. I felt I ought to tell someone about it since I was back from so far away! But I had no grip on what I had been through.

> ANTOINE DE SAINT EXUPÉRY, *Wind, Sand and Stars*

Numerous exclamatory or interrogative sentences or incomplete sentence fragments will affect the handling of a piece of prose for oral interpretation. Notice, for example, the vivacity and good humor suggested in this:

> God bless my soul! When do we find these contemptuous gentlemen lost to the world in the reading of Homer in his Greek or even of the bawdy Petronius in his Latin?

Not at all! We find them amusing themselves with bagatelles compared with which . . .

JOHN COWPER POWYS, Enjoyment of Literature

The exclamations give the writing speed and informality, while the question gives it intimacy and directness. The incomplete sentence, which in the complete essay is followed by a return to an earlier thought, leaves the reader to furnish the implied evaluation and again creates an atmosphere of conversation rather than of formal writing.

Longer sentences have more formality and must be broken down into speech phrases when read aloud. Long modifying phrases and clauses (italicized in the examples below) present the interpreter with a special challenge. Modifiers at the beginning of the sentence prepare the reader for the main idea and orient him toward it; and the interpreter has the problem of building up to the key words of the thought:

> *Wandering through clear chambers where the general effect made preferences almost as impossible as if they had been shocks, pausing at open doors where vistas were long and bland,* she would, *even if she had not already known,* have discovered for herself that Poynton was the record of a life.

HENRY JAMES, The Spoils of Poynton

When any of the elements occur out of the normal order in such a way that the meaning is held up until almost the very end of the sentence, we have a periodic construction. Because the periodic sentence defers the completion of meaning, it creates suspense; and because it breaks the usual sentence pattern and alters the normal stresses, it is especially emphatic. Although the inversion of normal word order is perhaps most effective in longer sentences where there is greater opportunity to arouse suspense by deferring completion of meaning, it is a device that can give special emphasis to a short sentence as well.

Modifiers in the middle of the sentence interrupt the main flow of the thought, even while explaining some elements within it. Here the interpreter must sustain the meaning, carrying the thread of the principal idea from one key word to another over the intervening material, without nullifying the contribution of those subordinate elements to the whole:

> The book in question, *which is at once a lasting contribution to English literature and a mere farrago of pretentious mediocrity,* was published about two months ago.

VIRGINIA WOOLF, The Common Reader

Modifiers at the end of the sentence continue the idea, expanding or qualifying it, although the skeletal frame of the thought is already complete without them:

I was at incredible pains in cutting down some of the largest trees for oars and masts, *wherein I was, however, much assisted by his Majesty's ship-carpenters, who helped me in smoothing them after I had done the rough work.*

JONATHAN SWIFT, *Gulliver's Travels*

Sentences with parallelisms and balanced constructions provide another challenge for the oral interpreter, since he must at once keep the parallel or coordinate elements equal in value and point the connection or contrast between them. A compound sentence, consisting of two independent clauses connected by a conjunction, is a very elementary example of syntactical parallelism; the clauses are so related in grammatical construction because the ideas are connected and have equal value. The connective "and," a usual signpost pointing out coordinations, as between parts of a compound subject or predicate, enables the interpreter to achieve a simple balance between parallel elements. The parallelism may be cast as a balanced construction, in which the parts are quite evenly set off against each other:

No man is an island, entire of itself; every man is a piece of the continent, a part of the main.

DONNE, *Devotions, XVII*

The parallelism here is easily and graphically shown by lining up the parts:

| No man | is an island, | entire of itself; |
| every man | is a piece of the continent, | a part of the main. |

Or it may be a series of elaborately wrought analogies and antitheses, reflected in the form in which the sentence is cast:

Harry, I do not only marvel where thou spendest thy time, but also how thou art accompanied; for though the camomile, the more it is trodden on the faster it grows, yet youth the more it is wasted the sooner it wears.

SHAKESPEARE, *Henry IV, Part I*

This sentence might be represented as follows:

Harry, I do	not only	marvel	where thou spendest thy time,
	but also		how thou art accompanied;
		for though	the camomile,
			the more it is trodden on
			the faster it grows,
		yet	youth
			the more it is wasted
			the sooner it wears.

The important thing for the interpreter to remember is that at the syntactical level parallelisms indicate parts of a sentence that are equal in value; at the stylistic level, ideas that are balanced against each other and mutually contribute to one another.

Too many sentences of similar construction or similar length result in a dead-level style that fails to hold the attention of the reader. Especially when read aloud, prose that repeats the same patterns and rhythms over and over falls monotonously on the ear. The skillful writer varies both the length and the structure of his sentences and lays claim to the reader's sustained attention by subtle shifts of emphasis and pattern. For instance, an uphill climb through three or four rather lengthy and difficult sentences may be broken by a short sentence which serves as a plateau on which one can catch one's breath and reorient oneself to the view. This is also a very effective climactic device. The problems of variety and rhythm in style must, of course, be solved first by the writer, but the interpreter must make himself aware of stylistic changes in pace, and in turn consciously use them to hold the attention of his audience and to point up shifts in tone.

Speech Phrases

In the discussion of sentences, we mentioned that long, grammatically complex sentences will probably need to be broken up into speech phrases when the material is read aloud to insure the clarity and relationship of the clauses and phrases.

This element of style is often more important to the interpreter than to the writer because the relative lengths of the units within the sentence and the location of stresses become an integral part of the sound pattern as the interpreter uses them. The division of a sentence into speech phrases is dictated by the punctuation and grammatical structure, and by the need to make mood and idea clear to an audience.

Punctuation is the first guide, even though it is meant for the eye rather than the ear. A comma, for example, prevents the eye from running ahead and mistaking the sense of the sentence, but in oral reading it need not always mean a pause; a change of the pitch, tempo, or volume of the voice can often serve the same purpose. For instance, in "a condition to be seen, in a lesser degree, in a turkey cock," it is unnecessary to pause before and after "in a lesser degree"; a slight drop of the voice, a change in rate of speech, or a combination of both will achieve the effect less obtrusively than a pause.

While commas are more frequently guides to possible speech phrases within a sentence than any other marks of punctuation, important clues are given also by semicolons, colons, parentheses, and dashes. A semicolon marks a turn of the thought, or a definite separation between two aspects of the same thought, and usually requires a slight pause to make the relationship clear to the listeners. Parentheses and dashes, in pairs, also mark off distinct speech phrases, often interpolative matter across which the main thought must be carried. (Long interpolations, of course, will need to be further subdivided for convenience and clarity in reading aloud.) A single dash, like the colon, often marks the pause that occurs just before a summing-up and implies a reference to some previous portion of the sentence.

But since punctuation is inserted as a visual aid in silent reading, it does not — unfortunately — prove an infallible or a complete guide to the oral interpreter in establishing his speech phrases. In fact, punctuation is often inadequate for aural comprehension, and the interpreter may need to insert slight pauses for clarity. Pauses are often necessary, likewise, to point up similar or contrasting ideas, as in

> The same cartoon humor that shows goats munching tin cans depicts ostriches swallowing alarm clocks, monkey wrenches, and cylinder heads.

> BERGEN EVANS
> *The Natural History of Nonsense*

Although the punctuation is correct in this sentence, a pause between "cans" and "depicts" helps to balance the parallel ideas when the sentence is read aloud.

Punctuation, of course, is a set of signposts for grammatical structure. In reading long, relatively complicated sentences, the interpreter will have some leeway in grouping his speech phrases. He will be guided by the need to simplify the long modifiers so that his audience will understand the meaning of the sentence at a single hearing. The speech phrases will tend to be longer because of the large number of phrases and clauses which must be kept in close relationship to the ideas they modify, and because of the need to bridge suspended thought across these modifiers. This single-sentence paragraph is an excellent example of the problem:

> There is an amusing belief among many country boys, for instance, that an owl has to turn his head to watch you and must watch you if you are near him, so that if you will only walk completely around him he will wring his own neck.

> BERGEN EVANS
> *The Natural History of Nonsense*

Read aloud without a pause or any attention to the author's punctuation, this involved sentence would quickly lose an audience in a maze of clauses and convey little of the idea intended. Read aloud a second time, with each mark of punctuation reflected in a change of pitch, pace, or volume, the sentence becomes much clearer. The punctuation, however, does not take care of the parallel values in "that an owl has to turn his head to watch you and must watch you if you are near him," or of the suspension of thought from "so that" to "he will wring his own neck." The interpreter, therefore, will need to break down these long units into shorter speech phrases, being careful, of course, not to destroy the relationship between the parts and the whole.

Choice of Words

Any discusion of words as an aspect of style will obviously overlap, to some extent, our earlier discussion of words as an aspect of content, for style and content are obviously inseparable. Nevertheless, the writer's choice of words is a vital part of his style and deserves special attention from that point of view.

We have already made a distinction between the denotations (dictionary meanings) and the connotations (suggestions, implications) of words. Now we should remind ourselves of another important aspect of literary style — the writer's use of allusions, similes, and metaphors. These three figures of speech are all means of comparing one thing to another; thus they are instruments of connotative meaning. They will contribute primarily to harmony by intensifying theme or underscoring attitude. This is certainly the function of the simile in "June Recital" (the studio "decorated like the inside of a candy box"), which sets the tone for the excerpt (page 197). Sometimes there is deliberate incongruity, as in Emily Dickinson's poem and Thurber's two fables, to mention only two earlier examples.

Another point to note is whether the words are abstract or concrete — whether they convey primarily an idea, like "sweetness," or an image, like "honeysuckle." Concrete terms appeal to our senses and muscle responses and predominate in descriptive and narrative prose. Abstractions appeal more directly to the intellect, without the mediation of the senses, and occur more often in expository prose, whose primary appeal is to the mind. But just as the appeal to the mind can be reinforced by appeals to the emotions and senses, so can concrete terms be used to flesh out abstract ideas and give them form and meaning. This was graphically illustrated in the comparison of the two poems examined earlier (pages 10–15).

The length of words is a practical concern for one who is to read aloud, but from the stylistic point of view the important thing is whether words are formal or informal or even colloquial in tone, whether they are unusual words or words common in everyday speech. In any case, the words should be evaluated in the light of the prevailing tone of the selection. An unusual word, for example, might reflect the highly intellectual tone of the selection, convey a deliberately romantic or archaic tone, or be used incongruously for the sake of humor or irony. The sentence from Virginia Woolf quoted on page 140 is a delightful example of shift of word choice within a single sentence to underscore attitude. She begins with the straightforward, factual "The book in question." This is also the tone of the closing phrase. Between the two, however, is the almost prime academic reference to "a lasting contribution to English literature" and the cutting, deliberately elaborate "mere farrago of pretentious mediocrity." It is amusing to know that "farrago" means a hotchpotch and comes from the Latin meaning mixed fodder for cattle. A very deadly criticism indeed! Although it will not often be necessary for the oral interpreter to delve into the origins and derivations of words, he must be prepared to do so if it seems helpful in bringing out complete meaning.

Finally, the repetition of words is an aspect of style that peculiarly concerns the oral interpreter. If words are repeated, the interpreter should decide why — and whether to play them up or down in reading aloud. If the writer repeated simply because repetition was unavoidable in communicating his idea lucidly, the interpreter might decide that a noticeable reiteration of the same sounds would distract his listeners and that the repeated words should not be given special stress in an oral reading. On the other hand, if the writer consciously repeated for emphasis or effectiveness, the rhetorical pattern will tell the interpreter so — and will enable him to decide that the repeated words should be read with marked emphasis. Powys uses an interesting repetition to describe the multiple personality of a bookseller:

> He is an ascetic hermit, he is an erotic immoralist, he is a papist, he is a Quaker, he is a communist, he is an anarchist, he is a savage iconoclast, he is a passionate worshipper of idols.

The parallel construction breaks this sentence into eight separate ideas, all of equal value. But perhaps more important to the interpreter is the fact that the repetition of the "he is" construction sets up a rhythm which allows the audience to complete each characteristic before moving on to the next, and at the same time alerts them for the one to come. In this way each quality is sharply pointed and the incongruity among them heightened.

The interpreter will not need to subject *all* words to such detailed scrutiny as that outlined above, but he will have to be constantly aware of all these possibilities for meaning and suggestion if he is to respond to his material at the deepest level of his consciousness.

We have not touched on the relationship of the sounds of the words as they are used together and will delay a consideration of this aspect until the next chapter, where it is discussed in some detail as it relates to description. We will only note in passing the sounds of the epithets which Powys uses for the bookseller. The softened sounds (and of course the connotation) of the first and last epithets bracket and help balance and control the "crackling" sounds of those between so that the effect is one of paradox rather than denunciation. This is a very subtle stylistic touch and evident only when the sentence is read aloud.

Prose Rhythm

Another important guide for the interpreter is the rhythm of the prose selection. All well-written prose has rhythm — not the formal, patterned rhythm of poetry, but a control of the flow of words that makes relationships clear and causes emphasis to fall on the important words.

We are already acquainted with rhythm of content, which is established by the organization of the thought progression and the emotional progression. It depends on the placement of key words and phrases and of the major and minor climaxes, both logical and emotional, throughout the entire selection.

There is also a rhythm in prose *structure* which becomes evident when it is read aloud. This prose rhythm is established by the length and grammatical construction of the sentences and speech phrases, and by the position of the stresses. As the interpreter groups words into thought units and speech phrases, separating them by pauses of varying duration, he is creating *cadences*. A cadence is a flow of sound. Obviously, then, words which are grouped form a flow of sound. A pause interrupts this flow, whether it be a terminal pause at the end of a sentence or a very brief pause to set off a speech phrase. Thus, length and frequency of pauses also become a part of prose rhythm.

Both the rate at which the flows of sound are uttered and the number of syllables within them affect the rhythm pattern. A mechanical measurement of the cadences in prose is usually not necessary, although it will prove interesting and helpful. The interpreter whose ear is trained will be aware of their existence and contribution.

Stress in prose is, of course, the result of a number of elements. It can result from the demands of proper pronunciation, the need for clarity, from contrast, or from a particular combination of sounds. The use of numerous one-syllable words in sequence, for instance, may very well produce a sharp staccato rhythm, especially if the content is forceful in meaning and the cadences established by the length of sentences and speech phrases are short. The brief excerpt from *Wind, Sand and Stars* (page 139), which we looked at earlier in relation to sentences, provides an interesting illustration. Since it is so brief we shall repeat it here, dividing the sentences as well as the speech phrases within the longer sentences by slashes and putting the number of syllables each contains directly above the phrase itself.

5   4   7

Had I been afraid? / I couldn't say. / I had witnessed a strange sight. /

3   4   4

What strange sight? / I couldn't say. / The sky was blue / and

5   11

the sea was white. / I felt I ought to tell someone about it / since

9   5   6

I was back from so far away! / But I had no grip / on what I had

been through.

It is immediately apparent even without counting that the sentences are quite short. But it is interesting to note that the longer sentences break into short speech phrases also, for clarity as well as to allow for the emotion they are expressing. Counting the syllables in the sentences and the speech phrases within the longer sentences reveals a very clear pattern, even in so brief an excerpt: the speech phrases within the longer sentences tend to correspond in length to the shorter, undivided sentences.

Add to this the fact that out of the sixty-three syllables in the excerpt thirty, or almost half, are stressed despite the presence of numerous monosyllabic words. Thus the stress results from meaning and attitude rather than from the demand of pronunciation. Only seven of the thirty stresses are required for proper pronunciation. The rhythm established, then, is sharp and almost staccato, which helps intensify the sense of nervous exhaustion and the unreality of what the speaker has "been through." If the interpreter uses this element of style, he will find his own and his audience's empathic response quickened and supported.

The single long sentence by Henry James quoted in the same discussion (page 140) provides a contrasting example.

7   12

Wandering through clear chambers / where the general effect made

13

preferences / almost as impossible as if they had been shocks, /

6   7

pausing at open doors / where vistas were long and bland, / she

2   10   7

would, / even if she had not already known, / have discovered for

3   7

herself / that Poynton / was the record of a life.

The sentence contains seventy-four syllables and divides into relatively long speech phrases. It is interesting to note that there are only two short speech phrases: "she would," the core on which the suspended syntax rests, along with the rest of the verb "have discovered," and "that Poynton," the beginning of the independent clause and the key to what "she would . . . have discovered."

Within these seventy-four syllables there are only twenty-six stresses, sixteen of which are required for proper pronunciation, leaving only ten which might be termed rhetorical stresses required for clarity and emphasis. Recall that the excerpt from *Wind, Sand, and Stars* had a much larger proportion. When the sentence from Henry James is read aloud, the easy, smooth flow of the longer speech phrases and the relatively few stresses within them underscore the leisurely pace of her "wandering."

A sensitive and attentive ear will usually catch the various rhythmic devices found in prose without needing to mark speech phrases and stresses. The purpose of the detailed attention here is to assure the interpreter that there is a rhythmic basis in effective prose and to encourage him to use all its elements fully as part of the "aesthetic entirety" he is working to share with his audience.

Factual Prose

The interpreter is not likely to be working extensively with strictly factual prose. Obviously, he would seldom choose to do a performance from an encyclopedia or a scientific work. Nevertheless, he may encounter passages or entire units in an essay which are technically factual and out of which the personal reflections of the author develop.

Factual prose, in the strictest definition of the term, is that in which the author gives verifiable information. It states that something is so. The writer's personal comment is kept at a minimum. Unadulterated examples of this type of writing are probably to be found only in books on science and mathematics, where one is told, for instance, that "in an isosceles triangle the angles opposite the equal sides are themselves equal," or in an encyclopedia which states on good authority that John Milton was born in England in 1608 and died in 1674. Objective journalistic reporting may also be considered factual when it limits itself to the simple formula of "who, where, when, what" and possibly "why."

In strictly factual material, the informative content and the logical development are of first importance. There is no emotional content, since the author is concerned with fact, not response to fact. It is, of course, possible for a fact to be so startling or shocking that even the unadorned statement will arouse emotional response in the reader, yet any arousal of emotion is due to subjective conclusions and associations on the part of the reader; it does not lie in the fact or in the writer's purpose. The content of factual writing depends for effectiveness on authoritative statements, logical progression of proofs, and exact denotation of the words. In short, factual prose informs, defines, explains. Facts need not be "sold" — only established; for anything that is demonstrated as true (and by definition a fact is something that is true) is accepted by the rational mind.

The interpreter is most likely to have occasion to deal with prose which is factual in the sense that it makes use of facts to support or explain a thesis — that is, prose in which the author is concerned with the implication or interpretation of the facts. In some cases, the facts will provide a touch of humor or satire, while in others the implied comment of the author is the desired end, and the factual content merely a means of achieving that end. In other words, the presentation of the facts themselves may be the basic purpose of the writing, or the facts may be merely the framework for an expression of attitude. It is the interpreter's responsibility to discover how the author uses the information he gives, and to make sure that he achieves the same purpose as he communicates the material to his audience.

The Personal Essay

We have seen that, in general, the writer of factual prose is primarily concerned with things outside himself — that even when his personal reaction to the facts comes through, his chief interest remains the communication of the factual information. However, the writer of an essay is less concerned with presenting facts than with developing ideas and sharing his personal opinions. He may use facts to support his conclusions, but what he thinks and how he feels, and why, are the pivots on which his writing turns. He may be olympian and instructive in setting forth his ideas, or detached and ironical, or humorous, or warmly personal; but whatever the tone of his remarks, he is speaking in his own person, and his attitude toward his subject is of primary importance.

As self-expression or self-revelation becomes the dominant motive for writing, the author puts more of himself as an individual into what he writes, the informative and instructional elements taper in importance, and attitude and mood become increasingly the handles by which the interpreter grasps the material. The writer's personality and his personal set of values are reflected in the facts and concrete objects he selects for setting up associations. This is especially true in accounts of travel and in autobiographical sketches. The associations or connotations lead the reader, and of course the listener, beyond the facts and the denotation of the words and phrases. For example, Jacques Barzun describes a certain mathematics teacher very sharply when he says that "he would put the chalk to his lips, make a noise like a straining gear box, and write out the correct result." We have no idea what the man looked like, nor do we need to. The selection of the characteristic gesture of putting chalk to lips calls up in almost everyone a complete mental picture of bemused, pedantic concentration. The "noise like a straining gear box" suggests that he is more a machine than a man, and when the gears start to move — out comes the answer!

Sometimes, especially in humorous essays, the writer will choose a speaker who may or may not be himself, or who may have been himself at some other time or place. Certainly we are not expected to believe that Thurber, for instance, actually experienced all the incidents he records in the first person! In such cases we are really not concerned about the actual physical identity of the speaker or the writer but with the wit and sense of the ridiculous which has exaggerated or played down the details of the incidents and ordered them for our enjoyment. We shall often be concerned with the age, sex, or social position of the speaker, but primarily as they relate to the situation the author has placed him in and the comments the speaker or the author makes by implication or direct statement.

The references the writer uses will grow out of his awareness of their probable universal appeal and also out of his own background and experiences. For understanding purely factual material, an examination of the author's life and background is useful only as it establishes his authority to write on his subject. The facts exist apart from the author, and it is the facts that are important, not the author's personal philosophy as it may relate to the facts, or his emotional response to them. But when facts are the framework for a theme, the author's principle of selection becomes very important. Only by careful scrutiny of all expressions and references that seem to carry a comment, an evaluation, or a judgment, by understanding what all words mean and what they suggest, not merely in themselves but in the context, can the interpreter come to a complete understanding of what the author is saying about his subject, explicitly or by implication, and be able to convey that attitude to an audience.

Didactic Prose

When the writer not only sets forth his opinions, but becomes preceptor and directly exhorts the reader to accept certain principles or ideas as guides to thought or conduct, we say that the writing is *didactic*.[1] In

[1] While much of literature is "didactic" in the sense of conveying certain ethical values, the term is most commonly applied to writing which is directly instructional or perceptual.

didactic writing the subject is, of course, important, but as in all prose of opinion, it is the author's attitude — the complex of ideas he has about the subject and his feelings toward it — that actually motivates the writing.

Because didactic prose is directive — that is, it instructs with the aim of persuading — the organization is dictated by the author's concept of what will best convert the reader to the way of thought or action which he himself considers good. Emotional connotations add their weight of persuasion and set up an interesting rhythm between the logical and emotional content, for a skilled writer knows that while man likes to think he is directed by his mind, his actions are in fact strongly influenced by his emotional response. This knowledge will be reflected also in the harmony between the idea and the way it is expressed. A writer of didactic literature has a specific audience in mind, and he selects his details for their associational value to that potential audience.

For example, in his essay "Of Revenge" Bacon wishes to instruct the reader on nobility of conduct and in so doing to dissuade him from vindictive action.

from *Of Revenge*

Revenge is a kind of wild justice, which the more man's nature runs to, the more ought law to weed it out; for as for the first wrong, it doth but offend the law; but the revenge of that wrong putteth the law out of office. Certainly, in taking revenge a man is but even with his enemy, but in passing it over he is superior; for it is a prince's part to pardon: and Solomon, I am sure, saith, *It is the glory of a man to pass by an offence.* That which is past is gone and irrevocable, and wise men have enough to do with things present and to come; therefore they do but trifle with themselves, that labor in past matters. . . . This is certain, that a man that studieth revenge keeps his own wounds green, which otherwise would heal and do well. Public revenges are for the most part fortunate; as that for the death of Caesar; for the death of Pertinax; for the death of Henry the Third of France; and many more. But in private revenges it is not so. Nay rather, vindictive persons live the life of witches; who, as they are mischievous, so end they infortunate.

FRANCIS BACON

Here Bacon appeals first to the logic of the law and to the unequivocal statement that revenge makes one "but even with his enemy." Immediately he transfers the appeal to the emotions by saying that it is a "prince's part to pardon," and by citing Solomon on the "glory" of overlooking an offense. His references to emperors and wise men, to princes and to Solomon, are appeals to the educated man who would like to think of himself as having something in common with such men. The next appeal is again directed to the mind; there can be no question of the logic of the statement that what "is past is gone." In the complete essay from which this excerpt is taken, the middle section continues this alternation of appeals to the mind and to the emotions, and the closing statement is clearly emotional. Didactic writing will probably have its climax where the emotional and logical appeals come together at their highest point. In the excerpt from Bacon, used here, this point comes in the sentence beginning, "This is certain . . . ." Here the certainty is obviously based on logic, while the reference to green wounds has a powerful empathic and connotative appeal.

Didactic prose confronts the interpreter with relatively few problems because it presents an easily discernible thesis and frankly attempts to persuade. The context makes the author's attitude abundantly clear, and all facts, specific examples, anecdotes, and emotional appeals are pointed toward one end — persuasion that this thesis should be accepted by right-thinking persons. For obvious reasons, the interpreter will normally choose for presentation a piece of didactic writing expressing a view with which he himself can sympathize, and to which his audience may be presumed to be at least not actively hostile. First, as interpreter it is his role to communicate to the audience exactly what the author intended to communicate to his readers. If he is out of sympathy with the material and shows it by intonation or gesture (in short, by tongue-in-cheek reading), he is not interpreting but commenting, even though he follows the printed page word for word. Second, if the writer has visualized an audience open to persuasion and the interpreter begins to battle his listeners, he may be going beyond the author's intent. This is oral delivery of a sort, but it is not interpretation.

Journals, Diaries, and Letters

Journals and diaries often make excellent selections for performance because they provide an intimate glimpse into special moments in the lives of interesting personalities. Ostensibly at least, most diaries were written for the private pleasure of the writer. They are likely to be less formal in style than the essay, which is intended for public consumption, and their organization is often dictated by highly subjective associations. A careful examination of the elements of style, however, will help the interpreter get at facets of the writer's personality and reveal attitudes and degrees of emotional involvement. In working with so personal a revelation as a diary or journal, it is also important to find out as much as possible about the writer and his times, since his motivation for recording certain details probably grew directly out of his relationship to his environment and the people in it.

The diarist may be said to be speaking as himself to himself. There is an element of danger in this idea, however. The interpreter who chooses to communicate such a record to an audience must not let his performance become so private that the audience feels it is intruding. Moreover, there must be sufficient projection, both mental and vocal, to hold their attention and interest. One of the ways of achieving this delicate balance between private and public thoughts is to allow the writer to "think aloud" as he puts his thoughts in order or as he rereads them aloud. This will help the interpreter keep his mind actively engaged in organizing and expressing the total entry.

It is not necessary or indeed usually desirable to try to re-create visually in performance the act of writing or the physical details of the writer or his immediate surroundings. Any strong suggestion of "pen-in-hand" action would slow the selection down unduly or strain the audience's willingness to believe. The interpreter's real concern is not how fast the diarist wrote or with which hand or what type of pen, but rather what he finally put down for readers to share.

In recent years there has been a wealth of published correspondence. Much of the appeal of letters is undoubtedly the same as that of diaries and journals. Letters, however, present an added problem for the interpreter. First, he will need to make a distinction between public and private letters. Public letters may be handled very much as one would approach an oration or a public address. They are usually designed to persuade a larger group of hearers or readers to a course of action or to the acceptance of an idea. The writer will have selected details which have strong universal appeal and refer to matters with which his intended audience is easily familiar. The letter of St. Paul at the end of this chapter is an excellent example of a public letter and is particularly interesting to examine for word choice and organization. Since the writer of a public letter is speaking to a specific audience, the interpreter may find it helpful to imagine that the specific audience and his own are identical. This will help achieve directness. He may address them in the person of the writer or, more probably, in the person of another selected to present the letter to the intended audience.

Because private letters involve a more complex relationship between writer and recipient, the interpreter will need to find out all he can about both parties concerned. Often the letter he has selected to read is a reply to one received earlier by the writer; consequently, a chain of references may have to be investigated. The method of organization and the style of writing will reflect the purpose of the letter and the relationship between the writer and the addressee. The Browning letters at the end of this chapter, for example, are by two poets who have never met but who know each other's work. Dylan Thomas is writing to a very close friend when he sends his apology and explanation to Vernon Watkins. Leonardo da Vinci's letter, on the other hand, is addressed to a nobleman with whom he is not on intimate terms — indeed, to a prospective employer! Again, as with diaries and journals, the interpreter may insure mental directness by assuming the attitude of the writer as he composes the letter or as he rereads it.

In some cases, of course, the interpreter is more interested in the reaction of the addressee than in the writer and will choose to handle the letter as if being read by the addressee. If this seems the more desirable approach, he must cope with the twofold problem of using the writer's style effectively and at the same time suggesting the reaction of another person. Obviously, such an approach is most useful when the relationship between the two people is clearly drawn or so well-known that the response is predictable. Letters are often used in this way within plays and narratives where the characters have already been established. In such situations the letter becomes virtually a part of the plot and motivation.

Selections for Analysis and Interpretation

Miss Moore is one of the most meticulous modern poets. The opening sentence refers to her famous poem, "Poetry," which begins, "I, too, dislike it." Her organization in this essay is loose and often interrupted by comments and quotations drawn from her vast knowledge of all kinds of literature, but it is unified by her continuing focus on what poetry should and should not be.

Subject, Predicate, Object / MARIANNE MOORE

Of poetry, I once said, "I, too, dislike it"; and say it again of anything mannered, dictatorial, disparaging, or calculated to reduce to the ranks what offends one. I have been accused of substituting appreciation for criticism, and justly, since there is nothing I dislike more than the exposé or any kind of revenge. Like Ezra Pound, I prefer the straightforward order of words, "subject, predicate, object"; in reverse order only for emphasis, as when Pope says:

> Men must be taught as if you taught them not,
> And things unknown proposed as things forgot.

Dazzled, speechless — an alchemist without implements — one thinks of poetry as divine fire, a perquisite of the gods. When under the spell of admiration or gratitude, I have hazarded a line, it never occurred to me that anyone might think I imagined myself a poet. As said previously, if what I write is called poetry it is because there is no other category in which to put it.

Nor is writing exactly a pastime — although when I was reading H. T. Parker's music page in the *Boston Evening Transcript*, in what it is not speaking too strongly to call an ecstasy of admiration, to be writing in emulation, anything at all for a newspaper, was a pleasure: no more at that time than woman's suffrage party notes, composed and contributed at intervals to the *Carlisle Evening Sentinel*.

I am reminded somewhat of myself by Arnold Toynbee's recital of his spiritual debts — indebtedness to his mother for awakening in him an interest in history, "to Gibbon for showing what an historian can do"; to "people, institutions . . . pictures, languages, and books" as exciting his "curiosity." Curiosity; and books. I think books are chiefly responsible for my doggedly self-determined efforts to write; books and verisimilitude; I like to describe things. I well understand the entrapped author of an autobiography in three volumes, who says he rewrote the first volume some twenty-six times "before I got it to sound the way I talk."

"Sweet speech does no harm — none at all," La Fontaine says of the song that saved the life of the swan mistaken by the cook for a goose. But what simple statement, in either prose or verse, really is simple? Wariness is essential where an inaccurate word could give an impression more exact than could be given by a verifiably accurate term. One is rewarded for knowing the way and compelling a resistful un-English-speaking taxi-driver to take it when he says upon arrival — dumfounded and gratified — "Ah, we did not suffer any lights."

It is for himself that the writer writes, charmed or exasperated to participate; eluded, arrested, enticed by felicities. The result? Consolation, rapture, to be achieving a likeness of the thing visualized. One may hang back or launch away. "With sails flapping, one gets nowhere. With everything sheeted down, one can go around the world" — an analogy said to have been applied by Woodrow Wilson to freedom.

Combine with charmed words certain rhythms, and the mind is helplessly haunted. In his poem, "The Small," Theodore Roethke says:

> A wind moves through the grass,
> Then all is as it was.

And from the following lines by Alberto da Lacerda (translated), one's imagination easily extends from the tiger to the sea, and beyond:

> The tiger that walks in her gestures
> Has the insolent grace of the ships.

Form is synonymous with content — must be — and Louis Dudek is perhaps right in saying, "The sound of the poem heard by the inner ear is the ideal sound," surely right in saying, "The art of poetry is the art of singular form." Poetry readings have this value, they assist one to avoid blurred diction. It should not be possible for the listener to mistake "fate" for "faith" — in "like a bulwark against fate." The five-line stanzas in my *Collected Poems* warn one to write prose or short-line verse only, since my carried-over long lines make me look like the fanciest, most witless rebel against common sense. Overruns certainly belong at the right — not left — of the page.

Translations suit no one; even so, I still feel that translated verse should have the motion of the original. La Fontaine says of the adder that lunged at its rescuer:

> *L'insecte sautillant cherche à réunir,*
> *Mais il ne put y parvenir.*

In

> The pestilent thirds writhed together to rear,
> But of course could no longer adhere

the word "insect," so pleasing, is sacrificed; but "r," important as sound, ends the line.

Poetry is the Mogul's dream: to be intensively toiling at what is a pleasure; La Fontaine's indolence being, as the most innocent observer must realize, a mere metaphor. As for the hobgoblin obscurity, it need never entail compromise. It should mean that one may fail and start again, never mutilate an auspicious premise. The objective is architecture, not demolition; grudges flower less well than gratitudes. To shape, to shear, compress, and delineate; to "add a hue to the spectrum of another's mind" as Mark Van Doren has enhanced the poems of Thomas Hardy, should make it difficult for anyone to dislike poetry!

This relatively long excerpt could conveniently be divided into smaller units for classroom use. It is so organized that each unit builds easily to its own conclusion and into the next unit. You might use paragraphs one through eight, or nine through eleven, or twelve to the end of the excerpt. Make careful use of the subtle style changes apparent within the basic unity.

FROM *Hidden Name and Complex Fate* / RALPH ELLISON

Once while listening to the play of a two-year-old girl who did not know she was under observation, I heard her saying over and over again, at first with questioning and then with sounds of growing satisfaction, "I am Mimi Livisay? . . . I am Mimi Livisay. I *am* Mimi Livisay . . . I am *Mimi* Li-vi-say! I am Mimi . . ."

And in deed and in fact she was — or became so soon thereafter, by working playfully to establish the unit between herself and her name.

For many of us this is far from easy. We must learn to wear our names within all the noise and confusion of the environment in which we find ourselves; make them the center of all of our associations with the world, with man and with nature. We must charge them with all our emotions, our hopes, hates, loves, aspirations. They must become our masks and our shields and the containers of all those values and traditions which we learn and/or imagine as being the meaning of our familial past.

And when we are reminded so constantly that we bear, as Negroes, names originally possessed by those who owned our enslaved grandparents, we are apt, especially if we are potential writers, to be more than ordinarily concerned with the veiled and mysterious events, the fusions of blood, the furtive couplings, the business transactions, the violations of faith and loyalty, the assaults; yes, and the unrecognized and unrecognizable loves through which our names were handed down unto us.

So charged with emotion does this concern become for some of us, that we have, earlier, the example of the followers of Father Divine and, now, the Black Muslims, discarding their original names in rejection of the bloodstained, the brutal, the sinful images of the past. Thus they would declare new identities, would clarify a new program of intention and destroy the verbal evidence of a willed and ritualized discontinuity of blood and human intercourse.

Not all of us, actually only a few, seek to deal with our names in this manner. We take what we have and make of them what we can. And there are even those who know where the old broken connections lie, who recognize their relatives across the chasm of historical denial and the artificial barriers of society, and who see themselves as bearers of many of the qualities which were admirable in the original sources of their common line (Faulkner has made much of this); and I speak here not of mere forgiveness, nor of obsequious insensitivity to the outrages symbolized by the denial and the division, but of the conscious acceptance of the harsh realities of the human condition, of the ambiguities and hypocrisies of human history as they have played themselves out in the United States.

Perhaps, taken in aggregate, these European names which (sometimes with irony, sometimes with pride, but always with personal investment) represent a certain triumph of the spirit, speaking to us of those who rallied, reassembled and transformed themselves and who under dismembering pressures refused to die. "Brothers and sisters," I once heard a Negro preacher exhort, "let us make up our faces before the world, and our names shall sound throughout the land with honor! For we ourselves are our *true* names, not their epithets! So let us, I say, Make Up Our Faces and Our Minds!"

Perhaps my preacher had read T. S. Eliot, although I doubt it. And in actuality, it was unnecessary that he do so, for a concern with names and naming was very much part of that special area of American culture from which I come, and it is precisely for this reason that this example should come to mind in a discussion of my own experience as a writer.

Undoubtedly, writers begin their *conditioning* as manipulators of words long before they become aware of literature — certain Freudians would say at the breast. Perhaps. But if so, that is far too early to be of use at this moment. Of this, though, I am certain: that despite the misconceptions of those educators who trace the reading difficulties experienced by large numbers of Negro children in Northern schools to their Southern background, these children are, in *their* familiar South, facile manipulators of words. I know, too, that the Negro community is deadly in its ability to create nicknames and to spot all that is ludicrous in an unlikely name or that which is incongruous in conduct. Names are not qualities; nor are words, in this particular sense, actions. To assume that they are could cost one his life many times a day. Language skills depend to a large extent upon a knowledge of the details, the manners, the objects, the folkways, the psychological patterns, of a given environment. Humor and wit depend upon much the same awareness, and so does the suggestive power of names.

"A small brown bowlegged Negro with the name 'Franklin D. Roosevelt Jones' might sound like a clown to someone who looks at him from the outside," said my friend Albert Murray, "but on the other hand he just might turn out to be a hell of a fireside operator. He might just lie back in all of that comic juxtaposition of names and manipulate you deaf, dumb and blind — and you not even suspecting it, because you're thrown out of stance by his name! There you are, so dazzled by the F.D.R. image — which you *know* you can't see — and so delighted with your own superior position that you don't realize that it's *Jones* who must be confronted."

Well, as you must suspect, all of this speculation on the matter of names has a purpose, and now, because it is tied up so ironically with my own experience as a writer, I must turn to my own name.

For in the dim beginnings, before I ever thought consciously of writing, there was my own name, and there was, doubtless, a certain magic in it. From the start I was uncomfortable with it, and in my earliest years it caused me much puzzlement. Neither could I understand what a poet was, nor why, exactly, my father had chosen to name me after one. Perhaps I could have understood it perfectly well had he named me after his own father, but that name had been given to an older brother who died and thus was out of the question. But why hadn't he named me after a hero, such as Jack Johnson, or a soldier like Colonel Charles Young, or a great seaman like Admiral Dewey, or an educator like Booker T. Washington, or a great orator and abolitionist like Frederick Douglass? Or again, why hadn't he named me (as so many Negro parents had done) after President Teddy Roosevelt?

Instead, he named me after someone called Ralph Waldo Emerson, and then, when I was three, he died. It was too early for me to have understood his choice, although I'm sure he must have explained it many times, and it was also too soon for me to have made the connection between my name and my father's love for reading. Much later, after I began to write and work with words, I came to suspect that he was aware of the suggestive powers of names and of the magic involved in naming.

I recall an odd conversation with my mother during my early teens in which she mentioned their interest in, of all things, prenatal culture! But for a long time I actually knew only that my father read a lot, and that he admired this remote Mr. Emerson, who was something called a "poet and philosopher" — so much so that he named his second son after him.

I knew, also, that whatever his motives, the combination of names he'd given me caused me no end of trouble from the moment when I could talk well enough to respond to the ritualized question which grownups put to very young children. Emerson's name was quite familiar to Negroes in Oklahoma during those days when World War I was brewing, and adults, eager to show off their knowledge of literary figures, and obviously amused by the joke implicit in such a small brown nubbin of a boy carrying around such a heavy moniker, would invariably repeat my first two names and then to my great annoyance, they'd add "Emerson."

And I, in my confusion, would reply, "No, *no, I'm* not Emerson, he's the little boy who lives next door." Which only made them laugh all the louder. "Oh no," they'd say, "*you're* Ralph Waldo Emerson," while I had fantasies of blue murder.

For a while the presence next door of my little friend, Emerson, made it unnecessary for me to puzzle too often over this peculiar adult confusion. And since there were other Negro boys named Ralph in the city, I came to suspect that there was something about the combination of names which produced their laughter. Even today I know of only one other Ralph who had as much comedy made out of his name, a campus politician and deep-voiced orator whom I knew at Tuskegee, who was called in friendly ribbing, *Ralph Waldo Emerson Edgar Allan Poe,* spelled Powe. This must have been quite a trial for him, but I had been initiated much earlier.

The expanded metaphors operating within this famous meditation help govern its organization and reveal the mind and attitude of its author. Be sure you understand the reference to the bell.

FROM *Devotions Upon Emergent Occasions* / JOHN DONNE

XVII

Perchance he for whom this bells tolls, may be so ill, as that he knows not it tolls for him; and perchance I may think myself so much better than I am, as that they who are about me, and see my state, may have caused it to toll for me, and I know not that. The Church is Catholic, universal, so are all her actions; all that she does belongs to all. When she baptizes a child, that action concerns me; for that child is thereby connected to that Head which is my Head too, engrafted into that body, whereof I am a member. And when she buries a man, that action concerns me: all mankind is of one Author, and is one volume; when one man dies, one chapter is not torn out of the book, but translated into a better language; and every chapter must be so translated; God employs several translators; some pieces are translated by age, some by sickness, some by war, some by justice; but God's hand is in every translation; and his hand shall bind up all our scattered leaves again, for the Library where every book shall lie open to one another: As therefore the bell that rings to a sermon, calls not upon the preacher only, but upon the congregation to come; so this bell calls us all: but how much more me, who am brought so near the door by this sickness. There was a contention as far as a suit (in which both piety and dignity, religion and estimation, were mingled), which of the religious orders should ring to prayers first in the morning; and it was determined, that they should ring first that rose earliest. If we understand aright the dignity of this bell that tolls for our evening prayer, we would be glad to make it ours, by rising early, in that application, that it might be ours, as well as his, whose indeed it is. The bell doth toll for him that thinks it doth; and though it intermit again, yet from that minute, that that occasion wrought upon him, he is united to God. Who casts not up his eye to the sun when it rises? but who takes off his eye from a comet when that breaks out? Who bends not his ear to any bell, which upon any occasion rings? but who can remove it from that bell, which is passing a piece of himself out of this world? No man is an island, entire of itself; every man is a piece of the continent, a part of the main; if a clod be washed away by the sea, Europe is the less, as well as if a promontory were, as well as if a manor of thy friends or of thine own were; any man's death diminishes me, because I am involved in mankind; and therefore never send to know for whom the bell tolls; it tolls for thee. Neither can we call this a begging of misery or a borrowing of misery, as though we were not miserable enough of ourselves, but must fetch in more from the next house, in taking upon us the misery of our neighbors. Truly it were an excusable covetousness if we did; for affliction is a treasure, and scarce any man hath enough of it. No man hath affliction enough that is not matured, and ripened by it, and made fit for God by that affliction. If a man carry treasure in bullion, or in a wedge of gold, and have none coined into current monies, his treasure will not defray him as he travels. Tribulation is treasure in the nature of it, but it is not current money in the use of it, except we get nearer and nearer our home, Heaven, by it. Another man may be sick too, and sick to death, and this affliction may lie in his bowels, as gold in a mine, and be of no use to him; but this bell, that tells me of his affliction, digs out, and applies that gold to me; if by this consideration of another's danger I take mine own into contemplation, and so secure myself by making my recourse to my God, who is our only security.

The travel accounts of these three writers vary as widely as the areas and events with which they deal. The style each uses is dictated in part, indeed, by the atmosphere of the location as well as by his personal response to concrete objects. Notice the change in style as the narrator gives way to another speaker in this excerpt.

FROM *Heart of Darkness* / JOSEPH CONRAD

"The reaches opened before us and closed behind, as if the forest had stepped leisurely across the water to bar the way for our return. We penetrated deeper and deeper into the heart of darkness. It was very quiet there. At night sometimes the roll of drums behind the curtain of trees would run up the river and remain sustained faintly, as if hovering in the air high over our heads till the first break of day. Whether it meant war, peace, or prayer we could not tell. The dawns were heralded by the descent of chill stillness; the wood-cutters slept, their fires burned low; the snapping of a twig would make you start. We were wanderers on a prehistoric earth, on an earth that wore the aspect of an unknown planet. We could have fancied ourselves the first of men taking possession of an accursed inheritance, to be subdued at the cost of profound anguish and of excessive toil. But suddenly, as we struggled round a bend, there would be a glimpse of rush

From *Heart of Darkness* by Joseph Conrad. Reprinted by permission of J. M. Dent & Sons, Ltd., and the Trustees of the Joseph Conrad Estate.

walls, of peaked grassroofs, a burst of yells, a whirl of black limbs, a mass of hands clapping, of feet stamping, of bodies swaying, of eyes rolling, under the droop of heavy and motionless foliage. The steamer toiled along slowly on the edge of a black and incomprehensible frenzy. The prehistoric man was cursing us, praying to us, welcoming us — who could tell? We were cut off from the comprehension of our surroundings; we glided past like phantoms, wondering and secretly appalled, as sane men would be before an enthusiastic outbreak in a madhouse. We could not understand because we were too far and could not remember, because we were traveling in the night of first ages, of those ages that are gone, leaving hardly a sign — and no memories.

"The earth seemed unearthly. We are accustomed to look upon the shackled form of a conquered monster, but there — there you could look at a thing monstrous and free. It was unearthly, and the men were — No, they were not inhuman. Well, you know, that was the worst of it — this suspicion of their not being inhuman. It would come slowly to one. They howled and leaped, and spun, and made horrid faces; but what thrilled you was just the thought of their humanity — like yours — the thought of your remote kinship with this wild and passionate uproar. Ugly. Yes, it was ugly enough; but if you were man enough you would admit to yourself that there was in you just the faintest trace of a response to the terrible frankness of that noise, a dim suspicion of there being a meaning in it which you — you so remote from the night of first ages — could comprehend. And why not? The mind of man is capable of anything — because everything is in it, all the past as well as all the future. What were there after all? Joy, fear, sorrow, devotion, valour, rage — who can tell? — but truth — truth stripped of its cloak of time. Let the fool gape and shudder — the man knows, and can look on without a wink. But he must at least be as much of a man as these on the shore. He must meet that truth with his own true stuff — with his own inborn strength. Principles won't do. Acquisitions, clothes, pretty rags — rags that would fly off at the first good shake. No; you want a deliberate belief. An appeal to me in this fiendish row — is there? Very well; I hear; I admit, but I have a voice, too, and for good or evil mine is the speech that cannot be silenced. Of course, a fool, what with sheer fright and fine sentiments, is always safe. Who's that grunting? You wonder I didn't go ashore for a howl and a dance? Well, no — I didn't. Fine sentiments, you say? Fine sentiments, be hanged! I had no time. I had to mess about with white-lead and strips of woollen blanket helping to put bandages on those leaky steampipes — I tell you. I had to watch the steering, and circumvent those snags, and get the tinpot along by hook or by crook. There was surface-truth enough in these things to save a wiser man. And between whiles I had to look after the savage who was fireman. He was an improved specimen; he could fire up a vertical boiler. He was there below me, and, upon my word, to look at him was as edifying as seeing a dog in a parody of breeches and a feather hat, walking on his hind-legs. A few months of training had done for that really fine chap. He squinted at the steam-gauge and at the water-gauge with an evident effort of intrepidity — and he had filed teeth, too, the poor devil, and the wool of his pate shaved into queer patterns, and three ornamental scars on each of his cheeks. He ought to have been clapping his hands and stamping his feet on the bank, instead of which he was hard at work, a thrall to strange witch-craft, full of improving knowledge. He was useful because he had been instructed; and what he knew was this — that should the water in that transparent thing disappear, the evil spirit inside the boiler would get angry through the greatness of his thirst, and take a terrible vengeance. So he sweated and fired up and watched the glass fearfully (with an impromptu charm, made of rags, tied to his arm, and a piece of polished bone, as big as a watch, stuck flat-ways through his lower lip), while the wooded banks slipped past us slowly, the short noise was left behind, the interminable miles of silence — and we crept on, towards Kurtz. But the snags were thick, the water was treacherous and shallow, the boiler seemed indeed to have a sulky devil in it, and thus neither that fireman nor I had any time to peer into our creepy thoughts."

Use all the richness of sound in this selection. Be sure to see and hear the various details as they are encountered. The final paragraph must be handled carefully so that it does not break the unity.

FROM *Prospero's Cell* / LAWRENCE DURRELL

Somewhere between Calabria and Corfu the blue really begins. All the way across Italy you find yourself moving through a landscape severely domesticated — each valley laid out after the architect's pattern, brilliantly lighted, human. But once you strike out from the flat and desolate Calabrian mainland towards the sea, you are aware of a change in the heart of things: aware of the horizon beginning to stain at the rim of the world: aware of *islands* coming out of the darkness to meet you.

In the morning you wake to the taste of snow on the air, and climbing the companion-ladder, suddenly enter the penumbra of shadow cast by the Albanian mountains — each wearing its cracked crown of snow — desolate and repudiating stone.

A peninsula nipped off while red hot and allowed to cool into an antarctica of lava. You are aware not so much of a landscape coming to meet you invisibly over those blue miles of water as of a climate. You enter Greece as one might enter a dark crystal; the form of things becomes irregular, refracted. Mirages suddenly swallow islands, and wherever you look the trembling curtain of the atmosphere deceives.

Other countries may offer you discoveries in manners or lore or landscape; Greece offers you something harder — the discovery of yourself.

This excerpt comprises several episodes which may be used separately. The style varies with the mood.

FROM *Travels with Charley* / JOHN STEINBECK

My plan was clear, concise, and reasonable, I think. For many years I have traveled in many parts of the world. In America I live in New York, or dip into Chicago or San Francisco. But New York is no more America than Paris is France or London is England. Thus I discovered that I did not know my own country. I, an American writer, writing about America, was working from memory, and the memory is at best a faulty, warpy reservoir. I had not heard the speech of America, smelled the grass and trees and sewage, seen its hills and water, its color and quality of light. I knew the changes only from books and newspapers. But more than this, I had not felt the country for twenty-five years. In short, I was writing of something I did not know about, and it seems to me that in a so-called writer this is criminal. My memories were distorted by twenty-five intervening years.

Once I traveled about in an old bakery wagon, double-doored rattler with a mattress on its floor. I stopped where people stopped or gathered, I listened and looked and felt, and in the process had a picture of my country the accuracy of which was impaired only by my own shortcomings.

So it was that I determined to look again, to try to discover this monster land. Otherwise, in writing, I could not tell the small diagnostic truths which are the foundations of the larger truth. One sharp difficulty presented itself. In the intervening twenty-five years my name had become reasonably known. And it has been my experience that when people have heard of you, favorably or not, they change; they become, through shyness or the other qualities that publicity inspires, something they are not under ordinary circumstances. This being so, my trip demanded that I leave my name and my identity at home. I had to be peripatetic eyes and ears, a kind of moving gelatin plate. I could not sign hotel registers, meet people I knew, interview others, or even ask searching questions. Furthermore, two or more people disturb the ecologic complex of an area. I had to go alone and I had to be self-contained, a kind of casual turtle carrying his house on his back.

With all this in mind I wrote to the head office of a great corporation which manufactures trucks. I specified my purpose and my needs. I wanted a three-quarter-ton pick-up truck capable of going anywhere under possibly rigorous conditions, and on this truck I wanted a little house built like the cabin of a small boat. . . . Although I didn't want to start before Labor Day, when the nation settles back to normal living, I did want to get used to my turtle shell, to equip it and learn it. It arrived in August, a beautiful thing, powerful and yet lithe. It was almost as easy to handle as a passenger car. And because my planned trip had aroused some satiric remarks among my friends, I named it Rocinante, which you will remember was the name of Don Quixote's horse. . . .

There was some genuine worry about my traveling alone, open to attack, robbery, assault. It is well known that our roads are dangerous. And here I admit I had senseless qualms. It is some years since I have been alone, nameless, friendless, without any of the safety one gets from family, friends, and accomplices. There is no reality in the danger. It's just a very lonely, helpless feeling at first — a kind of desolate feeling. For this reason I took one companion on my journey — an old French gentleman poodle known as Charley. Actually his name is Charles le Chien. He was born in Bercy on the outskirts of Paris and trained in France, and while he knows a little poodle-English, he responds quickly only to commands in French. Otherwise he has to translate, and that slows him down. He is a very big poodle, of a color called *bleu*, and he is blue when he is clean. Charley is a born diplomat. He prefers negotiation to fighting, and properly so, since he is very bad at fighting. Only once in his ten years has he been in trouble — when he met a dog who refused to negotiate. Charley lost a piece of his right ear that time. But he is a good watch dog — has a roar like a lion, designed to conceal from night-wandering strangers the fact that he couldn't bite his way out of a *cornet de papier*. He is a good friend and traveling companion, and would rather travel about than anything he can imagine. . . .

Equipping Rocinante was a long and pleasant process. I took far too many things, but I didn't know what I would find. Tools for emergency, tow lines, a small block and tackle, a trenching tool and crowbar, tools for making and fixing and improvising. Then there were emergency foods. I would be late in the northwest and caught by snow. I prepared for at least a week of emergency. Water was easy; Rocinante carried a thirty-gallon tank.

I thought I might do some writing along the way, perhaps essays, surely notes, certainly letters. I took paper, carbon, typewriter, pencils, note books, and not only those but dictionaries, a compact encyclopedia, and a dozen other reference books, heavy ones. I suppose our capacity for self-delusion is boundless. I knew very well that I rarely make notes, and if I do I either lose them or can't read them. I also knew from thirty years of my profession that I cannot write hot on an event. It has to ferment. I must do what a friend calls "mule it over" for a time before it goes down. And in spite of this self-knowledge I equipped Rocinante with enough writing material to take care of ten volumes. Also I laid in a hundred and fifty pounds of those books one hasn't got around to reading — and of course those are the books one isn't ever going to get around to reading. Canned goods, shotgun shells, rifle cartridges, tool boxes, and far too many clothes, blankets and pillows, and many too many shoes and boots, padded nylon sub-zero underwear, plastic dishes and cups and a plastic dishpan, a spare tank of bottled gas. The over-loaded springs sighed and settled lower and lower. I judge now that I carried about four times too much of everything. . . .

I crossed into New York State at Rouses Point and stayed as near to Lake Ontario as I could because it was my intention to look at Niagara Falls, which I had never seen, and then to slip into Canada, from Hamilton to Windsor, keeping Lake Erie on the south, and to emerge at Detroit — a kind of end run, a small triumph over geography. . . .

It rained in New York State, the Empire State, rained cold and pitiless, as the highway-sign writers would put it. Indeed the dismal downpour made my intended visit to Niagara Falls seem redundant. I was then hopelessly lost in the streets of a small but endless town in the neighbor-hood of Medina, I think. I pulled to the side of the street and got out my book of road maps. But to find where you are going, you must know where you are, and I didn't. The windows of the cab were tightly closed and opaque with steaming rain. My car radio played softly. Suddenly there was a knock on the window, the door was wrenched open, and a man slipped into the seat beside me. The man was quite red of face, quite whiskey of breath. His trousers were held up by red braces over the long gray underwear that covered his chest.

"Turn that damn thing off," he said, and then turned off my radio himself. "My daughter saw you out of the window," he continued. "Thought you was in trouble." He looked at my maps. "Throw those things away. Now, where is it you want to go?"

I don't know why it is a man can't answer such a question with the truth. The truth was that I had turned off the big highway 104 and into the smaller roads because the traffic was heavy and passing vehicles threw sheets of water on my windshield. I wanted to go to Niagara Falls. Why couldn't I have admitted it? I looked down at my map and said, "I'm trying to get to Erie, Pennsylvania."

"Good," he said. "Now throw those maps away. Now you turn around, go two traffic lights, that'll bring you to Egg Street. Turn left there and about two hundred yards on Egg turn right at an angle. That's a twisty kind of street and you'll come to an overpass, but don't take it. You turn left there and it will curve around like this — see? Like this." His hand made a curving motion. "Now, when the curve straightens out you'll come to three branching roads. There's a big red house on the left-hand branch so you don't take that, you take the right-hand branch. Now, have you got that so far?"

"Sure," I said. "That's easy."

"Well repeat it back so I'll know you're going right."

I had stopped listening at the curving road. I said, "Maybe you better tell me again."

"I thought so. Turn around and go two traffic lights to Egg Street, turn left for two hundred yards and turn right at an angle on a twisty street till you come to an overpass but don't take it."

"That clears it up for me," I said quickly. "I sure do thank you for helping me out."

"Hell," he said, "I ain't even got you out of town yet."

Well, he got me out of town by a route which, if I could have remembered it, let alone followed it, would have made the path into the Labyrinth at Knossos seem like a throughway. When he was finally satisfied and thanked, he got out and slammed the door, but such is my social cowardice that I actually did turn around, knowing he would be watching out the window. I drove around two blocks and blundered my way back to 104, traffic or not.

Niagara Falls is very nice. It's like a large version of the old Bond sign on Times Square. I'm very glad I saw it, because from now on if I am asked whether I have seen Niagara Falls I can say yes, and be telling the truth for once.

When I told my adviser that I was going to Erie, Pennsylvania, I had no idea of going there, but as it turned out, I was. My intention was to creep across the neck of Ontario, bypassing not only Erie but Cleveland and Toledo.

I find out of long experience that I admire all nations and hate all governments, and nowhere is my natural anarchism more aroused than at national borders where patient and efficient public servants carry out their duties in matters of immigration and customs. I have never smuggled anything in my life. Why, then, do I feel an uneasy sense of guilt on approaching a customs barrier? I crossed a high toll bridge and negotiated a no man's land and came to the place where the Stars and Stripes stood shoulder to shoulder with the Union Jack. The Canadians were very kind. They asked where I was going and for how long, gave Rocinante a cursory inspection, and came at last to Charley.

"Do you have a certificate of rabies vaccination on the dog?"

"No, I haven't. You see he's an old dog. He was vaccinated long ago."

Another official came out. "We advise you not to cross the border with him, then."

"But I'm just crossing a small part of Canada and re-entering the U.S."

"We understand," they said kindly. "You can take him into Canada but the U.S. won't let him back."

"But technically I am still in the U.S. and there's no complaint."

"There will be if he crosses the line and tries to get back."

"Well, where can I get him vaccinated?"

They didn't know. I would have to retrace my way at least twenty miles, find a vet, have Charley vaccinated, and then return. I was crossing only to save a little time, and this would wipe out the time saved and much more.

"Please understand, it is your government, not ours. We are simply advising you. It's the rule."

I guess this is why I hate governments, all governments. It is always the rule, the fine print, carried out by fine-print men. There's nothing to fight, no wall to hammer with frustrated fists. I highly approve of vaccination, feel it should be compulsory; rabies is a dreadful thing. And yet I found myself hating the rule and all governments that made rules. It was not the shots but the certificate that was important. And it is usually so with governments — not a fact but a small slip of paper. These were such nice men, friendly and helpful. It was a slow time at the border. They gave me a cup of tea and Charley half a dozen cookies. And they seemed genuinely sorry that I had to go to Erie, Pennsylvania, for the lack of a paper. And so I turned about and proceeded toward the Stars and Stripes and another government. Exiting I had not been required to stop, but now the barrier was down.

"Are you an American citizen?"

"Yes, sir, here's my passport."

"Do you have anything to declare?"

"I haven't been away."

"Have you a rabies vaccination certificate for your dog?"

"He hasn't been away either."

"But you are coming from Canada."

"I have not been in Canada."

I saw the steel come into eyes, the brows lower to a level of suspicion. Far from saving time, it looked as though I might lose much more than even Erie, Pennsylvania.

"Will you step into the office?"

This request had the effect on me a Gestapo knock on the door might have. It raises panic, anger, and guilty feelings whether or not I have done wrong. My voice took on the strident tone of virtuous outrage which automatically arouses suspicion.

"Please step into the office."

"I tell you I have not been in Canada. If you were watching, you would have seen that I turned back."

"Step this way, please, sir."

Then into the telephone: "New York license so-and-so. Yes. Pick-up truck with camper top. Yes — a dog." And to me: "What kind of dog is it?"

"Poodle."

"Poodle — I said poodle. Light brown."

"Blue," I said.

"Light brown. Okay. Thanks."

I do hope I did not sense a certain sadness at my innocence.

"They say you didn't cross the line."

"That's what I told you."

"May I see your passport?"

"Why? I haven't left the country. I'm not about to leave the country." But I handed over my passport just the same. He leafed through it, pausing at the entry-and-exit stamps of other journeys. He inspected my photograph, opened the yellow smallpox vaccination certificate stapled to the back cover. At the bottom of the last page he saw pencilled in a faint set of letters and figures. "What is this?"

"I don't know. Let me see. Oh, that! Why, it's a telephone number."

"What's it doing in your passport?"

"I guess I didn't have a slip of paper. I don't remember whose number it is."

By now he had me on the run and he knew it. "Don't you know it is against the law to deface a passport?"

"I'll erase it."

"You should not write anything in your passport. That's the regulation."

"I won't ever do it again. I promise." And I wanted to promise him I wouldn't lie or steal or associate with persons of loose morals, or covet my neighbor's wife, or anything. He closed my passport firmly and handed it back to me. I'm sure he felt better having found that telephone number. Suppose after all his trouble he hadn't found me guilty of anything, and on a slow day.

"Thank you, sir," I said. "May I proceed now?"

He waved his hand kindly. "Go ahead," he said.

And that's why I went toward Erie, Pennsylvania, and it was Charley's fault. I crossed the high iron bridge and stopped to pay toll. The man leaned out the window. "Go on," he said, "it's on the house."

"How do you mean?"

"I seen you go through the other way a little while ago. I seen the dog. I knew you'd be back."

"Why didn't you tell me?"

"Nobody believes it. Go ahead. You get a free ride one way."

He wasn't government, you see. But government can make you feel so small and mean that it takes some doing to build back a sense of self-importance. Charley and I stayed at the grandest auto court we could find that night, a place only the rich could afford, a pleasure dome of ivory and apes and peacocks and moreover with a restaurant, and room service. I ordered ice and soda and made a scotch and soda and then another. Then I had a waiter in and bespoke soup and a steak and a pound of raw hamburger for Charley, and I overtipped mercilessly. Before I went to sleep I went over all the things I wished I had said to that immigration man, and some of them were incredibly clever and cutting.

This journal entry is a glimpse of a famous person seen through the eyes of a great American poet who was also a newspaper man. Look for indications of Whitman's attitude toward Lincoln. Decide how you will handle his peculiar prose style so that it does not obscure this portrait.

Abraham Lincoln / WALT WHITMAN

August 12th — I see the President almost every day, as I happen to live where he passes to or from his lodgings out of town. He never sleeps at the White House during the hot season, but has quarters at a healthy location some three miles north of the city, the Soldiers' home, a United States military establishment. I saw him this morning at about 8½ coming in to business, riding on Vermont avenue, near L street. He always has a company of twenty-five or thirty cavalry, with sabres drawn and held upright over their shoulders. They say this guard was against his personal wish, but he let his counselors have their way. The party makes no great show in uniform or horses. Mr. Lincoln on the saddle generally rides a good-sized, easy-going gray horse, is dress'd in plain black, somewhat rusty and dusty, wears a black stiff hat, and looks about as ordinary in attire, &c., as the commonest man. A lieutenant, with yellow straps, rides at his left, and following behind, two by two, come the cavalry men, in their yellow-striped jackets. They are generally going at a slow trot, as that is the pace set them by the one they wait upon. The sabres and accoutrements clank, and the entirely unornamental *cortège* as it trots toward Lafayette square arouses no sensation, only some curious stranger stops and gazes. I see very plainly ABRAHAM LINCOLN'S dark brown face, with the deep-cut lines, the eyes, always to me with a deep latent sadness in the expression. We have got so that we exchange bows, and very cordial ones. Sometimes the President goes and comes in an open barouche. The cavalry always accompany him, with drawn sabres. Often I notice as he goes out evenings — and sometimes in the morning, when he returns early — he turns off and halts at the large and handsome residence of the Secretary of War, on K street, and holds conference there. If in his barouche, I can see from my window he does not alight, but sits in his vehicle, and Mr. Stanton comes out to attend him. Sometimes one of his sons, a boy of ten or twelve, accompanies him, riding at his right on a pony. Earlier in the summer I occasionally saw the President and his wife, toward the latter part of the afternoon, out in a barouche, on a pleasure ride through the city. Mrs. Lincoln was dress'd in complete black, with a long crape veil. The equipage is of the plainest kind, only two horses, and they nothing extra. They pass'd me once very closely, and I saw the President in the face fully, as they were moving slowly, and his look, though abstracted, happen'd to be directed steadily in my eye. He bow'd and smiled, but far beneath his smile I noticed well the expression I have alluded to. None of the artists or pictures has caught the deep, though subtle and indirect expression of this man's face. There is something else there. One of the great portrait painters of two or three centuries ago is needed.

Style underscores this satire on the sentimental novel of the early eighteenth century. Several sections within this excerpt may be used as units in themselves.

FROM *Tom Jones* / HENRY FIELDING

Mr. Western grew every day fonder and fonder of Sophia, insomuch that his beloved dogs themselves almost gave place to her in his affections; but as he could not prevail on himself to abandon these, he contrived very cunningly to enjoy their company together with that of his daughter by insisting on her riding a-hunting with him.

Sophia, to whom her father's word was a law, readily complied with his desires, though she had not the least delight in a sport which was of too rough and masculine a nature to suit with her disposition. She had, however, another motive besides her obedience to accompany the old gentleman in the chase; for by her presence she hoped in some measure to restrain his impetuosity, and to prevent him from so frequently exposing his neck to the utmost hazard.

The strongest objection was that which would have formerly been an inducement to her, namely, the frequent meeting with young Jones, whom she had determined to avoid; but as the end of the hunting season now approached, she hoped by a short absence with her aunt to reason herself entirely out of her unfortunate passion, and had not any doubt of being able to meet him in the field the subsequent season without the least danger.

On the second day of her hunting, as she was returning from the chase and was arrived within a little distance from Mr. Western's house, her horse, whose mettlesome spirit required a better rider, fell suddenly to prancing and capering in such a manner that she was in the most imminent peril of falling. Tom Jones, who was at a little distance behind, saw this, and immediately galloped up to her assistance. As soon as he came up, he immediately leapt from his own horse and caught hold of hers by the bridle. The unruly beast presently reared himself on end on his hind legs and threw his lovely burden from his back, and Jones caught her in his arms.

She was so affected with the fright that she was not immediately able to satisfy Jones, who was very solicitous to know whether she had received any hurt. She soon after, however, recovered her spirits, assured him she was safe, and thanked him for the care he had taken of her. Jones answered, "If I have preserved you, madam, I am sufficiently repaid; for I promise you I would have secured you from the least harm, at the expense of a much greater misfortune to myself than I have suffered on this occasion."

"What misfortune?" replied Sophia, eagerly. "I hope you have come to no mischief."

"Be not concerned, madam," answered Jones. "Heaven be praised you have escaped so well, considering the danger you was in. If I have broke my arm, I consider it as a trifle in comparison of what I feared upon your account."

Sophia then screamed out, "Broke your arm! Heaven forbid."

"I am afraid I have, madam," says Jones, "but I beg you will suffer me first to take care of you. I have a right hand yet at your service to help you into the next field, where we have but a very little walk to your father's house."

Sophia, seeing his left arm dangling by his side while he was using the other to lead her, no longer doubted of the truth. She now grew much paler than her fears for herself had made her before. All her limbs were seized with a trembling, insomuch that Jones could scarce support her; and as her thoughts were in no less agitation, she could not refrain from giving Jones a look so full of tenderness that it almost argued a stronger sensation in her mind than even gratitude and pity united can raise in the gentlest female bosom without the assistance of a third more powerful passion.

Mr. Western, who was advanced at some distance when this accident happened, was now returned, as were the rest of the horsemen. Sophia immediately acquainted them with what had befallen Jones and begged them to take care of him. Upon which Western, who had been much alarmed by meeting his daughter's horse without its rider, and was now overjoyed to find her unhurt, cried out, "I am glad it is no worse; if Tom hath broken his arm, we will get a joiner to mend un again."

The squire alighted from his horse, and proceeded to his house on foot with his daughter and Jones. An impartial spectator who had met them on the way would, on viewing their several countenances, have concluded Sophia alone to have been the object of compassion; for as to Jones, he exulted in having probably saved the life of the young lady at the price only of a broken bone; and Mr. Western, though he was not unconcerned at the accident which had befallen Jones, was, however, delighted in a much higher degree with the fortunate escape of his daughter.

The generosity of Sophia's temper construed this behaviour of Jones into great bravery, and it made a deep impression on her heart; for certain it is, that there is no one quality which so generally recommends men to women as this, proceeding, if we believe the common opinion, from that natural timidity of the sex, which is, says Mr. Osborne, so great that a woman is "the most cowardly of all the creatures God ever made" — a sentiment more remarkable for its bluntness than for its truth. Aristotle in his *Politics* doth them, I believe, more justice when he says, "The modesty and fortitude of men differ from those virtues in women; for the fortitude which becomes a woman would be cowardice in a man, and the modesty which becomes a man would be pertness in a woman." Nor is there, perhaps, more of truth in the opinion of those who derive the partiality which women are inclined to show to the brave from this excess of their fear. Mr. Bayle (I think in his article of Helen) imputes this, and with greater probability, to their violent love of glory; for the truth of which we have the authority of him who of all others saw farthest into human nature, and who introduces the heroine of his *Odyssey*, the great pattern of matrimonial love and constancy, assigning the glory of her husband as the only source of her affection towards him.

However this be, certain it is that the accident operated very strongly on Sophia; and indeed after much inquiry into the matter I am inclined to believe that at this very time the charming Sophia made no less impression on the heart of Jones; to say truth, he had for some time become sensible of the irresistible power of her charms.

It is very important to keep in mind occasion and recipient in analyzing these letters. This letter and Miss Barrett's reply, which follows, were mentioned within the chapter.

[A Letter to Miss Barrett]

New Cross, Hatcham, Surrey
[January, 10th 1845]

I love your verses with all my heart, dear Miss Barrett, — and this is no off-hand complimentary letter that I shall write, — whatever else, no prompt matter-of-course recognition of your genius, and there a graceful and natural end of the thing.

Since the day last week when I first read your poems, I quite laugh to remember how I have been turning and turning again in my mind what I should be able to tell you of their effect upon me, for in the first flush of delight I thought I would this once get out of my habit of purely passive enjoyment, when I do really enjoy, and thoroughly justify my admiration — perhaps even, as a loyal fellow-craftsman should, try and find fault and do you some little good to be proud of hereafter! — but nothing comes of it all — so into me has it gone, and part of me has it become, this great living poetry of yours, not a flower of which but took root and grew — Oh, how different that is from lying to be dried and pressed flat, and prized highly, and put in a book with a proper account at top and bottom, and shut up and put away . . . and the book called a 'Flora,' besides!

After all, I need not give up the thought of doing that, too, in time; because even now, talking with whoever is worthy, I can give a reason for my faith in one and another excellence, the fresh strange music, the affluent language, the exquisite pathos and true new brave thought; but in this addressing myself to you — your own self, and for the first time, my feeling rises altogether.

I do, as I say, love these books with all my heart — and I love you too. Do you know I was once not very far from seeing — really seeing you? Mr. Kenyon said to me one morning 'Would you like to see Miss Barrett?' then he went to announce me, — then he returned . . . you were too unwell, and now it is years ago, and I feel as at some untoward passage in my travels, as if I had been close, so close, to some world's-wonder in chapel or crypt, only a screen to push and I might have entered, but there was some slight, so it now seems, slight and just sufficient bar to admission, and the half-opened door shut, and I went home my thousands of miles, and the sight was never to be?

Well, these Poems were to be, and this true thankful joy and pride with which I feel myself,

Yours very faithfully,
ROBERT BROWNING

It is interesting to compare Miss Barrett's Victorian, lady-like restraint with Mr. Browning's exuberance.

[A Letter to Mr. Browning]

50 Wimpole Street
Jan. 11, 1845

I thank you, dear Mr. Browning, from the bottom of my heart. You meant to give me pleasure by your letter — and even if the object had not been answered, I ought still to thank you. But it is thoroughly answered. Such a letter from such a hand! Sympathy is dear — very dear to me: but the sympathy of a poet, and of such a poet, is the quintessence of sympathy for me! Will you take back my gratitude for it? — agreeing, too, that of all the commerce done in the world, from Tyre to Carthage, the exchange of sympathy for gratitude is the most princely thing!

For the rest you draw me on with your kindness. It is difficult to get rid of people when you once have given them too much pleasure — *that* is a fact, and we shall not stop for the moral of it. What I was going to say — after a little natural hesitation — is, that if ever you emerge without inconvenient effort from your 'passive state,' and will *tell* me of such faults as rise to the surface and strike you as important in my poems, (for of course, I do not think of troubling you with criticism in detail) you will confer a lasting obligation on me, and one which I shall value so much, that I covet it at a distance.

I do not pretend to any extraordinary meekness under criticism and it is possible enough that I might not be altogether obedient to yours. But with my high respect for your power in your Art and for your experience as an artist, it would be quite impossible for me to hear a general observation of yours on what appear to you my master-faults, without being the better for it hereafter in some way. I ask for only a sentence or two of general observation — and I do not ask even for *that*, so as to tease you — but in the humble, low voice, which is so excellent a thing in women — particularly when they go a-begging!

The most frequent general criticism I receive, is, I think, upon the style, — 'if I *would* but change my style'! But *that* is an objection (isn't it?) to the writer bodily? Buffon says, and every sincere writer must feel, that '*Le style c'est l'homme;*' a fact, however, scarcely calculated to lessen the objection with certain critics.

Is it indeed true that I was so near to the pleasure and honour of making your acquaintance? and can it be true that you look back upon the lost opportunity with any regret? But — you know — if you had entered the 'crypt,' you might have caught cold, or been tired to death, and *wished* yourself 'a thousand miles off;' which would have been worse than traveling them. It is not my interest, however, to put such thoughts in your head about its being 'all for the best;' and I would rather hope (as I do) that what I lost by one chance I may recover by some future one. Winters shut me up as they do dormouse's eyes; in the spring, *we shall see:* and I am so much better that I seem turning round to the outward world again. And in the meantime I have learnt to know your voice, not merely from the poetry but from the kindness in it. Mr. Kenyon often speaks of you — dear Mr. Kenyon — who most unspeakably, or only speakably with tears in my eyes, — has been my friend and helper, and my book's friend and helper! critic and sympathiser, true friend of all hours! You know him well enough, I think, to understand that I must be grateful to him.

I am writing too much, — and notwithstanding that I am writing too much, I will write of one thing more. I will say that I am your debtor, not only for this cordial letter and for all the pleasure which came with it, but in other ways, and those the highest: and I will say that while I live to follow this divine art of poetry, in proportion to my love for it and my devotion to it, I must be a devout admirer and student of your works. This is in my heart to say to you — and I say it.

And for the rest, I am proud to remain,

Your obliged and faithful
ELIZABETH B. BARRETT

Dylan Thomas writes intimately and informally in this second letter of apology, which he instructed Vernon Watkins to read first. Compare the organization and word choice in the two letters as clues to his increased penitence.

GRYPHON FILMS,
2–6 West Street, London, W.C. 2

TO BE READ FIRST

as from Majoda, New Quay, Cardiganshire
28 Oct. 1944

My dear Gwen and Vernon,

What on earth can you think of me? It is the last, last, last thing of all — on top of all the other things — that the hasty letter I should scribble in such a panic to you, while on the train away from London where we never met, should remain unposted until today: 26 days after your wedding. I have no excuses, but that I was so flurried and anxious, so tired, so miserable, that I put the train-letter into my pocket, arrived in New Quay after an 8 hour journey, imagined, in a kind of delirium, that it was posted, & then waited, perhaps without much hope of ever hearing, to hear from you that, though I was not forgiven, my explanation was understood. What can you think of me? Today I found the letter, crumpled, unposted, in my overcoat. Please, please do try to understand. I shall let you have these two letters now, & a poem I meant also to send weeks ago, without another word of apology or abasement. All our love to you both, for your happiness forever.

Your worst man,
DYLAN

[Sent with letter dated 28 October 1944]
[Pencil]   The Train to Wales, 1.30 Wed.

On Not Turning up to Be Best Man at the Wedding
of One's Best Friend

Reeking & rocking back from a whirled London where nothing went right, all duties were left, and my name spun rank in the whole old smoky nose, I try, to a rhythm of Manchester pocket-handkerchers, and Conk him on the mousetrap, Conk him on the mousetrap, from the London-leaving wheels, to explain to you both, clearly & sincerely, why I never arrived, in black overcoat & shiny suit, rose-lapelled, breathing cachous & great good will, at lunch and church. But the train's stacked tight, I'm tabling a bony knee for this little pad, and am stuck, in the windy corridor, between many soldiers, all twelve foot high & commando-trained to the last lunge of the bayonet. It's not easy to think, or write, or be, and my explanations, true as air, sound, when I try to marshall them, like a chapter of accidents written in a dream by a professor of mathematics who has forgotten all formulas but the wrong one that 2 & 2 make 5. First, then, I arrived in London on Thursday & was sent straitaway, that is, on Friday morning, to Coventry: the City of Coventry, where the company who pay me occasionally are making a film called 'Building The Future,' a subject on which I particularly should have no say. In Coventry I arranged to catch a train back on Sunday night, which would carry me to London in time to meet you both at the station. That train, owing to no fault of my own but to callous & diffident members of the hotel staff, who did not trouble to get the train-times straight, but only late, I missed. There was no other train until the next morning, which was Monday, & that train would reach London at an hour just convenient for me to be able to get into a cab & race for the church. I could not, at that hour of Sunday night, reach my office to leave a message for someone there to spend Monday morning ringing up you & your people & making my — by this time — frantic excuses; I could, indeed, have reached the office by telephone, but there would be no-one there to answer, except some celluloid rat or other. So I waited until Monday morning & then, before catching the train, rang up the office & told a secretary girl to ring Charing Cross Hotel straight away, get in touch with anyone called Watkins & explain the whole position to him or her. I had not, myself, got the time to ring up Charing X Hotel, as it wd take hours, & as my call to the office could be, & was, made Priority, thereby saving those hours during which, by the nicotine-stained skin of my few teeth, I caught the wedding-going & troop-crammed horrible slow train. On arriving in London I managed, by the fervour of my heart only, I am sure, to snatch a cab. I sat back, wheezing in it. "Where to?" the driver said. And — this is the real God-help-me — I couldn't remember the name of the church. It was after half past one. I looked in all my pockets but had left your last letter, I suppose, in wood-&-asbestos Majoda, New Quay. I tried, in my head, every church name I knew. I explained to the driver: "A Church in the City. Very old." Suddenly something came & I said, "I think it's Godolphin. Or something like that. Yes, Godolphin." We went to the City, the driver was dubious. We asked policemen: they were certain. By now, after two, & you too, I feared & hoped, married without my presence but with all my love, I went back to the office to find the secretary-girl out for lunch & the few people still there surprisingly cool and ignorant of all the infernal muddle that had been clotting up the wheels of the world for over a day. There was nothing to do. When the girl came in I asked her, though I was terrified to ask, if her little side of the whole business had gone well. She had tried the Charing X Hotel all morning. The Watkins were out. She had left my name. The Watkins were out.

Later that evening, feeling wretcheder than ever before, alone in my beast of a studio, I remembered the church. Of course I remembered the church. Not Godolphin but St. Bartholomew the Great — too late! O what a prize of prize pickles & I'll understand always if you never want to see me again. I know this hasty jumble can't explain all the somersaulting & backspinning of circumstances against my being where I most wanted to be: at your wedding. God bless you both, & do try to forgive me.

All my love,
DYLAN

One of the world's great artists writes a business letter.

Having, most illustrious lord, seen and considered the experiments of all those who pose as masters in the art of inventing instruments of war, and finding that their inventions differ in no way from those in common use, I am emboldened, without prejudice to anyone, to solicit an appointment of acquainting your Excellency with certain of my secrets.

1. I can construct bridges which are very light and strong and very portable, with which to pursue and defeat the enemy; and others more solid, which resist fire or assault, yet are easily removed and placed in position; and I can also burn and destroy those of the enemy.

2. In case of a siege I can cut off water from the trenches and make pontoons and scaling ladders and other similar contrivances.

3. If by reason of the elevation or the strength of its position a place cannot be bombarded, I can demolish every fortress if its foundations have not been set on stone.

4. I can also make a kind of cannon which is light and easy of transport, with which to hurl small stones like hail, and of which the smoke causes great terror to the enemy, so that they suffer heavy loss and confusion.

5. I can noiselessly construct to any prescribed point subterranean passages either straight or winding, passing if necessary underneath trenches or a river.

6. I can make armoured wagons carrying artillery, which shall break through the most serried ranks of the enemy, and so open a safe passage for his infantry.

7. If occasion should arise, I can construct cannon and mortars and light ordnance in shape both ornamental and useful and different from those in common use.

8. When it is impossible to use cannon I can supply in their stead catapults, mangonels, *trabocchi*, and other instruments of admirable effi-

ciency not in general use — In short, as the occasion requires I can supply infinite means of attack and defense.

9. And if the fight should take place upon the sea I can construct many engines most suitable either for attack or defense and ships which can resist the fire of the heaviest cannon, and powders or weapons.

10. In time of peace, I believe that I can give you as complete satisfaction as anyone else in the construction of buildings both public and private, and in conducting water from one place to another.

I can further execute sculpture in marble, bronze or clay, also in painting I can do as much as anyone else, whoever he may be. Moreover, I would undertake the commission of the bronze horse, which shall endue with immortal glory and eternal honour the auspicious memory of your father and of the illustrious house of Sforza. —

And if any of the aforesaid things should seem to anyone impossible or impracticable, I offer myself as ready to make trial of them in your park or in whatever place shall please your Excellency, to whom I commend myself with all possible humility.

LEONARDO DA VINCI

Both formality and warm sympathy are present in this famous novelist's letter to the widow of a beloved poet.

To Mrs. Robert Louis Stevenson

[Dec. 1894]

My dear Fanny Stevenson,
    What can I say to you that will not seem cruelly irrelevant or vain? We have been sitting in darkness for nearly a fortnight,[1] but what is *our* darkness to the extinction of your magnificent light? You will probably know in some degree what has happened to us — how the hideous news first came to us via Auckland, etc., and then how, in the newspapers, a doubt was raised about its authenticity — just enough to give one a flicker of hope; until your telegram to me via San Francisco — repeated also from other sources — converted my pessimistic convictions into the wretched knowledge. All this time my thoughts have hovered round you all, around *you* in particular, with a tenderness of which I could have wished you might have, afar-off, the divination. You are such a visible picture of desolation that I need to remind myself that courage, and patience, and fortitude are also abundantly with you. The devotion that Louis inspired —

From *The Selected Letters of Henry James*, edited by Leon Edel. Copyright © 1955 by Leon Edel. Reprinted by permission of Alexander R. James, Literary Executor.
[1] Robert Louis Stevenson had died suddenly in Samoa on December 3, 1894.

and of which all the air about you must be full — must also be much to you. Yet as I write the word, indeed, I am almost ashamed of it — as if anything could be 'much' in the presence of such an abysmal void. To have lived in the light of that splendid life, that beautiful, bountiful being — only to see it, from one moment to the other, converted into a fable as strange and romantic as one of his own, a thing that *has* been and has ended, is an anguish into which no one can enter with you fully and of which no one can drain the cup for you. You are nearest to the pain, because you were nearest the joy and the pride. But if it is anything to you to know that no woman was ever more felt *with* and that your personal grief is the intensely personal grief of innumerable hearts — know it well, my dear Fanny Stevenson, for during all these days there has been friendship for you in the very air. For myself, how shall I tell you how much poorer and shabbier the whole world seems, and how one of the closest and strongest reasons for going on, for trying and doing, for planning and dreaming of the future, has dropped in an instant out of life. I was haunted indeed with a sense that I should never again see him — but it was one of the best things in life that he was *there*, or that one had him — at any rate one heard him, and felt him and awaited him and counted him into everything one most loved and lived for. He lighted up one whole side of the globe, and was in himself a whole province of one's imagination. We are smaller fry and meaner people without him. I feel as if there were a certain indelicacy in saying it to you, save that I know that there is nothing narrow or selfish in your sense of loss — for himself, however, for his happy name and his great visible good fortune, it strikes one as another matter. I mean that I feel him to have been as happy in his death (struck down that way, as by the gods, in a clear, glorious hour) as he had been in his fame. And, with all the sad allowances in his rich full life, he had the best of it — the thick of the fray, the loudest of the music, the freshest and finest of himself. It isn't as if there had been no full achievement and no supreme thing. It was all intense, all gallant, all exquisite from the first, and the experience, the fruition, had something dramatically complete in them. He has gone in time not to be old, early enough to be so generously young and late enough to have drunk deep of the cup. There have been — I think — for men of letters few deaths more romantically right. Forgive me, I beg you, what may sound cold-blooded in such words — or as if I imagined there could be anything for you 'right' in the rupture of such an affection and the loss of such a presence. I have in my mind in that view only the rounded career and the consecrated work. When I think of your own situation I fall into a mere confusion of pity and wonder, with the sole sense of your being as brave a spirit as he was (all of whose bravery you shared) to hold on by. Of what solutions or decisions you see before you we shall hear in time; meanwhile please believe that I am most affectionately

with you. . . . More than I can say. I hope your first prostration and bewilderment are over, and that you are feeling your way in feeling all sorts
of encompassing arms — all sorts of outstretched hands of friendship.
Don't, my dear Fanny Stevenson, be unconscious of *mine*, and believe
me more than ever faithfully yours,

HENRY JAMES

*The letters of St. Paul are noted for their arresting figures of speech and their
organization. Some are straightforward and businesslike; others are distinctly
poetic. The following letter has a marked lyric quality, due in part to the
choice of words and images and in part to the rhythmic sentence structure.
The text is that of the King James Bible.*

FROM *The New Testament* / ST. PAUL

First Corinthians, Chapter 13

Though I speak with the tongues of men and of angels, and have not
charity, I am become as sounding brass, or a tinkling cymbal. And though
I have the gift of prophecy, and understand all mysteries, and all knowledge; and though I have all faith, so that I could remove mountains, and
have not charity, I am nothing. And though I bestow all my goods to
feed the poor, and though I give my body to be burned, and have not
charity, it profiteth me nothing. Charity suffereth long, and is kind; charity envieth not; charity vaunteth not itself, is not puffed up, Doth not
behave itself unseemly, seeketh not her own, is not easily provoked, think-
eth no evil; Rejoiceth not in iniquity, but rejoiceth in the truth; Beareth
all things, believeth all things, hopeth all things, endureth all things.
Charity never faileth: but whether there be prophecies, they shall fail;
whether there be tongues, they shall cease; whether there be knowledge,
it shall vanish away. For we know in part, and we prophesy in part. But
when that which is perfect is come, then that which is in part shall be
done away. When I was a child, I spake as a child, I understood as a
child, I thought as a child: but when I became a man, I put away childish things. For now we see through a glass, darkly; but then face to face:
now I know in part; but then shall I know even as also I am known. And
now abideth faith, hope, charity, these three; but the greatest of these is
charity.

Bibliography

Cowley, Malcolm (ed.). *Writers at Work: The "Paris Review" Interviews.*
New York: The Viking Press, 1961. Compass Books edition, C52.

A collection of interviews on "How Writers Write." Sixteen interviews
offer a range of styles and interests from E. M. Forster to Françoise Sagan.

Fiedler, Leslie (ed.). *The Art of the Essay: Edited with Introduction, Notes and Exercise Questions.* New York: Thomas Y. Crowell Company, 1958.

An extensive collection of essays and travel accounts.

Hook, J. N., and E. G. Matthews. *Modern American Grammar and Usage.* New York: The Ronald Press, 1956.

A textbook on grammar and modern American usage with particular attention to how language is used by contemporary writers.

Ludwig, Richard M. (ed.). *Essays Today, II.* New York: Harcourt, Brace and Company, 1956.

A collection of twenty-five essays from leading periodicals ranging from biographical sketches to reflective essays.

Reed, Herbert. *English Prose Style.* London: G. Bell and Son, Ltd., 1949.

Still the most complete discussion of prose style per se. *The approach is first from the standpoint of composition and then of rhetoric.*

Thomas, Wright, and Stuart Gerry Brown. *Reading Prose: An Introduction to Critical Study.* New York: Oxford University Press, 1952.

An extensive collection of essays grouped thematically, with a brief section on experimental prose. The final section is a compact directive for developing a critical approach. Helpful chronological index.

Thompson, Craig R., and John Hicks. *Thought and Experience in Prose.* New York: Oxford University Press, 1951.

A collection of essays ranging from Chesterfield's letters to his son to critical comments on selected literature.

Chapter 6

Though description sometimes exists for its own sake, it is most frequently found in conjunction with some other type of writing — as a means of implementing narrative, for example. Because it qualifies by expanding or limiting, a skilled writer uses description to control his readers' reactions and to focus their attention on selected facets of his subject. Description helps clarify factual prose and provides clear indications of attitude in more personal writing. It adds suggestion to both setting and character in narration. It makes an important contribution to rhythm of content and to harmony and is a chief source of variety and contrast. In short, without description a piece of literature lacks the full warmth and color of life.

Descriptive writing depicts the sensory qualities of a person, place, action, or object. It tells how something looks, sounds, smells, or tastes. It may describe texture or pressure, heat or cold. It may show how a person or thing moves. It can produce in the reader a feeling of tension or relaxation as an accompanying response to any one or a combination of these appeals to the senses and is, of course, a strong factor in empathy. It is a valuable asset to the interpreter because it encourages his audience to respond physically and emotionally as well as mentally and thus share the totality of the selection. Inexperienced interpreters are often tempted to skip the descriptive sections or to hurry over them as unimportant, but the skilled interpreter takes great care to use them as the author has to insure vividness and clarity and to help control and enrich suggestion.

Description

Factual Description

The strength of sensory appeal in description depends partly, of course, on the author's skill in selecting references which evoke sights, sounds, smells, tastes, and motor responses that are universal, rich in suggestion, and still highly individual. Of course, factual writing, which informs, defines, or explains, sometimes makes use of description as a practical means of presenting information and increasing understanding. In factual prose the descriptions will be much more neutral than in imaginative prose — that is, they will have less sensory appeal and will arouse little or no emotional response. Their purpose is to help the mind explore new material by reference to that with which it is already familiar.

Even when the words taken by themselves seem to have rather strong sensory connotations, the overall factual purpose for which they are used neutralizes the sensory appeal. For example, if one had occasion to read aloud from the *Encyclopaedia Britannica* the article on hydrogen sulphide, he would come across the following sentence: "Hydrogen sulphide, a colourless, poisonous gas having the odour of rotten eggs, is moderately soluble in water." Here, because of the context, the words "odour of rotten eggs" are not intended to arouse strong sensory response; rather, they serve the purpose of definition. The writer is concerned with telling what hydrogen sulphide is, not with conveying any feeling about it. For this reason, the person reading the passage aloud would properly present it in a straightforward fashion, and would not attempt to re-create a sensory response in his listeners. The oral interpreter is unlikely to be working with strictly factual prose.

Evocative Description

The interpreter's main concern will be with evocative description, by which the writer wants to arouse some feeling in the reader. When this is his purpose, the effectiveness of the description depends on the writer's ability to elicit the sensory response and on the reader's powers of perception — and further, in interpretation, on the interpreter's ability to re-create the sensory appeal for his listeners.

Description can be extremely persuasive, for it helps to make abstract ideas concrete so that they stir the emotions and encourage the reader to link the ideas to his own specific experiences. The skillful writer of didactic prose, therefore, is careful to condense his description so that it gains power by directness and does not distract the reader from the main theme. He usually chooses a familiar object which requires very little elaboration of detail to bring it well within the realm of any reader's experience. Bacon's reference to keeping wounds green, in the essay quoted in the preceding chapter, is an excellent example of this technique.

Description plays an especially important part in narration; indeed, narration without description is very rare. Description usually introduces character or setting or both and helps establish the relationship between them. It may create a mood or stir the reader's sympathy for a character's situation. All these factors come into play in the opening paragraph of a short story by Mark Schorer, "What We Don't Know Hurts Us."

> The midafternoon winter sun burned through the high California haze. Charles Dudley, working with a mattock in a thicket of overgrowth, felt as steamy and as moldy as the black adobe earth in which his feet kept slipping. Rain had fallen for five days with no glimmer of sunshine, and now it seemed as if the earth, with fetid animation, like heavy breath, were giving all that moisture back to the air. The soil, or the broom which he was struggling to uproot, had a disgusting, acrid odor, as if he were tussling with some obscene animal instead of with a lot of neglected vegetation, and suddenly an overload of irritations — the smell, the stinging sweat in his eyes, his itching skin, his blistering palms, made him throw the mattock down and come diving out of the thicket into the clearing he had already achieved.[1]

[1] From *The State of Mind* by Mark Schorer. Reprinted by permission of the author.

This description gives the setting, introduces the principal character, establishes the relationship between this character and the setting, and through that relationship sets a mood and creates an attitude toward the character. The reference to the "disgusting, acrid odor" is an emotion-arousing sense appeal that helps the reader share and sympathize with Charles Dudley's reaction to a hostile environment; it is not factual and definitive like "rotten eggs" in the *Britannica's* description of hydrogen sulphide.

Another function of description in narrative is to advance the action or stop it momentarily, to create suspense or relax the reader's tension for the sake of greater emphasis when the action is resumed. Edgar Allan Poe is an acknowledged master of this technique. The result is a rhythm of content which adds both variety and contrast to the total effect.

The oral interpreter needs to understand how description is used in the selection he is to present if he is to make full and proper use of it in re-creating the material for an audience. When he feels that he understands the relation of the descriptive elements to the purpose of the whole, he must then turn to a detailed analysis of the way descriptive writing appeals to the perceiver's senses.

Sensory Appeal Through Imagery

The sensory appeal of description is made through imagery. An image is inherent in any word or group of words which affects the senses and thus creates a sensory response. The amount, complexity, and vividness of imagery depend first of all on the author's purpose. In a piece of scientific writing that appeals primarily to the intellect, there will be relatively few images. On the other hand, in poetry, which of all forms of writing makes the strongest, most compressed appeal to the emotions and the senses, imagery reaches its highest development. The degree to which imagery is effectively used depends on the author's reservoir of experiences and his ability to recapture specific details of those experiences and put them into appropriate words.

Imagery has become a very popular — and occasionally confusing — word in the literary criticism of this century. In general it refers to language which describes, but within this category there are four common variations of usage. The first, and the one of primary concern to us, is language appealing to the senses and to motor responses. This we shall refer to as *sense imagery*. The second is language which gives concreteness to abstractions by describing them or endowing them with qualities which appeal to the senses, and will be referred to as *literary imagery*. The third broadens the term to include a condensation of a series of the first two, so that it becomes a *symbol*, such as Faulkner's frequent use of heat and dryness. The fourth commonly accepted meaning of imagery makes it synonymous with *idea or vision*. Although all four concepts are closely related, we shall give specific attention only to the first two.

The use of language to give concreteness to an abstraction, or literary imagery, was touched on briefly in Chapter 5 in our consideration of word choice. We shall return to it again in Chapter 10 where we will be discussing poetry, since it is in poetry that imagery is usually most basic and complex. We shall limit our consideration in this chapter to sense imagery, remembering, however, the close relationship between the two concepts.

The interpreter's skill in handling sense imagery depends first on his responsiveness to the words of the author. As the writer calls on his own memory for a concrete object which he can translate into sense-apprehended terms and thus enable the reader to create a similar image out of his own experience, so the interpreter, on encountering the word symbol that stands for the image, reaches back to a selected experience and recreates it in concrete terms. He then subjects that personal experience to the expansion or limitation dictated by the writer and makes a sensory response. Finally, he uses his physical and vocal techniques to convey that response to his hearers along with the image, so that they may complete the cycle by re-creating and responding in terms of *their* experiences.

This chain of perception and response is simply an extension of the process by which an actual object or sound stimulates a mental and emotional response. When a person sees a tree, for example, the stimulus of light, shade, color, and form which his eye receives produces the image of a tree in his mind. This process becomes automatic as his familiarity with the object increases. He begins to make classifications of trees, as pine tree or elm tree. As his experience increases, the likelihood of his mistaking a pine for an elm becomes negligible. Perhaps the image "pine tree" or "elm tree" has special, personal associations for him; if so, these too are carried over into his response. In short, he receives the stimulus through his senses, transmits it to his brain, classifies and perhaps enlarges it, and finally makes a response.

In the case of imagery in literature, a preliminary step is necessary. The stimulus comes from a word or group of words rather than from an object. This word stimulus strikes the eye of the reader or the ear of the listener. The symbols of the letters, in the former case, or the sounds in the latter must then be translated into the object or quality they represent to the perceiver. Thus the stimulus comes actually from a re-creation of the concrete object within the mind of the reader and of the listener. From this point, the process of translation, elaboration, classification, and evaluation is much as outlined above.

No two people will re-create an image in exactly the same terms. No two mental elm trees are quite the same or are visualized against the same background. But all images of "elm tree" will have enough elements in common so that all persons to whom the words "elm tree" mean anything at all can respond in similar fashion. The author will supply whatever qualifying elements are needed to direct the universal response to his individual purpose.

Varieties of Sensory Appeal

As we have noted, description achieves its effect through sensory images. Images that appeal predominantly to the sense of sight are called *visual*; to the sense of hearing, *auditory*; to the sense of taste, *gustatory*; to the sense of smell, *olfactory*. The sense of touch is appealed to in *tactual* (or tactile) imagery, which evokes a sensation of physical contact, pressure, or texture, and in *thermal* imagery, which refers to the feeling of heat and cold.

As we pointed out in Chapter 3, imagery can also appeal to the so-called motor sense. There are two types of imagery in this category. The first is *kinetic* imagery, a large, overt action of the muscles such as "ran," "jumped," "sat down," or "walked away." The second is *kinesthetic* imagery, which refers to muscle tension and relaxation. It is closely related to empathy and is likely to be present in any particularly rich sense appeal, although it can also stand alone and is found in references to height and distance, for example, or in qualified kinetic imagery, as in "sat down nervously," "walked away casually," or "ran breathlessly." Sometimes when a large kinetic action is being reported by an observer, such as a narrator, the effect on the one reporting is kinesthetic through empathy rather than kinetic, as his own action would have been.

Rarely does an image appeal to one and only one sense. In much of the best literature, certainly in all literature rich in suggestion, the images carry a complex of appeals. In addition to the primary sense appeal of a word, phrase, or thought unit, there will usually be one or more additional or secondary appeals as well. The senses of taste and smell, for example, are so closely allied that it is frequently impossible to affect one and not the other. Again, it is highly improbable that kinetic or action imagery would not be accompanied by kinesthetic or muscle-tension imagery. But complexity of appeal goes beyond these natural pairings. A skillful writer will frequently blend many secondary appeals with a primary appeal, or will allow the primary appeal to shift to secondary position within a single unit.

With this in mind, let us examine a portion of an essay by Lin Yutang. The phrases especially rich in imagery have been italicized.

> . . . To the soldier returning on leave the most common sights of city or country life — *a hot-dog stand, the neon lights at night,* even

the traffic lights — seem good and reassuring. Even *being a lazy louse lying in bed* without the *hallucination of the reveille* seems to constitute an august virtue and a permanent achievement of human civilization.

In fact, one suddenly realizes that all the good things of life — *the morning coffee, fresh air, a stroll in the afternoon*, even *dashing for the subway* or *dodging friends among commuters in the morning train* — constitute civilization because they constitute the very end of living. War makes us realize the importance of the things we ordinarily take for granted. No one values a *luxurious shave in a barber shop* more than a soldier returning from the front.[2]

By his use of the word "sights," the author indicates that he intends the primary appeal of the opening sentence to be visual. For example, the reader imagines a "hot-dog stand" primarily as an image to be seen. But out of his remembered experiences of hot-dog stands he summons associated imagery, though it is probably less strong than the primary visual image: olfactory, because of the smell of the hot dog sizzling on the grill; gustatory, because of the remembered taste, perhaps enhanced by pickle relish or mustard; thermal, not only because of the suggestion of "hot," but also because the perceiver's memories may be associated with summer; auditory, because of the voices of the customers, the rush of passing traffic and honking of horns on a state highway — or perhaps, if the remembered hot-dog stand is visualized at an amusement park, the music of a merry-go-round or the squeals of the roller-coaster riders in the background. In the same way, the primarily visual images "neon lights at night" and "traffic lights" carry associated secondary appeals to other senses. In the second sentence, the author abandons visual images and shifts his primary emphasis to motor response, the "lazy louse lying in bed," and to auditory appeal, "hallucination of the reveille," an image with strong secondary kinesthetic overtones.

The second paragraph presents a still more complex array of imagery, beginning with "morning coffee" (primary appeals, olfactory and gustatory; secondary appeals, thermal, visual, and kinesthetic, the last because of the suggestion of well-being) and continuing through a number of predominantly kinetic and kinesthetic images, to "among commuters in the morning train" (primary appeal, visual; secondary appeals, auditory and — more or less! — olfactory). The image of a "luxurious shave" is an excellent example of difference in point of view, depending, one may surmise, on whether or not one has ever had a shave. It is important to remember that Lin Yutang is a man, and the reader must attempt to make his, or more particularly her, response sympathetic with the

[2] From *With Love and Irony* by Lin Yutang. Reprinted by permission of the author.

author's. The feminine reader might derive approximately the same sensation of luxurious well-being from a facial or a scented bath — an interesting illustration of the fact that, though the details of the perceived images may differ, there can be enough basic similarity of sensation to arouse comparable responses.

Obviously, the interpreter cannot stop after each image and check to be sure his audience has had time to see, taste, smell, and hear all the accompanying appeals. All the images work together to produce the total effect. However, the more completely the interpreter has responded to the complexity of the appeals during preparation, and consequently during performance, the more force they will carry as he uses subtle variety of vocal technique and empathy to help the imagery fulfill its function of clarifying and making vivid.

An author's use of imagery will often affect his style and give important clues to his attitude. The writings of Thomas Wolfe contain innumerable examples of this relationship, including this fragment of remembered sense experience:

> . . . and the exciting smell of chalk and varnished desks; the smell
> of heavy bread-sandwiches of cold fried meat and butter . . .

and then the paragraph rushes on to other sense vignettes not connected with the schoolroom — and we become conscious of a vigorous personality, with an almost insatiable physical appetite for life, hurrying through a catalogue of remarkably sharp sense impressions, piling image on image as though striving desperately to pin down some of the heady, crowding sense memories before they escape.

By way of contrast, compare this with George Santayana's visual recall of a schoolroom out of his boyhood experiences:

> No blackboard was black; all were indelibly clouded with in-
> grained layers of old chalk; the more you rubbed it out, the more
> you rubbed it in. Every desk was stained with generations of ink-
> spots, cut deeply with initials and scratched drawings. What idle
> thoughts had been wandering for years through all those empty
> heads in all those tedious school hours![3]

In this description we sense the reflective mind of one who stands a little aloof from active participation in life, who uses images not so much as means of embracing life in all its physical manifestations but as spring-boards to reflection on the meaning that lies behind all that the senses apprehend.

Both Wolfe and Santayana have let their memories touch on similar aspects of experience, but each has selected the details to which he him-

---

[3] From *Persons and Places* by George Santayana. Reprinted by permission of Charles Scribner's Sons.

self responds most completely, the one as a voracious liver of life, the other as an esthete and philosopher.

Poets and prose writers alike use imagery not only to reveal their own attitudes toward what they are saying but often to create distinct and individual personalities for the speakers they choose when not speaking in their own persons. Robert Browning is a master of this technique, especially in his monologues, and Theodore Roethke uses it brilliantly in "Old Lady's Winter Words" (page 85). A playwright may also use sense imagery to tell us a good deal about a character's background and set of values.

Imagery and the Intrinsic Factors

When the interpreter begins to examine a selection in detail he will be aware that imagery contributes strongly to the intrinsic factors — that it helps to produce unity and harmony, variety and contrast, balance and proportion, and rhythm. Perhaps a few examples will be useful here.

One of the most obvious methods of achieving unity through imagery is the use of a single type of primary appeal throughout the unit. This is the technique used in the excerpt from *In Cold Blood* (pages 198–201); Capote allows us to see all the details through the eyes of the State's Attorney and adds only enough auditory appeal to provide variety. Sometimes a "camera" technique of progression toward objects is effective, as in "Kalymnos" (pages 205–206), where Durrell begins with a long view and gradually moves into the harbor. We are then able to focus on smaller details which were not discernible from a distance. It is at this point also that he introduces auditory imagery, completely absent in the first paragraph because we were too far away to hear the sounds that accompany the objects described. This progression toward place allows for an interesting accumulation and balance of sight and sound without distracting us from the panorama of the scene.

Sometimes the imagery displays very little unity of type but is held together by restrictions to a limited locale. This is true of the excerpt from "June Recital" (page 197). Or similarly, the imagery may all be slanted toward one person or object, as in "Dry September" (page 206), or to the parts of a series of details which relate to one object, place, or person. In the latter case, the effect is usually cumulative and must be handled so as to achieve the strongest ultimate impression. Charles Dickens uses this cumulative technique to describe a battle in *A Tale of Two Cities*:

> With a roar that sounded as if all the breath in France had been shaped into the detested word, the living sea rose, wave on wave, depth on depth, and overflowed the city to that point. Alarm-bells

ringing, drums beating, the sea raging and thundering on its new beach, the attack begun. . . .

Cannon, muskets, fire and smoke. . . . Flashing weapons, blazing torches, smoking waggon-loads of wet straw, hard work at neighboring barricades in all directions, shrieks, volleys, execrations, bravery without stint, boom, smash and rattle, and the furious sounding of the living sea. . . .

The author begins with the auditory appeal, to which he adds complexity that reaches its height in "cannon, muskets, fire and smoke"; then he shifts to the visual and kinetic imagery of "flashing weapons," returning almost at once to the auditory appeal in "shrieks, volleys," which comes to a climax in "boom, smash and rattle." Finally, he blends all this into "the furious sounding of the living sea."

Thomas Wolfe's "The Golden World" gives the interpreter a complex problem in unity through imagery. The following sentence illustrates his use of cumulative technique.

He knew the good male smell of his father's sitting-room; of the smooth worn leather sofa, with the gaping horse-hair rent; of the blistered varnished wood upon the hearth; of the heated calf-skin bindings; of the flat moist plug of apple tobacco, stuck with a red flag; of wood-smoke and burnt leaves in October; of the brown tired autumn earth; of honey-suckle at night; of warm nasturtiums; of a clean ruddy farmer who comes weekly with printed butter, eggs and milk; of fat limp underdone bacon and of coffee; of a bakery-oven in the wind; of large deep-hued stringbeans smoking-hot and seasoned well with salt and butter; of a room of old pine boards in which books and carpets have been stored, long closed; of Concord grapes in their long white baskets.[4]

In this one long sentence the imagery is predominantly olfactory, but within this unity of appeal there is a variety of place. The progression from interior to exterior and back to interior may prove troublesome to the interpreter unless he is careful to group the objects which appeal to the senses. The excerpt opens in the sitting room, where it remains through mention of the visual detail of "a red flag." Without warning or apparent motivation the scene shifts to the outdoors, but the olfactory motif remains strong and there is unity of appeal in the focus of attention on the earth and its produce. The "ruddy farmer" with his "butter, eggs and milk" sets up the train of thought which centers on the smell of food and calls up the rest of the images within the sentence, including the "room of old pine boards in which books and carpets have been stored,"

[4] From *Look Homeward, Angel* by Thomas Wolfe. Reprinted by permission of Charles Scribner's Sons.

an image which for the author belongs with these others, but to the interpreter may seem like an interpolation among the many references to food. The unifying factor here might best be classed as "stream of consciousness." The oral interpreter may experience some trouble in keeping the transitions clear and acceptable, unless he is careful to group the images by association of place or sense appeal, keeping in mind the importance of the primary olfactory appeal and the fact that the memories cluster around a single house. He must not forget or allow his listeners to forget that the sentence begins "He knew the . . . smell of. . . ."

Obviously, the type and vividness of the imagery must be in harmony with the total intention of the piece of literature: harmonious with the character and setting in a narrative, and with the tastes and experiences of the intended audience in didactic writing and essays. Even the adjectives used to give the objects added richness must be highly appropriate, such as "heated calf-skin bindings," "burnt leaves," and many others in the excerpt from "The Golden World." Books bound in watered silk would certainly not be harmonious with the "good male smell."

A skillful author is acutely aware, consciously or subconsciously, of the speed with which the senses tire. Everyone knows from experience that it is possible to become so accustomed to a smell, a sound, or a taste that it loses its initial impact or even passes into the realm of the subconscious and goes unnoticed. Thus, as Thomas Wolfe does here with his "red flag," an author will suddenly vary his appeal to allow the reader to shift his response to another sense. When he returns to the original appeal, the reader's response is heightened because of this momentary relief. The same relieving function can be accomplished by contrast as well. Thus imagery makes a particularly rich contribution to both variety and contrast and is itself intensified by variation and contrast. It is one of the interpreter's problems not to allow the variety to overshadow or violate the essential unity, but rather to use it to fulfill its purpose of relief.

Usually an author will provide help with this problem. On close observation, the interpreter will discover that the author has not really abandoned the primary appeal but has only allowed it to shift momentarily to a secondary position. He may also keep a fairly consistent relationship between the two types of imagery. This was done most successfully in the excerpt from *With Love and Irony* quoted earlier in this chapter (page 189), in which the visual and kinesthetic-kinetic images appear quite consistently in either the primary or secondary position, thus carrying out the author's intent of presenting familiar sights and implying their effect of muscle relaxation after the tension of a period of military service.

In the matter of balance and proportion, imagery is often used to weight a unit so that by its added vividness it is able to hold its own with a much larger unit. In this case, imagery is usually combined with other factors as well — especially to heighten a climax or sharpen a contrast.

In some selections imagery provides an interesting rhythm of logical content and emotional quality. In the excerpt quoted above, Lin Yutang neatly alternates imagistic appeals with statements directed primarily to the mind, so that the appeal to the reader is first intellectual, then sensory, then intellectual again. This rhythm is especially important in the case of kinetic and kinesthetic imagery.

Tone Color

For the interpreter the sounds of the words carrying the sensory appeal are especially important, since he will be translating the word symbols into sound symbols for his listeners. Writers who are concerned with appealing to the senses and emotions of their readers will take care that there is harmony between what they are describing and the sounds of the words they choose to describe it. Of course it is the words, not the separate sounds, which carry the meaning, and it is the connotation of the words themselves that influence the interpreter's pace, quality, and all the rest of the elements of vocal technique. There are, for instance, more things affecting the way one would say "sleep," "slap," "slip," and "slop" than the mere difference in the vowels. Nevertheless, certain combinations of sounds produce articulation problems which slow the pace or give a sharpness to separate words, while others lend themselves to smooth linking and help produce a flowing effect. The combination of sounds of vowels and consonants to help achieve a particular effect is called *tone color*.

Tone color is part of a writer's style, since how words sound when they are put together influences his choice of words, the way he arranges them in a sentence, and, ultimately, the rhythm of the entire section. We touched on this aspect of style without calling it by name when we noted the "crackling" sounds of Powys' description of a bookseller (page 145). It is the interpreter's responsibility to make full use of tone color to help support the imagery the author has provided. It is, moreover, a powerful aid to empathy since it underscores connotation and enriches suggestion. We shall return to a consideration of tone color when we discuss the sound patterns of poetry in Chapter 11.

The Interpreter's Use of Description

The interpreter's first response to imagery will probably be strongly subjective. This must be followed, however, by an examination which is as objective as possible, based on what is known of the author and his individual experiences, and on the organization and style of the piece of writing under analysis. Objective analysis will help the interpreter see the author's purpose and base his primary response on the author's obvious intent, but within the limits the writer has imposed it is the interpreter's part as a re-creative artist to color the imagery with his own experiences. For although no two people respond in exactly the same way to any phrases which carry sensory appeal, the perceivers' experiences seldom differ so widely as to destroy the basic purpose of the appeal. For example, we have seen that Lin Yutang's reference to a "luxurious shave in a barber shop" is definitely a masculine image, but that it matters very little whether the reader is a man or woman, since as perceiver he or she can draw on some experience that connotes the pleasant relaxation and well-being of the "luxurious shave."

In giving detailed consideration to each image and its related tone color, it is important to keep in mind the sense of the entire thought unit. Consider, for instance, the thermal implications of the word "hot." When used in a phrase like "hot bath after a cold walk," there is a natural tendency to let the accompanying suggestion of relaxation show in the muscles, in the slower tempo of the words, and in a more relaxed vocal tone. If, on the other hand, the word is used in such a context as "Ouch! That water is hot!" the muscles will become tense, the tempo of the words will quicken, and the vocal force and tension will increase. In short, the image-bearing word or phrase must never be divorced from the whole unit of thought.

Response to imagery will have a definite effect on the interpreter's muscle tone and consequently on the empathic and emotional response of his audience. This is particularly true in the case of appeals to the motor responses, but the attendant emotional associations the author has achieved through references to sights, sounds, tastes, and smells will also make an empathic contribution.

After the interpreter has worked out the description through the various images, the next step is to consider what aspects of the imagery contribute most to the whole — how to express particular images in such a way that they are not a catalogue of separate items but a unifying force instead. Having exhausted the possibilities of complexity in the appeals, the interpreter must next evaluate them in terms of the author's overall purpose. When the images are considered in relation to the whole, he will see that some contribute much more than others to the total effect and hence will need to be stressed, while those which provide variety within this unity may be played down. Against the desirablity of responding completely in order to make use of the vividness which imagery adds to the writing and hence to his performance, the interpreter must balance the ever-present danger of allowing this vividness of descriptive detail to destroy the essential unity of his material.

In performance, the descriptive elements, like every other aspect of content and form, must be used subtly and unobtrusively to achieve the overall effect of the entire selection. They are only part of the whole, and their importance will be dictated by the author's larger purpose. The interpreter must never forget that the final step in preparation is to put the material back together so that all parts are coordinated, and that the final test of his performance is its seeming artlessness and the completeness of his communication to his audience.

Selections for Analysis and Oral Interpretation

In addition to the following excerpts, you will find some interesting descriptive passages in the selections at the ends of earlier chapters and within the narratives in Chapter 7.

The style here is as packed as the recital room. Pay particular attention to the shift in imagery as you reach the last paragraph.

FROM *June Recital* / EUDORA WELTY

The night of the recital was always clear and hot; everyone came. The prospective audience turned out in full oppression.

In the studio decorated like the inside of a candy box, with "material" scalloping the mantel shelf and doilies placed under every movable object, now thus made immovable, with streamers of white ribbons and nosegays of pink and white Maman Cochet roses and the last MacLain sweetpeas dividing and re-dividing the room, it was as hot as fire. No matter that this was the first night of June; no electric fans were to whir around while music played. The metronome, ceremoniously closed, stood on the piano like a vase. There was no piece of music anywhere in sight.

When the first unreasoning hush — there was the usual series — fell over the audience, the room seemed to shake with the agitation of palmetto and feather fans alone, plus the occasional involuntary tick of the metronome within its doors. There was the mixture together of agitation and decoration which could make every little forthcoming child turn pale with a kind of ultimate dizziness. Whoever might look up at the ceiling for surcease would be floundered within a paper design stemming out of the chandelier, as complicated and as unavailing as a cut-out paper snowflake.

Now Miss Eckhart came into the room all changed, with her dark hair pulled low on her brow, and gestured for silence. She was wearing her recital dress which made her look larger and closer-to than she looked at any other times. It was an old dress: Miss Eckhart disregarded her own rules. People would forget that dress between times and then she would come out in it again, the untidy folds not quite spotlessly clean, gathered about her bosom and falling heavy as a coat to the sides; it was a tawny crepe-back satin. There was a bodice of browning lace. It was as rich and hot and deep-looking as a furskin. The unexpected creamy flesh on her upper arms gave her a look of emerging from it.

Miss Eckhart, achieving silence, stood in the shadowy spot directly under the chandelier. Her feet, white-shod, shod by Mr. Sissum for good, rested in the chalk circle previously marked on the floor and now, she believed, perfectly erased. One hand, with its countable little muscles so hard and ready, its stained, blue nails, went to the other hand and they folded quite still, holding nothing, until they lost their force by lying on her breast and made a funny little house with peaks and gables. Standing near the piano but not near enough to help, she presided but not with her whole heart on guard against disaster; while disaster was what remained on the minds of the little girls. Starting with the youngest, she called them out.

So they played, and except Virgie, all played their worst. They shocked themselves. Parnell Moody burst into tears on schedule. But Miss Eckhart never seemed to notice or to care. How forgetful she seemed at exactly the moments she should have been agonized! You expected the whip, almost, for forgetting to repeat before the second ending, or for failing to count ten before you came around the curtain at all; and instead you received a strange smile. It was as though Miss Eckhart, at the last, were grateful to you for *anything*.

Truman Capote received almost unanimous acclaim for the "coldly objective" reporting in this book, the account of the murder of an entire family. The skilled interpreter will be aware that, though the book is remarkably well done, the reporting is perhaps not so "coldly objective" after all. Capote allows Dewey, the State's Attorney, to be our witness to the hanging, but the description is, nevertheless, ostensibly factual. Keep the details unified within the specific room.

FROM *In Cold Blood* / TRUMAN CAPOTE

Dewey had watched them die, for he had been among the twenty-odd witnesses invited to the ceremony. He had never attended an execution, and when on the midnight past he entered the cold warehouse, the scenery had surprised him: he had anticipated a setting of suitable dignity, not this bleakly lighted cavern cluttered with lumber and other debris. But the gallows itself, with its two pale nooses attached to a crossbeam, was imposing enough; and so, in an unexpected style, was the hangman, who cast a long shadow from his perch on the platform at the top of the wooden instrument's thirteen steps. The hangman, an anonymous, leathery gentleman who had been imported from Missouri for the event, for which he was paid six hundred dollars, was attired in an aged double-breasted pin-striped suit overly commodious for the narrow figure inside it — the coat came nearly to his knees; and on his head he wore a cowboy hat which, when first bought, had perhaps been bright green, but was now a weathered, sweat-stained oddity.

Also, Dewey found the self-consciously casual conversation of his fellow witnesses, as they stood awaiting the start of what one witness termed "the festivities," disconcerting.

"What I heard was, they was gonna let them draw straws to see who dropped first. Or flip a coin. But Smith says why not do it alphabetically. Guess 'cause S comes after H. Ha!"

"Read in the paper, afternoon paper, what they ordered for their last meal? Ordered the same menu. Shrimp. French fries. Garlic bread. Ice cream and strawberries and whipped cream. Understand Smith didn't touch his much."

"That Hickock's got a sense of humor. They was telling me how, about an hour ago, one of the guards says to him, 'This must be the longest night of your life.' And Hickock, he laughs and says, 'No. The shortest.'"

"Did you hear about Hickock's eyes? He left them to an eye doctor. Soon as they cut him down, this doctor's gonna yank out his eyes and stick them in somebody else's head. Can't say I'd want to be that somebody. I'd feel peculiar with them eyes in my head."

"Christ! Is that *rain*? All the windows down! My new Chevy. Christ!'"

The sudden rain rapped the high warehouse roof. The sound, not unlike the rat-a-tat-tat of parade drums, heralded Hickock's arrival. Accompanied by six guards and a prayer-murmuring chaplain, he entered the death place handcuffed and wearing an ugly harness of leather straps that bound his arms to his torso. At the foot of the gallows the warden read to him the official order of execution, a two-page document; and as the warden read, Hickock's eyes, enfeebled by half a decade of cell shadows, roamed the little audience until, not seeing what he sought, he asked the nearest guard, in a whisper, if any member of the Clutter family was present. When he was told no, the prisoner seemed disappointed, as though he thought the protocol surrounding this ritual of vengeance was not being properly observed.

As is customary, the warden, having finished his recitation, asked the condemned man whether he had any last statement to make. Hickock nodded. "I just want to say I hold no hard feelings. You people are sending me to a better world than this ever was"; then, as if to emphasize the point, he shook hands with the four men mainly responsible for his capture and conviction, all of whom had requested permission to attend the executions: K.B.I. Agents Roy Church, Clarence Duntz, Harold Nye, and Dewey himself. "Nice to see you," Hickock said with his most charming smile; it was as if he were greeting guests at his own funeral.

The hangman coughed — impatiently lifted his cowboy hat and settled it again, a gesture somehow reminiscent of a turkey buzzard huffing, then smoothing its neck feathers — and Hickock, nudged by an attendant, mounted the scaffold steps. "The Lord giveth, the Lord taketh away. Blessed is the name of the Lord," the chaplain intoned, as the rain sound accelerated, as the noose was fitted, and as a delicate black mask was tied round the prisoner's eyes. "May the Lord have mercy on your soul." The trap door opened, and Hickock hung for all to see a full twenty minutes before the prison doctor at last said, "I pronounce this man dead." A hearse, its blazing headlights beaded with rain, drove into the warehouse, and the body, placed on a litter and shrouded under a blanket, was carried to the hearse and out into the night.

Staring after it, Roy Church shook his head: "I never would have believed he had the guts. To take it like he did. I had him tagged a coward."

The man to whom he spoke, another detective, said, "Aw, Roy. The guy was a punk. A mean bastard. He deserved it."

Church, with thoughtful eyes, continued to shake his head.

While waiting for the second execution, a reporter and a guard conversed. The reporter said, "This your first hanging?"

"I seen Lee Andrews."

"This here's my first."

"Yeah. How'd you like it?"

The reporter pursed his lips. "Nobody in our office wanted the assignment. Me either. But it wasn't as bad as I thought it would be. Just like jumping off a diving board. Only with a rope around your neck."

"They don't feel nothing. Drop, snap, and that's it. They don't feel nothing."

"Are you sure? I was standing right close. I could hear him gasping for breath."

"Uh-huh, but he don't feel nothing. Wouldn't be humane if he did."

"Well. And I suppose they feed them a lot of pills. Sedatives."

"Hell, no. Against the rules. Here comes Smith."

"Gosh, I didn't know he was such a shrimp."

"Yeah, he's little. But so is a tarantula."

As he was brought into the warehouse, Smith recognized his old foe, Dewey; he stopped chewing a hunk of Doublemint gum he had in his mouth, and grinned and winked at Dewey, jaunty and mischievous. But after the warden asked if he had anything to say, his expression was sober. His sensitive eyes gazed gravely at the surrounding faces, swerved up to the shadowy hangman, then downward to his own manacled hands. He looked at his fingers, which were stained with ink and paint, for he'd spent his final three years on Death Row painting self-portraits and pictures of children, usually the children of inmates who supplied him with photographs of their seldom-seen progeny. "I think," he said, "it's a helluva thing to take a life in this manner. I don't believe in capital punishment, morally or legally. Maybe I had something to contribute, something—" His assurance faltered; shyness blurred his voice, lowered it to a just audible level. "It would be meaningless to apologize for what I did. Even inappropriate. But I do. I apologize."

Steps, noose, mask; but before the mask was adjusted, the prisoner spat his chewing gum into the chaplain's outstretched palm. Dewey shut his eyes; he kept them shut until he heard the thud-snap that announced a rope-broken neck. Like the majority of American law-enforcement officials, Dewey is certain that capital punishment is a deterrent to violent crime, and he felt that if ever the penalty had been earned, the present instance was it. The preceding execution had not disturbed him, he had never had much use for Hickock, who seemed to him "a small-time chiseler who got out of his depth, empty and worthless." But Smith, though he was the true murderer, aroused another response, for Perry possessed a quality, the aura of an exiled animal, a creature walking wounded, that the detective could not disregard. He remembered his first meeting with Perry in the interrogation room at Police Headquarters in Las Vegas—the dwarfish boy-man seated in the metal chair, his small booted feet not quite brushing the floor. And when Dewey now opened his eyes, that is what he saw: the same childish feet, tilted, dangling.

This excerpt uses a unique approach to sense imagery. Flush was Elizabeth Barrett Browning's cocker spaniel, and Virginia Woolf allows us to share the sensations of his first arrival in the darkly Victorian Barrett household. Practically every type of imagery is used here, including appeals to muscle responses.

FROM *Flush: A Biography* / VIRGINIA WOOLF

. . . As Flush trotted up behind Miss Mitford, who was behind the butler, he was more astonished by what he smelt than by what he saw.

Up the funnel of the staircase came warm whiffs of joints roasting, or fowls basting, of soups simmering — ravishing almost as food itself to nostrils used to the meagre savour of Kerenhappock's penurious frys and hashes. Mixing with the smell of food were further smells — smells of cedarwood and sandalwood and mahogany; scents of male bodies and female bodies; of men servants and maid servants; of coats and trousers; of crinolines and mantles; of curtains of tapestry, of curtains of plush; of coal dust and fog; of wine and cigars. Each room as he passed it — dining-room, drawing-room, library, bedroom — wafted out its own contribution to the general stew; while, as he set down first one paw and then another, each was caressed and retained by the sensuality of rich pile carpets closing amorously over it. At length they reached a closed door at the back of the house. A gentle tap was given; gently the door was opened.

Miss Barrett's bedroom — for such it was — must by all accounts have been dark. The light, normally obscured by a curtain of green damask, was in summer further dimmed by the ivy, the scarlet runners, the convolvuluses and the nasturtiums which grew in the window-box. At first Flush could distinguish nothing in the pale greenish gloom but five white globes glimmering mysteriously in mid-air. But again it was the smell of the room that overpowered him. Only a scholar who has descended step by step into a mausoleum and there finds himself in a crypt, crusted with fungus, slimy with mould, exuding sour smells of decay and antiquity, while half-obliterated marble busts gleam in mid-air and all is dimly seen by the light of the small swinging lamp which he holds, and dips and turns, glancing now here, now there — only the sensations of such an explorer into the buried vaults of a ruined city can compare with the riot of emotions that flooded Flush's nerves as he stood for the first time in an invalid's bedroom, in Wimpole Street, and smelt eau de cologne.

Very slowly, very dimly, with much sniffing and pawing, Flush by degrees distinguished the outlines of several articles of furniture. That huge object by the window was perhaps a wardrobe. Next to it stood, conceivably, a chest of drawers. In the middle of the room swam up to the surface what seemed to be a table with a ring round it; and then the vague amorphous shapes of armchair and table emerged. But everything was disguised. On top of the wardrobe stood three white busts; the chest of drawers was surmounted by a bookcase; the bookcase was pasted over with crimson merino; the washing-table had a coronal of shelves upon it; on top of the shelves that were on top of the washing-table stood two more busts. Nothing in the room was itself; everything was something else. Even the windowblind was not a simple muslin blind; it was a painted fabric with a design of castles and gateways and groves of trees, and there were several peasants taking a walk. Looking-glasses further distorted these already distorted objects so that there seemed to be ten busts of ten poets instead of five; four tables instead of two. And suddenly there was a more terrifying confusion still. Suddenly Flush saw staring back at him from a hole in the wall another dog with bright eyes flashing, and tongue lolling! He paused amazed. He advanced in awe.

Thus advancing, thus withdrawing, Flush scarcely heard, save as the distant drone of wind among the tree-tops, the murmur and patter of voices talking. He pursued his investigations, cautiously, nervously, as an explorer in a forest softly advances his foot, uncertain whether that shadow is a lion, or that root a cobra. At last, however, he was aware of huge objects in commotion over him; and, unstrung as he was by the experiences of the past hour, he hid himself, trembling, behind a screen. The voices ceased. A door shut. For one instant he paused, bewildered, unstrung. Then with a pounce as of clawed tigers memory fell upon him. He felt himself alone — deserted. He rushed to the door. It was shut. He pawed, he listened. He heard footsteps descending. He knew them for the familiar footsteps of his mistress. They stopped. But no — on they went, down they went. Miss Mitford was slowly, was heavily, was reluctantly descending the stairs. And as she went, as he heard her footsteps fade, panic seized upon him. Door after door shut in his face as Miss Mitford went downstairs; they shut on freedom; on fields; on hares; on grass; on his adored, his venerated mistress — on the dear old woman who had washed him and beaten him and fed him from her own plate when she had none too much to eat herself — on all he had known of happiness and love and human goodness! There! The front door slammed. He was alone. She had deserted him.

Then such a wave of despair and anguish overwhelmed him, the irrevocableness and impalability of fate so smote him, that he lifted up his head and howled aloud. A voice said "Flush." He did not hear it. "Flush," it repeated a second time. He started. He had thought himself alone. He turned. Was there something alive in the room with him? Was there something on the sofa? In the wild hope that this being, whatever it was, might open the door, that he might still rush after Miss Mitford and find her — that this was some game of hide-and-seek such as they used to play in the greenhouse at home — Flush darted to the sofa.

"Oh, Flush!" said Miss Barrett. For the first time she looked him in the face. For the first time Flush looked at the lady lying on the sofa.

Each was surprised. Heavy curls hung down on either side of Miss Barrett's face; large bright eyes shone out; a large mouth smiled. Heavy ears hung down on either side of Flush's face; his eyes, too, were large and bright: his mouth was wide. There was a likeness between them. As they gazed at each other each felt: Here am I — and then each felt: But how different! Hers was the pale worn face of an invalid, cut off from air, light, freedom. His was the warm ruddy face of a young animal; instinct with health and energy. Broken asunder, yet made in the same mould, could it be that each completed what was dormant in the other? She might have been — all that; and he — But no. Between them lay the widest gulf that can separate one being from another. She spoke. He was dumb. She was woman; he was dog. Thus closely united, thus immensely divided, they gazed at each other. Then with one bound Flush sprang on to the sofa and laid himself where he was to lie for ever after — on the rug at Miss Barrett's feet.

Thomas Wolfe prepares us for complexity of imagery by mentioning "mixed odors and sensations." Take your cue from him. Use care in keeping the images, and the associations which lead from one to another, clearly unified.

The Golden World / THOMAS WOLFE

He had heard already the ringing of remote church bells over a countryside on Sunday night; he listened to the earth steeped in the brooding symphony of dark, and the million-noted little night things; and he had heard thus the far retreating wail of a whistle in a distant valley, and faint thunder on the rails; and he felt the infinite depth and width of the golden world in the brief seductions of a thousand multiplex and mixed mysterious odors and sensations, weaving, with a blinding interplay and aural explosions, one into the other.

He remembered yet the East India Tea House at the Fair, the sandalwood, the turbans, and the robes, the cool interior and the smell of India tea; and he felt now the nostalgic thrill of dew-wet mornings in Spring, the cherry scent, the cool clarion earth, the wet loaminess of the garden, the pungent breakfast smells and the floating snow of blossoms. He knew the inchoate sharp excitement of hot dandelions in young Spring grass at noon; the smell of cellars, cobwebs, and built-on secret earth; in July, of watermelons bedded in sweet hay, inside a farmer's covered wagon; of cantaloupe and crated peaches; and the scent of orange rind, bittersweet, before a fire of coals. He knew the good male smell of his father's sitting-room; of the smooth worn leather sofa, with the gaping horse-hair rent; of the blistered varnished wood upon the hearth;

From *Look Homeward, Angel* by Thomas Wolfe. Reprinted by permission of Charles Scribner's Sons.

of the heated calf-skin bindings; of the flat moist plug of apple tobacco, stuck with a red flag; of wood-smoke and burnt leaves in October; of the brown tired autumn earth; of honey-suckle at night; of warm nasturtiums; of a clean ruddy farmer who comes weekly with printed butter, eggs and milk; of fat limp underdone bacon and of coffee; of a bakery-oven in the wind; of large deep-hued stringbeans smoking-hot and seasoned well with salt and butter; of a room of old pine boards in which books and carpets have been stored, long closed; of Concord grapes in their long white baskets.

Kalymnos is one of the numerous islands in the Aegean Sea. Notice how skill-fully Durrell combines imaginative metaphor with almost factual description. Compare this description with the excerpt by the same author at the end of Chapter 5.

Kalymnos / LAWRENCE DURRELL

In Kalymnos the infant's paint-box has been at work again on the milky slopes of the mountain. Carefully, laboriously it has squared in a churchyard, a monastery, and lower down repeated the motif: a church, a monastery, a town; then, simply for the sake of appropriateness, a harbour with a shelf of bright craft at anchor, and the most brilliant, the most devastatingly brilliant houses. Never has one seen anything like it — the harbour revolving slowly round as one comes in. Plane after stiff cubistic plane of pure colour. The mind runs up and down the web of vocabulary looking for a word which will do justice to it. In vain. Under the church the half-finished caieques stand upon a slip — huge coops of raw wood looking for all the world like the skeletons of dis-membered whales.

Three little girls in crimson dresses stand arm in arm and watch us. The harbour liquefies under the keel as we throttle down and move towards the port, our engines now puffy and subdued, yet quickened like our heartbeats and we sit and watch the island. The echo of our passage — the hard *plam-plam-plam* of the exhaust — bounces gravely off the rusted iron hull of a steamer which lies on its side in the shallows, its funnels sticking up like nostrils, but all the rest of it submerged in water as clear as the purest white gin. This is Kalymnos. High up, under the walls of the Church of the Golden Hand a woman is singing, slowly, emphatically, while from the wharves across the way a man in a blue overall is hammering at a coffin. Uncanny isolation of sound and object, each dissimilar, each entire to itself. Detached from the temporal frame. A song and a hammering which exist together but never mix or muddle the hard outlines of each other.

There is remarkable unity of focus here. Notice how the descriptive details and the progress of time work together. The sentence structure is characteristic of Faulkner's style. Close attention to imagery and the relationship of descriptive words to each other will help untangle it.

FROM *Dry September* / WILLIAM FAULKNER

II

She was thirty-eight or thirty-nine. She lived in a small frame house with her invalid mother and a thin, sallow, unflagging aunt, where each morning between ten and eleven she would appear on the porch in a lace-trimmed boudoir cap, to sit swinging in the porch swing until noon. After dinner she lay down for a while, until the afternoon began to cool. Then, in one of the three or four new voile dresses which she had each summer, she would go downtown to spend the afternoon in the stores with the other ladies, where they would handle the goods and haggle over the prices in cold, immediate voices, without any intention of buying.

She was of comfortable people — not the best in Jefferson, but good people enough — and she was still on the slender side of ordinary looking, with a bright, faintly haggard manner and dress. When she was young she had had a slender, nervous body and a sort of hard vivacity which enabled her for a time to ride upon the crest of the town's social life as exemplified by the high school party and church social period of her contemporaries while still children enough to be unclassconscious.

She was the last to realize that she was losing ground; that those among whom she had been a little brighter and louder flame than any other were beginning to learn the pleasure of snobbery — male — and retaliation — female. That was when her face began to wear that bright, haggard look. She still carried it to parties on shadowy porticoes and summer lawns, like a mask or a flag, with that bafflement of furious repudiation of truth in her eyes. One evening at a party she heard a boy and two girls, all schoolmates, talking. She never accepted another invitation.

She watched the girls with whom she had grown up as they married and got homes and children, but no man ever called on her steadily until the children of the other girls had been calling her "aunty" for several years, the while their mothers told them in bright voices about how popular Aunt Minnie had been as a girl. Then the town began to see her driving on Sunday afternoons with the cashier in the bank. He was a widower of about forty — a high-colored man, smelling always faintly of the barber shop or of whisky. He owned the first automobile in town, a red runabout; Minnie had the first motoring bonnet and veil the town ever saw. Then the town began to say: "Poor Minnie." "But she is old enough to take care of herself," others said. That was when she began to ask her old schoolmates that their children call her "cousin" instead of "aunty."

It was twelve years now since she had been relegated into adultery by public opinion, and eight years since the cashier had gone to a Memphis bank, returning for one day each Christmas, which he spent at an annual bachelors' party at a hunting club on the river. From behind their curtains the neighbors would see the party pass, and during the over-the-way Christmas day visiting they would tell her about him, about how well he looked, and how they heard that he was prospering in the city, watching with bright, secret eyes her haggard, bright face. Usually by that hour there would be the scent of whisky on her breath. It was supplied her by a youth, a clerk at the soda fountain: "Sure; I buy it for the old gal. I reckon she's entitled to a little fun."

Her mother kept to her room altogether now; the gaunt aunt ran the house. Against that background Minnie's bright dresses, her idle and empty days, had a quality of furious unreality. She went out in the evenings only with women now, neighbors, to the moving pictures. Each afternoon she dressed in one of the new dresses and went downtown alone, where her young "cousins" were already strolling in the late afternoons with their delicate, silken heads and thin, awkward arms and conscious hips, clinging to one another or shrieking and giggling with paired boys in the soda fountain when she passed and went on along the serried store fronts, in the doors of which the sitting and lounging men did not even follow her with their eyes any more.

This description of a centuries-old Hopi ceremonial dance calls on every type of imagery. The Snake Dance is one of many religious dances honoring animals — the antelope, the deer, the eagle, and the buffalo, among others. It is not a typical tourist dance but is held in deep reverence by the Hopis. The snakes are not drugged nor are their sacs emptied of venom. The snake whips are of feathers and are used to coax the snake into uncoiling since it is believed that a snake strikes only when it is coiled. The speaker in this selection knows his Indians well, and it is important that the interpreter reflect his awe and fascination and not the white man's traditional revulsion toward snakes.

FROM *Masked Gods* / FRANK WATERS

The Snake Dance

It always seems sudden and unlooked for when at last they come. And it is always new, though it is essentially a duplicate of the Antelope Dance of the day before.

First come the Antelopes. Twelve men, a pair like prayer sticks for each of the six directions. But today more somber grey with black hands and feet, black chins, and a white line across their upper lips, their bodies dirty ash grey.

Then the Snakes. Today their faces are blackened with charcoal, with smears of red-brown on the cheeks, their black and red-brown bodies covered only with black kirtles.

Grotesque and horrible they file somberly around the plaza, their loose black hair flowing in the breeze. Short, heavy, powerfully built, as if compressed to the ground.

Ash grey and reddish black, they each in turn encircle the bower and cast their pinches of meal. Bend forward, shaking their rattles. Then stoop and stamp powerfully upon the plank resonator or foot drum, the *sipapu*. All call softly with a deep, somber, wordless chant.

This is the one supreme moment of mystery. Here, now, at the mouth of the cavern world where the power gushes up on call. Everything later is an anticlimax, even the snakes.

So it begins. The dull resonant stamp like distant thunder, like a faint rumble underground, sounds in the silent sunlit square. It is echoed by that deep, somber, thunderous chant. The sound is one we never hear, so deep and powerful it is. And it reveals how deep these men are in the mystery of its making. Calling to the deep cavern world below. Summoning the serpent power. Calling up the creative life force to the underground streams, to the roots of the corn, to the feet, the loins, the mind of man.

And the power does gush up. It shakes the two opposite lines of

Snakes and Antelopes into motion, into dance. And now it begins —
what the crowd has been waiting for.

A Snake stoops down into the *kisi*[1] and emerges with a snake in his
mouth. He holds it gently but firmly between his teeth, just below the
head. It is a rattlesanke. The flat birdlike head with its unmoving eyes
flattened against his cheek, its spangled body dangling like a long thick
cord. Immediately another Snake steps up beside him, a little behind,
stroking the rattlesnake with his snake whip with intense concentration.
Up and down they commence dancing, while another Snake emerges with
a giant bull snake between his teeth. At the end of the circle the Snake
dancer gently drops his snake upon the ground and goes after another.
The snake raises its sensitive head, darts out its small tongue like
antennae, then wriggles like lightning towards the massed spectators.
Now the yells and screams and scramble! But a third man, the snake
watcher, is waiting. He rushes up. Deftly he grabs the escaping snake,
waves the long undulating body over his head, and carries it to the Antelopes. They smooth it with their feathers and lay it down on a circle of
cornmeal.

Soon it is all confusion. The whole plaza is filled with Snake dancers
dancing with snakes in their mouths. Rattlesnakes, huge bull snakes
almost too heavy to carry, little whip, racer, and garter snakes curling
in a frenzy about one's ears. A loosely held rattler strikes a man on the
jowl and dangles there a moment before it is gently disengaged. The
dance goes on. Snakes wriggling on the ground, darting toward the
spectators. Brought back by the snake watchers, an armful at a time.
Until all of the snakes have been danced with and deposited in a great
wriggling mound by the ash-grey Antelopes.

Suddenly it is over. Two Hopi girls dressed in ceremonial mantles
sprinkle the writhing mass with baskets of meal. Then Snake priests
grab up the snakes in armfuls, like loose disjointed sticks of kindling, and
run out of the plaza. Down the trails into the stark Arizona desert to
four shrines where the snakes are freed. Released at last, after giving
up their dark potency, to carry the meal prayers sprinkled upon them,
the feather breaths of life, the ceremonial commands laid upon them,
back to the deep spinal core of the dark source.

The setting sun spreads its effulgence over the mesa, the farther mesas,
and distant buttes. The whole arid rock wilderness floods with twilight.
The clouds hang heavy, dark and somber. A few drops of rain sprinkle
the crowds. They hurry away swiftly. The motorcars start buzzing, filing
in a funeral cortege down the slope. Quickly, to "cross the wash," to
escape the coming flood.

---

[1] The enclosure in which the snakes are kept. It is usually made of willow
branches and shaped into a tepee.

The ash-grey Antelopes and the brown-black Snakes file ceremoniously back to their kivas. Each drinks a large bowl of emetic medicine concocted out of the root medicine and handsful of beetles and stinking tumblebugs. They go out to the edge of the cliff and vomit. If they didn't their bellies would swell up with the power like clouds and burst. Then they may eat and wash. But the dark power called up for nine nights and days is still within them. So tomorrow morning they must wash again: heads, bodies, necklaces, planting sticks. And again they must rub with the dry root medicine, must chew it and spit it in their hands and rub themselves. While the Snake Chief touches each with his snake whip, the last strike of the serpent, comes the vivid flame stroke of lightning which at last releases the sweet smelling rain, the torrential swishing floods.

Sometimes sights and sounds are deceptive. In this piece of literary journalism, the kinesthetic tension underlying the scarcity of kinetic imagery combines with the muted sounds of the terse comments to produce an effect of "silent violence" indeed. Release from the intensity is provided by the author's own comments, and the rhythm of content is interesting. Unity must be preserved by a clear focus on sense of place and on the unanimity of attitude among the various speakers.

FROM *La Raza:*[1] *The Mexican Americans* / STAN STEINER

The village of Antonchico is still. Not a goat goes out in the midday sun, it is too hot. Not a man walks on the street. The buzz of the flies and the whine of the supersonic jets are the only sounds in the white sky. Six men squat in the dust of the village. They talk, in whispers, of violent deeds that they intend to do to defend their ancestral lands and their manhood. They talk of murder. They talk, but not a man shifts an inch from his squat in the shadow of the adobe house.

"We are men of silent violence," says a farmer.

On a lazy old mare a young boy rides down the main street, the only street, of the village. The boy on the horse rides by in slow motion, as though he is asleep. The houses hide from the blazing sun. Even the gossiping women are sequestered behind the thick walls of adobe, for

From pp. 17–20, 21, 23–24, 25 in *La Raza: The Mexican Americans* by Stan Steiner. Copyright © 1969, 1970 by Stan Steiner. Reprinted by permission of Harper & Row, Publishers, Inc.

[1] When the conquistadors went out to find the "new Spain," the Pope is reported to have given them his blessing and said, "Go forth and create *la santa raza* — the holy race."

it is the time of siesta, and it is uncivilized to work, or walk, or talk loudly at the noon hour.

A priest squats in the dust beside the villagers. He is wearing an open shirt and dirty Western chinos. He balances himself expertly, so that the seat of his trousers is poised safely above the prickly sage-brush.

"It is so peaceful," I say to the priest.

"So is a volcano," he replies.

He is a hothead, this priest, so they say. I scoff at his intense words, but he merely smiles and says, "Do not be fooled by the silence."

The old farmer who squats beside us listens to our talk, but pretends not to hear. His eyes are alert as a small bird's and his face is innocent.

"He is peaceful," I say to the priest.

"In the village they say he has killed two men," the priest says matter-of-factly.

The old man gazes into my eyes with a kindly and distant look. He says nothing.

"Who did he kill?" I ask skeptically.

The priest whispers, "It is what they say. Some men tried to kill him. He killed two of them. Who knows?"

A young farmer who has heard this looks up. He breaks a twig in his hand and he jabs the broken ends into the earth, hard. "That is the way it is here," he says, then is silent once more.

"In the night I hear a rifle shot," the young farmer says, after a pause. He is answering a question no one has asked him. "And then there is this telephone call. A man says, 'If you don't watch your step we will kill your son.' He hangs up and they cut the telephone wire. My wife, she is frightened." His face is troubled by the memory. "That is how it is here."

"They cut my fences. And they steal two of my cows," says another farmer. He smiles with tight lips. "If they come again, I kill them."

A boy who has been silent among his elders — he is a student work-ing in the village during the summer — says very seriously, "If it were up to me I would go to them with a gun and kill them. Probably I would do that."

Who are *they*? None of the villagers will say.

"I do not say who," says a third farmer. He is taller than the others, maybe stronger, with a pebbly face and hands made of bones. "But I tell you this," and his words are hard. "The Spanish people are angry now. Now all the Spanish people have a good rifle. I visit many villages and I tell you this. Everyone has a rifle now."

The old man among them speaks. He speaks in quiet Spanish that cannot be translated. What he says is something like this: They have taken our land and stolen it. They have taken our crops and stolen them. They have taken our manhood, and broken it. They have taken our Spanish language, and dirtied it. They have taken our children into their schools, and made them rude.

"We have been under the feets of so many of the stranger," the old man suddenly says in English.

"The stranger?" I ask.

"Yes," he says, "the stranger who came from the East. Who took our land. Who pushes us around. They have done dirty things to the people of these villages. They did it to my ancestors. They keep on doing it to me. And they think that they are going to do it to my sons and grandsons, but they have another think coming. I tell you they will fight."

"Now, we will all fight," the old man says.

Each man is lost in his own shadow. In the other villages do the men feel this way? No one will say. How can they tell me what they think in another village? Every village is different. "Is any man like any other man?"

"Who can speak for me?" a farmer says. "No one but me. That's who I speak for."

In the city the officials tell me that these village men are not "typical" of the men of Antonchico and that the men of Antonchico are not "typical" of the men of the village. Some of the villagers are defeated, apathetic, and torn by self-anger and humiliation. Some of the villagers are easygoing, immune to the outside world, and tend to laugh off history. These things are more "typical" of the villagers' feelings, they say.

"Typical!" spits a farmer, when I tell him of this analysis. "You know who is typical? In the city *everybody* is typical, because you can't live in the city unless you are typical of everybody else."

"But not everybody is as angry as here."

"I am not angry." He laughs. "When I am angry I will not talk about it. Then it will be too late to talk. Angry? We are just thinking, how do you say, out loud? Yes, a man who talks about what he will do will not do it."

The farmer's words become a whisper. "We are not the black man. If we do something, we will not tell *you* about it first."

"What will you do?"

"Ah. Who knows?"

The haze of the sun diffuses the houses of the village. It looks unreal and faded. Quaint as a picturesque postcard the houses of Antonchico rise out of the adobe mud. But the adobe is cracking. Some of the houses are collapsing into the earth from which they emerged generations ago.

Hours of the afternoon fall upon the six men who squat and talk.

It grows later, it is three o'clock. Who knows the time? In the sky above the village the mirage of time shimmers and is gone. The wrath of the squatting men evaporates in the sun, but they hardly notice it vanish, for they are watching the village come to life again, as it always does after the noon.

El Viejo, the oldest man, is whittling the statue of a saint. Or is it the head of J.F.K.? He uses a daggerlike knife, almost as his grandfather did. The children run barefoot, for their sneakers are under a bush. On the adobe walls the strings of red chili ripen in the sun. The chili is hung from a television wire. In the yards of the houses the goats are separated by fences of twigs and branches tied by nylon cord. The road has been paved. But it is full of holes. Now the village has three stores and a not-quite-new school and some of the adobes have tin roofs and the inevitable television antennas. Since the old days things have changed. But not much.

· · · · ·

Ah, the sleepy villages of the Southwest. The life of the unhurried villagers is romantic to the dreamer. Most of all to the stranger.

· · · · ·

"Let them dream their dreams," says a farmer when we talk of this. "When you sleep on a dirt floor you dream a different dream. It is not so much romantic."

· · · · ·

"We live in a conspiracy of silence," says Fecundo Valdez. He is a rural organizer in the mountain villages of New Mexico. One of that new breed of university graduates, wearing a Pancho Villa mustache and a dashing sombrero on whose brim he has pinned a "Grapes of Wrath" button, Valdez travels the dirt roads to the hidden villages, for the agencies of the government and the universities. He comes from such a village himself.

"The people have a distaste, an anger, a hostility, to the things that have been done to them. But they say little," he says. "In the past these villages were not allowed to participate in real decision making. So they withdrew into their own circles, into silence. If you don't have the means to actively resist what is done to you, then what happens is that you become passively aggressive. It is a basic resistance. It may be dormant, it may be apathetic, but it may be harnessed.

"Silence is a way of resisting, you know," Valdez says. "It has been the way of the villages — until now."

The visitor who drives off U.S. Highway 84 into the village hears only the silence. He will think he has entered a valley of pastoral peace. He will not see the circle of men who squat in the dust of the adobes.

· · · · ·

"We are not people that believe in violence," the old man says. "I suppose that's why we have been pushed around so much. The Anglos might think we are coward. But the Spanish-speaking people have shown how coward they have been on the battlefields, in the First World War, the Second World War, Korea, and now Vietnam. We are not coward. But we are not people of violence. I hope that will never happen. For myself, I don't believe in that.

"I don't know, but the people in the future might have to get violent."

The young farmer inscribes a circle in the dust with his twigs; his circle grows smaller and smaller until he jabs the sticks into its heart, like two spears. No one says another word. Even the young and volatile priest is still.

Bibliography

Since description is an integral part of narration, the interpreter will find his best sources for further reading on descriptive prose in the books listed at the end of Chapter 7.

Chapter 7

Narration provides the interpreter with material which has a high degree of audience appeal. Myths, folk tales, and legends of every civilization testify to the fact that the enjoyment of a story is as old as human speech. The interpreter has no problem in finding narratives suitable for presentation. His only difficulty is in selecting one or two from the vast store of available material. In this he will be guided by his own interests and those of the audience he has in mind, and by his standards of literary excellence.

/ The primary purpose of narration, whether in prose or poetry, is to relate an incident or a series of incidents./ As always, the interpreter must thoroughly acquaint himself with the logical content, emotional quality, method of organization, and various aspects of literary craftsmanship peculiar to the form in which it is written. /When the narrative is in prose, he must evaluate it for style in the same manner he analyzes any other type of prose. He must consider the special problems of plot, setting, motivation, and characterization inherent in narration. The relative importance of these four factors — what happened, when and where, why and how, and to whom — will vary from selection to selection, but they are always present and require careful attention in preparation and special emphasis in presentation./

In its broadest sense, narration includes description of a single action, fables, allegories, parables, legends, fairy tales, anecdotes, diaries, history, biography and autobiography, travel and adventure, short stories, and novels. These various types of narration differ in length and complexity

Narration

and in degree of concentration on one or more of the factors of plot, setting, motivation, or character./The discussion in this chapter will be confined largely to the short story, a form that embodies many of the special problems to be found in the novel and yet is brief enough to be handled conveniently. It is more complex in structure and implication than the less sophisticated forms like the fable, the allegory, and the legend, and it does not require special attention to actual personalities as do histories, biographies, and autobiographies. Many of the selections at the ends of earlier chapters are basically narrative in structure, and occasional references will be made to some of them as well as to the material at the end of this chapter.

Action and Plot

Throughout this discussion we shall use the terms action and plot. *Action* is the sequence of visible or discernible physical happenings. *Plot* is the sequence of changes in human relations running parallel to the sequence of physical happenings that make up the action. Another term which must be mentioned in a consideration of fiction (or drama; see Chapter 8) is *crisis*, the turning point of the plot, like the fulcrum in a poem. It is that moment of development after which there can be only one credible outcome.

Some degree of conflict is essential to plot. This conflict may take place between man and an exterior force, such as another person, environment, society, nature, or even, in modern works, machinery. It may subsist between the main character and interior forces such as his will, his ideas, or his frustrations. Frequently external and internal conflict are combined, the one giving rise to the other. In any case, the writer selects and organizes his materials in a way that gives his plot speed, suspense, continuity, concreteness, and credibility. We do not ask for absolute realism or for factual logic in a plot. We ask only that it be acceptable and logical as it relates to the particular characters in the particular situation. The logic of events must always be tested in terms of each character's development and of the motivations which result from the kind of person he is and the kind of person he becomes.

We are already familiar with climaxes from our attention to them in Chapter 2. The major climax in fiction is the point of culmination in the complete selection, though there may be several minor climaxes preceding and following the main climax. These climaxes may be high points of action, character development, or emotional impact. Frequently the three types come together and are so closely interrelated that there is no need to consider them separately. Sometimes they follow each other very quickly, as in "A Banal Miracle" (pages 249–254). Often the climax of action sets up and motivates the highest point of emotional impact, as in the excerpt from *Deliverance* (pages 262–264). Or the arrangement may be reversed, with the highest point of emotional impact leading to the culmination of the action.

The writer may build his climax in numerous ways. In an extremely short narrative, he may open near the culmination of the action, set his background swiftly, and move immediately to the single climax. This gives the interpreter no particular problem except sustaining the steady build. A more common method of building climax is to use a series of incidents leading like stairs to the main incident. In this case, each minor incident will have its own beginning, its high point, and its conclusion. The interpreter must use these minor climaxes as focal points. They provide him with an interesting emotional rhythm and require him to give attention to the shifts in interest from one aspect of the story to another. Sometimes, for example, an author will follow one character for an entire incident, take another through the same process, and bring the two together for the final conflict and its resolution.

It would be impossible to mention here every type of problem which arises in the thousands of examples of narrative writing. The interpreter must examine each selection for its individual problems and make himself aware of the minor climaxes within each of the incidents in the plot, and of their relationship to the main climax of action and emotional tension. He will do well to take careful note of the kinetic and kinesthetic images present in the climactic moments. The former will help him communicate the feeling of speed and activity, the latter to create suspense and tension. Often a change in style of writing will help set off the climax. There may be a general tightening of thought units, shortening of sentences, and increase of words with high imagery content.

Point of View

The major controlling factor in any narrative is *point of view*. Point of view is a relatively modern critical term which refers to the physical and psychological position and degree of involvement the narrator takes in the events he is relating. Henry James calls it the "central intelligence." It can be simple and candid or complex, depending on the author's handling of it throughout the story, and it may vary within a basic unity from section to section. It embraces both the narrator's physical vantage point and his personal way of perceiving the events. These matters will affect his choice of details and the arrangement and amount of information he shares with us.

There are two important aspects of point of view: the person (first, second, or third) in which the narrator speaks, and the attitude and perception he adopts. In *first-person narration*, the person telling the story speaks in his own person as "I." This "I" may or may not be physically identified. He may be the author himself, an appropriate speaker, or a character involved in the action and plot. He may merely observe and report, or he may participate and evaluate. If he is physically identified, the interpreter must establish enough characterization to make him believable as one who could relate such a happening.

Frequently, the first-person narrator is one of the main characters in the plot. Such a use of "I," or sometimes "we," is an important aid to the interpreter not only because it unifies the story but also because it allows him to establish an appropriate character for the narrator and thus insure a high degree of vividness. There are almost limitless possibilities for variety within this area. A narrator who is a character in the plot may be an ordinary person, and our concern may be almost entirely with the sequence of events. On the other hand, he may be a character whose very complexities give credence to the events. In any case, whenever a story is told in the first person, it will be necessary for the interpreter to consider the physical and psychological background of the narrator. Whenever the narrator is a person involved in the action, certain specific qualities of characterization will need to be communicated to the audience by vocal and physical suggestion.

Second-person or "you" *narration* is rather rare, but it is effectively used in much travel literature. *Third-person narration* — "he," "she," or "they" — is probably the most frequently used of the three forms. Third-person narration, like first-person narration, may range from objective observation to a high degree of involvement. In any case, the author's control over what the narrator sees, hears, knows, and reports must not be overlooked or underestimated.

Thus the first question to be answered in considering point of view is "Who is telling the story?" The second is "Where and when is he telling it and where and when did it happen?" Most stories are told in the past tense, but the amount of time which has elapsed between the event and the telling is often important. Both Gibbs and Bowen, for example, have achieved considerable perspective as they look back on the performances they recount at the end of Chapter 4, as has Lowell in his memories of Revere Street in the same chapter. Likewise, events seen from afar differ from those in which we are actually involved. The degree of immediacy affects emotional response and attitude strongly. When distance in time and space increases, different relationships begin to emerge which were not so apparent at the moment or place of the incident itself.

The third question is "To whom is the story being told?" Frequently, it is being told to us, the readers, or in the interpreter's case, through him to his listeners. The expected audience will have a marked effect on all the elements of style and certainly on the amount and kind of detail the author includes.

The next two questions, "In what relation to the action does the narrator stand?" and "What kind of knowledge does he claim?" overlap the first three. More important, they lead us into the more sophisticated area of authority and reliability and the "central intelligence" to which Henry James refers, and into the second aspect of point of view, which is the attitude and perception the narrator adopts.

We mentioned earlier that the narrator is sometimes conceived of as an *objective observer*, but more often he identifies with one or more of the characters. There are, broadly speaking, four categories or degrees of this identification, and an author may use any or all of them within a story or a novel. When he is operating as an observer only, he stays outside the characters' minds to a large degree and gives us primarily action. This is what Truman Capote does through most of *In Cold Blood*, but it is interesting to note that in the excerpt used at the end of Chapter 6, where he is reporting on the hanging, he allows us to see it through the eyes of Mr. Dewey, whom he is observing. Mr. Dewey's reactions, implied rather than stated, are the ones we share. As an observer objectively reporting, Capote could not know what Dewey actually saw when he opened his eyes.

One of the most popular techniques in contemporary fiction is the *single-character point of view*, in which the narrator takes us only where a single character goes and lets us know only what he thinks and feels.

It is particularly effective in short stories because it allows for vividness and condensation. This is the technique Flannery O'Connor uses in "Everything That Rises Must Converge"; much of the impact lies in our seeing the mother and the action only through the eyes of her son Julian. Agee uses it in the excerpt from *A Death in the Family*, where we move into the little boy's mind; the man he encounters remains just someone he encounters — as do the boys who do not even cross the street. In the opening of Kafka's *The Metamorphosis* (page 87), the narrator becomes so closely identified with Gregor we almost forget that the technique is third person.

Sometimes a narrator uses *dual-character point of view*, and we are allowed to enter the minds and inner lives of two of the characters. One may dominate the other, they may be interwoven, or the narrator's focus may shift from one to the other. This, of course, enables an author to intensify conflict and is very effective when the story depends on the inability or unwillingness of the characters to communicate freely. It can become an important factor in rhythm of content as well.

Multiple-character point of view, in which several points of view are framed within the author's or narrator's own, is much more common in novels than in short stories because each character whose thoughts, feelings, and perspective we share must be developed. It is also more prevalent in nineteenth-century writing than in that of the twentieth century, when our psychological interest has become more highly developed.

There are infinite variations within each of these four categories and in the ways they can be combined. In "A Banal Miracle" we know very little about the minds of Angelo Vanelli and his children except that they were frightened of him. On the other hand, we are told, by reported rumor mostly, precisely what the townspeople thought, and we are allowed to enter briefly into Father Martin's mind as he pays his visit to the house. We know absolutely nothing about Mrs. Vanelli's thoughts or feelings, which adds considerably to our willingness to accept both the "miracle" and its banality.

Thus it is extremely important to consider the point of view adopted by the author to reveal background as well as to develop the events of the plot. Point of view helps dictate organization, selection of details, type of imagery, and style of writing. The resulting changes of pace help the interpreter achieve variety and sharpen contrasts; and the interesting interplay of rhythms is invaluable in holding attention and building to the climaxes. Point of view is the interpreter's clue to the relationship he will take to his audience, varying from objective, direct reporting to the sharing of an emotional experience through a character involved in the sequence of events. It is a basic consideration in Chamber Theatre (see pages 229–231).

Summary, Description, and Scene

The point of view the author adopts for his narrator is a controlling force in his handling of the three aspects of summary, description, and scene. A *summary* is a unit condensing and tying together significant moments of action. It may be used at the beginning of a story to sketch in important events leading up to the story (as in "A Banal Miracle"), at the end as an aftermath of the crisis, or one may be inserted from time to time within the narration to speed the action or form a transition from one unit to the next. It is without dialogue and may be done either by a character or by the narrator.

Description, on the other hand, extends or suspends the action. If it is used as a transition in time or place to establish setting, the action is momentarily suspended. But description has a unique and important function in fiction when it is used to describe action and thus extend it. It differs from a summary because it gives us a detailed look at some things along the way. It has the same opportunities for sensory appeal that we discussed in Chapter 6. Obviously, point of view is basic in any consideration of description within a story, because the narrator's personal perspective and sense of values dictate what we see and how we see it. Thus, description may be relatively objective, or it may share the subjective associations and responses of one or more of the characters or of a narrator. It is brilliantly combined with both plot and action in the excerpt from *Deliverance* at the end of this chapter.

Scene in fiction refers to a unit of the story which is primarily dialogue and is indeed comparable to a scene in drama. Father Martin's visit with Mrs. Vanelli is done "in scene" as is Julian's mother's encounter with the child and his mother on the bus. Units treated as scene give opportunities for heightened character suggestion. Style will probably vary from one character to another in the dialogue, and the indications of movement within the scene will provide important clues to kinetic and kinesthetic imagery. Care must be taken, however, not to let the units in scene overbalance the equally important sections of summary and description, a common failing with the beginning interpreter. Each element must be used fully and allowed to make its contribution to the aesthetic entirety.

An author's use of summary, description, and scene will establish rhythm of content throughout the story and provide important variety and contrast.

Setting

Keeping in mind the importance of point of view and of summary, description, and scene, let us look for a moment at some aspects of

setting in fiction. It is difficult to establish the setting subtly and unobtrusively. This difficulty must, of course, be solved first by the writer.
The interpreter in turn must be aware of its importance in the total
effect of the story.

The setting must bear a clear and acceptable relation to the action as
well as to the characters who are involved. Sometimes, especially in
travel and adventure stories, it is necessary to establish the geographical location and the physical aspects of the landscape and climate. In
biographies and histories as well as in historical fiction, the period in
which the action takes place is of vital importance. In modern stories
it is usually enough to establish the general geographical area, since
most contemporary writers are more concerned with the psychological
implications of the setting than with its physical details.

In any case, the scene must be created swiftly and concretely. Since
the author does not wish to delay the all-important action for detailed
description, he depends heavily on suggestion. He concentrates on aspects
of setting which will implement the action and character development.
They may be largely external, such as season, climate, urban or rural
locale, or a particular type of neighborhood or building. On the other
hand, they may be primarily psychological and depend on the characters' attitudes toward social customs, conventions, or atmosphere of
a locale not specifically identified. Almost always, however, the action is
motivated to a greater or lesser degree by the reaction of the character
to his environment, and the author will select details giving the surroundings their proper associational value for the characters he has in mind.

Consequently, the interpreter is likely to encounter a degree of condensation which makes it imperative to give careful attention to each
attribute mentioned. The author of a short story must create his
appeals to perception swiftly and accurately. He will most likely make
liberal use of sense imagery as a means of achieving this concreteness
and vividness. He may, of course, allow the setting to evolve gradually
as the story unfolds. In any event, the imagery serves to advance the story
and must be so used by the interpreter. The interpreter must perform
the same function for his audience as the narrator does for the reader.
He must make sure of the underlying motor responses and hence the
degree of tension or relaxation, activity or passivity, produced by all the
sensory appeals as they work together.

The details and the appeals to perception may be governed by the
unity of time or place, or both. Progression of time is a commonly used
method of unifying setting. A writer of narrative may have his clock
and his calendar move at any rate he chooses, backward as well as
forward. The progression may cover seconds, years, or generations. Unification by the passage of time is particularly useful because it can
combine subtly with the action and help keep the plot moving steadily.

Change of locale must be handled carefully in a piece of fiction as brief as most short stories. Bontemps does it effectively in "A Summer Tragedy" by combining change of place with time progression. Julian's attitude provides the unifying factor through change of place in "Everything That Rises Must Converge."

Character

As important as setting is, the delineation of character is even more important. Unless the interpreter and his audience know what kind of person is involved in the action of the story, setting becomes largely window dressing. The characters give the plot life and meaning.

The problem of providing information about character is much the same as that involved in creating the setting. It is, however, even more important to make the characters three-dimensional and credible because, though many stories could happen in almost any setting, very few situations would call up *exactly* the same response from different individuals. Thus it is important to establish clearly and concisely what traits of personality, habits of thought, and responses will motivate each character's reaction to the forces with which he will come in contact.

As we saw in our discussion of point of view, a narrator may tell us in the third person what he wants us to know about a character, describing his appearance, behavior, or speech, or recording his thoughts. Or the character may be described by another character, or even by himself. We may be given a unit in scene *showing* us the character in action; from that action we make our deductions about his personality, background, and attitudes.

Sometimes characters are deliberately underdeveloped and one-dimensional. This is almost always the case in fables and legends where certain broad, general characteristics are enough to establish the kind of person involved. Such "flat" characters can be very useful in statire, as in the excerpt from *Tom Jones* at the end of Chapter 5 and in Thurber's sketches; much of the humor grows out of stock, uncomplicated characters caught in exaggerated situations.

A character has two aspects: his inner responses — feelings, interests, and thoughts — and the exterior manifestations of these responses — his activities. He is complete only when the interior forces and the exterior manifestations are logically related. Sometimes the physical characteristics are the more important and sometimes the psychological characteristics are primary. Frequently they are interdependent, and the essential conflict of the plot depends on which is the driving force and determining factor for the other.

Although it is useful to examine setting and character as separate items, they cannot really be divorced. As soon as the interpreter puts the story back together, he is aware that the author, if he is skillful, has woven setting and character together in almost every instance. The interpreter's problem, then, becomes keeping the two in balance and putting the proper emphasis on whichever element the author has stressed.

Dialogue

Dialogue is almost always an integral part of a narrative. It is extremely useful in revealing what the writer wishes his readers to know. It provides variety by introducing different personalities and speech rhythms. It makes for vividness and aids in delineating character. Because it is fast-moving and condensed, it helps to speed the key situations along by eliminating the necessity for comment by the author. Certainly, then, dialogue is a convenient technique for the writer, but it occasionally proves troublesome for the interpreter.

Dialogue may be in the form of direct or indirect discourse. Direct discourse is easily recognized because it is set off by quotation marks. The interpreter cannot depend on this typographical device in communicating to his audience, however. Nor can he derive much help from dialogue tags, like "he said," for they do not always precede the speeches like warning bells. He must, then, use some other means of making it clear that a character is speaking. This he does by suggesting the personality of the character through skillful use of his body and voice and appropriate mental attitude.

Dialogue depends to a large extent on an interchange of comments or questions and answers. Whenever one character is addressing another, the audience must be aware that the speech is being directed to someone. This requires a focus of attention on the part of the interpreter which must be both physical and mental. He may wish to re-create in his own mind the person being addressed and place that person somewhere in the audience for greater directness. This device may help the interpreter feel and convey the illusion of direct address, but it may also embarrass the member of the audience who happens to occupy in the flesh the space where the interpreter has placed the character. Hence, it is better to establish the position of the character addressed somewhere on the back wall, between the heads of listeners and about shoulder level. This will help the interpreter to be sure that he is not appearing to single out any member of his audience, that his mental projection and his voice are strong enough to carry to the last row, and that he can differentiate between his role as narrator, when he includes the entire audience in his circle of concentration, and his role in presenting the speech of one character addressed to another. It might be helpful in this connection to review the material on projection in Chapter 4. When several characters are speaking in rapid succession, the interpreter may need to select a separate area of focus for each. This problem of focus of character will be developed in more detail in the section on drama, where it becomes a most essential technique.

Obviously, the degree of forcefulness intended will make a difference in the intensity of the physical and mental directness. If the speech is to carry great conviction or a suggestion of command, the eye contact will be sharply focused. If, however, the remark is more casual or of a general or reflective nature, it will be enough to locate an area for the character addressed, since in real-life situations one does not usually fix one's companions with a piercing and unwavering eye in ordinary conversation. It is important, however, to keep the mental focus sharp in order to convey spontaneity and proper motivation for reply.

If the speech is intended to be shouted at someone, the interpreter must also take the matter of distance into consideration. It is probably neither necessary nor desirable to shout as loudly as one might in a comparable real-life situation, but some suggestion of distance must be given in the combined mental and vocal projection.

In addition to direct address, the writer of narrative commonly uses indirect discourse, either in the ordinary grammatical sense of the term, in such instances as "He said that . . ." and others like it, or in somewhat more complex instances, such as "He thought that . . . ," "She hoped that . . . ," "She remembered having heard him say that . . . ," and innumerable others.

When a character speaks directly, he is usually projecting to one or more persons who are present. His speech is prompted by an immediate situation or remark. In indirect discourse, the degree of direct projection is less strong or may be absent altogether, as in the case of thoughts, fears, and hopes the character expresses to no one but himself. It must, however, be colored by the character's personality, his mental state, and the implied degree of reflection. A remembered remark, for example, would probably carry a hint of the attitude it carried originally, combined with the narrator's attitude at the time of repeating it.

Frequently, indirect discourse will be sharpened by an implication of activity to follow. In such a statement as "Finally he decided that he'd go and see for himself," there is clear appeal to muscle response. This particular example also indicates a positive decision, a turning point from passivity to activity, from reflection to immediacy.

Thus, style is also an important consideration in getting at the interior qualities of a character. His choice of words and the way they are put together help reveal his background, attitude, and degree of mental and emotional tension under the circumstances of the moment.

Any specific directions for projecting character and dialogue to the audience can plunge both giver and receiver into extremely deep and dangerous waters. This section should not, therefore, be interpreted as a collection of mechanical rules or tricks for dividing characters into categories and then drawing on the set of techniques which most neatly fits that category. All character suggestion must stem from what has been put down on the page. A writer of narrative will usually state his intentions more or less clearly, through what might be termed "stage directions." But to realize these intentions, the interpreter will need to understand the whole story; focusing on the whole, he will see dialogue in its proper perspective as a means of advancing the movement of plot and the revelation of character, not as an excuse for a display of virtuosity on the platform.

Probably the first things to consider about a character who is speaking are his sex and maturity. The next step is to discover personal characteristics which establish him as an individual — his attitudes, his degree of emotional intensity at the moment, and any significant vocal and physical traits. Usually the writer will supply specific clues, either explicitly by describing how the speech was said or what state of mind prompted it, or implicitly through the character's mode of speech.

Often the oral presentation will profit by omission of some phrases and sentences which the author included as a guide to characterization. The interpreter may be able to suggest a state of mind by his voice and body and thus make the explanation unnecessary. Extreme care must be used, however, not to eliminate important information about background, thus obscuring the relationships among characters and the motivation of the plot, or to do violence to the literary style.

It is usually wise to retain the dialogue tags until the character's individuality has been established. After this has been done, the interpreter may wish to eliminate most of the "he saids." This would certainly be possible in parts of "Everything That Rises Must Converge" where the dialogue is simple and the speeches brief. Where the author has given an indication of how the speech was said, the interpreter may choose to eliminate the "stage direction" and incorporate it into his manner of delivery.

As we have already said, these specific comments should be taken not as directives for interpreting dialogue but as guides for carrying out the author's intent in character suggestion through dialogue. If the interpreter does not understand or ignores the author's intent, he may be led into a display of his own virtuosity as an artist — and then, of course, he will be no artist at all. For instance, the interpreter might be tempted to exaggerate advanced age or youth to the point of caricature by too much vocal or physical characterization. These excesses must be avoided; they call attention to the interpreter and hence detract from the material.

In the chapters on drama, considerably more attention will be given to vocal and physical techniques to suggest age and sex as well as more individual aspects of character. For the moment, the interpreter should concentrate on communicating the mental attitude and degree of emotional tension the author has indicated, rather than being overly specific about physical characteristics.

In general, then, the interpreter must use his body and voice skillfully and unobtrusively in handling dialogue, so that the audience will be immediately aware that a certain character is speaking instead of the narrator. Moreover, he must communicate the mental attitude and distinguishing traits of that character. It is impossible to attempt to set down rules for the vocal and physical projection of a character who displays any degree of complexity and individuality. The final decision rests on the requirements of the material and on the skill of the interpreter, who will be guided by the principle that it is his responsibility to *suggest* through dialogue clearly enough for the audience to re-create both characters and situation in their proper relationship.

Cutting

Because of their brevity, most short stories need very little cutting. Mention has already been made of the possibility of eliminating some of the dialogue "tags" and "stage directions." Sometimes, of course, the interpreter may wish to use only a single key situation from a longer story. If so, he will usually need to tell his audience what takes place before the unit he is using so that they may pick up the story at the proper point of development. This is usually done most effectively by simply addressing them directly in one's own person and then taking up the thread of the story after the introductory remarks are completed.

The interpreter will not always wish to confine himself to short stories, however, for many longer narratives provide valuable and interesting material for an audience. Considerable abridgment is necessary in making a novel, a biography, or an autobiography suitable for oral presentation, since an audience will seldom be able to follow, mentally or physically, a performance lasting longer than an hour. Thus, the interpreter will need to limit his reading of a longer narrative to an abridgment of perhaps thirty or forty pages, depending on his natural rate of reading and the requirements of the material.

If a novel is so constructed that he can choose a single climactic episode, he will analyze the excerpt as a unit just as though it were a short story. He must be sure, however, to take care of whatever background information is necessary for understanding the incident he has chosen. If the excerpt does not in itself have an adequate introduction, he can provide his audience with this information by summarizing in his own words what has gone before. The episode must, of course, have a point of climax.

If the interpreter wishes to use an abridgment of the entire novel, he will first of all find the focal point without which the narrative would not achieve its purpose. He will then analyze and treat the climactic episode in the same way as any other narrative. Any details not relevant to that climactic unit should be cut. The next step is to time the unit carefully, to be sure it is within the prescribed time limit. The material should always be read aloud with as much attention to proper pace and other factors of performance as possible. Returning to a consideration of the total effect desired by the author, the interpreter will then decide what scenes or background material and which key situations must precede the climactic incident. They may be condensed, if necessary, and should then be timed by reading aloud, with particular attention to balance and proportion. The same procedure holds in preparing the concluding units. Finally, the story must again be considered as a whole and a decision made as to which transitions must be included to keep the introduction, climax, and conclusion logically and emotionally related. These transitions may be handled entirely in the interpreter's own words or they may be condensations of the transitions given by the writer.

Frequently, a long narrative will treat one or more subplots in addition to the main plot. The interpreter's decision to include or exclude these subplots will depend, first, on the length of time he has for performance, and second, on the effectiveness of the subplots in themselves and in their relation to the total effect. The same determinants will help him decide whether to eliminate any of the characters. It is usually wise, however, to keep the attention focused sharply on the main plot and on the principal characters involved in it.

All units to be eliminated should be clearly marked so that they cause no difficulty in performance. If many pages are to be omitted, they should be clipped together. Transitions should be typed and clipped to the page preceding the next unit to be read. The interpreter need only remember that all marking should help him move smoothly through the printed material. As he gains experience, he will inevitably work out his own system of marking.

Chamber Theatre

Although our concern in this book is primarily with the individual interpreter, some mention should be made of the method of handling narrative fiction called Chamber Theatre. It will be impossible to do more than touch on a few of the basic principles of this mode of performance here, but interpreters will find Chamber Theatre a useful, exciting area of group performance well worth investigating more fully.[1]

Earlier in this chapter, we noted that point of view is a basic consideration in Chamber Theatre. Indeed, since point of view controls and dictates the entire concept of a performance in this medium, Chamber Theatre has been defined as "a technique for dramatizing the point of view of narrative fiction."

In Robert Breen's words:

> The techniques of the Chamber Theatre were devised to present the novel, or narrative fiction, on the stage so that the dramatic action would unfold with full and vivid immediacy, as it does in a play, but at the same time allowing the sensibility of the narrator, or the central intelligence in the form of a character, to so condition our view of that action that we who listen and watch would receive a highly organized and unified impression of it.

The "dramatic action" of a piece of narration is, of course, made up of the dialogue and the discernible physical actions, those units of the story handled "in scene." Some description of action can be effectively adapted to scene as well in Chamber Theatre. These units are presented in dramatic form as if they were part of a play, with a separate "actor" for each character and appropriate but minimal properties, settings, and costumes. The characters move freely about the acting area. Their circle of concentration shifts from the scene created around them in direct discourse — during which they speak directly to each other and "play together" — to the audience area for much of the indirect discourse. Thus the dramatic devices of plot, character, action, dialogue, and climax "unfold with full and vivid immediacy."

The heart of Chamber Theatre, however, is the careful, intelligent use of the narrator through whom the author controls point of view. Not only does point of view govern the author's selectivity; it also conditions the listeners' responses to the characters and the action. When the narration is closely integrated with the action, there is an effect of simultaneity and a sharpening of motivation. Care must be taken to use the narrator — whatever his degree of involvement in plot and action — exactly as the author has used him. The tense in which he speaks of the action and the use of first, second, or third person should be retained.

When the narrator is expressing an objective point of view — observing and reporting without sharing the thoughts and responses of any of the characters — the interpreter might well move physically close to some scenes as he observes them. At other times he might work as far away

---

[1] I am indebted to Robert S. Breen for many of the ideas presented here. The quotations are from his unpublished manuscript and are used with his permission.

as outside a proscenium or down in the audience area as he reports transitions and descriptions of further action. It is often effective to have him allow a scene to run its full course without interruption as he and the audience watch. He can then pick up whatever thread is necessary and comment directly in the manner of a Greek chorus.

In the case of a single-character point of view, the narrator might well work physically close to that character whose attitudes and perceptions he shares. In dual-character point of view, he would be in close proximity to both, especially when they are engaged in a scene together, making visible the link between them. If the point of view is strictly his own and we are not taken into the inner life of any of the characters, he would probably work from outside the "acting area," perhaps moving closer to describe actions as the "actors" suggest them in pantomimes. He can act as stage manager and shift properties as he bridges locale and time. There are as many variations of his active physical involvement as there are stories, and good taste and effectiveness are the final tests.

Units of a story "in scene" may be used almost verbatim, with the narrator possibly handling the "stage directions" for the action and the characters speaking the direct discourse, eliminating the "he said" tags whenever practical. Some of the "stage directions" might be eliminated altogether and performed by the characters to whom they refer.

Indirect discourse is often given to the character doing the thinking or remembering or deciding. If third-person narration has been used, the character speaks of himself in that person, saying, "He was afraid and he thought he might betray his fear to those around him." Or the narrator might give us the first part of the statement with the character supplying the rest, or vice versa. A little experience and experimentation will soon show the cast and director which gives the best focus to the more important part of the sentence.

Chamber Theatre, then, allows for a great deal of flexibility in its method. But like all forms of interpretation, it must be based on a clear understanding of the principles involved in that particular mode of presentation, careful analysis of the author's achievement, and a high degree of artistic integrity. It is *not* making a novel into a play. It is the presentation of a piece of fiction on stage *as it was written*, with the narrator fulfilling his proper function so that point of view is made to operate vividly as it controls action and response. Summary, description, and scene must be allowed their usual functions, and literary style must be used to its fullest. In Breen's words,

> Chamber Theatre is dedicated to the proposition that the ideal literary experience is one in which the simultaneity of the drama, representing the illusion of actuality . . . be combined with the novel's privilege of examining human motivation at the moment of action.

Selections for Analysis and Oral Interpretation

All of the following selections require careful attention to the matters we have been discussing in this chapter. Each contains units brief enough for classroom use, but the interpreter should remember that any unit must be considered in its relationship to the entire story. When the selections are excerpts from longer works, some background is sketched in, which — though no substitute for an entire story or novel — will provide some guidance. Also, numerous selections at the ends of earlier chapters are basically narrative and could be used profitably as exercises in narration.

This is a fairly long excerpt from a full-length novel, but the excerpt is quite clear and complete in itself. It contains several shorter units which can be used separately. Agee has caught the combination of shy pride, bewilderment, and sense of isolation of a small boy whose father has been killed in an automobile accident. Point of view is particularly well handled. Let your muscles respond fully to help project the builds and drops of tension.

FROM *A Death in the Family* / JAMES AGEE

Chapter Sixteen

The air was cool and gray and here and there along the street, shapeless and watery sunlight strayed and vanished. Now that he was in this outdoor air he felt even more listless and powerful; he was alone, and the silent, invisible energy was everywhere. He stood on the porch and supposed that everyone he saw passing knew of an event so famous. A man was walking quickly up the street and as Rufus watched him, and waited for the man to meet his eyes, he felt a great quiet lifting within him of pride and of shyness, and he felt his face break into a smile, and then an uncontrollable grin, which he knew he must try to make sober again; but the man walked past without looking at him, and so did the next man who walked past in the other direction. Two schoolboys passed whose faces he knew, so he knew they must know his, but they did not even seem to see him. Arthur and Alvin Tripp came down their front steps and along the far sidewalk and now he was sure, and came down his own front steps and halfway out to the sidewalk, but then he stopped, for now, although both of them looked across into his eyes, and he into theirs, they did not cross the street to him or even say hello, but kept on their way, still looking into his eyes with a kind of shy curiosity, even when their heads were turned almost backwards on their necks, and he turned his own head slowly, watching them go by, but when he saw that they were not going to speak he took care not to speak either.

What's the matter with them, he wondered, and still watched them; and even now, far down the street, Arthur kept turning his head, and for several steps Alvin walked backwards.

What are they mad about?

Now they no longer looked around, and now he watched them vanish under the hill.

Maybe they don't know, he thought. Maybe the others don't know, either.

He came out to the sidewalk.

Maybe everybody knew. Or maybe he knew something of great importance which nobody else knew. The alternatives were not at all distinct in his mind; he was puzzled, but no less proud and expectant than before. My daddy's dead, he said to himself slowly, and then, shyly, he said it aloud: "My daddy's dead." Nobody in sight seemed to have heard it; he had said it to nobody in particular. "My daddy's dead," he said again, chiefly for his own benefit. It sounded powerful, solid, and entirely creditable, and he knew that if need be he would tell people. He watched a large, slow man come towards him and waited for the man to look at him and acknowledge the fact first, but when the man was just ahead of him, and still did not appear even to have seen him, he told him, "My daddy's dead," but the man did not seem to hear him, he just swung on by. He took care to tell the next man sooner and the man's face looked almost as if he were dodging a blow but he went on by, looking back a few steps later with a worried face; and after a few steps more he turned and came slowly back.

"What was that you said, sonny?" he asked; he was frowning slightly.

"My daddy's dead," Rufus said, expectantly.

"You mean that sure enough?" the man asked.

"He died last night when I was asleep and now he can't come home ever any more."

The man looked at him as if something hurt him.

"Where do you live, sonny?"

"Right here"; he showed with his eyes.

"Do your folks know you out here wandern round?"

He felt his stomach go empty. He looked frankly into his eyes and nodded quickly.

The man just looked at him and Rufus realized: He doesn't believe me. How do they always know?

"You better just go on back in the house, son," he said. "They won't like you being out here on the street." He kept looking at him, hard.

Rufus looked into his eyes with reproach and apprehension, and turned in at his walk. The man still stood there. Rufus went on slowly up his steps, and looked around. The man was on his way again but at the moment Rufus looked around, he did too, and now he stopped again.

He shook his head and said, in a friendly voice which made Rufus feel ashamed, "How would your daddy like it, you out here telling strangers how he's dead?"

Rufus opened the door, taking care not to make a sound, and stepped in and silently closed it, and hurried into the sitting room. Through the curtains he watched the man. He still stood there, lighting a cigarette, but now he started walking again. He looked back once and Rufus felt, with a quailing of shame and fear, he sees me; but the man immediately looked away again and Rufus watched him until he was out of sight.

How would your daddy like it?

He thought of the way they teased him and did things to him, and how mad his father got when he just came home. He thought how different it would be today if he only didn't have to stay home from school.

He let himself out again and stole back between the houses to the alley, and walked along the alley, listening to the cinders cracking under each step, until he came near the sidewalk. He was not in front of his own home now, or even on Highland Avenue; he was coming into the side street down from his home, and he felt that here nobody would identify him with his home and send him back to it. What he could see from the mouth of the alley was much less familiar to him, and he took the last few steps which brought him out onto the sidewalk with deliberation and shyness. He was doing something he had been told not to do.

He looked up the street and he could see the corner he knew so well, where he always met the others so unhappily, and, farther away, the corner around which his father always disappeared on the way to work, and first appeared on his way home from work. He felt it would be good luck that he would not be meeting them at that corner. Slowly, uneasily, he turned his head, and looked down the side street in the other direction; and there they were: three together, and two along the far side of the street, and one alone, farther off, and another alone, farther off, and, without importance to him, some girls here and there, as well. He knew the faces of all these boys well, though he was not sure of any of their names. The moment he saw them all he was sure they saw him, and sure that they knew. He stood still and waited for them, looking from one to another of them, into their eyes, and step by step at their several distances, each of them at all times looking into his eyes and knowing, they came silently nearer. Waiting, in silence, during those many seconds before the first of them came really near him, he felt that it was so long to wait, and be watched so closely and silently, and to watch back, that he wanted to go back into the alley and not be seen by them or by anybody else, and yet at the same time he knew that they were all approaching him with the realization that something had happened to him that had not happened to any other boy in town, and that now at last they were bound to think well of him; and the nearer they came but were yet at a distance, the more the gray, sober air was charged with the great energy and with a sense of glory and of danger, and the deeper and more exciting the silence became, and the more tall, proud, shy and exposed he felt; so that as they came still nearer he once again felt his face break into a wide smile, with which he had nothing to do, and, feeling that there was something deeply wrong in such a smile, tried his best to quieten his face and told them, shyly and proudly, "My daddy's dead."

This excerpt is approximately the last third of a longer story. Julian is taking his mother to the YWCA for her weekly reducing class, and the excerpt begins as they are on the bus. He considers himself far superior to his mother on every count and is disdainful of her values and her taste. For instance, the new hat she is wearing with such obvious pride strikes him as monstrously ugly. He refrained from saying so when she appeared in it not so much to spare her feelings as to avoid getting involved in the discussion he knew would follow. His mother, who considers herself tolerant and socially superior, explains her son's lack of employment with the excuse that he must have time to find himself after college. She reflects a number of white, middle-class attitudes toward members of the black community.

FROM *Everything That Rises Must Converge* / FLANNERY O'CONNOR

Behind the newspaper Julian was withdrawing into the inner compartment of his mind where he spent most of his time. This was a kind of mental bubble in which he established himself when he could not bear to be a part of what was going on around him. From it he could see out and judge but in it he was safe from any kind of penetration from without. It was the only place where he felt free of the general idiocy of his fellows. His mother had never entered it but from it he could see her with absolute clarity.

The old lady was clever enough and he thought that if she had started from any of the right premises, more might have been expected of her. She lived according to the laws of her own fantasy world, outside of which he had never seen her set foot. The law of it was to sacrifice herself for him after she had first created the necessity to do so by making a mess of things. If he had permitted her sacrifices, it was only because her lack of foresight had made them necessary. All of her life had been a struggle to act like a Chestny without the Chestny goods, and to give him everything she thought a Chestny ought to have; but since, said she, it was fun to struggle, why complain? And when you had won, as she had won, what fun to look back on the hard times! He could not forgive her that she had enjoyed the struggle and that she thought *she* had won.

What she meant when she said she had won was that she had brought him up successfully and had sent him to college and that he had turned out so well — good looking (her teeth had gone unfilled so that his could be straightened), intelligent (he realized he was too intelligent to be a success), and with a future ahead of him (there was of course no future ahead of him). She excused his gloominess on the grounds that he was still growing up and his radical ideas on his lack of practical experience. She said he didn't yet know a thing about "life," that he hadn't even entered the real world — when already he was as disenchanted with it as a man of fifty.

The further irony of all this was that in spite of her, he had turned out so well. In spite of going to only a third-rate college, he had, on his own initiative, come out with a first-rate education; in spite of growing up dominated by a small mind, he had ended up with a large one; in spite of all her foolish views, he was free of prejudice and unafraid to face facts. Most miraculous of all, instead of being blinded by love for her as she was for him, he had cut himself emotionally free of her and could see her with complete objectivity. He was not dominated by his mother.

The bus stopped with a sudden jerk and shook him from his meditation. A woman from the back lurched forward with little steps and barely escaped falling in his newspaper as she righted herself. She got off and a large Negro got on. Julian kept his paper lowered to watch. It gave him a certain satisfaction to see injustice in daily operation. It confirmed his view that with a few exceptions there was no one worth knowing within a radius of three hundred miles. The Negro was well dressed and carried a briefcase. He looked around and then sat down on the other end of the seat where the woman with the red and white canvas sandals was sitting. He immediately unfolded a newspaper and obscured himself behind it. Julian's mother's elbow at once prodded insistently into his ribs. "Now you see why I won't ride on these buses by myself," she whispered.

The woman with the red and white canvas sandals had risen at the same time the Negro sat down and had gone further back in the bus and taken the seat of the woman who had got off. His mother leaned forward and cast her an approving look.

Julian rose, crossed the aisle, and sat down in the place of the woman with the canvas sandals. From this position, he looked serenely across at his mother. Her face had turned an angry red. He stared at her, making his eyes the eyes of a stranger. He felt his tension suddenly lift as if he had openly declared war on her.

He would have liked to get in conversation with the Negro and to talk with him about art or politics or any subject that would be above the comprehension of those around them, but the man remained entrenched behind his paper. He was either ignoring the change of seating or had never noticed it. There was no way for Julian to convey his sympathy.

His mother kept her eyes fixed reproachfully on his face. The woman with the protruding teeth was looking at him avidly as if he were a type of monster new to her.

"Do you have a light?" he asked the Negro.

Without looking away from his paper, the man reached in his pocket and handed him a packet of matches.

"Thanks," Julian said. For a moment he held the matches foolishly. A NO SMOKING sign looked down upon him from over the door. This alone would not have deterred him; he had no cigarettes. He had quit smoking some months before because he could not afford it. "Sorry," he muttered and handed back the matches. The Negro lowered the paper and gave him an annoyed look. He took the matches and raised the paper again.

His mother continued to gaze at him but she did not take advantage of his momentary discomfort. Her eyes retained their battered look. Her face seemed to be unnaturally red, as if her blood pressure had risen. Julian allowed no glimmer of sympathy to show on his face. Having got the advantage, he wanted desperately to keep it and carry it through. He would have liked to teach her a lesson that would last her a while, but there seemed no way to continue the point. The Negro refused to come out from behind his paper.

Julian folded his arms and looked stolidly before him, facing her but as if he did not see her, as if he had ceased to recognize her existence. He visualized a scene in which, the bus having reached their stop, he would remain in his seat and when she said, "Aren't you going to get off?" he would look at her as at a stranger who had rashly addressed him. The corner they got off on was usually deserted, but it was well lighted and it would not hurt her to walk by herself the four blocks to the Y. He decided to wait until the time came and then decide whether or not he would let her get off by herself. He would have to be at the Y at ten to bring her back, but he could leave her wondering if he was going to show up. There was no reason for her to think she could always depend on him.

He retired again into the high-ceilinged room sparsely settled with large pieces of antique furniture. His soul expanded momentarily but then he became aware of his mother across from him and the vision shriveled. He studied her coldly. Her feet in little pumps dangled like a child's and did not quite reach the floor. She was training on him an exaggerated look of reproach. He felt completely detached from her. At that moment he could with pleasure have slapped her as he would have slapped a particularly obnoxious child in his charge.

He began to imagine various unlikely ways by which he could teach her a lesson. He might make friends with some distinguished Negro professor or lawyer and bring him home to spend the evening. He would be entirely justified but her blood pressure would rise to 300. He could not push her to the extent of making her have a stroke, and moreover, he had never been successful at making any Negro friends. He had tried to strike up an acquaintance on the bus with some of the better types, with ones that looked like professors or ministers or lawyers. One morning he had sat down next to a distinguished-looking dark brown man who had answered his questions with a sonorous solemnity but who had turned out to be an undertaker. Another day he had sat down beside a cigar-smoking Negro with a diamond ring on his finger, but after a few stilted pleasantries, the Negro had rung the buzzer and risen, slipping two lottery tickets into Julian's hand as he climbed over him to leave.

He imagined his mother lying desperately ill and his being able to secure only a Negro doctor for her. He toyed with that idea for a few minutes and then dropped it for a momentary vision of himself participating as a sympathizer in a sit-in demonstration. This was possible but he did not linger with it. Instead, he approached the ultimate horror. He brought home a beautiful suspiciously Negroid woman. Prepare yourself, he said. There is nothing you can do about it. This is the woman I've chosen. She's intelligent, dignified, even good, and she's suffered and she hasn't thought it *fun*. Now persecute us, go ahead and persecute us. Drive her out of here, but remember, you're driving me too. His eyes were narrowed and through the indignation he had generated, he saw his mother across the aisle, purple-faced, shrunken to the dwarf-like proportions of her moral nature, sitting like a mummy beneath the ridiculous banner of her hat.

He was tilted out of his fantasy again as the bus stopped. The door opened with a sucking hiss and out of the dark a large, gaily dressed, sullen-looking colored woman got on with a little boy. The child, who might have been four, had on a short plaid suit and a Tyrolean hat with a blue feather in it. Julian hoped that he would sit down beside him and that the woman would push in beside his mother. He could think of no better arrangement.

As she waited for her tokens, the woman was surveying the seating possibilities — he hoped with the idea of sitting where she was least wanted. There was something familiar-looking about her but Julian could not place what it was. She was a giant of a woman. Her face was set not only to meet opposition but to seek it out. The downward tilt of her large lower lip was like a warning sign: DON'T TAMPER WITH ME. Her bulging figure was encased in a green crepe dress and her feet overflowed in red shoes. She had on a hideous hat. A purple velvet flap came down on one side of it and stood up on the other; the rest of it was green and looked like a cushion with the stuffing out. She carried a mammoth red pocketbook that bulged throughout as if it were stuffed with rocks.

To Julian's disappointment, the little boy climbed up on the empty seat beside his mother. His mother lumped all children, black and white, into the common category, "cute," and she thought little Negroes were on the whole cuter than little white children. She smiled at the little boy as he climbed on the seat.

Meanwhile the woman was bearing down upon the empty seat beside Julian. To his annoyance, she squeezed herself into it. He saw his mother's face change as the woman settled herself next to him and he realized with satisfaction that this was more objectionable to her than it was to him. Her face seemed almost gray and there was a look of dull recognition in her eyes, as if suddenly she had sickened at some awful confrontation. Julian saw that it was because she and the woman had, in a sense, swapped sons. Though his mother would not realize the symbolic significance of this, she would feel it. His amusement showed plainly on his face.

The woman next to him muttered something unintelligible to herself. He was conscious of a kind of bristling next to him, a muted growling like that of an angry cat. He could not see anything but the red pocketbook upright on the bulging green thighs. He visualized the woman as she had stood waiting for her tokens — the ponderous figure, rising from the red shoes upward over the solid hips, the mammoth bosom, the haughty face, to the green and purple hat.

His eyes widened.

The vision of the two hats, identical, broke upon him with the radiance of a brilliant sunrise. His face was suddenly lit with joy. He could not believe that Fate had thrust upon his mother such a lesson. He gave a loud chuckle so that she would look at him and see that he saw. She turned her eyes on him slowly. The blue in them seemed to have turned a bruised purple. For a moment he had an uncomfortable sense of her innocence, but it lasted only a second before principle rescued him. Justice entitled him to laugh. His grin hardened until it said to her as plainly as if he were saying aloud: Your punishment exactly fits your pettiness. This should teach you a permanent lesson.

Her eyes shifted to the woman. She seemed unable to bear looking at him and to find the woman preferable. He became conscious again of the bristling presence at his side. The woman was rumbling like a volcano about to become active. His mother's mouth began to twitch slightly at one corner. With a sinking heart, he saw incipient signs of recovery on her face and realized that this was going to strike her suddenly as funny and was going to be no lesson at all. She kept her eyes on the woman and an amused smile came over her face as if the woman were a monkey that had stolen her hat. The little Negro was looking up at her with large fascinated eyes. He had been trying to attract her attention for some time.

"Carver!" the woman said suddenly. "Come heah!"

When he saw that the spotlight was on him at last, Carver drew his feet up and turned himself toward Julian's mother and giggled.

"Carver!" the woman said. "You heah me? Come heah!"

Carver slid down from the seat but remained squatting with his back against the base of it, his head turned slyly around toward Julian's mother, who was smiling at him. The woman reached a hand across the aisle and snatched him to her. He righted himself and hung backwards on her knees, grinning at Julian's mother. "Isn't he cute?" Julian's mother said to the woman with the protruding teeth.

"I reckon he is," the woman said without conviction.

The Negress yanked him upright but he eased out of her grip and shot across the aisle and scrambled, giggling wildly, onto the seat beside his love.

"I think he likes me," Julian's mother said, and smiled at the woman. It was the smile she used when she was being particularly gracious to an inferior. Julian saw everything lost. The lesson had rolled off her like rain on a roof.

The woman stood up and yanked the little boy off the seat as if she were snatching him from contagion. Julian could feel the rage in her at having no weapon like his mother's smile. She gave the child a sharp slap across his leg. He howled once and then thrust his head into her stomach and kicked his feet against her shins. "Be-have," she said vehemently.

The bus stopped and the Negro who had been reading the newspaper got off. The woman moved over and set the little boy down with a thump between herself and Julian. She held him firmly by the knee. In a moment he put his hands in front of his face and peeped at Julian's mother through his fingers.

"I see yoooooooo!" she said and put her hand in front of her face and peeped at him.

The woman slapped his hand down. "Quit yo' foolishness," she said, "before I knock the living Jesus out of you!"

Julian was thankful that the next stop was theirs. He reached up and pulled the cord. The woman reached up and pulled it at the same time. Oh my God, he thought. He had the terrible intuition that when they got off of the bus together, his mother would open her purse and give the little boy a nickel. The gesture would be as natural to her as breathing. The bus stopped and the woman got up and lunged to the front, dragging the child, who wished to stay on, after her. Julian and his mother got up and followed. As they neared the door, Julian tried to relieve her of her pocketbook.

"No," she murmured, "I want to give the little boy a nickel."

"No!" Julian hissed. "No!"

She smiled down at the child and opened her bag. The bus door opened and the woman picked him up by the arm and descended with him, hanging at her hip. Once in the street she set him down and shook him.

Julian's mother had to close her purse while she got down the bus step but as soon as her feet were on the ground, she opened it again and began to rummage inside. "I can't find but a penny," she whispered, "but it looks like a new one."

"Don't do it!" Julian said fiercely between his teeth. There was a streetlight on the corner and she hurried to get under it so that she could better see into her pocketbook. The woman was heading off rapidly down the street with the child still hanging backward on her hand.

"Oh little boy!" Julian's mother called and took a few quick steps and caught up with them just beyond the lamppost. "Here's a bright new penny for you," and she held out the coin, which shone bronze in the dim light.

The huge woman turned and for a moment stood, her shoulders lifted and her face frozen with frustrated rage, and stared at Julian's mother. Then all at once she seemed to explode like a piece of machinery that had been given one ounce of pressure too much. Julian saw the black first swing out with the red pocketbook. He shut his eyes and cringed as he heard the woman shout, "He don't take nobody's pennies!" When he opened his eyes, the woman was disappearing down the street with the little boy staring wide-eyed over her shoulder. Julian's mother was sitting on the sidewalk.

"I told you not to do that," Julian said angrily. "I told you not to do that!"

He stood over her for a minute, gritting his teeth. Her legs were stretched out in front of her and her hat was on her lap. He squatted down and looked her in the face. It was totally expressionless. "You got exactly what you deserved," he said. "Now get up."

He picked up her pocketbook and put what had fallen out back in it. He picked the hat up off her lap. The penny caught his eye on the sidewalk and he picked that up and let it drop before her eyes into the purse. Then he stood up and leaned over and held his hands out to pull her up. She remained immobile. He sighed. Rising above them on either side were black apartment buildings, marked with irregular rectangles of light. At the end of the block a man came out of a door and walked off in the opposite direction. "All right," he said, "suppose somebody happens by and wants to know why you're sitting on the sidewalk?"

She took the hand and, breathing hard, pulled heavily up on it and then stood for a moment, swaying slightly as if the spots of light in the darkness were circling around her. Her eyes, shadowed and confused, finally settled on his face. He did not try to conceal his irritation. "I hope this teaches you a lesson," he said. She leaned forward and her eyes raked his face. She seemed trying to determine his identity. Then, as if she found nothing familiar about him, she started off with a headlong movement in the wrong direction.

"Aren't you going on to the Y?" he asked.

"Home," she muttered.

"Well, are we walking?"

For answer she kept going. Julian followed along, his hands behind him. He saw no reason to let the lesson she had had go without backing it up with an explanation of its meaning. She might as well be made to understand what had happened to her. "Don't think that was just an uppity Negro woman," he said. "That was the whole colored race which will no longer take your condescending pennies. That was your black double. She can wear the same hat as you, and to be sure," he added gratuitously (because he thought it was funny), "it looked better on her than it did on you. What all this means," he said, "is that the old world is gone. The old manners are obsolete and your graciousness is not worth a damn." He thought bitterly of the house that had been lost for him. "You aren't who you think you are," he said.

She continued to plow ahead, paying no attention to him. Her hair had come undone on one side. She dropped her pocketbook and took no notice. He stooped and picked it up and handed it to her but she did not take it.

"You needn't act as if the world had come to an end," he said, "because it hasn't. From now on you've got to live in a new world and face a few realities for a change. Buck up," he said, "it won't kill you."

She was breathing fast.

"Let's wait on the bus," he said.

"Home," she said thickly.

"I hate to see you behave like this," he said. "Just like a child. I should be able to expect more of you." He decided to stop where he was and make her stop and wait for a bus. "I'm not going any farther," he said, stopping. "We're going on the bus."

She continued to go on as if she had not heard him. He took a few steps and caught her arm and stopped her. He looked into her face and caught his breath. He was looking into a face he had never seen before. "Tell Grandpa to come get me," she said.

He stared, stricken.

"Tell Caroline to come get me," she said.

Stunned, he let her go and she lurched forward again, walking as if one leg were shorter than the other. A tide of darkness seemed to be sweeping her from him. "Mother!" he cried. "Darling, sweetheart, wait!" Crumpling, she fell to the pavement. He dashed forward and fell at her side, crying, "Mamma, Mamma!" He turned her over. Her face was fiercely distorted. One eye, large and staring, moved slightly to the left as if it had become unmoored. The other remained fixed on him, raked his face again, found nothing and closed.

"Wait here, wait here!" he cried and jumped up and began to run for help toward a cluster of lights he saw in the distance ahead of him. "Help, help!" he shouted, but his voice was thin, scarcely a thread of sound. The lights drifted farther away the faster he ran and his feet moved numbly as if they carried him nowhere. The tide of darkness seemed to sweep him back to her, postponing from moment to moment his entry into the world of guilt and sorrow.

Be sure you understand the reason for including the name and vintage year of the wine. The climax will take careful handling to maintain balance and proportion.

Friends from Philadelphia / JOHN UPDIKE

In the moment before the door was opened to him, he glimpsed her thigh below the half-drawn shade. Thelma was home, then. She was wearing the Camp Winniwoho T shirt and her quite short shorts.

"Why, my goodness: Janny!" she cried. She always pronounced his name, John, to rhyme with Ann. Earlier that vacation, she had visited in New York City, and tried to talk the way she thought they talked there. "What on earth ever brings you to me at this odd hour?"

"Hello, Thel," he said. "I hope — I guess this is a pretty bad time." She had been plucking her eyebrows again. He wished she wouldn't do that.

Thelma extended her arm and touched her fingers to the base of John's neck. It wasn't a fond gesture, just a hostesslike one. "Now, Janny. You know that I — my mother and I — are always happy to see you. Mother, who do you ever guess is here at this odd hour?"

"Don't keep John Nordholm standing there," Mrs. Lutz said. Thelma's mother was settled in the deep red settee watching television and smoking.

A coffee cup being used as an ashtray lay in her lap, and her dress was hiked up so that her knees showed.

"Hello, Mrs. Lutz," John said, trying not to look at her broad, pale knees. "I really hate to bother you at this odd hour."

"I don't see anything odd about it." She took a deep-throated drag on her cigarette and exhaled through her nostrils, the way men do. "Some of the other kids were here earlier this afternoon."

"I would have come in if anybody had told me."

Thelma said, "Oh, Janny! Stop trying to make a martyr of yourself. Keep in touch, they say, if you want to keep up."

He felt his face grow hot and knew he was blushing, which made him blush all the more. Mrs. Lutz shook a wrinkled pack of Herbert Tareytons at him. "Smoke?" she said.

"I guess not, thanks a lot."

"You've stopped? It's a bad habit. I wish I had stopped at your age. I'm not sure I even *begun* at your age."

"No, it's just that I have to go home soon, and my mother would smell the smoke on my breath. She can smell it even through chewing gum."

"Why must you go home soon?" Thelma asked.

Mrs. Lutz sniffled. "I have sinus. I can't even smell the flowers in the garden or the food on the table any more. Let the kids smoke if they want, if it makes them feel better. I don't care. My Thelma, she can smoke right in her own home, her own living room, if she wants to. But she doesn't seem to have the taste for it. I'm just as glad, to tell the truth."

John hated interrupting, but it was close to five-thirty. "I have a problem," he said.

"A problem — how gruesome," Thelma said. "And here I thought, Mother, I was being favored with a social call."

"Don't talk like that," Mrs. Lutz said.

"It's sort of complex," John began.

"Talk like what, Mother? Talk like what?"

"Then let me turn this off," Mrs. Lutz said, snapping the right knob on the television set.

"Oh, Mother, and I was listening to it!" Thelma toppled into a chair, her legs flashing. John thought when she pouted, she was delicious.

Mrs. Lutz had set herself to give sympathy. Her lap was broadened and her hands were laid palms upward in it.

"It's not much of a problem," John assured her. "But we're having some people up from Philadelphia." He turned to Thelma and added, "If anything is going on tonight, I can't get out."

"Life is just too, too full of disappointments," Thelma said.

"Look, is there?"

"Too, too full," Thelma said.

Mrs. Lutz made fluttery motions out of her lap. "These Philadelphia people."

John said, "Maybe I shouldn't bother you about this." He waited, but she just looked more and more patient, so he went on. "My mother wants to give them wine, and my father isn't home from teaching school yet. He might not get home before the liquor store closes. It's at six, isn't it? My mother's busy cleaning, so I walked in."

"She made you walk the whole mile? Poor thing, can't you drive?" Mrs. Lutz asked.

"*Sure* I can drive. But I'm not sixteen yet."

"You look a lot taller than sixteen."

John looked at Thelma to see how she took that one, but Thelma was pretending to read a rented novel wrapped in cellophane.

"I walked all the way in to the liquor store," John told Mrs. Lutz, "but they wouldn't give me anything without written permission. It was a new man."

"Your sorrow has rent me in twain," Thelma said, as if she was reading it from the book.

"Pay no attention, Johnny," Mrs. Lutz said. "Now Frank will be home any time. Why not wait until he comes and let him run down with you for a bottle?"

"That sounds wonderful. Thanks an awful lot, really."

Mrs. Lutz's hand descended upon the television knob. Some smiling man was playing the piano. John didn't know who he was; there wasn't any television at his house. They watched in silence until Mr. Lutz thumped on the porch outside. The empty milk bottles tinkled, as if they had been nudged. "Now don't be surprised if he has a bit of a load on," Mrs. Lutz said.

Actually, he didn't act at all drunk. He was like a happy husband in the movies. He called Thelma his little pookie-pie and kissed her on the forehead; then he called his wife his big pookie-pie and kissed her on the mouth. Then he solemnly shook John's hand and told him how very, very happy he was to see him here and asked after his parents. "Is that goon still on television?" he said finally.

"Daddy, please pay attention to somebody else," Thelma said, turning off the television set. "Janny wants to talk to you."

"And *I* want to talk to *Johnny*," Thelma's father said. He spread his arms suddenly, clenching and unclenching his fists. He was a big man, with shaved gray hair above his tiny ears. John couldn't think of the word to begin.

Mrs. Lutz explained the errand. When she was through, Mr. Lutz said, "People from Philadelphia. I bet their name isn't William L. Trexler, is it?"

"No. I forget their name, but it's not that. The man is an engineer. The woman went to college with my mother."

"Oh. College people. Then we must get them something very, very nice, I should say."

"Daddy," Thelma said. "*Please*. The store will close."

"Tessie, you hear John. People from college. People with diplomas. And it is very nearly closing time, and who isn't on their way?" He took John's shoulder in one hand and Thelma's arm in the other and hustled them through the door. "We'll be back in one minute, Mamma," he said.

"Drive carefully," Mrs. Lutz said from the shadowed porch, where her cigarette showed as an orange star.

Mr. Lutz drove a huge blue Buick. "I never went to college," he said, "yet I buy a new car whenever I want." His tone wasn't nasty, but soft and full of wonder.

"Oh, Daddy, not *this* again," Thelma said, shaking her head at John, so he could understand what all she had to go through. When she looks like that, John thought, I could bite her lip until it bleeds.

"Ever driven this kind of car, John?" Mr. Lutz asked.

"No. The only thing I can drive is my parents' Plymouth, and that not very well."

"What year car is it?"

"I don't know exactly." John knew perfectly well it was a 1940 model. "We got it after the war. It has a gear shift. This is automatic, isn't it?"

"Automatic shift, fluid transmission, directional lights, the works," Mr. Lutz said. "Now, isn't it funny, John? Here is your father, an educated man, with an old Plymouth, yet at the same time I, who never read more than twenty, thirty books in my life . . . it doesn't seem as if there's justice." He slapped the fender, bent over to get into the car, straightened up abruptly, and said, "Do you want to drive it?"

Thelma said, "Daddy's asking you something."

"I don't know how," John said.

"It's very easy to learn, very easy. You just slide in there — come on, it's getting late." John got in on the driver's side. He peered out of the windshield. It was a wider car than the Plymouth; the hood looked wide as a boat.

Mr. Lutz asked him to grip the little lever behind the steering wheel. "You pull it toward you like *that*, that's it, and fit it into one of these notches. 'P' stands for 'parking' — I hardly ever use that one.

'N,' that's 'neutral,' like on the car you have, 'D' means 'drive' — just put it in there and the car does all the work for you. You are using that one ninety-nine per cent of the time. 'L' is 'low,' for very steep hills, going up or down. And 'R' stands for — what?"

"Reverse," John said.

"Very, very good. Tessie, he's a smart boy. He'll never own a new car. And when you put them all together, you can remember their order by the sentence, Paint No Dimes Light Red. I thought that up when I was teaching my oldest girl how to drive."

"Paint No Dimes Light Red," John said.

"Excellent. Now, let's go."

A bubble was developing in John's stomach. "What gear do you want it in to start?" he asked Mr. Lutz.

Mr. Lutz must not have heard him, because all he said was "Let's go" again, and he drummed on the dashboard with his fingertips. They were thick, square fingers, with fur between the knuckles.

Thelma leaned up from the back seat. Her cheek almost touched John's ear. She whispered, "Put it at 'D.' "

He did, then he looked for the starter. "How does he start it?" he asked Thelma.

"I never watch him," she said. "There was a button in the last car, but I don't see it in this one."

"Push on the pedal," Mr. Lutz sang, staring straight ahead and smiling, "and away we go. And ah, ah, waay we go."

"Just step on the gas," Thelma suggested. John pushed down firmly, to keep his leg from trembling. The motor roared and the car bounded away from the curb. Within a block, though, he could manage the car pretty well.

"It rides like a boat on smooth water," he told his two passengers. The metaphor pleased him.

Mr. Lutz squinted ahead. "Like a what?"

"Like a boat."

"Don't go so fast," Thelma said.

"The motor's so quiet," John explained. "Like a sleeping cat."

Without warning, a truck pulled out of Pearl Street. Mr. Lutz, trying to brake, stamped his foot on the empty floor in front of him. John could hardly keep from laughing. "I see him," he said, easing his speed so that the truck had just enough room to make its turn. "Those trucks think they own the road," he said. He let one hand slide away from the steering wheel. One-handed, he whipped around a bus. "What'll she do on the open road?"

"That's a good question, John," Mr. Lutz said. "And I don't know the answer. Eighty, maybe."

"The speedometer goes up to a hundred and ten." Another pause —

nobody seemed to be talking. John said, "Hell. A baby could drive one of these."

"For instance, you," Thelma said.

There were a lot of cars at the liquor store, so John had to double-park the big Buick. "That's close enough, close enough," Mr. Lutz said. "Don't get any closer, whoa!" He was out of the car before John could bring it to a complete stop. "You and Tessie wait here," he said. "I'll go in for liquor."

"Mr. Lutz. Say, Mr. Lutz," John called.

"Daddy!" Thelma shouted.

Mr. Lutz returned. "What is it, boys and girls?" His tone, John noticed, was becoming reedy. He was probably getting hungry.

"Here's the money they gave me." John pulled two wadded dollars from the change pocket of his dungarees. "My mother said to get something inexpensive but nice."

"Inexpensive but nice?" Mr. Lutz repeated.

"She said something about California sherry."

"What did she say about it? To get it? Or not to?"

"I guess to get it."

"You guess." Mr. Lutz shoved himself away from the car and walked backward toward the store as he talked. "You and Tessie wait in the car. Don't go off somewhere. It's getting late. I'll be only one minute."

John leaned back in his seat and gracefully rested one hand at the top of the steering wheel. "I like your father."

"You don't know how he acts to Mother," Thelma said.

John studied the clean line under his wrist and thumb. He flexed his wrist and watched the neat little muscles move in his forearm. "You know what I need?" he said. "A wrist-watch."

"Oh, Jan," Thelma said. "Stop admiring your own hand. It's really disgusting."

A ghost of a smile flickered over his lips, but he let his strong nervous fingers remain as they were. "I'd sell my soul for a drag right now."

"Daddy keeps a pack in the glove compartment," Thelma said. "I'd get them if my fingernails weren't so long."

"*I'll* get it open," John said, and did. They fished one cigarette out of the old pack of Luckies they found and took alternate puffs. "Ah," John said, "that first drag of the day, clawing and scraping its way down your throat."

"Be on the lookout for Daddy. They hate my smoking."

"Thelma."

"Yes?" She stared deep into his eyes, her face half masked by blue shadow.

"Don't pluck your eyebrows."

"I think it looks nice."

"It's like calling me 'Jan.'" There was a silence, not awkward, between them.

"Get rid of the 'rette, Jan. Daddy just passed the window."

Being in the liquor store had put Mr. Lutz in a soberer mood. "Here you be, John," he said, in a businesslike way. He handed John a tall, velvet-red bottle. "Better let me drive. You drive like a veteran, but I know the roads."

"I can walk from your house, Mr. Lutz," John said, knowing Mr. Lutz wouldn't make him walk. "Thanks an awful lot for all you've done."

"I'll drive you up. Philadelphians can't be kept waiting. We can't make this young man walk a mile, now can we, Tessie?" In the sweeping way the man asked the question there was an energy and a hint of danger that kept the young people quiet all the way out of town, although several things were bothering John.

When the car stopped in front of his house, he forced himself to ask, "Say, Mr. Lutz. I wonder if there was any change?"

"What? Oh. I nearly forgot. You'll have your daddy thinking I'm a crook." He reached into his pocket and without looking handed John a dollar, a quarter and a penny.

"This seems like a lot," John said. The wine must be cheap. His stomach squirmed; maybe he had made a mistake. Maybe he should have let his mother phone his father, like she had wanted to, instead of begging her to let him walk in.

"It's your change," Mr. Lutz said.

"Well, thanks an awful lot."

"Goodbye now," Mr. Lutz said.

"So long." John slammed the door. "Goodbye, Thelma. Don't forget what I told you." He winked.

The car pulled out, and John walked up the path. "Don't forget what I told you," he repeated to himself, winking. In his hands the bottle was cool and heavy. He glanced at the label; it read *Château Mouton-Rothschild 1937.*

Point of view and character suggestion make an interesting challenge here. The dialogue will take careful handling to keep it within the framework established by the point of view.

A *Banal Miracle* / TIM REYNOLDS

Linda Vanelli died suddenly and unobtrusively. She was seated at the foot of the kitchen table — she would never have assumed Angelo's chair,

"A Banal Miracle" by Tim Reynolds originally appeared in *New World Writing* 20. It is reprinted by permission of the author and J. B. Lippincott Company.

even when he was out on the boat — and the children were squabbling, yelling, whining, pecking at and mish-mashing spaghetti, squirming in their chairs, spilling milk down their already messy shirts, blouses and chests, when she made unexpectedly a curiously awkward movement, a wide stiff sweep of the right arm as though reaching clumsily for something she wanted, and knocked Jason's plate to the floor. For a moment the attention was all on the broken plate, and by the time the children looked up again their mother was dead.

There was no good reason for Mrs. Vanelli to die, that anyone could see; on the other hand, there was no particularly good reason for her not to. She had left no loose ends to speak of. Most of the housework in the past two years had been taken care of by Ginny and Vicky, since arthritis and two operations had left Mrs. Vanelli's right hand almost entirely useless and pretty well crippled the other too. She had brought up eleven out of fourteen born, kept clothes on their backs and food in their bellies most of the time, saw that each boy went to school as long as he wanted to, until he quit to get a job (hoping maybe that one of her children would go somewhere; but none ever did), protected them as well as she was able from her husband Angelo's infrequent but maniacally violent explosions; and had protected Angelo himself in his turn the time, three years before, when in such a rage he had beaten a child too hard and too long. She had been a good wife, then, and a good mother, and a good Catholic, and had spent most of her life unhappy, worried and in pain; so, although she was not yet fifty, people said or might have said, It was a blessing, as one says of old people or the incurably ill.

People felt that Angelo should have left it at that. He was out on the boat, which was a little seiner without a radio, so didn't know anything until he got home, the day after Linda Vanelli's sudden death. The neighbors had taken care of things; the house was pretty much in order, Ginny and Vicky were taking care of the little ones, and Mrs. Vanelli's body had been moved to the Boronis' where there was a bigger living room and fewer children.

Angelo walked in around ten in the morning. Right away the children felt not only frightened but guilty, as though they were responsible, as if they had broken something belonging to him while he was gone and were afraid to tell him but couldn't lie to him, could never conceive of defying Angelo.

Stinking of sardine, with four days' worth of beard on his face and two hours' worth of red wine in his belly, he looked ominously around the living room at the too-silent children. He felt threatened; they were always subdued when he came home, but he had never seen them so thoroughly chastened.

— Where's your ma, he asked them.

The little ones looked at the middle ones, the middle ones at the bigger ones, and finally everyone was looking at Ginny, who was oldest. Ginny took a deep breath.

— Ma's dead, she told her father.

— Hell you say, said Angelo.

— She's dead, Ginny said. They took her over to the Boronis'.

Angelo thought about it a while. Hell's bells, he said, and thought some more, and then said, She'll keep, and went on into the cluttered bedroom to lie down, as he always did when he came home. Mrs. Vanelli wasn't there to keep the children quiet while he slept, but it wasn't necessary. He slept until nine o'clock that evening.

When Angelo woke up he went over to the Boronis', three doors away, without even bothering to shave. The women, chatting over coffee, subsided when he came in. He paid no attention to them. Mrs. Vanelli was lying in a black coffin with silver handles lying across two chairs, and Angelo walked over and stood looking down at her.

Mrs. Boroni, later, maintained he had said it quietly, almost gently and lovingly; her daughter Frances claimed it was masterfully; Mrs. Corona thought it was desperate, as though he were pleading; of the other two ladies, one heard nothing and the other said Angelo had just said it, the way Angelo said anything, when he did, which was rarely; Get up and come home with me.

Then he turned and walked out the door. By the time Mrs. Vanelli had managed to scramble out of the coffin without overturning everything and hurriedly thank Mrs. Boroni and the other ladies for taking care of her, Angelo was almost halfway home. She had to run to catch up with him.

There was a good deal of talk at first; in a neighborhood where weddings were actively planned by everyone two months in advance and dissected for two weeks afterwards, it would have been odd if there hadn't been. But after a few days it was pretty well accepted; nothing had changed: Mrs. Vanelli's complexion, some said, was a little worse, but otherwise she was the same, and Angelo was as surly as ever and as little liked, so there was really nothing to talk *about*.

The general consensus initially inclined toward a "rare disease," but Doctor Karpov, who had examined Mrs. Vanelli and made out the certificates and such, denied it vehemently.

— There's no such disease, he said. I've made misdiagnoses, but I've never yet diagnosed a living woman as dead. It was heart failure pure and simple, not a rare disease or any disease. That woman was dead when I examined her, and if she was dead then she's dead now. But he refused to go see her, and after a time refused to talk about it any more.

That made it, evidently, a miracle. People looked oddly at Angelo

Vanelli in the streets: they recalled mutterings of "Mafista" when he had first come to Monterey — he was a Siciliano, while most of the others were second- and third-generation — and later mutterings concerning some unpleasantness with a child's death a few years back; they didn't think they'd ever seen him in church; there was nothing specific to say against him, at least out loud, but no one had anything to say in his favor either; it all seemed very odd. The two boys on the seiner started to call him Mr. Vanelli Sir instead of plain Mr. Vanelli when they spoke to him; and that was, and always had been, as little as they could help.

If it *was* a miracle, however, it was in Father Martin's department. He put it off as long as he could, but with a nagging certainty that it would eventually have to be tended to. As far as anyone seemed to know, this Angelo Vanelli had raised his wife from the dead. The worst of it was that there was apparently no question at all that it had taken place. Father Martin was certain there was a perfectly rational explanation, such as mass hypnosis or hysteria, but in the meantime he had what amounted to a miracle on his hands.

He went to speak with Linda Vanelli when most of the children were in school and Angelo out on the seiner, on a Tuesday. One of the little ones let him in, yelled over his shoulder *Maaaa!*, and returned immediately to the center of the floor, dropping cross-legged between two other children, one scantily diapered, and returned his attention to the massive television set in the corner by the kitchen door.

The room seemed perfectly familiar to the priest; although he had never been in this particular home, he had been in a hundred like it: a constellation of tinted photographs, children and weddings mostly, among whom Christ demonstrated his bleeding heart and Mary her sorrows as though members of the family, a blanket-swathed sofa, an armchair, an ungainly collection of rachitic chairs and stools, all aimed at the television set, a glimpse through the kitchen door of a cramped sink and a woodstove; and, he knew as well as if he had been conducted on a guided tour, beyond the closed door to his right a double bed, a crib and a cot to hold at night, with the sofa, an entire family of perhaps a dozen, tumbled like puppies in a cardboard carton. He noted, however, with approval, that although the furnishings were scuffed and worn everything was clean and moderately well ordered.

Mrs. Vanelli was a stout dull-eyed woman, like her house considerably frayed, considerably used, but well tended; although Father Martin had never had personal dealings with her save in the confessional, he knew her face well; she was a conscientious churchgoer.

— Coffee, Father? she asked hovering over the sofa, waiting his answer to either drop into it or retire to the kitchen for refreshments.

— No, thank you, Mrs. Vanelli. Mrs. Vanelli dropped. Father Martin leaned forward from the armchair, fingers interlaced. Mrs. Vanelli, I've come to speak to you in reference to an incident that occurred, I'm told, some two weeks ago. It appears that . . . He didn't quite know how to phrase it, and stopped, raising his eyebrows and leaning back to indicate that he was awaiting an answer more complete than the question.

— Oh, it's got nothing to do with you, Father. She seemed actually surprised. He waited. Mrs. Vanelli, eyes on the floor, or on her knees, searching ineptly for words. That's just between me and Mr. Vanelli, kind of, Father. You could talk to him, she added hopefully.

— I may have to, he answered. But right now I'd like to hear your view of the matter.

Mrs. Vanelli's brow creased thoughtfully. — It's just how Angelo *is*, she said at last. When he first came to town he was like that. He'd been here maybe a month, two months, and he came to my father's house and I was just sitting there, I was fifteen years old, almost sixteen, and he just looked at me and said, Get up and come home with me, and Pa was scared to say nothing on account of all the talk about Angelo, *you* know, so I went home with him.

— You mean, Father Martin interrupted, you mean . . . Just went home?

— Umhuh, she said. And maybe five years later I found out he was with another woman in Salinas and I was sick a lot and he'd get drunk and come home and be mean to me and the kids, *you* know, so I took the kids and went back home back to my pa. And a week, two weeks later, Angelo walks in and says, You get up and come home with me, so I did.

And that's how it is, Father, I mean how Angelo is. I just couldn't say no to him, ever. Did I do wrong, Father?

Father Martin considered. — I suppose not, he said.

— You see how it's got nothing to do with you, she pressed.

— I suppose not, he said again. Perhaps, as they say, love is stronger than death.

Mrs. Vanelli shrugged wearily. Her crushed and broken hands lay like gnarled cypress roots on her broad lap.

— Well, she said dubiously, anyway habits.

There was a long pause. There seemed nothing more to say. Father Martin rose from the armchair and Mrs. Vanelli walked three steps with him to the door. — Watch the step, she said, it's broken. But the priest stopped in the doorway and turned to her.

— What was it like? he asked cautiously.

— Being dead? I don't know, she said, holding the bellied-out rusty screen door open with one warped hand. It was like nothing; it wasn't so bad; it was like nothing at all. *You* know.

He stepped out and down, watching out for the broken step, and turned again. — Well, good-by, Mrs. Vanelli, he said; and thank you for talking with me.

— That's all right, she said. Her wide face looked dim and far away through the sagging mesh of the screen. Good-by. I'll tell Angelo you was here.

Point of view as it operates in this story was mentioned in the chapter. A large amount of the action is described here, while the units "in scene" are largely devoid of specific movement on the part of the characters.

A *Summer Tragedy* / ARNA BONTEMPS

Old Jeff Patton, the black share farmer, fumbled with his bow tie. His fingers trembled and the high stiff collar pinched his throat. A fellow loses his hand for such vanities after thirty or forty years of simple life. Once a year, or maybe twice if there's a wedding among his kinfolks, he may spruce up; but generally fancy clothes do nothing but adorn the wall of the big room and feed the moths. That had been Jeff Patton's experience. He had not worn his stiff-bosomed shirt more than a dozen times in all his married life. His swallow-tailed coat lay on the bed beside him, freshly brushed and pressed, but it was as full of holes as the overalls in which he worked on weekdays. The moths had used it badly. Jeff twisted his mouth into a hideous toothless grimace as he contended with the obstinate bow. He stamped his good foot and decided to give up the struggle.

"Jennie," he called.

"What's that, Jeff?" His wife's shrunken voice came out of the adjoining room like an echo. It was hardly bigger than a whisper.

"I reckon you'll have to he'p me wid this heah bow tie, baby," he said meekly. "Dog if I can hitch it up."

Her answer was not strong enough to reach him, but presently the old woman came to the door, feeling her way with a stick. She had a wasted, dead-leaf appearance. Her body, as scrawny and gnarled as a string bean, seemed less than nothing in the ocean of frayed and faded petticoats that surrounded her. These hung an inch or two above the tops of her heavy unlaced shoes and showed little grotesque piles where the stockings had fallen down from her negligible legs.

"You oughta could do a heap mo' wid a thing like that'n me—beingst as you got yo' good sight."

"Looks like I oughta could," he admitted. "But ma fingers is gone democrat on me. I get all mixed up in the looking glass an' can't tell wicha way to twist the devilish thing."

Jennie sat on the side of the bed and old Jeff Patton got down on one knee while she tied the bow knot. It was a slow and painful ordeal for each of them in this position. Jeff's bones cracked, his knee ached, and it was only after a half dozen attempts that Jennie worked a semblance of a bow into the tie.

"I got to dress maself now," the old woman whispered. "These is ma old shoes an' stockings, and I ain't so much as unwrapped ma dress."

"Well, don't worry 'bout me no mo', baby," Jeff said. "That 'bout finishes me. All I gotta do now is slip on that old coat 'n ves' an' I'll be fixed to leave."

Jennie disappeared again through the dim passage into the shed room. Being blind was no handicap to her in that black hole. Jeff heard the cane placed against the wall beside the door and knew that his wife was on easy ground. He put on his coat, took a battered top hat from the bedpost and hobbled to the front door. He was ready to travel. As soon as Jennie could get on her Sunday shoes and her old black silk dress, they would start.

Outside the tiny log house, the day was warm and mellow with sunshine. A host of wasps were humming with busy excitement in the trunk of a dead sycamore. Gray squirrels were searching through the grass for hickory nuts and blue jays were in the trees, hopping from branch to branch. Pine woods stretched away to the left like a black sea. Among them were scattered scores of log houses like Jeff's, houses of black share farmers. Cows and pigs wandered freely among the trees. There was no danger of loss. Each farmer knew his own stock and knew his neighbor's as well as he knew his neighbor's children.

Down the slope to the right were the cultivated acres on which the colored folks worked. They extended to the river, more than two miles away, and they were today green with the unmade cotton crop. A tiny thread of a road, which passed directly in front of Jeff's place, ran through these green fields like a pencil mark.

Jeff, standing outside the door, with his absurd hat in his left hand, surveyed the wide scene tenderly. He had been forty-five years on these acres. He loved them with the unexplained affection that others have for the countries to which they belong.

The sun was hot on his head, his collar still pinched his throat, and the Sunday clothes were intolerably hot. Jeff transferred the hat to his right hand and began fanning with it. Suddenly the whisper that was Jennie's voice came out of the shed room.

"You can bring the car round front whilst you's waitin'," it said feebly. There was a tired pause; then it added, "I'll soon be fixed to go."

"A'right, baby," Jeff answered. "I'll get it in a minute."

But he didn't move. A thought struck him that made his mouth fall open. The mention of the car brought to his mind, with new intensity, the trip he and Jennie were about to take. Fear came into his eyes; excitement took his breath. Lord, Jesus!

"Jeff . . . O Jeff," the old woman's whisper called.

He awakened with a jolt. "Hunh, baby?"

"What you doin'?"

"Nuthin. Jes studyin'. I jes been turnin' things round'n round in ma mind."

"You could be gettin' the car," she said.

"Oh yes, right away, baby."

He started round to the shed, limping heavily on his bad leg. There were three frizzly chickens in the yard. All his other chickens had been killed or stolen recently. But the frizzly chickens had been saved somehow. That was fortunate indeed, for these curious creatures had a way of devouring "Poison" from the yard and in that way protecting against conjure and black luck and spells. But even the frizzly chickens seemed now to be in a stupor. Jeff thought they had some ailment; he expected all three of them to die shortly.

The shed in which the old T-model Ford stood was only a grass roof held up by four corner poles. It had been built by tremulous hands at a time when the little rattletrap car had been regarded as a peculiar treasure. And, miraculously, despite wind and downpour it still stood.

Jeff adjusted the crank and put his weight upon it. The engine came to life with a sputter and bang that rattled the old car from radiator to taillight. Jeff hopped into the seat and put his foot on the accelerator. The sputtering and banging increased. The rattling became more violent. That was good. It was good banging, good sputtering and rattling, and it meant that the aged car was still in running condition. She could be depended on for this trip.

Again Jeff's thought halted as if paralyzed. The suggestion of the trip fell into the machinery of his mind like a wrench. He felt dazed and weak. He swung the car out into the yard, made a half turn and drove around to the front door. When he took his hands off the wheel, he noticed that he was trembling violently. He cut off the motor and climbed to the ground to wait for Jennie.

A few minutes later she was at the window, her voice rattling against the pane like a broken shutter.

"I'm ready, Jeff."

He did not answer, but limped into the house and took her by the arm. He led her slowly through the big room, down the step and across the yard.

"You reckon I'd oughta lock the do'?" he asked softly.

They stopped and Jennie weighed the question. Finally she shook her head.

"Ne' mind the do'," she said. "I don't see no cause to lock up things."

"You right," Jeff agreed. "No cause to lock up."

Jeff opened the door and helped his wife into the car. A quick shudder passed over him. Jesus! Again he trembled.

"How come you shaking so?" Jennie whispered.

"I don't know," he said.

"You mus' be scairt, Jeff."

"No, baby, I ain't scairt."

He slammed the door after her and went around to crank up again. The motor started easily. Jeff wished that it had not been so responsive. He would have liked a few more minutes in which to turn things around in his head. As it was, with Jennie chiding him about being afraid, he had to keep going. He swung the car into the little pencil-mark road and started off toward the river, driving very slowly, very cautiously.

Chugging across the green countryside, the small battered Ford seemed tiny indeed. Jeff felt a familiar excitement, a thrill, as they came down the first slope to the immense levels on which the cotton was growing. He could not help reflecting that the crops were good. He knew what that meant, too; he had made forty-five of them with his own hands. It was true that he had worn out nearly a dozen mules, but that was the fault of old man Stevenson, the owner of the land. Major Stevenson had the odd notion that one mule was all a share farmer needed to work a thirty-acre plot. It was an expensive notion, the way it killed mules from overwork, but the old man held to it. Jeff thought it killed a good many share farmers as well as mules, but he had no sympathy for them. He had always been strong, and he had been taught to have no patience with weakness in men. Women or children might be tolerated if they were puny, but a weak man was a curse. Of course, his own children —

Jeff's thought halted there. He and Jennie never mentioned their dead children any more. And naturally he did not wish to dwell upon them in his mind. Before he knew it, some remark would slip out of his mouth and that would make Jennie feel blue. Perhaps she would cry. A woman like Jennie could not easily throw off the grief that comes from losing five grown children within two years. Even Jeff was still staggered by the blow. His memory had not been much good recently. He frequently talked to himself. And, although he had kept it a secret, he knew that his courage had left him. He was terrified by the least unfamiliar sound at night. He was reluctant to venture far from home in the daytime. And that habit of trembling when he felt fearful was now far beyond his control. Sometimes he became afraid and trembled without knowing what had frightened him. The feeling would just come over him like a chill.

The car rattled slowly over the dusty road. Jennie sat erect and silent, with a little absurd hat pinned to her hair. Her useless eyes seemed very large, very white in their deep sockets. Suddenly Jeff heard her voice, and he inclined his head to catch the words.

"Is we passed Delia Moore's house yet?" she asked.

"Not yet," he said.

"You must be drivin' mighty slow, Jeff."

"We might just as well take our time, baby."

There was a pause. A little puff of steam was coming out of the radiator of the car. Heat wavered above the hood. Delia Moore's house was nearly half a mile away. After a moment Jennie spoke again.

"You ain't really scairt, is you, Jeff?"

"Nah, baby, I ain't scairt."

"You know how we agreed — we gotta keep on goin'."

Jewels of perspiration appeared on Jeff's forehead. His eyes rounded, blinked, became fixed on the road.

"I don't know," he said with a shiver. "I reckon it's the only thing to do."

"Hm."

A flock of guinea fowls, pecking in the road, were scattered by the passing car. Some of them took to their wings; others hid under bushes. A blue jay, swaying on a leafy twig, was annoying a roadside squirrel. Jeff held an even speed till he came near Delia's place. Then he slowed down noticeably.

Delia's house was really no house at all, but an abandoned store building converted into a dwelling. It sat near a crossroads, beneath a single black cedar tree. There Delia, a cattish old creature of Jennie's age, lived alone. She had been there more years than anybody could remember, and long ago had won the disfavor of such women as Jennie. For in her young days Delia had been gayer, yellower and saucier than seemed proper in those parts. Her ways with menfolks had been dark and suspicious. And the fact that she had had as many husbands as children did not help her reputation.

"Yonder's old Delia," Jeff said as they passed.

"What she doin'?"

"Jes sittin' in the do'," he said.

"She see us?"

"Hm," Jeff said. "Musta did."

That relieved Jennie. It strengthened her to know that her old enemy had seen her pass in her best clothes. That would give the old she-devil something to chew her gums and fret about, Jennie thought. Wouldn't she have a fit if she didn't find out? Old evil Delia! This would be just the thing for her. It would pay her back for being so evil. It would also pay her, Jennie thought, for the way she used to grin at Jeff — long ago when her teeth were good.

The road became smooth and red, and Jeff could tell by the smell of the air that they were nearing the river. He could see the rise where the road turned and ran along parallel to the stream. The car chugged on monotonously. After a long silent spell, Jennie leaned against Jeff and spoke.

"How many bale o' cotton you think we got standin'?" she said.

Jeff wrinkled his forehead as he calculated.

" 'Bout twenty-five, I reckon."

"How many you make las' year?"

"Twenty-eight," he said. "How come you ask that?"

"I's jes thinkin'," Jennie said quietly.

"It don't make a speck o' difference though," Jeff reflected. "If we get much or if we get little, we still gonna be in debt to old man Stevenson when he gets through counting up agin us. It's took us a long time to learn that."

Jennie was not listening to these words. She had fallen into a trance-like meditation. Her lips twitched. She chewed her gums and rubbed her gnarled hands nervously. Suddenly she leaned forward, buried her face in the nervous hands and burst into tears. She cried aloud in a dry cracked voice that suggested the rattle of fodder on dead stalks. She cried aloud like a child, for she had never learned to suppress a genuine sob. Her slight old frame shook heavily and seemed hardly able to sustain such violent grief.

"What's the matter, baby?" Jeff asked awkwardly. "Why you cryin' like all that?"

"I's jes thinkin'," she said.

"So you the one what's scairt now, hunh?"

"I ain't scairt, Jeff. I's jes thinkin' 'bout leavin' eve'thing like this — eve'thing we been used to. It's right sad-like."

Jeff did not answer, and presently Jennie buried her face again and cried.

The sun was almost overhead. It beat down furiously on the dusty wagon-path road, on the parched roadside grass and the tiny battered car. Jeff's hands, gripping the wheel, became wet with perspiration; his forehead sparkled. Jeff's lips parted. His mouth shaped a hideous grimace. His face suggested the face of a man being burned. But the torture passed and his expression softened again.

"You mustn't cry, baby," he said to his wife. "We gotta be strong. We can't break down."

Jennie waited a few seconds, then said, "You reckon we oughta do it, Jeff? You reckon we oughta go 'head an' do it, really?"

Jeff's voice choked; his eyes blurred. He was terrified to hear Jennie say the thing that had been in his mind all morning. She had egged him on when he had wanted more than anything in the world to wait, to reconsider, to think things over a little longer. Now she was getting cold feet. Actually there was no need of thinking the question through again. It would only end in making the same painful decision once more. Jeff knew that. There was no need of fooling around longer.

"We jes as well to do like we planned," he said. "They ain't nothin' else for us now — it's the bes' thing."

Jeff thought of the handicaps, the near impossibility, of making another crop with his leg bothering him more and more each week. Then there was always the chance that he would have another stroke, like the one that had made him lame. Another one might kill him. The least it could do would be to leave him helpless. Jeff gasped — Lord, Jesus! He could not bear to think of being helpless, like a baby, on Jennie's hands. Frail, blind Jennie.

The little pounding motor of the car worked harder and harder. The puff of steam from the cracked radiator became larger. Jeff realized that they were climbing a little rise. A moment later the road turned abruptly and he looked down upon the face of the river.

"Jeff."

"Hunh?"

"Is that the water I hear?"

"Hm. Tha's it."

"Well, which way you goin' now?"

"Down this-a way," he said. "The road runs 'long 'side o' the water a lil piece."

She waited a while calmly. Then she said, "Drive faster."

"A'right, baby," Jeff said.

The water roared in the bed of the river. It was fifty or sixty feet below the level of the road. Between the road and the water there was a long smooth slope, sharply inclined. The slope was dry, the clay hardened by prolonged summer heat. The water below, roaring in a narrow channel, was noisy and wild.

"Jeff."

"Hunh?"

"How far you goin'?"

"Jes a lil piece down the road."

"You ain't scairt, is you, Jeff?"

"Nah, baby," he said trembling. "I ain't scairt."

"Remember how we planned it, Jeff. We gotta do it like we said. Brave-like."

"Hm."

Jeff's brain darkened. Things suddenly seemed unreal, like figures in a dream. Thoughts swam in his mind foolishly, hysterically, like little blind fish in a pool within a dense cave. They rushed, crossed one another, jostled, collided, retreated and rushed again. Jeff soon became dizzy. He shuddered violently and turned to his wife.

"Jennie, I can't do it. I can't." His voice broke pitifully.

She did not appear to be listening. All the grief had gone from her face. She sat erect, her unseeing eyes wide open, strained and frightful.

Her glossy black skin had become dull. She seemed as thin, as sharp and bony, as a starved bird. Now, having suffered and endured the sadness of tearing herself away from beloved things, she showed no anguish. She was absorbed with her own thoughts, and she didn't even hear Jeff's voice shouting in her ear.

Jeff said nothing more. For an instant there was light in his cavernous brain. The great chamber was, for less than a second, peopled by characters he knew and loved. They were simple, healthy creatures, and they behaved in a manner that he could understand. They had quality. But since he had already taken leave of them long ago, the remembrance did not break his heart again. Young Jeff Patton was among them, the Jeff Patton of fifty years ago who went down to New Orleans with a crowd of country boys to the Mardi Gras doings. The gay young crowd, boys with candy-striped shirts and rouged-brown girls in noisy silks, was like a picture in his head. Yet it did not make him sad. On that very trip Slim Burns had killed Joe Beasley — the crowd had been broken up. Since then Jeff Patton's world had been the Greenbriar Plantation. If there had been other Mardi Gras carnivals, he had not heard of them. Since then there had been no time; the years had fallen on him like waves. Now he was old, worn out. Another paralytic stroke (like the one he had already suffered) would put him on his back for keeps. In that condition, with a frail blind woman to look after him, he would be worse off than if he were dead.

Suddenly Jeff's hands became steady. He actually felt brave. He slowed down the motor of the car and carefully pulled off the road. Below, the water of the stream boomed, a soft thunder in the deep channel. Jeff ran the car onto the clay slope, pointed it directly toward the stream and put his foot heavily on the accelerator. The little car leaped furiously down the steep incline toward the water. The movement was nearly as swift and direct as a fall. The two old black folks, sitting quietly side by side, showed no excitement. In another instant the car hit the water and dropped immediately out of sight.

A little later it lodged in the mud of a shallow place. One wheel of the crushed and upturned little Ford became visible above the rushing water.

This excerpt from the first novel of a distinguished contemporary poet contains an interesting problem in point of view and kinesthetic imagery as the speaker observes the death of his would-be attacker.

Four suburban businessmen, Lewis, Drew, Bobby, and Ed, the narrator, set out on a three-day canoe trip down a wild section of a river with the hope of doing some hunting with bow and arrow. In the early afternoon of the second day, Bobby and Ed, with Lewis and Drew some distance behind in a second canoe, pull into a secluded area to rest. They are surprised by two men (one with a shotgun) who resent their trespassing. Before they can escape, the two men tie Ed to a tree and force Bobby to submit to sodomy at gunpoint. This excerpt begins there.

Be sure to reflect the effect of what Ed has just seen and his terror as the men approach him.

FROM *Deliverance* / JAMES DICKEY

Then he turned to me, handing the gun off without looking. It stood in the middle of the air at the end of his extended arm. He said to me, "Fall down on your knees and pray, boy. And you better pray good."

I knelt down. As my knees hit, I heard a sound, a snap-slap off in the woods, a sound like a rubber band popping or a sickle-blade cutting quick. The older man was standing with the gun barrel in his hand and no change in the stupid, advantage-taking expression of his face, and a foot and a half of bright red arrow was shoved forward from the middle of his chest. It was there so suddenly it seemed to have come from within him.

None of us understood; we just hung where we were, the tall man in front of me unbuttoning his pants, me on my knees with my eyelids clouding the forest, and Bobby rolling back and forth, off in the leaves in the corner of my eye. The gun fell, and I made a slow-motion grab for it as the tall man sprang like an animal in the same direction. I had it by the stock with both hands, and if I could pull it in to me I would have blown him in half in the next second. But he only gripped the barrel lightly and must have felt that I had it better, and felt also what every part of me was concentrated on doing; he jumped aside and was gone into the woods opposite where the arrow must have come from.

I got up with the gun and the power, wrapping the string around my right hand. I swung the barrel back and forth to cover everything, the woods and the world. There was nothing in the clearing but Bobby and the shot man and me. Bobby was still on the ground, though now he was lifting his head. I could understand that much, but something kept blurring the clear idea of Bobby and myself and the leaves and the river. The shot man was still standing. He wouldn't concentrate in my vision; I couldn't believe him. He was like a film over the scene, gray and vague, with the force gone out of him; I was amazed at how he did everything. He touched the arrow experimentally, and I could tell that it was set in him as solidly as his breastbone. It was in him tight and unwobbling, coming out front and back. He took hold of it with both hands, but compared to the arrow's strength his hands were weak; they weakened more as I looked, and began to melt. He was on his knees, and then fell to his side, pulling his legs up. He rolled back and forth like a man with the wind knocked out of him, all the time making a bubbling, gritting sound. His lips turned red, but from his convulsions — in which there was something comical and unspeakable — he seemed to gain strength. He got up on one knee and then to his feet again while I stood with the shotgun at port arms. He took a couple of strides toward the woods and then seemed to change his mind and danced back to me, lurching and clog-stepping in a secret circle. He held out a hand to me, like a prophet, and I pointed the shotgun straight at the head of the arrow, ice coming into my teeth. I was ready to put it all behind me with one act, with one pull of a string.

But there was no need. He crouched and fell forward with his face on my white tennis shoe tops, trembled away into his legs and shook down to stillness. He opened his mouth and it was full of blood like an apple. A clear bubble formed on his lips and stayed there.

I stepped back and looked at the whole scene again, trying to place things. Bobby was propped up on one elbow, with his eyes as red as the bubble in the dead man's mouth. He got up, looking at me. I realized that I was swinging the gun toward him; that I pointed wherever I looked. I lowered the barrel. What to say?

"Well."

"Lord God," Bobby said. "Lord God."

"You all right?" I asked, since I needed to know even though I cringed with the directness.

Bobby's face expanded its crimson, and he shook his head. "I don't know," he said. "I don't know."

I stood and he lay with his head on his palm, both of us looking straight ahead. Everything was quiet. The man with the aluminum shaft in him lay with his head on one shoulder and his right hand relaxedly holding the barb of the arrow. Behind him the blue and silver of Lewis' fancy arrow crest shone, unnatural in the woods.

Nothing happened for ten minutes. I wondered if maybe the other man wouldn't come back before Lewis showed himself, and I began to compose a scene in which Lewis would step out of the woods on one side of the clearing with his bow and the tall man would show on the other, and they would have it out in some way that it was hard to imagine. I was working on the details when I heard something move. Part of the bark of a big water oak moved at leg level, and Lewis moved with it out into the open, stepping sideways into the clearing with another bright-crested arrow on the string of his bow. Drew followed him, holding a canoe paddle like a baseball bat.

Lewis walked out between me and Bobby, over the man on the ground, and put his bow tip on a leaf. Drew moved to Bobby. I had been holding the gun ready for so long that it felt strange to lower the barrels so that they were pointing down and could kill nothing but the ground. I did, though, and Lewis and I faced each other across the dead man. His eyes were vivid and alive; he was smiling easily and with great friendliness.

"Well now, how about this? Just . . . how *about* this?"

I went over to Bobby and Drew, though I had no notion of what to do when I got there. I had watched everything that had happened to Bobby, had heard him scream and squall, and wanted to reassure him that we could set all that aside; that it would be forgotten as soon as we left the woods, or as soon as we got back in the canoes. But there was no way to say this, or to ask him how his lower intestine felt or whether he thought he was bleeding internally. Any examination of him would be unthinkably ridiculous and humiliating.

There was no question of that, though; he was furiously closed off from all of us. He stood up and backed away, still naked from the middle down, his sexual organs wasted with pain. I picked up his pants and shorts and handed them to him, and he reached for them in wonderment. He took out a handkerchief and went behind some bushes.

Still holding the gun at trail, as the tall man had been doing when I first saw him step out of the woods, I went back to Lewis, who was leaning on his bow and gazing out over the river.

Without looking at me, he said, "I figured it was the only thing to do."

Bibliography

Bentley, Phyllis. *Some Observations on the Art of Narrative.* New York: The Macmillan Company, 1947.

Extensive treatment of summary, description, and scene. A standard reference work for analysis of narratives.

Booth, Wayne. *The Rhetoric of Fiction.* Chicago: The University of Chicago Press, 1961.

One of the classics in the criticism of prose fiction.

Brooks, Cleanth, and Robert Penn Warren. *Understanding Fiction.* New York: F. S. Crofts and Company, 1943.

Clear and usable approach to the analysis of fiction with an anthology of relevant stories.

Brown, E. K. *Rhythm in the Novel.* Toronto: University of Toronto Press, 1963.

A modern expansion of E. M. Forster's method of analysis.

Edel, Leon. *The Psychological Novel, 1900–1950.* Philadelphia: J. B. Lippincott Company, 1955.

Discussion of the psychological theories as they relate to the writer and the reader of modern fiction.

Isaacs, Neil D., and Louis Leiter (eds.). *Approaches to the Short Story.* San Francisco: Chandler Publishing Company, 1963.

A varied collection of short stories with critical comments on the thesis that the short story is a work of literary art.

James, Henry. *The Art of Fiction.* New York: Oxford University Press, 1948.

A classic work by an author who was himself a master in the field of fiction.

Mizener, Arthur. *The Sense of Life in the Modern Novel.* Boston: Houghton Mifflin Company, 1964.

An important study whose purpose is "to examine one aspect of the novel . . . the relation of the represented life to 'nature,' and the effects this relation has on the novel's expression of values." Novels by Trollope, Hardy, Cozzens, Faulkner, Fitzgerald, Hemingway, Salinger, Updike, and Tate are discussed.

Moffett, James and Kenneth R. McElheney. *Points of View: An Anthology of Short Stories.* New York: The New American Library, 1966.

Anthology arranged according to variations in point of view. A brief introduction precedes each of the eleven classifications.

Scholes, Robert. *Approaches to the Novel.* San Francisco: Chandler Publishing Company, 1961.

A collection of essays on the novel grouped under appropriate headings such as "Mimesis," "Plot," "Narrative Structure," etc.

Thompson, David W., and Virginia Fredricks. *Oral Interpretation of Fiction: A Dramatistic Approach.* Minneapolis: Burgess Publishing Company, 1964.

A brief text stressing a "dramatistic" approach to oral interpretation, based on the theory that "the total symbolic action in literature and in the reader's oral interpretation of it can be discovered only from exploring all the interacting relationships of Scene-Role-Gesture."

The Interpretation
of Drama

Part Three

Chapter 8

Many of the characteristics of narration are also common to drama. As a matter of fact, the elements of plot, character, and setting are as basic to one as to the other. Consequently, much of the discussion of narration in the previous chapter is equally applicable here. The chief difference for the interpreter lies in the form in which these three elements are presented. There are numerous highly literary definitions of "drama," but for the purposes of this chapter, attention will be focused on that type of writing which takes the form of a play.

Much stress has been laid, in previous chapters, on fidelity to the author's purpose. How, then, can one justify the use of drama for interpretation, since the material was obviously written to be presented on a stage with scenery, costumes, make-up, lights, and a number of actors? The justification rests on the interpreter's ability to suggest the visual aspects of a play so completely that the listeners will re-create the necessary details in their minds as he reads. A trained interpreter can accomplish this difficult feat so perfectly that the audience has the sense of knowing how the characters look and mentally seeing them move about in a clearly imagined setting.

Interpreting drama requires a particularly strong emphasis on technique, which, as always, must serve the literature and be so carefully and skillfully developed that it is completely unobtrusive in performance. Because of the form of the material, depending as it does on what the characters say and do, with no comment from the author to explain motivations and emotional responses, the interpreter must give particular attention to

The Interpreter's Approach to Drama

clear, unmistakable characterization. The audience must know immediately who is speaking, what prompted the speech, and to whom it is addressed. The interpreter cannot rely on a narrative device such as ". . . she said gently," or ". . . she said impatiently." He is on his own, with only the stage directions, his complete understanding of the material, and his body and voice to help him re-create *in the minds of his listeners* what actors, technicians, and director achieve in a dramatic performance.

Acting and Interpretation

The actor and the interpreter have many things in common, but they also have some basic differences. The printed page, as a medium for conveying the author's thought, is the point at which both interpreter and actor begin the process of re-creation. Both the actor and the oral interpreter of drama must study the characters and come to understand what kind of person each one is, how he thinks and feels, what motives drive him. Both must be aware of a character's language, speech rhythms, and choice of words, as all these things reflect personality and emotional state. Both must analyze the entire play carefully so that they will use their vocal and physical techniques to project the appropriate characterization to the audience. Thus the actor and the interpreter of drama have many responsibilities in common.

The actor completely memorizes his material and asks his audience to believe that he is actually the person to whom the events are happening. He normally portrays only one character and is aided in his portrayal by the other members of the cast, scenery, costumes, make-up, and properties. His scene is *on stage* and exists around him. He moves about the stage; he sits down; he enters and exits through doors that open and close; and in general, he strives for physically complete and explicit characterization. Theoretically, in a traditional play, he has no direct contact with the audience, for his circle of concentration is limited to the acting area. He is, of course, conscious of his audience to the degree that he senses their response, waits for laughs, and takes care to project so that his voice can be heard in the last row of the balcony. The audience, however, must not be aware that he is conscious of their presence; they should feel that a fourth wall has been removed from an actual location and that they are observing the events on that location without being observed.

The interpreter, on the other hand, does not necessarily memorize lines, and he places his scene *out front*. His area of concentration goes out from himself to include the entire audience. He focuses his speeches out front and receives his motivations, in terms of others' speeches and actions, from out front. He creates a scene in the minds of his audience, and through suggestion creates characters which move about that scene. He asks his audience to accept him as an instrument through which all the characters, their actions, their physical, mental, and vocal characteristics, and their relationships are *suggested*, not represented. Through his skill in suggestion, the audience re-creates mentally the action, scenery, costumes, make-up, and properties.

The interpreter, like the actor, is responsible for complete mental and emotional characterization. His presentation, however, must of necessity be less physically explicit. In the first place, he is not limiting himself to a single character. He may suggest a dozen or more during the course of a play. And he cannot change costumes and make-up for each line of dialogue. Moreover, he does not have doors to open and close; and if he did, he could not very convincingly take himself offstage as one character and then come bounding back, in the person of another character, to talk about himself after he had gone. After one or two such exhibitions, any audience would be reduced to a state of total confusion or uncontrollable laughter.

One of the most important problems for the interpreter of drama is audience contact. His circle of concentration is not limited to the reading stand, but must be wide enough to include all his listeners, although his direct eye contact is with the visualized character he is addressing. Some ways of communicating to the audience without losing the immediacy required in dialogue were mentioned briefly in direct discourse (Chapter 7) and will be given more attention in the next chapter. The important point here is that the interpreter's contact with his audience is conscious and constant, whereas the actor's is theoretically nonexistent.

It must now be apparent that the question which students often ask, "How far can you go in interpreting drama before it becomes acting?" is in reality putting the cart before the horse. Interpretation does not "come before" acting. Acting does not "go farther" than interpretation of drama. Both arts follow the same path in preparation. The actor and the interpreter of drama follow the same procedure of analysis and rehearsal, except that the interpreter must analyze all the characters and rehearse each one in turn until he has complete control of all of them, whereas an actor need concentrate on only one. The actor then puts himself physically and visibly into the scenery, costumes, and make-up, and begins to blend his performance with that of the other actors and with the concept of the entire production. His scene is around him. The interpreter, on the other hand, goes on to those details which will enable him to present a three-dimensional character, and incorporates into his muscle responses and vocal qualities whatever is important for *suggesting* character and action. His scene and characters are in the minds of his audience.

Thus the actor and the interpreter of drama differ primarily in degree of emphasis on certain techniques. In performance, the actor strives for the utmost physical explicitness, while the interpreter relies on suggestion.

Somewhere between acting and the oral interpretation of drama falls the art of impersonation, or monodrama. In this form of presentation, one person focuses attention on a single character in a single situation. He will probably use a minimum of properties, such as a chair or a table. He may suggest costume by a hat or a pair of gloves or some such article which will facilitate his business. This business will be limited, but he will be almost as explicit as the actor in handling properties and establishing entrances and exits. His circle of concentration, like the actor's, is limited to the area established by the set he has created, and his contact with the audience is secondary. The audience is allowed to overhear the scene. This differs from a soliloquy, in which a single actor in a play delivers a speech alone on the stage, for in a soliloquy a character thinks aloud, talks to himself, whereas a monologue or monodrama assumes the presence of other characters, who move in and out of the scene and motivate changes in the speaker's thoughts and actions. The minor characters are not, of course, seen by the audience, but the mono-actor must be aware of their presence and react to them.

In summary, then, an actor usually portrays only one character and is vocally and physically explicit in that portrayal, aided by make-up, costumes, scenery, and the presence of other actors. The mono-actor also concentrates on only one character, selects and uses appropriate properties, costumes, make-up, and scenery, and creates the other actors in imagination, while keeping the focus of attention constantly on the single character that is visible to the audience. The interpreter, on the other hand, presents many characters by suggesting them, basing his suggestion on complete understanding of the material and an intelligent selection of physical and vocal characteristics. He is the instrument through which the printed page comes alive and the means of re-creating in the mind of his audience the details which are physically present in a dramatic production.

It might be well to point out that although these three areas — acting, monoacting, and interpreting drama — are mutually related, each is a distinct art in itself. No one is "higher" than the others. The versatile artist will be able to handle all three. His decision as to which he wishes to use in approaching drama will be governed by practical considerations (such as the availability of other actors and the availability and physical equipment of a theater) and by his own interests and inclinations. But having decided which of these three dramatic arts he wishes to practice, he must be true to its principles.

Our concern here, obviously, is with interpretation. The basic principles of the interpretation of drama are the same as those of interpreting any other type of literature. The variations come in the degree and the mechanics of technique, always judged in terms of the vital word *suggestion*. The first step is to decide what elements are to be suggested; the second, to determine how these elements may best be handled by a voice and body governed by an alert, informed, and disciplined mind.

Structural Considerations

The interpreter who wishes to present a play will of course be guided by his standards of literary worth and by the interests of his audience in choosing one of the countless dramas available to him. After making his final choice, he must then undertake careful, objective analysis to discover all the aspects of content and form which make up the whole. His procedure in studying the content and organization of a play parallels, to some extent, the one he used with narrative prose. He follows the thread of the action and accepts the unifying principles of time, place, and character as the writer has established them.

Plays are organized on the principles of unity and probability, and their basic ingredient is conflict. The ways in which conflict is presented, developed, and resolved vary widely. In general, however, the opening scenes are devoted to exposition through action and dialogue. Following the clarification of the preliminary situation comes the challenge which introduces the inciting or exciting force. There may be several such units as the play develops. The primary challenge may already have been touched on in the exposition and be reintroduced and intensified by developing action or relationship so that it becomes more acute. This will usually be followed by moves and countermoves between the two characters most involved, thus producing a tightening of conflict and what is often termed the rising action. The rising action comes to a point of decision in the crisis. The *crisis* is the moment of recognition and limitation which directs the action to its final outcome. The crisis brings about the *climax*, the point of highest culmination of all the elements of conflict. This is followed by the dénouement or resolution, or, in tragedy, the inevitable catastrophe. Thus a play has an overall pattern of rhythm of content growing out of emotional builds, pace of action, and intensity of conflict.

The rhythm of a play is extremely interesting and somewhat complex. In the first place, at the stylistic level there is the individual speech rhythm of each character. Second, in terms of both content and form, there are the important fluctuations in emotional tension. Third, there is the inevitable alternation of "action" scenes and "static" scenes. This alternation is comparable to the rhythm of activity and passivity in other forms of writing, though, of course, no part of a good play is ever really passive inasmuch as a play depends on action for its development. Some scenes or portions of scenes may consist primarily of exposition and fulfill much the same function as transitional units in narrative writing. They may clarify cause and effect, present necessary relationships, allow the playwright to plead his case through one of his characters, or provide needed relaxation or suspense in preparation for a climax. This alternation between the active and the passive elements will affect the tempo at which the various scenes and speeches move, and the speed with which they build toward minor climaxes and finally toward the main climax, whether in terms of action, character development, or both. In a well-written modern play, these transitional "static" scenes are used sparingly and present nothing which does not bear on the ultimate outcome of the action. The playwright's arrangement of these scenes will probably be governed by the same principles influencing the writer of narrative prose; that is, he has to consider how much the audience must know about background and where added background material can be most effectively inserted. He also takes into account the need for relaxation from tension and intense activity.

The preceding discussion and much that follows is aimed at presenting a cutting of an entire play. Clearly, the average classroom situation will not permit a performance of this length, but the popularity of play cuttings for club audiences makes such a discussion valid. If the interpreter chooses only a single scene or a portion of a scene from a full-length play for his performance, he will be governed by principles of cutting and condensation similar to those suggested for the novel in Chapter 7. Although the time spent in preparation will be in proportion to the length of the selection, the general plan of working for complete understanding is basic, since it is impossible to do justice to a scene without knowing how it fits into the entire play.

Plot

In using drama, the interpreter's most important task, though probably not his most difficult one, is to keep the events which make up the plot in clear focus and in consecutive order, following whatever progression of time, place, and action the author has adopted. In narrative, it will be remembered, the action and the author's comments on background material are often woven together. In a play, the plot never begins until the curtain has gone up, because it depends on the speeches of the characters and their actions. Whereas the writer of narrative may devote several paragraphs to the introductory units of the story in careful preparation for his plot, a playwright cannot truly take up his job until the action begins. Consequently, the introductory units in a play or in a single scene, as they are presented by an interpreter to his audience, must be swifter and more sharply focused than is necessary in a narrative. They must be checked carefully for key speeches. The same is true of the conclusion. A writer of narrative may step in and explain how it all came out — that "they lived happily ever after." A playwright cannot take this direct approach, unless he is willing to have one of his characters speak an epilogue, as Tom does in Tennessee Williams' *The Glass Menagerie*.

Again, the main climax will be preceded by minor climaxes, just as in narrative. Early in his preparation the interpreter will become conscious of the focal points of meaning and emotion, and of the units forming the lead-in and conclusion to each. In drama, these focal points may consist of only single speeches or perhaps seemingly unimportant actions which nevertheless become steppingstones to the next unit of development or a means of resolving a much later episode. In narrative, the writer can, and often does, prepare the reader for the climaxes by his own comments or by detailed description. In drama, the writer must depend on his characters — their dialogue, which reflects their mental comment, and their actions, which are motivated by their complex responses. Consequently, the interpreter must keep in mind every signpost along the way and judge its importance in the light of the final outcome.

In analyzing a play for interpretation, it is necessary to be aware of two kinds of action. The first, which may be termed *practical business*, is intended primarily as guidance for a director when the play is presented on the stage. It is the action which moves a character from one area to another in order to free the first area for an entrance or to make a pictorially effective grouping for a climactic moment, or places a property where it will be needed for a later scene. The interpreter is not usually concerned with this sort of action, since he does not have to worry about getting the characters together or out of one another's way. Sometimes, however, such a piece of business will give him valuable clues to the degree of tension or focus of attention which he can and should incorporate into his empathic responses.

The second type of action, which we shall call *character business*, is used primarily to reveal mental attitude or emotional response. For instance, a playwright may indicate that a character is to pace nervously about the stage throughout the greater part of a scene. Obviously, in performance the interpreter will not pace about as one character, then stop in his tracks to reply to himself, then start pacing again. This explicit action would be both distracting and ridiculous; it would shatter the play his listeners are re-creating in their own minds. Certainly he need not stand glued to one spot. He may move about whenever such action helps project the scene, but he must be careful that his movement does not call attention to *him* rather than to the character and that he keeps his scene out front.

Moreover, much specific character business is completely unnecessary in performance, since by vocal quality, tempo, muscle tone, and mental comment as he reads the speeches of that character, the interpreter can suggest the nervous tension visually conveyed by the physical act of pacing. Usually he will not even need to tell his audience that the character is pacing about but will let his voice and body alone suggest the mental tension. In an important bit of action, however — something that motivates a climactic scene — it is usually safer and simpler to tell the audience directly, and as briefly as possible, that the business is taking place. Frequently, reading a printed stage direction to the audience in the interpreter's own person will be enough, *if* the growing mood and empathy are not broken.

Transitional scenes, or "static" scenes, must be kept in their proper relation to the whole so that they serve the intended purpose and no more. When the interpreter is cutting a long play, he might do well to include at least a few of them, since they contribute to the rhythm and allow the audience to relax before and after the more active scenes. Again, he may often summarize them in his own words and give them directly to the audience in his capacity as narrator. When he chooses the latter course, he should be careful to preserve the mood of the scene by keeping the style and choice of words close to the spirit of the original scenes. The summary must be truly transitional, both logically and emotionally, in order to prepare the listeners for whatever changes of place, time, train of thought, and emotional tone they will encounter in the scene to follow. A transition should bring the scene just read to a satisfying conclusion and "bridge into" the following one.

Character

After thoroughly examining the play as a whole and its individual scenes, it is time to consider character. Numerous ways of arriving at complete understanding of character are open to the interpreter, and he must find the one which best suits him. No matter what method he uses, however, he must investigate certain important factors, incorporate them into the presentation, and suggest them by body and voice, reflecting mental comment and attitude. The following method has proved useful and is offered as a suggestion until the interpreter feels able to establish his own.

The first steps in analyzing character must always be taken in terms of the entire play. This, of course, goes back directly to understanding logical content and the principles of organization. In short, what does each character say, in what circumstances does he say it, and how does what he says further the development of the plot?

After the relationship of the characters to the plot progression has been clearly established, it will be helpful to consider the relationship of characters to setting. Here again one starts with the play as a whole. The playwright had a definite purpose in placing his action in a particular setting. How does this locale affect the characters portrayed against it? Different people respond in different ways to the same environment, and a character's acceptance or rejection of the social standards and convictions of his milieu may be the motivating factor in the action and in the ultimate outcome of the plot. This is certainly important in *A Raisin in the Sun* (pages 307–312). A knowledge of the period and customs is often necessary to understand and appreciate a character — the old nurse in *Romeo and Juliet* (pages 346–347), for example, and indeed Juliet herself. Clothes affect manner and movement; hence some knowledge and awareness of period costume will help the interpreter in physically suggesting character and pacing some of the scenes.

Next comes the problem of the relationships among the characters. We shall delay for a moment the all-important psychological relationships and consider first simply how the characters compare, contrast, and balance in point of sex, maturity, and cultural background. These three elements contribute to the variety and contrast of the play as a whole and also help establish the prevailing emotional tone.

After the characters have been carefully considered in terms of the entire play and their relationships to each other, the interpreter begins his more detailed analysis. From his study of the play he should already have determined the important characters, especially the key character around whom the incidents revolve. He next evaluates the others by classifying them as those who are directly concerned in the plot, those who implement it, and those who can be eliminated in his cutting without interrupting the series of events. This last consideration is important, since it is not often practicable for the interpreter to do an unabridged performance of a full-length play. Before any characters are eliminated by cutting, however, an objective analysis should be made of the purpose of each in terms of the whole. This holds equally true for a single scene to be presented as a unit in itself. Frequently, of course, a character who might be important in the outcome of the plot can be eliminated from an isolated scene.

The next step is to focus attention on one character at a time in much the same way a cameraman brings his lens from a group picture to a close-up. Starting with the person around whom the plot — or the chosen scene — revolves, the interpreter applies to the speeches of that character the now-familiar process of understanding logical content, giving careful attention to the climaxes and focal points, style and rhythm, and the denotations and connotations of all the words. When he has the content of the speeches clear in his mind, he will be ready to study the character's exterior and interior traits.

Exterior or outward traits are the physical aspects immediately apparent to an observer, as: "young man, about twenty-three, blond, tall, rather frail physique, holds one shoulder higher than the other, moves with nervous, jerky motions." These traits include the character's sex, age, and any outstanding physical characteristics or mannerisms. In a play they are revealed by whatever stage directions the playwright has inserted, by what the character does, and by what others say about him. Obviously these physical characteristics provide only a skeleton of the character, but they must be examined to discover what they reflect of his inner qualities and how they affect his responses to his environment and to other characters. Moreover, they will help the interpreter suggest the character in performance, just as they guide the actor and director in representation when the play is staged.

Interior, psychological aspects of character are much more complex. They are sometimes touched on in the stage directions, especially of the more elaborate, analytical type, but they are more completely revealed by what the character does and says, how he says it, and by what other characters say about him. They include his point of view; his attitude toward himself, toward others, and toward his surroundings; his emotional stability; his habitual degree of tension; his reponses, both mental and emotional; and any variation from a "normal" set of values.

The writer of narrative can insert several paragraphs to tell about previous events and persons which have helped make his characters what they are. A playwright cannot allow himself this luxury unless he wishes to use a flashback technique. More frequently he must be content with drawing his characters so completely in dialogue and action that there can be no doubt about their earlier environment. The interpreter, in order to achieve this same completeness of characterization, must often go back and reconstruct much of the action which precedes the play proper. Sophocles does this for us in *Oedipus* (pages 293–297), but the flashback information must be kept in mind from the very beginning of Oedipus' speech to the Thebans. It accounts for his position and their respect for his wisdom. Davies gives us bits and scraps of highly prejudiced information about himself throughout *The Caretaker* (pages 287–292), but gradually we become aware that his speech and his standards betray a grasping self-centeredness rather than the cultural background he is trying so hard to wish onto his past. This becomes important as the play progresses. We must not allow our sympathy for his age and condition to blind us to his essential crudity and ruthlessness, or we will find ourselves as much victims of his pressure as the two brothers.

The interpreter of drama must follow much the same method of characterization as a conscientious actor. He will need to know how his character looked, lived, thought, and behaved long before the play or scene itself takes place. The playwright does not always give this complete information, and the interpreter may need to depend on his knowledge of human nature to supply him with the omitted details. He must develop an ability to observe life about him and then to go behind the exterior manifestations to discover motivations. He is dealing with human actions and reactions, and the more he knows of his fellow creatures the more easily he can understand and communicate to his audience the complexities of characters in a play.

Having filled in the physical, mental, and emotional background, the interpreter is ready to begin his study of each character as he is involved in the incidents of the play. What stage of development has the character reached by the time he makes his first entrance? What has he been doing immediately before his entrance? Has he been dozing in the garden, or attending a football game? Is he happy or depressed as the result of this activity? Does he expect to find the situation as it exists on stage and is he thus prepared to become a part of it immediately, or is he unprepared for the events which have taken place during his absence?

In the scene from *She Stoops to Conquer* (pages 357–360), for example, Kate is perfectly prepared for Marlow's behavior and thoroughly enjoys teasing him while playing her self-assigned role. Marlow has not had time to organize his thoughts or overcome his natural shyness with "ladies." Moreover, Kate is at home in her own house while Marlow thinks he is at a public inn. In the excerpt from *Oedipus* (pages 293–297), it is important to remember that Oedipus has sent for Teiresias, the blind prophet, and has been waiting for him with the citizens of Thebes, including a company of elders. It is a public, official occasion. Prior relationship is particularly vital in the scene from *Faust* (pages 305–307), as well. Obviously the Lord and Mephistopheles have met before! Each knows the other's position, power, and attitude toward mankind. Mephistopheles knows why he has been summoned and the Lord has a specific plan he wishes undertaken.

Because interrelationships play a vital part in character development, it is impractical to take a single character through an entire play while disregarding the others involved in the various scenes. Therefore, it might be well to follow the above procedure only to the end of the first key scene, and then go back to repeat it with the next most important character in that scene, evaluating his relation to the leading character and trying to discern what forces have shaped him over the years before the play begins and what attitude toward the main character he has already developed. The interpreter should note carefully how this attitude is revealed and whether or not it changes during the scene. Beginning interpreters often become so enamored of a favorite character in a play or scene that the rest of the characters never emerge at all. It is important to continue careful analysis of each character, studying each as an individual and evaluating his relationship to every other individual, so that in performance each segment will fit into the overall pattern and both plot and character development will reach their intended destinations.

After the interpreter has the first key scene firmly established in his mind and has considered all its aspects of content and form, he returns again to his main character and goes to the next key scene, repeating the process he used in analyzing the first one. This time he watches for any changes in the playwright's focus of attention, in the development of the separate characters, and in their relation to each other and to the setting; and in so doing he becomes aware, also, of the increase or decrease in emotional tension and in activity. As new characters are introduced, he catches them up, too, in his analysis and evaluation. Finally, after going through the entire play in this manner, focusing attention on the key scenes — those necessary to the development of the plot — first in terms of the most important character and then of the lesser characters, the interpreter turns his attention to the transitional scenes and analyzes them in the same way for character relationship and development.

The style of the dialogue often helps in character analysis. The language a character uses indicates a great deal about his background and his attitude, just as it does in narrative prose. This is a most important clue to character in *The Caretaker*, where each of the three men has not only highly individual rhythm of thought and dialogue but also widely varied word choice and syntax. The arrangement of ideas gives a clue to clarity of thinking and is likely to reflect intensity of emotion. The length of the thought units may also reveal much about a character's personality, forcefulness, and authority, as well as his degree of tension. This is an interesting aspect in *Rosencrantz and Guildenstern Are Dead* (pages 348–357). Through awareness of the harmony between content and style, the interpreter can establish an appropriate tempo and overall rhythm which will enable him to communicate a character's traits through his speeches. The language must always be considered in terms of the period in which the play was written, yet the well-written play of any time will convey strong indications of character through the length of the thought groups and the rhythms and stresses within the units.

Style is an interesting consideration in an "antidrama" like Ionesco's *Rhinoceros* (pages 361–367), where the language is deliberately reduced to its lowest level of suggestion to help achieve the dehumanization of the characters. As a matter of fact, many contemporary plays present interesting problems for the interpreter. Most of the so-called "absurd" plays have as their basic concept man's inability to communicate with his fellow man and even to put into words the frustrations and fears in his own mind. Thus, motivation and character interaction must be examined in quite a different fashion than in the traditional play. The motivation for both speech and action is often confined within the character's own mind and is formed by his sense of isolation from the world or the resultant acceptance of the belief that man, the world, life, love, and death are equally "absurd." The dialogue often takes the form of extremely long near-monologues or soliloquies. These are difficult to sustain, partly because they are subjectively motivated but also because they are highly repetitious, one of the devices for anticlimax in the structure of these plays. Likewise, the action is often either violent and almost stylized or statically impotent, and the shifts of muscle tone are swift and sharp. Very thorough analysis is necessary to make such scenes credible and dramatic.

Setting and Properties

The matter of setting is much simpler for the dramatist than for the writer of narrative prose, for the dramatist can put the necessary information into the stage directions which precede each scene. These notations of time and place are included on the printed program when the play is given on stage and are emphasized through the skill of the scene designer, costumer, and lighting expert. Playwrights differ in the number of details they give about period and locale. Shakespeare's plays, for example, frequently give no more indication of setting than "A public place" or "A room in ————'s house." Many contemporary playwrights, however, are more explicit in their directions and may include as many as a thousand words on setting and atmosphere. George Bernard Shaw was one of the most voluble, but even he was limited by the form in which he had chosen to work.

The author of a narrative has time and opportunity to dwell on the associational values he wishes to emphasize, and he gives the interpreter numerous clues to his intention by using various types of imagery. A playwright, on the other hand, relies heavily on visual appeal in his stage directions. He is primarily concerned with the scene as the audience is to see it, and he allows the characters to reveal their more complex reactions to it as the dialogue progresses. This formula is necessary for the practical reason that the audience does not see the complete set of stage directions. They are intended for the actors and technicians involved in staging the play.

How, then, does the interpreter of drama handle this background material and make it clear to his listeners? Obviously, since he does not have the help of technicians who design scenery and control lighting effects, and of actors who use stage properties and react to the setting, he must be, in a sense, actor, technician, and director, as well as narrator. In the role of narrator, he can easily and legitimately give most of the necessary stage directions directly to his audience before the curtain goes up on the action, as it were. The condensation and careful selection of detail that characterize most stage directions require him to make the most of his brief opportunity to create the scene. He therefore must emphasize important aspects of the time and place so that they etch themselves into the minds of the listeners, and he must give his listeners time to set up their own associational values. These values will result in part from the relationship of the setting to the social position, taste, and financial situation of the characters who are placed in it. Whenever a playwright has included abundant notes on production in his preliminary directions, the interpreter must decide which elements need to be presented directly to the audience and which ones can be handled by skillful suggestion of character as the play progresses.

In George Bernard Shaw's *Candida*, for example, nearly a thousand words of stage directions precede the rise of the curtain on Act I. Some of this information is of immediate interest to the audience, but a great deal of it is aimed primarily at establishing the background out of which the characters have come and against which they develop and can be revealed through the interpreter's mental comment as he handles the dialogue. Consequently, in giving the stage directions, the interpreter would do well to omit much of the detailed information and use it instead for his own guidance in showing plot motivation and character development. Since the scene cannot be presented visually to the listening audience, the interpreter, by selecting only the important details, can enable his listeners to focus on essential background information. On the other hand, the audience will need the description of the lion in the prologue from Shaw's *Androcles and the Lion* (pages 368–372), although the specific description of Androcles might well be omitted except for the last sentence.

The time or period in which a play is laid is of extreme importance when social customs and economic conditions play a vital part in making the plot credible. This is true of *Romeo and Juliet*, as mentioned. The love story is universal to all times and places; but the family enmity is emphasized by the period, and the duels, the famous potion scene, and the entombment of Juliet could hardly happen in modern times.

Occasionally, a playwright will allow much of the information about the setting to come from someone who speaks directly to the audience as a narrator. In Thornton Wilder's *Our Town*, for example, a "Stage Manager" explains the general location and atmosphere, sets each new scene, introduces the characters, establishes the time progression, and finally brings the play to its conclusion with:

> ... Mm ... Eleven o'clock in Grover's Corners. — You get a good rest, too. Good night.

Such devices as these simplify the interpreter's job because neither the "Stage Manager" nor the "Chorus" in a classic Greek play actually becomes a part of the play as a character caught up in the action, but is used only as a link between audience and actors. Hence the interpreter can assume the same relation to the audience and deliver the speeches directly to his listeners as narrator, suggesting only enough character to make the narrator fit into the spirit of the play while conveying the desired philosophical quality.

Another aspect of setting in drama which the interpreter must not overlook, either in preparation or performance, is the effect of the setting on the characters. The writer of narrative can and often does remind his readers, and consequently the interpreter and his audience, of the physical aspects and psychological impact of the surroundings. The playwright, on the other hand, does not ordinarily intrude after his play has begun but, rather, counts on the physical setting to keep itself and its effect on the characters in the consciousness of the audience. The interpreter, then, must see to it that he is as constantly aware of the surroundings he is attempting to suggest as the actor is of the set against which he plays. Suppose, for example, the character or characters are portrayed against an overcrowded room, elaborate with knickknacks, heavy draperies, and much furniture. It might well be that this atmosphere would produce a feeling of psychic suffocation in one character and a feeling of security in others. This will affect the mental attitude of each of them as well as their kinetic and kinesthetic responses. In *Romeo and Juliet*, for example, the lovers are affected by the gaiety and size of the ballroom; by the night, the distance between them, and the attendant details of setting in the balcony scene; by the intimacy and privacy of the bedchamber; and finally by the suffocating enclosure of the tomb.

Not only must the interpreter be aware of the area and specific location of the various scenes, he must also exercise some care in using the setting for whatever purpose it was intended — whether for realism, establishing a mood, motivating significant action, or all three. The more skillful the playwright, the more important this consideration is likely to be. The interpreter must remember that a play does not happen in a vacuum; although he does not have the actual scenery around him, he must nevertheless be constantly aware of its effect on the characters he is portraying. To be successful in creating the setting in the minds of others, he must first create it for himself. The playwright intended it to be a part of the whole, and the degree of emphasis placed on it is dictated by that intention.

Properties and various details of stage dressing may also play an important part in the action; the bed in *The Caretaker*, for example, takes on more than normal importance in Davies' mind and becomes a symbol of his aggressive grasping. In Ibsen's *Hedda Gabler*, with which you are probably familiar, the stove, included as a seemingly decorative detail in the description of Tesman's drawing room, assumes considerable importance when Hedda uses it to dispose of Lövborg's manuscript. If the interpreter has not mentioned the stove to his audience and thus enabled them to accept and visualize it as a part of the setting, it will be thrust too suddenly and confusingly into their consciousness in the manuscript-burning scene. The manuscript itself, first introduced when Lövborg takes it from his pocket and shows it to Hedda, is sufficiently pointed by the dialogue and will require no added emphasis. The next time the packet of papers is introduced as a property, the dialogue makes it clear that Tesman has brought it in, having found it and deliberately kept it from its owner. A stage direction says that Hedda places it, quite logically, in the bookcase. This action must be pointed slightly because it explains how she can fail to produce the manuscript when Lövborg returns and yet have it at hand to destroy immediately after his exit. Another property not emphasized when first introduced but increasingly significant as the play progresses is the pistol case. Hedda gives one of the pistols it contains to Lövborg for his suicide in the fourth act; and partly because it has been recognized by Judge Brack, she uses the other for her own self-destruction in the last act. In the theatre of the absurd, properties and settings underscore the mood of starkness and distortion. Therefore, the interpreter will want to describe them for his audience, though he will rarely "use" them in any practical sense.

The interpreter, then, must evaluate the details of setting and properties for their importance to plot and character motivation, as well as for their contribution to the visual aspects of time and place. Since he takes his cue from the playwright's objectivity, he will probably exhibit little or no muscular tension when he is giving stage directions, but will depend on tempo, pause, force, stress, and inflection to give the appropriate degree of pointing to the significant details. When, however, he is suggesting background — or its effect on the characters — through dialogue, he will make full use of muscle tone as well as voice to insure an empathic response from his audience.

Character Suggestion and Muscle Memory

The interpreter's primary concern is with what goes on *inside* the characters as they operate in relation to each other and to the events which take place. Nevertheless, as we have already seen, interior characteristics and responses are reflected in certain discernible exterior traits.

It is sometimes helpful to go through the entire cutting to be used and develop technique for one character at a time, concentrating wholly on his speeches and actions just as if one were going to act that part — and only that part — on the stage. In making this type of study, the interpreter uses the other characters merely as linefeeders until such time as he feels that the main character is clearly and lastingly instilled in his mind, muscles, and voice. Then, one by one, he allows the other characters to emerge with their individualities, progressions, and interrelationships. The interpreter will probably find it helpful to "walk" the main character, and the others in their turn — to rehearse relevant business exactly as if he were going to do it with properties and scenery. All this is an invaluable aid to timing, pace, and muscle tension, as well as to the motivation of changes in thought, his means for suggesting the character to his audience. Since this suggested procedure is time-consuming, the student should select for his classroom assignment a brief scene with relatively few characters, so that he may prepare thoroughly. After his habits of preparation are set, the process becomes less demanding because he knows what he is looking for and where to find it. Drama is built on complexity, and the interpreter who wishes to handle this type of material must be willing to discover the intricate shadings of the characters and their relationships to every other aspect of the play, and to use his technique to make those shadings clear to his audience.

After the characters are "set," the next step is vocal and physical selectivity. It is here that the paths of actor and interpreter of drama separate. The interpreter, like the actor, has created an explicit character with individual mental, emotional, physical, and vocal traits. He now decides which vocal elements — such as tempo, rhythm, inflection, range, and quality — will most accurately and swiftly suggest each character to the audience for whom he is preparing his performance. Abandoning the explicit, descriptive, overt actions he has been using, he depends primarily on posture, muscle tone, and kinesthetic response to suggest physical characteristics whenever they aid communication.

The time spent in rehearsing the actual business is by no means lost, however, because his *memory* of it will add to the vitality, pace, and general effectiveness of his performance. This principle of muscle memory is sometimes referred to as the theory of remembered action. Muscle memory affects the reader's empathy and allows him to suggest hurry or leisure, activity or passivity, tension or relaxation as the scenes progress, thus enabling him to build his climaxes more effectively.

To test the effectiveness of this theory of muscle memory, read the following scene aloud, ignoring the stage directions for the moment. Of course, it is necessary to consider this scene in the context of the entire play before complete character development will emerge. Nevertheless this excerpt as it stands will serve our purpose as an illustration.

BRACK: No. But you will have to answer the question: Why did you give Eilert Lövborg the pistol? And what conclusions will people draw from the fact that you did give it to him?

HEDDA (*Lets her head sink*): That is true. I did not think of that.

BRACK: Well, fortunately, there is no danger, so long as I say nothing.

HEDDA (*Looks up at him*): So I am in your power, Judge Brack. You have me at your beck and call, from this time forward.

BRACK (*Whispers softly*): Dearest Hedda — believe me — I shall not abuse my advantage.

HEDDA: I am in your power none the less. Subject to your will and your demands. A slave, a slave then! (*Rises impetuously.*) No, I cannot endure the thought of that! Never!

BRACK (*Looks half-mockingly at her*): People generally get used to the inevitable.

HEDDA (*Returns his look*): Yes, perhaps. (*She crosses to the writing table.*)[1]

After analyzing the elements of content and style and the relationship of the characters so that you are certain of their interplay, go through the excerpt again and follow fully the directions for action which Ibsen has given. Start perhaps with Brack since he does not change his position. Assume that he is standing, leaning against a chair. Get the feeling in your muscles of one who leans on a chair, perfectly in control

[1] From *Hedda Gabler* by Henrik Ibsen, translated by William Archer (1904). Reprinted with the permission of Charles Scribner's Sons from *The Collected Works of Henrik Ibsen,* Volume X.

of the situation. Let Brack look down at Hedda, who is seated. He will probably straighten slightly and shift his focus as she rises. Act out the business exactly as you would if you were rehearsing his lines for the stage. Next, take Hedda from a sitting position, through the drooping of her head and the upward look that follows, her sudden rising and her cross to the table. Repeat as often as necessary to perfect the timing. You will note that it is easier to vary pace and inflection, as well as muscle tone and emotional tension, when the action accompanies the words. Now, applying the theory of muscle memory, reread the scene without making the overt physical movements for either character. You will be able to retain the vocal variety as well as the physical variety for a strong degree of suggested activity.

Perhaps the most difficult thing about interpreting drama, aside from the purely mechanical or technical problems of suggesting character and action, is keeping the numerous threads of character development and reaction separated and yet related. This demands careful preparation and a high degree of concentration during performance. The interpreter must check carefully, especially during his preparation, to make sure that he is not doing merely a series of character sketches, each complete in itself but unrelated to the others. For besides a thorough knowledge of each character, a constant awareness of relationships and of progressions in these relationships is required. As the actor must learn to *hear* the speeches of other characters, the interpreter must learn to *have heard*. He must be sure each character is responding to what has gone before as it affects him. All the characters must stay "in scene" and ready to pick up the progression as they speak.

Thus the interpreter will need to select for each character enough significant physical and vocal details so that his hearers can themselves fill in the outline to make a three-dimensional, believable person. It is impractical and even dangerous to offer specific directions for achieving this final communication of character, because each personality in each play presents its own slightly different problems. Some suggestions for handling mechanical details — and they are suggestions only — will be given in the next chapter. For the moment, however, it is enough for the interpreter to be aware that he will need to spend considerable time and effort perfecting his control of voice and body, and that he will have to exert extreme care in performance to keep these techniques from calling attention to themselves.

Selections for Analysis and Oral Interpretation

This excerpt is the last part of the last act of Pinter's three-act play. Aston and Mick are brothers in their late twenties. Aston lives alone amid the clutter and decay of an old house, the setting of the play. Mick lives elsewhere in a manner more suited to his own taste. Davies, an old man, arrives one winter evening at Aston's with a long tale of abuse and persecution ending with his having been fired from his job. He has no clothes except his shabby overcoat and trousers, a waistcoat and vest, and a pair of worn sandals. During an early scene he persuades Aston to allow him to stay and help him build a shed. It is soon apparent that his garrulity and fawning mask acquisitiveness and vicious egocentricity. He moves in with Aston and within a fortnight has taken over his possessions.

Mick has been visiting the old house from time to time with the idea of doing some redecorating, and since Aston has told him that Davies claims to have had some experience with decorating, Mick allows him to remain. Just before this scene, Aston and Davies have quarreled and Aston tries to get Davies to leave. Davies pretends to go, and on the way out meets Mick. The scene begins there.

FROM *The Caretaker* / HAROLD PINTER

(*Voices on the stairs.* MICK *and* DAVIES *enter.*)

DAVIES: Stink! You hear that! Me! I told you what he said, didn't I? Stink! You hear that? That's what he said to me!

MICK: Tch, tch, tch.

DAVIES: That's what he said to me.

MICK: You don't stink.

DAVIES: No, sir!

MICK: If you stank I'd be the first one to tell you.

DAVIES: I told him, I told him he . . . I said to him, you ain't heard the last of this man! I said, don't you forget your brother. I told him you'd be coming along to sort him out. He don't know what he's started, doing that. Doing that to me. I said to him, I said to him, he'll be along, your brother'll be along, he's got sense, not like you —

MICK: What do you mean?

DAVIES: Eh?

MICK: You saying my brother hasn't got any sense?

DAVIES: What? What I'm saying is, you got ideas for this place, all this . . . all this decorating, see? I mean, he's got no right to order me about. I take orders from you, I do my caretaking for you, I mean, you look upon me . . . you don't treat me like a lump of dirt . . . we can both . . . we can both see him for what he is.

(*Pause*)

MICK: What did he say then, when you told him I'd offered you the job as caretaker?

DAVIES: He . . . he said . . . he said . . . something about . . . he lived here.

MICK: Yes, he's got a point, en he?

DAVIES: A point! This is your house, en't? You let him live here!

MICK: I could tell him to go, I suppose.

DAVIES: That's what I'm saying.

MICK: Yes. I could tell him to go. I mean, I'm the landlord. On the other hand, he's the sitting tenant. Giving him notice, you see, what it is, it's a technical matter, that's what it is. It depends how you regard this room. I mean it depends whether you regard this room as furnished or unfurnished. See what I mean?

DAVIES: No, I don't.

MICK: All this furniture, you see, in here, it's all his, except the beds, of course. So what it is, it's a fine legal point, that's what it is.

(*Pause*)

DAVIES: I tell you he should go back where he come from!

MICK (*turning to look at him*): Come from?

DAVIES: Yes.

MICK: Where did he come from?

DAVIES: Well . . . he . . . he. . . .

MICK: You get a bit out of your depth sometimes, don't you?

(*Pause*)

(*Rising, briskly.*) Well, anyway, as things stand, I don't mind having a go at doing up the place. . . .

DAVIES: That's what I wanted to hear!

MICK: No, I don't mind. (*He turns to face* DAVIES.) But you better be as good as you say you are.

DAVIES: What do you mean?

MICK: Well, you say you're an interior decorator, you'd better be a good one.

DAVIES: A what?

MICK: What do you mean, a what? A decorator. An interior decorator.

DAVIES: Me? What do you mean? I never touched that. I never been that.

MICK: You've never what?

DAVIES: No, no, not me, man. I'm not an interior decorator. I been too busy. Too many other things to do, you see. But I . . . but I could always turn my hand to most things . . . give me . . . give me a bit of time to pick it up.

MICK: I don't want you to pick it up. I want a first-class experienced interior decorator. I thought you were one.

DAVIES: Me? Now wait a minute — wait a minute — you got the wrong man.

MICK: How could I have the wrong man? You're the only man I've spoken to. You're the only man I've told, about my dreams, about my deepest wishes, you're the only one I've told, and I only told you because I understood you were an experienced first-class professional interior and exterior decorator.

DAVIES: Now look here —

MICK: You mean you wouldn't know how to fit teal-blue, copper and parchment linoleum squares and have those colours re-echoed in the walls?

DAVIES: Now, look here, where'd you get — ?

MICK: You wouldn't be able to decorate out a table in afromosia teak veneer, an armchair in oatmeal tweed and a beech frame settee with a woven sea-grass seat?

DAVIES: I never said that!

MICK: Christ! I must have been under a false impression!

DAVIES: I never said it!

MICK: You're a bloody impostor, mate!

DAVIES: Now you don't want to say that sort of thing to me. You took me on here as caretaker. I was going to give you a helping hand, that's all, for a small . . . for a small wage, I never said nothing about that . . . you start calling me names —

MICK: What is your name?

DAVIES: Don't start that —

MICK: No, what's your real name?

DAVIES: My real name's Davies.

MICK: What's the name you go under?

DAVIES: Jenkins!

MICK: You got two names. What about the rest? Eh? Now come on, why did you tell me all this dirt about you being an interior decorator?

DAVIES: I didn't tell you nothing! Won't you listen to what I'm saying? (*Pause.*) It was him who told you. It was your brother who must have told you. He's nutty! He'd tell you anything, out of spite, he's nutty, he's half way gone, it was him who told you.

MICK (*walks slowly to him*): What did you call my brother?

DAVIES: When?

MICK: He's what?

DAVIES: I . . . now get this straight. . . .

MICK: Nutty? Who's nutty? (*Pause.*) Did you call my brother nutty? My brother. That's a bit of . . . that's a bit of an impertinent thing to say, isn't it?

DAVIES: But he says so himself!

MICK (*walks slowly round* DAVIES' *figure, regarding him, once. He circles him, once*). What a strange man you are. Aren't you? Really strange. Ever since you come into this house there's been nothing but trouble.

Honest. I can take nothing you say at face value. Every word you speak is open to any number of different interpretations. Most of what you say is lies. You're violent, you're erratic, you're just completely unpredictable. You're nothing else but a wild animal, when you come down to it. You're a barbarian. And to put the old tin lid on it, you stink from arse-hole to breakfast time. Look at it. You come here recommending yourself as an interior decorator, whereupon I take you on, and what happens? You make a long speech about all the references you've got down at Sidcup, and what happens? I haven't noticed you go down to Sidcup to obtain them. It's all most regrettable but it looks as though I'm compelled to pay you off for your caretaking work. Here's half a dollar.

> (*He feels in his pocket, takes out a half-crown and tosses it at* DAVIES' *feet.* DAVIES *stands still.* MICK *walks to the gas stove and picks up the Buddha.*)

DAVIES (*slowly*): All right then . . . you do that . . . you do it . . . if that's what you want . . .

MICK: THAT'S WHAT I WANT! (*He hurls the Buddha against the gas stove. It breaks. Passionately.*) Anyone would think this house was all I got to worry about. I got plenty of other things I can worry about. I've got other things. I've got plenty of other interests. I've got my own business to build up, haven't I? I got to think about expanding . . . in all directions. I don't stand still. I'm moving about, all the time. I'm moving . . . all the time. I've got to think about the future. I'm not worried about this house. I'm not interested. My brother can worry about it. He can do it up, he can decorate it, he can do what he likes with it. I'm not bothered. I thought I was doing him a favour, letting him live here. He's got his own ideas. Let him have them. I'm going to chuck it in.

> (*Pause*)

DAVIES: What about me?

> (*Silence.* MICK *does not look at him. A door bangs. Silence. They do not move.* ASTON *comes in. He closes the door, moves into the room and faces* MICK. *They look at each other. Both are smiling, faintly.*)

MICK (*beginning to speak to* ASTON): Look . . . uh . . .

> (*He stops, goes to the door and exits.* ASTON *leaves the door open, crosses behind* DAVIES, *sees the broken Buddha, and looks at the pieces for a moment. He then goes to his bed, takes off his overcoat, sits, takes the screwdriver and plug and pokes the plug.*)

DAVIES: I just come back for my pipe.

ASTON: Oh yes.

DAVIES: I got out and . . . half way down I . . . I suddenly . . . found out . . . you see . . . that I hadn't got my pipe. So I come back to get it. . . . (*Pause. He moves to* ASTON.) That ain't the same plug, is it, you been . . . ? (*Pause.*) Still can't get anywhere with it, eh? (*Pause.*) Well, if you . . . persevere, in my opinion, you'll probably . . . (*Pause.*) Listen. . . . (*Pause.*) You didn't mean that, did you, about me stinking, did you? (*Pause.*) Did you? You been a good friend to me. You took me in. You took me in, you didn't ask me no questions, you give me a bed, you been a mate to me. Listen. I been thinking, why I made all them noises, it was because of the draught, see, that draught was on me as I was sleeping, made me make noises without me knowing it, so I been thinking, what I mean to say, if you was to give me your bed, and you have my bed, there's not all that difference between them, they're the same sort of bed, if I was to have yourn, you sleep, where-ever bed you're in, so you have mine, I have yourn, and that'll be all right, I'll be out of the draught, see, I mean, you don't mind a bit of wind, you need a bit of air, I can understand that, you being in that place that time, with all them doctors and all they done, closed up, I know them places, too hot, you see, they're always too hot, I had a peep in one once, nearly suffocated me, so I reckon that'd be the best way out of it, we swap beds, and then we could get down to what we was saying, I'd look after the place for you, I'd keep an eye on it for you, for you, like, not for the other . . . not for . . . for your brother, you see, not for him, for you, I'll be your man, you say the word, just say the word. . . . (*Pause.*) What do you think of this I'm saying?

(*Pause*)

ASTON: No, I like sleeping in this bed.

DAVIES: But you don't understand my meaning!

ASTON: Anyway, that one's my brother's bed.

DAVIES: Your brother?

ASTON: Any time he stays here. This is my bed. It's the only bed I can sleep in.

DAVIES: But your brother's gone! He's gone!

(*Pause.*)

ASTON: No. I couldn't change beds.

DAVIES: But you don't understand my meaning!

ASTON: Anyway, I'm going to be busy. I've got that shed to get up. If I don't get it up now it'll never go up. Until it's up I can't get started.

DAVIES: I'll give you a hand to put up your shed, that's what I'll do!

(*Pause.*) I'll give you a hand! We'll both put up that shed together! See? Get it done in next to no time! Do you see what I'm saying?

(*Pause.*)

ASTON: No. I can get it up myself.

DAVIES: But listen. I'm with you, I'll be here, I'll do it for you! (*Pause.*) We'll do it together! (*Pause.*) Christ, we'll change beds!

(ASTON *moves to the window and stands with his back to* DAVIES.)

You mean you're throwing me out? You can't do that. Listen man, listen man, I don't mind, you see, I don't mind, I'll stay, I don't mind, I'll tell you what, if you don't want to change beds, we'll keep it as it is, I'll stay in the same bed, maybe if I can get a stronger piece of sacking, like, to go over the window, keep out the draught, that'll do it, what do you say, we'll keep it as it is?

(*Pause.*)

ASTON: No.

DAVIES: Why . . . not?

(ASTON *turns to look at him.*)

ASTON: You make too much noise.

DAVIES: But . . . but . . . look . . . listen . . . listen here . . . I mean. . . .

(ASTON *turns back to the window.*)

What am I going to do? (*Pause.*) What shall I do? (*Pause.*) Where am I going to go? (*Pause.*) If you want me to go . . . I'll go. You just say the word. (*Pause.*) I'll tell you what though . . . them shoes . . . them shoes you give me . . . they're working out all right . . . they're all right. Maybe I could . . . get down. . . .

(ASTON *remains still, his back to him, at the window.*)

Listen . . . if I . . . got down . . . if I was to . . . get my papers . . . would you . . . would you let . . . would you . . . if I got down . . . and got my. . . .

(*Long silence.*)

CURTAIN

Oedipus, king of Thebes, who once answered the riddle of the Sphinx and thus destroyed her power, has been visited by the elders and townsmen begging him to deliver them once again from famine and pestilence. He tells them that

he has sent his brother-in-law, Creon, to the oracle to find out what he might
do to save the state. When Creon returns, he reveals that the oracle has said
the curse will not be lifted until the murderer of King Laius, who held the
throne before Oedipus, is found and driven from Thebes. Oedipus has issued
a proclamation to carry out this task. Moreover, he has sent for the blind
prophet Teiresias in the hope that he can help identify the murderer through
his powers of divination. Oedipus stands on the steps of his palace surrounded
by his citizens, waiting for the arrival of the revered man.

FROM *Oedipus the King* / SOPHOCLES

translated by Theodore Howard Banks

(*Enter* TIRESIAS, *led by a* BOY.)

OEDIPUS: You know all things in heaven and earth, Tiresias:
　Things you may speak of openly, and secrets
　Holy and not to be revealed. You know,
　Blind though you are, the plague that ruins Thebes.
　And you, great prophet, you alone can save us.
　Phoebus has sent an answer to our question,
　An answer that the messengers may have told you,
　Saying there was no cure for our condition
　Until we found the killers of King Laius
　And banished them or had them put to death.
　Therefore, Tiresias, do not begrudge your skill
　In the voice of birds or other prophecy,
　But save yourself, save me, save the whole city,
　Save everything that the pestilence defiles.
　We are at your mercy, and man's noblest task
　Is to use all his powers in helping others.
TIRESIAS: How dreadful a thing, how dreadful a thing is wisdom,
　When to be wise is useless! This I knew
　But I forgot, or else I would never have come.
OEDIPUS: What is the matter? Why are you so troubled?
TIRESIAS: Oedipus, let me go home. Then you will bear
　Your burden, and I mine, more easily.
OEDIPUS: Custom entitles us to hear your message.
　By being silent you harm your native land.
TIRESIAS: You do not know when, and when not to speak.
　Silence will save me from the same misfortune.
OEDIPUS: If you can be of help, then all of us
　Kneel and implore you not to turn away.

TIRESIAS: None of you know the truth, but I will never
    Reveal my sorrow — not to call it yours.
OEDIPUS: What are you saying? You know and will not speak?
    You mean to betray us and destroy the city?
TIRESIAS: I refuse to pain you. I refuse to pain myself.
    It is useless to ask me. I will tell you nothing.
OEDIPUS: You utter scoundrel! You would enrage a stone!
    Is there no limit to your stubbornness?
TIRESIAS: You blame my anger and forget your own.
OEDIPUS: No one could help being angry when he heard
    How you dishonor and ignore the state.
TIRESIAS: What is to come will come, though I keep silent.
OEDIPUS: If it must come, your duty is to speak.
TIRESIAS: I will say no more. Rage to your heart's content.
OEDIPUS: Rage? Yes, I will rage! I will spare you nothing.
    In the plot against King Laius, I have no doubt
    That you were an accomplice, yes, almost
    The actual killer. If you had not been blind,
    I would have said that you alone were guilty.
TIRESIAS: Then listen to my command! Obey the edict
    That you yourself proclaimed and never speak,
    From this day on, to me or any Theban.
    You are the sinner who pollutes our land.
OEDIPUS: Have you no shame? How do you hope to escape
    The consequence of such an accusation?
TIRESIAS: I have escaped. My strength is the living truth.
OEDIPUS: This is no prophecy. Who taught you this?
TIRESIAS: You did. You forced me to speak against my will.
OEDIPUS: Repeat your slander. Let me learn it better.
TIRESIAS: Are you trying to tempt me into saying more?
    I have spoken already. Have you not understood?
OEDIPUS: No, not entirely. Give your speech again.
TIRESIAS: I say you are the killer, you yourself.
OEDIPUS: Twice the same insult! You will pay for it.
TIRESIAS: Shall I say more to make you still more angry?
OEDIPUS: Say what you want to. It will make no sense.
TIRESIAS: You are living in shame with those most dear to you,
    As yet in ignorance of your dreadful fate.
OEDIPUS: Do you suppose that you can always use
    Language like that and not be punished for it?
TIRESIAS: Yes. I am safe, if truth has any strength.
OEDIPUS: Truth can save anyone excepting you,
    You with no eyes, no hearing, and no brains!

TIRESIAS: Poor fool! You taunt me, but you soon will hear
  The self-same insults heaped upon your head.
OEDIPUS: You live in endless night. What can you do
  To me or anyone else who sees the day?
TIRESIAS: Nothing. I have no hand in your destruction.
  For that, Apollo needs no help from me.
OEDIPUS: Apollo! Is this your trick, or is it Creon's?
TIRESIAS: Creon is guiltless. The evil is in you.
OEDIPUS: How great is the envy roused by wealth, by kingship,
  By the subtle skill that triumphs over others
  In life's hard struggle! Creon, who has been
  For years my trusted friend, has stealthily
  Crept in upon me anxious to seize my power,
  The unsought gift the city freely gave me.
  Anxious to overthrow me, he has bribed
  This scheming mountebank, this fraud, this trickster,
  Blind in his art and in everything but money!
  Your art of prophecy! When have you shown it?
  Not when the watch-dog of the gods was here,
  Chanting her riddle. Why did you say nothing,
  When you might have saved the city? Yet her puzzle
  Could not be solved by the first passer-by.
  A prophet's skill was needed, and you proved
  That you had no such skill, either in birds
  Or any other means the gods have given.
  But I came, I, the ignorant Oedipus,
  And silenced her. I had no birds to help me.
  I used my brains. And it is I you now
  Are trying to destroy in the hope of standing
  Close beside Creon's throne. You will regret
  This zeal of yours to purify the land,
  You and your fellow-plotter. You seem old;
  Otherwise you would pay for your presumption.
CHORUS: Sir, it appears to us that both of you
  Have spoken in anger. Anger serves no purpose.
  Rather we should consider in what way
  We best can carry out the god's command.
TIRESIAS: King though you are, I have a right to answer
  Equal to yours. In that I too am king.
  I serve Apollo. I do not acknowledge
  You as my lord or Creon as my patron.
  You have seen fit to taunt me with my blindness.
  Therefore I tell you this: you have your eyesight

And cannot see the sin of your existence,
Cannot see where you live or whom you live with,
Are ignorant of your parents, bring disgrace
Upon your kindred in the world below
And here on earth. And soon the double lash
Of your mother's and father's curse will drive you headlong
Out of the country, blinded, with your cries
Heard everywhere, echoed by every hill
In all Cithaeron. Then you will have learned
The meaning of your marriage, learned in what harbor,
After so fair a voyage, you were shipwrecked.
And other horrors you could never dream of
Will teach you who you are, will drag you down
To the level of your children. Heap your insults
On Creon and my message if you choose to.
Still no one ever will endure the weight
Of greater misery than will fall on you.

OEDIPUS: Am I supposed to endure such talk as this,
Such talk from him? Go, curse you, go! Be quick!

TIRESIAS: Except for your summons I would never have come.

OEDIPUS: And I would never have sent for you so soon
If I had known you would prove to be a fool.

TIRESIAS: Yes. I have proved a fool — in your opinion,
And yet your parents thought that I was wise.

OEDIPUS: What parents? Wait! Who was my father? Tell me!

TIRESIAS: Today will see your birth and your destruction.

OEDIPUS: You cannot speak unless you speak in riddles!

TIRESIAS: And yet how brilliant you are in solving them!

OEDIPUS: You sneer at me for what has made me great.

TIRESIAS: The same good fortune that has ruined you.

OEDIPUS: If I have saved the city, nothing else matters.

TIRESIAS: In that case I will go. Boy, take me home.

OEDIPUS: Yes, let him take you. Here, you are in the way.
Once you are gone, you will give no further trouble.

TIRESIAS: I will not go before I have said my say,
Indifferent to your black looks. You cannot harm me.
And I say this: the man whom you have sought,
Whom you have threatened, whom you have proclaimed
The killer of King Laius — he is here.
Now thought an alien, he shall prove to be
A native Theban, to his deep dismay.
Now he has eyesight, now his wealth is great;
But he shall make his way to foreign soil

Blinded, in beggary, groping with a stick.
In his own household he shall be shown to be
The father of his children — and their brother,
Son to the woman who bore him — and her husband,
The killer and the bedfellow of his father.
Go and consider this; and if you find
That I have been mistaken, you can say
That I have lost my skill in prophecy.

(*Exeunt* OEDIPUS *and* TIRESIAS.)

These scenes do not run consecutively in Archibald MacLeish's play about a modern Job. They do, however, all deal with his relationship with his wife and her involvement in his sufferings and struggle to accept God's will. With careful transitions they can work very well as a unit, or each can stand alone.

J.B. and Sarah have suffered a succession of tragedies. They have gone from wealth, prosperity, and a happy family life to degradation, poverty, illness, and the loss by horrible accident and murder of their five children. As a final catastrophe their whole world now lies in rubble around them, peopled only by a few survivors huddled on trash heaps.

Nickles, who has worn the Satan mask in the dramatic commentary on the story, operates almost as a Greek chorus, commenting to the audience, indeed to the world in general, rather than entering into the scene itself.

FROM **J.B.** / ARCHIBALD MACLEISH

Scene 8

(*There is no light but the glow on the canvas sky, which holds the looming, leaning shadows. They fade as a match is struck. It flares in* SARAH's *hand, showing her face, and glimmers out against the wick of a dirty lantern. As the light of the lantern rises,* J.B. *is seen lying on the broken propped-up table, naked but for a few rags of clothing.* SARAH *looks at him in the new light, shudders, lets her head drop into her hands. There is a long silence and then a movement in the darkness of the open door where four women and a young girl stand, their arms filled with blankets and newspapers. They come forward slowly into the light.*)

.   .   .   .   .

(The women settle themselves on their newspapers off at the edge of the circle of light. NICKLES has perched himself on a chair at the side.)

.   .   .   .   .   .

(Silence. Out of the silence, felt rather than heard at first, a sound of sobbing, a muffled, monotonous sound like the heavy beat of a heart.)

J.B.:   If you could only sleep a little
Now they're quiet, now they're still.

SARAH *(her voice broken)*:
I try. But oh I close my eyes and . . .
Eyes are open there to meet me!

(Silence. Then Sarah's voice in an agony of bitterness.)

My poor babies! Oh, my poor babies!

(J.B. pulls himself painfully up, sits huddled on his table in the feeble light of the lamp, his rags about him.)

J.B. *(gently)*:
Go to sleep.

SARAH: Go! Go where?
If there were darkness I'd go there.
If there were night I'd lay me down in it.
God has shut the night against me.
God has set the dark alight
With horror blazing blind as day
When I go toward it . . .
                close my eyes.

J.B.:   I know. I know those waking eyes.
His will is everywhere against us —
Even in our sleep, our dreams . . .

NICKLES *(a snort of laughter up toward the dark of the platform)*:
Your will, *his* peace!
Doesn't seem to grasp that, does he?
Give him another needling twinge
Between the withers and the works —
He'll understand you better.

J.B.:   If I
Knew . . . If I knew why!

NICKLES: If he knew
Why he wouldn't be there. He'd be
Strangling, drowning, suffocating,
Diving for a sidewalk somewhere . . .

J.B.:   What I *can't* bear is the blindness —
       Meaninglessness — the numb blow
       Fallen in the stumbling night.

SARAH (*starting violently to her feet*):
       Has death no meaning? Pain no meaning?

 (*She points at his body.*)

       Even these suppurating sores —
       Have they no meaning for you?

NICKLES: Ah!

J.B. (*from his heart's pain*):
       God will not punish without cause.

 (NICKLES *doubles up in a spasm of soundless laughter.*)

       God is just.

SARAH (*hysterically*): God is just!
       If God is just our slaughtered children
       Stank with sin, were rotten with it!

 (*She controls herself with difficulty, turns toward him, reaches her arms out, lets them fall.*)

       Oh, my dear! my dear! my dear!
       Does God demand deception of us? —
       Purchase His innocence by ours?
       Must we be guilty for Him? — bear
       The burden of the world's malevolence
       For Him who made the world?

J.B.:   *He*
       Knows the guilt is mine. He must know:
       Has He not punished it? He knows its
       Name, its time, its face, its circumstance,
       The figure of its day, the door,
       The opening of the door, the room, the moment ...

SARAH (*fiercely*):
       And you? Do you? You do not know it.
       Your punishment is all you know.

 (*She moves toward the door, stops, turns.*)

       I will not stay here if you lie —
       Connive in your destruction, cringe to it:
       Not if you betray my children ...
       I will not stay to listen ...
             They are
       Dead and they were innocent: I will not
       Let you sacrifice their deaths
       To make injustice justice and God good!

J.B. (*covering his face with his hands*):
      My heart beats. I cannot answer it.

SARAH: If you buy quiet with their innocence —
      Theirs or yours . . .
              (*Softly.*) I will not love you.

J.B.:   I have no choice but to be guilty.

SARAH (*her voice rising*):
      We have the choice to live or die,
      All of us . . .
             curse God and die . . .

(*Silence.*)

J.B.:   God is God or we are nothing —
      Mayflies that leave their husks behind —
      Our tiny lives ridiculous — a suffering
      Not even sad that Someone Somewhere
      Laughs at as we laugh at apes.
      We have no choice but to be guilty.
      God is unthinkable if we are innocent.

(SARAH *turns, runs soundlessly out of the circle of light, out of the door. The women stir.*)

. . . . . .

Gradually the women gather up their few belongings and leave the stage. J.B. is left alone lying on a pile of rubble. NICKLES crosses and stands looking down at him.

from Scene 10

. . . . . .

NICKLES: Oh come off it.
      You don't have to act with me.

(J.B. *is silent.*)

      O.K. Carry on.
      All I wanted was to help.
      Professional counsel you might call it . . .

(J.B. *is silent.*)

      Of course you know how all this ends? . . .

(J.B. *is silent.*)

      I wondered how you'd play the end.

J.B.:   Who knows what the end is, ever?

NICKLES: I do. You do.

J.B.:   Then don't tell me.

NICKLES: What's the worst thing you can think of?

J.B.:   I have asked for death. Begged for it. Prayed for it.

NICKELS: Then the worst thing can't be death.

J.B.:   Ah!

NICKLES: You know now.

J.B.:   No. You tell me.

NICKLES: Why should I tell you when you know?

J.B.:   Then don't. I'm sick of mysteries. Sick of them.

NICKLES: He gives it back to you.

J.B.:   What back?

NICKLES: All of it.
        Everything He ever took:
        Wife, health, children, everything.

J.B.:   I have no wife.

NICKLES: She comes back to you.

J.B.:   I have no children.

NICKLES (*a nasty laugh*):   You'll have better ones.

J.B.:   My skin is ...

(*He breaks off, staring at the skin of his naked arms.*)

NICKLES: Oh come on! I know the
        Look of grease paint!

J.B.:   ... whole! It's healed!

NICKLES (*heavily ironic*):
        You see? You see what I mean? What He plans for you?

(*J.B., staring at his arms, is silent.*)

NICKLES (*leaning forward, urgently*):
        Tell me how you play the end.
        Any man was screwed as Job was! ...

(*J.B. does not answer.*)

        I'll tell you how to play it. Listen!
        Think of all the mucked-up millions
        Since this buggered world began
        Said, No!, said, Thank you!, took a rope's end,
        Took a window for a door,
        Swallowed something, gagged on something ...

(*J.B. lifts his head: he is listening but not to* NICKLES.)

        None of them knew the truth as Job does.
        None of them had his cause to know.

J.B.:   Listen! Do you hear? There's someone ...

NICKLES (*violently*):
        Job won't take it! Job won't touch it!
        Job will fling it in God's face
        With half his guts to make it spatter!
        He'd rather suffocate in dung —
        Choke in ordure —
J.B. (*rising*):   There is someone —
        Someone waiting at the door.
NICKLES (*pulling his cap down, rising slowly*):
               I know.

(*The dangling lights dim out.*)

Scene 11

(*A light comes from the canvas door. It increases as though day were beginning somewhere.* NICKLES *has gone.*)

J.B.:   Who is it?

(*He crosses toward the door walking with his old ease. Stops.*)
        Is there someone there?

(*There is no answer. He goes on. Reaches the door.*)
    Sarah!

(*The light increases. She is sitting on the sill, a broken twig in her hand.*)

SARAH: Look, Job: the forsythia,
    The first few leaves . . .
            not leaves though . . .
                petals . . .

J.B. (*roughly*): Get up!
SARAH: Where shall I go?
J.B.:   Where you went!
    Wherever!

(*She does not answer.*)

(*More gently.*) Where?

SARAH: Among the ashes.
    All there is now of the town is ashes.
    Mountains of ashes. Shattered glass.
    Glittering cliffs of glass all shattered
    Steeper than a cat could climb
    If there were cats still . . .
        And the pigeons —
    They wheel and settle and whirl off

Wheeling and almost settling . . .
And the silence —
There is no sound there now — no wind sound —
Nothing that could sound the wind —
Could make it sing — no door — no doorway . . .
Only this.

(*She looks at the twig in her hands.*)

Among the ashes!
I found it growing in the ashes!
Gold as though it did not know . . .

(*Her voice rises hysterically.*)

I broke the branch to strip the leaves off —
Petals again! . . .

(*She cradles it in her arms.*)

But they so clung to it!

J.B.:   Curse God and die, you said to me.
SARAH: Yes.

(*She looks up at him for the first time, then down again.*)

You wanted justice, didn't you?
There isn't any. There's the world . . .

(*She begins to rock on the doorsill, the little branch in her arms.*)

Cry for justice and the stars
Will stare until your eyes sting. Weep,
Enormous winds will thrash the water.
Cry in sleep for your lost children,
Snow will fall . . .
snow will fall . . .

J.B.:   Why did you leave me alone?

SARAH:
I loved you.
I couldn't help you any more.
You wanted justice and there was none —
Only love.

J.B.:
He does not love. He
Is.

SARAH: But we do. That's the wonder.

J.B.:   Yet you left me.

SARAH:
Yes, I left you.
I thought there was a way away . . .
Water under bridges opens
Closing and the companion stars

Still float there afterwards. I thought the door
Opened into closing water.

J.B.: Sarah!

(*He drops on his knees beside her in the doorway, his arms around her.*)

SARAH: Oh, I never could!
I never could! Even the forsythia . . .

(*She is half laughing, half crying.*)

Even the forsythia beside the
Stair could stop me.

(*They cling to each other. Then she rises, drawing him up, peering at the darkness inside the door.*)

J.B.: It's too dark to see.

(*She turns, pulls his head down between her hands and kisses him.*)

SARAH: Then blow on the coal of the heart, my darling.
J.B.: The coal of the heart . . .
SARAH: It's all the light now.

(SARAH *comes forward into the dim room,* J.B. *behind her. She lifts a fallen chair, sets it straight.*)

Blow on the coal of the heart.
The candles in churches are out.
The lights have gone out in the sky.
Blow on the coal of the heart
And we'll see by and by . . .

(J.B. *has joined her, lifting and straightening the chairs.*)

We'll see where we are
The wit won't burn and the wet soul smoulders
Blow on the coal of the heart and we'll know . . .
We'll know . . .

(*The light increases, plain white daylight from the door, as they work.*)

CURTAIN

This translation of Goethe's Faust was made by Percy Bysshe Shelley in the early part of the nineteenth century. It combines Goethe's wit and skill in characterization and dialogue with the poet-translator's sensitivity to nuances of meaning.

FROM *Faust* / JOHANN WOLFGANG VON GOETHE

translated by Percy Bysshe Shelley

(*Enter* MEPHISTOPHELES.)

MEPHISTOPHELES: As thou, O Lord, once more art kind enough
    To interest Thyself in our affairs,
    And ask, 'How goes it with you there below?'
    And as indulgently at other times
    Thou tookest not my visits in ill part,
    Thou seest me here once more among Thy household.
    Though I should scandalize this company,
    You will excuse me if I do not talk
    In the high style which they think fashionable;
    My pathos certainly would make You laugh too,
    Had You not long since given over laughing.
    Nothing know I to say of suns and worlds;
    I observe only how men plague themselves; —
    The little god o' the world keeps the same stamp,
    As wonderful as on creation's day: —
    A little better would he live, hadst Thou
    Not given him a glimpse of Heaven's light
    Which he calls reason, and employs it only
    To live more beastily than any beast.
    With reverence to Your Lordship be it spoken,
    He's like one of those long-legged grasshoppers,
    Who flits and jumps about, and sings for ever
    The same old song i' the grass. There let him lie,
    Burying his nose in every heap of dung.

THE LORD: Have you no more to say? Do you come here
    Always to scold, and cavil, and complain?
    Seems nothing ever right to you on earth?

MEPHISTOPHELES: No, Lord! I find all there, as ever, bad at best.
    Even I am sorry for man's days of sorrow;
    I could myself almost give up the pleasure
    Of plaguing the poor things.

THE LORD: Knowest thou Faust?

MEPHISTOPHELES: The Doctor?

THE LORD: Ay; My servant Faust.

MEPHISTOPHELES: In truth
    He serves You in a fashion quite his own;
    And the fool's meat and drink are not of earth.
    His aspirations bear him on so far
    That he is half aware of his own folly,

For he demands from Heaven its fairest star,
And from the earth the highest joy it bears,
Yet all things far, and all things near, are vain
To calm the deep emotions of his breast.

THE LORD: Though he now serves Me-in a cloud of error,
I will soon lead him forth to the clear day.
When trees look green, full well the gardener knows
That fruits and blooms will deck the coming year.

MEPHISTOPHELES: What will You bet? — now I am sure of winning —
Only, observe You give me full permission
To lead him softly on my path.

THE LORD: As long
As he shall live upon the earth, so long
Is nothing unto thee forbidden — Man
Must err till he has ceased to struggle.

MEPHISTOPHELES: Thanks.
And that is all I ask; for willingly
I never make acquaintance with the dead.
The full fresh cheeks of youth are food for me,
And if a corpse knocks, I am not at home.
For I am like a cat — I like to play
A little with the mouse before I eat it.

THE LORD: Well, well! it is permitted thee. Draw thou
His spirit from its springs; as thou find'st power,
Seize him and lead him on thy downward path;
And stand ashamed when failure teaches thee
That a good man, even in his darkest longings,
Is well aware of the right way.

MEPHISTOPHELES: Well and good.
I am not in much doubt about my bet,
And if I lose, then 'tis Your turn to crow;
Enjoy Your triumph then with a full breast.
Ay; dust shall he devour, and that with pleasure,
Like my old paramour, the famous Snake.

THE LORD: Pray come here when it suits you; for I never
Had much dislike for people of your sort.
And, among all the Spirits who rebelled,
The knave was ever the least tedious to Me.
The active spirit of man soon sleeps, and soon
He seeks unbroken quiet; therefore I
Have given him the Devil for a companion,
Who may provoke him to some sort of work,
And must create forever. — But ye, pure
Children of God, enjoy eternal beauty; —

Let that which ever operates and lives
Clasp you within the limits of its love;
And seize with sweet and melancholy thoughts
The floating phantoms of its loveliness.

(*Heaven closes; the* ARCHANGELS *exeunt.*)

MEPHISTOPHELES: From time to time I visit the old fellow,
And I take care to keep on good terms with Him.
Civil enough is the same God Almighty,
To talk so freely with the Devil himself.

The setting of A Raisin in the Sun *is the crowded apartment of the Younger family on Chicago's South Side. Ruth and Walter Younger, about thirty, are husband and wife. Travis, their son, is a sturdy, handsome little boy of ten or eleven. Mama, to whom the apartment originally belonged, is his paternal grandmother. She is in her early sixties.*

During the first act we have learned that Mama has received a check for ten thousand dollars from a life insurance policy which her late husband somehow managed to keep up. The family has quarreled about the use of the money. Walter wants to invest it in a liquor store with his friend Willy Harris. Ruth insists the money is Mama's. Mama cannot bring herself to become involved in what seems to her a very questionable business. At the beginning of this scene Mama has gone out. Walter has obviously been drinking and is in a quarrelsome mood.

Make careful use of the rhythm of content and the sharp builds of emotion.

FROM A *Raisin in the Sun* / LORRAINE HANSBERRY

Act II, Scene 1

RUTH: Walter — (*She stops what she is doing and looks at him.*)

WALTER (*yelling*): Don't start!

RUTH: Start what?

WALTER: Your nagging! Where was I? Who was I with? How much money did I spend?

RUTH (*plaintively*): Walter Lee — why don't we just try to talk about it . . .

WALTER (*not listening*): I been out talking with people who understand me. People who care about the things I got on my mind.

RUTH (*wearily*): I guess that means people like Willy Harris.

WALTER: Yes, people like Willy Harris.

RUTH (*with a sudden flash of impatience*): Why don't you all just hurry up and go into the banking business and stop talking about it!

WALTER: Why? You want to know why? 'Cause we all tied up in a race of people that don't know how to do nothing but moan, pray and have babies! (*The line is too bitter even for him and he looks at her and sits down.*)

RUTH: Oh, Walter . . . (*Softly.*) Honey, why can't you stop fighting me?

WALTER (*without thinking*): Who's fighting you? Who even cares about you? (*This line begins the retardation of his mood.*)

RUTH: Well — (*She waits a long time, and then with resignation starts to put away her things.*) I guess I might as well go on to bed . . . (*More or less to herself.*) I don't know where we lost it . . . but we have . . . (*Then, to him.*) I — I'm sorry about this new baby, Walter. I guess maybe I better go on and do what I started . . . I guess I just didn't realize how bad things was with us . . . I guess I just didn't really realize — (*She starts out to the bedroom and stops.*) You want some hot milk?

WALTER: Hot milk?

RUTH: Yes — hot milk.

WALTER: Why hot milk?

RUTH: 'Cause after all that liquor you come home with you ought to have something hot in your stomach.

WALTER: I don't want no milk.

RUTH: You want some coffee then?

WALTER: No, I don't want no coffee. I don't want nothing hot to drink. (*Almost plaintively.*) Why you always trying to give me something to eat?

RUTH (*standing and looking at him helplessly*): What else can I give you, Walter Lee Younger?

> (*She stands and looks at him and presently turns to go out again. He lifts his head and watches her going away from him in a new mood which began to emerge when he asked her "Who cares about you?"*)

WALTER: It's been rough, ain't it, baby?

> (*She hears and stops but does not turn around and he continues to her back.*)

I guess between two people there ain't never as much understood as folks generally thinks there is. I mean like between me and you —

> (*She turns to face him.*)

How we gets to the place where we scared to talk softness to each other. (*He waits, thinking hard himself.*) Why you think it got to be

like that? (*He is thoughtful, almost as a child would be.*) Ruth, what
is it gets into two people ought to be close?

RUTH: I don't know, honey. I think about it a lot.

WALTER: On acount of you and me, you mean? The way things are with
us. The way something done come down between us.

RUTH: There ain't so much between us, Walter . . . Not when you come
to me and try to talk to me. Try to be with me . . . a little even.

WALTER (*total honesty*): Sometimes . . . sometimes . . . I don't even know
how to try.

RUTH: Walter —

WALTER: Yes?

RUTH (*coming to him, gently and with misgiving, but coming to him*):
Honey . . . life don't have to be like this. I mean sometimes people
can do things so that things are better . . . You remember how we used
to talk when Travis was born . . . about the way we were going to live
. . . the kind of house . . . (*She is stroking his head.*) Well, it's all
starting to slip away from us . . .

(MAMA *enters, and* WALTER *jumps up and shouts at her.*)

WALTER: Mama, where have you been?

MAMA: My — them steps is longer than they used to be. Whew! (*She
sits down and ignores him*) How you feeling this evening, Ruth?

(RUTH *shrugs, disturbed some at having been prematurely
interrupted and watching her husband knowingly.*)

WALTER: Mama, where have you been all day?

MAMA (*still ignoring him and leaning on the table and changing to more
comfortable shoes*): Where's Travis?

RUTH: I let him go out earlier and he ain't come back yet. Boy is he
going to get it!

WALTER: Mama!

MAMA (*as if she has heard him for the first time*): Yes, son?

WALTER: Where did you go this afternoon?

MAMA: I went downtown to tend to some business that I had to tend to.

WALTER: What kind of business?

MAMA: You know better than to question me like a child, Brother.

WALTER (*rising and bending over the table*): Where were you, Mama?
(*Bringing his fists down and shouting.*) Mama, you didn't go do
something with that insurance money, something crazy?

(*The front door opens slowly, interrupting him, and* TRAVIS
peeks his head in, less than hopefully.)

TRAVIS (*to his mother*): Mama, I —

RUTH: "Mama I" nothing! You're going to get it, boy! Get on in that
bedroom and get yourself ready!

TRAVIS: But I —

MAMA: Why don't you all never let the child explain hisself.

RUTH: Keep out of it now, Lena.

> (MAMA *clamps her lips together, and* RUTH *advances toward her son menacingly.*)

RUTH: A thousand times I have told you not to go off like that —

MAMA (*holding out her arms to her grandson*): Well — at least let me tell him something. I want him to be the first one to hear . . . Come here, Travis. (*The boy obeys, gladly.*) Travis — (*she takes him by the shoulder and looks into his face*) — you know that money we got in the mail this morning?

TRAVIS: Yes'm —

MAMA: Well — what you think your grandmama gone and done with that money?

TRAVIS: I don't know, Grandmama.

MAMA (*putting her finger on his nose for emphasis*): She went out and she bought you a house! (*The explosion comes from* WALTER *at the end of the revelation and he jumps up and turns away from all of them in a fury.* MAMA *continues, to* TRAVIS). You glad about the house? It's going to be yours when you get to be a man.

TRAVIS: Yeah — I always wanted to live in a house.

MAMA: All right, gimme some sugar then — (TRAVIS *puts his arms around her neck as she watches her son over the boy's shoulder. Then, to* TRAVIS, *after the embrace.*) Now when you say your prayers tonight, you thank God and your grandfather — 'cause it was him who give you the house — in his way.

RUTH (*taking the boy from* MAMA *and pushing him toward the bedroom*): Now you get out of here and get ready for your beating.

TRAVIS: Aw, Mama —

RUTH: Get on in there — (*Closing the door behind him and turning radiantly to her mother-in-law.*) So you went and did it!

MAMA (*quietly, looking at her son with pain*): Yes, I did.

RUTH (*raising both arms classically*): Praise God! (*Looks at* WALTER *a moment who says nothing. She crosses rapidly to her husband.*) Please, honey — let me be glad . . . you be glad too. (*She has laid her hands on his shoulders, but he shakes himself free of her roughly, without turning to face her.*) Oh, Walter . . . a home . . . a home. (*She comes back to* MAMA.) Well — where is it? How big is it? How much it going to cost?

MAMA: Well —

RUTH: When we moving?

MAMA (*smiling at her*): First of the month.

RUTH (*throwing back her head with jubilance*): Praise God!

MAMA (*tentatively, still looking at her son's back turned against her and* RUTH): It's — it's a nice house too . . . (*She cannot help speaking directly to him. An imploring quality in her voice, her manner, makes her almost like a girl now.*) Three bedrooms — nice big one for you and Ruth. . . . Me and Beneatha still have to share our room, but Travis have one of his own — and (*with difficulty*) I figure if the — new baby — is a boy, we could get one of them double-decker outfits . . . And there's a yard with a little patch of dirt where I could maybe get to grow me a few flowers . . . And a nice big basement . . .

RUTH: Walter honey, be glad —

MAMA (*still to his back, fingering things on the table*): 'Course I don't want to make it sound fancier than it is . . . It's just a plain little old house — but it's made good and solid — and it will be *ours*. Walter Lee — it makes a difference in a man when he can walk on floors that belong to *him* . . .

RUTH: Where is it?

MAMA (*frightened at this telling*): Well — well — it's out there in Clybourne Park —

> (RUTH's *radiance fades abruptly, and* WALTER *finally turns slowly to face his mother with incredulity and hostility.*)

RUTH: Where?

MAMA (*matter-of-factly*): Four o six Clybourne Street, Clybourne Park.

RUTH: Clybourne Park? Mama, there ain't no colored people living in Clybourne Park.

MAMA (*almost idiotically*): Well, I guess there's going to be some now.

WALTER (*bitterly*): So that's the peace and comfort you went out and bought for us today!

MAMA (*raising her eyes to meet his finally*): Son — I just tried to find the nicest place for the least amount of money for my family.

RUTH (*trying to recover from the shock*): Well — well — 'course I ain't one never been 'fraid of no crackers, mind you — but — well, wasn't there no other houses nowhere?

MAMA: Them houses they put up for colored in them areas way out all seem to cost twice as much as other houses. I did the best I could.

RUTH (*struck senseless with the news, in its various degrees of goodness and trouble, she sits a moment, her fists propping her chin in thought, and then she starts to rise, bringing her fist down with vigor, the radiance spreading from cheek to cheek again*): Well — well! — All I can say is — if this is my time in life — my time — to say good-bye — (*and she builds with momentum as she starts to circle the room with an exuberant, almost tearfully happy release*) — to these Goddamned cracking walls! — (*she pounds the walls*) — and these marching roaches! — (*she wipes at an imaginary army of marching roaches*) — and this cramped little closet which ain't now or never was no kitchen! . . . then I say it loud and good, *Hallelujah! and good-bye misery . . . I don't never want to see your ugly face again!* (*She laughs joyously, having practically destroyed the apartment, and flings her arms up and lets them come down happily, slowly, reflectively, over her abdomen, aware for the first time perhaps that the life therein pulses with happiness and not despair.*) Lena?

MAMA (*moved, watching her happiness*): Yes, honey?

RUTH (*looking off*): Is there — is there a whole lot of sunlight?

MAMA (*understanding*): Yes, child, there's a whole lot of sunlight.

(*Long pause.*)

RUTH (*collecting herself and going to the door of the room* TRAVIS *is in*): Well — I guess I better see 'bout Travis. (*To* MAMA.) Lord, I sure don't feel like whipping nobody today! (*She exits.*)

MAMA (*the mother and son are left alone now and the mother waits a long time, considering deeply, before she speaks*): Son — you — you understand what I done, don't you? (WALTER *is silent and sullen.*) I — I just seen my family falling apart today . . . just falling to pieces in front of my eyes . . . We couldn't of gone on like we was today. We was going backwards 'stead of forwards — talking 'bout killing babies and wishing each other was dead . . . When it gets like that in life — you just got to do something different, push on out and do something bigger . . . (*She waits.*) I wish you say something, son . . . I wish you'd say how deep inside you you think I done the right thing —

WALTER (*crossing slowly to his bedroom door and finally turning there and speaking measuredly*): What you need me to say you done right for? You the head of this family. You run our lives like you want to. It was your money and you did what you wanted with it. So what you need for me to say it was all right for? (*Bitterly, to hurt her as deeply as he knows is possible.*) So you butchered up a dream of mine — you — who always talking 'bout your children's dreams . . .

MAMA: Walter Lee —

(*He just closes the door behind him.* MAMA *sits alone, thinking heavily.*)

CURTAIN

Rosalind, disguised as a young boy, gives her lover a lesson in courting in this famous scene from Shakespeare's delightful sylvan comedy. The interpreter will want to assume some suggestion of male characteristics for Rosalind, but the audience must be aware that they are only a disguise, as Orlando conveniently is not. Celia is Rosalind's close companion and a party to her game.

FROM *As You Like It* / **WILLIAM SHAKESPEARE**

Act IV, Scene 1

ROSALIND: . . . Why, how now, Orlando! Where have you been all this while? You a lover! An you serve me such another trick, never come in my sight more.

ORLANDO: My fair Rosalind, I come within an hour of my promise.

ROSALIND: Break an hour's promise in love! He that will divide a minute into a thousand parts, and break but a part of the thousandth part of a minute in the affairs of love, it may be said of him that Cupid hath clapp'd him o' th' shoulder but I'll warrant him heart-whole.

ORLANDO: Pardon me, dear Rosalind.

ROSALIND: Nay, an you be so tardy, come no more in my sight. I had as lief be woo'd of a snail.

ORLANDO: Of a snail?

ROSALIND: Ay, of a snail; for though he comes slowly, he carries his house on his head; a better jointure, I think, than you make a woman. Besides, he brings his destiny with him.

ORLANDO: What's that?

ROSALIND: Why, horns, which such as you are fain to be beholding to your wives for. But he comes armed in his fortune and prevents the slander of his wife.

ORLANDO: Virtue is no horn-maker; and my Rosalind is virtuous.

ROSALIND: And I am your Rosalind.

CELIA: It pleases him to call you so; but he hath a Rosalind of a better leer than you.

ROSALIND: Come, woo me, woo me; for now I am in a holiday humour and like enough to consent. What would you say to me now, an I were your very very Rosalind?

ORLANDO: I would kiss before I spoke.

ROSALIND: Nay, you were better speak first; and when you were gravell'd for lack of matter, you might take occasion to kiss. Very good orators, when they are out, they will spit; and for lovers lacking — God warn us! — matter, the cleanliest shift is to kiss.

ORLANDO: How if the kiss be deni'd?

ROSALIND: Then she puts you to entreaty and there begins new matter.

ORLANDO: Who could be out, being before his beloved mistress?

ROSALIND: Marry, that should you if I were your mistress, or I should think my honesty ranker than my wit.

ORLANDO: What, of my suit?

ROSALIND: Not out of your apparel, and yet out of your suit. Am not I your Rosalind?

ORLANDO: I take some joy to say you are, because I would be talking of her.

ROSALIND: Well, in her person, I say I will not have you.

ORLANDO: Then in mine own person I die.

ROSALIND: No, faith, die by attorney. The poor world is almost six thousand years old, and in all this time there was not any man died in his own person, *videlicet*, in a love-cause. Troilus had his brains dash'd out with a Grecian club; yet he did what he could to die before, and he is one of the patterns of love. Leander, he would have liv'd many a fair year though Hero had turn'd nun, if it had not been for a hot mid-summer night; for, good youth, he went but forth to wash him in the Hellespont and being taken with the cramp was drown'd; and the foolish chronicles of that age found it was — Hero of Sestos. But these are all lies. Men have died from time to time and worms have eaten them, but not for love.

ORLANDO: I would not have my right Rosalind of this mind; for, I protest, her frown might kill me.

ROSALIND: By this hand, it will not kill a fly. But come, now I will be your Rosalind in a more coming-on disposition; and ask me what you will, I will grant it.

ORLANDO: Then love me, Rosalind.

ROSALIND: Yes, faith, will I, Fridays and Saturdays and all.

ORLANDO: And wilt thou have me?

ROSALIND: Ay, and twenty such.

ORLANDO: What sayest thou?

ROSALIND: Are you not good?

ORLANDO: I hope so.

ROSALIND: Why then, can one desire too much of a good thing? Come, sister, you shall be the priest and marry us. Give me your hand, Orlando. What do you say, sister?

ORLANDO: Pray thee, marry us.

CELIA: I cannot say the words.

ROSALIND: You must begin, "Will you, Orlando," —

CELIA: Go to. Will you, Orlando, have to wife this Rosalind?

ORLANDO: I will.

ROSALIND: Ay, but when?

ORLANDO: Why now; as fast as she can marry us.

ROSALIND: Then you must say, "I take thee, Rosalind, for wife."

ORLANDO: I take thee, Rosalind, for wife.

ROSALIND: I might ask you for your commission; but I do take thee, Orlando, for my husband. There's a girl goes before the priest; and certainly a woman's thought runs before her actions.

ORLANDO: So do all thoughts; they are wing'd.

ROSALIND: Now tell me how long you would have her after you have possess'd her.

ORLANDO: For ever and a day.

ROSALIND: Say "a day," without the "ever." No, no, Orlando. Men are April when they woo, December when they wed; maids are May when they are maids, but the sky changes when they are wives. I will be more jealous of thee than a Barbary cock-pigeon over his hen, more clamorous than a parrot against rain, more new-fangled than an ape, more giddy in my desires than a monkey. I will weep for nothing, like Diana in the fountain, and I will do that when you are dispos'd to be merry. I will laugh like a hyen, and that when thou art inclin'd to sleep.

ORLANDO: But will my Rosalind do so?

ROSALIND: By my life, she will do as I do.

ORLANDO: O, but she is wise.

ROSALIND: Or else she could not have the wit to do this. The wiser, the waywarder. Make the doors upon a woman's wit and it will out at the casement; shut that and 'twill out at the key-hole; stop that, 'twill fly with the smoke out at the chimney.

ORLANDO: A man that had a wife with such a wit, he might say, "Wit, whither wilt?"

ROSALIND: Nay, you might keep that check for it, till you met your wife's wit going to your neighbour's bed.

ORLANDO: And what wit could wit have to excuse that?

ROSALIND: Marry, to say she came to seek you there. You shall never take her without her answer, unless you take her without her tongue. O, that woman that cannot make her fault her husband's occasion, let her never nurse her child herself, for she will breed it like a fool!

ORLANDO: For these two hours, Rosalind, I will leave thee.

ROSALIND: Alas, dear love, I cannot lack thee two hours!

ORLANDO: I must attend the Duke at dinner. By two o'clock I will be with thee again.

ROSALIND: Ay, go your ways, go your ways; I knew what you would prove. My friends told me as much, and I thought no less. That flattering tongue of yours won me. 'Tis but one cast away, and so, come, death! Two o'clock is your hour?

ORLANDO: Ay, sweet Rosalind.

ROSALIND: By my troth, and in good earnest, and so God mend me, and by all pretty oaths that are not dangerous, if you break one jot of your promise or come one minute behind your hour, I will think you the most pathetical break-promise, and the most hollow lover, and the most unworthy of her you call Rosalind, that may be chosen out of the gross band of the unfaithful; therefore beware my censure and keep your promise.

ORLANDO: With no less religion than if thou wert indeed my Rosalind; so adieu.

ROSALIND: Well, Time is the old justice that examines all such offenders, and let Time try. Adieu.

(*Exit* ORLANDO.)

CELIA: You have simply misus'd our sex in your love-prate. We must have your doublet and hose pluck'd over your head, and show the world what the bird hath done to her own nest.

ROSALIND: O coz, coz, coz, my pretty little coz, that thou didst know how many fathom deep I am in love! But it cannot be sounded. My affection hath an unknown bottom, like the bay of Portugal.

CELIA: Or rather, bottomless; that as fast as you pour affection in, it runs out.

ROSILAIND: No, that same wicked bastard of Venus that was begot of thought, conceiv'd of spleen, and born of madness, that blind rascally boy that abuses every one's eyes because his own are out, let him be judge how deep I am in love. I'll tell thee, Aliena, I cannot be out of the sight of Orlando. I'll go find a shadow and sigh till he come.

CELIA: And I'll sleep.

(*Exeunt.*)

Bibliography

Since this chapter and the one which follows are so closely related in cause and effect, it seems wise to include here books which are applicable to both discussions.

Altenbernd, Lynn, and Leslie L. Lewis. *Introduction to Literature: Plays.* New York: The Macmillan Company, 1963.

One of a series of three books dealing with poetry, prose, and drama. An anthology of plays from Sophocles to Ionesco with an introduction covering the elements of drama, hints on the silent reading of plays, and a brief discussion of traditional and modern modes of dramatic writing.

Boleslavsky, Richard. *Acting: The First Six Lessons.* New York: Theatre Arts Books, 1949.

A delightful, sound book on the basic principles of observation and character analysis.

Brooks, Cleanth, and Robert B. Heilman (eds.). *Understanding Drama.* New York: Holt, Rinehart and Winston, Inc., 1945.

A companion to Understanding Fiction. Elementary but sound.

Coger, Leslie I., and Melvin R. White. *Readers Theatre Handbook: A Dramatic Approach to Literature.* Glenview, Ill.: Scott, Foresman & Company, 1967.

Corrigan, Robert W., and James L. Rosenberg. *The Art of the Theatre: A Critical Anthology of Drama.* San Francisco: Chandler Publishing Company, 1964.

Plays from Sophocles to Ionesco with selected critical essays preceding each play.

Corrigan, Robert W. *The Context and Craft of Drama: An Anthology of Critical Essays on the Nature of Drama and Theatre.* San Francisco: Chandler Publishing Company, 1964.

A collection of contemporary dramatic criticism presented in two divisions. Context includes discussions of the nature, language, structure, and criticism of drama; craft discusses the role of the playwright, actors, director, designer, and critic.

Gassner, John. *Form and Idea in Modern Theatre.* New York: Holt, Rinehart and Winston, Inc., 1956.

Considerations of dramatic structure and style within a historical development.

Kerr, Walter. *How Not to Write a Play.* New York: Simon and Schuster, 1955.

Witty, practical discussion of dramatic structure by a successful professional critic.

Magarshack, David. *Stanislavsky on the Art of the Stage.* New York: Hill and Wang, 1961.

A translation of this famous classic with an introductory essay on the Stanislavsky system.

McGaw, Charles. *Acting Is Believing: A Basic Method for Beginners.* Second Edition. New York: Holt, Rinehart and Winston, Inc., 1966.

Clear, practical statement on basic theories and techniques of acting. Exercises from well-known plays and two complete plays for analysis and practice.

Seyler, Athene, and Stephen Haggard. *The Craft of Comedy.* Second Edition. New York: Theatre Arts Books, 1957.

One of the standard books on structure and devices in comedy.

Wellwarth, George E. *The Theatre of Protest and Paradox: Developments in the Avant-Garde Drama.* New York: New York University Press, 1964.

Discussion of contemporary playwrights' use of the themes of protest developed through the techniques of paradox. Analyses of selected plays.

Chapter 9

In the preceding chapter we noted that during the early phases of preparation the interpreter of drama and the actor follow the same general procedure. Both first seek to understand and respond mentally, emotionally, and physically to all the aspects of the play. Then the actor goes forward into explicit physical and vocal representation, the interpreter into selectivity and suggestion. The question, then, for the interpreter of drama, is not so much how far to go as where to go. The accuracy of his selectivity will depend on the completeness of his understanding. The effectiveness of his suggestion will depend, in large measure, on the perfection of certain techniques. This chapter will be concerned with some specific technical problems inherent in the interpretation of drama. The brief suggestions for solving these problems are not, however, to be taken as rules. They are intended simply as practical suggestions which have been found effective. The only unbreakable rule is that there must be communication of the total achievement of the playwright, whether the entire play is being used or a single scene as an entity in itself.

The Role of Technique in the Interpretation of Drama

The interpretation of drama demands the utmost in alertness and in mental, emotional, vocal, and physical flexibility. Although a play usually revolves around one or two characters, the others are vitally important

Some Suggestions on Technique

in their relationship to the main characters and must emerge as individuals without any objective reminder from the author of the elements which make up that individuality. The threads of each character's development must remain unmistakable and unbroken and must be woven together to produce the whole fabric of the play. The interpreter must therefore be able to respond to every shade of mental and emotional activity for each character. Moreover, he must be able to pick up each character exactly as he has already suggested him in the previous scene or speech, taking into consideration whatever changes or development may have occurred in the meantime.

This extreme flexibility can be achieved only through careful, conscientious preparation. The process of analysis must be thorough and detailed. The interpreter must spend a great deal of time and effort in disciplining his voice and body to respond without visible coaching and with split-second timing to the dictates of the material. He may often have to go over and over a difficult speech or scene, working it out as a musician practices a complex passage or as a dancer perfects a complicated step. Only by such exercises can he bring his technique to the point where it becomes a tool to help him communicate rather than an embellishment to be exhibited. He must have his technique so completely under control that he can forget about it in performance, secure in the knowledge that his mind and muscles will respond. As experience increases, the degree of carry-over from preparation to performance will also increase. He will have reached his goal only when the audience is completely unaware of any effort on his part and is held by the material he is communicating to them. In performance, he must concentrate steadily on communication and on progressions and relationships.

Everything the interpreter chooses to do by way of technique must spring from an alert and disciplined mind. Mental discipline is perhaps more important in handling drama than in handling any other form of writing, both because of the special demands of drama, already noted, and because of the ever-present temptation to show off.

Techniques are not tricks. A trick deceives in order to puzzle or amuse. Technique, on the other hand, is skill in execution. The interpreter, who is an artist in his own right, is necessarily concerned with technique. It is wise to test one's artistic integrity from time to time in preparation to be sure one makes and observes the distinction. There is always a strong temptation to adopt certain physical and vocal mannerisms for their own sake, rather than allowing them to grow out of the needs of the material. A character is what he is because of numerous underlying mental and emotional qualities. He speaks and moves as he does because of those qualities. Only when the bases of characterization are clearly understood can the interpreter begin to work on the techniques which will honestly communicate the desired effects. Every interpreter who has a sense of performance and enjoys his position before his audience must occasionally ask himself, "Why am I doing this character in this particular way? Is it because of the demands of the material or because I am being tempted to charm or impress my audience?" The need to ask the question is no reflection on the interpreter's integrity. But strict honesty in answering it is absolutely imperative. Self-discipline and a firm set of artistic values will keep the interpreter from exhibitionism.

In no other area of interpretation is it more important to recall that "great art conceals art." The moment the audience becomes conscious of the way an interpreter is achieving an effect, the effect itself is weakened. It detracts from the total achievement by calling attention to the interpreter instead of to the play he is attempting to communicate. The effectiveness of his performance will depend directly on the interpreter's ease and unobtrusiveness. Ease will result from painstaking preparation and from discipline of vocal and physical technique. Unobtrusiveness, too, depends on thorough preparation and disciplined technique, and also on concentration and honesty of purpose in performance.

INTENSITY AND CONTROL OF EMOTION

These remarks on discipline and control should not be read as an indication that the interpreter of drama does not respond emotionally to his material. On the contrary, the intensity of his response is as great as the actor's. There is a difference between suppressing an emotion and controlling its outward manifestations. The intensity is present according to the demands of the material, but the control of that intensity is an important artistic discipline. An actor who became so caught up with his emotional responses to a scene that he neglected to give the proper cues to the other characters, or sank into a chair and wept when he was supposed to go offstage, would certainly be in for an after-performance lecture from the director, for he would have violated the principles of his art. In the same way, an interpreter who allows himself to be so completely caught up in one character that he neglects to give the others the proper degree of importance and clarity is not interpreting. He is not being true to the principles of any art. If he becomes so emotionally involved that his eyes fill with tears and his voice cannot be heard, he will embarrass the people close enough to see the tears and irritate those who cannot hear what he is saying. He will be calling attention to himself and concentrating on his own response instead of on the material and the audience's response to that material. As soon as he embarks on an emotional orgy, the audience becomes uneasy and embarrassed, for the emotion no longer belongs to the character but to the interpreter. A public display of personal emotion is in bad taste on any occasion, but in this case the interpreter is committing the further sin of forcing the audience to divide its attention between the character and the interpreter as a person.

The principle of controlled intensity is sometimes referred to as "aesthetic distance." It means, in the words of an old theatre axiom, keeping a cool head over a warm heart. It is a matter of increased control, not of lessened intensity. Emotional intensity must be strong when the material demands it, if the interpreter is to draw a suitable response from his audience. Yet this intensity must be kept under firm control, so that the audience will respond to the emotional impact of the material, not to the performer's extreme sensibility.

The interpreter's circle of emotional response, like his mental circle of concentration, is not limited to the reading stand but includes the entire audience in its sweep. The principle of emotional rapport with an audience is an extremely difficult one to define in words, but once the interpreter has experienced it he will never doubt its value and effectiveness in oral interpretation. We are all familiar with the process of projecting an emotion to a single person so that response is engendered in him and returns to us. The same process applies to a group of people. It is the interpreter's business to make his audience *feel* as well as *think* with the characters in a drama, and in this connection the already familiar principle of empathy is, of course, basic.

MEMORIZING

Closely allied with the interrelations among the interpreter, the dramatic materials he is presenting, and the audience is the question of memorizing. With drama, the interpreter needs to come closer to a complete memorization of his material than with any other type of writing, because of the speed with which he must handle the interplay of characters. He is without the prop of the explanatory dialogue tag, ". . . said Mr. So-and-So . . . ," such as he finds in narrative. He is given only the character's name at the beginning of each speech, which, of course, he does not repeat to the audience. Though the audience must always know who is speaking, identifying the character by name at the beginning of each speech would soon become tiresome. Moreover, it would constantly break the train of thought and emotion, and destroy the total effect. The interpreter, then, must be able to establish the character's identity immediately by a skillful use of technique. He must not only have the speeches and their progression clearly in mind, but who speaks them, what prompts them, and to whom they are addressed. He cannot afford to look down after each speech for his next cue. This would slow the performance — and worse still, it would break his own concentration on the continuity of the scene and destroy most of the necessary interplay between the characters. For these reasons, he would do best to have his material fairly well memorized, using the printed page only to refresh his memory from time to time.

Presenting the Cast

Each person who attends a theater performance is provided with a printed program listing the members of the cast. When an interpreter is doing a play, he must assume the responsibility of introducing the cast to his listeners directly as narrator.

If the cast is small, he may include all of them in his first remarks, perhaps indicating which ones appear somewhat later than the others. On the other hand, when a play has a large number of characters, it is neither practical nor necessary for the interpreter to attempt to introduce all of them. He will be guided by the cuts he has made in the material, and he will mention only those characters he will be using in his cutting. He may lump several together as "guests at the tea." When the cast is a large one, it is usually wise to introduce the minor characters when they appear, rather than to burden the audience with too many names at the outset. As a start, it will be enough to give only the names and a word or two of identification of the characters in the first key scene or two. The others may be introduced as they enter.

Many plays published in book form give on the cast page a notation of the date and place of first performance and the names of the complete original cast. This information will hardly be needed for the interpreter's purposes. Indeed, it is usually unwise to remind an audience that certain roles have been created or made famous by certain actors. After all, the interpreter is not attempting to suggest a famous portrayal of the main role, but rather the characters around whom the play revolves.

Stage Directions

The problem of handling preliminary stage directions was touched on in the preceding chapter in relation to establishing a play's background and setting. The interpreter can give the essential information directly to the audience before the action of the play begins and can incorporate other elements from the stage directions into his analysis of character and eventually into his handling of the dialogue.

When a play is divided into scenes and acts, it is usually simplest and clearest to make similar breaks in handling the material for interpretation. The interpreter normally does not leave the platform but indicates a division by general relaxation, an effective pause, and a return to conversational directness with his audience. Thus he makes the best possible use of the playwright's principles of organization by concluding large units of action and clearly establishing their conclusion for the audience. This technique, moreover, enables the interpreter and the listeners to relax momentarily and go smoothly into the next large unit.

Each scene and act will have its own indication of time and place. When the location remains the same throughout the play, the interpreter may establish that fact in his first narration to the audience and thereafter cope merely with time changes. When there are changes in location as well as time, it is most helpful to call them to the attention of the audience immediately before the units to which they apply.

It is smoother, more direct, and more conversational to use complete sentences for stage directions instead of the literal wording of the script, "Act One. Living room in the Martin home, Washington, D.C." Sometimes, of course, the stage directions may be used almost exactly as they are printed. If there are two or more scenes within a single act, these can be taken care of neatly and simply by a brief statement before each: "The first scene of Act Two takes place in John Martin's study"; "The second scene of Act Two is again in the living room."

The matter of time is handled in equally simple fashion. The cast page often gives the progression in terms of months, noting, for example, that the first act takes place in December, the second in January and February, and the last act in March. This information can most conveniently be given to the audience at the beginning of each scene and act. One may use the months as mentioned, or such phrases as "a few weeks later," "a month later," or any other wording which will make clear that enough time has elapsed to make the action and the development of character credible.

The same principles apply to stage directions at the end of an act. Just as a director times his curtain to harmonize with the mood of the scene, so an interpreter gives some attention to his choice of words in closing a scene. In *Androcles and the Lion* (page 368), for example, the prologue ends with a suggestion of continuing activity on the part of Androcles and his lion as well as a change of locale. Androcles' wife, however, has just revived from her faint and has a speech after their exit. The skilled interpreter who has already carefully established Megaera's character could probably suggest her revival without the stage direction, and indicate by vocal and mental projection that she is shouting after her husband and his waltzing partner. The closing stage direction, "She rushes off after them into the jungle," however, makes an excellent curtain line just as it stands. In *Rhinoceros* (page 361), on the other hand, most of the scenes conclude with a stage direction which must be included for both mood and clarity of action. Sometimes the playwright's words can be used almost verbatim, but the interpreter may need to smooth the transition to "Curtain" in such a close as this:

> (*He goes once more to the various exits, but the spectacle of the rhinoceros halts him. When he gets back to the bathroom door it seems about to give way.* BERENGER *throws himself against the back wall, which yields; the street is visible in the background; he flees, shouting:*)

Rhinoceros! Rhinoceros!

> (*Noises. The bathroom door is on the point of yielding.*)

CURTAIN

Entrances and exits during the course of a scene may occasionally cause some difficulty. If a character's exit occurs at the close of his speech and indicates the completion of a key scene, the interpreter may easily assume the role of narrator and tell his audience directly, "And he goes out." Sometimes it may be advisable to add some explanatory remark to maintain a mood or to complete an action, as "He hesitated for a moment, looking back at her, then went out, closing the door behind him." If the attention is to remain with the character or characters on stage, the wording can be changed slightly to accomplish this shift of focus: "He hesitated for a moment, looking back at her, then went out, closing the door behind him. As soon as she was left alone, Mary opened her eyes."

A character who enters will usually have to be identified — or reidentified. On a first entrance, the playwright will probably give a description of the character. The interpreter may use whatever he needs of that description to help identify the character for his audience. On later entrances, the character's name will probably be enough, with a brief reference to any relevant changes of costume or mood. Usually there is no need to specify the direction from which an entrance is made unless some definite plot motivation is involved. One might wish to say, "He enters from the porch," but it would not be necessary to say, "He enters from up center," because the interpreter's scene is not on stage and he is not concerned with physical layout beyond indicating an entrance into the scene.

Often the dialogue will identify the character who is entering or make perfectly clear that a character is leaving the scene, and the interpreter need not interrupt the scene to tell the audience directly that there has been an entrance or an exit. He will, however, need to be sure that the other characters show some reaction. At Mama's entrance in the excerpt from *A Raisin in the Sun* at the end of Chapter 8, for instance, Ruth and Walter have been having an intimate conversation. Obviously the mood is broken and the conversation comes to an abrupt end. Walter has the first speech after Mama's entrance. He identifies her by name, and the question "Where have you been?" makes the fact of her entrance perfectly clear. But Walter must see her and react sharply before he speaks. She must be visualized in the doorway and entering the room. The doorway, like the rest of the scene, is out front, and Walter watches her come toward him for a second while he adjusts his thoughts. The reverse process will work for exits. The character remaining on scene will visualize the departing character going out, and if he has a parting remark he will need to raise his projection, both mental and vocal, to reach over a greater distance. The first part of Juliet's speech (*Romeo and Juliet*, pages 346–347), for example, opens with "Farewell!" as Lady Capulet and the Nurse leave Juliet's room. Of course, the interpreter may assume that they have already gone and that the "Farewell!" is primarily reflective. The audience can be helped to visualize the scene more clearly, however, and the stage directions can be simplified as well, if Juliet calls this parting after them as they leave the room and then waits a moment, as she watches the door close behind them, before continuing with, "God knows when we shall meet again." Four lines later Juliet calls to the Nurse, and then immediately decides against having her return, something which can be suggested by attention to projection. The interpreter can suggest the decisions by the principle of muscle memory, which will motivate a change in muscle tone, and by appropriate timing and use of pauses.

Physical Action

In the case of a specific physical action, it is important to remember that suggestion rather than explicitness is the goal. It is never wise to underestimate the audience's ability and willingness to accept suggestion if it is clear and shows the proper motivation and empathic response. Listeners tend to accept a presentation on its own terms, so long as it is consistent and unobtrusive.

If an action is necessary to plot motivation, it is usually better to make use of the narrative technique, as was suggested in Chapter 8. If the action is primarily important for its revelation of an attitude or emotional state, then the audience should be made aware of the cause rather than the action itself. The action is the outward manifestation of an interior response, and this gives the interpreter an important clue to the way it should be handled. It is not so much *what* the character does as *how* he does it that will reveal what he is thinking and feeling. If, for example, a character sinks dejectedly into a chair, it is not the process of sitting down that is important but the dejection pointed up by the action. This dejection will show itself in the muscle tone of the interpreter's entire body, the pace of speech, the vocal quality, and numerous other ways. In preparation, the business should certainly be rehearsed in detail and the act of sitting synchronized with the speech so that voice and body are saying the same thing. In performance, however, the explicit act of sinking into a chair would pull the scene up on stage instead of keeping it out front. Moreover, it would be impractical and would cause needless complications. In the first place, the interpreter would need a chair to sink into. If he uses a chair, he may logically need a table, a mantel to lean against, a window to open, and a door to slam. To use one and not the others would be to meander back and forth between acting and interpretation, and the result would be an interruption of the audience's attention and an illogical if not ludicrous situation. Moreover, once the character was seated, there would always be the problem of getting him up again. This action, too, would need to be properly motivated by something the character said or thought, and the motivation might not occur for some time. And what about the characters who speak from another position? The safest plan is to continue standing throughout and to suggest repose not by an overt bodily act but by empathy, muscle tone, and whatever aspects of vocal technique are appropriate.

When an interpreter is confronted with a scene in which a character loses consciousness, effective presentation and good taste alike require of him a particular control and a nice discrimination. The end of the scene from *Romeo and Juliet* presents this problem. Obviously, any explicit action such as dropping the head and chest onto the lectern or relaxing in an exaggerated slump would be difficult to achieve subtly and would call attention to the interpreter. During the pause that follows Juliet's closing words, the physical tension can be held for a moment, then visibly relaxed and the head dropped forward. The pause should be long enough to enable the audience to complete the piece of action *in their own minds* before the interpreter closes his manuscript or speaks directly as a narrator to tell them "the curtain falls," or some such appropriate phrase to end the scene.

PROPERTIES

Properties which must be suggested can also cause difficulty. In fact, the whole matter of properties requires of the interpreter a sure sense of degree of suggestion. The characters in many modern plays, for example, use a telephone. The excerpt from *Rhinoceros* depends in part on effective handling of this property. Placing one clenched hand to the ear and the other below the chin, which for some reason seems to be a popular way to suggest a telephone conversation, can be ludicrous and create unnecessary complications — especially if one hand is occupied with a book or script. If the interpreter wishes to suggest so explicitly that he is holding a telephone, then he must also pick it up from somewhere and put it back on the hook when he has finished the conversation. Instead of going through these motions in mid-air, it is far better to insert the word "Operator" or "Hello" before giving the number. The audience will immediately know that a telephone is being used. When a dial telephone is indicated, it is simpler to translate the action into words as if the connection were being made through an operator. The type of telephone being used is, after all, a matter of very little consequence. More important is the difference in degree of directness between a telephone conversation and a conversation with someone who is present. The quality of attention and the manner of speaking will help set the telephone speeches off from the others better than mime, as will the handling of the pauses to indicate the other half of the dialogue which the audience does not hear.

But the problem of properties is by no means confined to modern plays. In one of the most familiar scenes from *Romeo and Juliet* — Scene 3 of Act IV, in which Juliet drinks the potion Friar Laurence has given her — the interpreter must cope with both a vial and a dagger. In the passage beginning "Come, vial," in which Juliet voices her doubts as she looks at the mixture, she clearly picks up the vial with the intention of drinking it. It is traditional and practical for an actress on the stage to hold the vial high enough to be seen by the audience. But the interpreter does not have a vial. For this reason, it is enough — and considerably more effective — to keep the hand low, on the reading stand or level with the book, and visualize a small vial lying in the palm of the hand, or even lying on the stand itself. The interpreter is not trying to make the audience believe he actually is holding a vial; he is merely establishing the idea of the vial in the minds of the audience since it is essential to the plot. The barely sketched gesture of holding it in his palm will help him visualize it and project the muscle response which will enable the audience to accept the idea that Juliet has a potion in her hand and is about to drink it. Muscle tone and emotional tensions are the important considerations, not an overt manipulation of an imaginary object.

A few lines later attention turns to the dagger. Juliet does not mention it specifically, but it is logically implied by the words "This shall forbid it. Lie thou there." When the play is staged, the weapon is held so that the audience can see it. But again, the interpreter does not have a dagger. A slight gesture comparable to the one used to indicate the vial will satisfy a desire for action on the line and will establish the presence of the dagger in the minds of the listeners. If it is assumed that Juliet picks up the dagger, looks at it a moment, and then lays it down, the interpreter will need to draw on his muscle memory for his timing. His hand, kept low on the reading stand or level with the book, may merely turn from palm up while holding the dagger to palm down on "Lie thou there." Attention focuses for a moment on the dagger and then returns to the vial.

If the interpreter has fallen into the trap of the too-explicit gesture, he will find himself in trouble as he shuttles his imaginary properties from hand to hand, or plucks them from mid-air and lays them down on nothingness — especially if he has no reading stand and has one hand occupied with an all too solid book! Since much activity and a high degree of tension in this scene must be allowed to come through, the interpreter is very likely to feel the need for some bodily expression that goes beyond muscle tension. Even so, he should guard against overt representation. He wants to catch the audience up with him, enable them to see the scene in their minds and feel it in their muscles. But he does not want to step across the boundary from suggestion to explicitness, presenting not Juliet in her agonized moment of decision but the spectacle of himself plucking at the air. *Suggestion, empathy,* and *controlled intensity* are the keynotes.

The last words of the speech, and of the scene, "This do I drink to thee," make it very clear that the vial has been lifted to Juliet's lips and that she swallows the potion. This is a dramatic moment for the actress. But the interpreter is not physically *being* Juliet; he is helping the audience to *see* Juliet. Because it is the close of a scene and a high point, and because Juliet is the only character to be considered, the interpreter may be unendurably tempted to raise the vial to his mouth in a grand final gesture. The effectiveness of such a gesture will depend on his control, his timing, and his specificness. Certainly raising the hand holding the vial to the level of the mouth will be most helpful in making the important action clear to the audience. But it must be done swiftly and with precisely the appropriate degree of tension, and with his concentration on *Juliet's* emotional state, not on his own execution of the action. To clutch a vial of a certain size and shape, lift it to the lips, and then obtrusively gulp the liquid is too elaborate and physically descriptive, and would distract from the scene the audience is holding in its minds. They would become involved in watching the *interpreter* swallow, in the size of the vial, the amount he consumes, and various other irrelevant matters, and lose the dramatic impact of the result. The gesture should describe the way the action made Juliet feel rather than the action itself. As the interpreter grows in skill, he will become increasingly able to distinguish between valid bodily action and the tension it conveys and the explicit physical representation of the action for its own sake.

Immediately after the vial has been raised there must be a second of tense suspension followed by a suggestion, at least, of loss of consciousness — probably by slackening the muscle tone and dropping the head. As we noted earlier, this can be accomplished during the pause which must follow the speech and can be perfectly timed for climactic effect. It requires maximum concentration and control. The interpreter will need to rehearse the full action in his early preparation to get the feel and timing of coordinated bodily action and speech, but he will be wise to experiment until he can do the scene in performance without the overt action of drinking the poison. After he has learned to work without the overt action, he will be aware of the functioning of muscle memory and the pull and tension that go into the complete cycle of deciding to drink, drinking, experiencing the effect of the potion, and finally losing consciousness. He may then go back to the action itself and use whatever parts of it seem necessary, remembering that the action itself is less important to his audience's comprehension than the build-up to it and its effect. The lines make the action clear. The important thing is its effect on Juliet.

PHYSICAL CONTACT

Action requiring physical contact with another character should probably be translated into narration. A handshake, for example, is most difficult to make convincing when only one hand is involved. To reach out into space as one character, grasp a hand that is not there and give it a firm clasp, then jump into the other character and complete the greeting is both awkward and unnecessary. A straightforward manner of speaking, an increased directness, and a sharpening of focus are enough to suggest the greeting.

A kiss, which is more difficult to suggest, cannot always be cut, since it is often a key action; when retained, however, it can usually be translated into narration. In no case should a kiss be an explicit action, for an interpreter who purses his lips and closes his eyes for a fond caress with empty air can most charitably be described as an amusing spectacle.

Usually the playwright provides stage directions to indicate the physical contact and to serve as a guide to actors and director. When these can be appropriately used, the interpreter may give them directly to the audience as narration. In Tennessee Williams's *The Glass Menagerie*, for example, the Gentleman Caller has been telling Laura what she should do about her inferiority complex, and he comes to the conclusion that

> Somebody — ought to —
> Ought to — *kiss* you, Laura!
> (*His hand slips slowly up her arm to her shoulder. He suddenly turns her about and kisses her on the lips. When he releases her,* LAURA *sinks on the sofa with a bright, dazed look.* JIM *backs away and fishes in his pocket for a cigarette.*)

The playwright has successfully maintained the proper mood through these brief directions. He reaches the climax swiftly in the second parenthetical sentence. The interpreter would probably hold this climax for a moment to allow the audience to complete the picture and the emotional implications. The playwright provides for a gradual release of tension in the next sentence, keeping the attention focused on Laura. The last sentence comes back to reality, as attention turns to the Gentleman Caller. When the playwright's stage directions do not coincide so happily with the interpreter's needs as Williams's do in this case, the interpreter had best rewrite the directions so that they preserve the mood established and prepare the audience for whatever change is to follow.

Physical contact growing out of anger usually comes at a climactic moment. Thus, to interrupt a speech with the parenthetical information that "He slapped her" or "He hit him" would often break the build-up. This type of action, of course, carries with it a high degree of muscle tension and a sharp kinetic imagery. The interpreter's mental comment, emotional intensity, facial expression, and entire posture will help considerably in suggesting not only the anger which motivates the action but even the thrust of the blow. The character receiving the blow will react with a sudden muscle reflex, and with either increased muscle tension or total relaxation depending on the force and effect of the blow. Because they depend on the visual spectacle for their effectiveness and are longer in duration, duels and wrestling are best covered by narration. The narration can help create suspense and eliminate the problem of simultaneous activity by two characters.

It is impossible and impractical to formulate general rules to be applied to every example of physical contact. Each instance presents its own problem, depending on its importance in the overall effect and on the interpreter's experience and skill in suggestion and his taste and discrimination. The only rule that can guide him may be summed up in two questions. The first is: "How explicit *must* (not *may*) I be so that the audience will understand what I am doing and accept the action as an integral part of the total effect?" In answering this question, the interpreter must take care not to underestimate his audience. That is, he should think in terms not of how much action he can get away with, but of how little he needs to use. The second question is: "Will this technique of suggested action call attention to itself and to me and thus detract from the material?"

The interpreter is by no means to infer that he should stand like a totem pole, not daring to move his hands. Any action he feels *necessary* for communication is to be used without apology or self-consciousness. He will find it useful to go to both extremes in preparation. On the one hand, specific action will insure muscle memory and thus help him establish his timing and motivate empathy. On the other, it is only through trying the scene without any specific action at all that he can put his artistic standards to the test. Somewhere between these extremes he will hit upon the mean which seems right to him. His decision will rest on his ultimate purpose: communicating the *total* scene with all its elements in proper proportion.

Portrayal of Character

Drama, by its very nature and form, does not tell explicitly *about* the characters, except in brief stage directions; hence it imposes on the interpreter a greater responsibility for suggestion than do some other literary forms. All outward manifestations suggesting character must spring directly from an understanding of the mental and emotional characteristics of the person being suggested. A character moves and speaks as he does largely because of what he thinks and feels. Certain physical aspects, however, are important in establishing a three-dimensional character, and sex, age, and infirmity can play a strong part in forming the inner response. The following suggestions are offered to help the interpreter handle these and other physical aspects of character. Obviously, the complexity of the characters and the importance of their physical attributes will vary from play to play. The interpreter of drama must be guided by the playwright's achievement and his own knowledge of the relationship between the interior and exterior aspects of each character. He must always remember that his aim is to *suggest* and not to *represent* character. Some of these matters were touched on briefly in relation to narratives in Chapter 7, but they will bear repeating here.

SEX

One of the most troublesome problems in handling drama arises out of the interpreter's need to suggest characters of both sexes. It is a common mistake to begin character analysis with the generalization that all men are alike and all women are alike. Nothing, of course, could be further from the truth. The most important character elements to start with are individual differences in attitude and style, just as they are in any character analysis. The next steps in preparation should follow the pattern already suggested in Chapter 8. Only after all the individual traits are discovered and coordinated will the interpreter turn his attention specifically to sex differentiation. Certainly sex accounts for some of these individual traits and cannot be ignored even in the first steps of analysis, but the physical and vocal suggestion of male or female characteristics will grow most easily out of a study of individual differences. Certain characters, and indeed certain pieces of nondramatic literature, are easier for a man than a woman, and vice versa. But any interpreter worthy of the name can suggest either sex quite satisfactorily to the audience. He is not asking them to believe that he *is* physically that character; he is asking them to imagine a character who behaves and thinks in such-and-such a fashion.

As to techniques of voice, the male interpreter will do well to underplay rather than overplay his suggestion of feminine character. He need not raise his voice above its natural pitch for the women's speeches. He can put across the idea of feminine speech more effectively by merely lightening the quality of his voice and allowing most of the sound to come from the top of his throat, and by establishing individual rhythms of speech for the feminine as well as for the masculine characters.

To suggest a feminine character physically, a man may allow his weight to shift very slightly forward on one foot, as women tend to stand with the weight centered on the balls of the feet rather than back on the heels. He should be very careful, however, not to go beyond the point of merely helping the audience to identify the character speaking. He is not attempting to assume the role of a woman, and he certainly does not want to set up a rhythmic rocking motion — swaying forward for a woman, back again for a man. Awareness of the part played by the smaller muscles of the neck, the waist, and the ankles and wrists may also help achieve a feeling of delicacy.

A woman interpreter will have comparable difficulties with male characters. She must also remember that she is *suggesting* and that her audience will accept even slight distinctions between masculine and feminine characters if she is consistent and sufficiently clear in establishing that difference in their minds. She, too, should underplay rather than overplay the physical and vocal attributes of a male character. An exaggerated bass voice convinces no one of masculinity; indeed, it is ridiculous to assume that a violent change in pitch or volume indicates anything to the listeners except the reader's vocal range, which is of interest only as it promotes understanding and enjoyment of the material at hand. But quality of voice as a means of suggesting a male character is a different matter. A fuller sound can be achieved by allowing the throat to relax so that the undertones of the voice are put to use, and by breathing fully and deeply so that a steady stream of air sustains the richer quality. Physically, the woman interpreter can suggest a male character by reversing the procedure a man uses to suggest a woman. That is, she may let the large muscles of the shoulders, legs, and upper arms give her a feeling of solidness, and allow her weight to shift backward a little more onto her heels. Few men stand with their feet extremely far apart, but they do tend to keep their weight evenly balanced, a fact which gives them a firmer stance than women usually have. This simple change in balance, combined with an almost imperceptible squaring of the shoulders, is ordinarily all that is needed for physical suggestion.

AGE AND INFIRMITY

The outward manifestations of age and vitality or infirmity are important if the hearers are to re-create a three-dimensional character as they listen to and watch the interpreter of drama. A subtle suggestion of age, however, is most difficult to achieve. It is neither necessary nor desirable to hump the shoulders, curl the hands helplessly across the breast, and speak in an exaggerated tremolo and falsetto. Indeed, few old people speak and hold themselves that way unless they are extremely feeble and emaciated. A person beyond middle age is not necessarily in the last stages of debility. Further, when a pattern so devoid of vitality is set up, it is almost impossible to achieve any strength or climactic builds within the development of the character. Age, like so many other things, is a relative matter. Some people are mentally and emotionally antiquated at fifty; others retain their vitality through a long and vigorous old age. The degree of vitality should be dictated by the individual character involved, and should be related less to his chronological age as indicated in the stage directions than to his responsiveness and individuality.

Age can be suggested by muscle memory and certain aspects of vocal technique. An old person will move more deliberately, more cautiously than one in his prime. Consequently, his scenes are likely to be paced more slowly and evenly than those of a younger character. By responding empathically to the idea of stiffened joints, insecure footing, and generally decreased vigor, the interpreter can convey an impression of age to the audience; and he may also sketch a suggestion, through his body, of the physical pattern of age — the shoulders slightly drooped, the head thrust almost imperceptibly forward. In preparation, when the specific actions are rehearsed, the hands rather than full arm movements should be used wherever possible, since the big muscles of the arms and shoulders no longer have the strength of youth. The interpreter should watch old people carefully to note how they handle things without putting their arm and shoulder muscles into play, and how they minimize the use of muscles in the back and thighs. In performance, this impression of diminished muscular activity can be put across by means of muscle tone and a shift in the balance of the whole frame. The interpreter must always remember that the audience is not interested in seeing how quickly he can snap from an aged stoop to the erect posture of youth. Underemphasis on physical details is the safer part, for any abrupt change in stance calls attention to itself and destroys the overall effect of the material. In like manner, individual characteristics of age — indecisiveness, pomposity, or any other quality which would show itself physically — must be treated with the same restraint as diminished vitality.

Vocally old people tend to use a narrow range of inflection, partly because their responses are slower and partly because the mental attitude of age reflects less enthusiasm than does that of youth. The rate of speech may also be slower and the rhythm less staccato than that of a younger person. This will be apparent in the style of their speeches.

Interplay of Characters

The interpreter who wants to work out the full values in drama will find it helpful, at least until he becomes experienced, to take one character at a time and perfect the technique to be used in suggesting him, as outlined in the previous chapter. Then comes the problem of getting all the characters together so that they are contributing parts of the whole and reacting to each other as the play progresses. The actor must learn not only how to speak and move in his part but also how to listen. The interpreter of drama obviously cannot listen as one character while he is speaking as another. Therefore, we may say that the interpreter must instead learn to "have heard." He must develop the ability to pick up the thread of thought in the person of the character who has heard the speech or seen the action. This requires a split-second response possible only when he has all the characters so completely under control that they seem ready and waiting to step immediately into the center of attention. In short, the interpreter is not to develop a split personality but to build a compound one. He cannot let half his mind, voice, and body lie dormant while one character speaks, thinks, and acts. He must use all his faculties for each character. He must have a clear focus of attention when he is speaking and a sharp and immediate response in the person of the character who replies. When he has developed the art of interpreting drama to its highest point, his reaction will be as complete mentally and emotionally as the actor's, and his empathic response as genuine.

There is no quick way to accomplish this difficult feat. The only sure method is careful, painstaking preparation and complete concentration during performance. No character should be allowed to drop out of the scene or out of the fabric of the whole. Furthermore, his outlines must not become blurred; he must emerge complete and individual the moment he picks up his cue. Developing this technique takes time, effort, and experience, and the beginner can only work toward it as a goal, but it lies at the heart of a well-paced, successful performance of drama.

PICKING UP CUES

The interpreter should recall that a cue can be picked up mentally and physically as well as vocally. The character need not begin to speak the second his cue is given. Pauses are often effective and necessary. Moreover, they give the audience time to assimilate the previous speech if it has been an important or complex one. Care should be taken, however, not to let the pace become labored. It is important to keep a careful check on the rhythm of the entire scene. A cue can be picked up by a glance or a facial expression or a change of muscle tone.

The interpreter's control and precision must be highly developed to avoid two common pitfalls in the shift from one character to another. One of these is the danger of allowing a sag in characterization between speeches. Inexperienced readers are sometimes guilty of completing one character and then reverting to their own personalities in the fraction of a second before they pick up another character. This slows the scene and makes the total effect labored and heavy-handed. The student should practice picking up each of the characters cleanly and sharply, as they are rehearsed individually, until his mind and muscles react without conscious prompting.

The other pitfall is the danger of a too-hurried transition, the result of imperfect timing and coordination between mind and muscles. When the interpreter leaves one character and picks up another a fraction of a second before a speech has been completed, his listeners may lose the final words of the speech. What is even more serious, they may become aware that the interpreter is anticipating the other character, and this awareness will split their attention. Thorough preparation, time and effort spent on technique, and a sure sense of timing will help the interpreter avoid either of these extremes in the transition from one character to another.

The vocal technique must become so much a part of the characterization that it is almost automatic as the mind and muscles pick up the character. This cannot be achieved in a few minutes of preparation. It is far better to begin preparation well in advance of performance, and keep working at it so that there is time to evolve the habit of each character, than to attempt the work in one long, sustained session just before a presentation. The interpreter must live with his characters; they must become part of him, and he of them.

Physical Focus

The degree and direction of physical focus on the characters must spring out of the interpreter's concept of his material as a whole and not be imposed on the material by external rules. There are, however, a few general techniques that may prove helpful.

It is usually safest, for example, to assume that a character being addressed is approximately one's own height, with an eye level about even with one's own. Even when a discrepancy in height may be assumed, any exaggerated angle of focus should be avoided. When a short person and a tall one converse, unless they are standing very close together the angle at which their eyes meet is not a marked one. Thus, in suggesting a tall character addressing a short one, an adult speaking to a child, or a standing character addressing a seated character, the interpreter must take care not to reduce the shorter person to a spot on the floor. For best results, he should rehearse each character specifically, and then let muscle memory dictate the angle of eye focus.

Sometimes it is necessary to indicate that the character being addressed is approaching or going away from the speaker. This situation was mentioned in connection with the "Farewell" in Juliet's speech and with Mama's entrance in A Raisin in the Sun. Since the interpreter's scene is out front, the characters approach and depart out front — not behind or beside him as they would on stage. When the person to whom a speech is directed is entering or leaving the room, descending or ascending stairs, or moving about in other ways which change the distance between him and the speaker, it is well to visualize his movement in the area of the back wall, allowing the eyes to follow the direction and rate of his movement. The increase or decrease of vocal and mental projection thus required will help to indicate the logical eye movements, too.

ANGLE OF PLACEMENT

It must be borne in mind that, like the other technical suggestions in this chapter, the following suggestions on angle of placement are not rules but devices that have been found useful. If the suggestions do not fit the demands of the material and the needs of the interpreter, they need not be followed.

On stage, people move about from one area to another; consequently, speeches addressed to a character must be directed to the place where he is stationed at the moment. Many interpretive artists follow this same principle and allow the direction of address to change as the character being addressed moves about. This is a logical procedure and is often handled most skillfully. It does, however, impose an added burden on the interpreter, who must remember not only which character is speaking, what prompted the speech, and to whom it is addressed, but also where the character being addressed has moved to since his earlier scenes.

It is less complicated and more effective to follow the principle that the angle of address should be dictated by the character speaking, not by the hypothetical position of the character being addressed. In the first place, an audience quickly becomes accustomed to having a certain character speak at a certain angle. It helps identify him. This is especially important when there are several characters who are hard to distinguish in terms of vocal and physical characteristics. Further, the interpreter can more easily accustom himself to the nearly automatic pickup of focus and muscle set for each character when he retains the same relative position for all the speeches of each one.

In other words, a specific character always speaks in the same direction no matter whom he is addressing. This does not mean that he keeps his eyes glued on a single spot on the back wall. If he is addressing several people simultaneously or in succession, he will let his eye focus shift slightly to indicate that he is doing so. In actual conversation, one does not stare steadily into the eyes of another unless the degree of emotional intensity demands such concentration. Locating the character as to area of address is enough unless there is an unusually large cast of characters.

Since the angle widens as it extends to the rear of the audience, the interpreter should keep his areas of address close enough together so that he can shift from one to the other easily. An almost imperceptible change of angle, combined with the other changes in posture, muscle tone, facial expression, and vocal characteristics, will make it clear that another character is speaking. When the characters are placed too far apart the interpreter must turn his whole head, and the result, in fast dialogue, is much the same as the head movement of a spectator at a tennis match. Moreover, the danger of a lag between speeches is increased because the interpreter has so far to go physically before he can pick up the next speech. Any movement of this kind may become unpleasantly noticeable and detract from the effectiveness of the performance.

In deciding on the angle of address or the area toward which each character will direct his speeches, it is usually more practical to retain exact center position for narration to the audience in the interpreter's own person. The characters may then be placed on either side of that center line, as close together as possible without confusing the audience. The principal characters, who carry much of the dialogue and have the most important speeches, may be placed on either side of the center line to facilitate their interplay. It is sometimes practical to separate similar characters so that they will not overlap as they might if placed side by side. Minor characters who play a scene together should all be placed in the same general direction to prevent any wide gap between them.

It is recommended that the interpreter adopt this method of character placement until he is experienced enough to develop his own method without the danger of confusing his audience and adding needless complications to the already complex process of interpreting drama. The most important consideration is that the audience know immediately who is speaking.

AUDIENCE CONTACT

Establishing and maintaining contact with the audience is one of the most troublesome problems in handling drama. Clearly, the interpreter can easily maintain immediate contact during his direct narrative and explanatory material. The problem manifests itself in dialogue. Some authorities suggest selecting a member of the audience and addressing the speeches to him. Though this helps a beginner achieve directness, we assume here that the interpreter who is ready to handle drama has already passed that stage in his development. And, as we have remarked, it often embarrasses a listener to have highly emotional speeches directed at him, and he will tend to pull away. Moreover, a direct meeting of eyes can sometimes throw the interpreter off stride for a moment and break his concentration. It is simpler and safer to visualize the characters addressed as somewhere toward the back of the room, only a few inches above the heads of the audience. In this way the interpreter can achieve direct focus on character without seeming to single out any member of the audience. During a long or particularly reflective speech, the interpreter may include an entire section of his audience in his eye contact. When one carries on a conversation in real life, the eyes ocasionally move about during the speech, and the same can be true in interpretation. Care should be taken, however, to start and end the speech with the angle of address already established for the character in question, so that his identity will never merge with that of another character. The interpreter's sense of communication must remain as direct for this as for any other type of material.

The Reading Stand

An interpreter who wishes to use dramatic material outside the class-room must be adaptable. He may have a large auditorium complete with stage and reading stand. Or he may find himself in a small living room or behind a banquet table. He should practice working with and without the reading stand so that he can adapt himself to any set of circumstances without detriment to his performance. He will find, too, that reading stands vary in height, width, and lighting facilities, and he may need to remind himself that the stand is to hold the manuscript, not to prop up the interpreter!

An interpreter is free to use a reading stand or not, as he prefers. The only difficulty arises if he has come to depend on one and is then placed in a situation where none is provided. If he uses a reading stand, he must guard against the temptation to remain too long behind it. He should use it as the center for whatever changes of position he may find helpful. Most of these changes can usually be made during the direct, informal, less demanding narrative sections. When the interpreter uses no reading stand, he may move as he pleases for variety and relief, being careful only to avoid any movement that might distract the audience. Any repeated pattern of movement will soon become obtrusive.

Cutting

It is extremely dangerous to try to establish set rules for cutting a play since each script presents its own opportunities and difficulties. Moreover, to cut any piece of literature is to sacrifice some of its aesthetic entirety. Nevertheless, it is seldom practical, even for a full hour's program, to read a complete full-length play. Cutting is painful when you are fond of the play, but it is usually necessary. We shall assume that you have read the entire play several times before you begin to cut and that you know the location and function of key scenes and climaxes, as well as the rhythm of builds and drops, active and static scenes, and character development.

A play is usually cut to preserve the plot line and its attendant conflict. After you are thoroughly familiar with the entire play, spend a short time sorting out in your mind what must be retained to enable the audience to follow the plot line and the character development. Start with the essential scenes and eliminate whatever you can within them, such as minor characters and subplot. Having done that, examine the scenes carefully to ascertain what the audience will need to know to make them credible. Then go back and insert units or speeches from the eliminated scenes which will provide this information.

At this point, read your cutting aloud and time it. You will probably discover that it is still too long, because a well-written play is tightly woven. The next step is to decide which scenes you can condense into transitions, which you will give directly in your own person to bridge time or place or some action begun in a key scene and concluded later. Sometimes, though not always, part of the exposition at the beginning of the first act can be handled in this fashion. Occasionally, however, threads are introduced in it which will be needed later, so it must be used as it is. Sometimes the second act is devoted primarily to completing action begun in the first act and to preparing for the culmination in the third act. In such plays, much of the second act can be condensed into a bridge, leaving the first and last acts almost intact.

After deciding which scenes to keep and which to eliminate, you should write out the transitions and introductory units you will do in your own person so that you will not forget an important point and will choose the right style for the mood. Next, you should decide which stage directions can be effectively used as they stand and which may be suggested by empathy and muscle memory.

In general, the same procedure is followed when a single scene is used. The scene selected must contain at least a minor climax and must come to a conclusion that will make the audience feel they have experienced a complete unit of the development of the whole. It will always be necessary, except for an opening scene, to sketch in briefly what has gone on before so that the audience knows who the characters are and what has led up to this particular unit.

The last and most difficult step in cutting is taking out the favorite speech or scene that does not contribute directly to the purpose of your cutting! After every step the cutting must be read aloud and timed carefully. When an interpreter is asked to give a program of specific length, it is part of his responsibility to fill the time allotted. It is poor form and bad manners to continue the program long past the time set aside for it. A selection should always be timed as it is read aloud because of the tendency to skim and omit pauses in silent reading.

The marks used in cutting a play must be particularly clear because of the speed with which the performance moves. Sometimes portions of speeches will be cut or several speeches run together. Many experienced interpreters draw a line through the cut material or put it in brackets, and connect the end of one portion to be read to the beginning of the next by an arrow. If for some reason the book cannot be marked, pieces of blank paper may be clipped over the speeches to be omitted. When whole speeches are cut, the character names preceding them should be crossed out so that they will not cause confusion at a quick glance. If several pages are to be omitted, they should be clipped together for ease in turning. In any case, the interpreter should mark his book or typescript so that it is clear and unmistakable. He should not depend on chance; the mind does strange things under the stress of performance. Once he has established his own method of marking, he should use it consistently.

Readers Theatre

In recent years there has been an increased interest in group interpretation of drama, sometimes referred to as Readers Theatre. Readers Theatre uses all the techniques we have been discussing for the individual interpreter. The difference is that a separate interpreter takes each role just as in a fully staged production. Though each interpreter is responsible for only one character, he must, of course, make a thorough study of the entire play so that he is aware of relationships and of the contribution of each scene to the total effect.

There is no "one way" to do Readers Theatre. The cast and the director must always be guided by the demands of the selection they are using. Many directors place the readers on stage in groups suggesting the psychological relationship of the characters. They may be either standing or sitting, in chairs or on stools. Some use reading stands; others do not. If reading stands are used, they must not be so high that they obscure the view for the people in the front row. Manuscripts may be placed on the stands or held in the hands just as in individual interpretation.

Some directors prefer to play the scenes in Readers Theatre with the focus on stage rather than out front as is done in individual readings. The on-stage focus allows the characters to move about the stage area much as they would in a fully staged production. This technique has been used in some very successful productions, but it should certainly be reserved for a highly experienced cast or for experimental purposes. Otherwise the production can look like a dress rehearsal in which the cast has not yet learned its lines, since the participants usually carry their books and refer to them from time to time.

The more usual procedure is to keep the scene out front and specific action at a minimum. It must be remembered, however, that empathy and muscle memory are as important to group work as to the single interpreter of drama. The members of the cast do not stand like wax figures behind the reading stands. They may feel free to move about the stand as the individual interpreter does.

At first the technique of playing the scene out front despite the use of separate readers for the various parts may feel awkward and artificial to the actor accustomed to playing on stage. He is naturally tempted to turn and look at the person whose speech he is answering, but doing so brings the scene up on stage. It is often helpful during the rehearsal period to divide the cast so that half of them are working at the back of the auditorium and the members on stage can address them directly. After a few rehearsals the positions can be reversed. This encourages good visualization and directness. When all members of the cast are again on stage, they simply remember how they handled the scene when the other characters were at the back of the auditorium and continue to visualize them there.

Since the interpreter in Readers Theatre is handling only one role, he need not be so concerned about angle of placement as he would be if he were handling several characters. He may feel free to use the whole back of the house in dialogue, allowing the angle of focus to shift according to whom he is addressing. If he is playing a scene with a character whose interpreter is on his right, he will turn slightly in that direction, for instance. The angles of focus on the characters addressing each other will cross about two-thirds of the way back in the auditorium.

Entrances and exits may be suggested effectively in several ways. Usually the reader does not leave the stage when the character for whom he is responsible exits. Nevertheless, the audience must know who is present during the various scenes. If the readers are to stand during their scenes and be seated when they are out of scene, entrances become very simple. Each reader simply rises *in character*, assuming whatever physical characteristics will best suggest his character. He brings his attention into sharp focus by visualizing the action and other characters out front. If the cast is to remain seated, a lift of the head and widening of the circle of concentration will achieve the desired effect. If the stools revolve, a reader may turn slightly away from the audience until the entrance of his character, at which time he faces front and either remains seated or rises. Exits, of course, can be handled in the reverse of any of these ways. With a large cast it is often more practical to have most or all of the readers seated well upstage and bring them downstage to handle their scenes. Readers may also enter from and exit to the off-stage area. Practical considerations such as the size of the cast, the area available for staging, and the number and length of scenes will influence the decisions on all these matters.

However the entrances and exits are handled, timing is extremely important, as are muscle tone, the "sense of performance," and empathy. If the entrance is a sudden one, the reader will rise quickly and "take scene" in the mood of the lines he is about to speak. For such an exit he will sit or turn quickly and then "drop scene." When the character for whom he is responsible is offstage, the reader remains absolutely quiet with his head slightly down so as to resist the temptation to look at the audience and draw attention to himself. He narrows his circle of concentration so that he is, as it were, mentally isolated. Of course, he must be careful not to become so comfortable in his isolation that he is not ready for his cue. When he "takes stage," he widens his circle of concentration to include the entire audience and directs his thoughts and voice to the back of the auditorium. His exits reverse the procedure. This change in mental directness, and consequently in physical and vocal projection, is an extremely important part of Readers Theatre technique. When it is neglected, the audience is distracted from the scene in progress.

Drama in which the literary style is especially strong adapts itself well to Readers Theatre and can often be used exactly as written. Greek dramas are especially effective. Plays with a great deal of stage business are more difficult to handle. When explanations must be made, many directors use a narrator at one side and in front of the proscenium who speaks directly to the audience in his own person. Such a device is very effective, but it must be carefully timed and coordinated in mood so that the narration does not break the dramatic progression. Most play scripts will need little or no alteration for a Readers Theatre production.

Though a pleasing stage picture is valuable in Readers Theatre, scenery, costumes, and makeup may be kept at a minimum. It would be impossible to cover all the examples which might be considered because each play and each cast will have its own requirements and limitations. On the whole, it is safest to remember that in Readers Theatre, as in individual interpretation of drama, the speakers are not attempting to look like the characters, but rather to project the mental and emotional complexities of the characters so that the audience will create the scene and action in their minds. It is wise not to place too many obstacles in their way, however. Medea in a cocktail dress might be unduly distracting and ask more adjustment of the audience than is wise.

Although we have been discussing Readers Theatre as group readings of dramatic scripts, the term itself is popularly used to include as well programs in which several readers present an integrated thematic montage of selections. It is still a new mode of performance and allows for a great deal of flexibility.

The interpreter should not make the mistake of thinking that Readers Theatre takes less time and effort on the part of the participants than a fully staged production. The interpreter must be as well prepared as the actor. Since he will have his manuscript before him, whether he memorizes his lines or not is unimportant. Nevertheless, he must be completely in control of all the elements of the entire play and alert to the contribution his scenes make to the total performance. Though difficult and challenging, Readers Theatre is an effective and satisfying technique.

Selections for Analysis and Oral Interpretation

All the following scenes, and indeed the complete plays from which they are taken, would make interesting Readers Theatre productions.

The beginning of this famous scene, with its entrances and exits, will require some care to keep the abrupt stage directions from interrupting the dialogue. Juliet's speech, with its problem of properties and her loss of consciousness at the end, has been mentioned within this chapter. Watch the build of hysteria toward the end of the speech and the resultant problem of balancing the climactic "This do I drink to thee."

FROM *Romeo and Juliet* / WILLIAM SHAKESPEARE

Act IV, Scene 3

(*Enter* JULIET *and* NURSE.)

JULIET: Ay, those attires are best; but, gentle nurse,
I pray thee, leave me to myself to-night;
For I have need of many orisons
To move the heavens to smile upon my state,
Which, well thou know'st, is cross and full of sin.

(*Enter* LADY CAPULET.)

LADY CAPULET: What, are you busy, ho? Need you my help?
JULIET: No, Madame; we have cull'd such necessaries
As are behoveful for our state to-morrow.
So please you, let me now be left alone,
And let the nurse this night sit up with you;
For, I am sure, you have your hands full all,
In this so sudden business.
LADY CAPULET: Good-night.
Get thee to bed, and rest; for thou hast need.

(*Exeunt* LADY CAPULET *and* NURSE.)

JULIET: Farewell! God knows when we shall meet again.
I have a faint cold fear thrills through my veins,
That almost freezes up the heat of life.
I'll call them back again to comfort me.
Nurse! What should she do here?
My dismal scene I needs must act alone.
Come, vial.

What if this mixture do not work at all?
Shall I be married then to-morrow morning?
No, no; this shall forbid it. Lie thou there. (*Laying down her dagger.*)
What if it be poison, which the friar
Subtly hath minist'red to have me dead,
Lest in this marriage he should be dishonour'd
Because he married me before to Romeo?
I fear it is; and yet, methinks, it should not,
For he hath still been tried a holy man.
How if, when I am laid into the tomb,
I wake before the time that Romeo
Come to redeem me? There's a fearful point!
Shall I not then be stifled in the vault,
To whose foul mouth no healthsome air breathes in,
And there die strangled ere my Romeo comes?
Or, if I live, is it not very like
The horrible conceit of death and night,
Together with the terror of the place, —
As in a vault, an ancient receptacle,
Where, for this many hundred years, the bones
Of all my buried ancestors are pack'd;
Where bloody Tybalt, yet but green in earth,
Lies fest'ring in his shroud; where, as they say,
At some hours in the night spirits resort; —
Alack, alack, is it not like that I,
So early waking, — what with loathsome smells,
And shrieks like mandrakes' torn out of the earth,
That living mortals, hearing them, run mad; —
O, if I wake, shall I not be distraught,
Environed with all these hideous fears,
And madly play with my forefathers' joints,
And pluck the mangled Tybalt from his shroud,
And, in this rage, with some great kinsman's bone
As with a club, dash out my desperate brains?
O, look! methinks I see my cousin's ghost
Seeking out Romeo, that did spit his body
Upon a rapier's point. Stay, Tybalt, stay!
Romeo, I come! This do I drink to thee. (*She falls upon her bed, within the curtains.*)

Rosencrantz and Guildenstern open this play with a game of tossing coins, which Rosencrantz always wins. They have been summoned to Hamlet's uncle's court. They do not know why they are there but soon discover they are to accompany the "mad" Hamlet to England where he will be given into custody of the king. As the play progresses they become increasingly aware that they are involved in a plot from which they have no chance of emerging alive. This scene opens the third act when they, Hamlet, and, interestingly enough, the Players are on shipboard.

As the dialogue reveals, Rosencrantz and Guildenstern are here given specific differences in sophistication and intelligence which they do not have in Shakespeare's Hamlet. This difference is vital to the tension within this scene. The dialogue is witty, but the characters' response to their environment and developing situation must not be lost. The interpreter will need to decide which stage directions to use as they are and which to omit or suggest by action. Units within the long scene may, of course, be used for classroom work, but cutting within the remarkably tight dialogue would seriously threaten the rhythm of building tension.

FROM *Rosencrantz and Guildenstern Are Dead* / TOM STOPPARD

Act III

(*Opens in pitch darkness. Soft sea sounds. After several seconds of nothing, a voice from the dark . . .*)

GUILDENSTERN: Are you there?

ROSENCRANTZ: Where?

GUILDENSTERN (*bitterly*): A flying start. . . .

(*Pause.*)

ROSENCRANTZ: Is that you?

GUILDENSTERN: Yes.

ROSENCRANTZ: How do you know?

GUILDENSTERN (*explosion*): Oh-for-God's-sake!

ROSENCRANTZ: We're not finished, then?

GUILDENSTERN: Well, we're here, aren't we?

ROSENCRANTZ: Are we? I can't see a thing.

GUILDENSTERN: You can still *think*, can't you?

ROSENCRANTZ: I think so.

GUILDENSTERN: You can still *talk*.

ROSENCRANTZ: What should I say?

GUILDENSTERN: Don't bother. You can *feel*, can't you?

ROSENCRANTZ: Ah! There's life in me yet!

GUILDENSTERN: What are you feeling?

ROSENCRANTZ: A leg. Yes, it feels like my leg.

GUILDENSTERN: How does it feel?

ROSENCRANTZ: Dead.

GUILDENSTERN: Dead?

ROSENCRANTZ (*panic*): I can't feel a thing!

GUILDENSTERN: Give it a pinch! (*Immediately he yelps.*)

ROSENCRANTZ: Sorry.

GUILDENSTERN: Well, that's cleared that up.

> (*Longer pause: the sound builds a little and identifies itself — the sea. Ship timbers, wind in the rigging, and then shouts of sailors calling obscure but inescapably nautical instructions from all directions, far and near: A short list:*)

Hard a larboard!
Let go the stays!
Reef down me hearties!
Is that you, cox'n?
Hel-llo! Is that you?
Hard a port!
Easy as she goes!
Keep her steady on the lee!
Haul away, lads!
(*Snatches of sea shanty maybe.*)
Fly the jib!
Tops'l up, me maties!

> (*When the point has been well made and more so:*)

ROSENCRANTZ: We're on a boat. (*Pause.*) Dark, isn't it?

GUILDENSTERN: Not for night.

ROSENCRANTZ: No, not for *night*.

GUILDENSTERN: Dark for day.

> (*Pause.*)

ROSENCRANTZ: Oh yes, it's dark for *day*.

GUILDENSTERN: We must have gone north, of course.

ROSENCRANTZ: Of course?

GUILDENSTERN: Land of the midnight sun, that is.

ROSENCRANTZ: Of course.

> (*Some sailor sounds. A lantern is lit upstage — in fact by HAMLET. The stage lightens disproportionately — enough to see: ROSENCRANTZ and GUILDENSTERN sitting downstage. Vague shapes of rigging, etc., behind.*)

I think it's getting light.

GUILDENSTERN: Not for night.

ROSENCRANTZ: This far north.

GUILDENSTERN: Unless we're off course.

> (*A better light — Lantern? Moon? . . . Light. Revealing, among other things, three large man-sized casks on deck, upended,*

with lids. Spaced but in line. Behind and above — a gaudy striped umbrella, on a pole stuck into the deck, tilted so that we do not see behind it — one of those huge six-foot-diameter jobs. Still dim upstage. ROSENCRANTZ *and* GUILDENSTERN *still facing front.*)

ROSENCRANTZ: Yes, it's lighter than it was. It'll be night soon. This far north. (*Dolefully.*) I suppose we'll have to go to sleep. (*He yawns and stretches.*)

GUILDENSTERN: Tired?

ROSENCRANTZ: No . . . I don't think I'd take to it. Sleep all night, can't see a thing all day. . . . Those eskimos must have a quiet life.

GUILDENSTERN: Where?

ROSENCRANTZ: What?

GUILDENSTERN: I thought you ——— (*Relapses.*) I've lost all capacity for disbelief. I'm not sure that I could even rise to a little gentle scepticism.

(*Pause.*)

ROSENCRANTZ: Well, shall we stretch our legs?

GUILDENSTERN: I don't feel like stretching my legs.

ROSENCRANTZ: I'll stretch them for you, if you like.

GUILDENSTERN: No.

ROSENCRANTZ: We could stretch each other's. That way we wouldn't have to go anywhere.

GUILDENSTERN (*pause*): No, somebody might come in.

ROSENCRANTZ: In where?

GUILDENSTERN: Out here.

ROSENCRANTZ: In out here?

GUILDENSTERN: On deck.

ROSENCRANTZ (*considers the floor: slaps it*): Nice bit of planking, that.

GUILDENSTERN: Yes, I'm very fond of boats myself. I like the way they're —contained. You don't have to worry about which way to go, or whether to go at all — the question doesn't arise, because you're on a *boat*, aren't you? Boats are safe areas in the game of tag . . the players will hold their positions until the music starts. . . . I think I'll spend most of my life on boats.

ROSENCRANTZ: Very healthy.

(ROSENCRANTZ: *inhales with expectation, exhales with boredom.* GUILDENSTERN *stands up and looks over the audience.*)

GUILDENSTERN: One is free on a boat. For a time. Relatively.

ROSENCRANTZ: What's it like?

GUILDENSTERN: Rough.

(ROSENCRANTZ *joins him. They look out over the audience.*)

ROSENCRANTZ: I think I'm going to be sick.

GUILDENSTERN (*licks a finger, holds it up experimentally*): Other side, I think.

> (ROSENCRANTZ *goes upstage: Ideally a sort of upper deck joined to the downstage lower deck by short steps. The umbrella being on the upper deck.* GUILDENSTERN *meanwhile has been resuming his own theme — looking out over the audience —*)

Free to move, speak, extemporise, and yet. We have not been cut loose. Our truancy is defined by one fixed star, and our drift represents merely a slight change of angle to it: we may seize the moment, an exploration there, but we are brought round full circle to face again the single immutable fact — that we, Rosencrantz and Guildenstern, bearing a letter from one king to another, are taking Hamlet to England.

> (*By which time,* ROSENCRANTZ *has returned, tiptoeing with great import, teeth clenched for secrecy, gets to* GUILDENSTERN, *points surreptitiously behind him — and a tight whisper.*)

ROSENCRANTZ: I say — *he's there!*

GUILDENSTERN (*unsurprised*): What's he doing?

ROSENCRANTZ: Sleeping.

GUILDENSTERN: It's all right for him.

ROSENCRANTZ: What is?

GUILDENSTERN: He can sleep.

ROSENCRANTZ: It's all right for him.

GUILDENSTERN: He's got us now.

ROSENCRANTZ: He can sleep.

GUILDENSTERN: It's all done for him.

ROSENCRANTZ: He's got us.

GUILDENSTERN: And we've got nothing. (*A cry.*) All I ask is our common due!

ROSENCRANTZ: For those in peril on the sea. . . .

GUILDENSTERN: Give us this day our daily cue.

> (*Beat, pause. Sit. Long pause.*)

ROSENCRANTZ (*after shifting, looking around*): What now?

GUILDENSTERN: What do you mean?

ROSENCRANTZ: Well, nothing is happening.

GUILDENSTERN: We're on a boat.

ROSENCRANTZ: I'm aware of that.

GUILDENSTERN (*angrily*): Then what do you expect? (*Unhappily.*) We act on scraps of information . . . sifting half-remembered directions that we can hardly separate from instinct.

(ROSENCRANTZ *puts a hand into his purse, then both hands behind his back, then holds his fists out.* GUILDENSTERN *taps one fist.* ROSENCRANTZ *opens it to show a coin. He gives it to* GUILDENSTERN. *He puts his hand back into his purse. Then both hands behind his back, then holds his fists out.* GUILDENSTERN *taps one.* ROSENCRANTZ *opens it to show a coin. He gives it to* GUILDENSTERN. *Repeat. Repeat.* GUILDENSTERN *getting tense. Desperate to lose. Repeat.* GUILDENSTERN *taps a hand, changes his mind, taps the other, and* ROSENCRANTZ *inadvertently reveals that he has a coin in both fists.*)

GUILDENSTERN: You had money in both hands.

ROSENCRANTZ (*embarrassed*): Yes.

GUILDENSTERN: Every time?

ROSENCRANTZ: Yes.

GUILDENSTERN: What's the point of that?

ROSENCRANTZ (*pathetic*): I wanted to make you happy.

(*Beat.*)

GUILDENSTERN: How much did he give you?

ROSENCRANTZ: Who?

GUILDENSTERN: The King. He gave us some money.

ROSENCRANTZ: How much did he give you?

GUILDENSTERN: I asked you first.

ROSENCRANTZ: I got the same as you.

GUILDENSTERN: He wouldn't discriminate between us.

ROSENCRANTZ: How much did you get?

GUILDENSTERN: The same.

ROSENCRANTZ: How do you know?

GUILDENSTERN: You just told me — how do *you* know?

ROSENCRANTZ: He wouldn't discriminate between us.

GUILDENSTERN: Even if he could.

ROSENCRANTZ: Which he never could.

GUILDENSTERN: He couldn't even be sure of mixing us up.

ROSENCRANTZ: Without mixing us up.

GUILDENSTERN (*turning on him furiously*): Why don't you say something original! No wonder the whole thing is so stagnant! You don't take me me up on anything — you just repeat it in a different order.

ROSENCRANTZ: I can't think of anything original. I'm only good in support.

GUILDENSTERN: I'm sick of making the running.

ROSENCRANTZ (*humbly*): It must be your dominant personality. (*Almost in tears.*) Oh, what's going to become of us!

GUILDENSTERN (*comforts him, all harshness gone*): Don't cry . . . it's all right . . . there . . . there, I'll see we're all right.

ROSENCRANTZ: But we've got nothing to go on, we're out on our own.

GUILDENSTERN: We're on our way to England — we're taking Hamlet there.

ROSENCRANTZ: What for?

GUILDENSTERN: What for? Where have you been?

ROSENCRANTZ: When? (*Pause.*) We won't know what to do when we get there.

GUILDENSTERN: We take him to the King.

ROSENCRANTZ: Will *he* be there?

GUILDENSTERN: No — the king of England.

ROSENCRANTZ: He's expecting us?

GUILDENSTERN: No.

ROSENCRANTZ: He won't know what we're playing at. What are we going to *say?*

GUILDENSTERN: We've got a letter. You remember the letter.

ROSENCRANTZ: Do I?

GUILDENSTERN: Everything is explained in the letter. We count on that.

ROSENCRANTZ: Is that it, then?

GUILDENSTERN: What?

ROSENCRANTZ: We take Hamlet to the English king, we hand over the letter — what then?

GUILDENSTERN: There may be something in the letter to keep us going a bit.

ROSENCRANTZ: And if not?

GUILDENSTERN: Then that's it — we're finished.

ROSENCRANTZ: At a loose end?

GUILDENSTERN: Yes.

(*Pause.*)

ROSENCRANTZ: Are there likely to be loose ends? (*Pause.*) Who is the English king?

GUILDENSTERN: That depends on when we get there.

ROSENCRANTZ: What do you think it says?

GUILDENSTERN: Oh . . . greetings. Expressions of loyalty. Asking of favours, calling in of debts. Obscure promises balanced by vague threats. . . . Diplomacy. Regards to the family.

ROSENCRANTZ: And about Hamlet?

GUILDENSTERN: Oh yes.

ROSENCRANTZ: And us — the full background?

GUILDENSTERN: I should say so.

(*Pause.*)

ROSENCRANTZ: So we've got a letter which explains everything.

GUILDENSTERN: You've got it.

(ROSENCRANTZ *takes that literally. He starts to pat his pockets, etc.*)

What's the matter?

ROSENCRANTZ: The letter.

GUILDENSTERN: Have you got it?

ROSENCRANTZ (*rising fear*): Have I? (*Searches frantically.*) Where would I have put it?

GUILDENSTERN: You can't have lost it.

ROSENCRANTZ: I must have!

GUILDENSTERN: That's odd — I thought he gave it to me.

ROSENCRANTZ (*looks at him hopefully*): Perhaps he did.

GUILDENSTERN: But you seemed so sure it was *you* who hadn't got it.

ROSENCRANTZ (*high*): It *was* me who hadn't got it!

GUILDENSTERN: But if he gave it to me there's no reason why you should have had it in the first place, in which case I don't see what all the fuss is about you *not* having it.

ROSENCRANTZ (*pause*): I admit it's confusing.

GUILDENSTERN: This is all getting rather undisciplined. . . . The boat, the night, the sense of isolation and uncertainty . . . all these induce a loosening of the concentration. We must not lose control. Tighten up. Now. Either you have lost the letter or you didn't have it to lose in the first place, in which case the King never gave it to you, in which case he gave it to me, in which case I would have put it into my inside top pocket, in which case (*calmly producing the letter*) . . . it will be . . . here. (*They smile at each other.*) We mustn't drop off like that again.

(*Pause.* ROSENCRANTZ *takes the letter gently from him.*)

ROSENCRANTZ: Now that we have found it, why were we looking for it?

GUILDENSTERN (*thinks*): We thought it was lost.

ROSENCRANTZ: Something else?

GUILDENSTERN: No.

(*Deflation.*)

ROSENCRANTZ: Now we've lost the tension.

GUILDENSTERN: What tension?

ROSENCRANTZ: What was the last thing I said before we wandered off?

GUILDENSTERN: When was that?

ROSENCRANTZ (*helplessly*): I can't remember.

GUILDENSTERN (*leaping up*): What a shambles! We're just not getting anywhere.

ROSENCRANTZ (*mournfully*): Not even England. I don't believe in it anyway.

GUILDENSTERN: What?

ROSENCRANTZ: England.

GUILDENSTERN: Just a conspiracy of cartographers, you mean?

ROSENCRANTZ: I mean I don't believe it! (*Calmer.*) I have no image. I try to picture us arriving, a little harbour perhaps . . . roads . . . inhabitants to point the way . . . horses on the road . . . riding for a day or a fortnight and then a palace and the English king. . . . That would be the logical kind of thing. . . . But my mind remains a blank. No. We're slipping off the map.

GUILDENSTERN: Yes . . . yes. . . . (*Rallying.*) But you don't believe anything till it happens. And it *has* all happened. Hasn't it?

ROSENCRANTZ: We drift down time, clutching at straws. But what good's a brick to a drowning man?

GUILDENSTERN: Don't give up, we can't be long now.

ROSENCRANTZ: We might as well be dead. Do you think death could possibly be a boat?

GUILDENSTERN: No, no, no . . . Death is . . . not. Death isn't. You take my meaning. Death is the ultimate negative. Not-being. You can't not-be on a boat.

ROSENCRANTZ: I've frequently not been on boats.

GUILDENSTERN: No, no, no — what you've been is not on boats.

ROSENCRANTZ: I wish I was dead. (*Considers the drop.*) I could jump over the side. That would put a spoke in their wheel.

GUILDENSTERN: Unless they're counting on it.

ROSENCRANTZ: I shall remain on board. That'll put a spoke in their wheel. (*The futility of it, fury.*) All right! We don't question, we don't doubt. We perform. But a line must be drawn somewhere, and I would like to put it on record that I have no confidence in England. Thank you. (*Thinks about this.*) And even if it's true, it'll just be another shambles.

GUILDENSTERN: I don't see why.

ROSENCRANTZ (*furious*): He won't know what we're talking about. — What are we going to *say*?

GUILDENSTERN: We say — Your majesty, we have arrived!

ROSENCRANTZ (*kingly*): And who are you?

GUILDENSTERN: We are Rosencrantz and Guildenstern.

ROSENCRANTZ (*barks*): Never heard of you!

GUILDENSTERN: Well, we're nobody special ——

ROSENCRANTZ (*regal and nasty*): What's your game?

GUILDENSTERN: We've got our instructions ——

ROSENCRANTZ: First I've heard of it ——

GUILDENSTERN (*angry*): Let me finish —— (*Humble.*) We've come from Denmark.

ROSENCRANTZ: What do you want?

GUILDENSTERN: Nothing — we're delivering Hamlet ——

ROSENCRANTZ: Who's he?

GUILDENSTERN (*irritated*): You've heard of *him* ——

ROSENCRANTZ: Oh, I've heard of him all right and I want nothing to do with it.

GUILDENSTERN: But ——

ROSENCRANTZ: You march in here without so much as a by-your-leave and expect me to take in every lunatic you try to pass off with a lot of unsubstantiated ——

GUILDENSTERN: We've got a letter ——

ROSENCRANTZ (*snatches it and tears it open. Efficiently*): I see . . . I see . . . well, this seems to support your story such as it is — it is an exact command from the king of Denmark, for several different reasons, importing Denmark's health and England's too, that on the reading of this letter, without delay, I should have Hamlet's head cut off ——!

(GUILDENSTERN *snatches the letter.* ROSENCRANTZ, *double-taking, snatches it back.* GUILDENSTERN *snatches it half back. They read it together, and separate. Pause. They are well downstage looking front.*)

The sun's going down. It will be dark soon.

GUILDENSTERN: Do you think so?

ROSENCRANTZ: I was just making conversation. (*Pause.*) We're his *friends*.

GUILDENSTERN: How do you know?

ROSENCRANTZ: From our young days brought up with him.

GUILDENSTERN: You've only got their word for it.

ROSENCRANTZ: But that's what we depend on.

GUILDENSTERN: Well, yes, and then again no. (*Airily.*) Let us keep things in proportion. Assume, if you like, that they're going to kill him. Well, he is a man, he is mortal, death comes to us all, etcetera, and consequently he would have died anyway, sooner or later. Or to look at it from the social point of view — he's just one man among many, the loss would be well within reason and convenience. And then again, what is so terrible about death? As Socrates so philosophically put it, since we don't know what death is, it is illogical to fear it. It might be . . . very nice. Certainly it is a release from the burden of life, and, for the godly, a haven and a reward. Or to look at it another way — we are little men, we don't know the ins and outs of the matter, there are wheels within wheels, etcetera — it would be presumptuous of us to interfere with the designs of fate or even of kings. All in all, I think we'd be well advised to leave well alone. Tie up the letter — there — neatly — like that. — They won't notice the broken seal, assuming you were in character.

ROSENCRANTZ: But what's the point?

GUILDENSTERN: Don't apply logic.

ROSENCRANTZ: He's done nothing to us.

GUILDENSTERN: Or justice.

ROSENCRANTZ: It's awful.

GUILDENSTERN: But it could have been worse. I was beginning to think it
was. (*And his relief comes out in a laugh.*)

*This scene is from the second act of Goldsmith's comedy of manners. Marlow,
a young man of wealth and social position, has come to visit his father's old
friend, Mr. Hardcastle, and, at his father's insistence, to pay court to Miss
Kate Hardcastle as well. However, he and his friend Hastings become lost on
the way and stop at a tavern where Tony, Mrs. Hardcastle's son, gives them
directions to the house but tells them it is an inn. Since neither Marlow nor
Hastings has ever met the Hardcastles, they have no reason to suspect the
trick. Mr. Hardcastle, who has been expecting them, makes them welcome
but is unaware of their confusion. Since Kate and her cousin, Miss Neville,
pretend to be at the "inn" quite by chance, the following interview can be
arranged without Marlow being any the wiser. Marlow has confessed to Hastings that though he is very much at ease with barmaids, he finds conversation
with a lady excruciating. Kate has been warned of Marlow's shyness by her
father and enjoys herself immensely during the interview.*

Take care to handle the entrances and exits smoothly.

FROM *She Stoops to Conquer* / OLIVER GOLDSMITH

(*Enter* MARLOW *alone.*)

MARLOW: The assiduities of these good people tease me beyond bearing.
My host seems to think it ill manners to leave me alone, and so he
claps not only himself, but his old-fashioned wife on my back. They
talk of coming to sup with us, too; and then, I suppose, we are to run
the gauntlet through all the rest of the family. — What have we got
here? —

(*Enter* HASTINGS *and* MISS NEVILLE.)

HASTINGS: My dear Charles! Let me congratulate you! — The most fortunate accident! — Who do you think is just alighted?

MARLOW: Cannot guess.

HASTINGS: Our mistresses, boy, Miss Hardcastle and Miss Neville. Give
me leave to introduce Miss Constance Neville to your acquaintance.
Happening to dine in the neighbourhood, they called, on their return,
to take fresh horses here. Miss Hardcastle has just stepped into the next
room, and will be back in an instant. Wasn't it lucky? eh!

MARLOW (*aside*): I have just been mortified enough of all conscience, and
here comes something to complete my embarrassment.

HASTINGS: Well! but wasn't it the most fortunate thing in the world?

MARLOW: Oh! yes. Very fortunate — a most joyful encounter. — But our dresses, George, you know, are in disorder. — What if we should postpone the happiness till tomorrow? — Tomorrow at her own house. — It will be every bit as convenient — and rather more respectful. — Tomorrow let it be. (*Offering to go.*)

MISS NEVILLE: By no means, sir. Your ceremony will displease her. The disorder of your dress will shew the ardour of your impatience. Besides, she knows you are in the house, and will permit you to see her.

MARLOW: Oh! the devil! how shall I support them? Hem! hem! Hastings, you must not go. You are to assist me, you know. I shall be confoundedly ridiculous. Yet, hang it! I'll take courage. Hem!

HASTINGS: Pshaw, man! it's but the first plunge, and all's over. She's but a woman, you know.

MARLOW: And of all women, she that I dread most to encounter!

(*Enter* MISS HARDCASTLE, *as returned from walking.*)

HASTINGS (*introducing them*): Miss Hardcastle. Mr Marlow. I'm proud of bringing two persons of such merit together, that only want to know, to esteem each other.

MISS HARDCASTLE (*aside*): Now, for meeting my modest gentleman with a demure face, and quite in his own manner. (*After a pause, in which he appears very uneasy and disconcerted.*) I'm glad of your safe arrival, sir — I'm told you had some accidents by the way.

MARLOW: Only a few, madam. Yes, we had some. Yes, madam, a good many accidents, but should be sorry — madam — or rather glad of any accidents — that are so agreeably concluded. Hem!

HASTINGS (*to him*): You never spoke better in your whole life. Keep it up, and I'll insure you the victory.

MISS HARDCASTLE: I'm afraid you flatter, sir. You that have seen so much of the finest company can find little entertainment in an obscure corner of the country.

MARLOW (*gathering courage*): I have lived, indeed, in the world, madam; but I have kept very little company. I have been but an observer upon life, madam, while others were enjoying it.

MISS NEVILLE: But that, I am told, is the way to enjoy it at last.

HASTINGS (*to him*): Cicero never spoke better. Once more, and you are confirmed in assurance for ever.

MARLOW (*to him*): Hem! Stand by me, then, and when I'm down, throw in a word or two to set me up again.

MISS HARDCASTLE: An observer, like you, upon life, were, I fear, disagreeably employed, since you must have had much more to censure than to approve.

MARLOW: Pardon me, madam. I was always willing to be amused. The folly of most people is rather an object of mirth than uneasiness.

HASTINGS (*to him*): Bravo, bravo. Never spoke so well in your whole life. Well, Miss Hardcastle, I see that you and Mr Marlow are going to be very good company. I believe our being here will but embarrass the interview.

MARLOW: Not in the least, Mr Hastings. We like your company of all things. (*To him.*) Zounds! George, sure you won't go? How can you leave us?

HASTINGS: Our presence will but spoil conversation, so we'll retire to the next room. (*To him.*) You don't consider, man, that we are to manage a little *tête-à-tête* of our own.

(*Exeunt.*)

MISS HARDCASTLE (*after a pause*): But you have not been wholly an observer, I presume, sir: the ladies, I should hope, have employed some part of your addresses.

MARLOW (*relapsing into timidity*): Pardon me, madam, I — I — I — as yet have studied — only — to — deserve them.

MISS HARDCASTLE: And that some say is the very worst way to obtain them.

MARLOW: Perhaps so, madam. But I love to converse only with the more grave and sensible part of the sex. — But I'm afraid I grow tiresome.

MISS HARDCASTLE: Not at all, sir; there is nothing I like so much as grave conversation myself: I could hear it for ever. Indeed, I have often been surprised how a man of sentiment could ever admire those light airy pleasures, where nothing reaches the heart.

MARLOW: It's — a disease — of the mind, madam. In the variety of tastes there must be some who, wanting a relish for — um-a-um.

MISS HARDCASTLE: I understand you, sir. There must be some, who, wanting a relish for refined pleasures, pretend to despise what they are incapable of tasting.

MARLOW: My meaning, madam, but infinitely better expressed. And I can't help observing — a —

MISS HARDCASTLE (*aside*): Who could ever suppose this fellow impudent upon some occasions. (*To him.*) You were going to observe, sir —

MARLOW: I was observing, madam — I protest, madam, I forget what I was going to observe.

MISS HARDCASTLE (*aside*): I vow and so do I. (*To him.*) You were observing, sir, that in this age of hypocrisy — something about hypocrisy, sir.

MARLOW: Yes, madam. In this age of hypocrisy, there are few who upon strict inquiry do not — a — a — a —

MISS HARDCASTLE: I understand you perfectly, sir.

MARLOW (*aside*): Egad! and that's more than I do myself!

MISS HARDCASTLE: You mean that in this hypocritical age there are few that do not condemn in public what they practise in private, and think they pay every debt to virtue when they praise it.

MARLOW: True, madam; those who have most virtue in their mouths, have least of it in their bosoms. But I'm sure I tire you, madam.

MISS HARDCASTLE: Not in the least, sir; there's something so agreeable and spirited in your manner, such life and force — pray, sir, go on.

MARLOW: Yes, madam. I was saying — that there are some occasions — when a total want of courage, madam, destroys all the — and puts us — upon a — a — a —

MISS HARDCASTLE: I agree with you entirely, a want of courage upon some occasions assumes the appearance of ignorance, and betrays us when we most want to excel. I beg you'll proceed.

MARLOW: Yes, madam. Morally speaking, madam — but I see Miss Neville expecting us in the next room. I would not intrude for the world.

MISS HARDCASTLE: I protest, sir, I never was more agreeably entertained in all my life. Pray go on.

MARLOW: Yes, madam. I was — but she beckons us to join her. Madam, shall I do myself the honour to attend you?

MISS HARDCASTLE: Well then, I'll follow.

MARLOW (*aside*): This pretty smooth dialogue has done for me. (*Exit.*)

MISS HARDCASTLE (*alone*): Ha! ha! ha! Was there ever such a sober sentimental interview? I'm certain he scarce looked in my face the whole time. Yet the fellow, but for his unaccountable bashfulness, is pretty well, too. He has good sense, but then so buried in his fears, that it fatigues one more than ignorance. If I could teach him a little confidence, it would be doing somebody that I know of a piece of service. But who is that somebody? — that, faith, is a question I can scarce answer. (*Exit.*)

As this play has progressed, all the characters except the two we meet here have been dehumanized. They have become rhinoceroses, some of them before our very eyes. The metamorphosis is painful and horrible, terminating in animal noises and violence. Daisy and Berenger are alone now. The animals have taken charge of the world.

This excerpt will divide into separate scenes for class exercises, but the steady build of disintegration must be constantly realized. The deliberate starkness of the style was mentioned in our earlier discussion. Notice how it increases as Daisy's human fear turns to spiritual and mental lethargy. The telephone and the abundance of stage directions offer a nice challenge to the interpreter.

FROM *Rhinoceros* / EUGENE IONESCO

Act III

(*The telephone rings.*)

BERENGER: Who could that be?

DAISY (*fearful*): Don't answer.

BERENGER: Why not?

DAISY: I don't know. I just feel it's better not to.

BERENGER: It might be Mr. Papillon, or Botard, or Jean or Dudard ringing to say they've had second thoughts. You did say it was probably only a passing phase.

DAISY: I don't think so. They wouldn't have changed their minds so quickly. They've not had time to think it over. They're bound to give it a fair trial.

BERENGER: Perhaps the authorities have decided to take action at last; maybe they're ringing to ask our help in whatever measures they've decided to adopt.

DAISY: I'd be surprised if it was them.

(*The telephone rings again.*)

BERENGER: It is the authorities, I tell you, I recognize the ring — a long drawn-out ring, I can't ignore an appeal from them. It can't be anyone else. (*He picks up the receiver.*) Hallo? (*Trumpetings are heard coming from the receiver.*) You hear that? Trumpeting! Listen!

DAISY (*puts the telephone to her ear, is shocked by the sound, quickly replaces the receiver. Frightened*): What's going on?

BERENGER: They're playing jokes now.

DAISY: Jokes in bad taste!

BERENGER: You see! What did I tell you?

DAISY: You didn't tell me anything.

BERENGER: I was expecting that; it was just what I'd predicted.

DAISY: You didn't predict anything. You never do. You can only predict things after they've happened.

BERENGER: Oh yes, I can; I can predict things all right.

DAISY: That's not nice of them — in fact it's very nasty. I don't like being made fun of.

BERENGER: They wouldn't dare make fun of you. It's me they're making fun of.

DAISY: And naturally I come in for it as well because I'm with you. They're taking their revenge. But what have we done to them?

(The telephone rings again.)

Pull the plug out.

BERENGER: The telephone authorities say you mustn't.

DAISY: Oh you never dare to do anything — and you say you could defend me!

BERENGER *(darting to the radio)*: Let's turn on the radio for the news!

DAISY: Yes, we must find out how things stand!

(The sound of trumpeting comes from the radio. BERENGER peremptorily switches it off. But in the distance other trumpetings, like echoes, can be heard.)

Things are getting really serious! I tell you frankly, I don't like it! *(She is trembling.)*

BERENGER *(very agitated)*: Keep calm! Keep calm!

DAISY: They've taken over the radio stations!

BERENGER *(agitated and trembling)*: Keep calm, keep calm!

(DAISY runs to the up-stage window, then to the down-stage window, and looks out; BERENGER does the same in the opposite order, then the two come and face each other centre-stage.)

DAISY: It's no joke any longer. They mean business!

BERENGER: There's only them left now; nobody but them. Even the authorities have joined them.

(They cross to the windows as before, and meet again centre-stage.)

DAISY: Not a soul left anywhere.

BERENGER: We're all alone, we're left all alone.

DAISY: That's what you wanted.

BERENGER: You mean that's what you wanted!

DAISY: It was you!

BERENGER: You!

(Noises come from everywhere at once. Rhinoceros heads fill the up-stage wall. From left and right in the house, the noise of rushing feet and the panting breath of the animals. But all these disquieting sounds are nevertheless somehow rhythmical, making a kind of music. The loudest noises of all come from above; a noise of stamping. Plaster falls from the ceiling. The house shakes violently.)

DAISY: The earth's trembling! *(She doesn't know where to run.)*

BERENGER: No, that's our neighbours, the Perissodactyles! *(He shakes his fist to left and right and above.)* Stop it! You're preventing us from working! Noise is forbidden in these flats! Noise is forbidden!

DAISY: They'll never listen to you!

(*However the noise does diminish, merely forming a sort of musical background.*)

BERENGER (*he, too, is afraid*): Don't be frightened, my dear. We're to-gether — you're happy with me, aren't you? It's enough that I'm with you, isn't it? I'll chase all your fears away.

DAISY: Perhaps it's all our own fault.

BERENGER: Don't think about it any longer. We mustn't start feeling remorse. It's dangerous to start feeling guilty. We must just live our lives, and be happy. We have the right to be happy. They're not spite-ful, and we're not doing them any harm. They'll leave us in peace. You just keep calm and rest. Sit in the armchair. (*He leads her to the armchair.*) Just keep calm! (DAISY *sits in the armchair.*) Would you like a drop of brandy to pull you together?

DAISY: I've got a headache.

BERENGER (*taking up his bandage and binding* DAISY's *head*): I love you, my darling. Don't you worry, they'll get over it. It's just a passing phase.

DAISY: They won't get over it. It's for good.

BERENGER: I love you. I love you madly.

DAISY (*taking off the bandage*): Let things just take their course. What can we do about it?

BERENGER: They've all gone mad. The world is sick. They're all sick.

DAISY: We shan't be the ones to cure them.

BERENGER: How can we live in the same house with them?

DAISY (*calming down*): We must be sensible. We must adapt ourselves and try and get on with them.

BERENGER: They can't understand us.

DAISY: They must. There's no other way.

BERENGER: Do you understand them?

DAISY: Not yet. But we must try to understand the way their minds work, and learn their language.

BERENGER: They haven't got a language! Listen . . . do you call that a language?

DAISY: How do you know? You're no polyglot!

BERENGER: We'll talk about it later. We must have lunch first.

DAISY: I'm not hungry any more. It's all too much. I can't take any more.

BERENGER: But you're the strong one. You're not going to let it get you down. It's precisely for your courage that I admire you so.

DAISY: You said that before.

BERENGER: Do you feel sure of my love?

DAISY: Yes, of course.

BERENGER: I love you so.

DAISY: You keep saying the same thing, my dear.

BERENGER: Listen, Daisy, there *is* something we can do. We'll have children, and our children will have children — it'll take time, but together we can regenerate the human race.

DAISY: Regenerate the human race?

BERENGER: It happened once before.

DAISY: Ages ago. Adam and Eve . . . They had a lot of courage.

BERENGER: And we, too, can have courage. We don't need all that much. It happens automatically with time and patience.

DAISY: What's the use?

BERENGER: Of course we can — with a little bit of courage.

DAISY: I don't want to have children — it's a bore.

BERENGER: How can we save the world, if you don't?

DAISY: Why bother to save it?

BERENGER: What a thing to say! Do it for me, Daisy. Let's save the world.

DAISY: After all, perhaps it's we who need saving. Perhaps we're the abnormal ones.

BERENGER: You're not yourself, Daisy, you've got a touch of fever.

DAISY: There aren't any more of our kind about anywhere, are there?

BERENGER: Daisy, you're not to talk like that!

(DAISY *looks all around at the rhinoceros heads on the walls, on the landing door, and now starting to appear along the footlights.*)

DAISY: Those are the real people. They look happy. They're content to be what they are. They don't look insane. They look very natural. They were right to do what they did.

BERENGER (*clasping his hands and looking despairingly at* DAISY): We're the ones who are doing right, Daisy, I assure you.

DAISY: That's very presumptuous of you!

BERENGER: You know perfectly well I'm right.

DAISY: There's no such thing as absolute right. It's the world that's right — not you and me.

BERENGER: I *am* right, Daisy. And the proof is that you understand me when I speak to you.

DAISY: What does that prove?

BERENGER: The proof is that I love you as much as it's possible for a man to love a woman.

DAISY: Funny sort of argument!

BERENGER: I don't understand you any longer, Daisy. You don't know what you're saying, darling. Think of our love! Our love . . .

DAISY: I feel a bit ashamed of what you call love — this morbid feeling, this male weakness. And female, too. It just doesn't compare with the ardour and the tremendous energy emanating from all these creatures around us.

BERENGER: Energy! You want some energy, do you? I can let you have some energy! (*He slaps her face.*)

DAISY: Oh! I never would have believed it possible . . . (*She sinks into the armchair.*)

BERENGER: Oh forgive me, my darling, please forgive me! (*He tries to embrace her, she evades him.*) Forgive me, my darling. I didn't mean it. I don't know what came over me, losing control like that!

DAISY: It's because you've run out of arguments, that's why.

BERENGER: Oh dear! In the space of a few minutes we've gone through twenty-five years of married life.

DAISY: I pity you. I understand you all too well . . .

BERENGER (*as* DAISY *weeps*): You're probably right that I've run out of arguments. You think they're stronger than me, stronger than us. Maybe they are.

DAISY: Indeed they are.

BERENGER: Well, in spite of everything, I swear to you I'll never give in, never!

DAISY (*she rises, goes to* BERENGER, *puts her arm round his neck*): My poor darling, I'll help you resist — to the very end.

BERENGER: Will you be capable of it?

DAISY: I give you my word. You can trust me.

(*The rhinoceros noises have become melodious.*)

Listen, they're singing!

BERENGER: They're not singing, they're roaring.

DAISY: They're singing.

BERENGER: They're roaring, I tell you.

DAISY: You're mad, they're singing.

BERENGER: You can't have a very musical ear, then.

DAISY: You don't know the first thing about music, poor dear — and look, they're playing as well, and dancing.

BERENGER: You call that dancing?

DAISY: It's their way of dancing. They're beautiful.

BERENGER: They're disgusting!

DAISY: You're not to say unpleasant things about them. It upsets me.

BERENGER: I'm sorry. We're not going to quarrel on their account.

DAISY: They're like gods.

BERENGER: You go too far, Daisy; take a good look at them.

DAISY: You mustn't be jealous, my dear.

(*She goes to* BERENGER *again and tries to embrace him. This time it is* BERENGER *who frees himself.*)

BERENGER: I can see our opinions are directly opposed. It's better not to discuss the matter.

DAISY: Now you mustn't be nasty.

BERENGER: Then don't you be stupid!

DAISY (*to* BERENGER, *who turns his back on her. He looks at himself closely in the mirror*): It's no longer possible for us to live together. (*As* BERENGER *continues to examine himself in the mirror she goes quietly to the door, saying:*) He isn't very nice, really, he isn't very nice. (*She goes out, and is seen slowly descending the stairs.*)

BERENGER (*still looking at himself in the mirror*): Men aren't so bad-looking, you know. And I'm not a particularly handsome specimen! Believe me, Daisy! (*He turns round.*) Daisy! Daisy! Where are you, Daisy? You can't do that to me! (*He darts to the door.*) Daisy! (*He gets to the landing and leans over the banister.*) Daisy! Come back! Come back, my dear! You haven't even had your lunch. Daisy, don't leave me alone! Remember your promise! Daisy! Daisy! (*He stops calling, makes a despairing gesture, and comes back into the room.*) Well, it was obvious we weren't getting along together. The home was broken up. It just wasn't working out. But she shouldn't have left like that with no explanation. (*He looks all around.*) She didn't even leave a message. That's no way to behave. Now I'm all on my own. (*He locks the door carefully, but angrily.*) But they won't get me. (*He carefully closes the windows.*) You won't get me! (*He addresses all the rhinoceros heads.*) I'm not joining you; I don't understand you! I'm staying as I am. I'm a human being. A human being. (*He sits in the armchair.*) It's an impossible situation. It's my fault she's gone. I meant everything to her. What'll become of her? That's one more person on my conscience. I can easily picture the worst, because the worst can easily happen. Poor little thing left all alone in this world of monsters! Nobody can help me find her, nobody, because there's nobody left.

(*Fresh trumpetings, hectic racings, clouds of dust.*)

I can't bear the sound of them any longer, I'm going to put cotton wool in my ears. (*He does so, and talks to himself in the mirror.*) The only solution is to convince them — but convince them of what? Are the changes reversible, that's the point? Are they reversible? It would be a labour of Hercules, far beyond me. In any case, to convince them you'd have to talk to them. And to talk to them I'd have to learn their language. Or they'd have to learn mine. But what language do I speak? What is my language? Am I talking French? Yes, it must be French. But what is French? I can call it French if I want, and nobody can say it isn't — I'm the only one who speaks it. What am I saying? Do I understand what I'm saying? Do I? (*He crosses to the middle of the room.*) And what if it's true what Daisy said, and they're the ones in the right? (*He turns back to the mirror.*) A man's not ugly to look at, not ugly at all! (*He examines himself, passing his hand over his face.*) What a funny-looking thing! What do I look like? What? (*He darts to a cupboard, takes out some photographs which he examines.*) Photographs? Who are all these people? Is it Mr. Papillon — or is it Daisy? And is that Botard or Dudard or Jean? Or is it me? (*He rushes to the cupboard again and takes out two or three pictures.*) Now I recognize me: that's me, that's me! (*He hangs the pictures on the back wall, beside the rhinoceros heads.*) That's me, that's me! (*When he hangs the pictures one sees that they are of an old man, a huge woman, and another man. The ugliness of these pictures is in contrast to the rhinoceros heads which have become very beautiful.* BERENGER *steps back to contemplate the pictures.*) I'm not good-looking, I'm not good-looking. (*He takes down the pictures, throws them furiously to the ground, and goes over to the mirror*). They're the good-looking ones. I was wrong! Oh, how I wish I was like them! I haven't got any horns, more's the pity! A smooth brow looks so ugly. I need one or two horns to give my sagging face a lift. Perhaps one will grow and I needn't be ashamed any more — then I could go and join them. But it will never grow! (*He looks at the palms of his hands.*) My hands are so limp — oh, why won't they get rough! (*He takes his coat off, undoes his shirt to look at his chest in the mirror.*) My skin is so slack. I can't stand this white, hairy body. Oh I'd love to have a hard skin in that wonderful dull green colour — a skin that looks decent naked without any hair on it, like theirs! (*He listens to the trumpetings.*) Their song is charming — a bit raucous perhaps, but it does have charm! I wish I could do it! (*He rises to imitate them.*) Ahh, Ahh, Brr! No, that's not it! Try again, louder! Ahh, Ahh, Brr! No, that's not it, it's too feeble, it's got no drive behind it. I'm not trumpeting at all; I'm just howling. Ahh, Ahh, Brr. There's a big difference between howling and trumpeting. I've only myself to blame; I should have gone with them while there was still time. Now it's too late! Now I'm a monster, just a monster. Now I'll never become a rhinoceros, never, never! I've gone past changing. I want to, I really do, but I can't, I just can't stand the sight of me. I'm too ashamed! (*He turns his back on the mirror.*) I'm so ugly! People who try to hang on to their individuality always come to a bad end! (*He suddenly snaps out of it.*) Oh well, too bad! I'll take on the whole of them! I'll put up a fight against the lot of them, the whole lot of them! I'm the last man left, and I'm staying that way until the end. I'm not capitulating!

CURTAIN

The interpreter will need to decide which of the stage directions he wishes to read and which he can incorporate into character suggestion. There are also some interesting problems of physical action and proximity. Style and rhythm in the dialogue add to the humor.

FROM *Androcles and the Lion* / GEORGE BERNARD SHAW

Prologue

(*Overture: forest sounds, roaring of lions, Christian hymn faintly.*

A jungle path. A lion's roar, a melancholy suffering roar, comes from the jungle. It is repeated nearer. The LION *limps from the jungle on three legs, holding up his right forepaw, in which a huge thorn sticks. He sits down and contemplates it. He licks it. He shakes it. He tries to extract it by scraping it along the ground, and hurts himself worse. He roars piteously. He licks it again. Tears drop from his eyes. He limps painfully off the path and lies down under the trees, exhausted with pain. Heaving a long sigh, like wind in a trombone, he goes to sleep.*

ANDROCLES *and his wife* MEGAERA *come along the path. He is a small, thin, ridiculous little man who might be any age from thirty to fifty-five. He has sandy hair, watery compassionate blue eyes, sensitive nostrils, and a very presentable forehead; but his good points go no further: his arms and legs and back, though wiry of their kind, look shrivelled and starved. He carries a big bundle, is very poorly clad, and seems tired and hungry.*

His wife is a rather handsome pampered slattern, well fed and in the prime of life. She has nothing to carry, and has a stout stick to help her along.)

MEGAERA (*suddenly throwing down her stick*): I won't go another step.

ANDROCLES (*pleading wearily*): Oh, not again, dear. What's the good of stopping every two miles and saying you won't go another step? We must get on to the next village before night. There are wild beasts in this wood: lions, they say.

MEGAERA: I don't believe a word of it. You are always threatening me with wild beasts to make me walk the very soul out of my body when I can hardly drag one foot before another. We haven't seen a single lion yet.

ANDROCLES: Well, dear, do you want to see one?

MEGAERA (*tearing the bundle from his back*): You cruel brute, you don't care how tired I am, or what becomes of me (*she throws the bundle on the ground*): always thinking of yourself. Self! self! self! always yourself! (*She sits down on the bundle.*)

ANDROCLES (*sitting down sadly on the ground with his elbows on his knees and his head in his hands*): We all have to think of ourselves occasionally, dear.

MEGAERA: A man ought to think of his wife sometimes.

ANDROCLES: He can't always help it, dear. You make me think of you a great deal. Not that I blame you.

MEGAERA: Blame me! I should think not indeed. Is it my fault that I'm married to you?

ANDROCLES: No, dear: that is my fault.

MEGAERA: That's a nice thing to say to me. Aren't you happy with me?

ANDROCLES: I don't complain, my love.

MEGAERA: You ought to be ashamed of yourself.

ANDROCLES: I am, my dear.

MEGAERA: You're not: you glory in it.

ANDROCLES: In what, darling?

MEGAERA: In everything. In making me a slave, and making yourself a laughing stock. It's not fair. You get me the name of being a shrew with your meek ways, always talking as if butter wouldn't melt in your mouth. And just because I look a big strong woman, and because I'm goodhearted and a bit hasty, and because you're always driving me to do things I'm sorry for afterwards, people say 'Poor man: what a life his wife leads him!' Oh, if they only knew! And you think I don't know. But I do, I do, (*screaming*) I do.

ANDROCLES: Yes, my dear: I know you do.

MEGAERA: Then why don't you treat me properly and be a good husband to me?

ANDROCLES: What can I do, my dear?

MEGAERA: What can you do! You can return to your duty, and come back to your home and your friends, and sacrifice to the gods as all respectable people do, instead of having us hunted out of house and home for being dirty disreputable blaspheming atheists.

ANDROCLES: I'm not an atheist, dear: I am a Christian.

MEGAERA: Well, isn't that the same thing, only ten times worse? Everybody knows that the Christians are the very lowest of the low.

ANDROCLES: Just like us, dear.

MEGAERA: Speak for yourself. Don't you dare to compare me to common people. My father owned his own public-house; and sorrowful was the day for me when you first came drinking in our bar.

ANDROCLES: I confess I was addicted to it, dear. But I gave it up when I became a Christian.

MEGAERA: You'd much better have remained a drunkard. I can forgive a man being addicted to drink: it's only natural; and I don't deny I like a drop myself sometimes. What I can't stand is your being addicted to Christianity. And what's worse again, your being addicted to animals. How is any woman to keep her house clean when you bring in every stray cat and lost cur and lame duck in the whole countryside? You took the bread out of my mouth to feed them: you know you did: don't attempt to deny it.

ANDROCLES: Only when they were hungry and you were getting too stout, dearie.

MEGAERA: Yes: insult me, do. (*Rising.*) Oh! I won't bear it another moment. You used to sit and talk to those dumb brute beasts for hours, when you hadn't a word for me.

ANDROCLES: They never answered back, darling. (*He rises and again shoulders the bundle.*)

MEGAERA: Well, if you're fonder of animals than of your own wife, you can live with them here in the jungle. I've had enough of them and enough of you. I'm going back. I'm going home.

ANDROCLES (*barring the way back*): No, dearie: don't take on like that. We can't go back. We've sold everything: we should starve; and I should be sent to Rome and thrown to the lions —

MEGAERA: Serve you right! I wish the lions joy of you. (*Screaming.*) Are you going to get out of my way and let me go home?

ANDROCLES: No, dear —

MEGAERA: Then I'll make my way through the forest; and when I'm eaten by the wild beasts you'll know what a wife you've lost. (*She dashes into the jungle and nearly falls over the sleeping* LION.) Oh! Oh! Andy! Andy! (*She totters back and collapses into the arms of* ANDROCLES, *who, crushed by her weight, falls on his bundle.*)

ANDROCLES (*extracting himself from beneath her and slapping her hands in great anxiety*): What is it, my precious, my pet? What's the matter? (*He raises her head. Speechless with terror, she points in the direction of the sleeping* LION. *He steals cautiously towards the spot indicated by* MEGAERA. *She rises with an effort and totters after him.*)

MEGAERA: No, Andy: you'll be killed. Come back.

(*The* LION *utters a long snoring sigh.* ANDROCLES *sees the* LION, *and recoils fainting into the arms of* MEGAERA, *who falls back on the bundle. They roll apart and lie staring in terror at one another. The* LION *is heard groaning heavily in the jungle.*)

ANDROCLES (*whispering*): Did you see? A lion.

MEGAERA (*despairing*): The gods have sent him to punish us because you're a Christian. Take me away, Andy. Save me.

ANDROCLES (*rising*): Meggy: there's one chance for you. It'll take him pretty nigh twenty minutes to eat me (I'm rather stringy and tough) and you can escape in less time than that.

MEGAERA: Oh, don't talk about eating. (*The* LION *rises with a great groan and limps toward them.*) Oh! (*She faints.*)

ANDROCLES (*quaking, but keeping between the* LION *and* MEGAERA): Don't you come near my wife, do you hear? (*The* LION *groans.* AN-DROCLES *can hardly stand for trembling.*) Meggy: run. Run for your life. If I take my eye off him, it's all up. (*The* LION *holds up his wounded paw and flaps it piteously before* ANDROCLES.) Oh, he's lame, poor old chap! He's got a thorn in his paw. A frightfully big thorn. (*Full of sympathy.*) Oh, poor old man! Did um get an awful thorn into um's tootsums wootsums? Has it made um too sick to eat a nice little Christian man for um's breakfast? Oh, a nice little Christian man will get um's thorn out for um; and then um shall eat the nice Christian man and the nice Christian man's nice big tender wifey pifey. (*The* LION *responds by moans of self-pity.*) Yes, yes, yes, yes, yes. Now, now (*taking the paw in his hand*), um is not to bite and not to scratch, not even if it hurts a very very little. Now make velvet paws. That's right. (*He pulls gingerly at the thorn. The* LION, *with an angry yell of pain, jerks back his paw so abruptly that* ANDROCLES *is thrown on his back.*) Steadee! Oh, did the nasty cruel little Christian man hurt the sore paw? (*The* LION *moans assentingly but apologetically.*) Well, one more little pull and it will be all over. Just one little, little, leetle pull; and then um will live happily ever after. (*He gives the thorn another pull. The* LION *roars and snaps his jaws with a terrifying clash.*) Oh, mustn't frighten um's good kind doctor, um's affectionate nursey. That didn't hurt at all: not a bit. Just one more. Just to show how the brave big lion can bear pain, not like the little crybaby Christian man. Oopsh! (*The thorn comes out. The* LION *yells with pain, and shakes his paw wildly.*) That's it. (*Holding up the thorn.*) Now it's out. Now lick um's paw to take away the nasty inflammation. See? (*He licks his own hand. The* LION *nods intelligently and licks his paw industriously.*) Clever little liony-piony! Understands um's dear old friend Andy Wandy. (*The* LION *licks his face.*) Yes, kissums Andy Wandy. (*The* LION, *wagging his tail violently, rises on his hind legs, and embraces* ANDROCLES, *who makes a wry face and cries*) Velvet paws! Velvet paws! (*The* LION *draws in his claws.*) That's right. (*He embraces the* LION, *who finally takes the end of his tail in one paw, places that tight round* ANDROCLES' *waist, resting it on his hip.* ANDROCLES *takes the other paw in his hand, stretches out his arm, and the two waltz rapturously round and round and finally away through the jungle.*)

MEGAERA (*who has revived during the waltz*): Oh, you coward, you haven't danced with me for years; and now you go off dancing with a great brute beast that you haven't known for ten minutes and that wants to eat your own wife. Coward. Coward! Coward! (*She rushes off after them into the jungle.*)

The story of the controversy between Henry VIII and Sir Thomas More is too well known to need reviewing here. This scene takes place some months after Thomas has been condemned to prison for high treason because he will not accept the Act of Parliament declaring Henry's first marriage illegal and his marriage to Anne acceptable to the church. Thomas has not yet been sentenced to death, but, knowing the workings of the political leaders, he has no doubt that this will be his fate. Alice is Thomas's wife, and Margaret, in her middle twenties, is their daughter.

FROM A *Man for All Seasons* / ROBERT BOLT

(*Enter* JAILER *and* MARGARET.)

JAILER: Wake up, Sir Thomas! Your family's here!

MORE (*starting up. A great cry*): Margaret! What's this? You can visit me? (*Thrusts his arms through the cage.*) Meg. Meg. (*She goes to him. Then horrified.*) For God's sake, Meg, they've not put *you* in here?

JAILER (*reassuringly*): No-o-o, sir. Just a visit; a short one.

MORE (*excited*): Jailer, jailer, let me out of this.

JAILER: Yes, sir. I'm allowed to let you out.

MORE: Thank you. (*Goes to the door of the cage, gabbling while* JAILER *unlocks it.*) Thank you, thank you.

(*He comes out. He and she regard each other; then she drops into a curtsy.*)

MARGARET: Good morning, Father.

MORE (*ecstatic, wraps her to him*): Oh, good morning — Good morning. (*Enter* ALICE, *supported by* ROPER. *She, like* MORE, *has aged and is poorly dressed.*) Good morning, Alice. Good morning, Will.

(ROPER *is staring at the rack in horror.* ALICE *approaches* MORE *and peers at him technically.*)

ALICE (*almost accusatory*): Husband, how do you do?

MORE (*smiling over* MARGARET): As well as need be, Alice. Very happy now. Will?

ROPER: This is an awful place!

MORE: Except it's keeping me from you, my dears, it's not so bad. Remarkably like any other place.

ALICE (*looks up critically*): It drips!

MORE: Yes. Too near the river.

 From A *Man For All Seasons*, by Robert Bolt. Copyright © 1962 by Robert Bolt. Reprinted by permission of Random House, Inc.

(ALICE *goes apart and sits, her face bitter*).

MARGARET (*disengages from him, takes basket from her mother*): We've brought you some things. (*Shows him. There is constraint between them.*) Some cheese. . . .

MORE: Cheese.

MARGARET: And a custard. . . .

MORE: A custard!

MARGARET: And, these other things . . . . (*She doesn't look at him.*)

ROPER: And a bottle of wine. (*Offering it.*)

MORE: Oh. (*Mischievously.*) Is it good, son Roper?

ROPER: I don't know, sir.

MORE (*looks at them, puzzled*): Well.

ROPER: Sir, come out! Swear to the Act! Take the oath and come out!

MORE: Is this why they let you come?

ROPER: Yes. . . . Meg's under oath to persuade you.

MORE (*coldy*): That was silly, Meg. How did you come to do that?

MARGARET: I wanted to!

MORE: You want me to swear to the Act of Succession?

MARGARET: "God more regards the thoughts of the heart than the words of the mouth." Or so you've always told me.

MORE: Yes.

MARGARET: Then say the words of the oath and in your heart think otherwise.

MORE: What is an oath then but words we say to God?

MARGARET: That's very neat.

MORE: Do you mean it isn't true?

MARGARET: No, it's true.

MORE: Then it's a poor argument to call it "neat," Meg. When a man takes an oath, Meg, he's holding his own self in his own hands. Like water. (*He cups his hands.*) And if he opens his fingers *then* — he needn't hope to find himself again. Some men aren't capable of this, but I'd be loath to think your father one of them.

MARGARET: In any State that was half good, you would be raised up high, not here, for what you've done already. It's not your fault the State's three-quarters bad. Then if you elect to suffer for it, you elect yourself a hero.

MORE: That's very neat. But look now. . . . If we lived in a State where virtue was profitable, common sense would make us good, and greed would make us saintly. And we'd live like animals or angels in the happy land that *needs* no heroes. But since in fact we see that avarice, anger, envy, pride, sloth, lust and stupidity commonly profit far beyond humility, chasity, fortitude, justice and thought, and have to choose, to be human at all . . . why then perhaps we *must* stand fast a little — even at the risk of being heroes.

MARGARET (*emotionally*): But in reason! Haven't you done as much as God can reasonably *want*?

MORE: Well . . . finally . . . it isn't a matter of reason; finally it's a matter of love.

ALICE (*hostile*): You're content, then, to be shut up here with mice and rats when you might be home with us!

MORE (*flinching*): Content? If they'd open a crack that wide (*between finger and thumb*) I'd be through it. (*To* MARGARET.) Well, has Eve run out of apples?

MARGARET: I've not yet told you what the house is like, without you.

MORE: Don't, Meg.

MARGARET: What we do in the evenings, now that you're not there.

MORE: Meg, have done!

MARGARET: We sit in the dark because we've no candles. And we've no talk because we're wondering what they're doing to you here.

MORE: The King's more merciful than you. He doesn't use the rack.

(*Enter* JAILER.)

JAILER: Two minutes to go, sir. I thought you'd like to know.

MORE: Two minutes!

JAILER: Till seven o'clock, sir. Sorry. Two minutes. (*Exit* JAILER.)

MORE: Jailer! (*Seizes* ROPER *by the arm.*) Will — go to him, talk to him, keep him occupied — (*Propelling him after* JAILER.)

ROPER: How, sir?

MORE: Anyhow! Have you got any money?

ROPER (*eagerly*): Yes!

MORE: No, don't try and bribe him! Let him play for it; he's got a pair of dice. And talk to him, you understand! And take this — (*He hands him the wine.*) and mind you share it — do it properly, Will! (ROPER *nods vigorously and exits.*) Now listen, you must leave the country. All of you must leave the country.

MARGARET: And leave you here?

MORE: It makes no difference, Meg; they won't let you see me again. (*Breathlessly, a prepared speech under pressure.*) You must all go on the same day, but not on the same boat; different boats from different ports —

MARGARET: After the trial, then.

MORE: There'll be no trial, they have no case. Do this for me, I beseech you?

MARGARET: Yes.

MORE: Alice? (*She turns her back.*) Alice, I command you!

ALICE (*harshly*): Right!

MORE (*looks into the basket*): Oh, this is splendid; I know who packed this.

ALICE (*harshly*): I packed it.

MORE: Yes. (*He eats a morsel.*) You still make superlative custard, Alice.

ALICE: Do I?

MORE: That's a nice dress you have on.

ALICE: It's my cooking dress.

MORE: It's very nice anyway. Nice color.

ALICE (*turns. Quietly*): By God, you think very little of me. (*Mounting bitterness.*) I know I'm a fool. But I'm no such fool as at this time to be lamenting for my dresses! Or to relish complimenting on my custard!

MORE (*regarding her with frozen attention. He nods once or twice*): I am well rebuked. (*He holds out his hands.*) Al——

ALICE: No! (*She remains where she is, glaring at him.*)

MORE (*he is in great fear of her*): I am faint when I think of the worst that they may do to me. But worse than that would be to go with you not understanding why I go.

ALICE: I don't!

MORE (*just hanging on to his self-possession*): Alice, if you can tell me that you understand, I think I can make a good death, if I have to.

ALICE: Your death's no "good" to me!

MORE: Alice, you must tell me that you understand!

ALICE: I don't! (*She throws it straight at his head.*) I don't believe this had to happen.

MORE (*his face is drawn*): If you say that, Alice, I don't see how I'm to face it.

ALICE: It's the truth!

MORE (*gasping*): You're an honest woman.

ALICE: Much good may it do me! I'll tell you what I'm afraid of: that when you've gone, I shall hate you for it.

MORE (*turns from her, his face working*): Well, you mustn't, Alice, that's all. (*Swiftly she crosses the stage to him; he turns and they clasp each other fiercely.*) You mustn't, you —

ALICE (*covers his mouth with her hand*): S-s-sh. . . . As for understanding, I understand you're the best man that I ever met or am likely to; and if you go — well, God knows why I suppose — though as God's my witness God's kept deadly quiet about it! And if anyone wants my opinion of the King and his Council they've only to ask for it!

MORE: Why, it's a lion I married! A lion! A lion! (*He breaks away from her, his face shining.*) Say what you may — this custard's very good. It's very, very good.

> (*He puts his face in his hands;* ALICE *and* MARGARET *comfort him;* ROPER *and* JAILER *erupt onto the stage above, wrangling fiercely*).

JAILER: It's no good, sir! I know what you're up to! And it can't be done!

ROPER: Another minute, man!

JAILER (*descending; to* MORE): Sorry, sir, time's up!

ROPER (*gripping his shoulder from behind*): For pity's sake!

JAILER (*shaking him off*): Now don't do that, sir! Sir Thomas, the ladies will have to go now!

MORE: You said seven o'clock!

JAILER: It's seven now. You must understand my position, sir.

MORE: But one more minute!

MARGARET: Only a little while — give us a little while!

JAILER (*reprovingly*): Now, miss, you don't want to get me into trouble.

ALICE: Do as you're told. Be off at once!

(*The first stroke of seven is heard on a heavy, deliberate bell, which continues, reducing what follows to a babble.*)

JAILER (*taking* MARGARET *firmly by the upper arm*): Now come along, miss; you'll get your father into trouble as well as me. (ROPER *descends and grabs him.*) Are you obstructing me, sir? (MARGARET *embraces* MORE *and dashes up the stairs and exits, followed by* ROPER. *Taking* ALICE *gingerly by the arm.*) Now, my lady, no trouble!

ALICE (*throwing him off as she rises*): Don't put your muddy hand on me!

JAILER: Am I to call the guard then? Then come on!

(ALICE, *facing him, puts foot on bottom stair and so retreats before him, backwards.*)

MORE: For God's sake, man, we're saying goodbye!

JAILER: You don't know what you're asking, sir. You don't know how you're watched.

ALICE: Filthy, stinking, gutter-bred turnkey!

JAILER: Call me what you like, ma'am; you've got to go.

ALICE: I'll see you suffer for this!

JAILER: You're doing your husband no good!

MORE: Alice, goodbye, my love!

(*On this, the last stroke of the seven sounds,* ALICE *raises her hand, turns, and with considerable dignity, exits.* JAILER *stops at the head of the stairs and addresses* MORE, *who, still crouching, turns from him, facing audience.*)

JAILER (*reasonably*): You understand my position, sir, there's nothing I can do; I'm a plain, simple man and just want to keep out of trouble.

MORE (*cries out passionately*): Oh, Sweet Jesus! These plain, simple men!

Edward Albee's The American Dream has been described as a comic nightmare. The author says it is "an examination of the American Scene, an attack on the substitution of artificial for real values in our society, a condemnation of complacency, cruelty, emasculation and vacuity; it is a stand against the fiction that everything in this slipping world of ours is peachy-keen."[1]

Prior to this scene, Grandma has revealed to a Mrs. Barker that years ago Mommy and Daddy "adopted" what she calls a "bumble of joy." As the child matured, they mutilated him to prevent tendencies from developing which would disrupt their moral and social patterns. Throughout the play Grandma is aware that Mommy and Daddy plan to send her away to a home. She is expecting the van man to come for her belongings at any moment, so when the Young Man enters, she assumes he is the van man until he disabuses her. In the scene immediately preceding this one, Grandma, who admires the young man's physical attractiveness and coldly factual agreement that he is indeed "something," dubs him The American Dream.

FROM *The American Dream* / EDWARD ALBEE

GRANDMA: Well, let's see. If you're not the van man, what are you doing here?

YOUNG MAN: I'm looking for work.

GRANDMA: Are you! Well, what kind of work?

YOUNG MAN: Oh, almost anything . . . almost anything that pays. I'll do almost anything for money.

GRANDMA: Will you . . . will you? Hmmmm. I wonder if there's anything you could do around here?

YOUNG MAN: There might be. It looked to be a likely building.

GRANDMA: It's always looked to be a rather unlikely building to me, but I suppose you'd know better than I.

YOUNG MAN: I can sense these things.

GRANDMA: There *might* be something you could do around here. Stay there! Don't come any closer.

YOUNG MAN: Sorry.

GRANDMA: I don't mean I'd *mind*. I don't know whether I'd mind, or not. . . . But it wouldn't look well; it would look just *awful*.

YOUNG MAN: Yes; I suppose so.

GRANDMA: Now, stay there, let me concentrate. What could you do? The folks have been in something of a quandary around here today, sort of a dilemma, and I wonder if you mightn't be some help.

YOUNG MAN: I hope so . . . if there's money in it. Do you have any money?

[1] Edward Albee, "Preface to *The American Dream*." In *Two Plays by Edward Albee* (New York: The New American Library, Inc., 1964), pp. 53–54.

GRANDMA: Money! Oh, there's more money around here than you'd know what to do with.

YOUNG MAN: I'm not so sure.

GRANDMA: Well, maybe not. Besides, I've got money of my own.

YOUNG MAN: You have?

GRANDMA: Sure. Old people quite often have lots of money; more often than most people expect. Come here, so I can whisper to you . . . not too close. I might faint.

YOUNG MAN: Oh, I'm sorry.

GRANDMA: It's all right, dear. Anyway . . . have you ever heard of that big baking contest they run? The one where all the ladies get together in a big barn and bake away?

YOUNG MAN: I'm . . . not . . . sure. . . .

GRANDMA: Not so close. Well, it doesn't matter whether you've heard of it or not. The important thing is — and I don't want anybody to hear this . . . the folks think I haven't been out of the house in eight years — the important thing is that I won first prize in that baking contest this year. Oh, it was in all the papers; not under my own name, though. I used a *nom de boulangère*; I called myself Uncle Henry.

YOUNG MAN: Did you?

GRANDMA: Why not? I didn't see any reason not to. I look just as much like an old man as I do like an old woman. And you know what I called it . . . what I won for?

YOUNG MAN: No. What did you call it?

GRANDMA: I called it Uncle Henry's Day-Old Cake.

YOUNG MAN: That's a very nice name.

GRANDMA: And it wasn't any trouble, either. All I did was go out and get a store-bought cake, and keep it around for a while, and then slip it in, unbeknownst to anybody. Simple.

YOUNG MAN: You're a very resourceful person.

GRANDMA: Pioneer stock.

YOUNG MAN: Is all this true? Do you want me to believe all this?

GRANDMA: Well, you can believe it or not . . . it doesn't make any difference to me. All *I* know is, Uncle Henry's Day-Old-Cake won me twenty-five thousand smackerolas.

YOUNG MAN: Twenty-five thou——

GRANDMA: Right on the old loggerhead. Now . . . how do you like them apples?

YOUNG MAN: Love 'em.

GRANDMA: I thought you'd be impressed.

YOUNG MAN: Money talks.

GRANDMA: Hey! You look familiar.

YOUNG MAN: Hm? Pardon?

GRANDMA: I said, you look familiar.

YOUNG MAN: Well, I've done some modeling.

GRANDMA: No . . . no. I don't mean that. You look familiar.

YOUNG MAN: Well, I'm a type.

GRANDMA: Yup; you sure are. Why do you say you'd do anything for money . . . if you don't mind my being nosy?

YOUNG MAN: No, no. It's part of the interviews. I'll be happy to tell you. It's that I have no talents at all, except what you see . . . my person; my body, my face. In every other way I am incomplete, and I must therefore . . . compensate.

GRANDMA: What do you mean, incomplete? You look pretty complete to me.

YOUNG MAN: I think I can explain it to you, partially because you're very old, and very old people have perceptions they keep to themselves, because if they expose them to other people . . . well, you know what ridicule and neglect are.

GRANDMA: I do, child, I do.

YOUNG MAN: Then listen. My mother died the night that I was born, and I never knew my father; I doubt my mother did. But, I wasn't alone, because lying with me . . . in the placenta . . . there was some- one else . . . my brother . . . my twin.

GRANDMA: Oh, my child.

YOUNG MAN: We were identical twins . . . he and I . . . not fraternal . . . identical; we were derived from the same ovum; and in *this*, in that we were twins not from separate ova but from the same one, we had a kinship such as you cannot imagine. We . . . we felt each other breathe . . . his heartbeats thundered in my temples . . . mine in his . . . our stomachs ached and we cried for feeding at the same time . . . are you old enough to understand?

GRANDMA: I think so, child; I think I'm nearly old enough.

YOUNG MAN: I hope so. But we were separated when we were still very young, my brother, my twin and I . . . inasmuch as you can separate one being. We were torn apart . . . thrown to opposite ends of the continent. I don't know what became of my brother . . . to the rest of myself . . . except that, from time to time, in the years that have passed, I have suffered losses . . . that I can't explain. A fall from grace . . . a departure of innocence . . . loss . . . loss. How can I put it to you? All right; like this: Once . . . it was as if all at once my heart . . . became numb . . . almost as though I . . . almost as though . . . just like that . . . it had been wrenched from my body . . . and from that time I have been unable to love. Once . . . I was asleep at the time . . . I awoke, and my eyes were burning. And since that time I have been unable to see anything, *anything*, with pity, with affection . . . with anything but . . . cool disinterest. And my groin . . . even there . . . since one time . . . one specific agony . . . since then I have not been able to *love* anyone

380 / Oral Interpretation

with my body. And even my hands . . . I cannot touch another person
and feel love. And there is more . . . there are more losses, but it all
comes down to this: I no longer have the capacity to feel anything. I
have no emotions. I have been drained, torn asunder . . . disembow-
eled. I have, now, only my person . . . my body, my face. I use what
I have . . . I let people love me . . . I accept the syntax around me, for
while I know I cannot relate . . . I know I must be related *to*. I let
people touch me . . . I let them draw pleasure from my groin . . . from
my presence . . . from the fact of me . . . but, that *is* all it comes to.
As I told you, I am incomplete . . . I can feel nothing. I can feel nothing. And so . . . here I am . . . as you see me. I am . . . but this . . .
what you see. And it will always be thus.

GRANDMA: Oh, my child; my child. (*Long pause; then*) I was mistaken
. . . before. I don't know you from somewhere, but I knew . . . once
. . . someone very much like you . . . or, very much as perhaps you were.

YOUNG MAN: Be careful; be very careful. What I have told you may not
be true. In my profession . . .

GRANDMA: Shhhhhh. (*The* YOUNG MAN *bows his head, in acquiescence.*)
Someone . . . to be more precise . . . who might have turned out to be
very much like you might have turned out to be. And . . . unless I'm
terribly mistaken . . . you've found yourself a job.

The Interpretation
of Poetry

Part Four

Chapter 10

Broadly speaking, poetry differs from prose in the emotional weight of its content and the importance of its sound pattern. In poetry, perhaps more than in any other kind of literature, the content and the form are inseparable in achieving the total effect. The one intensifies the other. A poet's ear is attuned to the sound of words as a composer's is to tone and the effect of tone sequences, and the poet tests his words for sound as well as for denotation and connotation. Consequently, poetry may be said to be the particular province of the oral interpreter because it reaches its ultimate objective only when it is read aloud.

The high degree of emotion in poetry requires that the interpreter make full use of all the sense imagery, usually more abundant than in other types of writing. Complete response to this imagery will affect his posture and muscle tone and help him draw an appropriate empathic response from his listeners. The principle of empathy lies at the very heart of poetry, since emotion produces and in turn is intensified by physical response. Because poetry is so condensed, an audience profits considerably from the trained interpreter's knowledge and control of vocal quality, inflection, force, and timing that help to clarify the meaning and add richness to the associational values of the words.

The structure of poetry, examined in detail in the next chapter, has its traditional requisite of rhythm, based on an effective combination of sounds and silences and of light and heavier stresses. This pattern of sound and stress can of course be fully realized and appreciated only when it strikes the ear. If the poet had not been concerned with the heightened

The Language of Poetry

contribution of patterned sound, he might well have put his idea into prose. The interpreter will discover that poetry demands the utmost vocal flexibility and control, for it is his responsibility to keep in harmonious balance the content and the sound pattern so that neither obscures the other. His audience's response to a poem is influenced by this harmony, and the total effect of the poem is achieved only when content and structure are perfectly coordinated. Nevertheless, each presents some specific problems which may be considered separately during the process of objective analysis.

Poetic Content

In previous chapters, logical content (what a piece of writing "says") and emotive content (what causes the reader's pleasure or pain, relaxation or tension) have sometimes been considered separately, although they can never actually be divorced in either prose or poetry. As we have noted, emotive content may be found even in predominantly factual prose, where, however, it is not an end in itself but a means of reinforcing or making more vivid the idea being developed. Descriptive prose has an accompanying emotive response which intensifies and adds effectiveness to the description itself. In drama, a high degree of emotive response may grow out of the conflict and character reactions. However, the development of the characters and the situation are things which hold the attention of the writer and consequently of the interpreter, with emotion used to implement and motivate the plot.

In poetry, the logical content and the emotive content are blended so completely that it is nearly impossible to tell where the one ends and the other begins. Poetry is characterized by the greatest possible condensation. It leaves much unsaid. Nevertheless, the poet must give his readers enough clues to guide their responses; consequently, he selects every word with the utmost care. Moreover, the syntactical relationship of the words is vitally important. This principle of selectivity operates, of course, in other forms of writing, but in poetry each word must carry specific denotative and rich connotative meaning, and make a harmonious contribution to the sound pattern as well. It is partly by this careful selectivity that condensation is achieved. The condensation, in turn, sharpens the emotional impact and allows the poem to move on several levels simultaneously, providing the reader with strong suggestion so that he may personally identify with the experience of the poem.

Since the poet is intent on emotive response, he uses his organization and whatever aspects of progression, character suggestion, and description he finds effective to implement and establish that emotion. The experience he wishes to share may call up a response as pleasant and delicate as Cummings' "Spring is like a perhaps hand" (page 469), or as disturbing as the Emily Dickinson poem we looked at in Chapters 1 and 2 and Eliot's "The Love Song of J. Alfred Prufrock" (page 420).

It may be necessary, therefore, to reconsider the established concept of content, or what the author has said. Obviously, a poet must have something to say and must say it so that his audience will understand. This does not mean, however, that a poem must be as immediately clear and factual as an essay or a newspaper article. If the poet had wished simply to inform, he would have put his idea into a prose essay or article — that is, into a form which lends itself much more easily to developing a purely logical idea. But the poet intends to communicate something beyond fact or opinion. Indeed, much poetry does not require an opinion at all. It asks of the reader merely the acceptance of an attitude. It is not necessary that he accept this attitude as a philosophy of life. It is only necessary that he grant the poet the right to hold it and begin his evaluation from there. Enjoying poetry is comparable to enjoying music or any other art. It requires a degree of cooperation from the perceiver.

Some people distrust poetry because they feel it does not say anything. Their distrust, of course, is based on their own personal opinion of what is worth saying. The pseudo-realists of this century tend to insist that all literature must present information, an answer to some problem of living or a logical explanation of some contemporary phenomenon. They are so accustomed to reading for information that they fall into the trap of "message hunting."

Poetry is a record of experience to be shared. This does not mean experience to be explained, nor does it always mean totality of experience. A poet may give us only a segment of his experience, translatable into terms of the reader's own experiences. He may certainly write of facts, but he interprets them in the wider areas of human life. He may have been motivated to write by an "idea"; but if the "idea" had been his whole concern, he would not have needed the additional suggestion and richness of sound which are characteristic of poetry. He is usually concerned rather with an emotional or aesthetic response to the idea. Even in didactic poetry, where the idea is probably of first importance, provoking emotive response is the force behind the idea. Sometimes the poet's intention is primarily to express and give aesthetic pleasure, or he may wish merely to create a mood of excitement or repose, or to recapture the effects of a specific emotion, such as love, hate, joy, or fear. In any case, he will go beyond the confines of strictly logical content. A poet's achievement must be judged in terms of what he has chosen to do, not what the reader thinks he should have done.

Archibald MacLeish says in his "Ars Poetica" that

> A poem should not mean
> But be.

This statement implies not that a poem needs only to exist without meaning anything, but rather that a poem must be a complete, harmonious entity — that it does not *only* "mean" something but has an existence beyond purely logical meaning. It goes far beyond definition into connotation. As soon as the reader has accepted the fact that poetry is not only what it means but what it does with meaning, he will be ready to let the poet and his poem begin their communication to him.

The first step in understanding and evaluating any piece of literature is, of course, reading it over in its entirety to get a general idea of what it says. And this is the first thing to be done with a poem. This first step may be less objective, less purely "mental," with poetry, however, than with most prose or even with drama. The initial response to a poem may not be in terms of idea or logical content at all, but rather in terms of pleasure or pain, activity or repose — in short, of emotive content. The interpreter should read the poem aloud — several times over — and permit himself the luxury of a completely subjective response before beginning the objective analysis. He should give full play to the sound and to the harmony between content and form. Instead of beginning at once to work on the poem, he should let the poem work on him. Enjoyment is a good starting point for appreciation, even if the reason for liking the poem cannot be put into words immediately.

The student interpreter should not be discouraged if he finds only a very simple, obvious meaning in a poem and someone else finds a great quantity of implication. As his experience with life and with poetry increases, he will be better able to enrich the core of meaning with appropriate marginal and associational implications. Above all, he should be careful not to get so preoccupied with reading between the lines that he loses sight of the lines themselves.

Poetry has been classified by types according to innumerable systems — some based on content, some on structure, and some on combinations of both. Many of the classifications overlap, and the student will find differences of opinion as to the precise category in which certain poems should be placed. The interpreter is not concerned with technical names and categories, except as they provide him with handles for grasping his material. From this standpoint, however, he will find it helpful to consider briefly some of the more common classifications in order to discover their advantages and special problems. He will, of course, always go beyond these generalizations to the special qualities of the individual selection.

For our purposes, poetry may be classified under three major headings: narrative, lyric, and dramatic. These distinctions are based largely on a consideration of the *persona* — the speaker in the poem. This consideration is, of course, important to the interpreter as a guide to his relation to his audience. He must know who is speaking in the poem, to whom he is speaking, and whether the experience is being revealed directly (as in a narrative poem), is overheard (as in a dramatic poem), or is the highly personal utterance of a single speaker to anyone who can share his response (as in a lyric poem). This consideration closely parallels the concern with point of view in narrative prose in Chapter 7.

Narrative Poetry

Narrative poetry tells a story or relates a series of events leading up to a climax. In this respect it resembles narrative prose, and many of the steps suggested in Chapter 7 for understanding narrative prose are equally applicable here. It will be necessary to discover the key situations, their focal points, and their relationship to the main climax. Attention must be given to the progression of time and place, the development of character, and the relationships between characters, whenever these elements are important in furthering the plot. Setting, situation, and physical and psychological traits of character — and the interdependence of these factors — must also be considered, if the poet has made use of them. The *persona* is the narrator, and the interpreter will be very much concerned with his point of view, just as he was in prose fiction. When dialogue occurs in narrative poetry, as it often does, the interpreter must solve the problem of handling it, just as he did in narrative prose. And as in narrative prose, there may or may not be descriptive passages where imagery is used to reinforce setting or effect a transition from one key situation to the next.

When the interpreter elects to present a narrative poem, he accepts a twofold responsibility. He must be, first of all, a story-teller — that is, the progression of events leading to the climax must be his primary concern. He must analyze the content carefully to become thoroughly aware of all the aspects of organization. He must remember that he is telling *a story in poetry*, and that it is his obligation to use the poetic aspects to implement the story and enhance its movement and emotional impact.

Communicating a story in condensed poetic form, with all its suspense and activity, demands a high degree of directness. The interpreter must keep his attention on the unity of the incident or incidents which make up the plot, and he must allow the descriptions and transitions to provide the needed variety and emotional rhythm. He must use his knowledge of balance and proportion so that the climax will achieve its purpose. The incidents must retain their proper proportion, hold suspense, and move with speed. These two attributes, suspense and speed, can be enhanced by the condensation and high degree of suggestivity of poetry.

If it is necessary to cut a long narrative poem, the interpreter follows much the same procedure as in cutting narrative prose, except that he has to be very careful not to violate the poem's structural pattern. That is, he may, if absolutely necessary, cut complete sections but not lines or parts of lines within stanzas. For example, the tag "he said" might easily be eliminated from a sentence of prose without any loss, but cutting it out of a line of poetry would destroy the pulse of the line and break the pattern of sound.

Of the three commonly accepted types of narrative poetry, possibly the oldest in English is the *popular ballad,* a folk product and always anonymous. Simple in plot and metrical structure, it is a short, swift, stark narrative told in unadorned language. The narrator's point of view is completely objective, and he injects no comment or personal attitude. The modern interpreter will need a strong sense of performance to give these stark and often bloody stories the gusto to make them convincing and interesting.

The speed of the ballad is due in part to the omission of transitions of time, place, and character development. Consequently, the interpreter will need to establish these transitions for himself in order to retain the unity of progression. Dialogue is usually a prominent characteristic of ballads and must be handled with precision and clarity. The question-and-answer technique is quite common and requires a sure sense of "interplay" to keep the progression alive. This dependence on dialogue,

388 / Oral Interpretation

of course, takes the interpreter into aspects of technique which belong primarily to drama but which are also important in handling direct discourse in any type of narrative writing.

Ballads usually have a refrain which may help to implement the plot, but whose contribution is often primarily rhythmic. Refrains present the interpreter with a challenging problem in unity; they must not be allowed to break the progress of the story, yet they must be made to serve their purpose of repetition.

Even the modernized versions of the old ballads retain traces of dialect or archaic words and spellings. The extent to which the modern interpreter uses dialect depends partly on his own ability to make it convincing, but even more on his hearers' background and their willingness and ability to follow it without finding it an annoying barrier to understanding. The safest path is probably to give just a *suggestion* of dialect, pronouncing the words as they are written in order to preserve the rhythm and rhyme, but concentrating on overall flavor and lilt rather than on individual sounds. The ballad must have an easy flow of sound, but it must also tell a fast-moving and exciting story.

The second important type of narrative poetry is the *metrical tale*, a full-length novel or short story in verse. It may be a medieval tale such as those in *The Canterbury Tales* or a modern product like Keats's "The Eve of St. Agnes," John Masefield's "Dauber," or Robert Frost's "The Death of the Hired Man." In any case, the process of analyzing content and organization will be comparable to that used for the short story. The characters may be romanticized types, as in "The Eve of St. Agnes," and thus exhibit little more complexity than those in some of the ballads, or they may be completely realized individuals, like Mary, Warren, and Silas in "The Death of the Hired Man." Descriptions of the setting are likely to be fairly explicit, and the relationship between the characters and the setting takes on a good deal of importance. Moreover, the poet does not hesitate to express his own attitude and sympathies from time to time while still retaining his position as observer.

The third type of narrative poetry is the *epic*; it differs from an ordinary narrative in its extreme length and elevated tone and more particularly in the type of events it relates. An epic centers on a hero of superhuman proportions, both morally and physically, whose exploits are of great significance to a tribe, race, or nation. Art epics like the *Aeneid* and folk epics like *Beowulf* are examples of this type of poetry. Another kind of epic concerns mankind's battle with the forces of evil and his struggle for a divine victory; *Paradise Lost* is the prime example. Finally, the mock epic, like Pope's "The Rape of the Lock," applies the grand epic scope and manner to trivial circumstances with amusing satirical effect.

The style of an epic is lofty, the language highly poetic and exalted, and the sentences usually complex and elaborate, with numerous clauses and inversions. The interpreter must use these aspects of style to help suggest the scope of the episodes and the heroic proportions of the participants. Epics are not written about common men in everyday situations. They involve whole nations and heroes who are larger than life, and they must be given their proper dimension in performance.

Lyric Poetry

The *lyric* is most typically a short poem, though it may be a long, sustained emotional utterance. It is strongly unified poetry, for all aspects of content are shaped toward the emotional focal point. The *persona* in a lyric poem is usually a single speaker whose primary purpose is to share an emotional experience. Whether or not the speaker is the poet himself is a matter of debate among contemporary critics. The differences of opinion grow in part out of a semantic problem. For our purposes we shall assume that the poet is speaking in a lyric poem, remembering that poets, like the rest of us, have varying moods and attitudes and complex and many-sided personalities. We shall handle the problem of someone who thinks and feels like the poet but who is a clearly distinguishable character in his own right when we come to the dramatic lyric (page 393). It might be well to point out, however, that we are not concerned in a lyric with the poet as a man with brown hair and blue eyes wearing a sport shirt, but rather with his emotional and psychological personality as it is revealed in the particular poem under consideration.

A lyric poem has been compared to a flash of lightning which illuminates some object with a moment of vividness, in this case emotional vividness. The lyric poet usually gives little or no account of what leads up to the emotional experience or what follows it, since his concern is with *sharing* the experience, not *explaining* it. The interpreter, however, will find that sketching in some relevant background in his own mind enhances his appreciation and helps him set the appropriate mood, since these poems, especially the shorter ones, provide him with practically no introductory material. The high degree of association and the intensity of emotion make it imperative for him to be in complete control of his techniques before he even begins reading the poem to an audience: the extreme condensation will allow him no time to "warm up" or to find his equilibrium. Thus his introduction becomes unusually important.

If a lyric is to achieve its purpose, the interpreter must allow himself to respond to it completely. Only through his complete response will his audience be moved. This does not mean, of course, that he becomes so carried away by his own emotions that he neglects his responsibility to his listeners. In his earliest phases of preparation he may indulge in complete subjectivity, but in performance he must remember that his purpose is to share an experience, not to display his own sensitivity. He will attempt to call forth from his audience the emotional response the poet obviously intended, and to this end he will keep intelligent control of his techniques. The more the listeners are moved by the material and the less they are aware of the interpreter's presence, the greater is his success.

The reader may not have had the exact experience the poet is sharing, but he can apply the principle of remembered or transferred emotion, calling on his own experience to guide him into the area of the poet's intention. The intensity of response desired by the poet may vary all the way from gentle relaxation to passionate mystical experience. Full appreciation of the kinesthetic imagery will help produce the proper empathy that will intensify the audience's response. In the lyric, the poet usually speaks his own thoughts, aspirations, and fears; hence it is useful to know as much as possible about the man who felt the impact of that particular experience.

Most lyric poetry demands slower reading than other forms of writing, partly because imagery is less easy to assimilate than story, and partly because a swiftly paced reading does not permit the sound pattern to make its full contribution to both music and emotion. The audience must have time to hear the words, re-create the images, and set up the response. Lyric poetry requires less directness in presentation than narrative writing, but the interpreter must be careful not to withdraw completely from his audience and read as though he were lost in the clouds. On the other hand, direct eye contact with the members of the audience may inhibit their response and make them self-conscious. The happy mean is to adopt an attitude of *sharing* the *experience*. The interpreter can help intensify the audience's response by skillful technique and by control. He is aware of his power to stimulate his listeners' emotions, but he knows that he cannot compel them.

The emotion that characterizes a lyric poem is often expressed in terms of reflection or description. Thus, the *reflective lyric*, as its name suggests, is the poet's emotional response through recall and reflection or contemplation. This element of an emotional experience remembered in tranquillity is important to the interpreter because it gives him a clue to the degree of activity — or, more precisely, absence of immediate physical activity — in the poem. Wordsworth's famous poem, popularly called "Daffodils," is an outstanding example of the reflective lyric.

The *elegy* is a lyric that expresses grief at death, usually the death of an individual. In Greek verse, the elegy had a definite structural form, but it was brought over into English poetry not as a form but as a quality of emotional expression. Thus an elegy may assume any conventional metrical pattern or may even be written in free verse. Usually, however, there is a formality of language and structure which lends dignity to the expression of grief and harmonizes with the solemn mystery of death and the sense of personal loss. Auden's "In Memory of W. B. Yeats" (page 474) is an elegy which uses a combination of structural patterns that change with the tone of the separate sections.

Like the elegy, the *ode* was a recognized lyrical form in Greek verse. Designed to be accompanied by music and a highly stylized dance, it consisted of three movements, two of which had identical music and dance patterns. But although these Greek structures have been imitated in English verse, the term "ode" has come to be applied to any sustained lyric utterance of exalted theme, often in commemoration of some important event or experience. An ode, then, is a dignified, relatively long lyric poem, formal in language, and formal though not necessarily regular in structure.

In harmony with the dignity of its inspiration, the ode moves steadily to a single philosophic-emotional focal point. The progress is often achieved by elaborating various details or attributes of the person, object, or circumstance that serves as the motivation, and the climax occurs when these are given a universal and philosophical implication. This is the method Keats used in his famous "Ode on a Grecian Urn" (page 416). The interpreter must make full use of the imagery and keep a careful check on unity so that all details may lead to the final culmination. In general tone, the ode is more contemplative than active and suggests a restraint of movement similar to a reflective lyric — though by no means a complete passivity, for a sense of movement in the particularly strong kinesthetic imagery accompanies response to an exalted theme.

Perhaps the most familiar type of lyric is the *sonnet*. This poetic form is interesting to the interpreter for several reasons. In the first place, it is widely used — with varying degrees of success, of course — even by contemporary writers. The sonnet by tradition deals with dignified subject matter — although not necessarily so exalted as that treated in the ode — and its greatest challenge to both poet and interpreter lies in its fixed form.

A sonnet is a fourteen-line poem, written in predominantly iambic meter, with five feet to the line. It has, moreover, a prescribed rhyme scheme. The two most common types of sonnet are the Petrarchan and the Shakespearean, which differ primarily in the arrangement of their rhyme sounds. The distinction between them is important, but it need not concern the interpreter unduly except as it gives him certain guides to the organization of content and to the intricacy of the sound pattern. Both in content and structure, the Petrarchan sonnet is very strictly organized. The first four lines introduce the subject and the next four develop it. In a true Petrarchan sonnet each of these quatrains completes a unit of thought, and the sentences are allowed to "run on." The next three lines introduce a new but related theme, and the last three lines bring the observation to its conclusion. The rhyme scheme, which is *abba, abba, cdc, cdc,* or *cdcdcd,* reinforces the division of content. A true Petrarchan sonnet is somewhat rare in English, however, as most poets have chosen to vary the strict form. The Shakespearean sonnet follows the same principle of organization through the first eight lines, but departs from it in devoting the last six lines to the conclusion, with the focal point occurring in the two final lines. There is also greater flexibility in the rhyme scheme of the Shakespearean sonnet — *abab, cdcd, efef, gg.* This variation in rhyme pattern concerns the interpreter because it corresponds to the divisions of the content and helps bring the poem to a firm close by introducing a rhyming couplet for the last two lines.

When a poet has accepted such traditional restrictions of organization and structure, the interpreter must also give particular attention to the way the sonnet form augments the emotion being expressed and to the determination of his own responsibilities in retaining the sound pattern established by the rhyme scheme and the five-foot iambic lines. He will be greatly aided in his analysis by the sonnet's prescribed principles of organization of content, and he must use some care in preserving the balance and proportion.

Dramatic Poetry

Many contemporary critics take the position that all poetry is dramatic in that it is an action in itself concerning a person or persons and that it contains a distinct development or revelation. This is, of course, true, and this approach to poetry can prove very helpful. Nevertheless, in line with our early classifications of literature we shall limit our discussion of dramatic poetry to those works centering on a character in conflict with a force within or outside himself, whose development is revealed without a third-person narrator.

Dramatic poetry includes the *dramatic narrative, dramatic lyric, dramatic monologue,* and *soliloquy.* Although these terms are often used interchangeably, the four types vary slightly in emphasis on character and situation, and some attempt to differentiate them will help the interpreter in making his analysis and in deciding on the degree of characterization which will be necessary in his performance. In each case, the *persona* is an identifiable character speaking directly to an audience, to himself as he thinks aloud, or to other characters involved in a dramatic situation.

A *dramatic narrative* is a poem in which the incidents or series of incidents are related by a participant affected by the events he relates. Byron's "The Prisoner of Chillon" is such a poem. It opens with Bonivard's brief description of his present physical state, and the purpose of this unit is obviously first, to establish the flashback technique that will reveal the plot, and second, to indicate the point of view which will give the incidents greater vividness. After the introductory statement, Bonivard begins to draw the story out of the past. His attention is on the story, and his own reactions to events are used primarily as transitions from one key situation to the next. Thus the interpreter may assume that the personality of Bonivard is in reality a device for revealing the plot and not a motivating force for its progression, and he will suggest only enough of the prisoner's broken health and spirit to make the plot credible and prepare for the closing phrase

> — even I
> Regain'd my freedom with a sigh.

The *dramatic lyric*, like any other lyric poetry, is a reflection of the poet's subjective responses, thoughts, and aspirations. It is dramatic because the poet has put his thoughts and emotions into the mouth of an appropriate character who speaks for him, so that there is added force and vividness to the expression. Tennyson's "Ulysses" (page 73) and Eliot's "The Love Song of J. Alfred Prufrock" (page 420) fall into this general classification, although they also share some of the characteristics of dramatic monologues or soliloquies. The interpreter will emphasize in his suggestion of character those qualities which make the speaker an appropriate exponent of the philosophy being expressed. The essential qualities in Ulysses, for instance, are his mental vigor, maturity, and wisdom, and his authority and leadership. It is unwise to take too literally his phrase, "you and I are old," because he turns immediately to the belief that

> Old age hath yet his honor and his toil,

which he reinforces with

> . . . but something ere the end,
> Some work of noble note, may yet be done,
> Not unbecoming men that strove with Gods.

The poem closes on the positive note that Ulysses is still

> . . . strong in will
> To strive, to seek, to find, and not to yield.

Prufrock's ironic awareness of his own inability to "disturb the universe" is carefully concealed by his meticulous grooming and "a face [prepared] to meet the faces that you meet."

The *dramatic monologue* is spoken by a single character created outside the poet's own personality. The speaker directly addresses other characters, who are also affected by the incident taking place and who help motivate the speaker's reactions and train of thought. The other characters do not speak, but they are nevertheless rather fully developed as personalities, or at least as forces in relation to the speaker. Browning's "My Last Duchess" is an excellent example of this type of dramatic poetry. Anyone who knows the love story of Elizabeth and Robert Browning will be aware that Browning is not expressing his own ideas of marriage in this famous poem. The ideas are the Duke's and reflect his time and his attitude toward himself and others. He is not acting as an appropriate mouthpiece for the poet's subjective response, but is created outside the poet and speaks for himself. Therefore, the interpreter must give the audience a clear, three-dimensional picture of him so that they will understand his thoughts and feelings.

The *soliloquy* is also spoken by a single character created outside the poet's own personality. The principal difference is that no other characters are being addressed. Since the speaker in a soliloquy is alone, his degree of directness is likely to be less pronounced. However, as in "Soliloquy of the Spanish Cloister" (page 434), he may receive direct and immediate motivations from some exterior source. Though the monk is speaking only to himself, Brother Lawrence's actions direct his thoughts.

The Poet's Attitude

Methods of discovering the author's attitude have been touched on in previous chapters. All the things we have already said are equally useful when applied to poetry. However, because of its extreme condensation as well as its highly personal implications, poetry needs particulary close attention to every clue.

Poetry is probably most often inspired by an emotional urge on the part of the writer. A man's emotions are closely tied up with his philosophy of life, his set of values about himself and the people with whom he associates, and the things with which he is surrounded. It is, therefore, helpful to know as much about a poet as possible if one is to understand what he considers worth saying. Information about the poet does not mean knowing mere biographical facts. It means, rather, realizing what effect the time in which he lived and the circumstances of his life had on his attitude and interests.

A poet's attitude, or that of the speaker if it is not the poet himself, is discovered first of all by careful attention to all the details of the poem being studied. It is also helpful to read some other things the poet has written and to find out as much as possible about what interested him and why. Some poets have expressed their theories in essays and books of criticism. Others have been more reticent and left only their poems to speak for them. Those who achieve a degree of fame, however, often have friends and acquaintances to publish what they know or think they know about the poets and their ways of life, or biographers and scholars to reconstruct the stories of their lives and interpret their thoughts. Contemporary poets, most of whom do not insist on an ivory tower but take part in the world around them, are frequently quite articulate about their intentions and attitudes. Despite all the things the interpreter can find out "about" the poem, however, his most valuable source of information is the poem itself.

One of the clearest indications of attitude is often to be found in the title. For example, the irony of the entire poem is foreshadowed in the title "The Love Song of J. Alfred Prufrock." The combination of "Love Song" with the somewhat pretentious "J. Alfred Prufrock" clearly indicates that this is not a love song in the usual sense. One signs a legal document or formal social note "J. Alfred Prufrock" — not a love song! Another equally effective title is "To His Coy Mistress." "Coy" is a very important word; she is not, obviously, merely reluctant or unalterably opposed. She is being "coy." Poets choose their titles with great care to help us in deciding what the poem is about as well as the way we are to take it.

Admittedly, some poets do not use titles. Then we must depend on the elements of style within the poem itself. Choice of words and figures of speech and the way they are combined into phrases, line units, sentences, and stanzas must be carefully considered. Method of organization and the resultant balance and proportion will give us valuable clues to the weight attached to the various phases of thought development. The sound pattern supporting the content will often indicate the degree of seriousness and dignity inherent in the attitude. We will give this aspect more attention in the next chapter, but a look at the last three lines of each stanza of John Donne's "Go and Catch a Falling Star" (page 468) will convince any reader that this is not a poem of tragic love. The opening lines with their abrupt and impossible commands indicate this as well.

Exaggeration or hyperbole characterizes the poetry of satire and wit, numerous examples of which are to be found in sixteenth- and seventeenth-century poems. It is also a useful device for the contemporary poet, who is often primarily interested in reflecting a complex and highly subjective set of psychological associations.

It is extremely important that the interpreter be willing to let the poet have his way. He must examine every word of the poem in its relationship to every other word and let them operate as they *must* within the whole — not as he wishes they did. If there is a line or phrase which will not fit into his concept of the poem, he must reconsider his analysis. He must share with the audience the poet's attitude toward love, death, childhood, or the passing years, not his own. If he does not like the philosophy being expressed, he should find another selection. He is responsible for the totality of the poem as the poet put it down.

Figurative Language

Poetry is, as we have said, a highly condensed form of expression. The poet has neither the time within the poem nor the inclination for literal explanations and logical expositions. Although he may seem to communicate less directly than the prose writer, he is actually making a more direct appeal, for he is not talking *about* something but attempting to present the essence of that something. He does this by reaching the reader at as many points of contact as possible — striking at him through his senses, his emotions, his intellect, his imagination, and calling forth a blended response that gives new insight into experience. Hence, he must find the exact word which will carry with it not only the precise denotation but, perhaps more important, the right connotation as well.

The word the poet uses does not *define* his concept so much as it *expands* it in the reader's consciousness, just as a pebble tossed into a pool sends ever-widening circles rippling out from the point of surface contact. The implications of the word take the reader beyond the narrow confines of exact definition into the area of suggested meaning and into the complex realm of the experiences the poet is writing about and the reader is perceiving. In examining a poet's choice of words, then, an interpreter must remember that just as a poem not only *means* something but *is* something beyond meaning, so the words that make it up go beyond fact and information. To accomplish this, they must be in complete harmony with the tone and mood of the poem and must make their contribution to the sound pattern as well as to logical and emotive meaning. In spite of good intentions, many people never learn to read poetry so that it has meaning for them or for others. This failure often stems from the reader's inability to untangle certain complexities present in all but the most direct poetic expression. One of the most common of these complexities is the use of figurative language.

A poet often achieves condensation and emotional impact by using references or allusions that embody a wealth of implication. These allusions may contribute materially to the logical meaning of the poem, but they are likely to be most valuable for the associations they set up by implied comparison. Very often they are references to mythical or historical persons or places; and although, with the passing of the classical tradition, their associational value may be lessened for the modern reader, he readily recognizes them as allusions and knows that he can clarify them by consulting an encyclopedia or other appropriate reference book.

In some modern poetry, however, the connotative literary allusion may prove more difficult, since it involves the deliberate echo of a phrase or line from the work of another poet in order to reinforce mood or emotion by inviting comparison or ironic contrast. Archibald MacLeish, for example, in his poem, "You, Andrew Marvell" (page 412), reinforces his own sense of the crowding and closing of time,

> ... the always coming on
> The always rising of the night,

by suggesting through his title that the reader hold simultaneously in mind the seventeenth-century poet's lines on the same subject; and the reader who takes the allusion finds that his immediate response to Mac-Leish's poem is intensified by his remembered or re-evoked response to Marvell's "Coy Mistress," and particularly, no doubt, to the famous lines,

> But at my back I always hear
> Time's wingèd chariot hurrying near . . .

And yet MacLeish's poem has meaning and emotion quite independent of Marvell's poem and conveys that meaning and emotion to one who has never heard of Andrew Marvell or of the "Coy Mistress." For a literary allusion says something directly, in its context, even though it passes undetected as an allusion. Hearing literary echoes brings an added level of understanding and delight and a more complex response — it strengthens the impact of the poem — but it is always the poem itself that speaks, not the source of the allusion.

How does all this affect the interpreter? Obviously, he is not going to explain the references to the audience, to stand between poem and audience as a sort of *Bulfinch's Mythology* or *Bartlett's Familiar Quotations.* He is, however, concerned with the quality of his own understanding and response, for he cannot share the poem with his hearers if he has not first assimilated it himself. The more thoroughly he understands the allusions, the more fully he will appreciate the purpose for which the poet has used them — and the more intelligently he himself can use them in communicating the whole intent of the poem to others. He must, therefore, make himself familiar enough with the allusions to understand the *type of response* they are intended to arouse or reinforce; and by integrating them into the poem as it stands, as a self-contained whole, use them as a means of drawing the proper empathic response from the audience.

Three of the most common figures of speech, mentioned earlier as part of literary imagery (page 144) — the *simile*, the *metaphor*, and the *analogy* — are all based on comparing one thing to another. These comparisons appeal to our senses and our motor responses. Therefore, they depend on sense imagery, discussed at some length in Chapter 6.

A *simile* is easily recognized because it makes an explicit comparison, generally using the word "like." It simply compares two objects of common nature or the particular qualities of one thing to the general qualities of another, as when Keats compares Autumn's activity to that of a gleaner:

> And sometimes like a gleaner thou dost keep
> Steady thy laden head across a brook . . .

A quite different effect is achieved in "The Love Song of J. Alfred Prufrock" by the simile

> When the evening is spread out against the sky
> Like a patient etherized upon a table. . . .

A *metaphor* states that something *is* something else, based on some related but not identical factor. It establishes a relationship between two elements which may be dissimilar in their basic components and yet have attributes in common. Sometimes a metaphor expresses a synthesis of thought and feeling so subtle and complex that it becomes organic or structural in the whole poem. Indeed, contemporary critics often use the term "metaphor" or "metaphorical" to describe any writing which goes beyond fact and obvious relationships.

An *analogy* is an extended metaphor and may serve to implement an entire poem. In Francis Thompson's "The Hound of Heaven," for example, God's pursuit of man is compared to a hound's pursuit in the hunt, and the poem ends with the final triumph of the pursuer over the pursued. This particular poem, as it happens, is also especially rich in similes and metaphors within the analogy.

These three types of figurative language, all means of making comparisons, are important to the oral interpreter for several reasons. First, of course, he must understand what they are and how they function if he is to find the real meaning of the poem. More particularly, however, he needs to be aware not only of the objects being compared but of the attributes of those objects which make their comparison acceptable. Finally, he must use his knowledge of sense imagery and empathy to make the comparisons work effectively for his audience.

Two other figures of speech — *metonymy* and *synecdoche* — carry associational values somewhat different from those of the three "comparison" figures mentioned above. *Metonymy* is the use of one word for another which it suggests, such as "a good table" for "good food." *Synecdoche* is the use of a part for a whole, such as "sail" for "boat." The technical difference between these two figures is of minor importance for our discussion here, and in any case they are not likely to present the interpreter with any very real difficulties once he is aware of their function. They are useful to him whenever they suggest certain characteristics emphasized by the part chosen for the whole. For example, "sail" is a more picturesque word than "boat" and could be used to imply majesty, in which case the interpreter would wish to make some use of the visual and kinesthetic imagery that might be less vivid without the synecdoche.

But the interpreter's concern, as always, is not with putting a name to what the poet did or classifying a figure of speech, but with understanding why that figure was used, what it is intended to convey, and what it demands of him when he presents the material to an audience. The poet achieves concreteness and vividness of suggestion by using figures which indicate or imply a comparison or an association. They must be understood for what they are and for the purpose they serve before the interpreter can proceed with his job of doing justice to the poetry.

In addition to the five figures of speech already mentioned, two others directly affect the interpreter's communication. They are *personification* and *apostrophe*.

Personification is the attributing of human qualities to an abstract or inanimate object. This figure of speech is closely related to the "comparison" figures discussed above, because the poet treats some inanimate object or an abstraction as if it were a person, and thus gives it definite human characteristics. Keats, for example, uses personification throughout "To Autumn" (page 401), from the second line, in which he calls Autumn the "close bosom-friend of the maturing sun," to the final stanza. The personification is most vivid in the second stanza where Autumn is visualized as "sitting careless on a granary floor," or "on a half-reaped furrow sound asleep," or "by a cider-press" watching "the last oozings hours by hours."

The interpreter will find personification a great aid in visualizing. It is easier to re-create a person than an abstraction. Moreover, this device allows for more kinetic and kinesthetic imagery than if the abstraction were dealt with in some other way. The interpreter must not overlook the animate quality this figure of speech provides.

Frequently, personification is combined with the figure of speech known as *apostrophe* — direct address to an abstraction or to an absent or inanimate object. "To Autumn" makes consistent use of this combination of personification and apostrophe. The opening line,

> Season of mists and mellow fruitfulness,

might be taken merely as a reflective thought about the season, if considered by itself. On close examination, however, it is evident that the poet becomes more direct in his approach to the season as the poem progresses, and there can be no doubt as to the directness of address in the opening lines of the final stanza,

> Where are the songs of Spring? Ay, where are they?
> Think not of them, thou hast thy music too . . .

An awareness of apostrophe will help the interpreter keep the unity, as well as bring out variety, by adding vitality to the words and enhancing the effect of the imagery. It should be remembered, however, that apostrophe is not so direct as address to an actual person from whom a reply is expected. Even so, the complex train of imagery that develops out of the personification and apostrophe in the two lines just quoted is worth noting.

Thus, figurative language enables a writer to express an abstract idea in concrete terms, to make it more vivid and more readily grasped by comparing it or relating it to a concrete object or a specific quality. Again, through a figure of speech the poet may bring together things which are not ordinarily seen in relation to one another, and by thus relating separate areas of experience, open the way to new insights.

Clearly then, sense imagery and figurative language, or literary imagery, are interdependent, and the motor responses to literary and sensory imagery are inseparably tied up with emotional response and empathy. Sense imagery in poetry is usually much more prevalent and complex than in prose; where the prose writer explains or elaborates or describes, the poet suggests. He sends the image vibrating along the reader's consciousness to touch off all sorts of emotive, imaginative, and intellectual associations.

The complexity and urgency of poetic imagery results partly from the condensation of content in poetry, partly from the central importance of the poet's own emotion and attitude, and partly from the poet's use of figures of speech. Because the image comes in through the door of the senses, the poet is likely to select objects or qualities that seem to him particularly rich in sensory suggestion in order to express most completely the experience he is attempting to share. Hence the interpreter, both in preparing his material and in presenting it to an audience, makes the most of the empathic response set up by these appeals to the senses in order to reinforce the emotional and intellectual content of the poem.

Imagery was discussed previously in terms of the primary and secondary strength of the appeals. The primary appeal was fairly easy to isolate in the excerpts used as examples of descriptive prose. In poetry, however, the appeals are often so blended and many-sided that this separation is not possible. Even when the primary appeal in individual units is immediately identifiable, the secondary appeals assume an almost equal importance in the total effect. Frequently a type of imagery, such as kinesthetic, or a combination of types, will be used in a secondary position throughout the poem and will provide an important clue to unity.

Many poems depend almost completely on sensory appeals for their final achievement. When this is so, the interpreter must accept and use all the clues the writer has given him. Such a poem is Keats's "To Autumn." One of the characteristics of Keats's writing is its strong sensory quality, and his skill in blending and even combining words to intensify the appeal to the senses makes this poem one of his most famous.

The chief purpose of "To Autumn" is to record the sights, sounds, smells, and rich texture of the season. This poem makes no significant comment about life, except perhaps to imply the satisfaction to be found in inevitable change, in

> Where are the songs of Spring? Ay, where are they?
> Think not of them, thou hast thy music too . . .

The poet devotes his entire attention to a series of descriptions of autumn, and the poem lays claim to emotional response through the pleasure this season gives to the senses.

To Autumn

Season of mists and mellow fruitfulness,
 Close bosom-friend of the maturing sun;
Conspiring with him how to load and bless
 With fruit the vines that round the thatch-eaves run;
To bend with apples the mossed cottage-trees,
 And fill all fruit with ripeness to the core;
  To swell the gourd, and plump the hazel shells
 With a sweet kernel; to set budding more,
And still more, later flowers for the bees,
Until they think warm days will never cease,
  For Summer has o'er-brimmed their clammy cells.

Who hath not seen thee oft amid thy store?
 Sometimes whoever seeks abroad may find
Thee sitting careless on a granary floor,
 Thy hair soft-lifted by the winnowing wind;
Or on a half-reaped furrow sound asleep,
 Drowsed with the fume of poppies, while thy hook
  Spares the next swath and all its twined flowers:
And sometime like a gleaner thou dost keep
 Steady thy laden head across a brook;
 Or by a cider-press, with patient look,
  Thou watchest the last oozings hours by hours.

Where are the songs of Spring? Ay, where are they?
 Think not of them, thou hast thy music too, —
While barred clouds bloom the soft-dying day,
 And touch the stubble-plains with rosy hue;
Then in a wailful choir the small gnats mourn
 Among the river sallows, borne aloft
  Or sinking as the light wind lives or dies;
And full-grown lambs loud bleat from hilly bourn;

Hedge-crickets sing; and now with treble soft
The red-breast whistles from a garden-croft;
And gathering swallows twitter in the skies.

JOHN KEATS

The opening lines have a characteristic complexity of appeals. Since the title is "To Autumn," the "season of mists" has a strong thermal appeal which combines at once the warmth of the sun and the coolness of the mists. "Mellow fruitfulness" carries with it olfactory, gustatory, visual, and kinesthetic appeal, as well as a continuation of thermal and a possibility of tactual. The second line brings in a still stronger thermal appeal. The effect is one of warmth, and it enhances the feeling of drowsiness and almost static heaviness which recurs in each stanza. The next three lines contain all these previous appeals to sensory perception, but with kinetic appeals added — in fact, with special appeal to kinetic and kinesthetic response — "load with fruit," "vines that run," "to bend with apples."

Because the appeals are so complex and so closely interwoven, it is almost impossible, and probably unnecessary, to decide which is primary within a unit of thought. The strength of the appeals shifts from one type to another almost within a single word. Indeed, the first five lines include every type of imagery except auditory, and even that is suggested later in the stanza by "the bees."

As the poem progresses, the visual and auditory appeals become increasingly important. The second stanza indicates the poet's concern with the visual by its opening question, "Who hath not seen thee . . . ?" The third stanza is strongly auditory with its references to "songs" and "music." Within this framework, the sensory appeals remain complex. The interpreter will find that the imagery not only guides him in making the descriptions vivid, but also contributes significantly to the unity, harmony, and variety of the poem. Attention to the kinesthetic imagery and the kinetic imagery, both of which are made more vivid through personification, will help keep this poem from becoming merely a lush combination of beautiful sounds. Awareness of the shift to visual and then to auditory imagery in the second and third stanzas will help unravel the complicated sentences and keep the poem moving.

The Stanzas

Paragraphs are the major organizational signposts in the progress of the thought in prose writing (Chapter 5). A stanza often serves the same purpose in a poem. In blank verse and free verse, the stanzas or unit divisions (if they exist) are often of irregular length, dictated by the amount of attention the author wished to devote to each unit of content; hence they may be considered in the same light as prose paragraphs as far as progression of content is concerned. The stanza divisions in "The Love Song of J. Alfred Prufrock" are interesting in this regard, for although the unifying principle of the whole poem may be said to be Prufrock's stream of consciousness, each stanza develops or negates an already considered question or admission. In other types of poetry, however, the poet usually limits his stanzas to a specific length and condenses or expands each unit of thought to coincide with this structural restriction. Nevertheless, even in the most tightly structured poetry, a stanza usually operates as a major thought unit, and this entity is intensified if a formal rhyme scheme is used.

Stanley Kunitz' poem "Open the Gates" (page 430) progresses chronologically and in giant steps from one four-line stanza to the next. MacLeish is meticulous in his use of four-line units in "You, Andrew Marvell" until he reaches the closing lines, where he changes the pattern. It must not be assumed that he just forgot what he started out to do — or that he could not make those last four lines work as a stanza! His setting off the single line increases its importance, adds strength to the next line — a near-repetition of the opening line — and brings the poem full circle to its conclusion.

The interpreter will find considerable help in achieving variety as well as rhythm of content in a careful consideration of stanzaic divisions. He must not, of course, let these separate units of thought break off from each other, and he must keep the transitions from stanza to stanza clear in his mind so that the audience receives a unified experience. Transitions in poetry are often abrupt and implied rather than explicitly stated. They may be transitions of time or place, of course, but often, as in "To Autumn," they simply move us into another aspect of the same subject or provide a subtle shift in mood. In any case, the order of the stanzas is not an accident, and the stanza "breaks" must be in reality "links."

In "Soliloquy of the Spanish Cloister" (page 434), for example, some of the stanzas are linked by the monk's observations of some action by Brother Lawrence as he moves about in his garden; others are connected only by the monk's stream of consciousness as he muses on his "heart's abhorrence" and their daily contacts. Sometimes, as in "Poem in October" (page 414), a single word or phrase provides the link to the next stanza, as in the use of "still sleeping town" at the end of the first stanza and the progression to "the town awoke" in the second. Also, the bird motif and "set forth" and "walked abroad" early in the poem prepare us for the larks and blackbirds in the "roadside bushes" so that we move easily with the poet as he climbs the hill. The third and fourth stanzas are clearly linked by "rain wringing," "Pale rain," "sea-wet" and "mist." The warmth of the sun "On the hill's shoulder" has already been introduced in contrast to the dampness and cold wind "faraway under me" so that we move with no surprise to spring and summer and the "fond climates." The fifth and sixth stanzas are not separated by terminal punctuation and are closely connected by "and" as well as by similar references in "legends" and "twice told fields." The final stanza is introduced by "And" followed by a repetition. Thus, the continuity is remarkably clear and carries us smoothly along up to the "high hill" and back into time until we are brought once more to the present by the repeated line — and then turned at once to the future with the final

O may my heart's truth
Still be sung
On this high hill in a year's turning.

Syntax and Line Length

The stanzas of a poem provide the main divisions of organization and content, and within this structure sentences are minor units of thought progression. The length and grammatical structure of the sentences play an important part in the organization of the content, just as they do in prose style. In poetry, moreover, the sentences are related to the line lengths.

In some forms of poetry, both the stanza pattern and the metrical length of the lines are prescribed by tradition. Further, although the point should not be too rigidly insisted on, it may be said in a general way that some patterns, like the ballad stanza or the heroic couplet, more commonly lend themselves to sentences that make partial or full stops at the line-ends; other patterns, such as blank verse, to sentences whose pauses and stops occur variously within the lines as well as at the line ends. The presence and the prominence of rhyme, the simplicity or complexity of the stanza pattern, the relation of the line length to the natural speech phrase, and the tone and purpose of the poem are all factors that enter into an explanation of why this is so and will be dealt with more explicitly in the next chapter. For the moment, we shall limit our consideration to some aspects of sentence structure and to the relationship between sentences and line lengths as units of content.

In Chapter 5 attention was given to the associative function of syntax in prose style. These considerations operate in poetry as well, and are complicated by the condensation and weight of suggestion in poetry and by the poet's own heightened subjectivity. Poets often achieve condensation in part by using long, involved sentences in which there are numerous dependent clauses and descriptive phrases. These clauses and phrases are not always adjacent to the words they modify, with the result that some care in analysis and in performance may be required to keep the thread of thought from becoming hopelessly entangled and the poem from seeming to consist merely of unrelated sets of words "signifying nothing." The interpreter will need to give some detailed attention to this aspect of content in order to make the necessary relationships clear to his audience when reading the poem aloud.

Perhaps the best approach to an involved sentence is simply to recast it in normal order, identifying the subject, the verb, and the object, if any, and arranging the clauses and phrases to modify the appropriate parts of the sentence. One must not, however, insist that poetry display the same clarity and syntactical precision as factual prose. Often parts of speech are omitted and references implied rather than stated. Normal word order is frequently changed for emotional effect or heightening of sound qualities, or both.

The opening sentence of Hopkins' "The Windhover" (page 410) is an excellent example of this ellipsis or omission of words.

> I CAUGHT this morning morning's minion, king-
>> dom of daylight's dauphin, dapple-dawn-drawn Falcon, in
>>> his riding
>> Of the rolling level underneath him steady air, and striding
> High there, how he rung upon the rein of a wimpling wing
> In his ecstasy! then off, off forth on swing,
>> As a skate's heel sweeps smooth on a bow-bend: the hurl
>>> and gliding
>> Rebuffed the big wind. . . .

The sentence begins reasonably enough with the simple "I caught" (meaning, of course, "caught sight of" rather than "captured"), and the adverbial phrase "this morning" tells us when the event took place. After this comes the object of the sentence, the windhover, which the poet calls "minion," "dauphin," and "Falcon," and we are told what the bird was doing. He was riding and striding, and he rung upon the rein of a wimpling wing — that is, he flew upward in spirals by folding or "pleating" or tipping one wing. And then he was off as smoothly as an ice skate cuts a curve, and the hurl and gliding rebuffed, snubbed, refused to consider the big wind. This, then, is the syntactical skeleton of the sentence. The next step is to attempt to find the proper relationship of the words fleshing out this skeleton by eliminating the elliptical quality. In the process we shall obviously destroy much of the beauty of the sound, but that too may help prove our point. The sentence might now read: This morning I caught [sight of] morning's minion [in his] kingdom of [which he is] daylight's dauphin [and] dapple-dawn-drawn Falcon, in his riding of the rolling level [which was] underneath him [and which was] steady air and [when he was] striding high there [you should have seen] how he rung upon the rein of a wimpling wind in his ecstasy [and] then [he was] off, off forth on a swing as [smoothly as] a skate's heel sweeps on a bow-bend [and] the hurl and gliding rebuffed the big wind.

Admittedly, this is an extremely awkward sentence, plodding heavily from one detail to the next. We have lost all the "hurl and gliding," the sense of lift and freedom, and much of the beauty of the sound combinations. Harmony has almost completely disappeared. The insertion of "and" after the exclamation point defeats the poet's own ecstasy at the sight. The substitution of "and" for the colon before the last clause robs it of its conclusive value by making it just one more item rather than a culmination of several. The interpreter must, of course, fully understand the grammatical relationships, but he then must go back to the sentence as the poet wrote it. If his response is full, his audience will have no difficulty in catching the essential images and the totality of the experience.

Dylan Thomas uses characteristically complex syntax in the opening stanza of "Poem in October" (page 414), where "woke" operates on several levels. His "thirtieth year" woke to his hearing and the hearing woke him, and he himself woke to "set foot" and "set forth." Another effective use of syntax is to be found in "The Love Song of J. Alfred Prufrock" (page 420), where Eliot uses the simple, direct statement, "No! I am not Prince Hamlet, . . ." followed by the balancing "nor was meant to be," in which the "I" is not repeated. Omitting it very subtly negates the importance of Prufrock as an individual. The effect is forcefully underscored in the next line, "Am an attendant lord, one that will do." Inserting the personal pronoun each time produces a noticeably different effect. Poetry is full of innumerable instances of this sort of thing, and the interpreter must watch carefully for clues to attitude as well as suggestion and the intrinsic factors. The way a poet puts his words together into sentences is a highly specialized discipline.

A still more subtle relationship of words can be discovered by attention to the *line* as a unit of thought within the larger unit of the sentence. Dylan Thomas is particularly skillful in his use of this aspect of writing. The second stanza of "Poem in October," for instance, begins

My birthday began with the water-
Birds and the birds of the winged trees flying my name

The separation of the hyphenated word "water-birds" is not an accident. His birthday, as he has told us in the opening stanza, began with the water and the water-birds. If the lines are read

My birthday began with the water-birds
And the birds of the winged trees flying my name

we get two separate kinds of birds instead of a synthesis of water and water-birds and birds of the winged trees. This last phrase, incidentally, is an interesting transfer of the characteristic of the birds to the trees in which they settle and is continued as the birds "fly" his name. Appreciating the contribution of the line as a closely related unit of thought requires sophistication and experience, as well as a trained ear and a willingness to allow the poet to have his own way with his poem. It cannot always be explained logically, but it operates effectively as one of the many complexities which make poetry a challenge to the interpreter.

Tone Color

In addition to connotative values and sensory appeals, another very important factor in poetry is the choice and arrangement of words. A poet strives for the perfect union of sense and sound and is acutely aware of the contribution each makes to the other. This attention to the sounds of words separately and in combination is called *tone color*. It was mentioned briefly in Chapter 6 in the section on descriptive prose, but it is so basic to the sound pattern of a poem that it requires some added consideration here.

Tone color is the combination of vowels and consonants to help achieve a particular effect. Clearly, poets do not simply scramble together assorted vowels and consonants. They must, of course, use words. But the choice of a word and its position in relation to other words is partially dictated by the way the sounds go together. Cummings' poem "Spring is like a perhaps hand" (page 469) owes part of its effectiveness to tone color. The two words "perhaps hand" are characteristic of his remarkable freedom with syntax, using "perhaps" as an adjective to modify "hand." The connotation is helped, however, by juxtaposing "haps" and "hand," both of which must be said carefully to pronounce the aspirate *h* and the vowel *a*. The *p* and *s* of "haps" slow the rate, and a slight pause is necessary before the *h* of "hand." This is a subtle effect, but to be aware of its importance one need only consider what a difference it would make if the line read

Spring is perhaps like a hand

in which meaning, rhythm, and sound values are quite changed.

Tone color is another of the elements which make poetry so satisfying to and in turn so dependent on the artist-interpreter. Obviously, there is no way to appreciate tone color or permit it to achieve its purpose except to give the words their sounds. To make full use of tone color, the interpreter must be sure that he is enunciating clearly and that he is forming all sounds properly. The poet had a purpose in combining the sounds as he did, and the interpreter must accept the responsibility of reproducing them accurately.

The general term *tone color* embraces *onomatopoeia* and *alliteration*, *assonance* and *consonance*.

Onomatopoeia is the use of words whose sounds suggest or reinforce their meaning, such as "hiss," "thud," "crack," and "bubble."

Alliteration is the close repetition of identical or nearly identical sounds, usually consonants, at the beginning of adjacent words. The phrase "*m*orning *m*orning's *m*inion" in "The Windhover" is a classic example, as are many other combinations in the poem. Prufrock's question "Do I *d*are/*D*isturb . . ." and Thomas' "That *s*econd/In the *s*till *s*leeping town and *s*et forth" are other examples. Modern writers are likely to use alliteration even more widely spaced and operating throughout a large unit or indeed an entire brief poem.

The use of identical or closely approximated vowels within words is called *assonance*, while the close repetition of identical or approximate consonants within or at the ends of words is called *consonance*. These two techniques are also found in the opening Hopkins lines: assonance in the repeated "o's," consonance very strong in the *n* sounds of "morning morning's minion," and both assonance and consonance in "minion," "dauphin," and "Falcon" in the long first line.

Tone color performs several functions in poetry. The amount and richness of it vary with the purpose of the writing. The more marked the aesthetic and emotional effect desired, the richer and more complex the tone color is likely to be. One of the most important uses of tone color is to enrich the emotional content. Most authorities agree that it is nearly impossible to divorce the connotation of a word from the sound of it. Even in everyday conversation, words are colored and their meanings intensified or depreciated by the elongation or shortening of the vowel sounds and by the softening or sharpening of the consonants. This coloring or intensification through sound is even more marked in poetry, when a word is used with others to strengthen the associational values. Thus, it makes an important contribution to suggestion.

Tone color is also important in implementing sense imagery and intensifying empathy. "To Autumn" offers a particularly good example. The opening lines, or indeed any lines chosen at random, provide unmistakable proof of Keats's concern with sounds:

> *Sea*son of *m*ists and *m*ellow fruitfu*l*ness,
> C*l*ose bo*s*om-friend of the *m*aturing *s*un;

Within these lines, the consonants *s*, *m*, *n*, and *l* predominate, skillfully combined with rich "oo" and "u" sounds, while the lighter vowels in "mists," "mell," "ness," and "friend" keep the effect from becoming monotonous. With such a strong hint from the poet in the opening lines, the interpreter will do well to pay particular attention to the combination of sounds in the rest of the poem. He will find that they vary as the content varies and that in every case sound, connotation, and sense imagery reinforce each other.

Another extremely important function of tone color is to provide for change of tempo and give clues to variation in vocal quality. Certain combinations of vowels and consonants allow and even encourage the reader to speak more rapidly or slowly than other combinations. If the poet is a skilled craftsman, he is aware of variety of tempo and has probably used it in his poem. The interpreter will do well to look for it and use it, too. Variations in tempo will, of course, also depend on the content, both emotional and logical, and on the type of imagery they augment.

The last stanza of "To Autumn" contains an excellent example of the use of tone color to provide variety of tempo and vocal quality. The short speech phrases in the form of the questions

Where are the songs of Spring? Ay, where are they?

help the interpreter achieve needed variety after the rich, slow sounds of

Thou watchest the last oozings hours by hours.

which closed the preceding stanza. "Think not of them" is likewise light and almost crisp in its sound and its implication of dismissal. Immediately, however, the tempo slows again with "thou hast thy music too," and even more in the next line with "barred clouds bloom." The pace picks up slightly on "touched the stubble-plains" but immediately slows again on "rosy hue." This alternation continues throughout the entire stanza. The contrast between "lambs loud bleat from hilly bourn" and the following "hedge-crickets sing" is particularly effective. Attention to subtle changes indicated by the sounds will allow the interpreter to make the most of the needed variety.

Articulation plays an important part in the effectiveness of tone color as it reinforces content or helps achieve a particular effect. Not only is it important that the interpreter enunciate clearly and correctly (albeit without obvious effort), but the process of forming the sounds in combination can have a very subtle effect on his own intensity of response. J. Alfred Prufrock" (page 420). "Yellow fog" seems to constrict the back Many interesting examples are to be found in Eliot's "The Love Song of of the mouth cavity in a way that "a gray mist" would not, and indeed yellow fog in a smoky city does just that. When Prufrock states that he is "not Hamlet," he goes on to say "Am an attendant lord." Here the omission of "I" is significant both in sound and implication of anonymity. The juxtaposition of "am" and "an" and "*attendant*" forces the mouth into an open frontal position which slackens the jaw and gives a feeling of slight distaste and rejection, a little like spitting out the "withered apple seed," to borrow a phrase from another Eliot poem. And certainly ease or difficulty in articulating any specific series of words is a factor in control and variety of pace and vocal quality.

Tone color usually does not make its primary contribution to unity except within small units or stanzas. An entire poem richly laden with the same sound combinations would be extremely difficult to handle. But tone color is certainly basic to harmony and valuable in achieving variety and contrast. Its primary function is supportive, and it must be used in its proper relationship with all the other elements the interpreter discovers in his analysis.

What, then, is the secret of a poem's effectiveness? It is impossible to answer that question satisfactorily. We only know from our own experience that the poet has somehow expressed and lifted out of time the transient moment — the universal moment — that may not, cannot be prolonged. The blending of the logical and the emotional is certainly one of the important factors, but it is not the whole answer. Nor will we find the *whole* answer even after the most careful analysis. An objective study of the component parts will enable the interpreter to make the best possible use of the poet's technique as a guide to interpretation. But the essence of a poem is not quantitative; its whole is more than the sum of its parts. We must accept the fact that at the heart of every good poem there is something beyond objective analysis — just as there is always something "beyond" the laboratory or the scalpel.

Selections for Analysis and Oral Interpretation

Let the full richness of the sounds come through to increase the lift and sweep of this poem. The dedication will help you understand the poet's attitude. The two stresses in line eleven were put there by the poet.

The Windhover / GERARD MANLEY HOPKINS

To Christ our Lord

I CAUGHT this morning morning's minion, kingdom of daylight's dauphin, dapple-dawn-drawn Falcon, in
      his riding

Of the rolling level underneath him steady air, and striding
High there, how he rung upon the rein of a wimpling wing
In his ecstasy! then off, off forth on swing,
    As a skate's heel sweeps smooth on a bow-bend: the hurl
      and gliding
    Rebuffed the big wind. My heart in hiding
Stirred for a bird, — the achieve of, the mastery of the thing!

Brute beauty and valour and act, oh, air, pride, plume, here
    Buckle! AND the fire that breaks from thee then, a billion
Times told lovelier, more dangerous, O my chevalier!

    No wonder of it: shéer plód makes plough down sillion
Shine, and blue-bleak embers, ah my dear,
    Fall, gall themselves, and gash gold-vermilion.

This seventeenth-century poem, a famous example of the use of hyperbole, served as the springboard for MacLeish's "You, Andrew Marvell." Contrast it with the MacLeish poem in attitude and use of figures of speech. The rhyme reinforces the sophisticated light touch.

To His Coy Mistress / ANDREW MARVELL

Had we but world enough, and time,
This coyness, lady, were no crime.
We would sit down, and think which way
To walk, and pass our long love's day.
Thou by the Indian Ganges' side
Should'st rubies find: I by the tide
Of Humber would complain. I would
Love you ten years before the Flood,
And you should, if you please, refuse
Till the conversion of the Jews.
My vegetable love should grow
Vaster than empires, and more slow.
An hundred years should go to praise
Thine eyes, and on thy forehead gaze:
Two hundred to adore each breast:
But thirty thousand to the rest;
An age at least to every part,
And the last age should show your heart.

For, lady, you deserve this state,
Nor would I love at lower rate.
    But at my back I always hear
Time's wingèd chariot hurrying near:
And yonder all before us lie
Deserts of vast eternity.
Thy beauty shall no more be found;
Nor, in thy marble vault, shall sound
My echoing song: then worms shall try
That long-preserved virginity,
And your quaint honour turn to dust,
And into ashes all my lust.
The grave's a fine and private place,
But none, I think, do there embrace.
    Now, therefore, while the youthful hue
Sits on thy skin like morning dew,
And while thy willing soul transpires
At every pore with instant fires,
Now let us sport us while we may;
And now, like amorous birds of prey,
Rather at once our Time devour,
Than languish in his slow-chapt power.
Let us roll all our strength and all
Our sweetness up into one ball,
And tear our pleasures with rough strife
Thorough the iron gates of life.
Thus, though we cannot make our sun
Stand still, yet we will make him run.

This poem, mentioned on page 397 in the discussion of literary allusions, will require some attention to geographical allusions and syntax, as well. The use of "And" will need careful handling in order to achieve the very subtle effect of the extremely long, complex sentence and the broken final stanza.

You, Andrew Marvell / ARCHIBALD MACLEISH

And here face down beneath the sun
And here upon earth's noonward height
To feel the always coming on
The always rising of the night:

To feel creep up the curving east
The earthly chill of dusk and slow
Upon those under lands the vast
And ever-climbing shadow grow

And strange at Ecbatan the trees
Take leaf by leaf the evening strange
The flooding dark about their knees
The mountains over Persia change

And now at Kermanshah the gate
Dark empty and the withered grass
And through the twilight now the late
Few travellers in the westward pass

And Baghdad darken and the bridge
Across the silent river gone
And through Arabia the edge
Of evening widen and steal on

And deepen on Palmyra's street
The wheel rut in the ruined stone
And Lebanon fade out and Crete
High through the clouds and overblown

And over Sicily the air
Still flashing with the landward gulls
And loom and slowly disappear
The sails above the shadowy hulls

And Spain go under and the shore
Of Africa the gilded sand,
And evening vanish and no more
The low pale light across the land

Nor now the long light on the sea:

And here face downward in the sun
To feel how swift how secretly
The shadow of the night comes on . . .

The reversed organization of content in the second stanza must be carefully coordinated with the opening stanza to allow this "credo" to come full circle. Pay close attention to the kinesthetic imagery, the slight alteration of the repeated lines, and the parallel grammatical structure.

In My Craft or Sullen Art / DYLAN THOMAS

> In my craft or sullen art
> Exercised in the still night
> When only the moon rages
> And the lovers lie abed
> With all their griefs in their arms,
> I labour by singing light
> Not for ambition or bread
> Or the strut and trade of charms
> On the ivory stages
> But for the common wages
> Of their most secret heart.
>
> Not for the proud man apart
> From the raging moon I write
> On these spindrift pages
> Nor for the towering dead
> With their nightingales and psalms
> But for the lovers, their arms
> Round the griefs of the ages,
> Who pay no praise or wages
> Nor heed my craft or art.

The lines as units of thought make a very important contribution to the progression of this poem. Observe them carefully. Notice the number of "lifting" images.

Poem in October / DYLAN THOMAS

> It was my thirtieth year to heaven
> Woke to my hearing from harbour and neighbour wood
> And the mussel pooled and the heron
> Priested shore
> The morning beckon
> With water praying and call of seagull and rook
> And the knock of sailing boats on the net-webbed wall
> Myself to set foot

That second
In the still sleeping town and set forth.

My birthday began with the water-
Birds and the birds of the winged trees flying my name
Above the farms and the white horses
And I rose
In rainy autumn
And walked abroad in a shower of all my days.
High tide and the heron dived when I took the road
Over the border
And the gates
Of the town closed as the town awoke.

A springful of larks in a rolling
Cloud and the roadside bushes brimming with whistling
Blackbirds and the sun of October
Summery
On the hill's shoulder,
Here were fond climates and sweet singers suddenly
Come in the morning where I wandered and listened
To the rain wringing
Wind blow cold
In the wood faraway under me.

Pale rain over the dwindling harbour
And over the sea-wet church the size of a snail
With its horns through mist and the castle
Brown as owls,
But all the gardens
Of spring and summer were blooming in the tall tales
Beyond the border and under the lark-full cloud.
There could I marvel
My birthday
Away but the weather turned around.

It turned away from the blithe country,
And down the other air and the blue altered sky
Streamed again a wonder of summer
With apples
Pears and red currants,
And I saw in the turning so clearly a child's
Forgotten mornings when he walked with his mother
Through the parables
Of sunlight
And the legends of the green chapels

And the twice told fields of infancy
That his tears burned my cheeks and his heart moved in mine.
These were the woods the river and sea
Where a boy
In the listening
Summertime of the dead whispered the truth of his joy
To the trees and the stones and the fish in the tide.
And the mystery
Sang alive
Still in the water and singing birds.

And there could I marvel my birthday
Away but the weather turned around. And the true
Joy of the long-dead child sang burning
In the sun.
It was my thirtieth
Year to heaven stood there then in the summer noon
Though the town below lay leaved with October blood.
O may my heart's truth
Still be sung
On this high hill in a year's turning.

Keats tells us clearly in the title that this poem will have at least some of the
characteristics of the traditional ode. Remember that the poet is contemplating the urn, and that kinetically this is an almost completely static poem.
Nevertheless, numerous details give it variety. It is, of course, a classic example
of apostrophe.

Ode on a Grecian Urn / JOHN KEATS

Thou still unravished bride of quietness,
Thou foster-child of silence and slow Time,
Sylvan historian, who canst thus express
A flowery tale more sweetly than our rime:
What leaf-fringed legend haunts about thy shape
Of deities or mortals, or of both,
In Tempe or the dales of Arcady?
What men or gods are these? What maidens loath?
What mad pursuit? What struggle to escape?
What pipes and timbrels? What wild ecstasy?

Heard melodies are sweet, but those unheard
Are sweeter; therefore, ye soft pipes, play on;

Not to the sensual ear, but, more endeared,
　Pipe to the spirit ditties of no tone:
Fair youth, beneath the trees, thou canst not leave
　　Thy song, nor ever can those trees be bare;
　　Bold Lover, never, never canst thou kiss,
Though winning near the goal — yet, do not grieve;
　　She cannot fade, though thou hast not thy bliss,
　　For ever wilt thou love, and she be fair!

Ah, happy, happy boughs! that cannot shed
　Your leaves, nor ever bid the Spring adieu:
And, happy melodist, unweariéd,
　　For ever piping songs for ever new;
More happy love! more happy, happy love!
　　For ever warm and still to be enjoyed,
　　For ever panting, and for ever young;
All breathing human passion far above,
　　That leaves a heart high-sorrowful and cloyed,
　　A burning forehead, and a parching tongue.

Who are these coming to the sacrifice?
　To what green altar, O mysterious priest,
Lead'st thou that heifer lowing at the skies,
　　And all her silken flanks with garlands drest?
What little town by river or sea shore,
　　Or mountain-built with peaceful citadel,
　　Is emptied of this folk, this pious morn?
And, little town, thy streets for evermore
　　Will silent be; and not a soul to tell
　　Why thou art desolate, can e'er return.

O Attic shape! Fair attitude! with brede[1]
　Of marble men and maidens overwrought,
With forest branches and the trodden weed;
　　Thou, silent form, dost tease us out of thought
As doth eternity: Cold Pastoral!
　　When old age shall this generation waste,
　　Thou shalt remain, in midst of other woe
　　Than ours, a friend to man to whom thou say'st,
"Beauty is truth, truth beauty," — that is all
　　Ye know on earth, and all ye need to know.

---

[1] Braid or garland.

This is one of a series of poems by the contemporary Greek poet who won the Nobel Prize for literature in 1963. The title is a combination of "myth" and the Greek word meaning "novel" or "tale." Watch carefully for important clues in the syntax and line units.

Mythistorema X / GEORGE SEFERIS

Our country is a shut-in place, all mountains
And the mountains roofed by a low sky, day and night.
We have no rivers, we have no wells, we have no fountains,
Only some cisterns, empty; they ring and are to us
Objects of worship.
A sound stagnant, hollow, like our solitude,
Like our love and like our bodies.
It seems to us strange that once we were able to build
These houses of ours, these huts, these sheep-folds.
And our marriages, — the dewy garlands, the marriage fingers,
Have become insoluble riddles for our souls.
How were they born
Our children? How then did they grow up?

Our country is a shut-in place. It is enclosed
By the two black Clashing Rocks. And when we go
On Sundays down to the harbour for a breath of air,
We see, lit by the sunset,
The broken timbers of unfinished journeys,
Bodies that know no longer how to love.

This psalm on the glory of God and the dignity of man is a prayer of exaltation. Make careful use of the parallel constructions, a basis of rhythm in Hebrew poetry. They function in much the same way in this translation taken from the King James Bible.

Psalm 8

O Lord our Lord,
how excellent is thy name in all the earth!
who hast set thy glory above the heavens.
Out of the mouth of babes and sucklings hast thou ordained

strength because of thine enemies,
  that thou mightest still the enemy and the avenger.

When I consider thy heavens, the work of thy fingers,
  the moon and the stars, which thou hast ordained;
What is man, that thou art mindful of him?
  and the son of man, that thou visitest him?
For thou hast made him a little lower than the angels,
  and hast crowned him with glory and honor.
Thou madest him to have dominion over the works of thy hands;
  thou hast put all things under his feet:
  All sheep and oxen,
  yea, and the beasts of the field;`
  The fowl of the air, and the fish of the sea,
  and whatsoever passeth through the paths of the sea.

O Lord our Lord,
  how excellent is thy name in all the earth!

Allusions are important here within the context of the ancient city of Byzantium. Some research on its position in the antique world of art and material wealth will help clarify the implied analogy.

Sailing to Byzantium / WILLIAM BUTLER YEATS

That is no country for old men. The young
In one another's arms, birds in the trees
— Those dying generations — at their song,
The salmon-falls, the mackerel-crowded seas,
Fish, flesh, or fowl, commend all summer long
Whatever is begotten, born, and dies.
Caught in that sensual music all neglect
Monuments of unaging intellect.

An aged man is but a paltry thing,
A tattered coat upon a stick, unless
Soul clap its hands and sing, and louder sing
For every tatter in its mortal dress,
Nor is there singing school but studying

Monuments of its own magnificence;
And therefore I have sailed the seas and come
To the holy city of Byzantium.

O sages standing in God's holy fire
As in the gold mosaic of a wall,
Come from the holy fire, perne in a gyre,
And be the singing-masters of my soul.
Consume my heart away; sick with desire
And fastened to a dying animal
It knows not what it is; and gather me
Into the artifice of eternity.

Once out of nature I shall never take
My bodily form from any natural thing,
But such a form as Grecian goldsmiths make
Of hammered gold and gold enameling
To keep a drowsy Emperor awake;
Or set upon a golden bough to sing
To lords and ladies of Byzantium
Of what is past, or passing, or to come.

We gave some attention to this poem in the preceding chapter. Make careful use of the sentence structure and length, and of the lines as units. The allusions are immediately identifiable but important. Notice particularly the frequent questions, the use of negatives and the past subjunctive.

The Love Song of J. Alfred Prufrock / T. S. ELIOT

S'io credesse che mia risposta fosse
A persona che mai tornasse al mondo,
Questa fiamma staria senza piu scosse.
Ma perciocche giammai di questo fondo
Non torno vivo alcun, s'i'odo il vero,
Senza tema d'infamia ti rispondo.[1]

Let us go then, you and I,
When the evening is spread out against the sky
Like a patient etherised upon a table;

[1] "If I thought my answer were to one who could ever return to the world, this flame should shake no more; but since, if what I hear is true, no one ever returned alive from this depth, I answer you without fear of shame." A statement made by a spirit in hell to Dante in the twenty-seventh canto of the *Inferno*.

Let us go, through certain half-deserted streets,
The muttering retreats
Of restless nights in one-night cheap hotels
And sawdust restaurants with oyster-shells:
Streets that follow like a tedious argument
Of insidious intent
To lead you to an overwhelming question . . .
Oh, do not ask, "What is it?"
Let us go and make our visit.

In the room the women come and go
Talking of Michelangelo.

The yellow fog that rubs its back upon the window-panes,
The yellow smoke that rubs its muzzle on the window-panes
Licked its tongue into the corners of the evening,
Lingered upon the pools that stand in drains,
Let fall upon its back the soot that falls from chimneys,
Slipped by the terrace, made a sudden leap,
And seeing that it was a soft October night,
Curled once about the house, and fell asleep.

And indeed there will be time
For the yellow smoke that slides along the street,
Rubbing its back upon the window-panes;
There will be time, there will be time
To prepare a face to meet the faces that you meet;
There will be time to murder and create,
And time for all the works and days of hands
That lift and drop a question on your plate;
Time for you and time for me,
And time yet for a hundred indecisions,
And for a hundred visions and revisions,
Before the taking of a toast and tea.

In the room the women come and go
Talking of Michelangelo.

And indeed there will be time
To wonder, "Do I dare?" and, "Do I dare?"
Time to turn back and descend the stair,
With a bald spot in the middle of my hair —
[They will say: "How his hair is growing thin!"]
My morning coat, my collar mounting firmly to the chin,
My necktie rich and modest, but asserted by a simple pin —

[They will say: "But how his arms and legs are thin!"]
Do I dare
Disturb the universe?
In a minute there is time
For decisions and revisions which a minute will reverse.

For I have known them all already, known them all: —
Have known the evenings, mornings, afternoons,
I have measured out my life with coffee spoons;
I know the voices dying with a dying fall
Beneath the music from a farther room.
    So how should I presume?

And I have known the eyes already, known them all —
The eyes that fix you in a formulated phrase,
And when I am formulated, sprawling on a pin,
When I am pinned and wriggling on the wall,
Then how should I begin
To spit out all the butt-ends of my days and ways?
    And how should I presume?

And I have known the arms already, known them all —
Arms that are braceleted and white and bare
[But in the lamplight, downed with light brown hair!]
Is it perfume from a dress
That makes me so digress?
Arms that lie along a table, or wrap about a shawl.
    And should I then presume?
    And how should I begin?

                .   .   .   .   .

Shall I say, I have gone at dusk through narrow streets
And watched the smoke that rises from the pipes
Of lonely men in shirt-sleeves, leaning out of windows? . . .

    I should have been a pair of ragged claws
Scuttling across the floors of silent seas.

                .   .   .   .   .

And the afternoon, the evening, sleeps so peacefully!
Smoothed by long fingers,
Asleep . . . tired . . . or it malingers,
Stretched on the floor, here beside you and me.
Should I, after tea and cakes and ices,
Have the strength to force the moment to its crisis?
But though I have wept and fasted, wept and prayed,

Though I have seen my head [grown slightly bald] brought in upon
    a platter,
I am no prophet — and here's no great matter;
I have seen the moment of my greatness flicker,
And I have seen the eternal Footman hold my coat, and snicker,
And in short, I was afraid.

   And would it have been worth it, after all,
After the cups, the marmalade, the tea,
Among the porcelain, among some talk of you and me,
Would it have been worth while,
To have bitten off the matter with a smile,
To have squeezed the universe into a ball
To roll it toward some overwhelming question,
To say: "I am Lazarus, come from the dead,
Come back to tell you all, I shall tell you all" —
If one, settling a pillow by her head,
   Should say: "That is not what I meant at all.
   That is not it, at all."

   And would it have been worth it, after all,
Would it have been worth while,
After the sunsets and the dooryards and the sprinkled streets,
After the novels, after the teacups, after the skirts that trail along
    the floor —
And this, and so much more? —
It is impossible to say just what I mean!
But as if a magic lantern threw the nerves in patterns on a screen:
Would it have been worth while
If one, settling a pillow or throwing off a shawl,
And turning toward the window, should say:
   "That is not it at all,
   That is not what I meant, at all."

           · · · ·

No! I am not Prince Hamlet, nor was meant to be;
Am an attendant lord, one that will do
To swell a progress, start a scene or two,
Advise the prince; no doubt, an easy tool,
Deferential, glad to be of use,
Politic, cautious, and meticulous;
Full of high sentence, but a bit obtuse;
At times, indeed, almost ridiculous —
Almost, at times, the Fool.

I grow old . . . I grow old . . .
I shall wear the bottoms of my trousers rolled.

Shall I part my hair behind? Do I dare to eat a peach?
I shall wear white flannel trousers, and walk upon the beach.
I have heard the mermaids singing, each to each.
  I do not think that they will sing to me.

I have seen them riding seaward on the waves
Combing the white hair of the waves blown back
When the wind blows the water white and black.

We have lingered in the chambers of the sea
By sea-girls wreathed with seaweed red and brown
Till human voices wake us, and we drown.

*Sentence lengths provide variety within the philosophical attitude of this poem.
Keep careful control of the "who" references.*

I Think Continually of Those Who Were Truly Great / STEPHEN SPENDER

I think continually of those who were truly great.
Who, from the womb, remembered the soul's history
Through corridors of light where the hours are suns,
Endless and singing. Whose lovely ambition
Was that their lips, still touched with fire,
Should tell of the spirit clothed from head to foot in song.
And who hoarded from the spring branches
The desires falling across their bodies like blossoms.

What is precious is never to forget
The delight of the blood drawn from ageless springs
Breaking through rocks in worlds before our earth;
Never to deny its pleasure in the simple morning light,
Nor its grave evening demand for love;
Never to allow gradually the traffic to smother
With noise and fog the flowering of the spirit.

Near the snow, near the sun, in the highest fields
See how those names are fêted by the wavering grass,

And by the streamers of white cloud,
And whispers of wind in the listening sky;
The names of those who in their lives fought for life,
Who wore at their hearts the fire's centre.
Born of the sun they traveled a short while towards the sun,
And left the vivid air signed with their honour.

E. E. Cummings uses his own distinctive syntax in this love poem. Let the sounds support the mood by making full use of them. The line entities must be carefully and faithfully observed.

anyone lived in a pretty how town / E. E. CUMMINGS

> anyone lived in a pretty how town
> (with up so floating many bells down)
> spring summer autumn winter
> he sang his didn't he danced his did.
>
> Women and men(both little and small)
> cared for anyone not at all
> they sowed their isn't they reaped their same
> sun moon stars rain
>
> children guessed(but only a few
> and down they forgot as up they grew
> autumn winter spring summer)
> that noone loved him more by more
>
> when by now and tree by leaf
> she laughed his joy she cried his grief
> bird by snow and stir by still
> anyone's any was all to her
>
> someones married their everyones
> laughed their cryings and did their dance
> (sleep wake hope and then)they
> said their nevers they slept their dream
>
> stars rain sun moon
> (and only the snow can begin to explain

how children are apt to forget to remember
with up so floating many bells down)

one day anyone died i guess
(and noone stooped to kiss his face)
busy folk buried them side by side
little by little and was by was

all by all and deep by deep
and more by more they dream their sleep
noone and anyone earth by april
wish by spirit and if by yes.

Women and men(both dong and ding)
summer autumn winter spring
reaped their sowing and went their came
sun moon stars rain

Wallace Stevens believed that art is the highest product of the imagination because it orders disordered nature. For him imagination and what we call reality
were of equal importance in life and were interdependent. You will find that
this poem contains overlapping analogies to support this theme. Ramon is
probably just a name for his companion rather than an allusion to any historical figure.

The Idea of Order at Key West / WALLACE STEVENS

She sang beyond the genius of the sea.
The water never formed to mind or voice,
Like a body wholly body, fluttering
Its empty sleeves; and yet its mimic motion
Made constant cry, caused constantly a cry,
That was not ours although we understood,
Inhuman, of the veritable ocean.

The sea was not a mask. No more was she.
The song and water were not medleyed sound
Even if what she sang was what she heard,
Since what she sang was uttered word by word.
It may be that in all her phrases stirred

The grinding water and the gasping wind;
But it was she and not the sea we heard.

For she was the maker of the song she sang.
The ever-hooded, tragic-gestured sea
Was merely a place by which she walked to sing.
Whose spirit is this? we said, because we knew
It was the spirit that we sought and knew
That we should ask this often as she sang.

If it was only the dark voice of the sea
That rose, or even colored by many waves;
If it was only the outer voice of sky
And cloud, of the sunken coral water-walled,
However clear, it would have been deep air,
The heaving speech of air, a summer sound
Repeated in a summer without end
And sound alone. But it was more than that,
More even than her voice, and ours, among
The meaningless plungings of water and the wind,
Theatrical distances, bronze shadows heaped
On high horizons, mountainous atmospheres
Of sky and sea.

       It was her voice that made
The sky acutest at its vanishing.
She measured to the hour its solitude.
She was the single artificer of the world
In which she sang. And when she sang, the sea
Whatever self it had, became the self
That was her song, for she was the maker. Then we,
As we beheld her striding there alone,
Knew that there never was a world for her
Except the one she sang and, singing, made.

Ramon Fernandez, tell me, if you know,
Why, when the singing ended and we turned
Toward the town, tell why the glassy lights,
The lights in the fishing boats at anchor there,
As the night descended, tilting in the air,
Mastered the night and portioned out the sea,
Fixing emblazoned zones and fiery poles,
Arranging, deepening, enchanting night.

Oh! Blessed rage for order, pale Ramon,
The maker's rage to order words of the sea,

Words of the fragrant portals, dimly-starred,
And of ourselves and of our origins,
In ghostlier demarcations, keener sounds.

The thirteen units within this poem are oriental in feeling and technique.
They will need to be set off from each other; yet care must be taken to keep
them all within the thirteen ways of looking at the same thing.

Thirteen Ways of Looking at a Blackbird / WALLACE STEVENS

I

Among twenty snowy mountains,
The only moving thing
Was the eye of the blackbird.

II

I was of three minds,
Like a tree
In which there are three blackbirds.

III

The blackbird whirled in the autumn winds.
It was a small part of the pantomime.

IV

A man and a woman
Are one.
A man and a woman and a blackbird
Are one.

V

I do not know which to prefer,
The beauty of inflections
Or the beauty of innuendoes,
The blackbird whistling
Or just after.

VI

Icicles filled the long window
With barbaric glass.
The shadow of the blackbird
Crossed it, to and fro.
The mood
Traced in the shadow
An indecipherable cause.

VII

O thin men of Haddam,
Why do you imagine golden birds?
Do you not see how the blackbird
Walks around the feet
Of the women about you?

VIII

I know noble accents
And lucid, inescapable rhythms;
But I know, too,
That the blackbird is involved
In what I know.

IX

When the blackbird flew out of sight,
It marked the edge
Of one of many circles.

X

At the sight of blackbirds
Flying in a green light,
Even the bawds of euphony
Would cry out sharply.

XI

He rode over Connecticut
In a glass coach.
Once, a fear pierced him,
In that he mistook
The shadow of his equipage
For blackbirds.

XII

The river is moving.
The blackbird must be flying.

XIII

It was evening all afternoon.
It was snowing
And it was going to snow.
The blackbird sat
In the cedar-limbs.

The strength of the words and images, combined with the starkness and near-brutality of syntax, helps keep this brief poem moving fiercely and swiftly to its conclusion.

Open the Gates / STANLEY KUNITZ

Within the city of the burning cloud,
Dragging my life behind me in a sack,
Naked I prowl, scourged by the black
Temptation of the blood grown proud.

Here at the monumental door,
Carved with the curious legend of my youth,
I brandish the great bone of my death,
Beat once therewith and beat no more.

The hinges groan: a rush of forms
Shivers my name, wrenched out of me.
I stand on the terrible threshold, and I see
The end and the beginning in each other's arms.

Sylvia Plath made several attempts at suicide in her short life. Some of the near-rhymes in the short, irregularly stressed lines are so discordant they set the teeth on edge. Use her line units faithfully. Watch for the sentences that do not conform to the stanza lengths. The abrupt shifts in line lengths and cadence lengths often jar. Trust her and this poem will move with a terrifying swiftness. But do not neglect the pauses where there is a sharp twist of attitude. Check the Biblical reference in the title.

Lady Lazarus / SYLVIA PLATH

I have done it again.
One year in every ten
I manage it ——

A sort of walking miracle, my skin
Bright as a Nazi lampshade,
My right foot

A paperweight,
My face a featureless, fine
Jew linen.

Peel off the napkin
O my enemy.
Do I terrify? ——

The nose, the eye pits, the full set of teeth?
The sour breath
Will vanish in a day.

Soon, soon the flesh
The grave cave ate will be
At home on me

And I a smiling woman.
I am only thirty.
And like the cat I have nine times to die.

This is Number Three.
What a trash
To annihilate each decade.

What a million filaments.
The peanut-crunching crowd
Shoves in to see

Them unwrap me hand and foot ——
The big strip tease.
Gentleman, ladies,

These are my hands,
My knees.
I may be skin and bone,

Nevertheless, I am the same, identical woman.
The first time it happened I was ten.
It was an accident.

The second time I meant
To last it out and not come back at all.
I rocked shut

As a seashell.
They had to call and call
And pick the worms off me like sticky pearls.

Dying
Is an art, like everything else.
I do it exceptionally well.

I do it so it feels like hell.
I do it so it feels real.
I guess you could say I've a call.

It's easy enough to do it in a cell.
It's easy enough to do it and stay put.
It's the theatrical

Comeback in broad day
To the same place, the same face, the same brute
Amused shout:

"A miracle!"
That knocks me out.
There is a charge

For the eyeing of my scars, there is a charge
For the hearing of my heart ——
It really goes.

And there is a charge, a very large charge,
For a word or a touch
Or a bit of blood

Or a piece of my hair or my clothes.
So, so, Herr Doktor.
So, Herr Enemy.

I am your opus,
I am your valuable,
The pure gold baby

That melts to a shriek.
I turn and burn.
Do not think I underestimate your great concern.

Ash, ash —
You poke and stir.
Flesh, bone, there is nothing there ——

A cake of soap,
A wedding ring,
A gold filling.

Herr God, Herr Lucifer,
Beware
Beware.

Out of the ash
I rise with my red hair
And I eat men like air.

This elegy for a little girl contains some interesting problems of balance and proportion. Look carefully at the structure of the three middle stanzas. Keep the speaker and his attitude clear.

Bells for John Whiteside's Daughter / JOHN CROWE RANSOM

There was such speed in her little body,
And such lightness in her footfall,
It is no wonder her brown study
Astonishes us all.

Her wars were bruited in our high window.
We looked among orchard trees and beyond,
Where she took arms against her shadow,
Or harried unto the pond

The lazy geese, like a snow cloud
Dripping their snow on the green grass,

Tricking and stopping, sleepy and proud,
Who cried in goose, Alas,

For the tireless heart within the little
Lady with rod that made them rise
From their noon apple-dreams, and scuttle
Goose-fashion under the skies!

But now go the bells, and we are ready;
In one house we are sternly stopped
To say we are vexed at her brown study,
Lying so primly propped.

This poem presents a character study not only of the monk who is speaking but of Brother Lawrence as well. Remember that it is a soliloquy, an indication that the speaker is alone. Evidently, however, Brother Lawrence is moving within sight of the speaker, and his actions provide the motivations for the swift changes of thought. Notice the spite the monk who follows the letter of the law feels for the man who lives by the spirit. The structure of the poem helps to underscore this feeling.

Soliloquy of the Spanish Cloister / ROBERT BROWNING

Gr-r-r — there go, my heart's abhorrence!
   Water your damned flower-pots, do!
If hate killed men, Brother Lawrence,
   God's blood, would not mine kill you!
What? Your myrtle-bush wants trimming?
   Oh, that rose has prior claims —
Needs its leaden vase filled brimming?
   Hell dry you up with its flames!

At the meal we sit together:
   Salve tibi![1] I must hear
Wise talk of the kind of weather,
   Sort of season, time of year:
Not a plenteous cork-crop: scarcely
   Dare we hope oak-galls, I doubt:
What's the Latin name for "parsley"?
   What's the Greek name for Swine's Snout?

Whew! We'll have our platter burnished,
   Laid with care on our own shelf!

[1] Hail.

With a fire-new spoon we're furnished,
   And a goblet for ourself,
Rinsed like something sacrificial
   Ere 'tis fit to touch our chaps —
Marked with L for our initial
   (He-he! There his lily snaps!)

Saint, forsooth! while brown Dolores
   Squats outside the Convent bank
With Sanchicha, telling stories,
   Steeping tresses in the tank,
Blue-black, lustrous, thick like horse-hairs,
   — Can't I see his dead eye glow,
Bright as 'twere a Barbary corsair's?
   (That is, if he'd let it show!)

When he finishes refection,
   Knife and fork he never lays
Cross-wise, to my recollection,
   As do I, in Jesu's praise.
I the Trinity illustrate,
   Drinking watered orange-pulp
In three sips the Arian[2] frustrate;
   While he drains his at one gulp.

Oh, those melons! If he's able
   We're to have a feast! so nice!
One goes to the Abbot's table,
   All of us get each a slice.
How go on your flowers? None double?
   Not one fruit-sort can you spy?
Strange! — And I, too, at such trouble
   Keep them close-nipped on the sly!

There's a great text in Galatians,
   Once you trip on it, entails
Twenty-nine distinct damnations,
   One sure, if another fails:
If I trip him just a-dying,
   Sure of heaven as sure can be,
Spin him round and send him flying
   Off to hell, a Manichee![3]

[2] The Arian heresy held that Christ was created by God, and was inferior to Him in nature and dignity.

[3] A sect that combined Persian and Christian beliefs.

Or, my scrofulous French novel
    On gray paper with blunt type!
Simply glance at it, you grovel
    Hand and foot in Belial's gripe:
If I double down its pages
    At the woeful sixteenth print,
When he waters his greengages,
    Ope a sieve and slip it in't?

Or there's Satan! One might venture
    Pledge one's soul to him, yet leave
Such a flaw in the indenture
    As he'd miss till, past retrieve,
Blasted lay that rose-acacia
    We're so proud of! *Hy, Zy, Hine* . . .[4]
'St, there's Vespers! *Plena gratia,*
    Ave, Virgo![5] G-r-r-r — you swine!

This is an interesting variation on the traditional ballad form. The repetitions and lack of transitions are deliberate. There is simplicity and dignity within this brief poem.

A Ballad of Trees and the Master / SIDNEY LANIER

Into the woods my Master went,
Clean forspent, forspent.
Into the woods my Master came,
Forspent with love and shame.
But the olives they were not blind to Him,
The little gray leaves were kind to Him:
The thorn-tree had a mind to Him
When into the woods He came.

Out of the woods my Master went,
And He was well content.
Out of the woods my Master came,
Content with death and shame.
When Death and Shame would woo Him last,

---

[4] This series of sounds has caused considerable dissension among critics. It may be the beginning of a curse on Brother Lawrence.
[5] Full of grace, Hail, Virgin!

From under the trees they drew Him last:
'Twas on a tree they slew Him — last
When out of the woods He came.

This soft-spoken poem is completely devoid of sentimentality. The negation of the meaning of life is clearly set up by the opening references to the routine and mundane, and it is summed up in the single-line second stanza. The third stanza moves to the stars, which should carry meaning but do not. Again, a single-line stanza offers a summation. The fulcrum turns the poem gently but ironically toward its conclusion.

Preface to a Twenty Volume Suicide Note / LEROI JONES

Lately, I've become accustomed to the way
The ground opens up and envelops me
Each time I go out to walk the dog.
Or the broad edged silly music the wind
Makes when I run for a bus —

Things have come to that.

And now, each night I count the stars,
And each night I get the same number.
And when they will not come to be counted
I count the holes they leave.

Nobody sings anymore.

And then last night, I tiptoed up
To my daughter's room and heard her
Talking to someone, and when I opened
The door, there was no one there . . .
Only she on her knees,
Peeking into her own cupped hands.

Bibliography

Since, as noted at the beginning of this chapter, content and structure must ultimately be considered in combination, the bibliography for Chapters 10 and 11 appears at the end of Chapter 11.

Chapter 11

The statement was made in the preceding chapter that poetry carries order to its highest degree. This order is apparent in the condensation and organization of the content and in the close interaction of content and form. It is even more apparent, however, in the discipline poetic structure places on the writer and consequently on the interpreter. In good poetry, structure and content are in perfect harmony, and neither may be considered without the other in an evaluation of the whole. Poetry depends for its full meaning on the perfect blend of sound and sense.

The prose writer is disciplined by the need to present his materials with clarity and to find the most effective method of organizing them in order to achieve the purpose for which he is writing. The dramatist has the added problem of expressing himself entirely in dialogue, with only the brief, occasional aid of stage directions to keep his plot believable and make the progression clear and motivated. The poet also accepts the need for clarity and effective organization. If he is dealing with dramatic elements, as in the dramatic monologue or verse drama, he must also be aware of the restrictions under which the dramatist writes. In addition, his writing must be characterized by certain elements of structure inherent in poetry and affected by the above considerations.

The study of the structure of poetry is called prosody. The term *structure* is used in different ways by different critics, but it is generally taken to mean the way the component parts of a piece of literature are formed into a whole. This, of course, includes all the elements of the

The Structure of Poetry

language of poetry we have been discussing. Sense imagery, paradoxes, allusions, and other literary imagery are all part of structuring. But we shall use the term to apply specifically to devices which produce the sound pattern in a poem. Obviously, this must include a careful consideration of tone color, covered in the previous chapter, because it is part style, or language, and part sound patterning.

In this chapter we shall focus on stanzaic form, composition and length of lines, rhythm as established by both stress and flow of sound, and rhyme. These are the bases of the sound pattern on which much of the poem's effectiveness depends. These component parts of the sound pattern depend in a very special way on the services of the interpreter, because they can be thoroughly appreciated and allowed to fulfill their function only when the poem is read aloud.

Since the late nineteenth century, it has been convenient to make a distinction between conventional poetry and free verse. The structure of *conventional poetry* is based on a clearly discernible pattern of light and heavier stresses grouped into a traditional system of metrical feet, and on a fixed pattern of stanza and line length. The same pattern, with only slight variation, usually recurs from stanza to stanza, both in length of lines and arrangement of stresses within those lines. Moreover, the number of lines per stanza is usually consistent. Within this fixed structural framework, however, there may be numerous variations in stress pattern and in the location of pauses in a line to keep the fall of the words from becoming monotonous. Finally, conventional poetry — with the notable exception of blank verse — has the added element of rhyme, with the corresponding sounds in the line-end positions arranged in an easily perceived pattern called the rhyme scheme.

Blank verse is a special type of conventional poetry. It is unrhymed and has no recurring stanza pattern, for the stanzas divide according to the development of the thought and hence are irregular in length. It has, however, a definitely prescribed line length of five metrical feet, and a prescribed prevailing foot, the iamb. Blank verse is of particular interest to the interpreter because it is so often used in material inherently attractive to an audience. The absence of rhyme and the lack of restriction on stanzaic structure permit the skillful poet to use this form effectively with narrative and dramatic materials. Shakespeare, an acknowledged master of blank verse in poetic drama, used it to wed nobility of utterance to acceptable rhythms of speech; poets as diverse as Robert Browning and Robert Frost, to sustain the dramatic quality of a long poem and to achieve the difficult feat of making poetry sound like conversation and conversation like poetry.

Free verse is often considered a recent addition to the realm of poetry. At least the term is modern, and the genre has developed during the last hundred years or less, though it is not impossible to find earlier examples. Free verse is a term adopted from the French *vers libre*. *Vers* in French refers to a *line* of poetry; hence *vers libre* actually means a "free line." Thus it is from the varying lengths of the lines and the arrangement of stresses within them that we get our surest indication that a poem is in free verse.

Free verse differs in many ways from conventional poetry. If the free-verse poem is divided into stanza units at all, they are often irregular in length, although a free-verse poem *may* have quite regular stanzaic division. The free-verse line may vary in length from a single syllable to fifty or more — if the author feels that he needs to use so long a line and that he can bring it off successfully. Free verse often makes no use of rhyme, though the poet may choose to introduce it in order to achieve some special effect. It exhibits no significant pattern of metrical feet, and its rhythm is based on cadence rather than meter.

Successful free verse is not, as the term might suggest, completely lacking in form and discipline. It is a subjective discipline imposed by the poet without strict adherence to regular, traditional forms. There must be, however, a discoverable rhythmic basis. Sometimes it will be found in the number of syllables in the speech phrases within the lines, or in the number of heavier stresses within those speech phrases. Sometimes it will be discovered by careful analysis of the number of heavier stresses per line regardless of their relative positioning with lighter stresses. The important point is to find out what the *poet* has done and then see how it works with the content to produce a successful whole.

The strict dichotomy between conventional verse and free verse is becoming much less important in contemporary poetry. Most poets today work *from* rather than *within* strict metrical patterns so that we often find an interesting combination of the two modes within a single poem. The traditional lines set up an expectation for us which, when it is denied a few lines later by insertion of free verse, helps underscore variety and contrast. Or, on the other hand, the strictly regular line may surprise us with its steady beat and help point up a climax. Stanley Kunitz' poem "Open the Gates" has an interesting example of this effect (page 430). William Van O'Connor, speaking of T. S. Eliot's prosody, quotes the poet when he says, "Even in the 'freest' of free verse there should lurk the ghost of some simple meter 'which should advance menacingly as we doze, and withdraw as we arouse.' "[1] And Robert Frost once remarked that writing what some people called free verse was like playing tennis with the net down. Thus contemporary free verse is more accurately "freed verse," but the interpreter must make a careful study to find out how freed it is from traditional patterns, and how this freedom is coordinated with the content to produce the whole.

The Stanza

As we saw in the last chapter, a stanza of poetry is comparable to a paragraph in prose, in that it is often a major unit of thought, and as such, it is an important factor in the organization. But a stanza may also be a unit of sound, just as a line of poetry is not only a line of print but also a unit of sound, and a word is not only a symbol for meaning but a sound or combination of sounds as well. That is, the stanzaic structure may contribute significantly to the poem's pattern of sound. The recurrence of the same stanza pattern throughout, together with the poet's skill in making his thought units coincide with the stanzas, may divide the poem into nearly identical units of sound when the poem is read aloud, since the interpreter tends to separate major divisions in thought by appropriate use of pause and to establish terminations by both pause and vocal inflection.

A stanza in conventional poetry is measured by the number of lines it contains. The normal stanza ranges from units of two lines (couplets) to nine lines or more. Without going into technical details, we may note that the stanza may be named with reference to the number of lines it contains, as a *quatrain* (four-line unit); or with reference not only to the number of lines it contains but also to the measure and rhyme scheme

[1] William Van O'Connor, *Sense and Sensibility in Modern Poetry* (Chicago: The University of Chicago Press, 1948), p. 58.

of the lines, as the *heroic quatrain* (four lines of iambic pentameter with the lines rhyming alternately, *abab*); or the *Spenserian stanza* (nine lines in the meter and rhyme scheme of Spenser's stanzas in *The Faerie Queene*).

The contribution of stanzaic length to the sound pattern of the poem varies considerably in importance from one selection to another. In general, the shorter the stanzas and the tighter the rhyme scheme, the more apparent is the sound effect. For example, a poem written entirely in two-line stanzas sets up a very close pattern of sounds and silences, especially if each pair of lines completes a thought division. This would constitute an important aspect of structural unity but might seriously threaten the variety unless the poet has been very skillful in his handling. Gwendolyn Brooks's poem "We Real Cool" (page 474) is an excellent example of effective use of the couplet made even more tight by the brief lines and packed rhymes. In blank verse, on the other hand, the contribution of stanzaic structure to sound pattern is almost negligible, partly because of the absence of rhyme but primarily because the stanzas are of unequal length and may run to a hundred lines or more.

Sometimes the division of the poem into regular stanzas is emphasized by repetition of the opening or closing line. We are familiar, of course, with this characteristic of the ballad form. The villanelle, the form of Theodore Roethke's "The Waking" (page 461), is particularly restrictive in the use of repetition and stanzaic structure, limited as it is to only nineteen lines and demanding the *aba* rhyme scheme throughout. Moreover, the first and third lines of the opening stanza must be repeated at the close of alternating stanzas and must be brought together for the closing two lines of the poem. The following poem exhibits the use of refrain within a regular but less traditional framework.

The Dead in Europe

After the planes unloaded, we fell down
Buried together, unmarried men and women;
Not crown of thorns, not iron, not Lombard crown,
Not grilled and spindle spires pointing to heaven
Could save us. Raise us, Mother, we fell down
Here hugger-mugger in the jellied fire:
Our sacred earth in our day was our curse.

Our Mother, shall we rise on Mary's day
In Maryland, wherever corpses married

Under the rubble, bundled together? Pray
For us whom the blockbusters marred and buried;
When Satan scatters us on Rising-day,
O Mother, snatch our bodies from the fire:
Our sacred earth in our day was our curse.

Mother, my bones are trembling and I hear
The earth's reverberations and the trumpet
Bleating into my shambles. Shall I bear,
(O Mary!) unmarried man and powder-puppet,
Witness to the Devil? Mary, hear,
O Mary, marry earth, sea, air and fire;
Our sacred earth in our day was our curse.

ROBERT LOWELL

Here each seven-line stanza presents a new plea built on and growing out of the one before it, yet each is terminated by the same cry:

> Our sacred earth in our day was our curse.

Further, the recurrence of the word "fire" immediately preceding the refrain line serves subtly to intensify the repetition and mark off each stanza as a distinct unit. Since in this poem the thought units are identical with the structural units, the interpreter should take pains to use the stanza and its emphasized termination to point up the poem's quality of prayer and lament.

Frequently in modern poetry of regular stanza pattern the thought units are not identical with the stanzas, but run on from one to another. A comma or other mark of punctuation not indicative of a full stop — or, indeed, the absence of any punctuation at all — at the end of the last line of the stanza, as we find in the fifth stanza of "Poem in October" (page 414) and throughout MacLeish's poem "You, Andrew Marvell" (page 412), serves as a warning that the thought is unfinished and that the break imposed by the stanza pattern is a suspended one. The poet has chosen to set himself a discipline but has reserved the right to take liberties within it whenever he feels justified by his overall purpose.

Stanza length and composition can be strong factors in unity, harmony, and rhythm of both content and structure, as we have seen in "The Dead in Europe." Variety and contrast are also served by this aspect of structure, as is clearly indicated in W. H. Auden's poem "In Memory of W. B. Yeats" (page 474), to note only one of many examples. A change in stanzaic pattern is sometimes used to point the fulcrum or the climax, as it is John Ciardi's "As I Would Wish You Birds" (page 462).

Thus the interpreter must be aware of whatever contribution the stanza length may make to the sound pattern the poet has adopted. In evaluating its importance, he must take his cue from the poet. When the poet has made a point of adhering to brief, regular stanzas, or has emphasized stanza divisions by repetition, the interpreter must assume that this strict discipline serves a definite purpose. On the other hand, when the stanzas are long or irregular in length, the interpreter may assume that the stanzas function primarily as means of organizing the logical or emotional content.

The Line

The three main types of prosody, all based on the composition of the individual lines within the stanzas, are usually designated as *metrical* or *foot* prosody, *stress* prosody, and *syllabic* prosody. We shall discuss metrical or foot prosody first since it is the most familiar and, at least until the last few decades, the most commonly used in poetry in English.

FOOT PROSODY

The structural rhythm of conventional poetry is based on meter, the pattern set up by a reasonably regular recurrence of an identifiable combination of light and heavier stresses within a line. In Chapter 5 we spoke of the contribution of stresses to the rhythm of prose. Poetry, however, is characterized in part by a high degree of regularity in the pattern of structural rhythm not found in other forms of writing. This pattern in conventional poetry is discovered through scansion, the division of the poetic line into metrical feet. A metrical foot is a grouping of light and heavier stresses into a unit. The most common feet in English poetry are these:

1. the *iamb* — an unstressed syllable followed by a stressed syllable $(\smile\prime)^2$

When Ĭ | hăve feárs | thăt Ĭ | măy ceáse | tŏ bé

2. the *anapest* — two unstressed syllables followed by a stressed syllable $(\smile\smile\prime)$

Ŏf mў dár | lĭng — mў dár | lĭng — mў lífe | ănd mў bríde

3. the *trochee* — a stressed syllable followed by an unstressed syllable $(\prime\smile)$

Téll mĕ | nót ĭn | moúrnfŭl | númbĕrs

---

[2] (´) indicates a stressed syllable; (˘) an unstressed syllable. A vertical line (|) is used here to mark off the feet.

4. the *dactyl* — a stressed syllable followed by two unstressed syllables (´˘˘)

Cánnŏn tŏ | right ŏf thĕm

5. the *spondee* — two heavy stresses (´´), usually used in combination with other types of feet

Beát ońce | thĕrewíth | aňd beát | nŏ moŕe.

6. the *pyrrhic* — two light stresses (˘˘), also usually found within another basic pattern

Thĕ eńd | aňd thĕ | begín | nĭng ĭn | eăch oth | eř's arḿs.

There are some other combinations such as the *amphibrach* (˘´˘) and the *amphimacer* (´˘´), but the six types above are the most usual.

A line is classified according to its prevalent foot as iambic, anapestic, trochaic, or dactylic; and according to the number of feet it contains as a monometer (one foot), dimeter (two), trimeter (three), tetrameter (four), pentameter (five), hexameter (six), and so on. Thus, a line of five iambic feet is spoken of as an iambic pentameter.

In almost all conventional poetry, one type of metrical foot will prevail. In English poetry, the iamb is the most common foot, due in part to our pronunciation. It is often varied by the trochee, its reversed counterpart. The next most common is probably the anapest and then the dactyl. The spondee and pyrrhic are used, as we have noted, primarily for variation within a framework of the other more common patterns. Certain harmonies are sometimes achieved most successfully by strict consistency in meter, or by approximate consistency (as in the combination of iamb and anapest), but most poets make effective use of variations in the prevalent measure, since variety-in-unity is the keystone of all art.

A detail that may clarify the process of scanning a conventional poem is relative stress. Not all stressed syllables receive the same degree or value of stress. Thus, though the following line might be scanned

Nót már | blĕ, nór | thĕ gíld | ĕd món | ŭménts

as a regular iambic pentameter, except for the irregularity of the emphatic opening spondee, in an oral reading the relative values of the stresses would be something like this, where (´) indicates a heavy stress, (`) a lighter one, and (˘) no discernible stress:

Nòt már | blĕ, nòr | thĕ gíld | ĕd món | ŭmènts

A most interesting study can be made of the relative values of stresses, but for our purposes we shall use only two degrees, lighter and heavier;

that is, a syllable receives a lighter or heavier stress than the syllables on either side of it.

How does one begin to scan a poem? Since stress in poetry, as in prose, results from the demands of proper pronunciation and of the total meaning, mood, and purpose of the literature, it is simplest to start with the words of more than one syllable, putting the stress where it must fall for pronunciation. If the interpreter is not sure of syllabication, he should check a dictionary; it is imperative that every syllable be accounted for.

The next step, which cannot be undertaken until the poem has been analyzed and the interpreter is familiar not only with what it says but how it means what it says, is to mark key words which must be emphasized for clarity and general comprehension. The attitude of the author or speaker is an important consideration here. This step is followed by a careful look at words which create mood or contribute sharply to needed variety and contrast. For instance, when a new type of sense imagery is introduced, it may need to be pointed slightly so it will serve its purpose for later lines. The interpreter scans a poem the way it must be read to achieve its total effect. He scans to find what the poet has actually done, not to make the lines fit a preconceived pattern.

After these first two steps he may discover that a *fairly* regular pattern of light and heavier stresses in traditional feet has begun to emerge. He then completes the pattern by filling in whatever syllables have not yet been assigned a degree of stress to conform as nearly as possible to the predominant type of foot. If no such pattern emerges, he examines further to determine whether or not he is dealing with free verse and must look to line lengths, speech phrases, and the number of stresses within them for his structural unity.

The relative degree of stress is a matter the interpreter must work out for himself from his understanding of the poem, for no one "right way" of reading a poem can be imposed from without. Not to submerge meaning in meter, not to lose sight of pattern in an attempt to communicate expressively — these are the twin channel markers the interpreter must watch in steering his course. He must let the poet have his way. He must find out what he did with meter if that was his basis of rhythm and allow him his variations. If the poet can best achieve the rhythmic effect he wants by following a regular meter very closely, he will keep to that meter; if by departing from a regular meter, he will do that. Eliot uses some very conventional metrical units within "The Love Song of J. Alfred Prufrock." One of the most effective is the repeated couplet

In the room | the wom | en come | and go

Talking | of Mich | elan | gelo.

OVERRIDES

One of the subtle effects of prosody, apparent only after the scansion has been completed, is *overrides*. As we know, strict scansion often splits words and combines the last syllable of one word with the first syllable of another to form a foot. Thus, scansion is a method of dividing verse into metrical units regardless of the sense units formed by words and speech phrases. The point for the interpreter to remember is that he is not concerned with the individual foot and is not going to be called on to deal with a nonsensical entity like "en come" or "of Mich," but with the combination of feet that produce the characteristic rhythm of the whole. Here, once again, it cannot be too strongly emphasized that it is the overall pattern that is important to the interpreter in bringing content and structure together.

Often, therefore, when a line is read aloud the word as a sense unit *overrides* the foot division and helps control a too-regular beat. Modern poets frequently use this device to produce a sort of counter-rhythm and increase mood and connotation. Theodore Roethke is a master of this technique as may be seen in these two lines from "The Waking" (page 461), where the overrides impose a falling rhythm on the strictly iambic lines.

Ĭ wáke | tŏ sléep, | ănd táke | mŷ wák | ĭng slów.

Ĭ leárn | bŷ gó | ĭng whére | Ĭ háve | tŏ gó.

Without scanning the lines, one would be instinctively aware of this effect, for certainly it reads itself out. But having found it used with such deliberate skill, as a close analysis of the whole poem will reveal, the interpreter can certainly assume it is no accident and use it confidently as a guide to his own technique. It would, of course, be impossible to discover the overrides without first scanning the poem and grouping the lighter and heavier stresses into the traditional feet.

STRESS PROSODY

If the interpreter finds no significant pattern of traditional feet emerging from his scansion, he explores the possibility that he is dealing with *stress prosody*. Stress prosody finds its rhythmic base in the number of stresses per line, regardless of their position in relation to each other; thus it is often impossible or at least impractical to group the lighter and heavier stresses into traditional metrical feet. But despite the number of syllables in a line, the number of stresses remains consistent or varies only occasionally for a specific effect. This concept of rhythm will be important in the discussion of cadences and the effectiveness of stresses within flows of sound. Dylan Thomas makes excellent use of a nearly consistent number of stresses per line in "In My Craft or Sullen Art."

SYLLABIC PROSODY

Syllabic prosody is somewhat less common in English although it is the basis of French prosody. Since the turn of this century, many poets have used it most effectively in combination with foot or stress prosody. *Syllabic prosody* measures flow of sound rather than stresses and depends quite simply on the number of syllables per line. Thomas combines this technique with a consistency of stresses in "In My Craft or Sullen Art" (page 414); all but three lines contain seven syllables. And, incidentally, two of those three lines are used to terminate stanzas.

The interpreter, then, must be aware of how the poet has used whatever basis of rhythm he has chosen and where he has varied it. We have repeatedly stated that classifications are important to the interpreter only insofar as he needs them to analyze and communicate his material more effectively. How, then, is he to use meter or stress prosody or syllabic prosody? First, of course, he must find out how the *poet* has used prosody. He does this by scansion, to learn where and in what relationship to each other the lighter and heavier stresses are placed. If he discerns a pattern of traditional feet, he looks for overrides. If not, he moves at once to either stress or syllabic examination for the basic rhythmic pattern and its variations. The length and composition of the individual lines is only one aspect of the poem, however. It must be synthesized and blended with every other aspect to achieve a total effect. In short, the interpreter never forgets that his concern is communicating meaning and emotion in poetry, not meter: when the poet uses the pattern in order to intensify meaning or emotion, the interpreter will do the same; and when the poet departs from the pattern, the interpreter must understand why and use the irregularities to carry out the poet's intent. Sometimes the break in the established pattern reinforces a particularly strong turn of emotion, a change of thought, attitude, or imagery, to bring structure and content into harmony. This the interpreter must recognize and reflect. The important thing, then, is not for him to say, "This is iambic — or trochaic — or anapestic — or dactylic," but rather for him to be aware of the *particular* metrical pattern, with all its variations, of the *particular* poem, and to reflect sensitively the unique mixture of pattern and irregularity the poet has produced.

The interpreter may find a combination of all three types of prosody in many contemporary poems. When he is working with precontemporary poetry, he may find a history of prosody valuable for learning whether his selection belongs to an experimental period of English literary development when stress or syllabic poetry was in vogue. Usually, however, his awareness that such systems exist will guide him into the appropriate method of analysis. He then uses what he finds exactly as the poet used it, remembering that a poem depends for its effectiveness on the blend of sound and sense.

Stanley Kunitz' lyric "Open the Gates" (page 430) is an excellent example of how at least two of the three systems work within a single contemporary poem. Since it is so brief, we shall repeat it here, with the lines numbered for convenient reference and the light and heavy stresses marked, ignoring for the moment the problem of relative strength of stress. The overrides are italicized.

Open the Gates

1 Withín | the *ci* | *ty* of | the *burn* | ing cloud,

2 Dragging | my life | behind | me in | a sack,

3 Nakĕd | I prowl, | scourged by | the black

4 Temptá | *tion* of | the blood | grown proud.

5 Here at | the *mon* | *ument* | *al* door,

6 Carved with the | curious | legend of | my youth,

7 I *brand* | *ish* the great | bone of | my death,

8 Beat once | therewith | and beat | no more.

9 The *hing* | *es* groan: | a rush | of forms

10 Shivĕrs | my name, | wrenched out | of me.

11 I stand | on the *ter* | *rible thresh* | old, and | I see

12 The end | and the | beginning | in each *oth* | er's arms.

STANLEY KUNITZ

Admittedly, there is more than one way to group the light and heavy stresses into traditional feet, particularly in lines 6, 11, and 12. This is a problem which plagues a prosodist, but our concern is basically with the relative positioning of the stresses within the line. For the interpreter, the grouping of stresses into traditional feet is largely a convenient way of clarifying the pattern. The scansion reveals that the meter is basically iambic with a great many variations. As a matter of fact, Kunitz uses each of the other five common types of feet at least twice. The only purely iambic line is line 9, immediately following the fulcrum.

From our preliminary marking, then, we discover that the first two lines and the last two lines of "Open the Gates" have five feet, the others four. The four pentameter lines all have a pyrrhic foot, however, so that the stresses per line are consistently four, except for lines 8 and 10 where spondees add a fifth stress. Thus, despite the greater length of the opening and closing lines, unity of stress is carefully preserved. It is important to note that line 8 is clearly the fulcrum of the poem, and that line 10 contains the emotional climax.

Some interesting details immediately become apparent. For instance, line 6 contains eleven syllables and yet contains only four heavy stresses, as does the nine-syllable line which follows it. These two lines immediately preceding the fulcrum are the only ones with an uneven number of syllables.

The two overrides in the first line, "city" and "burning," help to control the force of the opening image. Line 4, which closes the stanza, has one override, "temptation." The second stanza opens with a double override, "monumental," and line 7 has a single override in precisely the same position as the one in line 4 of the first stanza. The opening line of the third stanza again has an override in the same position as lines 4 and 7. There are two almost precisely in the middle of line 11, and the override of "other's" in the last line is in the same position as "burning" in the first line of the poem.

Six of the twelve lines open on a stress, and three of them then revert immediately to a rising meter. Line 3 has a sort of double reversal of rising and falling meter which the poet has divided neatly by his comma. This division of the line into two separate units is right for the heaviness of "Naked . . . prowl . . . scourged . . . black." Although line 4 opens on a light stress, it has a spondee balanced by a pyrrhic to bring the stanza to a pounding conclusion with "blóod grówn próud" and yet retains the four-stress line. Lines 8 and 10 have no compensating pyrrhic. Line 10 (the third line from the end, incidentally) has a reversal in the first half identical to that in line 3, and the line is also divided in the middle by a comma.

An examination of the scansion of this brief poem assures us that there is more to poetic rhythm than a "da-dá da-dá" alternation of light and heavy stresses. Stanley Kunitz has achieved remarkable variety-within-unity, always a mark of the best English poetry.

THE INTERPRETER'S USE OF LINE LENGTHS

Early in our discussion of the three types of prosody we mentioned the importance of the line as a structural unit. A line of poetry, it must be remembered, is not just a line of print. It is a unit of sound as well as a minor unit of thought. Because it functions as both sound and sense, it is important to consider in some detail the twofold discipline the poet has imposed on himself — and consequently on the interpreter — with specific line lengths.

A poet who writes conventional poetry consistently divides his stanzas into lines whose length is prescribed by or appropriate to the form of stanza he is using, and he combines this measure with a more or less regular arrangement of stresses, and perhaps with rhyme, to achieve his pattern of sound. Obviously, then, the line units must not be ignored. After all, the poet has put his content into units of a specific length, and the interpreter may assume that he had some reason for selecting the particular line length, or at least that, having selected it, he made some effort to fit his thought units — which will also become sound units when the poem is read aloud — into that pattern. We mentioned in the previous chapter the two-way effect of "water-Birds" in "Poem in October" in which "water-" is allowed to operate in the line it ends and then link into the following line. Often a poet breaks his thought into separate lines to point up either the last word of a line or the opening word of the next line. "The Dead in Europe" has frequent examples of this use of line division.

Blank verse affords the greatest temptation to ignore line length, partly because the line-ends do not have the added reinforcement of rhyme. Yet one of the accepted requisites of the best blank verse is that there be an opportunity to establish the line length when the poem is read aloud. The degree or value of the pause will vary, but the line length must be given special consideration, since it is one of the components of the rhythmic pattern. The extent to which the poet is able to conform to this discipline, while achieving variety within it, is one standard for measuring the excellence of his achievement. On the other hand, the interpreter must remember that verse is written in sentences as well as lines, and that he should not emphasize lines at the expense of sentences and overall sense. Not only would a drop of the voice or a distinct pause at the end of every line produce monotony; it would also distort the sense (since we are accustomed to consider a marked pause as signifying the completion of a thought) and cancel out one of the chief advantages of the blank-verse line — its approximation of the rhythms of conversational speech.

A writer of free verse often uses long sentences so that the flow of sound may be technically uninterrupted for an entire unit (T. S. Eliot does this repeatedly in most of his poems). One may certainly assume, then, that since he may arrange these sentences in lines as long or as short as he wishes, he had a reason for the line division he used. Some critics contend that a line of free verse ends where it is convenient to take a breath— that it is written with the scope of a breath in mind. We may invert this statement and say that for the interpreter's practical purposes it is convenient to take a breath where the free verse line ends. It is logical, too, because the breath comes at a division of the thought, or at a point where the poet wishes to reinforce feeling or establish a relationship or progression. There is an excellent example of such subtle progression in Eliot's "Journey of the Magi" (page 463). In the last stanza we find the lines

> All this was a long time ago, I remember,
> And I would do it again, but set down
> This set down
> This: . . .

Such a line arrangement gives a far different effect when read aloud than if the words were arranged

> All this was a long time ago,
> I remember, and I would do it again,
> But set down this, set down this:

It must be remembered that pauses vary greatly in duration. The line end as a line end (that is, apart from punctuation, sentence construction, and overall meaning) does not require a terminal pause of the kind used to end a sentence. Indeed, if the sentence or speech phrase runs over into the next line — a device technically known as *enjambment*[3] — there will be no *obvious* hesitation. Nevertheless, the line length imposes a sense of the boundaries or "shape" of the poem, to be marked by the eye in silent reading and carried over into the voice in oral interpretation, though not to the point where the physical pattern of the poem obtrudes into the listener's consciousness at the expense of meaning, sound, and feeling.

Thus the length, force, and terminal effect of the line-end pauses will vary, from a barely perceptible pause or a slight drawing out or suspension of the terminal vowel sound, to a semistop or "breath pause," to a full pause at then end of the sentence or thought unit. The interpreter, accordingly, should be alert to make the most of these opportunities for variety in treating line lengths by his use of pauses and voice inflections at the line-ends. In a caution to poets, Ezra Pound once wrote: "Don't make each line stop dead at the end, and then begin every next line with a heave. Let the beginning of the next line catch the rise of the rhythm

[3] From the French *enjambement*, meaning "straddling."

wave, unless you want a definite longish pause." The interpreter, too, can apply this advice to his own art.

Line length, especially in free verse, will be considered further in the following section on cadence. For the moment, however, it is enough to acknowledge its importance and to give the poet credit for being able to fit his thoughts into whatever restrictions of structure he has set for himself. Obviously, the audience should not be made aware of each line length any more than of any other single aspect of the material. Each element makes its contribution to the whole and must be carefully blended with and properly related to all the other elements.

Cadences

Analyzing cadences is a way of making graphic the length and stress composition of the separate flows of sound within a poem. It brings together considerations of syllabic prosody (the number of syllables in each line) and stress prosody (the number rather than location of stresses in each line).

A cadence, as we shall use the term here, is simply an uninterrupted flow of sound. Pauses of varying duration and prominence break the flow and thus establish the cadence pattern. Since the syllable is the smallest functional unit of sound, cadences are measured by the number of syllables they contain.

When we mentioned syllabic and stress prosody earlier, we were concerned only with the line as a unit of measure. In analyzing cadences, we shall again be concerned with the line, but we shall also give attention to the way the individual lines may be divided into speech phrases when the poem is read aloud, and to the length of entire sentences whether or not they continue past the line-end. We touched on these matters in our examination of prose style. Here we shall apply the same approach to poetic style, but we shall find a greater similarity in line length and in speech phrases within the lines because of the tighter structural demands of poetry. Analyzing the length and composition of speech phrases and sentences is useful in studying prose rhythm, but it is absolutely essential in examining poetic rhythm. This is partly because of the importance of line lengths in poetic structure, but also because cadences are part of the essential sound pattern all poetry depends on and because they must be coordinated with all the other sound factors.

A *primary cadence* is the number of syllables in an entire sentence. *Secondary cadences* are made up both of line lengths and of the speech phrases within the lines. It is, of course, immediately obvious that merely counting syllables will not give us the total picture. Cadences must always be considered in relation to two other elements within them. The first of these is number and arrangement of stresses, especially within lines. This consideration, of course, overlaps scansion in conventional poetry, and it is of considerable importance in free verse even though a clear, consistent metrical pattern cannot be established. The second element is partly a matter of tone color and has to do with the length or duration of the sounds within syllables. Thus, a duration pattern as well as a stress pattern is at work within the syllables in secondary cadences. We shall not go into detail on the duration aspect here because the interpreter is already familiar with tone color and its effect on tempo and quality.

There can be no question about the length of the primary cadences in a given poem. A primary cadence is the number of syllables in the sentence, from its beginning to its end as marked by terminal punctuation. The line lengths are also immediately evident. The lengths of the speech phrases, however, are somewhat more subjectively determined, since not all interpreters would pause at precisely the same places. Sometimes there can be little question about the need for a pause and hence for establishing a cadence, as when the poet has inserted appropriate punctuation. Beyond these restrictions, however, the interpreter may make his own decisions about pauses, guided by the requirements of content (both logical and emotive), by the relationship of phrases and clauses to the terms they modify and to the complete sentence, and by opportunities for variety and contrast within unity and for the communication of imagery and tone color. His pauses, however slight, will break the line into speech phrases.

Meter is, of course, the basis of the rhythmic structure in foot prosody, but a consideration of the cadences may open up unsuspected possibilities for variety and harmony. Frequently a poet will achieve a large part of his rhythm by manipulating the cadences within a strict pattern of scansion. This is one of the important attributes of successful blank verse. Tennyson uses cadences most effectively, for instance, in "Ulysses" (page 73): a large proportion of the lines are broken near the middle either by terminal punctuation or by a colon or semicolon. This provides variety, of course, without breaking the unity of the iambic pentameter line. Such a significant pause within a line is called a *caesura*. In numerous other lines, a balanced syntax or the need to point a comparative phrase will cause the interpreter to insert a somewhat less distinct pause which will nevertheless interrupt the flow of sound within the line as a unit.

Primary cadences — that is, complete sentences — usually tell us less by their specific length than by their relation to each other. In T. S. Eliot's "Journey of the Magi" (page 463), where most of the primary cadences are long and cover several lines, the final sentence forms an interesting contrast and brings the poem to a firm close. He skillfully blends long and short primary cadences in "The Love Song of J. Alfred Prufrock" as well.

The line-length cadences are probably most fundamental in poetry, since all types of prosody take the line as a basic measure. Keeping this in mind, we then look at speech phrases *within* the separate lines, knowing that even an enjambment line has some kind of pause, however unobtrusive, at its end. In extremely long lines, as in Walt Whitman's poems, these speech phrases often provide the surest basis for the rhythm.

Since analyzing cadences brings together syllabic prosody and stress prosody, the interpreter must also be aware of any consistency in the number of stresses per secondary cadence. The number of stresses in the primary cadences is not likely to help much since they are often long and overflow or interrupt the line.

In "Open the Gates," an interesting example of carefully controlled variation from traditional metrics, the cadences contribute to unity and harmony as well as to variety and contrast. Counting the syllables and major stresses within lines and speech phrases and noting the sentence lengths, we discover the following pattern:

LINE NO.	SYLLABLES PER LINE	STRESSES PER LINE	*Secondary Cadence* SYLLABLES PER SPEECH PHRASE	STRESSES PER SPEECH PHRASE	*Syllables per Primary Cadence*
1	10	4	10	4	36
2	10	4	7–3	3–1	
3	8	4	4–1–3	2–1–1	
4	8	4	3–3–2	1–1–2	
5	8	4	1–7	1–3	36
6	11	4	1–7–3	1–2–1	
7	9	4	9	4	
8	8	5	4–4	3–2	FULCRUM
9	8	4	4–4	2–3	16
10	8	5	4–4	2–3	CLIMAX
11	12	4	9–3	3–1	24
12	12	4	2–5–5	1–1–2	

The primary cadences, as usual, tell us less by their specific length than by their relation to each other. Though they are of minor significance in this poem, they are obviously a unifying factor in the first two stanzas.

Furthermore, the change from the established thirty-six syllables to sixteen syllables helps set off the climax.

Turning to the secondary cadences, we notice that lines of identical length are used in pairs or threes, except for the two center lines. These two are neatly bracketed by eight-syllable lines serving as a steadying force in the middle of the poem. The stresses per line are a strong unifying force, with the added stress in lines 8 and 10 providing contrast to reinforce the fulcrum and the climax.

The speech phrases provide needed variety within this unity. They too, however, tend to cluster, with three predominating near the opening, varied by units of seven, four, one, and two. The one and seven combination is apparent in line 5, and one and seven and three in line 6. The even four-and-four division in lines 8, 9, and 10, mentioned in relation to scansion, helps reinforce the emotional weight of the content. Again, despite the opening two-syllable phrase, there is an even division in the five and five of the last line.

Further analysis will reveal even more subtle effects in this remarkable poem, but we have perhaps proved well enough that the line-length and speech-phrase cadences and their stresses and elongated syllables are important in the pattern of a successful poem, and that such analysis is basic in discovering the rhythmic elements of free verse. A careful analysis of the cadences and stresses in a poem will convince the interpreter that conventional poetry need not be read like a nursery rhyme, and that the discipline inherent in free verse will safeguard him from the danger of reading this type of poetry as if it were prose. Free verse, properly written, is probably the most demanding type of poetry to read aloud, and any interpreter who chooses it must be prepared to analyze its structure painstakingly. Such analysis will greatly increase his own artistic ability and his appreciation of the poet's artistic achievement.

Clearly, no audience could be expected to appreciate the subtlety of this rhythmic pattern for itself when the poem is read aloud. Indeed, it would be most unfortunate if attention were called to the pattern. Nevertheless, the interpreter must understand what the poet has done in order to communicate the total effect.

Rhyme

Closely allied to line length is another important aspect of poetic structure: rhyme and other correspondences of sound in the terminal syllables of two or more words. By now it must be abundantly clear that poetry is not "something that rhymes"; that rhyme, unlike rhythm and cadence, is not an essential element of poetry, and that when it is used it is important because it reinforces rhythm, cadence, pattern, and tone color rather than because it is itself the stuff of poetry.

Although correspondences of sound strike the mind's ear in silent reading, they emerge for complete appreciation, like so many other factors in poetry, only when a poem is read aloud. Rhyme satisfies the ear because it is like a chime of music, and it pleases the mind by affording the delights of repetition and anticipation. But the purpose of rhyme is not to decorate but rather to bind the poem more closely together. For one thing, it unifies the pattern of sound. It reinforces the stanza pattern by establishing a recurring rhyme scheme. It emphasizes the line lengths by creating an expectation of repeated sounds at regular intervals. Thus, rhyme reinforces content and rhythm by helping to establish cadences and thought divisions. On the other hand, skillful poets and interpreters know that rhyme, unwisely used, can shatter rather than intensify the unity of a poem, and they therefore exhibit great care and variety in handling it. An interpreter who bears down hard on every rhyme will make the physical shape of the poem block out everything else. He will give his audience the sensation of being taken for a ride on a rocking-horse instead of on a Pegasus.

Rhyme is the exact correspondence of both vowel and final consonant sounds; *assonance* is the correspondence of vowel sounds only, regardless of the final consonant sounds (*place-brave*). There are many kinds of rhyme: half-rhymes, like *pavement-gravely* and *river-weather*, in which only half of a two-syllable word rhymes; double rhymes, in which the two final syllables correspond (*crying-flying, arrayed-afraid*); and even triple rhymes (*din afore-pinafore*), though these are usually too jingling and ingenious for anything but humorous verse. And there is approximate rhyme or rhyme by *consonance*, when the final consonant sounds are identical but the vowel sounds are not (*rock-luck*).

A rhyme scheme is indicated in prosodic analysis by letters standing for the terminal rhyme sounds, with *a* representing that of the first line and of every line corresponding to it, *b* the next terminal sound and its corresponding lines, and so on; thus, in this stanza from Shelley's "Adonais":

Most musical of mourners, weep anew!	*a*
Not all to that bright station dared to climb;	*b*
And happier they their happiness who knew,	*a*
Whose tapers yet burn through that night of time	*b*
In which suns perished; others more sublime,	*b*
Struck by the envious wrath of man or God,	*c*
Have sunk, extinct in their refulgent prime;	*b*
And some yet live, treading the thorny road,	*c*
Which leads, through toil and hate, to Fame's serene abode.	*c*

This gives a rhyme scheme designated by *ababbcbcc,* the characteristic pattern of the Spenserian stanza.

Rhyme is an essential part of all conventional poetry except, of course, blank verse. The rhyme of a poem has several important functions to fulfill. It can be a strong factor in the harmony between what is being said and the way it is expressed. It is of vital importance in both unifying the poem and providing appropriate variety and contrast, while at the same time it enriches and intensifies tone color. It invariably tends to emphasize the line ends and make the harmony between structure and content more apparent.

Rhyme can also cause an interpreter some trouble, however, if the poet has not used it skillfully. Even the best poets are sometimes unable to cope with too strict a pattern, and then the rhyme begins to manage the poet instead of the other way around. Sometimes the form the poet has adopted becomes too rigid for effective oral reading. When this is true and the poem is nonetheless worthy of presentation on other counts, the interpreter must attempt to compensate for the weakness. He will be able to do this by close attention to every opportunity for variety in his use of pauses and inflection at the line ends. Particular attention to tone color within the line can bring some of the interior words to a prominence which will challenge that of the rhyming words, and emphasis on imagery will add variety.

The interpreter ought first to be very sure, however, that the poem really does have structural imperfections. He must be very certain that the repeated sounds do not serve an important purpose as they certainly do in Gwendolyn Brooks's poem "We Real Cool" (page 474). Tight rhyme is also an excellent device for humor, as Keats demonstrates in "A Song About Myself" (page 464). If the poem is good on other counts, it is safe to assume, until a careful objective analysis disproves the assumption, that the poet was at least competent in handling rhyme. It is always wise to give the poet the benefit of the doubt and use what he has given you.

The problem of rhyme does not, as we have said, arise in blank verse. But the very absence of it affects the interpreter: on the one hand, he is released from one of the disciplines he often must consider in interpreting poetry; on the other, he is deprived of a significant means of communicating structural unity. For these reasons, the interpreter of blank verse should pay particular attention to other elements in the sound pattern — alliterations, harsh or liquid vowel and consonant combinations, the echoing of mood or sense in sound. He will find his surest guide to structural unity, however, in the prevalent iambic meter and the consistent line length.

The writer of free verse may or may not use rhyme, as he sees fit. He may use it more or less consistently throughout a poem, although such a technique is not common. Sometimes rhyme will appear, if at all, only in brief units of the poem. When the interpreter finds such units, he should examine carefully their contribution to the whole, for the poet will have used rhyme consciously, not as part of a conventional pattern but out of a subjective decision to use rhyme at that point. The sounds of the rhymes and the length of the lines containing them are of considerable importance in intensifying certain aspects of the content. T. S. Eliot makes very skillful use of rhyme in "The Love Song of J. Alfred Prufrock."

To draw on another familiar example, Robert Lowell uses an intricate and effective combination of rhymes in "The Dead in Europe." In each stanza, the first, third, and fifth lines correspond in terminal sounds and the final syllables are firmly stressed, helping to intensify the correspondence. The second and fourth lines end with two-syllable words in which the last syllable receives a lighter stress. Moreover, only the lightly stressed syllables agree exactly in sound since the first syllable of "women" only approximates the first syllable of "heaven." Here the intentionally minor rhyme keeps the poem from becoming ponderous in its sound pattern. It is interesting to notice, though, that all the lines end in "n" until the last two. The last two lines do not rhyme at all, though "fire" and the entire last line are repeated at the end of every stanza and thus set up a pattern of their own. Moreover, the "r" is common to both "fire" and "curse." The numerous repetitions of the rhyme words within adjacent lines and the use of "buried" with "married" and "unmarried," as well as the near-identity with "Mary," deserve attention.

Modern writers are most sophisticated in their use of rhymes and near-rhymes. Again, Stanley Kunitz provides us with an excellent example in "Open the Gates." On reading it aloud, we find rhyme sounds woven intricately throughout the poem. (Although it is not technically a rhyme, we cannot resist pointing out the pun of "grown" and "groan.") The terminal rhymes are identical and therefore satisfying, except for the paradoxical rhyme of "youth" and "death" immediately preceding the fulcrum, and the slight variance between "forms" and "arms" in the last stanza. Moreover, their identity is emphasized because all but three of the lines are wholly or partially end-stopped by punctuation. Of the three enjambent lines, the first is the inescapable, harsh rhyme of "black" and "sack." The other two are found in the last stanza, one softening "forms," the other softening "see."

Another extremely subtle manipulation of rhyme sounds, which will probably escape an audience but delight an interpreter, may or may not have been accidental, although in a poem so meticulously constructed we can take nothing for granted. Kunitz repatterns the same sounds in successive rhymes, as in "proud" and "door" and "more" and "forms."

Also, the "d" of "cloud" and "proud" introduces "door" and "death" in the second stanza; the "m" of "more" carries over into "forms," "me," and "arms"; and the "s" introduces the fourth rhyme word, "see."

An additional aspect of line-end sounds is not, strictly speaking, a matter of rhyme but is worthy of the interpreter's attention. We touched on it but did not identify it in examining rhyme in "The Dead in Europe" a few paragraphs earlier. This is the use of masculine and feminine line endings. A *masculine* line ending has a discernible stress. All the line endings in "Open the Gates," for example, are masculine. A *feminine* line end terminates on a lighter stress. In each of the three stanzas of "The Dead in Europe," the second and fourth lines have feminine endings. Lowell has used "women" and "heaven," "married" and "buried," "trumpet" and "puppet." All the other lines have masculine endings. Lowell has also added to this poem the emphasis of close rhyme, but T. S. Eliot, in "Journey of the Magi," uses masculine and feminine endings without rhyme. Sometimes feminine endings are used to weaken or soften the line end, especially when they are combined with enjambment. Modern poets frequently use them to reinforce a feeling of instability, as Eliot often does. They are effective psychologically because the added light stress denies our expectation. Certainly they help build tension as they work against the masculine endings in "The Dead in Europe."

Careful, detailed analysis of the structure of a poem will provide the interpreter with a sure basis for using his own techniques. Poetry is an art, but it is also a kind of science, and the intricacies of a successful poem are amazing.

Having discovered the aspects of structure the poet has used and so far as possible his purpose in using them, the interpreter must carefully relate them to content. He must then evaluate both content and structure in the light of the touchstones for judging a piece of literature: the extrinsic factors of universality, individuality, and suggestion; the intrinsic factors of unity and harmony, variety and contrast, balance and proportion, and rhythm. Finally, in oral presentation the interpreter must remember that no single aspect of structure is to be exhibited for its own sake, but must be skillfully blended with every other aspect to communicate the aesthetic entirety of the poem.

Selections for Analysis and Oral Interpretation

It will be interesting to compare the structure and syntax of these two Roethke poems with "Old Lady's Winter Words" at the end of Chapter 3. They offer sharply contrasting physical responses. The first is held at a fairly steady level and builds to the final triumph a child would feel at having undivided attention. Keep it unified without sacrificing the excitement of the separate thought units within the single primary cadence. Let the numerous overrides fulfill their function.

Child on Top of a Greenhouse / THEODORE ROETHKE

The wind billowing out the seat of my britches,
My feet crackling splinters of glass and dried putty,
The half-grown chrysanthemums staring up like accusers,
Up through the streaked glass, flashing with sunlight,
A few white clouds all rushing eastward,
A line of elms plunging and tossing like horses,
And everyone, everyone pointing up and shouting.

This villanelle uses a highly restrictive structure. Examine it carefully for the patterning of the overrides. Let the stanzaic structure help keep the cadences from becoming abrupt. Make full use of the remarkable tone color, especially assonance.

For Roethke all of life was a waking toward the sleep of death. He reminds one of Thomas in his affirmation of life.

The Waking / THEODORE ROETHKE

I wake to sleep, and take my waking slow.
I feel my fate in what I cannot fear.
I learn by going where I have to go.

We think by feeling. What is there to know?
I hear my being dance from ear to ear.
I wake to sleep, and take my waking slow.

Of those so close beside me, which are you?
God bless the Ground! I shall walk softly there,
And learn by going where I have to go.

Light takes the Tree; but who can tell us how?
The lowly worm climbs up a winding stair;
I wake to sleep, and take my waking slow.

Great Nature has another thing to do
To you and me; so take the lively air,
And, lovely, learn by going where to go.

This shaking keeps me steady. I should know.
What falls away is always. And is near.
I wake to sleep, and take my waking slow.
I learn by going where I have to go.

The stanzaic structure is interesting here. There is also a good deal of ellipsis. Be sure you understand the seemingly simple allusions as they are used to reflect attitude. The line lengths as units of thought are particularly important; use them as the poet has.

As I Would Wish You Birds / JOHN CIARDI

Today — because I must not lie to you —
there are no birds but such as I wish
for. There is only my wish to wish you
birds. Catbirds with spatula tails up
jaunty. Jays, gawky as dressed-up toughs.
Humming birds, their toy engines going.
Turkeys with Savonarola heads. Bitchy
Peacocks. The rabble of Hens in their
stinking harems — these three (and
Ostriches and Dodos) a sadness to think
about. But then Gulls — ultimate bird
everywhere everything pure wing and wind
are, there over every strut, flutter, cheep,
coo. At Dover over the pigeon-cliffs.
At Boston over the sparrows. Off tropics
where the lyre-tails and the green-
iridescent heads flash. And gone again.

You never see Gulls in aviaries. Gulls are
distance. Who can put distance in a cage?

Today — and I could never lie to you —
there is no distance equal to what I wish

for. There is only my wish to wish you
a distance full of birds, a thronged air
lifting above us far, lifting us, the sun
bursting in cloud chambers, a choir there
pouring light years of song, its wings
flashing. See this with me. Close your eyes
and see what air can do with more birds in it
than anything but imagination can put there.
There are not enough birds in the eyes we
open. There are too many hens, turkeys, and
that peacock seen always on someone else's
lawn, the air above it wasted unused, songless.
Birds cannot be seen in fact. Not enough
of them at once, not now nor any day. But think
with me what might be, but close your eyes and see.

In this poem the line-length cadences are not only important for structural rhythm but provide clues to emotional content and connotations. The first five lines are quoted from a famous sermon. Notice how skillfully Eliot moves into his own comment. The quote must not be set off too obviously from the rest of the stanza. Eliot uses capital letters for spiritual birth and death as opposed to physical birth and death.

Journey of the Magi / T. S. ELIOT

"A cold coming we had of it,
Just the worst time of the year
For a journey, and such a long journey:
The ways deep and the weather sharp,
The very dead of winter."
And the camels galled, sore-footed, refractory,
Lying down in the melting snow.
There were times we regretted
The summer palaces on slopes, the terraces,
And the silken girls bringing sherbet.
Then the camel men cursing and grumbling
And running away, and wanting their liquor and women,
And the night-fires going out, and the lack of shelters,

And the cities hostile and the towns unfriendly
And the villages dirty and charging high prices:
A hard time we had of it.
At the end we preferred to travel all night,
Sleeping in snatches,
With the voices singing in our ears, saying
That this was all folly.

Then at dawn we came down to a temperate valley,
Wet, below the snow line, smelling of vegetation;
With a running stream and a water-mill beating the darkness,
And three trees on a low sky,
And an old white horse galloped away in the meadow.
Then we came to a tavern with vine-leaves over the lintel,
Six hands at an open door dicing for pieces of silver,
And feet kicking the empty wine-skins.
But there was no information, and so we continued
And arrived at evening, not a moment too soon
Finding the place; it was (you may say) satisfactory.

All this was a long time ago, I remember,
And I would do it again, but set down
This set down
This: were we led all that way for
Birth or Death? There was a Birth, certainly,
We had evidence and no doubt. I had seen birth and death,
But had thought they were different; this Birth was
Hard and bitter agony for us, like Death, our death.
We returned to our places, these Kingdoms,
But no longer at ease here, in the old dispensation,
With an alien people clutching their gods.
I should be glad of another death.

Even the most serious of Romantic poets had their lighter moments. Use the rhymes and line units as candidly as Keats did.

A Song About Myself / JOHN KEATS

I

There was a naughty Boy,
And a naughty boy was he,

He would not stop at home,
  He could not quiet be —
    He took
    In his Knapsack
    A Book
    Full of vowels
    And a shirt
    With some towels —
    A slight cap
    For night cap —
    A hair brush,
    Comb ditto,
    New Stockings
    For old ones
    Would split O!
    This Knapsack
    Tight at's back
    He rivetted close
And followéd his nose
    To the North
    To the North,
And follow'd his nose
    To the North.

II

There was a naughty boy,
  And a naughty boy was he,
For nothing would he do
  But scribble poetry —
    He took
    An ink stand
    In his hand
    And a pen
    Big as ten
    In the other,
    And away
    In a Pother
    He ran
    To the mountains
    And fountains
    And ghostes
    And Postes
    And witches

And ditches
And wrote
In his coat
When the weather
Was cool,
Fear of gout,
And without
When the weather
Was warm —
Och the charm
When we choose
To follow one's nose
To the north,
To the north,
To follow one's nose
To the north!

III

There was a naughty boy,
And a naughty boy was he,
He kept little fishes
In washing tubs three
In spite
Of the might
Of the Maid
Nor afraid
Of his Granny-good —
He often would
Hurly burly
Get up early
And go
By hook or crook
To the brook
And bring home
Miller's thumb,
Tittlebat
Not over fat,
Minnows small
As the stall
Of a glove,
Not above
The size
Of a nice

Little Baby's
Little fingers —
O he made
'Twas his trade
Of Fish a Pretty Kettle
A Kettle —
A Kettle
Of Fish a pretty Kettle
A Kettle!

IV

There was a naughty Boy,
And a naughty Boy was he,
He ran away to Scotland
The people for to see —
Then he found
That the ground
Was as hard,
That a yard
Was as long,
That a song
Was as merry,
That a cherry
Was as red —
That lead
Was as weighty,
That fourscore
Was as eighty,
That a door
Was as wooden
As in England —
So he stood in his shoes
And he wonder'd,
He wonder'd,
He stood in his shoes
And he wonder'd.

Like Roethke's "The Waking," this poem is a villanelle. Compare the structure with the equally meticulous but more varied structure of the two Thomas poems at the end of Chapter 10. Thomas's use of line lengths must be respected.

468 / Oral Interpretation

Do Not Go Gentle Into That Good Night / DYLAN THOMAS

Do not go gentle into that good night,
Old age should burn and rave at close of day;
Rage, rage against the dying of the light.

Though wise men at their end know dark is right,
Because their words had forked no lightning they
Do not go gentle into that good night.

Good men, the last wave by, crying how bright
Their frail deeds might have danced in a green bay,
Rage, rage against the dying of the light.

Wild men who caught and sang the sun in flight,
And learned, too late, they grieved it on its way,
Do not go gentle into that good night.

Grave men, near death, who see with blinding sight
Blind eyes could blaze like meteors and be gay,
Rage, rage against the dying of the light.

And you, my father, there on the sad height,
Curse, bless, me now with your fierce tears, I pray.
Do not go gentle into that good night.
Rage, rage against the dying of the light.

Much of the wit in this poem is underscored by the rhymes and feminine
line ends. Use the structure confidently.

Go and Catch a Falling Star / JOHN DONNE

Go and catch a falling star,
    Get with child a mandrake root,
Tell me where all past years are,
    Or who cleft the devil's foot,
Teach me to hear mermaids singing,
Or to keep off envy's stinging,
            And find
            What wind
Serves to advance an honest mind.

If thou beest born to strange sights,
   Things invisible to see,
Ride ten thousand days and nights,
   Till age snow white hairs on thee,
Thou, when thou return'st, wilt tell me
All strange wonders that befell thee,
       And swear
       No where
Lives a woman true, and fair.

If thou find'st one, let me know,
   Such a pilgrimage were sweet;
Yet do not, I would not go,
   Though at next door we might meet;
Though she were true when you met her,
And last till you write your letter,
       Yet she
       Will be
False, ere I come, to two or three.

Trust this poet completely and use his line lengths exactly as he has put them down. He uses capital letters for a shade of emphasis. Make the most of the kinesthetic imagery implied. Keep the thought suspended across the parentheses, which make a sort of "subpoem" in themselves.

Spring is like a perhaps hand / E. E. CUMMINGS

Spring is like a perhaps hand
(which comes carefully
out of Nowhere)arranging
a window,into which people look(while
people stare
arranging and changing placing
carefully there a strange
thing and a known thing here)and

changing everything carefully

spring is like a perhaps
Hand in a window

(carefully to
and fro moving New and
Old things,while
people stare carefully
moving a perhaps
fraction of flower here placing
an inch of air there)and

without breaking anything.

Speech-phrase cadences provide much of the basic rhythm in this selection.

FROM *Song of Myself* / WALT WHITMAN

A child said *What is the grass?* fetching it to me with full hands,
How could I answer the child? I do not know what it is any more than
he.

I guess it must be the flag of my disposition, out of hopeful green stuff
woven.

Or I guess it is the handkerchief of the Lord,
A scented gift and remembrancer designedly dropt,
Bearing the owner's name some way in the corners, that we may see and
remark, and say *Whose?*

Or I guess the grass is itself a child, the produced babe of the vegetation.

Or I guess it is a uniform hieroglyphic,
And it means, Sprouting alike in broad zones and narrow zones,
Growing among black folks as among white,
Kanuck, Tuckahoe, Congressman, Cuff, I give them the same, I receive
them the same.

And now it seems to me the beautiful uncut hair of graves.

Tenderly will I use you curling grass,
It may be you transpire from the breasts of young men,
It may be if I had known them I would have loved them,
It may be you are from old people, or from some offspring taken soon out
of their mothers' laps,
And here you are the mothers' laps.

This grass is very dark to be from the white heads of old mothers,
Darker than the colorless beards of old men,
Dark to come from under the faint red roofs of mouths.

O I perceive after all so many uttering tongues,
And I perceive that they do not come from the roofs of mouths for nothing.

I wish I could translate the hints about the dead young men and women,
And the hints about old men and mothers, and the offspring taken soon
out of their laps.

What do you think has become of the young and old men?
And what do you think has become of the women and children?

They are alive and well somewhere,
The smallest sprout shows there is really no death,
And if ever there was it led forward life, and does not wait at the end to
arrest it,
And ceas'd the moment life appear'd.

All goes onward and outward, nothing collapses,
And to die is different from what any one supposed, and luckier.

*Parodies must be read with almost exaggerated seriousness. The fun lies in
the awareness on the part of the interpreter, the poet, and the audience of the
characteristic style of the one being parodied.*

Jack and Jill / CHARLES BATTELL LOOMIS

(As Walt Whitman Might Have Written It)

I celebrate the personality of Jack!
I love his dirty hands, his tangled hair, his locomotion blundering.
Each wart upon his hands I sing,
Paeans I chant to his hulking shoulder blades.
Also Jill!
Her I celebrate.
I, Walt, of unbridled thought and tongue,
Whoop her up!
What's the matter with Jill!
Oh, she's all right!
Who's all right?
Jill.
Her golden hair, her sun-struck face, her hard and reddened hands;

So, too, her feet, hefty, shambling.
I see them in the evening, when the sun empurples the horizon, and
    through the darkening forest aisles are heard the sounds of myriad
    creatures of the night.
I see them climb the steep ascent in quest of water for their mother.
Oh, speaking of her, I could celebrate the old lady if I had time.
She is simply immense!

But Jack and Jill are walking up the hill.
(I didn't mean that rhyme.)
I must watch them.
I love to watch their walk,
And wonder as I watch;
He, stoop-shouldered, clumsy, hide-bound,
Yet lusty,
Bearing his share of the 1-lb. bucket as though it were a paperweight.
She, erect, standing, her head uplifting,
Holding, but bearing not the bucket.
They have reached the spring.
They have filled the bucket.
Have you heard the "Old Oaken Bucket"?
I will sing it: —

Of what countless patches is the bed-quilt of life composed!
Here is a piece of lace. A babe is born.
The father is happy, the mother is happy.
Next black crêpe. The beldame "shuffles off this mortal coil."
Now brocaded satin with orange blossoms,
Mendelssohn's "Wedding March," an old shoe missile,
A broken carriage window, the bride in the Bellevue sleeping.
Here's a large piece of black cloth!
"Have you any last words to say?"
"No."
"Sheriff, do your work!"
Thus it is: from "grave to gay, from lively to severe."

I mourn the downfall of my Jack and Jill.
I see them descending, obstacles not heeding.
I see them pitching headlong, the water from the pail outpouring, a noise
    from the leathern lungs out-belching.
The shadows of the night descend on Jack, recumbent, bellowing, his pate
    with gore besmeared.
I love his cowardice, because it is an attribute, just like
Job's patience or Solomon's wisdom, and I love attributes.
Whoop!!!

The following sonnet contains some difficulties in the denotation and connotation of words and in the involved sentence structure. Remember that a sonnet requires certain organization of content. Variety in unity is apparent in the structure.

Sonnet 29 / WILLIAM SHAKESPEARE

When, in disgrace with Fortune and men's eyes,
I all alone beweep my outcast state,
And trouble deaf heaven with my bootless cries,
And look upon myself and curse my fate,
Wishing me like to one more rich in hope,
Featured like him, like him with friends possess'd,
Desiring this man's art, and that man's scope,
With what I most enjoy contented least;
Yet in these thoughts myself almost despising,
Haply I think on thee; and then my state,
Like to the lark at break of day arising
From sullen earth, sings hymns at heaven's gate;
   For thy sweet love rememb'red such wealth brings
   That then I scorn to change my state with kings.

This famous sonnet uses a different but equally conventional rhyme scheme and division of content.

On His Blindness / JOHN MILTON

When I consider how my light is spent
Ere half my days, in this dark world and wide,
And that one talent which is death to hide
Lodged with me useless, though my soul more bent
To serve therewith my Maker, and present
My true account, lest he returning chide,
"Doth God exact day-labor, light denied?"
I fondly ask. But Patience, to prevent
That murmur, soon replies: "God doth not need
Either man's work or his own gifts; who best
Bears his mild yoke, they serve him best. His state
Is kingly: thousands at his bidding speed,

And post o'er land and ocean without rest;
They also serve who only stand and wait."

We mentioned the contribution of rhyme in this poem within the chapter.
The rhythm is unmistakable and vital to the tone and mood. Use the line
lengths exactly as they are given you and the rhythm will emerge. Contrast
this selection with Keats's "A Song About Myself" (with its short lines and
close rhymes) and you will be aware of the contribution here of clustered
heavy stresses and corresponding cadences.

We Real Cool / GWENDOLYN BROOKS

> The Pool Players
> Seven at the Golden Shovel

> We real cool. We
> left school. We

> Lurk late. We
> Strike straight. We

> Sing sin. We
> Thin gin. We

> Jazz June. We
> Die soon.

The three sections of this modern elegy vary in their structure rather markedly. Use everything the poet has given you to insure the proper changes of
tone.

In Memory of W. B. Yeats / W. H. AUDEN

> (d. Jan. 1939)

> 1

He disappeared in the dead of winter:
The brooks were frozen, the airports almost deserted,

And snow disfigured the public statues;
The mercury sank in the mouth of the dying day.
O all the instruments agree
The day of his death was a dark cold day.

Far from his illness
The wolves ran on through the evergreen forests,
The peasant river was untempted by the fashionable quays;
By mourning tongues
The death of the poet was kept from his poems.

But for him it was his last afternoon as himself,
An afternoon of nurses and rumours;
The provinces of his body revolted,
The squares of his mind were empty,
Silence invaded the suburbs,
The current of his feeling failed: he became his admirers.

Now he is scattered among a hundred cities
And wholly given over to unfamiliar affections;
To find his happiness in another kind of wood
And be punished under a foreign code of conscience.
The words of a dead man
Are modified in the guts of the living.

But in the importance and noise of tomorrow
When the brokers are roaring like beasts on the floor of the Bourse,
And the poor have the sufferings to which they are fairly accustomed,
And each in the cell of himself is almost convinced of his freedom;
A few thousand will think of this day
As one thinks of a day when one did something slightly unusual.
O all the instruments agree
The day of his death was a dark cold day.

2

You were silly like us: your gift survived it all;
The parish of rich women, physical decay,
Yourself; mad Ireland hurt you into poetry.
Now Ireland has her madness and her weather still,
For poetry makes nothing happen: it survives
In the valley of its saying where executives
Would never want to tamper; it flows south
From ranches of isolation and the busy griefs,
Raw towns that we believe and die in; it survives,
A way of happening, a mouth.

3

Earth, receive an honoured guest;
William Yeats is laid to rest:
Let the Irish vessel lie
Emptied of its poetry.

Time that is intolerant
Of the brave and innocent,
And indifferent in a week
To a beautiful physique,

Worships language and forgives
Everyone by whom it lives;
Pardons cowardice, conceit,
Lays its honours at their feet.

Time that with this strange excuse
Pardoned Kipling and his views,
And will pardon Paul Claudel,
Pardons him for writing well.

In the nightmare of the dark
All the dogs of Europe bark,
And the living nations wait,
Each sequestered in its hate;

Intellectual disgrace
Stares from every human face,
And the seas of pity lie
Locked and frozen in each eye.

Follow, poet, follow right
To the bottom of the night,
With your unconstraining voice
Still persuade us to rejoice;

With the farming of a verse
Make a vineyard of the curse,
Sing of human unsuccess
In a rapture of distress;

In the deserts of the heart
Let the healing fountain start,
In the prison of his days
Teach the free man how to praise.

Hyperbole in the selection of allusions sets the cavalier tone of this love poem. The rhymes will help as well, especially in the closing couplet.

Since There's No Help / MICHAEL DRAYTON

Since there's no help, come let us kiss and part.
Nay, I have done; you get no more of me,
And I am glad, yea, glad with all my heart,
That thus so cleanly I myself can free;
Shake hands for ever, cancel all our vows,
And when we meet at any time again,
Be it not seen in either of our brows
That we one jot of former love retain.
Now at the last gasp of Love's latest breath,
When, his pulse failing, Passion speechless lies,
When Faith is kneeling by his bed of death,
And Innocence is closing up his eyes,
Now if thou wouldst, when all have given him over,
From death to life thou mightst him yet recover.

Notice the tightening of the rhyme in the last two lines of this poem. Allow time between the brief stanzas and lines for the quick shifts in sense imagery.

Dream Deferred / LANGSTON HUGHES

What happens to a dream deferred?

Does it dry up
like a raisin in the sun?
Or fester like a sore —
And then run?
Does it stink like rotten meat?
Or crust and sugar over —
like a syrupy sweet?

Maybe it just sags
like a heavy load.

Or does it explode?

The same poet handles the same theme quite differently in the following poem. Take his direction in the title and use the rhythm fully. Make the shifts sharp as you come to the question.

Dream Boogie / LANGSTON HUGHES

Good morning, daddy!
Ain't you heard
The boogie-woogie rumble
Of a dream deferred?

Listen closely:
You'll hear their feet
Beating out and beating out a —

You think
It's a happy beat?

Listen to it closely:
Ain't you heard
something underneath
like a —

What did I say?

Sure,
I'm happy!
Take it away!

Hey, pop!
Re-bop!
Mop!

Y-e-a-h!

The use of capital letters is an immediate clue to the attitude of the poet in this brief selection. Use the stanza divisions and the line lengths to help point the barbed wit.

Reprinted by permission of Harold Ober Associates Incorporated. Copyright 1951 by Langston Hughes.

Status Symbol / MARI EVANS

i
Have Arrived

i
am the
New Negro

i
am the result of
President Lincoln
World War I
and Paris
the
Red Ball Express
white drinking fountains
sitdowns and
sit-ins
Federal Troops
Marches on Washington
    and
prayer meetings . . .

today
They hired me
it
is a status
job . . .
along
with my papers
They
gave me my
Status Symbol
the
key
to the
White . . . Locked . . .
John

Rhythm and sound accumulation help achieve the effect of this poem. The line lengths must be carefully observed to catch the rhythm and especially to control or accelerate the pace. Let the last five lines operate exactly as they are divided to accentuate the ending.

But He Was Cool or: he even stopped for green lights / DON L. LEE

        super-cool
        ultrablack
        a tan/purple
        had a beautiful shade.

        he had a double-natural
        that wd put the sisters to shame.
        his dashikis were tailor made
        & his beads were imported sea shells
                (from some blk/country i never heard of)
        he was triple-hip.

        his tikis were hand carved
        out of ivory
        & came express from the motherland.
        he would greet u in swahili
        & say good-by in yoruba.
        woooooooooooo-jim he bes so cool & ill tel li gent
                        cool-cool is so cool he was un-cooled by
                                other niggers' cool
                        cool-cool ultracool was bop-cool/ice box
                                cool so cool cold cool
                        his wine didn't have to be cooled, him was
                                air conditioned cool
                        cool-cool/real cool made me cool — now
                                ain't that cool
                        cool-cool so cool him nick-named refrig-
                                erator.

        cool-cool so cool
        he didn't know,
        after detroit, newark, chicago &c.,
        we had to hip
                        cool-cool/ super-cool/ real cool
                that
        to be black
        is
        to be
        very-hot.

Bibliography

Bateson, F. W. *English Poetry and the English Language*. New York: Russell and Russell, 1961.

A careful examination of a wide variety of poetic devices.

Bloom, Edward A., Charles H. Philbrick, and Elmer M. Blistein. *The Order of Poetry: An Introduction*. New York: The Odyssey Press, Inc., 1961.

A clear and direct approach to the critical analysis of poetry with representative selections used for illustrations. Contains a chapter on versification and a glossary of critical terms.

Bodkin, Maud. *Archetypal Patterns in Poetry*. New York: Oxford University Press, 1963.

Poetry analyzed in terms of Jung's theory of the collective unconscious. Psychological studies in imagination.

Brooks, Cleanth. *The Well Wrought Urn*. New York: Harcourt, Brace and World, Inc., 1947.

Based on the theory of poetry as dramatic discourse and on the organic relationship of art and meaning in poetry. Essays on specific poems.

Brooks, Cleanth, and Robert Penn Warren. *Understanding Poetry*. Third Edition. New York: Holt, Rinehart and Winston, Inc., 1960.

A good introductory book. An anthology with critical discussions and commentaries on representative poems.

Cane, Melville. *Making a Poem: An Inquiry into the Creative Process*. New York: Harcourt, Brace and World, Inc., 1962. Harvest Book edition, HB44.

An informal, readable book on how a poem is written.

Ciardi, John. *How Does a Poem Mean?* Boston: Houghton Mifflin Company, 1959.

An excellent discussion of reading poetry, with particularly good examples. Covers many aspects of content and structure.

Ciardi, John (ed.). *Mid-Century American Poets*. New York: Twayne Publishers, 1950.

A collection of poems and essays by fifteen contemporary American poets expressing their attitudes toward writing poetry. Particular attention to the need to read poetry orally.

Crane, R. S. *The Languages of Criticism and the Structure of Poetry*. Toronto: University of Toronto Press, 1953. Alexander Lecture Series.

A highly scholarly discussion of the complexities of poetic criticism.

Daiches, David. *Poetry and the Modern World: A Study of Poetry in English Between 1900 and 1939*. Chicago: The University of Chicago Press, 1940.

Specific poets examined with emphasis on the phenomenon of culture and the effect on their poetry. The range is from the Victorians to Spender and Auden.

Davie, Donald. *Articulate Energy: An Enquiry into the Syntax of English Poetry*. London: Routledge and Kegan Paul, 1955.

A somewhat specialized but stimulating examination of syntactical manipulations in a variety of poems.

Deutsch, Babette. *Poetry Handbook: A Dictionary of Terms*. New York: Funk and Wagnalls, 1957.

A complete, concise sourcebook of poetic terminology.

Dickey, James. *Babel to Byzantium*. New York: Farrar, Straus and Giroux, 1968.

A series of brief essays and criticism about the work of a wide variety of modern poets.

Dolman, John, Jr. *The Art of Reading Aloud*. New York: Harper and Row, 1956.

Devoted exclusively to the problems of reading poetry aloud. Somewhat uneven but of interest to the interpreter.

Drew, Elizabeth. *Discovering Poetry*. New York: W. W. Norton and Company, Inc., 1962. The Norton Library Series, N-110.

Readable and sound introductory book. Contains an appendix of terms and a bibliography of principal English and American poets.

Drew, Elizabeth, and George Connor. *Discovering Modern Poetry*. New York: Holt, Rinehart and Winston, Inc., 1961.

A thematic approach to an excellent selection of modern poems. The second section includes additional poems for study. The third section is a compilation of significant comments of poets on the nature and function of poetry.

Eliot, T. S. *On Poetry and Poets*. New Edition. New York: Farrar, Straus and Company, 1957.

Essays on poetry, poetic drama, and poetic criticism with chapters on specific poets from Virgil to Yeats.

Empson, William. *Seven Types of Ambiguity*. Third Edition. London: Chatto and Windus, Ltd., 1956.

A scholarly consideration of imaginative language as it functions to convey several meanings simultaneously.

Frye, Northrop. *The Well-Tempered Critic*. Bloomington, Indiana: Indiana University Press, 1963.

A refreshing reevaluation of some traditional and contemporary modes of criticism.

Fussell, Paul, Jr. *Poetic Meter and Poetic Form*. New York: Random House, Inc., 1965.

Clear and sound discussion of the elements of prosody.

Geiger, Don. *The Dramatic Impulse in Modern Poetics*. Baton Rouge: Louisiana State University Press, 1967.

An important book for its intelligent and readable consideration of the problem of persona, written by a poet and teacher of interpretation.

Hemphill, George (ed.). *Discussions of Poetry: Rhythm and Sound*. Boston: D. C. Heath and Company, 1961.

A collection of essays on prosody of the last four centuries.

Hollander, John. *Modern Poetry: Essays in Criticism*. New York: Oxford University Press, 1968.

Twenty-five essays by established critics arranged chronologically to highlight changes in critical approaches from 1913 to 1968.

Ostroff, Anthony (ed.). *The Contemporary Poet as Artist and Critic: Eight Symposia*. Boston and Toronto: Little, Brown and Company, 1964.

A collection of twenty-four essays on eight contemporary poems and the responses of the poets themselves. The poets include Richard Wilbur, Theodore Roethke, Stanley Kunitz, Robert Lowell, John Crowe Ransom, Richard Eberhart, W. H. Auden, and Karl Shapiro.

Sanders, Gerald. *A Poetry Primer*. New York: Farrar, Straus and Company, 1935.

Brief, explicit definitions and examples of the nature and forms of poetry and the elements of poetic structure.

Sebeok, Thomas A. (ed.). *Style in Language*. New York: John Wiley and Sons, Inc., 1960.

Numerous essays dealing with linguistic and psychological approaches to literature with special attention to modern theories of prosody.

Shapiro, Karl. *A Bibliography of Modern Prosody*. Baltimore: The Johns Hopkins Press, 1948.

A valuable sourcebook for detailed study of critical and practical discussions of poetic techniques.

Spender, Stephen. *The Making of a Poem*. New York: W. W. Norton and Company, Inc., 1962.

A collection of readable and penetrating essays on various aspects of the contemporary literary situation with a comparative look at the Romantics. Also includes discussions of novels and autobiographies.

Stauffer, Donald A. *The Nature of Poetry*. New York: W. W. Norton and Company, Inc., 1962. The Norton Library Series, N-167.

Sound introductory study of poetry and poetic language.

Thompson, John. *The Founding of English Metre*. New York: Columbia University Press, 1961.

An historical survey of the basic meters and variations in English poetry.

Wimsatt, W. K., Jr. *The Verbal Icon: Studies in the Meaning of Poetry*. New York: Farrar, Straus and Company, 1954. Noonday Press edition, N-123, 1958.

One of the classics of modern criticism with particular attention to some of the fallacies of poetic criticism.

Wright, George T. *The Poet in the Poem: The Personae of Eliot, Yeats and Pound*. Berkeley and Los Angeles: University of California Press, 1960.

Excellent discussion of Eliot, Yeats, and Pound, plus a sound, provocative analysis of poetry in general.

In addition to the books listed above, you will find much to interest you in the letters, notebooks, and critical essays of a large number of poets both pre-modern and contemporary.

Appendix A

Building and Presenting a Program

Throughout this text an attempt has been made to keep a balance between the demands for detailed literary analysis and the techniques necessary to communicate the literature in its entirety to an audience. It will be assumed in this discussion of program building that the interpreter will do his analysis and preparation thoroughly and that his physical and vocal techniques are under control.

There are, however, some special aspects of building a sustained and well-integrated program that should be mentioned. Although our primary focus has not been on training the professional recitalist, there is considerable pleasure and satisfaction in presenting a program or lecture recital to an audience outside the classroom. Certainly much of the discussion which follows is equally applicable to the longer class performance, such as a final reading, or to the increasingly popular reading hours being offered on many campuses. After all, the techniques used in performance are dictated by the demands of the material rather than the length or circumstances of the presentation.

The difference between a program and a lecture recital is primarily one of proportion and degree. A *program* uses a minimum of transitional material and focuses almost entirely on the literature itself. A *lecture recital*, by contrast, has a strong central unity, uses the critics' opinions and historical data as transitions, and arranges the selections to illustrate whatever technical or thematic development the speaker has chosen. It emphasizes evaluation more than appreciation per se. For example, a program designed to show the scope and variety of Browning's work might include letters, shorter poems, and selections from *The Ring and the Book*, the verse play *Pippa Passes,* or his unsuccessful play *Stafford.* If it also included critical comments and references to Browning's early Romanticism and his position as one of the great Victorians, it would be termed a lecture recital. A program on Browning, on the other hand, would be less concerned with the range of his writing than with selections the audience would enjoy as pieces of literature. As a rule, it would contain more selections and far less interpretive and evaluative comment. As we have said, the difference is largely one of degree. We shall give primary attention to the program since the lecture recital appeals to a more specialized audience and is much less practical for the beginning interpreter.

Cuttings of novels and plays are very popular for out-of-classroom programs, but they are probably too ambitious for most beginning interpreters. For this discussion we shall concentrate on building the program of varied selections, referring to material in the text as well as to selections you will find in your library.

Selecting Material

The first consideration in selecting the material you will present is its literary worth. Do not read something you consider markedly inferior because you think your audience will not accept anything better. It is your job to present the selection so well that it will not seem difficult. Moreover, it is completely foolhardy to underestimate the members of a group. They are often better informed and more sophisticated than the title of their organization might suggest.

Sometimes you will be asked to do a special program for a specific group or occasion. Perhaps the group is following a particular course of study, such as contemporary theatre, the Old Testament, human relations, ecology, or any one of a number of interest areas, and they wish you to add a new dimension or an introductory or concluding unit. You will, of course, select material to follow their theme. The time of year may influence your selection. A Christmas program, for example, is not the place for nihilism or irreverence. A spring luncheon is not the ideal occasion for a reading from *Medea.* February offers the opportunity to read love poems, love letters, and love scenes from plays. Since it marks the birthdays of two famous Americans, it also offers the opportunity to present historical material, patriotic selections, or perhaps a scene from *The Crucible* or Robert Sherwood's *Abe Lincoln in Illinois.* Selections from Walt Whitman's journals and his "When Lilacs Last in the Dooryard Bloom'd" are particularly appropriate for a program on Lincoln. In short, almost any topic of human interest can become the focal point of a program. The range of possibilities is limited only by the interpreter's skill and imagination.

Occasionally you may be asked to read selections written by a member of the group. Do so with good grace, and bring your art to bear on all the strong points you can find in the writing. Generally, however, insist on the right to select your own material. Consider first your own standards and your own abilities. Read something you enjoy and know you can handle in the time allowed.

Selecting a Unifying Theme

Whatever the occasion, your program should have a unifying theme. As we have said, this unity may be dictated by what you know about your audience, the time of year, the purpose of the organization you are reading for, or any number of other factors. It may also be — and most often is — determined by your personal taste. In any case, the program must hold together as a total experience. Indeed, the intrinsic factors of unity and harmony, variety and contrast, balance and proportion, and rhythm of emotional impact and focus of interest are doubly important.

Working toward a unified program is important, but it may or may not be the place to start in making your selection. Often it is more practical to begin with what you like to read and can get ready and then see what thematic unity your preferences offer.

For example, suppose you wish to start with Robert Frost's "Wild Grapes" (pages 114–116). This poem is "about" a good many things, all operating within a harmonic unity: memory of childhood, a young girl and her brother, an experience with nature, wisdom, and letting go with the hands but not with the heart, among other things. Any one of this cluster of meanings could become your unifying theme. If you choose memories of childhood, you might wish to include "Child on Top of a Greenhouse" (page 461), "June Recital" (pages 197–198), a section from *A Death in the Family* (pages 232–235), "Ring Out, Wild Bells" (pages 119–122), or *The Little Girls* (pages 123–126), and perhaps something from Robert Lowell's *91 Revere Street* and some of Dylan Thomas' autobiographical prose in *Portrait of the Artist as a Young Dog,* or Truman Capote's *A Christmas Memory.* Mark Twain's work, now enjoying a revival, evokes warm memories for many people. Theodore Roethke's poems are rich in memories of his childhood in Michigan, and Gwendolyn Brooks's *Annie Allen* and *A Street in Bronzeville* contain many examples of a black girl's memories. Walt Whitman's "A Child Went Forth" would be useful, as would certain selections from Wordsworth or Housman's "When I was one-and-twenty." The list of available material is practically endless; only time and interest are necessary to provide the interpreter with an extremely wide choice.

Perhaps you decide to set the theme by Jaques' speech from *As You Like It* and move from very early childhood to old age, closing with "Old

Lady's Winter Words" and using "I Dreamed that I was Old" and "Ulysses" within the sequence. Edith Sitwell's poem "Colonel Fantock" and D. H. Lawrence's short story "The Lovely Lady" would add interesting variety, as would units from Edgar Lee Masters' *Spoon River Anthology* or scenes from such widely divergent plays as Ibsen's *A Doll's House*, Shaw's *Caesar and Cleopatra*, or Shakespeare's *King Lear*. There are innumerable variations on the theme of youth and age. The readings might have a strongly humorous tone or a rhythm set up by the gently humorous and the deeply moving.

Interesting programs can be arranged around people and places. The material may be about rural life or urban life, or both in contrast. You might choose regional American literature or descriptive and dramatic writing about foreign places. The letters, travel accounts, and diaries of famous people present fascinating pictures of other times and cultures.

The works of one author may serve as a unifying device. You could concentrate on his treatment of a theme, such as Shakespeare's kings, or on his method of revealing character, as in Browning's monologues. Or you could show some developmental trend, beginning with his early works and concluding with his later ones.

A most successful ninety-minute program was presented recently at a D. H. Lawrence festival. It was unique in that all the transitional material came from Lawrence's own writing or from books and letters written about him by other people. The audience was made up of scholars of Lawrenciana and people of Taos, New Mexico, where he lived and wrote for a considerable period. Thus the material included items showing his literary development and "human interest" material about his months in that area. The four men and four women used as readers held their manuscripts and sat on stools of various heights. The women wore simple white blouses and long, full denim skirts in vivid colors. The men wore light khaki trousers, solid-color sports shirts, and corduroy jackets. Because of its length, the program was presented in two acts, with a brief intermission between.

The program opened with a comment from one of Lawrence's letters: "The world is as it is. I am as I am. We don't fit very well." This was followed by about two minutes of brief quotes from his letters and essays establishing his attitude toward sex, love, women, the necessity of harmony between the mind and the body, and his interest in the animalistic aspects of man, religion, and nature. These were the themes to be touched on as the program progressed. The Lawrence quotes were divided among the four men; there was no attempt to characterize him specifically or to make one reader play the role of D. H. Lawrence.

This introductory montage was followed by an autobiographical paragraph in which Lawrence tells when and where he was born and gives his early impressions of the countryside. The material that followed was taken from *Sons and Lovers*, considered by most critics to be highly autobiographical, and continued through the description of the mother and father, including one of their many quarrels, into an abridged account of Paul's courtship and ultimate rejection of Miriam. This unit closed with Lawrence's poem "Last Words to Miriam" and a paragraph from *Sons and Lovers* about Paul's return to his mother and his devotion to her.

The next section included some of Lawrence's letters dealing with his mother's illness and death and closed with two short poems written in her memory, "Sorrow" and "Brooding Sorrow."

A short biographical paragraph made the bridge into his meeting with Frieda Weekley. For this unit, material was drawn from *Frieda Lawrence: Memoirs and Correspondences*, edited by E. W. Tadlock, Jr., and from the letters Lawrence wrote her before they went off to Bavaria together. His poem "Fröhnleichnam" was used to epitomize their period of happiness there. This was followed by four excerpts from letters which described the difficult period of adjustment and formed the lead-in to "The Song of a Man Who has Come Through."

The next section, again drawn from Lawrence's letters and Frieda's memoirs, took up their travels and carried them to Sicily, which Lawrence found fascinating. One of his letters provided the perfect introduction to the famous poem "Snake." More excerpts from letters led into a section from *Sea and Sardinia*. One of Frieda's letters describing how this account of their travels was written led quite nicely into Mabel Dodge's account, found in her *Lorenzo in Taos*, of her invitation to Lawrence to come to New Mexico after she had read *Sea and Sardinia*. The first act ended with Mabel's comment on the Lawrences' acceptance of the invitation and their later postponement of the trip. It sets the tone for their future relationship: "I knew what it meant. They were scared. . . . Someone had warned them. I was used to that. People were always warning people about me. No matter if it was justified, and I knew it was, still it always hurt my feelings and stiffened my backbone. I'd had the idea of having him come to Taos, and I'd sit there and draw him until he came. I'd go down inside myself and call that man until he would come."

The second act began with Mabel's account of the Lawrences' arrival in New Mexico and moved quickly into the series of minor conflicts which developed almost immediately. This provided an opportunity to include some humor — from Frieda's and Lawrence's letters to friends, Mabel's comments, and Dorothy Brett's *Lawrence and Brett: A Friendship*.

Because it was written in Taos and dealt with people Lawrence knew there, the fragment of a play *Altitude* was used at this point. Mabel Dodge introduces it in her book with: "One day Lorenzo began, for the first time in his life, to write a comedy: a Taos comedy. He laid the opening scene in the morning in our house, with the usual anomalous mixture of people . . . and he started to write it." Since much of the humor of the fragment depends on the pointless but amusing activity of preparations for breakfast when the cook failed to appear, it was decided to stage it rather than continue the reading technique. The readers simply put down their books, moved their stools around to suggest a stove and a grouping around a table, and the play began. It broke abruptly, with a quote from Mabel Dodge to end it: "But he never went on with it." The readers moved rapidly to replace the stools and retrieve their books, and the reading continued, resuming with the Lawrences' move to Lobo Ranch and the long winter that followed. Dorothy Brett's account furnished most of the material here and led into Lawrence's poem "Mountain Lion," which was arranged for three voices. This was followed by more accounts of Lawrence's experiences with the Indians, drawn from his letters and his essays "Taos," "New Mexico," "Indians and an Englishman." Other letters and Frieda's memoirs provided the transition for their move to Mexico and the account of his writing *Mornings in Mexico* and *Plumed Serpent*, from which brief paragraphs were used.

The period of the Lawrences' further travels and sojourn in England was omitted to save time. Besides, the accounts available emphasize the gradual failure of Lawrence's health and tend to be repetitious and nondramatic. An excerpt from one of Lawrence's letters tells enough about his declining health to bridge into Frieda's letter about his death, a letter interspersed with brief sections from Lawrence's "The Ship of Death." The program concluded with his famous poem "Bavarian Gentians."

This program has been treated in some detail to show how the works of one author can form the organizing theme and how a variety of written materials can be blended effectively. The Lawrence program had strong unity and remarkable variety both in type of writing and in range of mood and feeling. The rhythm of emotional impact was carefully considered so that the entire evening moved smoothly and without monotony.

Using Multiple Readers and Art Forms

Using more than one reader for a program often helps to solve the problems of short preparation time and inexperience. Moreover, using two or more interpreters adds variety and thus increases the program's audience appeal. This is not to suggest that several people just read whatever they have ready. There must be some central unity, of course. The several readers must rehearse together so that transitions serve their proper function and the material is arranged to provide variety and contrast, rhythm of emotional impact, and effective use of climactic selections. Multiple readers may be used in a program as elaborate as the one just described or in a format as simple as having them alternate selections and/or use scenes or dialogue in which two or more work together.

The opportunities for experimentation in program building are great. Much literature combines well with dance, either as an accompaniment to the reading or inserted at various places in the program to underscore, sustain, or alter mood. Music may be used whenever it is appropriate, and slides can be most effective if they are well-handled and if the equipment is dependable. William Blake and E. E. Cummings, for example, were both artists of some distinction as well as poets, and some of their drawings and paintings might well be combined with their writing for an enjoyable program. The drawings and prose writings in Gerard Manley Hopkins' *Notebooks* might be skillfully combined with his poetry to provide a novel and interesting program.

The possibilities for using readers in combination and other art forms with literature are practically endless. And of course units of Readers Theatre and Chamber Theatre may be combined with the performance of single readers when the material seems suitable for the techniques. Care must be taken, however, not to let the variety thus achieved overpower the essential unity. Innovations must always contribute to the total experience of the program and never be allowed to distract from the literature or become an end in themselves.

Arranging and Linking the Selections

Unless you know your audience well or the special occasion demands particular selections, it is usually wise to mix prose and poetry, and perhaps a scene or two from a play, into an hour's program. This provides variety and does not require sustaining any one set of special techniques too long. If at all appropriate, include some lighter pieces to provide rhythm of emotional response. In arranging the selections in sequence, this becomes an important consideration. If possible, long, medium, and short selections should be intermingled for a proper balance of sustained experiences and condensed ones. If you do not know how sophisticated your audience is, open your program with a disarming selection. The most difficult selections should probably come slightly past the middle of the program, before your audience tires but after you have won them to the mood and direction of your theme. Close on the note you wish them to take home with them. This may be a culmination of your theme or the climax of a sequence of units of that theme. Frost's "For Once, Then, Something," Ciardi's "As I Would Wish You Birds," or Roethke's "The Waking" might serve such a purpose, as would innumerable other pieces of poetry, prose, or drama.

The important thing to remember is that the performance as a whole must have both unity and variety. It should have an introductory unit, a climax (usually the longest selection and the one most clearly exemplifying your theme), and a conclusion. When you have selected and arranged your material, look at the whole program and check it against each of the intrinsic factors.

The introduction and the transitions between selections are vitally important and must be handled so that they underscore the unity and add dimension to the variety. They need not be long or elaborate. Review the suggestions on introductions in Chapter 2. The introduction will, of course, set the tone for the entire performance.

If you are doing the program alone or if you are the first of two or more performers, your introduction should contain a word of appreciation for the remarks the program chairman made in introducing you to the audience. Sometimes a simple "Thank you, Mrs. —" will do nicely. It is courteous to express some pleasure in being with that particular group if it can be done gracefully and briefly. Keep the introduction short. The audience came to hear the program, not a long-winded preamble. If you are not the first speaker, your introductory remarks should form a bridge from the previous performers' work to the mood and train of thought you wish to establish. In either case, the opening words are primarily useful in establishing rapport — in allowing your audience to focus its attention and you to adjust to the place in which you are speaking. After the first sentence or two, you begin to turn their thoughts and yours in the direction you want them to go.

The transitions between selections should allow the listeners a few seconds to complete their emotional response to the preceding selection and should lead them economically and subtly into the mood and area of response of the one to follow. They should be brief, relevant, and keyed to your unifying theme, although you need not mention it specifically every time. Do not tell your audience what the next selection is going to say. The author has done that, and if you do your job well, the audience will know. Instead, prepare them and yourself for the *experience* of the selection.

Transitions make it possible to use wide variety and sharp contrast in selections without breaking the unity of the program. For example, suppose you want to use Frost's "Wild Grapes" and Kunitz's "I Dreamed That I Was Old." Or suppose you are following an interpreter whose selection was heavy and you wish to lighten the tone and introduce a touch of humor. You can simply say that you are going to take quite a different view of a similar time of life, episode, or character. If the process is to be reversed, you may need a little longer transition to turn the audience from laughter to a more serious mood. Empathy will play a large part in any such change of mood, of course.

Introductions and transitions are vital parts of the whole performance. They must be carefully worked out for thought progression and mood. When several readers are working together, it is particularly important that they rehearse with the total performance in mind, not as soloists who just happen to be on the same program.

Adapting to the Audience

It is impossible to know exactly what the interests of your audience will be unless, of course, the group has a special purpose, but it is possible to make some generalizations. The sex of the audience makes less difference than one would at first imagine. Both men and women are interested in people and places and a wealth of other things as well. Men are less likely to admit an interest in love themes or selections about home and children. They are, however, frankly if secretly sentimental about patriotism, fellowship, adventure, and family life. Women are somewhat more flexible, partly because they carry fewer business and practical considerations with them into their meetings. As a rule, men's service organizations prefer short programs, preferably humorous to provide a break in the business day) or highly relevant to current events. An audience of men and women is usually the easiest to handle because it is more candidly social than business.

Age is an important factor to consider in audience adaptation. In general, a younger audience of either sex is more open to experimental material and a wider range of subject matter. An audience of the very elderly usually wants traditional, familiar material. They like being reminded of happier times and being reassured that there is still beauty and gentleness in a chaotic world. They are not primarily interested in old age, illness, and death. They come together for companionship and encouragement. In a group where the age spread is wide there should, of course, be something for everyone, but if you are in doubt about the suitability of a selection for even a segment of the audience, it is better to omit it than to offend them.

Children are a wonderful audience. They like material about people, animals, clouds, birds, and anything they can visualize, whether real or imaginary. They like poetry with a clear rhythm and a rhyme. The selections should be relatively short and the transitions handled with care in order to connect what they know with what the literature is saying. Stories, of course, are great favorites, and children enjoy having the characters made vivid by more explicit vocal and physical characterization than would be appropriate for a mature audience. Nor need you limit yourself to children's literature exclusively. Children enjoy the sounds and the basic references in Hopkins' "The Starlight Night" or "Pied Beauty," Carroll's "Jabberwocky," de la Mare's "The Listeners," or even Frost's "Choose Something Like a Star."

These brief statements on audience adaptation are not to be construed as a suggestion that you sacrifice your own standards of literary worth to audience expectation. There are dozens of ways to write about every subject under the sun. Your audience outside the classroom will be interested *first* in what your material is about and second in how it is presented.

For a final recital in the classroom you may assume an audience with more specialized interest in your performance and greater willingness to accept a narrower range of material. Because the audience will be keenly aware of technique, your introductory remarks and transitions may be more obviously analysis-oriented. Remember, however, the admonition in Chapter 2 (pages 35–36) about putting the selections back together again. Your classmates do not want to hear your analysis. They want to experience the literature in its logical, emotional, and aesthetic entirety. They already know you and are ready to accept you as a peer and performer. They will be critical but highly receptive.

The image the audience has of you is related to the preceding discussion. An out-of-classroom audience expects you to be young, skilled, intelligent, attractive, and interesting. Otherwise they would not have asked you to present the program. But "young" does not mean childish or even childlike. It means fresh and vital. Four-letter words and risqué dialogue are not compatible with their ideal of youth and intelligence. They may read them themselves, but they do not like hearing them from you. They expect you to be well prepared and are often highly critical if your performance is rough at the edges. You are an artist in their eyes, and they came to enjoy your art. They have invited you because you can do something they themselves cannot do as well. Accept this responsibility. Use your intelligence and education, but do not flaunt them. You are their guest artist. Live up to their expectations on both counts. If you have been sent by your school, you are responsible for the reputation and prestige of your instructor and your school. If you have been asked because your parents belong to the organization or because you are back in your home town again, what you do reflects your home life and your family's standards and taste.

Timing the Program

One consideration which applies to every performance is the amount of time you have been allowed. Only a beginner or a rank egoist permits a program to run past its allotted time by more than a very few minutes. On television or radio, such a reader finds himself talking to a dead microphone. In the live-audience situation, his listeners often become ill at ease and distracted if the meeting runs long. It is always better to leave an audience wishing for more than to risk the sigh of relief and the hurried exit.

Time your selections and transitions several times during your preparation. You will find that you consume more time as you progress. It is probably safe to add at least ten minutes an hour to your early reading time; audience response and your own increased control of the selections will tend to slow your pace in final performance. If you are sharing a program with other readers or with musicians, find out how much time you have been allotted and stick to it precisely.

A program of varied selections is particularly difficult to time because it is likely to be lengthened by applause between selections. This is, of course, a phenomenon no performer wishes to prevent! Nevertheless, enthusiastic applause can add five minutes or more to a fifty-minute program af relatively short selections. Be sure to consider this in your planning. In general, applause permits the audience to complete their response to what you have just given them. Accept it graciously and with poise.

On some occasions applause is, of course, inappropriate. If you sense that this is the situation, a moment's pause after each selection and before the next transition will be helpful. Do not prolong the pause so that your audience thinks you are waiting for applause. This sense of timing will develop as your experience increases. Occasionally, applause would break a mood you are trying to establish, especially if you are using a group of short selections. In that case, you might indicate in your transition that you will be using a group of short poems all touching on the same aspect of your theme. Hold your performance dimension for a brief pause after each one and then move directly into the next selection or brief transition. When you finish the group, drop your directness slightly and allow the audience to show its appreciation before moving into the next unit. Audiences are remarkably sensitive to your wishes and will take your cue easily.

Some Practical Considerations

Earlier in this discussion we mentioned the reading hours so popular on numerous campuses. They provide an excellent opportunity for experience before an audience and establish good public relations with the community. Reading hours are usually set up in a series and are very simple to inaugurate. They may occur as often as suitable material can be prepared and may include every mode of performance from the highly experimental to the traditional program of single readers. It is wise to have them at regular intervals so your audience will know when to expect them and thus set up the habit of attending. Once a month is a common schedule, keeping the same hours and day of the week. Reading hours should not last over sixty minutes. A complete schedule may be sent out to the community and to other departments on campus at the beginning of the series and then be followed by a simple reminder about two weeks before the date, such as a postcard or mimeographed announcement giving the details of the program. Each program must be carefully rehearsed and have a unifying theme even if it is no more restricting than "Victorian Literature," "Modern Thoughts on Peace and War," "Black Heritage," or "Experiments in Words and Movement."

Requests for programs frequently come from those attending the regular reading hours. More often, however, program chairmen call the college or department to request readers for a specific date. An interesting group project for a speech organization or club is to set up and staff a program bureau to handle such requests. Clubs, church groups, and nearby high schools and colleges would be interested in a listing of the programs you have to offer. In large cities there are regularly scheduled auditions where you may present ten or fifteen minutes of a longer program for an audience of club presidents and program chairmen. There is a great need for brief programs for children's wards in hospitals, and the time spent on such volunteer projects can be highly rewarding. The same holds true for retirement centers and veterans' hospitals. Libraries often have reading hours for children and adults which offer the opportunity to do public service and gain valuable experience as well.

It is always wise to get in touch with the program chairman early to find out what he would like as far as tone and message are concerned, how long the program should be, and what time you should arrive. Most organizations can provide a reading stand, but if you need other special equipment, be sure to find out well in advance whether it is available. If you will need stools or other properties, you will probably have to supply your own. Be sure to check on the lighting and lighting equipment. If you need special effects, or if you are to bring your own equipment, make an early check on outlets, extension cords, and the capacity of the wiring. The same holds true for slide projectors. If you will need transportation, indicate this in an early conversation with the program chairman. Once you have agreed to do a program, nothing short of a serious emergency should prevent you from being there on time and fully prepared.

It is helpful to the program and publicity chairman if you give him a title for your program. The title should be brief and should announce the theme without disclosing too much of the program content. Ideally, it should contain only three or four words. If it is alliterative or otherwise easy to remember, so much the better.

It is usually wise to have an encore ready, but it should be brief and should continue the tone of your final selection and your theme. Except in unusual circumstances, the encore should take not more than two minutes. Unless you are remarkably successful, one selection will suffice. Remember! It is better to leave your audience wishing for more than wishing you had stopped five minutes sooner. If there are several readers, you might plan an encore which can be done in unison or with alternating voices.

In short, wherever you do a program remember your role as an interpreter whose duty and privilege it is to *share* a piece of interesting literature with an audience. Remember that your art and your technique must serve the author's intentions. As we pointed out in the opening chapter, the better your technique the less apparent it will be, and the more completely the audience can focus on the experience of the literature you are sharing with them.

Out-of-classroom performances require effort, time, intelligence, imagination, and the willingness to do a great deal of research to find exactly the right kind of material. Putting it together and arranging it effectively takes time and energy, as does the analysis and preparation necessary for a polished performance. Even so, the experience of sharing good literature with an audience is always rewarding and exciting.

Appendix B

A Brief History of
Theories of Interpretation

From earliest times the spoken word has attracted audiences and influenced their thinking. The history of public speaking has been traced by numerous authorities, who have shown that its thread is unbroken from the fourth century B.C. down to the present. The theatre enjoys a similarly clear history. Oral interpretation, too, even though its genesis and growth as a distinct art may be less easy to define, has a long lineage of its own.

The art of interpretation probably had its beginnings with the rhapsodies of ancient Greece, when poets gathered to read their works in public competition. However, the emergence of interpretation as a field of study in its own right was delayed because it was long confused with oratory and rhetoric. Some of the works dealing in detail with the history of interpretation are listed in the general bibliography at the end of this appendix. It will be enough to sketch the outlines very lightly here, in order to note the development of certain theories and to see where we now stand in relation to those theories.

The colleges of America were already giving some attention to the oral interpretation of literature by the beginning of the nineteenth century. As early as 1806, when John Quincy Adams assumed the chair of Rhetoric and Oratory, Harvard, which from its founding had carried on the medieval tradition of "declamations" and "disputations," was offering a few courses that included the interpretative approach to literary materials. As the century progressed, more and more colleges offered specific courses in spoken English — courses that carried such titles as "Declamation and

Composition," "Declamation," "Elements of Orthoëpy and Elocution," or simply "Elocution."

The word *elocutio* (Latin, *eloqui, elocutus* = speak out) orginally referred to effective literary or oratorical style. Between 1650 and 1750, however, a shift in connotation took place, and the term *elocution* began to be applied to the manner of oral delivery rather than to the written style of a composition. *Pronuntiatio*, which had meant primarily the management of voice and body, gradually took on our modern meaning of pronunciation as the correct phonation of individual words. By 1750 then, these shifts in meaning had taken place, and the term *elocution* had come to connote a considerable degree of emphasis on delivery. By this time, also, a renewed interest in reading aloud and in oratory had developed, especially in England where an important group of writer-speakers known as the English Elocutionists had come into being. Outstanding among them were Thomas Sheridan (1719–1788) and John Walker (1732–1807), whose books and lectures had great bearing on the development in America of what we now call interpretation.

Thomas Sheridan, father of the famous dramatist Richard Brinsley Sheridan and himself an actor, published his *Course of Lectures on Elocution* in 1763. This book came out strongly against artificialities and laid much stress on the method of natural conversation in the oral presentation of literature. Sheridan thus became known as the leader of the "natural school." His thesis was that elocution should follow the laws of nature. He held that body and voice were natural phenomena and were thus subject to the laws of nature. He pointed out that nature gave to the passions and emotions certain tones, looks, and gestures which are perceived through the ear and the eye. Therefore, he contended, the elocutionist should reproduce these tones, looks, and gestures as nearly as possible in presenting literature orally to an audience. Basically, this theory was sound.

As often happens in the application of a theory, however, Sheridan became trapped in his efforts to be specific, and he began to evolve a system of markings and cues for the discovery and reproduction of these "natural" tones and gestures. Hence, by the end of his career he had become the exponent of a method which, judged by modern standards, was much more mechanical than natural. Nevertheless, the term "natural school" has persisted to the present day.

The other famous English Elocutionist, John Walker, published his *Elements of Elocution* almost twenty years later, in 1781. He, too, professed to take his cues from nature. However, he could not (or at least did not) resist the urge to set down specific rules and markings for the slightest variations of vocal tempo, inflection, and force, and for the various aspects of gesture. These markings caught the public fancy because they were more concrete than anything that had been offered before. (It is always so much easier to be told exactly how to do a thing than to put one's own intelligence to work to solve each individual problem as it arises!) Walker must be given credit for stating clearly that these markings were intended as helps toward the satisfactory projection of the material at hand; and perhaps he is not to be held wholly responsible for the fact that future generations were to place more emphasis on the markings and other mechanical devices than on the projection of material. Walker and his imitators, then, established what has been called the "mechanical school" in seeming opposition to Sheridan's "natural school." Thus began a schism which is only now disappearing.

Two other names must be mentioned in connection with the English Elocutionists of the eighteenth century. Although they were less prolific and influential than Sheridan and Walker, John Mason (1706–1763) and James Burgh (1714–1775) both wrote books which enjoyed considerable popularity. Mason's *An Essay on Elocution, or Pronunciation* (1748), the first book to include the word "Elocution" in its title, put heavy emphasis on the "right" management of the voice.

James Burgh was primarily a political philosopher whose interest in speech probably grew out of his political activities. In his book *The Art of Speaking* (1762), he discussed with some vehemence the rules for expressing "the principal Passions and Humors." This volume, which contained an anthology of readings, with the passions and humors carefully documented, was based on the theory that nature had given every passion its proper physical expression and that only by careful attention to the physical features, such as the eye, could the proper passion be projected.

To sum up, the closing years of the eighteenth century saw an increased interest in the use of voice and body in the oral presentation of literature. Sheridan had set up a "natural school," purportedly based on the "laws of nature"; Walker had established a "mechanical school," based in fact on the same premises but more preoccupied with markings and charts. It is understandable that the followers of these men would tend to emphasize their differences rather than their similarities, and that some degree of confusion and dissension would result.

In the nineteenth century two names stand out above all others in the history of interpretation. The first is that of an American, James Rush (1786–1869), a medical man turned speech teacher and lecturer. Dr. Rush confined himself almost entirely to the study of vocal projection. He believed that the management of the voice was in reality not an art but a science, and he went to great lengths to develop an appropriate vocabulary for that science. Indeed, much of his terminology has become standard among modern teachers of speech. He also went to great lengths in the title of his book, published in 1827: *The Philosophy of the Human Voice: Embracing Its Physiological History: Together with a System of Principles by Which Criticism in the Art of Elocution May Be Rendered Intelligible, and Instruction, Definite and Comprehensive, to Which Is Added a Brief Analysis of Song and Recitative.*

Dr. Rush developed elaborate charts and markings for pitch, force, abruptness, quality, and time. He was convinced that rules could be developed to govern the analysis of vocal technique, although he was careful to point out that the practice of these rules must be accompanied by concentration on the literature being read. This last bit of advice, however, was often forgotten by his more zealous and less discriminating followers; as a result, attention was focused even more sharply on markings and symbols. Nevertheless, Dr. Rush's use of appropriate scientific method and vocabulary and his studies of the mechanisms of the human voice were valuable contributions to the field of speech.

The second significant name in nineteenth-century interpretation is François Delsarte (1811–1871). About the time Dr. Rush's method was making its way in America, Delsarte was delivering lectures in France on elocution and calisthenics. He left no writings, but so strong was his influence that many of his students recorded his philosophy and system in great detail. The Delsarte system concerned itself entirely with bodily action, and it became an accepted complement to Dr. Rush's treatises on vocal management. Delsarte based his system on a philosophy of the interrelation of man's soul, mind, and body, and on a complicated and highly mystical concept of a corresponding triune relationship throughout the entire universe. Despite this philosophical premise, the system became mechanical in the extreme. The writings reflecting and interpreting it are filled with elaborate charts and diagrams.

Delsarte, like Walker and Rush, suffered somewhat at the hands of his followers. One example of the perversion of a basically sound but inadequately expressed theory — that gestures must spring from the heart — was the notion that all gestures must start from the breastbone and sweep out in a graceful curve. This misconception persisted for generations. Although Delsarte's system in practice took on mechanical aspects that had some unfortunate results, modern teachers of speech have been greatly influenced by his concept of mind, soul (heart or emotions), and body working together.

Thus, almost simultaneously, Rush in America was setting up a scientific approach to vocal technique and Delsarte in France was teaching a philosophical approach to bodily action. Although both men were originally concerned with the artistic projection of materials, those whom they influenced tended often to concentrate on the techniques rather than on the reasons for the techniques. In this way the mechancial school, well established under the aegis of Walker's disciples, became even more firmly entrenched.

Near the close of the nineteenth century, the natural school received new impetus under the leadership of Samuel Silas Curry (1847–1921).

His first book, *The Province of Expression*, published in Boston in 1891, was based on the major premise that the mind, in order to express an idea, must actively hold that idea and thus dictate the appropriate means of expression. This theory he summed up in the admonition, "Think the thought!" It is understandable that such a phrase would catch the fancy of those who read his books and heard of his teachings — and equally understandable that it would lead to oversimplification, to the extent that Curry's fundamentally sound theory came to be popularized as "Think the thought and all things else will be added unto you." As a result, many teachers began to assert that the training of voice and body consisted of wholly artificial and mechanical procedures, and that comprehension of thought and active concentration on that thought would insure adequate projection of any material to an audience.

Admittedly, this idea came as a relief to those who had become weary of the exhibitionism that prevailed among the second- and third-generation advocates of the mechanical method. In an attempt to break more completely with the earlier artificialities, teachers even began to shy away from the term "elocution," with all its connotations, and to adopt instead Curry's term "expression." Thus, lessons in "elocution" became lessons in "expression."

One of the most interesting and influential teachers in America at the close of the century was Charles Wesley Emerson (1837–1908), founder of the Emerson College of Oratory, now Emerson College in Boston. His *Evolution of Expression* (1905) stressed vocal technique and gymnastics for their therapeutic value as well as for their contribution to the techniques of communicating literature.

By the end of the nineteenth century, then, three distinct groups had emerged: one militantly carried on the traditions of the mechanical school; another distrusted mechanics, relied on the natural method, and developed in the direction of "think-the-thought"; and a third composed of a few independents who found some values in each camp and who attempted to blend the two approaches.

By the turn of the twentieth century, a number of colleges were offering courses in elocution or expression, but the average student did not usually include speech in his program of studies unless he was preparing himself for the ministry, politics, or law. Most of those who wished to do "platform work" as "readers" enrolled in private schools or studios. There they worked under teachers often three or four times removed from the originators of basically sound theories, and received instruction which, having filtered through several personalities, was strongly flavored by the individual teacher's own taste and understanding.

The first three decades of the twentieth century were the era of the private, highly specialized school or studio of speech. Each had its own staff of teachers, most of whom had been trained by the head of that particular school. Each had its own course of study and its own special emphasis. And each prided itself on its independence and its difference from the others. Consequently, they had no common philosophy or methodology. Each school tended to emphasize its individuality rather than to work with the others toward solidarity and a unity of purpose among all teachers in the field.

Many who studied at these schools returned to their homes, framed their certificates, hung them on their walls, and opened their own studios, where they taught to the best of their ability what they had learned. Their students, in turn, acquired certificates and went out to spread the gospel as they understood it. Thus, of the thousands of teachers who were conducting classes and giving private lessons, very few had had an opportunity to receive sound training under the great leaders. As a result, the original principles and practices were continually watered down. Not only were teachers often imperfectly prepared, but they worked in comparative isolation, without professional associations and strong university departments of speech to serve as centers for the exchange of ideas. The better informed and more progressive teachers who studied under Curry and his contemporaries grew with the entire educational system to become the outstanding men and women in the field of speech as a whole and in the more specialized area of interpretation. Others, however, continued to teach specific gesture, highly obtrusive vocal technique, and the use of materials of questionable literary merit, thus perpetuating to our own day not only the more regrettable excesses and misconceptions in vogue in the early years of the century, but also a confusion in terminology and in standards of performance.

An important link between the theorists and teachers of the nineteenth century and the present is *Principles of Vocal Expression* (1897), by William B. Chamberlain (1847–1903) and Solomon H. Clark (1861–1927). This book, acknowledging a deep indebtedness to Curry, stressed the interaction of mind and body and the control of "instincts" by reason. Clark was to make a more important contribution in his *Interpretation of the Printed Page* (1913), which helped to turn the attention of teachers and students from the mechanical techniques to the appreciation and analysis of the literature itself. His concept of "impression" as distinct from and prerequisite to "expression" was to become the basis of *The Art of Interpretative Speech* by Charles H. Woolbert and Severina E. Nelson, published in 1929.

Another popular book of the early twentieth century was *Natural Drills in Expression with Selections* (1909). The author, Arthur Edward Phillips (1867–1932), reflects much of Chamberlain's interest in paraphrase and tone drills, and the book was used extensively for many years in schools and colleges.

With the advance of the twentieth century, departments of speech grew in stature in the colleges and universities and became fully accepted members of the academic family. Many private schools also moved with the times, some of them burgeoning into degree-granting colleges. Speech training, freed from the cultist studio, flourished under the stimulating crosswinds of professional associations and the spur of more homogeneous standards. Ideas were pooled, theories argued, heritages reevaluated. Interpretation emerged from the strait jacket of the "reading" (which was not a reading at all, but a virtuoso exhibition of memory and technique) and reoriented itself to the printed page.

The fourth decade of this century was one of transition and stabilization. Interest increased in history and research, as shown by Mary Margaret Robb's history of oral reading in the colleges and universities and the establishment of doctoral programs in the field.

Cornelius Carman Cunningham, Gertrude Johnson, Wayland Maxwell Parrish, Solomon Henry Clark, and Maud May Babcock published texts which had an important effect on the whole area of study. Although they differed somewhat in emphasis, all firmly insisted on the primacy of the literature and the importance of the demands it made. The present generation of interpreters and teachers is deeply indebted to them for their ability to come to grips with critical and aesthetic principles and to formulate standards applicable to both analysis and performance.

The modern interpreter believes in training both voice and body. He knows that his voice must be flexible and strong and his articulation clear if he is to do full justice to the material he has chosen. He knows, too, that his body must be trained to respond in harmony with his voice. He is no longer afraid of the word "technique" because he understands what it is and what he must do with it.

He also believes in carefully analyzing his material and actively concentrating on it when he presents it to an audience. In a sense, he reverts to the classical tradition of rhetoric in his insistence on the importance of understanding the elements of literary craftsmanship in the selection to be interpreted. He is concerned with the author's art — how he shapes the whole out of its parts.

Happily, differences still exist in degrees of emphasis on one or another aspect of the field. However, the isolationism and long list of "thou-shalt-nots" which characterized oral interpretation in the early part of the century no longer prevail. The modern interpreter opens his mind to the aesthetician, the literary critic, the linguist, the psychologist, and the social behaviorist. He realizes that the more he knows about related studies the more he learns about literature. He is no longer afraid to experiment because he knows precisely where his first dependence lies — on the elements present in the work of literature he has chosen. Excellent books present a strong rhetorical approach, a dramatistic approach, or a primary emphasis on applied and theoretical literary criticism. The contemporary interpreter is aware of the complexity of good literature, and he is eager to bring to it whatever is needed for its full comprehension and appreciation, whether for his own enjoyment or that of an audience.

Bibliography

This bibliography is selective and does not include all the contemporary texts. Its emphasis is on the historical, with only those present-day texts listed which differ significantly in emphasis or approach from this one.

Aggertt, Otis J., and Elbert R. Bowen. *Communicative Reading.* Second Edition. New York: The Macmillan Company, 1963.

Bacon, Wallace A. *The Art of Interpretation.* New York: Holt, Rinehart and Winston, Inc., 1966.

Bacon, Wallace A., and Robert S. Breen. *Literature as Experience.* New York: McGraw-Hill Book Company, 1959.

Beloof, Robert. *The Performing Voice in Literature.* Boston: Little, Brown and Company, 1966.

Chaytor, H. J. *From Script to Print: An Introduction to Medieval Vernacular Literature.* Second Impression. Cambridge, England: W. Heffer and Sons, Ltd., 1950.

Clark, Solomon Henry, and Maud May Babcock. *Interpretation of the Printed Page.* New York: Prentice-Hall, Inc., 1940.

Cunningham, Cornelius Carman. *Literature as a Fine Art.* New York: The Ronald Press Company, 1941.

Curry, Samuel Silas. *Foundations of Expression, Studies and Problems for Developing the Voice, Body, and Mind in Reading and Speaking.* Boston: Expression Company, 1907.

Emerson, Charles Wesley. *Evolution of Expression. A Compilation of Selections Illustrating the Four Stages of Development in Art as Applied to Oratory.* 4 vols. Boston: Emerson College of Oratary, Publishing Department, 1905.

Geiger, Don. *Oral Interpretation and Literary Study.* San Francisco: Peter Van Vloten, 1958.

Geiger, Don. *The Sound, Sense, and Performance of Literature.* Chicago: Scott, Foresman and Company, 1963.

Joseph, B. L. *Elizabethan Acting.* London: Oxford University Press, 1951.

Kenyon, Frederic G. *Books and Readers in Ancient Greece and Rome.* Second Edition. Oxford: The Clarendon Press, 1951.

Lowrey, Sara, and Gertrude E. Johnson. *Interpretative Reading.* Revised Edition. New York: Appleton-Century-Crofts, Inc., 1953.

Lynch, Gladys E., and Harold C. Crain. *Projects in Oral Interpretation.* New York: Henry Holt, 1959.

Mattingly, Alethea Smith, and Wilma H. Grimes. *Interpretation: Writer-Reader-Audience.* Second Edition. San Francisco: Wadsworth Publishing Company, Inc., 1970.

Mouat, Lawrence H. *Reading Literature Aloud.* New York: Oxford University Press, 1962.

Parrish, Wayland Maxwell. *Reading Aloud.* Fourth Edition. New York: The Ronald Press Company, 1966.

Phillips, Arthur Edward. *Natural Drills in Expression, with Selections, a Series of Exercises Colloquial and Classical, Based Upon the Principles of Reference to Experience and Comparison, and Chosen for their Practical Worth in Developing Power and Naturalness in Reading and Speaking. With Illustrative Selections for Practice.* Chicago: The Newton Company, 1920.

Robb, Mary Margaret. *Oral Interpretation of Literature in American Colleges and Universities.* New York: H. W. Wilson Company, 1941.

Sloan, Thomas O. (ed.) *The Oral Study of Literature.* New York: Random House, Inc., 1966.

Wallace, Karl R. (ed.). *History of Speech Education in America: Background Studies.* New York: Appleton-Century-Crofts, Inc., 1954.

Woolbert, Charles H., and Severina E. Nelson. *The Art of Interpretative Speech: Principles and Practices of Effective Reading.* Fifth Edition. New York: Appleton-Century-Crofts, Inc., 1968.

Index

abridgment, 228–229

acting, and interpretation, 269–272, 320

action: in narrative, 217–219; physical, 328–333, 368–372[1]; of players, 274–275; and problems of physical contact, 331–333; theory of remembered, 285

action, bodily, 62–63; to identify characters, 225, 227; of interpreter, 3–4, 87–89

address, angle of. *See* placement, angle of.

"aesthetic distance," 322–323

age, characterizing, 335–336

Agee, James
From *A Death in the Family*, 221, 232–235[2], 487

Albee, Edward
From *The American Dream*, 377–380

alliteration in poetry, 408

allusions, 18–19, 20, 46, 48–49, 70–71, 118–119, 412–413, 419–420, 420–424, 462–463, 477; function in poetry, 396–397; and style, 144

ambiguity, 13, 14

amphibrach, 445

amphimacer, 445

analogy, 31, 39–40, 419–420, 426–428; in poetry, 398

anapest, 444, 445

apostrophe, 399, 416–417

Arnold, Matthew
"Dover Beach," 130–131

art, intrinsic factors of, 24–30

articulation: defined, 108–109; and intensity of response, 409; in poetry reading, 409

assonance, 408, 457, 461–462

attitude, 22–24, 38, 39, 51, 71–73, 132–133, 149, 479; author's, 130–131, 170–171; and character business, 275; and choice of words, 52–54; poet's, 37–38, 394–395, 410–411; interpreter's 61–62, 100–101, 225; and style, 23, 49–50; and unity, 25

Auden, W. H.
"In Memory of W. B. Yeats," 391, 443, 474–476
"Musée des Beaux Arts," 20, 23, 48–49

audience: adapting to, 493–494; hold-

---

[1] Italicized page numbers in a topic entry show where the topic is illustrated with one or more references to literary works.

[2] Italicized page numbers in an author/selection entry show where the selection is reprinted or quoted directly; Roman page numbers indicate where the selection is referred to in the text.

audience (*cont'd.*)
ing attention of, 29; interpreter's contact with, 270–271, 340; response, 62, 69

background, through point of view, 221
Bacon, Francis
From *Of Revenge, 151,* 186
balance, 27–28, 31, 33, 35, 38, 39, *46, 51, 79, 83–84,* 133, *192–195, 433–434*
ballad, 387, 404, *436–437*
Bartlett's Familiar Quotations, 397
Barzun, Jacques, 149–150
Bennett, Arnold, 137–138
Beowulf, 388
The Bible
1 Corinthians XIII, *182*
Daniel V, *128–130*
Genesis I, 29
Psalm 8, *418–419*
blank verse, 404, 440; and cadences, 454; and line length, 451
Bodenheim, Maxwell
"Death," 100, *127–128*
Bolt, Robert
From *A Man for All Seasons,* 372–376
Bontemps, Arna
"A Summer Tragedy," 224, *254–261*
Bowen, Elizabeth, 220
From *The Little Girls, 123–126,* 487
breath control, 95–100; exercises, 97–99
Breen, Robert, 230, 231
Brooks, Gwendolyn, 487
"Love Note I: Surely," *126–127*
"Love Note II: Flags," 127
"We Real Cool," 442, 458, *474*
Browning, Elizabeth Barrett
Letter to Mr. Browning, *175–176*
Browning, Robert, 192, 440, 485–486
"Andrea del Sarto," 23
Letter to Miss Barrett, *174–175*
"My Last Duchess," 393–394

From "The Pied Piper of Hamelin," 98–99
"Soliloquy of the Spanish Cloister," 23, 394, 403, *434–436*
Bulfinch's Mythology, 397
business: character, 275; practical, 274–275
Byron, George Gordon: "The Prisoner of Chillon," 392

cadences, 146, 453–456, *461–462, 463–464;* primary, 453–455, *461;* and rhyme, 457; and rhythm, 454, 470–471; secondary, 453–456, *455–456;* and sound pattern, 453
caesura, 454
Capote, Truman, 487
From *In Cold Blood, 192, 198–201,* 220
Carroll, Lewis
"Jabberwocky," *110–111,* 494
cast, introduction by reader, 324–325
Chamber Theatre, 221, 229–231, 491; point of view in, 231
characterization: in drama, 268–269; pitfalls in, 337–338; by suggestion, 333–336
character(s), 224–225; business, 275; cutting from play, 277; in drama, 276–280; focus of, 225–226, 338–340; interplay of, 336–337; portrayal by suggestion, 284–285, 333–336; relationship to plot, 276
Chaucer, Geoffrey: *The Canterbury Tales,* 388
Ciardi, John
"As I Would Wish You Birds," 443, *462–463*
climax, 21–22, 29, 42–43, 46–48, 75–78, 83–84, 128–130, 133, 443, 455–456; in didactic prose, *152;* in drama, 273; emotional, 21, 22, 27, 29–30, *35,* 450; in fiction, 218; logical, 21, 22, 27, 31, 35; and pause, 106. *See also* crisis.
communication, 4; bodily action as, 64–65; interpreter's attitude toward, 100–101